HISTORY OF
PUBLIC SPEAKING
IN AMERICA

Books by Robert T. Oliver

FOUR WHO SPOKE OUT: BURKE, FOX, SHERIDAN, AND PITT

SYNGMAN RHEE: THE MAN BEHIND THE MYTH

KOREA: FORGOTTEN NATION

WHY WAR CAME IN KOREA

THE TRUTH ABOUT KOREA

VERDICT IN KOREA

PSYCHOLOGY OF PERSUASIVE SPEECH

PERSUASIVE SPEAKING: PRINCIPLES AND METHODS

TRAINING FOR EFFECTIVE SPEECH

EFFECTIVE SPEECH (with R. L. Cortright)

COMMUNICATIVE SPEECH (with H. P. Zelko and P. D. Holtzman)

EFFECTIVE SPEECH FOR DEMOCRATIC LIVING

EFFECTIVE SPEECH NOTEBOOK (with V. Anderson, et al.)

CONVERSATION: THE DEVELOPMENT AND EXPRESSION OF PERSONALITY

THE HEALTHY MIND IN COMMUNION AND COMMUNICATION (with D. A. Barbara)

CULTURE AND COMMUNICATION: THE PROBLEM OF PENETRATING NATIONAL AND CULTURAL BOUNDARIES

BECOMING AN INFORMED CITIZEN

DEVELOPING IDEAS FOR ESSAYS AND SPEECHES (with H. W. Robbins)

Editor, KOREA, MY COUNTRY, by Yung Tai Pyun

Editor (with M. Bauer), RE-ESTABLISHING THE SPEECH PROFESSION: THE FIRST FIFTY YEARS

HISTORY OF PUBLIC SPEAKING IN AMERICA

HISTORY OF PUBLIC SPEAKING IN AMERICA

Robert T. Oliver

The Pennsylvania State University

Allyn and Bacon, Inc.

Boston

first printing . . . *December, 1964*
second printing . . . *May, 1966*

PS
40°
Ø 4

LIBRARY OF CONGRESS CATALOG CARD NUMBER: 65–11628

PRINTED IN THE UNITED STATES OF AMERICA.

Dedicated to

THE PENNSYLVANIA STATE UNIVERSITY

Which Values and Fosters

The Inquiring Mind, Advancement of Learning,

and Service

By the Campus to the Community

PREFACE

No ONE can write a history of broad scope without a devout sense of obligation to the multitude of specialists who have provided the building blocks with which the general structure is erected. This debt which I owe to the careful labors of many are in part indicated in the footnotes and the Bibliography. I have not attempted, however, to spell out this indebtedness in full—for in the academic community facts and ideas are the stuff of life and they are present in abundance on every hand. He who does not feast cannot complain of the lack of opportunity.

At the same time, it would be both timorous and inexact to suggest that I have taken refuge behind the findings of industrious colleagues. My method has been to borrow widely and, I hope, wisely, but always to serve my own needs and intent. Many of those upon whose work I have drawn might feel that they themselves would give a slightly different emphasis or interpretation to the speakers and speeches and events and results. For one thing, whether one is intent upon a specific scene or upon a broad perspective makes a considerable difference in the impression that is gained. For another, each of us brings to the process of judgment his own system of values—or, if you will, his own prejudices and biases.

Aside from the enormous debt any historian owes to his predecessors and colleagues in the field, my gratitude is extended most feelingly to specific individuals who have gone far beyond the call of duty or friendship to render special assistance. To Harry Hayden Clark, Professor of American Literature of the University of Wisconsin, and to Dr. Lionel Crocker of Denison University, I am indebted for their encouragement to commence this work, some twenty five years ago. Dr. Anthony Hillbruner, of the Los Angeles State College, read the initial drafts of the first several chapters and did much to help guide the work toward its present form. My older brother, Dr. Egbert S. Oliver, Chairman of the Department of English of the Portland State College, and a specialist in the Transcendental period of American literature, patiently and generously read large portions of the early drafts, and with tact and considerateness helped to shape the direction which has been taken. Dr. Ira Brown, Professor of American History at the Pennsylvania State University, and a specialist in American religious development, graciously took time from his own busy program to read a large portion of the finished manuscript and make cogent suggestions for its improvement.

Other colleagues in my own Department have been exceedingly generous in assisting with the discovery and interpretation of source materials—notably Dr. Iline Fife, Dr. Eugene White, Dr. Carroll Arnold, and Dr. Thomas Olbricht. Dr. White, in particular, has very helpfully read and criticized the entire manuscript.

The dedication of the book to the Pennsylvania State University is intended to indicate a sincere and heartfelt appreciation for generous and understanding help of a very tangible nature. From the Central Research Fund, year after year, I have received limited but helpful sums to assist with the inevitable expenses of such an undertaking. Special provision has been made to engage the services of two excellent graduate assistants, David Jabusch and David Butt, who worked with zeal and skill at the endless task of verifying and tabulating bibliographical details. I am grateful also for the effective help of Mrs. Patricia Collier in the preparation of the index. Even more significantly, the administration of the University has consistently maintained the view that time expended in the advancement of knowledge was fully as consonant with the purposes of the institution as time devoted to more immediate duties of the classroom or office. Meanwhile, secretaries in the departmental office and staff members of the University Library have invariably acted as though their particular pleasure was to be of the utmost service.

In the writing of books, as in much else, no man is an island, entire unto himself, but each is a part of the main . . . And the headlands on every side loom impressively high.

RTO

State College, Penna.

CONTENTS

INTRODUCTION

PUBLIC SPEAKING AND HISTORY

WHEN HENRY FORD said "History is bunk!" he probably meant much the same as did a schoolgirl in one of Agatha Christie's detective novels: "Such a lot of things seem to me such rot. History, for instance. Why, it's quite different out of different books." History, as a written record, is not and cannot be a reproduction of what has happened; it can only be a record of what particular historians feel must be understood and remembered. History-as-written is a product not only of past events but also of the predilections of the historical writer. Whenever a volume of history comes to hand, the first question always is: "What message is this writer trying to convey?" History is what the historian makes of it. The readers are entitled to be told what a particular historian is trying to do. The standards which I have sought to follow in selecting and interpreting the facts presented in this history constitute a series of convictions.

The first is that what matters principally in history is what relates to the minds, the emotions, and the behavior of people. My concern is with individuals and with the reasons why and the means by which they form into groups. Carlyle with his hero-worship and Emerson with his dictum that "an institution is but the lengthened shadow of one man" no doubt pushed individualism beyond its attainable bounds. But it seems to me at least equally true that history loses sound perspective when written as though economic trends, or geographic and climatic factors, or any other kinds of blind and insensate forces, somehow have dominated and shaped human development. Whether or not man has free will may, in this context, be irrelevant. At least men organize and conduct society as *though* there is individual responsibility for choices that are made; and rewards and punishments are meted out on this basis. Besides, as human beings we are interested in human beings.

Second, it is presumed that what people do or what they reject doing is ultimately decided or at least declared by those who speak for and to the people. This is not to claim that American history has been directed in its course by a succession of persuasive speakers. On the contrary, the following chapters depict time and again the futility and sometimes the folly of much that was said. Moreover, often the speech that has principal significance is not that which diverts or directs the public will but that which senses and represents what the people believe and feel, though often but dimly and imperfectly until they hear moving words which unveil their own sentiments better than they have been able to do for themselves.

Third, I have sought as best I could to understand and think and feel my way *inside* the events and situations depicted, with the view that each deserves to be interpreted on its own terms. This means that I have tried to give a sympathetic interpretation of all the speakers and movements, *up to the point of final evaluation.* There is no need to brand the Southern slavocrats as being inhumane or insincere or unintelligent; but their tragedy was that they were attached to the wrong side of the controversy. The pursuit of financial success in the heyday of the lecture platform stimulated exciting performances of great skill; but awareness of this fact does not prevent assessment of the lecturers and their managers as caricatures of the Elder Cato's ideal of the "good man skilled in the arts of speech."

Fourth, the aim has been to apply critical standards that reflect what the speaker was trying to do—or what, in view of the taste and the problems of his period, he had to do—rather than to judge in terms of what might be suitable today. It makes little sense to evaluate Webster's orations in terms of how they might sound coming from the television set in today's living rooms. Lincoln's attitude toward racism is anachronistic for our day but not necessarily for his. Jonathan Edwards was old-fashioned even for his own time, but he was far closer to the religious sentiments of his listeners than he is to present-day readers. It is a cheap victory over our great forebears to ridicule them for not having had an enlightenment that could only derive from an understanding of conditions developed after their death.

Fifth, I have tried to avoid extravagance of praise. The few histories of oratory hitherto written (as distinguished from scholarly studies of individual orators) have been little more than uncritical encomiums. Even merited praise cloys when unrelieved; and it contributes little except to emphasize that the speaker being praised does apparently deserve a critical examination which he is not receiving.

Sixth, on the other hand, I have not sought to sensationalize this history by excessive ridicule of demagogues and platform buffoons. Every great art has its low imitators. Platform pretenders must, of course, be unmasked and on occasion (to discourage continuance of the example they set) should even be pilloried; and cleverness that masks want of substance should be distinguished from the eloquence that is rooted in deep convictions. But there is little need to dwell on the inconsequential. Normally the best criticism of the trivial is merely to brush it aside.

Seventh, while striving to avoid both adulation and ridicule, I have felt that a true history of American eloquence demands an assessment of its failures and excesses along with its accomplishments. When George Mason sought to justify American violation of the Treaty of Ghent by demanding, "If we pay the debts owing to British merchants, what were we fighting for?", it is a nice question whether he was revealing himself a demagogue or was granting to history an oblique view into the motivation of his auditory. When Benjamin Harrison, waving the "bloody shirt" in his efforts to win the governorship in Indiana, was decisively rejected by the voters, it was a heartening indication that some listeners, at least, resented the pandering by politicians to the least responsible elements in the community.

Eighth, while trying to be essentially true to the nature of each speaking situation, I have not found it practical, within the limits of space and considering the breadth of scope of this work, to delve into the kinds of details that are the proper concern of particularized studies of individuals. It is quite true that the minutiae of specific situations are very far from being insignificant. My effort, generally, has been to try to profit from the interpretations of such details that have been made by the specialists and to refer the readers to them for elaboration and verification. What is aimed for here is the sound depiction of broad movements and general characteristics.

Ninth, concerning the authenticity of the extant texts of the speeches, this has not been assumed to be the critical question for this study. Most of the available speech texts, as a matter of fact, are far from exact representations of the words spoken by the orators. But even when the printed text is verbatim, this does not mean it is an authentic reproduction of what was said. The printer had no way of capturing the gestures, or the pauses, or the facial expressions, or the vocal inflections that did so much to give the remarks a meaning that was indissolubly wedded to the moment of delivery. The lines of argument, the level of style, the kinds of illustrations used, the nature of motivation appealed to, the type of relationship assumed or represented to exist between speaker and listeners—all these are cardinal questions which may be dealt with even when the remnant texts of the speeches are no more than close paraphrases to what was said. The focus of attention in this history has been upon the totality of the speaking situation rather than a minute examination of the texts of speeches.

Finally, the effort has been made to present the history of public speaking in America as a central core around which to depict the general flow of the history itself. Readers who find certain approaches to history dull, or lifeless, or seemingly unduly technical, will, it is hoped, find in the debates and speeches which are here presented a succession of vivid dramas that will attract interest while illuminating the democratic processes by which our institutions have been built and our national ideas and ideals developed.

What is brought to the platform on great public occasions is usually important and usually controversial. Perhaps nowhere better than in a history of public speaking can there be found a depiction of the pros and cons of history, the arguments for and against, by which the crucial decisions have been reached. On occasion an idea has failed because it was not effectively presented; and sometimes a shabby solution has won support because it was upheld with persuasive skill. What mattered greatly to our ancestors (as it does to us) was that the problems confronting them could be and were freely and vigorously debated before being decided. The story of these discussions is in effect the story of our national growth into increasingly broad democratic participation. Whatever else has happened in our history, the democratization of our society has steadily advanced. And one reason is that when once the principle is admitted that issues affecting the public may be publicly discussed, the compass of the discussion always expands, and never contracts.

It is not without significance that in these United States public speaking has flourished as it has nowhere else—with the possible exception of the democratic "upper-crust" society of ancient Athens. We as a people have developed orators, have valued oratory as an art, and have listened and talked back to multitudes of speakers far more than has any other portion of the globe. Our communities are governed by the consent of the people themselves. The spirit of the Town Meeting once unloosed (like the genie that escaped from Aladdin's lamp) cannot be cabined again.

Americans, and all others who "live" democracy as well as value it, talk out their mutual concerns. There is no substitute for face-to-face confrontation. This is the principal theme of this book. *Man speaking* is the prototype American democrat. How he speaks, why, and with what results, are matters worthy of our constant concern.

⚏⚏ HISTORY OF
PUBLIC SPEAKING
IN AMERICA ⚏⚏

"The talent for effective oratory is much more common in America . . . where laws are made, controversies are settled, and proselytes are gained by it every day. . . . Crowds of listeners are continually collected in all parts of this country to hear eloquent speeches and sermons. The legislature, the court house, and the church are thronged with auditors of both sexes, attracted by that talent which was the intense study and great power of the ancient orators." Charles Jared Ingersoll, "A Discourse Concerning the Influence of America on the Mind," 1823.

* * * * * * *

"The dangers of popular oratory are always great, and unhappily ours is nearly all of this kind. Even a speaker in Congress addresses his real hearers through the reporters and the post-office. The merits of the question at issue concern him less than what he shall say about it so as not to ruin his own chance of re-election, or that of some fourth-cousin, to a tidewaitership. Few men have any great amount of gathered wisdom, still fewer of extemporary, while there are unhappily many who have a large stock of accumulated phrases, and hold their parts of speech subject to immediate draft." James Russell Lowell, in his Works, Riverside edition, Vol. V, p. 265.

GROPING TOWARD
INDEPENDENCE
1609—1765

The Seeds of Independence

THEY CAME, our earliest American ancestors, not so much seeking as escaping—from debt, from poverty, from religious persecution, from military conscription. They left homelands described by the French émigré Michel-Guillaume de Crèvecoeur, in his *Letters from an American Farmer* (1782), as "a continual scene of sore affliction or pinching penury." Here in the Atlantic Colonies, Crèvecoeur exulted, the transplanted Europeans "are melted into a new race of men . . . . The American is a new man, who acts upon new principles; he must therefore entertain new ideas, and form new opinions . . . It is in consequence of that change, that he becomes an American."[1]

The transformation was less explosive, less radical than Crèvecoeur suggests. The England that was alive with the imaginative genius of the Age of Elizabeth and the renovating zeal of the Cromwellian Reformation was not, as Crèvecoeur charged, "a vegetative mould." While settlers in America were gradually developing into individualists with a bent for independence, their relatives and friends who remained at home were undergoing a similar kind of transformation. In England the tradition of the divine right of kings died when Charles I was beheaded in 1649; the Bill of Rights was enacted in 1689; John Locke brought forth his revolutionary doctrine of human equality; in succeeding decades Lord Chatham, Edmund Burke, Charles James Fox, and others argued with eloquent courage for parliamentary rights and an end of monarchal absolutism. In France the Encyclopedists were preaching progress, and the ideas of Rousseau and Voltaire were undermining the Bourbons.

[1] Michel-Guillaume de Crèvecoeur, *Letters from an American Farmer*, London, 1782. Letter III, "What Is An American?", in Robert Spiller, *The Roots of National Culture*, New York: Macmillan, 1933, pp. 451–454.

The Declaration of Independence would seem to have had European as well as American roots.[2]

Even so, something special was happening in America. Settlers arrived as "free-born Englishmen," loyal to their sovereign, proud of their tradition, conservatively intent upon building a greater future on the foundations of a great past. Between 1609 and 1775 five or six generations succeeded one another. Children were born to whom England was only a romantic tale of far away and long ago. Taverns, churches, gristmills, farmsteads, and towns gradually filled the space from Marblehead in Massachusetts to Charleston, South Carolina. Men and women who had never seen the Old World begat children, and grandchildren, and great grandchildren, who were first of all Massachusetts men or Pennsylvanians, or Virginians, but who gradually developed into Americans. For a long time they remained Englishmen, too, but ever more remotely, more distantly, more mistily, as time and space, new settings, new customs, new needs, new opportunities, and new challenges worked their pervasive and creative effects.[3]

Before the musket shots were fired at Lexington and Concord, the American Revolution was essentially complete. John Adams, who knew it well, phrased it properly in a letter to Hezekiah Niles, on February 13, 1818: "But what do we mean by the American Revolution? Do we mean the American War? The Revolution was effected before the war commenced. The Revolution was in the minds and hearts of the people . . . . *This radical change in the principles, opinions, sentiments, and affections of the people was the real American Revolution.*"[4]

In a sense, the Revolution was talked into being—not only by the harangues of Sam Adams and Patrick Henry, but, long before, in the sermons that asserted the equality of all men in the sight of God; in the town meetings where common problems were discussed in free debate; in the colonial assemblies where delegates dared to challenge the prerogatives of Royal Governors; and in homes and taverns where families and friends conversed about problems that they themselves had to solve in their own way.

Edmund Burke, speaking in the House of Commons, was right in

[2] Cf. J. Bronowski and Bruce Mazlish, *The Western Intellectual Tradition: From Leonardo to Hegel*, New York: Harper, 1960, particularly Part II, "The Age of Reasoned Dissent: From Cromwell to Rousseau, 1630–1760," pp. 153–304; and E. J. Hobsbawm, *The Age of Revolution: Europe, 1789–1848*, London: Weidenfeld and Nicolson, 1962, particularly Chapter I, "The World in the 1780's," pp. 7–26.
[3] Cf. R. L. Bruckberger, *Image of America*, New York: Viking, 1959, particularly Chapter IV, "The Pride of Being English," pp. 29–37, and Chapter VIII, "Thomas Jefferson and Saint-Just," pp. 57–69.
[4] John Adams, *The Life and Works of John Adams*, Boston: Little, Brown, 1865, X:282.

tracing the causes of the "fierce spirit of Liberty"[5] manifested by the Colonials to their geographical distance from England; to the natural tendency of every people to seek its own welfare; to religious separatism; to the expansion of education in New England; to the determination of the Colonists to claim for themselves the political rights of free Englishmen. These were facts. Nevertheless, oratory had a great function to perform. On both sides of the Atlantic, minds and actions were shaped in part by the dominant few who proved skillful in pinpointing the issues and in dramatizing their own partial and prejudiced interpretations of events. There is truth in the observation of William Norwood Brigance that "Whether men shall pursue an immediate want or a remote one, whether they shall accept the satisfaction of a high idealistic desire or of a low material one, has always been, and so long as this planet supports human life will continue to be, dependent in part on how vividly and impellingly these alternatives are revealed to them by leaders, thinkers, writers, and speakers."[6]

One theory is that the Revolution was engendered by impersonal economic forces—that the wrath of the Colonists was aroused as their pockets were picked by the Navigation Acts, the Molasses Act, the Stamp Tax, and a whole series of other "Intolerable Acts." Countering this theory are the facts that the standard of living in the Colonies was high, was steadily rising, and was definitely superior to that in England. Colonial wage earners received more pay, for shorter hours, under more humane working conditions than did English workers. The public debt in England amounted, in 1765, to eighteen pounds per capita, in the Colonies to only eighteen shillings.[7] Americans did not rebel because of poverty.

Another theory is that political rather than economic injustice underlay the rebellion. *Taxation without representation*, however, was a wrong suffered in the unfranchised manufacturing cities of England, such as Birmingham and Manchester, as truly as in the Colonies. On most local and on many Colony-wide problems the Colonials enjoyed more self-government than did the citizenry of their European homelands. This is not to deny that the Lords of Trade sought to exploit the Colonies through crassly self-interested mercantile policies; nor that George III and his Tory advisers had little concern for the rights of the

[5] Edmund Burke, *The Works of Edmund Burke*, New York: Harper, 1859, I:228.
[6] William Norwood Brigance, "Can We Redefine the James Winans Theory of Persuasion?" *Quarterly Journal of Speech*, XXI (Feb., 1935):24.
[7] Cf. J. Franklin Jameson, *The American Revolution Considered as a Social Movement*, Boston: Beacon Press, 1956, based on his 1925 lectures, particularly Chapter III, "Industry and Commerce," pp. 47–75; and Clinton Rossiter, *The First American Revolution*, New York: Harcourt, Brace, Harvest Books, 1956, particularly Chapter II, "Soil, Sea, and Forest: The Economy of the Colonies," pp. 29–64.

Americans. Nevertheless, the growing dissatisfaction with England that spread through the Atlantic seaboard was less a matter of economics or of politics than of the spirit. Protest and eventual revolt did not arise inevitably. They were aroused by dissatisfied individuals.[8]

As Adam Smith shrewdly pointed out in his *Wealth of Nations* (1776): "The leading men of America, like those of other countries, desire to preserve their own importance."[9] Thomas Jefferson, in his *Summary View of the Rights of British America* (1774), asserted that Americans ought not to be ruled by Britons when "every individual of [the Colonies] is equal to them in virtue, in understanding, and in bodily strength."[10] Benjamin Franklin, in his *Rules by Which a Great Empire May be Reduced to a Small One* (1773), chiefly charged the Royal Governors with being "ignorant, wrong headed, and insolent."[11] Governor Hutchinson, in his royalist history of Massachusetts, reversed the complaint, saying that the Colonials refused to "doff their hats to their betters."

This was the long road that was travelled from Jamestown to Bunker Hill. Somehow, as Crèvecoeur said, Americans became "a new race of men." But the transformation did not just happen; it was brought about. How it was caused is our present theme.

The Beginnings of Self-Government

THE FIRST charter of Virginia, granted by King James I on April 10, 1606, provided that "each of the said Colonies shall have a Council." And the second charter, drawn three years later, guaranteed that all emigrants to Virginia and all their descendents "shall Have and Enjoy all Liberties, Franchizes, and Immunities of Free Denizens and natural Subjects." In accordance with these provisions, the first representative government in America was convened as the Assembly of Virginia on July 30, 1619, and consisted of "two Burgesses out of every Town, Hundred, or other particular Plantation, to be respectively chosen by the

---

[8] For a detailed development of this theme cf. George V. Bohman, "The Colonial Period," in W. N. Brigance, editor, *The History and Criticism of American Public Address*, New York: McGraw-Hill, 1943, I:3–54.
[9] Adam Smith, *An Inquiry into the Nature and Causes of the Wealth of Nations*, ed. Edwin Cannan, New York: Modern Library, 1937, p. 586; cf. also pp. 556 and 581–582.
[10] Thomas Jefferson, *The Complete Jefferson*, ed. Saul K. Padover, New York: Duell, Sloan and Pearce, 1943, p. 11.
[11] Benjamin Franklin, "Rules By Which a Great Empire May Be Reduced to a Small One," in Spiller, *op. cit.*, p. 230.

Inhabitants, . . . wherein . . . all Matter shall be decided, determined, and ordered, by the greater Part of the Voices then present; reserving to the Governor always a Negative Voice."[1]

The priority in self-government, then, clearly belongs to the South. The twenty members of the First House of Burgesses were elected by vote of every male seventeen years of age or older. In 1658, since slaves and bondmen were by then becoming numerous, the suffrage was changed to include only adult freemen—still without property or religious restrictions. Even so, democracy in Virginia was more a form than a fact. The plantation system, the slave labor that forced the poor whites out into sub-marginal communities, the lack of a public school system, and domination by a few wealthy families, encouraged an assertive individualism by the few but discouraged representative democracy. The many could vote but only the few were eligible for election.

A Southern scholar, W. J. Cash, in *The Mind of the South*, depicted the region as "beset by the specters of defeat, of shame, of guilt,"[2] as its tobacco, rice, indigo, and cotton culture made inevitable a slavocracy which its proponents very well understood to be an archaic evil. Under such circumstances, wrote Cash, "rhetoric flourished here far beyond even its American average." Forced to rationalize a system that exploited the Negroes and defrauded the majority of the whites, the Southern leader, Cash believed, developed a "remarkable tendency to seize on lovely words, to roll them in his throat, to heap them in redundant profusion one upon another until meaning vanishes and there is nothing left but the sweet, cancerous drunkenness of sound, nothing but the play of primitive rhythm upon the secret springs of emotion."

There were other significant factors restricting the early growth of democracy in the South. In the early years, perhaps the most crucial fact was that the men who founded Virginia came as adventurers rather than as settlers. They brought no women; they established no real homes. Their aim was to find gold and spices, to discover the Northwest Passage, and to commence profitable enterprises that would insure an income for themselves and their families back in England. As another factor of consequence, those who were religious at all belonged chiefly to the Established Church, in which ritual was more important than

---

[1] The first and second charters and the Ordinance for Virginia are in Henry Steele Commager, editor, *Documents of American History*, New York: Crofts, 1946, Two Vols. in one, I:8–14.

[2] W. J. Cash, *The Mind of the South*, New York: Doubleday Anchor Book, 1954, pp. 63, 90. For a balanced pro and con view, see Waldo W. Braden, "Southern Oratory Reconsidered: A Search for an Image," *Southern Speech Journal*, XXIX (Summer, 1964):303–315.

preaching.[3] Instead of a free and compulsory school system, education was largely in the hands of tutors hired by plantation owners for their own children. Most of the settlers came as indentured servants or as bondsmen from debtors' prisons. The system did not encourage a town meeting communal spirit of joint decision-making.

New England democracy commenced with the compact drawn on the deck of the *Mayflower*, on November 11, 1620. Since the Pilgrims were not under the jurisdiction of the Virginia Company, they had no instrument of government and therefore agreed to "covenant and combine ourselves together into a civil Body Politick, for our better Ordering and Preservation." Nine years later Charles I chartered the Massachusetts Bay Colony, providing that "once every Moneth, or oftener at their Pleasures" the settlers should "assemble and houlde and keepe a Courte or Assemblie of themselves, for the better ordering and directing of their Affaires."[4]

Unlike the Virginia adventurers, the immigrants into Massachusetts arrived as complete families, searching for a place to build homes. They came as free men, with their own destinies to carve. And because the land was stony and the climate inhospitable, the only farming that proved to be practical was that of small plots, each cultivated by its owner. This kind of land tenure led to the formation of towns; and the clustering together of families of equals encouraged the building of schools. Moreover, their religion emphasized dissent and thereby required the preaching of lengthy sermons that dealt with intellectual reasons for their beliefs. Finally, living closely together as they were, they found themselves confronted with many local problems which could best be solved by discussion in regular town meetings. All these factors combined to make New England the real founder of both our democracy and the spirit of independence.

The New Englanders came as proud people, stiffly self-assertive. "God hath sifted a nation," declared one of their early preachers, William Stoughton, "that he might send choice grain into this wilderness."[5] It was a sentiment that was to be repeated often in the years and the centuries ahead. These Americans, like the Israelites of old, calmly assumed that they were God's own anointed people. But with the special grace of God to bless them, there came also special responsibilities. "Wee shall be as a Citty upon a Hill," warned John Winthrop, in a

[3] Cf. Rossiter, *op. cit.*, Chapter III, "The Dissidence of Dissent: Religion in the Colonies," pp. 65–99, particularly pp. 73–74; and Jameson, *op. cit.*, Chapter IV, "Thought and Feeling," pp. 74–100.
[4] Commager, *op. cit.*, I:15–16.
[5] William Stoughton, "New England's True Interests," a sermon in Boston, April 29, 1668, in *Works of William Stoughton*, Cambridge: S. Green and M. Johnson, 1670.

sermon he preached aboard the *Arabella*, during its journey to Boston, in the spring of 1630. "The eies of all people are upon us; so that if wee shall deale falsely with our god in his workes wee have undertaken and soe cause him to withdraw his present help from us, wee shall be made a story and a by-word through the world."[6] The relentless Puritan conscience, a heavier task-master than any government, was early born.

It was not true, however, that religion was the sole force dominating the life of early New England. "New England is originally a Plantation of Religion, not a Plantation of Trade," the Reverend John Higginson felt constrained to remind his congregation, in an election sermon preached in 1663.[7] When a Boston preacher took one of his "dogmatical" sermons to a meetinghouse in Marblehead, he was startled to have his solemn review of their godly duties interrupted by an impatient cry from the assembly, "Sir, you are mistaken . . . ; our main end was to catch fish."[8] Within twenty years after the landing at Plymouth Rock, Thomas Lechford was complaining that "three parts of the people of the Country remain out of the Church."[9]

By and large, the New England settlers were a disputatious lot. They were Separatists and Independents, Calvinists and Baptists, Quakers, Seekers, and Congregationalists. On the sanctity of the Scriptures they were agreed; but how God's words were to be interpreted was a subject of continual dispute. The communities that rapidly spread out from Boston Bay were shaken by "hellish revilling," as Cotton Mather sorrowfully recorded in his *Magnalia Christi Americana*. Even the Quakers, who arrived in New England with their "poison of error" in 1656, were accused by Mather of freely using such epithets as: "thou fiery fighter and greenheaded trumpeter; thou hedgehog and grinning dog; thou bastard that tumbled out of the mouth of the Babilonish bawd; thou mole; thou tinker; thou lizard; thou bell of no metal, but the tone of a kettle; thou wheelbarrow; thou whirlpool; thou whirligig. O thou firebrand; thou adder and scorpion; thou louse; thou cow-dung; thou mooncalf; thou ragged tatterdemalion; thou Judas; thou livest in philosophy, and logick, which are of the devil."[10]

People of this sort required stern government, and the churchmen set

---

[6] John Winthrop, sermon aboard the *Arabella*, 1630, *Massachusetts Historical Collection*, 3rd Series, VII:31–48; abstracted in R. C. Winthrop, *Life and Letters of John Winthrop*, Boston: Ticknor and Fields, 1866, p. 19.
[7] John Higginson, "The Cause of God and His People in New England," May 27, 1663, pamphlet publication, Cambridge: S. Green, 1663.
[8] Cotton Mather, sermon, July 12, 1713; cf. *Diary of Cotton Mather*, New York: Frederick Unger, 1957, II:206, 221.
[9] Thomas Lechford, *Plain Dealing*, cited by J. B. Felt in *Ecclesiastical History of New England*, Boston: Congressional Library Association, 1855–62, II:3.
[10] Cotton Mather, *Magnalia Christi Americana*, Hartford: Silas Andrus and Son, 1855, II:531.

about providing it for them. Gradually they hammered out a theocratic form of government that placed the ruling power firmly in the hands of the ministers. Eleven years after the *Mayflower* landed, the Bay Colony decided to limit the ballot to church members. This was not because everyone belonged to the church, but, rather, because three-fourths of the people did not. The danger was becoming acute that the godly nature of the new settlements might be lost. Religious dissension was severely punished precisely because it was becoming so widespread as to be dangerous. In 1631 one Philip Ratliffe was sentenced to "be whipped, have his ears cut of, fyned 40 shillings and banished" for "uttering malitious & scandalous speeches against the government & the church of Salem."[11] In 1635 church attendance was made compulsory; and the next year it was ordained that no new church could be established without the approval of the magistrates.

What was happening, with profound significance in the development of the American dream, was a strange intermingling of liberalism and conservatism. On the one hand the people were being taught that their first duty no longer was to the absolutist power centered in faraway England. On the other hand their nascent liberties were being tightly restrained by the rising power of their own communal church.

With great skill the preachers worked out and implanted a theocratic form of government that made the pulpit the main source of authority. Few disagreed with John Winthrop's judgment that "Democritie is, among most Civill nations accounted the meanest & worst of all forms of Governm't."[12] Few quarrelled with John Cotton's conclusion that "Democracy, I do not conceyve that ever God did ordeyne as fit government eyther for church or commonwealth."[13] The constitution by which God meant for men to be ruled was the Bible. Somewhere in its pages was to be found an answer for every problem, a rule for all conduct. But its meaning had to be interpreted—and this could only be by God's elect, the ordained. As Thomas Hutchinson noted in his *History of Massachusetts Bay Colony*, "it be a divine truth, that none are to be trusted with public permanent authority but godly men."[14]

For a hundred and fifty years the leaders of colonial New England were preachers. In all our history no other vocational group has ever equalled the record of dominance achieved by the Massachusetts pulpiteers. Their task was never easy, for what they asked was surrender by

[11] Ratliffe Trial, June 14, 1631, *Records of the Governor and Company of the Massachusetts Bay Colony in New England*, N. B. Shurtleff, editor, Boston: William White, 1853, I:88.
[12] Winthrop, *Life and Letters*, op. cit., II:430.
[13] John Cotton, "Letter to Lord Say and Sele," T. Hutchinson, *History of Massachusetts Bay Colony*, Cambridge: Harvard University Press, 1936, I:497.
[14] *Ibid.*, Appendix 2.

the whole community to their rule. Their victory at no time was complete. Like other types of leaders in later periods—plantation owners, politicians, generals, industrialists, businessmen—they found that entire control of the whole society was impossible to achieve. Often the greatest of the preachers were near despair as they viewed the enormity of the obstacles of worldliness and lust that stood between them and the heavenly city of their goal. As Cotton Mather dolefully complained, "God indeed has the *Devil* in a *Chain*, but has horribly lengthened out the *Chain*."[15] Yet despite discouragements they persisted. And what they achieved was notable.

The declaration of the *Mayflower* Compact that sovereignty rested in the whole adult male population was quickly amended. John Cotton revised the rule to read "church members": for "none should be Electors . . . except such as were *visible subjects* of our Lord, Jesus Christ, personally *confederated* in our churches."[16] After property qualifications were also added, fully ninety-five percent of New Englanders in the Theocratic period were disenfranchised. But this was in full accord with the only history they knew. Every generation is limited by its own heritage of tradition. Who could doubt the pronouncement of John Winthrop that among the "body of the people . . . the best part is always the least, & of that best part the wiser part is always the lesser." At least they had made the advance over their brethren in England that their rulers should be "chosen of God," rather than be a hereditary aristocracy.[17]

The Role of the Preachers

THE INFLUENCE of preachers in early New England is understandable only in terms of problems that confronted them in the kind of community in which they spoke. To the Puritans the preacher was literally a *teacher*. The sermon was the most typical and influential of the early American culture-shaping institutions. The content of the sermons was theological, yet it was theology with an immediately practical application. The Word of God was for the people their guide, constitution, and rule-book for everyday life, as well as their map to salvation. In most churches there were two sermons every Sunday and another on Thurs-

[15] Cotton Mather, *Wonders of the Invisible World*, Boston: John Dunton, 1693, p. 63.
[17] John Winthrop, *Journal*, Hartford: Elisha Babcock, 1790, II:428.
[16] C. Mather, *Magnalia, op. cit.*, I:266.

day morning or afternoon. Additional sermons were preached for hangings, elections, the muster of militiamen, fast days, Thanksgiving, and on any and all special occasions. In the absence of newspapers, "the publick ministry of the word" was the chief means of explaining events and of exhorting the people to do their full duty as citizens and as children of God. It is noteworthy that the church buildings were also used for town meetings. It is even more notable that there were no clear distinctions between secular and religious topics or attitudes. Only later did the notion emerge that there is one ethic for church, another for business. Under the Theocracy, church and state were one.

By 1775 there were in the thirteen Colonies 3105 churches serving a population of 2.5 million.[1] Congregations varied in size from a few listeners to the two thousand who could crowd into Boston's South Church.[2] The sermons commonly ran for an hour, though the minister sometimes turned the hourglass over to "take another glass." Normally the sermons were written out, or based on full notes, and delivered from partial or complete memorization. Many, however, were completely extemporaneous. The popularity of the sermons is indicated by the fact that during the colonial period more than two thousand of them were published.[3] Their composition was guided chiefly by William Perkins's *Art of Prophecying*, an English homiletic rhetoric found on most New England booklists. The generality of Puritan sermons consisted of three parts, like a lawyer's brief: first the "doctrine," which the preacher "found" when he "opened" the text; then the "reasons," which were arguments demonstrating the truth of the doctrine; finally, the "uses," which were practical applications of the doctrine to the daily lives of the parishioners.

The length of the sermon presented special problems because of the physical discomfort suffered by the listeners. For many years, no church had either artificial light or any method of heating. Despite the icy blasts of winter, which easily penetrated the thin walls and the bare boards laid upon the ground, even foot-warmers were frowned upon during the early decades. Fireplaces were not admitted to the sanctuary until well into the eighteenth century. The preacher could keep himself warm with the ardor of his feeling and the physical activity of his speaking. But he had to warm his auditors with vivid exhortation. Since the taste of the Puritans demanded a plain style, liveliness was achieved primarily by sensational descriptions of hellfire for those not saved by predestined salvation, and, secondly, by the use of homely illustrations.

[1] Jameson, *op. cit.*, p. 85.
[2] Bohman, *op. cit.*, I:8.
[3] *Ibid.*, I:5.

Thomas Hooker, for example, compared the human body in process of resurrection to an onion, with the earthly residues being peeled off in successive layers until only the soul is left. Cotton Mather was fond of the image of the devil bound in God's chains, from which he was forever struggling to break free, and which could be kept tight only through the faith of true believers.[4] Repetition was a frequent device to make sure no one missed the point through nursing his cold hands. And to aid further in clarity, the framework of the ideas was indicated by a succession of *firstlies, secondlies,* and so on. The style was usually not distinguished, but it was vivid, personalized, and clear. Each listener was helped to feel, "This is for me."

The congregations took the preaching seriously,[5] for theology was as important to them as business and politics are to us. Moreover, the church was in itself the first school of the new settlers. Children, as well as adults, were expected to learn from the sermons how to think clearly and soundly, as well as what to believe. Families would discuss at the dinner table the sermon they had just heard; and parents often would ask their children to summarize and illustrate further the ideas the minister had expressed. The educational values of increasing perception in listening, of thinking clearly, of developing retentive memories, and of attaining practice in oral reporting, should not be discounted. There was much gained in the colonial churches besides religious reassurance.

Nevertheless, the definitive roles of the church were to provide spiritual consolation and to interpret theological doctrines.[6] Heaven and Hell were to the Puritans real places and inescapable final destinations. God and the devil were an intimate part of their thoughts and more important to their welfare than were their own family members. Preaching was first and foremost a guide to their eternal well-being and, secondly, a prescription for fulfilling their day-by-day duties. Through the sermons they heard, discussed, and read, supplemented by their morning, mealtime, and evening prayers at home, the devout colonials found solace for their all-too-prevalent troubles, strength for confronting their

[4] Vernon Louis Parrington, *Main Currents of American Thought*, New York: Harcourt, Brace, 1927, 1930, III Vols., I:114, 116. Nathaniel Ward, in *The Simple Cobbler of Aggawam*, London: J. Dever and R. Ibbitsen, 1647, wrote: "It seems it is a fashion with you to sugar your papers with Carnation phrases, and spangle your speeches with new quodled words." He admitted this made for "a pleasing eloquence" but warned that it gave "bangled ears" to listeners. *Ibid.,* I:77.
[5] Perry G. Miller, *New England Mind in the Seventeenth Century*, New York: Macmillan, 1939; and Herbert W. Schneider, *The Puritan Mind*, New York: Holt, 1930.
[6] The idea that the preachers incited political rebellion was popularized by Alice Baldwin, *New England Clergy and the Revolution*, Durham: University of North Carolina Press, 1931; this view, however, has been questioned by Harry P. Kerr, "The Character of Political Sermons Preached at the Time of the American Revolution," unpublished Ph.D. thesis, Cornell University, 1962.

trials, and reassurance in their faith. The devout were always the minority; but even the unchurched majority respected the learning of the clergy, generally feared hellfire, and sought to maintain good relations with the godly. The church was, consequently, not only the meeting place and center of social life but also the active agent of the divine will, and colonial preachers were the chief agents of power and influence.

With few exceptions, the preachers were also men of intellect, integrity, dedication, and humane sympathy. In view of the nature of their role, it was inevitable that many of them were proud; more than a few were vain; and they generally tended to be dictatorial. In part this was because their own superiority was manifest even to themselves. In part it was also because the whole community was organized around them and was largely subject to their direct or indirect influence. Beyond this, several times a week they experienced the heady stimulation of standing before packed congregations to tell them, in God's name, what and how to think and how to behave. Few significant matters of life and death were not brought to them for judgment. Few public occasions ever occurred in which they were not the center of attention.

The First Generation of Preachers

THE FIRST decade after the chartering of Massachusetts Bay Colony in 1629 was intellectually turbulent. There was, perhaps, an excess of leadership. Such strong minds and spirits as John Winthrop (1588–1649), John Cotton (1585–1652), Roger Williams (1603?–1683), Anne Hutchinson (1591–1643), and Thomas Hooker (1586–1647), could not escape contention, especially in a society just forming and dependent upon leadership to establish its traditions. Their lives became far too closely intertwined to be dealt with separately, but we shall examine the several strands.

Dr. John Cotton had already won fame in London as the scholarly pastor of St. Botolph Church when, at the age of forty six, he moved to Massachusetts Bay because he valued a free mind in a crude wilderness more than bodily comforts with intellectual restraints. However, the minds he encountered in contentious Boston were too free. He had reached his own conclusions by hard study; and in the wilderness of New England it irritated him to be questioned and even contradicted by uneducated farmers. Cotton Mather called him "A most *universal* scholar, a living system of the liberal arts, and a walking library.[1] The devout opined that "God would not allow Mr. Cotton to err."[2] John Cotton began to believe it himself, and concluded that in this raw land a society should be constructed based on rule by the divines.

"A most excellent casuist," as his grandson wrote of him, he was kindly and tolerant in personal affairs, profoundly learned, a scholar who spent twelve hours daily with his books, and a preacher of such power that his listeners likened him to a prophet of ancient Israel. Yet, for all the sweetness of his temper, he distrusted the people and decided upon Theocracy as the best form of government. "It is better," he declared, "that the commonwealth be fashioned to the setting forth of God's house, which is his church: than to accommodate the church frame to the civill state."[3] The question in his mind was simple: "If the people be governors, who shall be governed?" In sermons and in town meetings, he argued for basic principles that gave ministers control of the state. First, ministerial salaries should be paid from taxation. Next, no one but church members should be allowed to vote for civil officers. Third, as Scripture teaches, the parishioners must yield their own judgment to that of their chosen ministers. Finally, once a preacher was named to a pulpit, he could not be removed, for he became not an agent of his people but a vice-regent of God. This was the pattern of Theocracy established by John Cotton, and it was fully acceptable to John Winthrop, who became the first Governor of Massachusetts Bay Colony.

The first truly notable speech on the North American continent was made by Winthrop in 1635; but in order to assess its significance we shall have to examine individuals and conditions that were already, by then, threatening the stability of the Theocracy John Cotton had advocated.

Roger Williams shocked Boston, upon his arrival in 1631, first by refusing the proferred post of teacher in the church and, second, by asserting that "God requireth not a uniformity of religion."[4] During the next four years he became increasingly troublesome as a critic of the theocratic tenets. Persecutions for heresy he denounced as "high blasphemy." Then, striking directly at the privileges monopolized by church members, he attacked the "Machiavellism" which "makes religion but a cloak or a stalking horse to policy and private ends."[5] For four years the orthodox struggled to bring him into conformity, then ordered his banishment. In midwinter, 1635, he fled to Providence Bay, in Rhode Island,

[1] C. Mather, *Magnalia*, *op. cit.*, I:273.
[2] Parrington, *op. cit.*, I:28.
[3] John Cotton, *op. cit.*, I:497.
[4] Roger Williams, *The Works of Roger Williams*, edited by members of the Narragansett Club, Providence, 1867, III:3.
[5] *Ibid.*, III:15–240.

where he established a new Colony in which "Opinionists" of every sort were welcomed. Williams founded the Baptist Church in America, then left it to become a "Seeker." He set up a town-meeting democracy in which he often found himself outvoted. Before his death Rhode Island outlawed trials for witchcraft and forbade imprisonment for debt. Providence became a center of dissention, smuggling, piracy, and all manner of equalitarian virtues and vices. The name of Roger Williams was a byword in Massachusetts; some admired, most condemned.

Mistress Anne Hutchinson was even more troublesome to Boston Bay. She followed John Cotton to America because she could not bear to be separated from the sweetness of his discourse. But she was a woman of strong will who preferred talking to listening. Her first sin was to argue that God's will could be known to every individual through direct revelation. Then she even more directly challenged the rule of the clergy by holding Wednesday evening meetings in her home, in which she taught that preachers are not necessary since "God's sheep know his voice."[6] She taught also that regenerated Christians could do no wrong, which some who thronged to her meetings interpreted as meaning that they were free to do whatever they wished. The number of her followers increased so greatly that by 1634 she was able to defeat Winthrop's bid for re-election to the Governorship. Moreover, she tried, though without success, to oust the Reverend John Wilson from the pulpit of Boston Church, so that her brother-in-law John Wheelright could be appointed to the position.

The rebelliousness stirred by Williams and Hutchinson aroused the more than one hundred Bay area alumni of English universities to decide to found a college in which their own children could be educated. If the clergy were to be the power in the community, they wanted their own sons to become preachers. Thus were drawn the plans that, in 1636, culminated in the founding of Harvard College, which in turn became a growing threat to the monopoly of power exercised by the ruling clique.

This was the situation in which John Winthrop, in 1635, after being defeated for re-election as Governor, was haled into court by the heretical followers of Roger Williams and Anne Hutchinson, charged with illegal arbitrariness in his rule. The evidence was heard in a crowded courtroom, while Winthrop sat grimly silent, refusing to speak in his own defense. It was only after the judges brought in a verdict of innocence that Winthrop arose and delivered his "little speech on liberty," which he afterwards transcribed from memory into his *Journal*.

"There is a twofold liberty," he said with cold dignity. ". . . The first is common to man with beasts and other creatures. By this, man, as he

6 Hutchinson, History, *op. cit.*, II:482–520.

stands in relation to man simply, hath liberty to do what he lists; it is a liberty to evil as well as to good. This liberty," he went on (and he must have glared stonily at his tormenters), "is incompatible and inconsistent with authority. The exercise and maintaining of this liberty makes men grow more evil, and in time to be worse than brute beasts . . . This is the great enemy of truth and peace . . . which all the ordinances of God are bent against, to restrain and subdue it." In this opening Winthrop was simply stating a traditional view that had been largely unquestioned for centuries—and which was symbolized even after the American Revolution in the famous declaration ascribed to Alexander Hamilton, that "The people, Sir, are a great beast." To Winthrop and also to most of his listeners the principle that the people could not be allowed to do as they wished without great harm to themselves was simply axiomatic. It was the challenge to this view by the Williams-Hutchinson clique that was eccentric. Winthrop went on:

"The other kind of liberty I call civil or federal; and it may also be termed moral, in reference to the covenant between God and man, in moral law, and the political covenants and constitutions amongst men themselves. This liberty is the proper end and object of authority, and cannot subsist without it; and it is a liberty to that only which is good, just, and honest."

Then he made his point:

> If you stand for your natural corrupt liberties, and will do that which is good in your own eyes, you will not endure the least weight of authority, but will murmur and oppose, and be always striving to shake off that yoke; and if you will be satisfied to enjoy such civil and lawful liberties, such as Christ allows you, then you will quietly and cheerfully submit unto that authority which is set over you, in all the administrations of it, for your own good.[7]

In a sense, Winthrop was arguing for government itself, against nihilism. Laws, he was saying, must be obeyed even when they are disapproved. More significant, however, was the fact that he derived the source of authority from the ordinances of Christ as interpreted by the ordained ministers. As for the result of the trial, Mrs. Hutchinson, like Williams, was expelled from the Colony and followed him to Providence. Winthrop was three times afterwards re-elected to the Governorship, in which post he died in 1649. The Theocracy retained its supremacy, but not without additional troubles.

[7] John Winthrop, *The History of New England from 1630 to 1649*, edited by James Savage, Boston: Little, Brown, 1853, II:279–282; reprinted in Marvin Meyers, Alexander Kern, and John G. Cawelti, editors, *Sources of the American Republic*, Chicago: Scott, Foresman, n. d., I:38–39.

Thomas Hooker, who came to Boston Bay in 1633 because his independence was causing him difficulty in England, was an even abler adversary than the Theocrats had yet encountered. Archbishop Laud, the stoutest defender of the Stuart principle of monarchal absolutism, became alarmed when Hooker "blew the bellows of his sedition" so effectively that he became a center of revolutionary liberalism. As Laud was informed in a special report on Hooker in 1629: "His genius will still haunte all ye pulpits in ye country, where any of his scholars may be admitted to preach." Then the report, which was written by one of Laud's many undercover agents, continued: "I have lived in Essex to see many changes, and have seene the people idolizing many new ministers and lecturers, but this man surpasses them all for learning and some other considerable partes and . . . gains more and far greater followers than all before him."[8] Success proved for Hooker, as it has for many others, more costly than mediocrity; to avoid constant harassment by Laud, he was forced to leave.

In the Bay Colony, Hooker proved as troublesome to the Theocracy as he had been back home to King Charles; for, "After Mr. Hooker's coming over, it was observed that many of the freemen grew to be very jealous of their liberties."[9] Unlike the Providence rebels, Hooker did not attack orthodoxy. Instead, he took the political position that the majority had the right to govern themselves. Striking directly at Winthrop's view that "the lesser is always the wiser," he declared that "in matters of greater importance, the most suitable to rule and the most safe is a general counsel chosen by all."[10] This was a blow struck against the most essential link in the chain of logic by which John Cotton had established the Theocracy: a denial that voting should be restricted to members of the church.

For five years Hooker nurtured his ideas of equalitarianism with quiet propriety, demonstrating his respect for individualism through careful attention to his pastoral work rather than in inflammatory sermons. It was an article of faith with him that "Time, Place, Outward Decency and Comeliness"[11] were to be carefully observed in all public affairs. Then, on May 31, 1638, he was invited to deliver a sermon before the General Court. In a crowded room in which expectancy and simmering antagonisms created tensions among the listeners, and confronting all the principal leaders of the Theocracy, Hooker chose as his text *Deuteronomy* i:13: "The Lord hath promised to take away the veil from all

[8] George Leon Walker, *Thomas Hooker: Preacher, Founder, Democrat*, New York: Dodd, Mead, 1891, p. 46.
[9] Parrington, *op. cit.*, I:57.
[10] R. C. Winthrop, *op. cit.*, II:237.
[11] Parrington, *op. cit.*, I:57.

faces." The text may be ambiguous, but Hooker's interpretation of it was not. "The foundation of authority," he declared, "is laid, firstly, in the free consent of the people." Accordingly, "The choice of public magistrates belongs to the people by God's own allowance." Furthermore, the right of election carries with it the right "to set bounds and limitations upon the power and place unto which they call them."[12] The full text of the sermon was not preserved and the remaining notes reveal little more than the main stream of the ideas. Yet even this is enough to indicate the effect it must have had upon its listeners.

Conciliatory as he always was, Hooker was content to state his ideas constructively, rather than to launch an attack against the Theocrats for their renunciation of popular sovereignty. He might have remained in Boston to battle Cotton and Winthrop for control of the Colony. Instead, he took his congregation with him to the site of Hartford, Connecticut, where, on January 14, 1639, he defined his political theories in a set of Fundamental Orders which have been called the first written constitution in America.

What Hooker advocated was not what we today would call democracy. "The government of the Church in regard to the body of the people," he explained, "is Democraticall; in regard to the Elders Aristocraticall; in regard to Christ, Monarchicall."[13] The diction is strange to us, but it was clear to his associates. What Hooker advocated was delegated or representative government. The Elders, selected by the people, would govern the church in accordance with their own understanding of Scriptures; but their power was limited by the fact that they were always subject to re-election.

This was a major assault against the Cotton-Winthrop foundation of the Theocracy. By intimating that even uneducated people could understand God's meaning in the Scriptures, Hooker's views invited argumentation. As the years passed, the individual interpretations of Scripture hardened into the creeds and doctrines of the multiplying denominations. Meantime, during the seventeenth and eighteenth centuries, the intellectual disputation began to deal less with man's preparation for eternity than with adjustments needed during this temporal life. The secularization of the church did not proceed, however, without considerable resistance. A notable family of preachers who for four generations impressed their personalities upon the whole community was the Mather dynasty. They repay study for their own sake and also as an illustration of how preaching helped to shape the character of colonial New England.

12 *Ibid.*, I:59.
13 *Ibid.*, I:60.

📖 The Mather Dynasty

RICHARD MATHER (1596–1669), the first of the dynasty in America, came over in his fortieth year after a career of high success as student, teacher, and preacher in England. With typical Mather thoroughness, he drew up in his diary a long list of reasons for emigrating: chiefly, to be able to preach and practice his own religion without interference. Upon the advice of John Cotton and Thomas Hooker he accepted a call to the dormant church at Dorchester, only a mile from the heart of Boston.[1] Most of the congregation had followed Hooker to Connecticut, and a new beginning was required. Richard Mather put tremendous energy into his sermons, speaking with the powerful voice and great forcefulness which he bequeathed to his descendents. His learning was great, but he wore it lightly. He did not need (though he doubtless received) the advice of Dr. Cotton against using "swelling words," which make preachers "blubber-lipt." Like Cotton, he felt the good preacher to be one who "lets fly poynt blanck." In the opinion of his son Increase, his "way of Preaching . . . was plain, aiming to shoot his Arrows not over his peoples heads, but into their Hearts and Consciences." Above all, "The Lord gave him an excellent faculty in making abstruse things plain."[2]

Despite these rhetorical abilities, Richard Mather is not remembered as a great speaker. He deserves a place in a history of oratory primarily because of two major contributions toward changing the conditions affecting the relations of preachers and their congregations. The first of these was his principal authorship of *A Platform of Church Discipline*, commonly known as "the Cambridge Platform," which was adopted by the Synod of 1649. This platform, like his second contribution, the advocacy of "the Half-Way Covenant," had the primary effect of liberalizing the means of attaining to church membership.[3]

In keeping with the Theocracy, the Cambridge Platform reiterated that only church members might vote; that these members should in effect yield their right of judgment to their chosen minister; and that admission to church membership must be carefully regulated. However, the Platform provided that a candidate for church membership might plead his cause before the Elders of the Church, and afterwards, if they

[1] Increase Mather, *The Life and Death of Mr. Richard Mather*, in *Collections* of the Dorchester Antiquarian and Historical Society, Boston, 1850, III:74.
[2] *Ibid.*, III:75, 81–83, 85.
[3] Schneider, *op. cit.*, pp. 19–24 and *passim*. Cf. also *Papers of the American Society of Church History*, New York: Christian Literature Co., 1894, Vol. V.

agreed, would make "a solemne speech" to the congregation. This process by itself might not have opened the doors to wider membership: indeed, the necessity it imposed of being skillful in speaking might have reduced the numbers. But Richard Mather devised the concept of the "half-way covenant," by which a person who did not wholly believe the orthodoxies might be admitted on the basis of partial conviction, on the theory that through being a member the remainder of the doctrine would gradually become acceptable to him.

These achievements would have been impossible had not this first Mather been a man not only of indomitable will and strong intellect but also of warm human sympathies. His manner was conciliatory and he alone, of the four generations of the dynasty, concluded his ministry without making numerous and powerful enemies. His grandson, Cotton Mather, wrote of him in the *Magnalia Christi Americana* that "His voice was loud and big, and uttered with a deliberate vehemency, it procured unto his ministry an awful and very taking majesty; nevertheless, the substantial and rational matter delivered by him, caused his ministry to take yet more."[4] The judgment was probably sound; but, correct or not, it is significant as indicating that to the Mathers both the "manner" and the "matter" of their speaking were important.

The fifth son of Richard Mather was Increase (1638–1723), named in honor of the rapid growth of New England. This son soon became the favorite of his mother, and both parents labored hard to help him develop all his abilities. As a child Increase loved the fields better than his books, though he was well versed in Greek and Latin when he entered Harvard at the age of twelve. Upon his graduation six years later, he preached in his father's church so effectively that "The whole Auditory were greatly Affected with the *Light and Flame*, in which the Rare Youth Appear'd unto them."[5] Increase then went to Dublin, where, through "exercises in Disputations, Orations, &c," he earned his Master's degree. He accepted a call to a church on the island of Guernsey, where he expected to spend the remainder of his life. But after the Restoration he returned to Boston, where, in 1664, he became the preacher of the Second Church in Boston.

His fame as a preacher spread, as he was invited to speak in various pulpits. His appearance—tall, with finely chiselled features, a long straight nose, and expressive hands with slender fingers—was so striking that a contemporary observed: "It is a very Edifying Thing, only to see him in our Public Assemblies; His very Countenance carried the Force

---

[4] Cotton Mather, *Magnalia*, op. cit., p. 452.
[5] Cotton Mather, *Parentator, Memoirs of Remarkables in the Life and Death of Ever-Memorable Dr. Increase Mather*, Boston: B. Green, 1724, p. 15.

of a sermon with it." According to the biography written by his son Cotton: "His Delivery had something Singular in it. He spoke with a Grave and Wise *Deliberation:* But on some Subjects, his Voice would rise for the more *Emphatical Clauses,* as the Discourse went on: and anon come on with such a *Tonitrous Cogency,* that the Hearers would be struck with an *Awe,* like what would be Produced by the Fall of *Thunderbolts.*" He never read his sermons and though he made notes he seldom referred to them. "He wished," Cotton Mather wrote, "there were more *Speaking* and less *Reading* in our *Sermons* . . . that the Necessary *Vigour* and *Address,* of proper *Preaching,* might not be lost." Like his father, Increase forebore to parade his learning in his sermons but took great care to use plain language and clear exposition, aimed "to the Lowest and Meanest Capacity" of his hearers. "He was very careful to be *understood,* and *concealed* every other *Art,* that he might Pursue and Practise that one *Art* of *Being Intelligible.*"

The enormous industry of the man is indicated by his publication of one hundred and seventy-five books on religion, politics, and science. "*He never Preached a Sermon but what was worthy of the Press,*"[6] wrote Cotton Mather. Meanwhile, he was so active in the affairs of the community that he was familiarly referred to as "the uncrowned king of Massachusetts." To Kenneth Murdock he appeared "The Foremost American Puritan."[7] He became a manager of the Boston press, a member of the Harvard Board of Overseers, and served as president of Harvard from 1685 to 1701. For four years, 1688–1692, he represented the Colony in England as its ambassador, negotiating for the new charter that was granted in 1691.

Increase returned to Boston from London just in time to become involved in the Salem witchcraft trials, in which nineteen men and women were hanged and one man was pressed to death for refusing to plead. Increase could not miss the opportunity for a timely book on the subject. Like practically all his contemporaries, he believed in witches and believed also that they should be destroyed. But he pleaded for the utmost care in examining the evidence. "It were better," he wrote, "that ten suspected Witches should escape, than that one innocent Person should be Condemned."[8] Nevertheless, in the aftermath of public remorse for the hangings, his reputation suffered. Because of his prominence, even his moderation, in support of error, was condemned while the extremism of lesser men was forgiven.

[6] *Ibid.,* pp. 210–220.
[7] Kenneth Murdock, *Increase Mather: The Foremost American Puritan,* Cambridge: Harvard University Press, 1926.
[8] Increase Mather, "The Cases of Conscience," pamphlet, London, 1639; included in Cotton Mather, *The Wonders of the Invisible World,* London: John Russell Smith, 1862, p. 282.

The next decade was a period of defeat for ambitions he dearly cherished. His son Cotton had taken over his church while he was in London. The four years of absence separated him from direct leadership in community affairs. Politics were stirring and so were changes in religious belief and practices. Increase ranged himself on the side of old ideas, especially for the dominance of religion in daily life. His greatest disappointment came in 1701, when he was defeated in his bid for re-election as president of Harvard. In great bitterness he wrote in his diary: "Doubtless there is not any government in the world that has been laid under greater obligations by a greater man than this government has by me. Nevertheless, I have received more discouragement in the work of the Lord, by those in government, than all the men in the world besides. Let not my children put too much trust in men."[9]

For the remaining two decades of his life, Increase devoted himself to writing, to controversies, and to the moody seclusion of semi-retirement. Secularism and rationalistic deism were entering into fashion, to his intense dislike. He died as he lived, secure in his faith. While he lay on his deathbed a friend wrote to ask if he were still in the land of the living. "No," Increase retorted, "tell him I am going to it; this Poor World is the Land of the Dying."[10]

Many of his ideas were surprisingly liberal. In *Some Important Truths about Conversion*, a collection of his sermons published in 1674, he spoke neither of hellfire nor of predestination, but stressed the reshaping of one's life through the redeeming power of the love of Christ. "There never was any man did believe," he said, "but he found hard work of it . . . Carnal hearts would be well pleased with it, if Ministers would sew pillows under mens elbows, and tell them that they might easily get to Heaven. But Truth saith otherwise, God saith otherwise."[11]

Similarly forward-looking was his Wo[e] to Drunkards, two sermons published in 1673, which mark him as a pioneer in the temperance movement. "Drink is in itself a good creature of God," he said, "and to be received with thankfulness, but the abuse of drink is from Satan." His argument was both homely and realistic. "The Drunkards credit is crackt, and lost amongst all sober men . . . ," he reminded his listeners. "Trust a Drunkard with an Estate, and when he is in his Cups hee'll send it going: Trust him with a Secret, and when he is drunken hee'll

[9] Increase Mather, *Autobiography*, American Antiquarian Society; quoted by Murdock, *op. cit.*, p. 373.
[10] Cotton Mather, *Parentator*, *op. cit.*, p. 209.
[11] Increase Mather, *Some Important Truths about Conversion*, London: Richard Chiswell, 1674.

discover it; Trust him, and when he is drunken he will undo himself and his friend too." His conclusion was a plea for decision: "Kill this serpent, before it be grown too big for you."[12]

To be the son and grandson of indubitably great men may be either an insuperable handicap or a spur to unusual achievement. For Cotton Mather (1663–1728) the effect was incredible stimulation of great abilities. To avoid being overshadowed by his father, he labored prodigiously —and wrote some four hundred books, most of them sermons, collections of sermons, or sermon-like tracts. Among them, his diary is the most interesting, revealing a mind hungry for facts, indomitable in courage, vain almost to the verge of insanity, morbidly suspicious, dedicated to service, and delighting in self-abasement to God. One of Cotton Mather's psychological oddities was a propensity for seeing visions—that is, for losing himself so completely in his daydreams that he believed them to be real. At the beginning of his twenty third year, while he was serving with honor and success in the pulpit of his father's church, he recorded in his diary a vision that dramatizes his ambitions:

> A strange and memorable thing. After outpouring of prayer, with the utmost fervor and fasting, there appeared an Angel, whose face shone like the noonday sun. His features were those of a man, and beardless; his head was encircled by a splendid tiara; on his shoulders were wings; his garments were white and shining; his robe reached to his ankles; and about his loins was a belt not unlike the girdles of the peoples of the East. And this Angel said that he was sent by the Lord Jesus to bear a clear answer to the prayers of a certain youth, and to bear back his words in reply. Many things this Angel said which is not fit to be set down here. But among other things not to be forgotten he declared that the fate of this youth should be to find expression for what in him was best; . . . . And in particular this Angel spoke of the influence his branches should have, and of the books this youth should write and publish, not only in America but in Europe. And he added certain special prophecies of the great works this youth should do for the Church of Christ in the revolutions that are now at hand. Lord Jesus! What is the meaning of this marvel? From the wiles of the Devil, I beseech thee, deliver and defend Thy most unworthy servant.[13]

Cotton Mather possessed to the full the restless energy, the pride, and the fierce temper of his father. To these qualities he added a painful sensitivity and a narrowness in his range of interests. Unlike Increase, Cotton never left the New England Colonies, and there is doubtless truth in Parrington's judgment that "his mind was dwarfed by a village

---

[12] Increase Mather, Wo[e] to Drunkards, *Two Sermons Testifying against the Sin of Drunkenness,* Cambridge: Marmaduke Johnson, 1673.
[13] Cotton Mather, *Diary, op. cit.,* I:87.

world."[14] He was acutely aware of the shortcomings and needs of his crude environment and esteemed himself as being especially charged to deliver New England into enlightenment and godliness. In his compendium of Massachusetts history and biography called *Magnalia Christi Americana*, he explained his reluctance to spend time in pastoral duties and admitted that he greeted visitors by saying: "You'll excuse me if I ask you to be short with me, for my work is great and my time is but little."[15] His enemies, who were many—for he had not a shred of tact—were, in his view, "all strangely and fiercely possessed of the Devil." His sermons in North Church became so abusive of the congregation that a group of them took the unprecedented step of withdrawing, to establish a new Brattle Street Church—in order, as Cotton's diary records, "to delude many better-meaning Men of their own Company."[16]

His regular Sunday congregation dwindled in size until on occasion there were only a score or so of worshippers. Nevertheless, when he put his mind to his speaking he was a powerful and moving orator. He rose to his greatest power on special occasions, when he could be the dramatic center of the attention of the whole community. In his diary he describes one such sermon, delivered at the hanging of an unfortunate girl who had murdered her illegitimate baby. The chief significance of the event to Cotton Mather was the opportunity it afforded him for a magnificent display of his eloquence. He wrote a lengthy sermon and, immediately after the hanging, while public interest was still intense, he rushed to the printer with it, to which he appended "An History of Criminals executed in this Land, and effectually, an Account of their dying Speeches, and my own Discourses with them in their last Hours."

As for the sermon, he recounted the winsomeness of it and the glory it reflected upon his ministry. He tells, too, of his good fortune in getting this speaking appointment for himself, after it already had been assigned to another:

> The Execution of the miserable Malefactor, was ordered to have been the last Week, upon the lecture of another. I wondered then what would become of my Particular Faith, of her condition being so ordered in the Providence of God, that it should furnish me, with a *special Opportunity* to glorify Him. While I was entirely resigning to the wisdome of Heaven all such Matters, the Judges, wholly without my seeking, altered and allow'd her Execution to fall on the Day of *my Lecture.* The General Court then sitting, ordered the Lecture to bee held in a larger

[14] Parrington, *op. cit.,* I:106–117, specifically, p. 107.
[15] *Ibid.,* I:108.
[16] Cotton Mather, *Diary, op. cit.,* I:326.

and stronger House, than that old one, where 'tis usually kept. For my own part, I was weak, and faint, and spent; but I humbly gave myself up to the *Spirit* of my Heavenly Lord and Hee assured mee that Hee would send His good angel to strengthen mee. The greatest Assembly, ever in this Countrey preach'd unto, was now come together; It may bee four or five thousand Souls. I could not gett unto the *Pulpit* but by climbing over *Pues* and *Heads:* and there the Spirit of my dearest Lord came upon mee. I preached with a more than ordinary Assistance, and enlarged, and uttered the most awakening Things, for near two hours together. My Strength and Voice failed not; but when it was near failing, a silent Look to Heaven strangely renew'd it. In the whole I found Prayer answered and Hopes exceeded, and Faith encouraged, and the Lord using mee, the vilest of all that great Assembly, to glorify Him. Oh! what shall I render to the Lord![17]

As New England's leading preacher, Cotton Mather never forgot that he was a "Person whom the Eye and the Talk of the People is very much upon."[18] Never did he shrink from the limelight, even when to stand in its glare proved costly. In 1709 he launched a fierce attack against Governor Dudley, who had been appointed to the governorship upon Cotton's own recommendation. As a result, Cotton was omitted from the invitation lists for the social revels held by the leading socialites of Boston. Although he claimed to "rejoice in my Liberty from the Temptations,"[19] in truth his vanity was much injured. His reaction was to switch again and become once more so stout a defender of the Governor and of the power of the English Parliament over the Colonies that Judge Samuel Sewall feared his debasement of colonial rights "might be an Invitation to the Parliament to take away our Charter."[20] So strongly did Cotton Mather believe that the people must be held in "*Submission* unto a lawful Government"[21] that, when the Theocracy had become a dead letter, he devoted his last years to defense of the secular rule. For this cause he spoke zealously and often.

In his diary he noted with satisfaction that in a typical year he delivered seventy two "publick Sermons,"[22] and half as many more in private gatherings. Meanwhile, he prided himself upon being an assiduous, and, as he thought, an entrancing conversationalist, never missing a chance to say something spiritually uplifting. In the biography written

[17] *Ibid.*, I:279; quoted by Parrington, *op. cit.*, I:110.
[18] Parrington, *op. cit.*, I:111.
[19] Cotton Mather, *Diary, op. cit.*, II:15.
[20] Samuel Sewall, *Diary of Samuel Sewall,* Collections of Massachusetts Historical Society, II:214.
[21] Barrett Wendell, *Cotton Mather: Puritan Priest,* New York: Dodd, Mead, 1891, p. 82.
[22] Samuel Mather, *The Life of the Very Reverend and Learned Cotton Mather,* Boston: Samuel Gerrish, 1729, p. 24.

by his son, Samuel, it is recorded that "His *Conversation* he endeavor'd to render extremely entertaining; and it was so . . ." Samuel then dutifully presented Cotton's "rules" for good table talk. "First, He would not affect *Loquacity* in his Discourses, but, on the contrary, much *Deliberation*," which he found to be impressive. "Second, He would studiously decline to utter anything, that he foresaw might be *useless* . . . Third, He would with all the nice *Contrivance* imaginable, improve Opportunities to say something or other that might particularly set off *some Glories* for his Lord . . ."[23]

It was, indeed, a "Remarkable Providence" that Cotton Mather was enabled to become a preacher; for, as Samuel relates, "There was one Thing, which, from his Cradle, seem'd to have a dark and sad Aspect upon his Usefulness, and that was an *uncommon Impediment in his Speech*."[24] Increase Mather used to gather the whole family about to pray for a removal of this stuttering; and Cotton, while a student at Harvard, attempted to overcome it by meeting with other young men in a series of Sunday evening discussions; "and unto these Matters he ascribed his *first* Rise and Improvements in the Art of *Speaking*." For a time Cotton abandoned thoughts of the ministry and decided to become a physician. However, a schoolmaster named Corlet advised "a dilated *Deliberation in Speaking* . . . so by prolonging your Pronunciation *you will get an habit of Speaking without Hesitation*."[25] This method worked so well that never, thereafter, do we find reference to his stutter—and never did he abandon the habit of slow and emphatic utterance.

His ideas were a curious mixture of reactionism, liberalism, and self-seeking opportunism. In the Salem Witch Trials he was representative of his age, neither better nor worse. His most courageous stand was his defense of inoculation against smallpox, even though this seemed to many to be an interference with God's plans for man. He refused to be daunted even when a bomb, fortunately a dud, was thrown into his living room, together with a note: "may this enoculate you."[26] In religion, he clung as long as he could to the past, trying valiantly to shore up the secular power of the church until the cause was wholly lost. Never did he abandon his view that God watches over the most minute affairs of every individual and that every portion of life must be lived strictly according to God's rules. His view that he was a very special vessel of the Lord is well illustrated in his account of an affliction of stomach cramps while he was offering an opening prayer, preparatory to

[23] *Ibid.*, pp. 19, 20.
[24] *Ibid.*, p. 26.
[25] *Ibid.*, p. 26.
[26] Cotton Mather, *Diary, op. cit.*, II:657.

preaching on the "Wiles of the Devil." In Cotton's view, the devil, afraid of the power of the discourse, "horribly buffetted me,"[27] but God's grace gave him strength to recover.

A parishioner noted that "In his Style, indeed, he is somewhat singular, and not so agreeable to the Gust of the Age. But *like* his *manner of speaking*, it was very *emphatical*." The emphasis derived in part from his own conviction that he was particularly called by God "to countermine the whole *Plot* of the Devil against New England."[28]

What he did accomplish was astounding: perhaps as many as four hundred and fifty books and tracts, besides regular preaching and constant intervention into every public question that arose. He tried unsuccessfully to maneuver control over the presidency of Harvard and, as Harvard drifted into increasing liberalism, he helped to establish Yale as a conservative counterforce. He was elected a Fellow of the Royal Society, to which he contributed far more papers than any other American, and was awarded an honorary degree by the University of Aberdeen. Finally, in his advanced years, he achieved such tolerance of view that he actually helped in the ordination of a Baptist minister. Eccentric, opinionated, and vain though he undoubtedly was, he was also enormously vital, intellectual, and capable of reflecting in his own mind the changes that were making New England a seedbed of individual differences.

Samuel Mather (1706–1785) deserves little attention except to note that he was the last member of this remarkable dynasty. At twenty six he was chosen to succeed his distinguished father and grandfather as pastor of North Church, by 69 votes out of 112. Nine years later, amidst dissention caused by his reactionism and the growing liberalism of the congregation, he was given his dismissal, with a year's salary. Taking ninety three members of the congregation with him, he founded a new church; but his preaching was so feeble that attendance dropped to twenty or thirty. Samuel authored twenty books, of which the most interesting is a didactic but somehow stirring life of his father, Cotton Mather. The most courageous period of his life was near the end, when he resisted the temptation to stay with the Tories and followed the leaner road of Whiggish revolutionism.

Undoubtedly, the Mather dynasty was an important influence in the formation of the American character. No other family, not excluding the Adamses and Roosevelts, labored more exhaustively to try to shape the destiny of their countrymen. So far as their understanding went, they tried to be liberal and forward-looking. Always and most urgently,

---

[27] Cotton Mather, *Wonders of the Invisible World, op. cit.,* pp. 63ff.
[28] Parrington, *op. cit.,* I:114–115.

they sought to shape men's minds and behavior in accordance with the will of God as they saw it.

A very revealing commentary upon the dynasty and upon the intellectual quality of the Theocracy is a paragraph from the diary of Cotton Mather, dated January 3, 1725 (New Style), and relating to his son. Samuel had been promised a voyage to the West Indies, which he strongly desired, but

> A Gracious God . . . marvellously interposed . . . to prevent his going . . . . Then he shipp'd himself upon a Vessel bound more directly for *London*. Here also the divine Providence ordered something to fall out, which putt a Delay and a Defeat upon his Intentions. This is the Effect of my Cries unto the glorious Lord, that if the Child's Voyage might not be for the service of His Kingdom, and the welfare of the Child himself, He would graciously put a stop unto it. The calm Resignation and Satisfaction, with which the Child entertains the Disappointment of a Matter in which his Heart was exceedingly and passionately sett upon is a token for Good . . . . I hope to improve the Occurence, as great Obligations upon both of us, to apply ourselves unto such Things, as may effectually demonstrate, that God meant them unto Good.[29]

The lesson is clear. Whatever may happen is good. Whatever may happen is God's plan. The evidence may be absent and the logic obscure; but there was no lack of faith. The faith itself, however, was bolstered by a complex system of theology that only the learned could hope to understand. Therefore, the interpretation of what God intends must rest finally and securely in the hands of the ecclesiastical elect. This was the view of the Theocracy. This was the faith of the Mather dynasty.

New Dimensions in the Pulpit

WITH THE passage of years, growth of population, establishment of towns, expansion of trade, and stabilization of agriculture, new generations of settlers were developing new ideas. The pulpit continued to be the principal influence in the communities; but the preaching, like the rest of colonial life, became increasingly diversified. A few strong preachers did a great deal to influence the development of the later colonial ideas and institutions—and, conversely, the new commercialism and the crystallization of New World traditions also exercised a considerable influence upon the content and manner of preaching. Following

[29] Cotton Mather, *Diary, op. cit.*, II:779.

the Mathers, whose influence declined after 1700, the ministers of most general import were Solomon Stoddard, Jonathan Edwards, and George Whitefield, together with half a dozen others whose influence was more localized or particularized but was also genuinely significant.

Out in the broad valley of the Connecticut, in western Massachusetts, in the town of Northampton, Solomon Stoddard (1643–1729) commenced as a rebel and lived to the patriarchal age of eighty six, preaching to the end, with a power so absolute that he was familiarly known as "Pope Stoddard."

He entertained a view very different from that of the Mather dynasty concerning the relation of the church to the people. As we have seen, the Theocracy narrowly limited church membership, guarding it with careful and strict requirements. Stoddard, on the contrary, viewed the church as completely inclusive, taking in even the unregenerate and unconverted. So broad was his conception that he even opened the ministry to the unlearned and, when the need seemed great, to unconverted or "ungodly" preachers. In defiance of one of the most sacred rules of the Theocrats, Stoddard opened the sacrament of the Lord's Supper to all who chose to partake of it, whether or not they were members of the church. To the charge levelled against him by Increase and Cotton Mather that he was betraying the faith of the founders of the New England Church, Stoddard replied boldly: "It may possibly be a fault, and the aggravation of a fault, to depart from the ways of our fathers; but it may also be a vertue . . . . He that believes principles, because they affirm them, makes idols of them: and it would be no humility, but baseness of spirit, for us to judge ourselves uncapable, to examine the principles that have been handed down to us."[1]

Stoddard's view of the people, and of the ministerial relation to them, was liberal in terms of his time but was also in some respects stubbornly conservative. He believed implicitly in original sin and in the abject unworthiness of all humanity. This meant, to him, that parishioners must not be held to an unrealistically high level of spiritual attainment; for "piety is not natural to a people, and so they do not hold it long."[2] Wherever one may look, "the world lies in wickedness; all countries are over-run with iniquity: there is swearing and cursing, & killing, & thefts, and adulteries, & lying, & incest, & witchcraft . . . . : and this is the cause of them, men love themselves more than God."[3]

[1] Solomon Stoddard, *The Inexcusableness of Neglecting the Worship of God, under a Pretence of Being in an Unconverted Condition,* Boston: B. Green, 1708, preface, pp. ii–iii.
[2] Eugene E. White, "Solomon Stoddard's Theories of Persuasion," *Speech Monographs,* XXIX (Nov., 1962):238.
[3] Williston Walker, *The Creeds and Platform of Congregationalism,* New York: Christian Literature Co., 1893, pp. 409–440. Cf. Stoddard, *Three Sermons Preach'd at Boston:* B. Green, 1717.

From this view of human unworthiness, Stoddard reasoned, first, that all men should be brought into the church, regardless of their beliefs or conduct; and, secondly, that their ministers should rule over them with unquestioned authority, for "their authority is established by God."[4] He recognized that his theory would bring into the church many hypocrites, who sought its advantages without accepting its principles, but he thought even the pretense of religion better than the open flouting of it:

> For hypocrites . . . are not destructive to the state of the church: but on the contrarie do great service to the church, they help to maintain the church and ordinances of God, they do defend the church, they do incourage the church, they are serviceable by their gifts, by their authority, by their prudence & zeal, by their estates; and it would be exceedingly difficult for the church to subsist without them.[5]

In its straightforward practicality, this comment tells us more about Solomon Stoddard than we ever learn about many of his contemporaries. In truth, his opinion of mankind was so low that he found little reason to make any special differentiation between the "good" and the "bad." Men are "vermin," "dead fish," "worms," and "polluted creatures," in his view. "Every natural man is over-run with the leprosy of sin from head to foot," he preached; "has not one spark of goodness in him; all his faculties are corrupted utterly . . . . His whole soul is like a dead carcass, like a heap of carrion, loathsome and noisom, and God may justly abhor him."[6]

This description is not of hypocrites, or of any special class of sinners; it is meant to depict natural man in his natural state—the human creature as he stands revealed in the sight of God. The judgment of Stoddard on this matter did not differ essentially from that of the more orthodox Puritans of Boston Bay. But he followed his reasoning from this premise to the conclusion that the gradations of virtue found amongst such miserable sinners are so slight that it is rather futile to try to separate the good from the evil. Why, therefore, make it difficult for any particular class to enter the church?

This low view of human nature was one of the foundation stones upon which Stoddard erected his theology. Another was the belief in absolute predestination, and in the doctrine that God had from the beginning of time already determined who would be saved and who damned—another view which he shared with the Theocrats. Unlike

---

[4] Solomon Stoddard, "An Examination of the Power of the Fraternity," appended to *The Presence of Christ with the Ministers of the Gospel*, Boston: B. Green, 1718, pp. 10–16.
[5] Solomon Stoddard, *An Appeal to the Learned . . . Against the Exceptions of Mr. Increase Mather*, Boston: B. Green, 1709.
[6] Solomon Stoddard, *Three Sermons Preach'd at Boston*, op. cit.

them, however, Stoddard decided that it is a part of God's will that all humanity should be won to a belief in Christ. He could not overlook the famous verse in the Gospel of John promising that "whosoever believeth on His name shall be saved." Stoddard felt keenly the injunction to preach repentance and conversion to all—and in this faith he became the first American evangelist, with great "harvests" of souls in 1679, 1683, 1696, 1712, and 1718.

Why he sought converts is not in doubt: bringing people into the church placed them under the discipline of the ministers, restrained them from immoralities, and caused them to "walk uprightly" as orderly and responsible citizens. What the converts themselves were to get from their conversion could not be "salvation," for this was a matter of predestination; but they would attain satisfaction in living in accordance with God's ordinances. Beyond this, there was little gain. If a person came to be a very model of piety, God realizes that this is only because he "is frightened into reformation: he don't know how to bear the flames of hell; he would be as bad as the worst, but he dare not."[7]

As this judgment suggests, Stoddard's evangelical method was the skillful use of fear. "Fear and dread of hell," he told his congregation, "make men do what they do in religion." He went on: "Ministers are faulty when they speak to them of gentleness . . . . Men need to be terrified and have the arrows of the Almighty in them that they may be converted. Ministers should be sons of thunder: men need to have storms in their hearts, before they will betake themselves to Christ . . . . Reason will govern men in other things; but it is fear that must make them diligently seek salvation."[8] Thus, in his preaching he would cry: "What will you think of it when the devil will lay hold of you to drag you down to hell? How will you cry out when tumbling into the lake that burns with fire and brimstone? . . . . You will wring your hands, and tear your hair, and gnash your teeth, and curse your day, and fill hell with outcries and lamentations!"[9]

As for what the truly converted could hope to get from their religion, the first and certain reward was "inward peace and quietness." Beyond this, Stoddard appears to have weakened in his later years in his belief in predestination and began to preach of "the safety of coming to Christ."[10] He spoke far less of heaven than of hell, but he did assure true believers that their acceptance of Christ would confirm them in the company of

[7] Solomon Stoddard, *An Appeal to the Learned,* op. cit. Cf. White, op. cit., pp. 235–259.

[8] Solomon Stoddard, *The Defects of Preachers Reproved,* New London: T. Green, 1724.

[9] Solomon Stoddard, *The Safety of Appearing at the Day of Judgment,* Boston: D. Herchman, 1729.

[10] White, op. cit., p. 258.

the elect, who "will spend an eternity in praising & magnifying God" and in "making melody to the Lord."[11]

As we noted earlier, Stoddard welcomed into the ministry, to serve the growing number of churches in the valley, men of little special theological training, and even men who could not qualify themselves by belief in all the doctrines of the church. The blessing of religion, he pointed out, "doth not depend upon the piety of him that doth administer it."[12] Learning in itself was of no avail, for it was not by theological argumentation that men could be won to God. "The *life* and *zeal* that is in the delivery [of the sermon] is of special use, and a great means to affect the heart." "Some ministers," he added scornfully, "affect rhetorical strains of speech, as if they were making an oration in the schools; this may tickle the fancies of men, and scratch itching ears; but we have men's consciences to deal with: men need to be frightened and not to be pleased."[13] He went on: "We are not sent into the pulpit to show our wit and eloquence, but to set the consciences of men on fire: . . . the word is as an hammer and we should use it to break the rocky hearts of men."[14]

For sixty years Stoddard preached from the pulpit in Northampton and dominated the churches and the life of the Connecticut Valley, with frequent trips to Boston where he spoke every year at Harvard and preached on special days, teaching other ministers his goal and his methods of evangelism. Then, as he neared his eighty sixth year, he looked about among the young ministers who were eager to become his successor and chose his grandson, Jonathan Edwards (1703–1758), a graduate of Yale, whose genius was already evident in his youth. In 1727, two years before Stoddard's death, Edwards commenced his own twenty-three-year pastorate in Northampton. At first he enjoyed great success, following closely in his grandfather's footsteps; but as he launched forth upon a new theology of his own, he was found guilty by his congregation of "having separated and departed from the principles of the great Mr. Stoddard,"[15] and was summarily dismissed. Edwards is generally accounted one of the greatest intellects to be produced in the New World; but somehow he went awry and ended his ministry in defeat.

11 *Ibid.*, p. 259.
12 Solomon Stoddard, *The Presence of Christ, op. cit.*, pp. 27–28.
13 Solomon Stoddard, *The Defects of Preachers Reproved, op. cit.*, pp. iv–v and 23–24.
14 Solomon Stoddard, *The Efficiency of the Fear of Hell to Restrain Men from Sin*, Boston: Thomas Fleet, 1713, p. 37.
15 Serno Edwards Dwight, editor, *The Works of President Edwards, With a Memoir of His Life*, New York: S. Converse, 1829, I:327.

Like his mentor, Solomon Stoddard, Edwards believed strongly that men are wholly lost in original sin and are helpless to salvage their own souls. With a logic that was more inexorable than Stoddard's, he saw clearly that if God is absolutely sovereign, man must be inescapably subject to His will; if God is absolute goodness, sin must be so remote from God as to have no means of access to him; if God is both omnipotent and omniscient, all eternity must be unalterably predetermined. With unremitting integrity he undertook to spell out the consequences of this chain of logic.

To Edwards, the government of the universe was not democratic but totalitarian. God did not bargain with man and had no covenant with him. "The unfettered will of God," one of his favorite phrases, was the sole ruling power. God, being compacted of goodness, had trustfully created man in His own image; but the devil had seduced the original parents of the human race and led them into the fundamental error of preferring their own wisdom to subservience to God. The sinfulness of having deliberately chosen to be separated from God was thereby implanted in the human psyche. In order to fulfill His original purpose of maintaining a creature to worship and glorify His eminence, God ordained that a small proportion of mankind should arbitrarily be selected to enjoy the perpetual bliss of heaven. The vast majority were inexorably fore-ordained to eternal hellfire to burn for their sin of willfullness. The sacrifice of Jesus was God's supreme effort to provide a way by which sinful humanity could reconcile themselves to His governance; but not even the crucifixion of Christ could alter the everlasting fact that man had departed from God so decisively that there was no way by which he could return. The justice of God was so incorruptible that it could not avoid the hard necessity of punishing man for his departure from his original purity.[16] This was the message which Jonathan Edwards preached in his twelve hundred sermons, all written out in full or in detailed outline, during his Northampton ministry.[17]

The farmers and villagers of Northampton were far from amenable to the harshness of this doctrine. For sixty years they had listened to the Reverend Stoddard preach the terrors of hellfire; but he opened church membership to any who wished it and, toward the end, he indicated that acceptance of Christ as the redeemer was an assurance of getting into heaven. Edwards decisively closed the door of hope, insisting inexorably upon the doctrine of predestined election as the only means of rescue from hell.

[16] Cf. the interpretation by Herbert W. Schneider, *The Puritan Mind, op. cit.,* in Chapter IV, "The Great Awakening," pp. 102–155.
[17] Orville A. Hitchcock, "Jonathan Edwards," in Brigance, *History and Criticism, op. cit.,* pp. 213–237, specifically p. 214 and pp. 232–233.

From Edwards's chain of logic, the process of conversion which he demanded was inevitable. First, the sinner must recognize his own utter worthlessness and vileness as a creature separated from God. Second, he must accept the fact that not even the utmost purity of thought and conduct could ever in the slightest degree wipe out this sin of separation; nothing can restore the sinner to the bosom of God except God's own arbitrary choice—which had been made once and for all aeons before the individual was born. Third, the sinner must come to feel a sense of ecstatic happiness in subjecting himself to God's will, fully realizing that this meant almost inevitably his condemnation to an eternity of hell.[18]

The power of Edwards as a preacher is evident in the fact that he brought four hundred new converts into his church through this hard route during his ministry.[19] Each of them was required to believe himself utterly depraved and God wholly good, with the understanding that such evil and such goodness could no more be reunited than can oil and water. Man's entire duty is that of reconciling himself to the full consequences of Adam's fall. In many of his sermons Edwards spoke of God's mercy and of the peace and comfort that is felt by the sinner when he accepts unquestioningly and joyously God's plan for humanity. Through conversion, he told his congregation, you will have "all your sins forgiven, your greatest and most aggravated transgressions blotted out as a cloud, and buried as in the depths of the sea, that they may never be found more." Following in the evangelical footsteps of his grandfather, he told them: "Now God stands ready to pity you; this is the day of mercy; you may cry now with some encouragement of obtaining mercy."[20] Hearing this message, "the assembly were, from time to time, in tears while the word was preached; some weeping with sorrow and distress, others with joy and love, others with pity."[21] Another effect was at least one suicide; and, as Edwards reported in a sermon, since many "pious persons" felt the urge to "Cut your own throat, now is a good opportunity."[22]

The mercy of God which Edwards promised to true converts, it must be kept in mind, was not salvation; it was not reconciliation with God; it was instead the solemnly joyful acceptance by the sinner of the fact that in facing damnation he was enacting the role God had destined for him.

[18] C. H. Faust and T. H. Johnson, editors, *Jonathan Edwards: Representative Selections, with Introduction, Bibliography and Notes*, New York: American Book Co., 1935, pp. 155–161.
[19] Hitchcock, *op. cit.*, I:235n.
[20] "Sinners in the Hands of an Angry God," in Faust and Johnson, *op. cit.*, p. 167.
[21] S. E. Dwight, *op. cit.*, I:161.
[22] Perry Miller, *Jonathan Edwards*, New York: Wm. Sloane Associates, 1949, p. 140, and Hitchcock, *op. cit.*, I:235.

The best known of Jonathan Edwards's sermons is "Sinners in the Hands of an Angry God,"[23] which he preached not in his own pulpit but at Enfield, Massachusetts, on July 8, 1741, from the foreboding text of *Deuteronomy*, xxxii: 35: "Their foot shall slide in due time." The fact that Edwards chose this message when he was a guest in another man's pulpit indicates that it represents what he most wanted to have identified as his particular message; in any event, it corresponds closely with his general theme to his own congregation.

"The bow of God's wrath is bent," he told his hearers, "and the arrow made ready on the string, and justice bends the arrow at your heart, and strains at the bow, and it is nothing but the mere pleasure of God, and that of an angry God, without any promise or obligation at all, that keeps the arrow one moment from being drunk with your blood." Here was his central theme; but lest any should think themselves safe from such wrath, he went on: "However you may have reformed your life in many things, and may have had religious affections, and may keep up a form of religion in your families and closets, and in the house of God, it is nothing but his mere pleasure that keeps you from being this moment swallowed up in everlasting destruction."

Then he proceeded into one of the most dreadful passages from the whole library of Christian preaching:

> The God that holds you over the pit of hell, much as one holds a spider, or some loathsome insect over the fire, abhors you, and is dreadfully provoked: His wrath toward you burns like fire; He looks upon you as being worthy of nothing else, but to be cast into the fire; He is of purer eyes than to bear to have you in His sight; you are ten thousand times more abominable in His eyes, than the most hateful venomous serpent is in ours. You have offended Him infinitely more than ever a stubborn rebel did his prince; and yet it is nothing but His hand that holds you from falling into the fire every moment. It is to be ascribed to nothing else, that you did not go to hell the last night; that you was suffered to awake again in this world, after you closed your eyes to sleep. And there is no other reason to be given, why you have not dropped into hell since you arose in the morning, but that God's hand has held you up. There is no other reason to be given why you have not gone to hell, since you have sat here in the house of God, provoking His pure eyes by your sinful wicked manner of attending His solemn worship. Yea, there is nothing else to be given as a reason why you do not this very moment drop down into hell.[24]

Aside from the content of his sermons, Edwards was deliberately unsensational in his preaching. In appearance he was delicate, almost

[23] The text is in Faust and Johnson, *op. cit.*, pp. 155–172.
[24] *Ibid.*, pp. 155, 163, 164, 165.

effeminate: six feet tall, thin, and meticulously neat in dress. His voice was low but clear, easily heard in an auditorium that, with balconies on three sides, was normally crowded with more than a thousand parishioners. His inflectional pattern was level and unvaried, with a uniform pattern of stress on the parallel phrases that marched like soldiers out across the heads of his hearers. Deliberately he refrained from any personalization, either in content or in delivery. He refused to pander to the farmer-auditors who were restive to "every thing but noise and nonsense, and cannot be content to sit quiet," as a contemporary preacher complained, "unless their auditory nerves are drummed upon with a voice like thunder."[25] Edwards further muted his delivery by refraining from the use of any gestures and kept his eyes so fixed upon the upper wall in the back of the sanctuary that one of his parishioners said "he looked on the bell rope until he looked it off."[26] Edwards apparently never received any explicit training in speech and, whether from inclination or temperament, did not develop any personalized warmth or fervor in delivery. He did, however, display considerable skill in the clear organization of his ideas, and his style sparkled with specific illustrations as well as developing a trip-hammer force from the repetition of key words and the close succession of brief parallel phrases. His preparation was exhaustive, keeping him in his study twelve hours a day; and even during his daily after-lunch horseback ride, he carried pen and ink with him to jot down ideas as they occurred. In a spirit of humility that ill fitted his intellectual assurance, he described himself in 1757 as having "a kind of childish weakness and contemptibleness of speech, presence, and demeanor, with a disagreeable dulness and stiffness, much unfitting me for conversation . . ."[27]

The astounding fact is, however, that this stiff man with his unbendingly harsh message accomplished in 1735 (and then again in 1741) an evangelical revival that far outmatched the "harvests" reaped by Stoddard. New England Puritanism traditionally stressed restraint and privacy in worship; but in a series of revival sermons in 1735 Edwards swept not only his own congregation but the whole Valley, and much beyond, into a veritable public purgation of mass emotionalism and confession of sin. In 1736 he published an account of this feat, in a work entitled *A Faithful Narrative of the Surprising Work of God in the Conversion of Many Hundred Souls in Northampton, and the Neighboring Towns and Villages.* Within three years the book went through twenty printings, and a hundred years later it was still in use as a guide

---

[25] Miller, *op. cit.*, p. 9; cf. also, Hitchcock, *op. cit.*, I:233.
[26] Miller, *op. cit.*, p. 51.
[27] *Ibid*, p. 47.

to evangelical preaching. The method he advocated consisted primarily of making inescapably vivid to the listeners their utter sinfulness and the immediate need to cast themselves without restraint into the hands of God. What he sought was not to appeal to their understanding but to give them a direct experience of confrontation with their unworthiness and God's power. As for the result, he wrote that "This Town never was so full of Love, nor so full of Joy, nor so full of Distress as it has Lately been."[28] Edwards assured the congregations that "Unconverted men walk over the pit of hell on a rotten covering . . . ,"[29] and they reached out for the support of his upholding hand.

A second Great Awakening was achieved in 1741; but thereafter for four full years there was not a single addition to his church. In December, 1748, when he refused membership to a convert who was unwilling to make a public profession of faith, the Northampton congregation rebelled and dismissed him. What Jonathan Edwards left to posterity is the regrettable memory of a vastly gifted man who used his gifts prodigally in trying in vain to support a view of man's destiny that was yielding inevitably to new ideas.

The new ideas, theologically, were primarily of two sorts: the liberating emotionalism of Wesleyan Methodism and the liberal rationality of Deism. In the Gospel of John there stands the verse promising eternal salvation to whomsoever would believe in the redeeming power of Christ; but the Wesley brothers were the first to stress its importance, and George Whitefield (1714–1770) was the first to spread widely in the American colonies this evangelical message of salvation through love.[30] In contrast to the predestined gloom and damnation of Presbyterianism, in August of 1737 the young Whitefield published in England his first sermon, on *The Nature and Necessity of our New Birth in Christ Jesus, in Order to Salvation.*

The new doctrine was astoundingly and fundamentally radical. By it, together with the very different stream of rationalistic Deism, the old totalitarian religion of a sovereign God dealing arbitrarily with a helpless humanity was replaced by a new concept of free enterprise religion whereby man could escape from his bondage in original sin by earning (and thence inevitably receiving) the gift of salvation. According to the Wesleyans, eternal bliss could be attained by an act of will: the acceptance of Christ as a Redeemer. According to the Deists, salvation was to

---

[28] Faust and Johnson, *op. cit.*, p. 78; S. E. Dwight, *op. cit.*, I:137.
[29] Faust and Johnson, *op. cit.*, p. 159.
[30] Stuart C. Henry, *George Whitefield: Wayfaring Witness*, New York: Abingdon Press, 1957. John and Charles Wesley preceded Whitefield in America (1735–38); their evangelism was not very fruitful, and their preaching was confined to Georgia.

be gained by leading a Christ-inspired life of rationality and goodness. In either case, God ceased to be an irresponsible dictator and became rather a force amenable to control through an established and clearly defined methodology. Democracy, once abolished from religion, was now entrenched as its central characteristic. The doctrine of special election was a form of aristocracy renounced in favor of the new doctrine that every individual is master of his own fate, and that God Himself could not prevent the dominance of man's free will.

The apotheosis of this new religious teaching was not to be achieved until the mid-nineteenth century, when it was given climactic expression in the conclusion of a sermon on "The Love of God," preached by Henry Ward Beecher in Plymouth Church, Brooklyn:

> When I come up before the eternal Judge and say all aglow, "My Lord and my God," will he turn to me and say: "You did not come up the right road . . . go down"? I, to the face of Jehovah, will stand and say: "God! I won't go to hell; I will go to heaven; I love Thee. Now, damn me if Thou canst. I love Thee." And God shall say, and the heavens flame with double and triple rainbows, and echo with joy: "Dost thou love? Enter in and be blessed forever." Let us pray.[31]

This was the inevitable result: the subjection of God Himself to principles reflecting the emergent political emphasis upon equality and justice for all. In this sense John Locke (among others) profoundly influenced theology; then, cumulatively, the new preaching came to exercise a very considerable political effect. In the pulpit new egalitarian ideas could be experimented with in an atmosphere safely impractical and remote from immediate political effect; but as the minds of men were reshaped by the preaching to a new concept of individual responsibility and privilege, the consequences inevitably spilled over into the political realm.

In 1738 George Whitefield, filled with the fervor of evangelism, came from England to spend some eight months in Georgia, experimentally preaching the new gospel of salvation through the redemptive power of Christ's martyrdom. Then, after a return to England, where he tried out the daring plan of preaching in open fields, without the ritualistic support of the church's sanctuary, he made a second trip, this time of seventeen months, in which he travelled through New England, Pennsylvania, and Georgia, raising the Great Awakening to a fever-pitch of optimistic enthusiasm. During another three-year span in England he

[31] Paxton Hibben, *Henry Ward Beecher: An American Portrait*, New York: Press of the Readers Club, 1942, p. 301. The passage gains added interest when considered in the light of Beecher's advice to his brother Charles on how to win success in the pulpit: "Preach little doctrine except what is of mouldy orthodoxy." *Ibid.*, p. 89.

reasserted an allegiance to Calvinism, but with a most uncalvinistic interpretation. Convinced now of the absolute sovereignty of God, he could no longer doubt either predestination or election. However, he felt that God had predestined a possible route to salvation for all who might choose to follow it; and he decided that as many could join the "elect" as accepted the redemption offered by Christ. This was a new Calvinism, deeply tinged with Methodism, dealing the old theology a blow from which it never recovered.

On Whitefield's third trip to America (in 1744) he accepted a call to Charleston, where he was given a plantation equipped with slaves, and devoted himself to defending slavery as being sanctioned by the Bible.[32] During the remainder of his life he commuted back and forth between England and the colonies, until his death at the age of fifty six in Newburyport, Massachusetts.

His preaching was unmatched both in quantity (for he preached over eighteen thousand sermons) and in emotional power. With simplicity of language and a message that merely called sinners to repent and to permit Jesus to bear their burdens, he spoke to enormous crowds several times a day, sometimes for two hours or more at a time. For many years he preached at least forty hours a week.[33] In the entire history of religious propagation, it is doubtful that anyone else ever preached to so many, for so long, under such varied conditions, or with such measurable effect. The numbers of his converts were in the scores of thousands, and they varied from illiterate farmers to prime ministers and leading men in government, education, and business. His strong musical voice could be heard by thousands, and the great actor David Garrick is reputed to have exclaimed, "I would give one hundred guineas if I could say 'O' like Mr. Whitefield."[34] When in one sermon he dramatically pictured an elderly traveller unknowingly coming closer and closer to the edge of a high cliff in the dark of night, so sophisticated an auditor as Lord Chesterfield jumped up and exclaimed, "By heavens, he is gone!"[35] Benjamin Franklin recorded that he was at first scornful of Whitefield but became more and more impressed as the sermon continued.[36] Nevertheless, the Pennsylvania Deist did not abandon his

---

[32] Henry, *op. cit.*, pp. 116–118.
[33] Eugene E. White, "The Preaching of George Whitefield During the Great Awakening in America," unpublished doctoral thesis, Louisiana State University, May, 1947.
[34] Henry, *op. cit.*, p. 61.
[35] *Ibid.*, 62.
[36] In his *Autobiography*, Franklin relates the incident: "I happened soon after to attend one of his sermons, in the course of which I perceived he intended to finish with a collection, and I silently resolved he should get nothing from me. I had in my pocket a handful of copper money, three or four silver dollars, and five pistoles in gold. As he proceeded I began to soften, and concluded to give the coppers. Another

scepticism. The effects of the preaching, Franklin insisted, were short-lived.[37] In one sermon Whitefield commenced fourteen successive short sentences with the exclamation, "Oh," and found this ritualistic repetition effective in breaking down the spirit of resistance. In general Whitefield's style was conversational and exceedingly direct, with much personalization, and with a skillful intermingling of pathos and humor. The content stressed the tortures of hellfire as contrasted with the eternal bliss to be won through the simple act of coming forward to attest publicly a belief in Jesus as Saviour.

By preaching sometimes outside of churches, by denying denominationalism, and by undermining the old orthodoxy, Whitefield created considerable ill will. On the other hand, his travels up and down the Colonies helped greatly to break up the sense of separateness of the colonials. Wherever he spoke, in Massachusetts, Pennsylvania, or in the deep South, he interlarded his sermons with references to experiences throughout the settlements, thus helping to create a sense of one indissoluble American community. Furthermore, as has been noted and is worth repeating, his emphasis upon personal salvation within the reach of all inevitably helped to develop a sense of individual rights and of revolt against confining external authority.

The period from 1609 to 1765 was a time of vast and stirring changes in the colonies. The early efforts of the Theocrats to secure a static theological and social climate failed in the face of new conditions, expanding opportunities, and the spirit of rationalistic empirical inquiry. Both inside and outside the church new ideas were astir, mostly spread and made effective by men of fearless and pungent speech.[38] The pulpit was the classroom of early America, and its diverse and challenging lessons were eagerly learned.

stroke of his oratory made me asham'd of that, and determin'd me to give the silver; and he finish'd so admirably, that I empty'd my pocket wholly into the collector's dish, gold and all." Benjamin Franklin, *Representative Selections*, ed. Frank Luther Mott and Chester Jorgenson, New York: American Book Co., 1936, p. 90.

[37] On July 6, 1749, Franklin wrote Whitefield a suavely discourteous letter, in which he expressed approval "that you have frequent opportunities of preaching among the great" since "there are numbers who, perhaps, fear less the being in hell, than out of the fashion." He then commented on the number of conversions achieved by Whitefield, and added: "O that some method could be found to make them lasting! He who discovers that will, in my opinion, deserve more, ten thousand times, than the inventor of the longitude." *Ibid.*, p. 198.

[38] Cf. George V. Bohman, "The Colonial Period—Religious Speaking," in Brigance, ed., *History and Criticism, op. cit.*, I:22–27; and John C. Miller, *Origins of the American Revolution*, Boston: Little, Brown, 1943, Chapter VIII, Section III, pp. 186–197.

II

BETTER TO LIVE FREE
1761‿1788

─────────────────────────────

📖 *From Localism Toward Unity*

FOUR PATTERNS of stress were affecting the political ideas of the American colonials in the period preceding the War of Independence. Two of these were loyalty toward and resentment against the crown and parliament of Great Britain. The other two were the forces of localism and of union in and among the Colonies themselves. The four patterns were related in ways sometimes clear, sometimes confusing. Some speakers knew and some did not which of the forces they wished to represent. Most of them in one way or another and at one time or another were proponents for all four.

In 1643, "for offence and defence, mutuall advice and succore,"[1] the four Colonies of Plymouth, Massachusetts, Connecticut, and New Haven joined together in "The New England Confederacy," with Rhode Island explicitly omitted; and their commissioners continued to meet to discuss their common problems until 1684. In 1661 the General Court of Massachusetts Bay adopted a bold resolution claiming "full power and authoritie, both legislative & executive, for the gouvernement of all the people heere . . . "[2] And in 1678 the even more assertive position was assumed that "the lawes of England are bounded within the fower seas, and doe not reach America."[3] The four different patterns now seem to be really one, for pushing away from England meant pulling together.

The earliest colonial to become really an American was a Bostonian who chose to be a Philadelphian, Benjamin Franklin (1706–1790). He was also a skilled and effective speaker who refused to be an orator.[4]

Philadelphia was congenial to his temperament and beliefs. Quaker piety was no obstacle to business success in a city that valued com-

[1] "The New England Confederation, May 19, 1643," *Basic Documents in American History*, ed. Commager, *op. cit.*, I:26.
[2] *Ibid.*, I:34.
[3] *Ibid.*, I:34.
[4] For a discussion of Franklin's ideas about speaking see Sandra Lewis, "Franklin's Advice to Speakers," *Today's Speech*, VII (Nov., 1959):18–21.

mercialism and financial achievement. The spirit of the community was well reflected in the advice the prosperous Quaker merchant John Reynell gave to his apprentices: "If thou finds out a place where they sell cheap, keep it to thyself, for if thou ships off goods cheaper than others, it will increase business."[5] The mellow practicality of Franklin's political philosophy found ready acceptance in Quakerland, where the early quarrelsomeness (which had led William Penn to write to one of his tormenters: "For the love of God, me, and the poor country, do not be so litigious and brutish!"[6]) was yielding to the gentle influence of the inner light doctrine, and where business acumen favored conciliation of present and potential customers.

Both Franklin's humble origin and his rationalistic deism barred him from intimacy with the First Families of Pennsylvania. But his persuasive skill in "humble inquiry" and his avoidance of "abrupt contradiction" helped him to reap quick and substantial advantage from his diligence and talents: "for I was but a bad speaker, never eloquent, subject to much hesitation in my choice of words, hardly correct in language, and yet I generally carried my point."[7] By 1727 Franklin was joined by a congenial group of young men in founding the Junto, a club dedicated to the improvement of its members through weekly debate and discussion. "Tart words make no friends," he observed, but "a spoonful of Honey will catch more flies than a Gallon of Vinegar."[8] With a keen sense of practicality, Franklin advised, "Would you persuade, speak of interest, not of reason."[9] His critique of the evangelist George Whitefield reflected the high value Philadelphians placed upon propriety: ". . . every accent, every emphasis, every modulation of voice, was so perfectly well turn'd and well plac'd, that, without being interested in the subject, one could not help being pleased with the discourse."[10] The statement came perilously close to asserting that what a man professes is less important than how he phrases it. Such a conclusion was soundly consonant with the business ethic that was developing in Philadelphia, New York, and other centers of commercialism. What was important was to be tolerant and even uncritical of differences of opinion—to live together amicably in a social unity which subordinated con-

[5] Frederick B. Tolles, *George Logan of Philadelphia*, New York: Oxford University Press, 1953, pp. 15–16.
[6] For a discussion of the controversies between William Penn and his adversaries, see Jon Hopkins, "A Rhetorical Analysis of the Oratory of William Penn," unpublished Ph. D. thesis, The Pennsylvania State University, 1961.
[7] *The Writings of Benjamin Franklin*, ed. A. H. Smyth, New York: Macmillan, 1905–1907, I:338.
[8] Benjamin Franklin, *The Sayings of Poor Richard*, ed. Paul Leicester Ford, New York: Knickerbocker Press, 1890.
[9] *Ibid.*
[10] From the *Autobiography*, in *Writings, op. cit.*, I:359.

tradictory beliefs or contrasting manners. Such an approach was the needed key to attaining unity amidst the colonial diversity.

In 1754, trouble with the Iroquois Indians led to the calling of an inter-colonial Congress at Albany, in which Chief Hendrick of the Mohawks argued cogently against the land speculation that was confining the Indians to "the very spot we live upon and scarcely that,"[11] and also against the greed that led white traders to sell guns and ammunition to French-allied Indian tribes in return for beaver pelts. Benjamin Franklin seized upon the opportunity to present his Plan of Union for the Colonies, supported by the famous cartoon in his *Pennsylvania Gazette*, for May 9, showing a snake cut in pieces, with the slogan, "Join or Die." Franklin's speech to the Congress pleading for confederation was based on his view that people and groups may disagree and yet combine, provided they exercise a decent tolerance. Disagreements, Franklin noted, are inevitable but should not be disturbing. His view was well summarized in a letter to a friend: "Since I cannot govern my own tongue tho' within mine own teeth, how can I hope to govern the tongue of others?"[12] The effort to unite the Colonies proved to be premature; but the seed was sown that eventuated in the First Continental Congress, in Philadelphia, twenty years later.

Between the Southerners and the New Englanders, the merchant-traders of the Middle Colonies exercised an influence tending to de-emphasize differences and encourage a sense of commonality. After all, trade knows no reason for barriers and gold bears no mark of the Colony from which it comes. Despite the scattering of Swedes, Dutchmen, Germans, and French Huguenots, the vast majority of the colonists came from Great Britain. As Noah Webster exultantly noted in 1800: "North America will be Peopled with a hundred millions of men, *all speaking the same language.*"[13] To observers familiar with the diversity of languages in Europe and the widely variant dialects in Great Britain, the relative uniformity of colonial speech was both surprising and indicative of a generic unity. John Witherspoon, coming from Scotland to assume the presidency of Princeton near the close of the Revolution, noted with satisfaction that "The vulgar in America speak much better than the vulgar in Great-Britain."[14] In the preface to a *Vocabulary of American-*

[11] Theodore Atkinson, "Memo Book," in *Colonial Manuscripts*, LXXIX, No. 23, *Archives of the State of New York.* Cf. Robert C. Wenkold, *The Albany Congress and Plan of Union of 1754*, New York: Vantage Press, 1955.
[12] *Selected Works of Benjamin Franklin*, ed. Epes Sargent, Boston: Phillips, Sampson, 1853, p. 420.
[13] Noah Webster, "Preface" to *The American Dictionary of the English Language*, Springfield, Mass.: Merriam, 1860, p. xiii.
[14] *The Works of the Reverend John Witherspoon*, ed. J. Rogers, Philadelphia: William Woodward, 1802, IV:459.

isms, by John Pickering, published in 1816, the lexicographer noted "a greater uniformity of dialect throughout the United States . . . than is to be found in England"; and he ascribed it to the "frequent removals of people from one part of our country to another."[15]

With an ocean that stretched three thousand miles behind them, and that required three months to cross, the new immigrants were able to turn from their old heritage and to strive quickly to take on the idiom as well as the habits of thought of this New World. The results were noted by the cosmopolitan William Eddis, in a letter he wrote on June 8, 1770:

> In England, almost every county is distinguished by peculiar dialect; even different habits, and different modes of thinking, evidently discriminate inhabitants, whose local situation is not far remote: but in Maryland, and throughout adjacent provinces, it is worthy of observation, that a striking similarity of speech universally prevails; and it is strictly true, that the pronunciation of the generality of the people has an accuracy and elegance, that cannot fail of gratifying the most judicious ear . . . .
>
> For my part, I confess myself totally at a loss to account for the apparent difference, between the colonists and persons under equal circumstances of education and fortune, resident in the mother country. This uniformity of language prevails not only on the coast, where Europeans form a considerable mass of the people, but likewise in the interior parts, where population has made slow advances; and where opportunities seldom occur to derive any great advantages from an intercourse with intelligent strangers.[16]

Along with their commonality of language, the inhabitants of the thirteen Colonies also possessed a common pride in their heritage of English liberties. The universities in Peru and Mexico City were established a hundred years before Harvard; and the Spaniards were firmly based in Florida, New Orleans, and the Pacific Southwest before the English settlers arrived at Jamestown and Cape Cod. In the north the French Canadians were establishing missions and building an extensive fur trade while the residents of the thirteen Colonies were struggling to scratch a living from the soil. What was it that led the mid-colonials to unite? Why did they prosper far beyond their southern and northern neighbors? The reasons are complex, extending far beyond the scope of this particularized history.

But there was one institution to be found in all the Colonies which helped to give the settlers a sense of fellow-feeling. This was the famous

---

[15] John Pickering, *Vocabulary of Americanisms*, Boston: Cummings and Hillard, 1816.
[16] William Eddis, *Letters from America*, London: C. Dilley, 1792, pp. 59–61.

Town Meeting. It took so many forms that historical summary is difficult. Nevertheless, whether among the Quakers of Pennsylvania, the Huguenots of Charleston, the planters of Virginia, the rebels of Providence, or the townsmen of New England, the town meetings constituted a valuable medium through which public opinion could be formulated and communicated. The basic pattern was established in 1641, in the "Body of Liberties" granted to Massachusetts Bay, which provided:

> Everyone whether Inhabitant or Forreiner, free or not free, shall have libertie to come to any publique Court, Councel, or Town Meeting, and either by speech or writeing to move any lawfull, seasonable, and materiall question, or to present any necessary motion, complaint, petition, Bill or information, whereof that meeting hath proper cognizance, so it be done in convenient time, due order, and respective manner.[17]

The discussions must have been vigorous, for by 1645 it was found expedient to create the office of Moderator, to keep the members "attentive to the business of the assembly." Meetings apparently were poorly attended, for a system of fines was adopted to prevent members from entering late or leaving early. Even so, the minutes are replete with such phrases as "after a very long debate," or, "after a full debate," indicating that the questions were seriously discussed.

In New England the Town Meetings elected the Constable and a board of twelve men who advised the Magistrate between meetings. They also discussed questions of community importance, such as school affairs, management of the common grazing lands, problems of conduct and delinquency; and improvement of the roads. Until the mid-eighteenth century most of the Town Meetings were held only once or twice a year—although in Providence the meetings were conducted weekly.

Gordon, in his *History of the Independence of the United States*, described the pre-revolutionary pattern: "Every town is an incorporated republic. The selectmen by their own authority, or upon the application of a certain number of townsmen, issue a warrant calling for a town meeting. The warrant mentions the business to be engaged in, and no other can be legally executed. The inhabitants are warned to attend; and they that are present, though not a quarter nor a tenth of the whole, have a right to proceed. They choose a president by the name of Moderator, who regulates the proceedings of the meetings. Each individual has an equal liberty of delivering his opinion, and is not liable to be silenced or brow-beaten by a richer or greater townsman than himself. Every freeman or freeholder gives his vote or not, and for or against, as

[17] *The Laws and Liberties of Massachusetts*, ed. Max Farrand, Cambridge: Harvard University Press, 1929, p. 35.

he pleases; and each vote weighs equally, whether that of the highest or lowest inhabitant . . . . All the New England towns are on the same plan in general."[18]

In Charleston, South Carolina, the Huguenot immigrants from their earliest settlement made this institution an important center of their political and social activities. In Williamsburg, Virginia, the planters zealously guarded their political privileges and met regularly to discuss them. In Pennsylvania—and wherever else the Quakers went—the religious meetings of the Friends were always in the form of discussions, in which the sanction of religious approval or disapproval was freely brought to bear upon a wide variety of community questions.[19] In all the Colonies, as grievances against the Crown accumulated, Town Meetings came increasingly to be utilized as centers of agitation and as a focal point for drawing up and presenting petitions.

Like so much else in democracy, the Town Meetings were sometimes disorderly and irregular in procedure. Often they were poorly attended and the quality of discussion varied from eloquent to dull. Nevertheless, they deserve their reputation as a seedbed of independence. Any society needs an apparatus for developing a "network of agreements" among its members. Through the Town Meetings the people became accustomed to meeting together, to talking over their problems, to forming courses of action, and to judging the quality of their leadership. It was largely through them that there evolved gradually the working philosophy and methodology that made national independence possible. Faneuil Hall was even more important to the formation of the new nation than was Bunker Hill.

The Boston Radicals: Sam Adams and James Otis

IT IS a truism that a patriot is a traitor whose rebellion has proved successful. Until success is achieved the men who rebel (and most particularly the agitators who arouse and guide the rebelliousness) can scarcely be expected to measure up to standards of social respectability.

---

[18] William Gordon, *The History of the Independence of the United States,* New York: Hodge, Allen, and Campbell, 1794, I:250–251. Cf. David Potter, "Some Aspects of Speaking in the Town Meetings of Colonial New England," *Southern Speech Journal,* XXII (Spring 1957):157–163.
[19] John Woolman, for example, travelled up and down the Colonies from 1746 until his death in 1772, discussing with them, among other things, the evils of slavery. Cf. John Woolman, *The Journals and Essays,* ed. A. M. Gummere, New York: Macmillan, 1922, pp. 380–381.

In Virginia, Patrick Henry's radicalism was relatively sedate, for in that Colony the rebels were first of all the heads of the great families. In Massachusetts the spirit of independence was born in the middle class and spilled downward, with the aristocracy by and large remaining with the Tories. It is only natural, then, that violence, and even vindictiveness, marked the feverish and often demagogic oratory of the two principal Boston radicals: Sam Adams (1722–1803) and James Otis (1725–1783).

Both men were outwardly ultra-conservative. Otis was a man of wealth and social status, and eccentric to the ultimate point of insanity. Sam Adams belonged to the respectable branch of the great Adams family; his father, a lifelong opponent of authoritarianism in government, was a Deacon, a banker, and a man of both social and economic substance. The younger Adams was a devout churchgoer, puritanical in behavior, and typically middle-class in his tastes. Nevertheless, beneath the surface respectability there boiled a pitch-pot of fanatic zeal.

After his cause had been won, Sam Adams could say with becoming modesty: "It is often said that I am at the head of the Revolution, whereas a few of us merely lead the way as the people follow, and we can go no further than we are backed by them; for, if we advance any further, we make no progress, and may lose our labor in defeat."[1] The fact is that without Sam Adams there might have been no Revolution. Certainly he fanned the embers of discontent to white-hot heat and cared little for either principles of morality or temperance in his methods. He himself accurately and adequately defined his basic tenet of propaganda: "Put your adversary in the wrong and keep him there."[2]

The chief fallacy of Adams's case against British tyranny is the fact that he was left free by the authorities to carry on his campaign of vituperation and incitement to rebellion. Through his voluminous journalistic writings, he pushed to the utmost the limits of freedom of the press; in his speeches and organizational activities he strained the boundaries of legitimate political opposition. Even in his private life he surely strayed beyond the law; for, as colonial tax collector for Boston, he misappropriated several thousand pounds of public revenue and was saved from imprisonment largely through public favor won by laxness in collecting taxes. By all these means his skill in arousing united resistance to British rule was so great that a succession of Royal Governors found themselves helpless to deal with him. "Unquestionably," says Miller, his

[1] James Speer Loring, *The Hundred Boston Orators*, Boston: J. P. Jowett, 1853, p. 13.
[2] Quoted by John C. Miller, *Sam Adams: Pioneer in Propaganda*, Boston: Little, Brown, 1936, p. 24.

ablest biographer, "he was a master of stagecraft, deeply versed in the art of swaying the popular mind."[3]

After Adams was elected to the Assembly—and from there elevated to the influential office of Clerk—his followers succeeded in having installed a public gallery, so that the public could hear him and Otis "thunder from the Rostrum." Since Sam Adams spoke always extemporaneously, few samples of his vocal diatribes remain; but it is well attested that his talk was even more violent than his writings. In the Assembly, the Adams and Otis team, through "inflammatory Speeches within doors and parades of the mob without,"[4] began "driving on at a furious rate" in their campaign to arouse resentment against English rule. A Tory journalist wrote: "This dog [Sam Adams] is very artful, loves babbling, especially when he gets in a large room."[5] A master organizer and winner of converts, Adams was "ever going about, seeking whom he might devour." Within the Caucus Club he found receptive dissidents already assembled by his father. He himself founded new clubs the way a farmer sows grain: Sons of Liberty, Mohawks, Fire Companies, even Singing Societies—over all of which Adams presided and "embraced such Opportunities to ye inculcating Sedition, 'till it ripened into Rebellion!"[6] Even fast days and prayer meetings were converted by Adams into occasions for patriotic consecration.

Arousing Bostonian fervor was not, Sam Adams realized, sufficient to create revolution. Somehow the widely separated and quarrelsome Colonies must be induced to unite in resentment. The task seemed impossible. When Benjamin Franklin had proposed Union at Albany in 1754, the effort failed totally. Andrew Burnaby, travelling through the Middle Colonies in the early 1760's, concluded that "Fire and water are not more heterogeneous than the different colonies in North America."[7] As we have seen, Burnaby's observation was wide of the mark. Nevertheless, when Otis and Adams persuaded the Massachusetts Assembly to send a Circular Letter to the other colonial legislatures in opposition to the Stamp Tax, the results were meager. With an instinct for local ward politics, however, Sam Adams hit upon the device of establishing Committees of Correspondence from Boston to Charleston; and this personalized type of organization proved more fruitful.

When the British sought to dampen the growing colonial resentment

---

[3] *Ibid.*, p. 24.
[4] *Bernard Papers*, "Bernard to General Conway, Nov. 25, 1765," and "Bernard to Powell, Oct. 26, 1765," Vol. IV. Cf. Miller, *op. cit.*, p. 60.
[5] *Boston Evening Post*, Nov. 23, 1767; cf. Miller, *op. cit.*, p. 98.
[6] *The Works of John Adams*, ed. Charles Frances Adams, Ten Vols., Boston: Little, Brown, 1850–56, X:251.
[7] Andrew Burnaby, *Travels Through the Middle Settlements in North America*, London: T. Payne, 1798, p. 121.

by repealing the Stamp Tax, Adams was not mollified but was encouraged to hope for even greater success. The quartering of British troops in Boston in September, 1768, gave him a master opportunity. To a mob in the south end of Boston, "trembling and in great agitation," Adams cried: "If you are Men, behave like Men; let us take up arms immediately and be free to seize all the King's Officers: we shall have thirty thousand Men to join us from the Country."[8] Soon he had his Mohawk Boys organized to jeer and stone the Redcoats whenever they appeared on the streets. To a Boston Town Meeting in 1769 he exclaimed: "Independent we are, and independent we will be." Tension and ill-will mounted.

On the night of March 4, 1770, Adams had Boston plastered with handbills declaring the Redcoats were about to attack the citizenry. The next morning, as a jeering mob gathered about the lone British sentry in Dock's Square, off King's Street, Captain Preston, commanding the Twenty-Ninth Regiment of British troops, decided to confront the mob with a platoon. Sam Adams was ready for his major triumph. As John Adams described the scene: "The multitude was shouting and huzzaing, and threatening life, the bells ringing, the mob whistling, screaming and rending like an Indian yell, the people from all quarters throwing every species of rubbish they could pick up in the streets."[9] Finally one of the soldiers was knocked down by a brickbat; when he got up he fired into the crowd. The mob surged forward and Preston ordered his troops to fire. Five civilians fell dead or mortally wounded.

The next day Sam Adams called a mammoth meeting in Faneuil Hall, to which he made a violent speech, "enough to fire any heart with a desire to become a patriot."[10] Heading a committee to the Governor's mansion to demand withdrawal of all British troops from Boston, Adams threatened that fifteen thousand fighting men were ready to pour into Boston to annihilate the Redcoats. Governor Hutchinson yielded and promised quick removal of the troops. Adams's next demand was for a speedy trial of Preston and his soldiers, with the charge to be murder. When Hutchinson managed to get the trial postponed for six months, and as opinion in Boston swung toward moderation, Adams established a committee to organize an annual Massacre Day, complete with parades and an oration.

For the next three years Adams's efforts seemed futile. He attempted to organize American-wide boycotts of English goods, but the conflict-

[8] Miller, *op. cit.*, p. 144.
[9] Frederic Kidder, *The Boston Massacre*, Albany: Joel Munsell, 1870, pp. 255–257.
[10] *The New York Journal*, March 29, 1770; cf. Miller, *op. cit.*, pp. 80ff.

ing interests of the Colonies proved too great a barrier. In 1773, however, the decree of an East India Company monopoly for the import of tea provided a better opportunity. In a mass meeting on December 16, when Hutchinson refused to order the departure of three ships loaded with tea, Sam Adams arose and announced portentously: "This meeting can do nothing further to save the country."[11] That night his Mohawk Boys dumped the tea in the harbor. The Rubicon had been crossed. As Adams said, it was now "Neck or Nothing." The British could not ignore such an act of flagrant rebellion, and Boston was closed to all shipping. Here, at last, was an issue on which the Colonies could unite.

When the First Continental Congress convened in Philadelphia to deal with the emergency, Sam Adams led the delegation from Boston. Joseph Galloway was ready with a proposal that foreshadowed the later Dominion plan for the British Commonwealth. To counter this moderation, Sam and his colleagues acted with "uncommon prudence and discretion," saying little, contenting themselves with hinted aspersions against "half-way patriots." Sam was pinpointed in the Congress as "the most extravagent partisan of democracy," and the "Greatest Republican in America." He recognized this doubtful praise as evidence that for the moment his radicalism was too far in advance of the public sentiment. Nevertheless, he had the satisfaction of seeing the Congress adopt the measure he had long advocated of an all-American "association" against the import or the consumption of English-made goods and also against the export of goods to England. Galloway wrote of Adams: "He eats little, drinks little, sleeps little, thinks much, and is most decisive and indefatigable in the pursuit of his objects."[12]

Back in Boston, Adams's next opportunity came on Massacre Day, March 5, 1775, when he touched off a near riot with his remarks as Moderator. The war was now gathering. Six months later came the "shot heard round the world" at Concord; and that night, in Lexington, Adams fled in his nightdress to escape capture. No soldier, his work was largely done.

Although he lived until 1803, his days of greatness ended with the start of the war he did so much to instigate. In 1788 he opposed the Federal Constitution, believing it an instrument of centralizing tyranny; but his words smacked too much of the past to carry significant influence. When Daniel Shays led a farmers' rebellion against taxation policies of the new government in 1786–87, Sam Adams uttered the (for

[11] Miller, op. cit., p. 294; cf. Massachusetts Historical Proceedings, VIII:325.
[12] Joseph Galloway, Historical and Political Reflections of the Rise and Progress of the American Revolution, London: G. Wilkie, 1780, p. 67.

him) astonishing dictum that "republics could only exist by a due submission to the laws."[13] This was his requiem: an anticlimactic conclusion to a life that persisted after its purpose had been achieved.

A close partner of Sam Adams in revolutionary agitation was the able and well-to-do lawyer James Otis, Jr. Otis was both brilliant and emotionally unstable. It was he, as the Tories said, "who first broke down the barriers of Government to let in the Hydra of Rebellion."[14] The occasion was a trial, on February 24, 1761, in which he defended a group of Boston merchants (actually smugglers) against the application of Writs of Assistance, or unlimited search warrants. To a crowded courtroom Otis made a five-hour speech, commencing at two o'clock in the afternoon, and appealing in effect from parliamentary authority to "natural rights," which he described as the basis of English Common Law. "The laws of God and nature," he declared, are supreme. "No parliament could stand against them, and no king."[15] The Court listened in silence as Governor Hutchinson could find no better recourse than to refer the matter back to London for reconsideration. "Here this day, in the old Council Chamber," John Adams wrote fifty years later, "the child independence was born." No text of the speech was preserved. Notes were made by John Adams, which were expanded into a quasi-text by G. R. Minot, and this is the best we have.[16]

In the Assembly James Otis ruled as Speaker, and his "mobbish eloquence," so the Tories charged, had "Superior Powers of inflaming and distracting an infatuated People." Had he not carried in his nervous system the seeds of a developing insanity, Otis might well have been the true father of the Revolution. His ability to inflame passions in his talks to the Boston mobs was offset by his "mad pranks" and periods of alternating wild gaiety and deep depression. Governor Thomas Hutchinson thought him "more fit for a madhouse than the House of Representatives."[17] Because of his tremendous popular appeal, Tories called him the "Mad Dictator" of Boston. His methods are well illustrated by the Boston Town Meeting in 1765 in which he challenged Prime Minister George Grenville to a personal duel to solve the problems between England and the Colonies. Otis jeered at the members of the House of Commons as "those mighty Men that affect to give Law to the Colonies

[13] *The Works of John Adams, op. cit.,* IX:551.
[14] Miller, *op. cit.,* p. 32.
[15] William Tudor, *The Life of James Otis,* Boston: Wells and Lilly, 1823, pp. 62–88.
[16] Both the Adams' notes and the Minot text are included in Commager, *Documents of American History, op. cit.,* I:45–47.
[17] *Works of John Adams, op. cit.,* II:179–180.

. . . , a parcel of Button-makers, Pin-makers, Horse Jockeys, Gamesters, Pensioners, Pimps, and Whore Masters."[18] Ten years before the revolution he was saying he "hoped and believed we should one and all resist even unto Blood."[19]

Despite his occasional bursts of uncontrollable violence, Otis was basically much more conservative than his friend Sam Adams. "If I have one ambitious wish," he declared earnestly, "it is to see Great Britain at the head of the world, and to see my King, under God, the father of mankind."[20] What he most desired was establishment of colonial representation in Parliament—upon which aim, so he insisted, "I placed my foot, and built my only hope and desire."[21] Rather than independence, what he sought was justice within the Empire—for the Colonies as political units and for the "necessitous" poor. When the Revolution commenced, he had already lost his mind wholly and was living under the care of a sister in Boston. Nevertheless, during the battle of Bunker Hill he somehow made his way to the scene of action and was found crouching in a trench, his eyes staring vacantly along the barrel of a wavering rifle. Friends led him quietly away. Like Sam Adams, his contribution was considerable and his end anticlimactic. His life closed like a speech that lasts too long.

John Adams: The Atlas of Independence

ON A FARM outside the small town of Braintree, ten miles south of Boston, was born John Adams (1735–1826), whose parents, both uneducated, destined him from birth, as their eldest son, for Harvard College and the Congregational ministry. The boy lived up to every expectation—except that he studied law instead of theology, and in 1758 was admitted to the Boston bar. It was in 1761, listening to James Otis speak against the Writs of Assistance, that John (a cousin of Sam Adams) became converted to the defense of colonial rights. Unlike Sam, he was not fitted for popular leadership, partly because he took himself too seriously. Nevertheless, his abilities and courage combined to give him considerable influence among the Massachusetts Whigs.

In December, 1765, he spoke boldly before the Governor and Coun-

---

[18] Miller, *op. cit.*, p. 143.
[19] *Ibid.*, p. 143. Cf. *Chalmers Papers*, II, which records the speech by Otis in June, 1768.
[20] "James Otis to the Earl of Buchan, July 18, 1768," *Otis Papers*, Ms., Massachusetts Historical Society; cf. Miller, *op. cit.*, p. 93.
[21] Miller, *op. cit.*, p. 91.

cil, declaring the Stamp Act invalid on the grounds that the Colonies were not represented in Parliament. Even more bravely he accepted, in 1770, a plea to defend Captain Preston and the British soldiers accused of murder in the "Boston Massacre" case—though this meant defiance of his cousin Sam, of whom he was fond, and of the most articulate Boston public opinion. John Adams was steeled to expect the criticism engendered by his decision from the Sons of Liberty; but he was appalled by the congratulations that poured in upon him from the conservatives. "Nine Tories out of ten," he told his wife Abigail, despondently, "are convinced I have come over to their side."[1] It was small consolation when, before the trial the next Spring, he was elected to the Massachusetts House of Representatives by a vote of 418 to 118. Too many of the votes came from Tories. Too many were in doubt as to which side he was on.

In the trial of the eight indicted soldiers, Adams had to attack his fellow Bostonians in order to defend the accused. Blaming the incident on the crowd that commenced the violence, Adams told the jury: "Why we should scruple to call such a set of people a mob I cannot conceive, unless the name is too respectable for them." He admitted that all Boston wished for a verdict of guilt. But "Facts," he said, "are stubborn things . . . . Nor is the law less stable than the fact." Then he concluded, slowly and soberly: "The law on the one hand is inexorable to the cries and lamentations of the prisoners. On the other it is deaf, deaf as an adder to the clamors of the populace." The jury was out two and a half hours before it returned with the verdict: "Not guilty of murder, but Guilty of manslaughter." Six of the defendants were released; the other two were branded on the thumb and then set free. John Adams, so weary that he felt his career was at an end, wrote in his diary: "For the remainder of my days I shall decline in sense, spirit, and activity." When Sam Adams, holding out a gesture of reconciliation, came months later to invite him on behalf of the Sons of Liberty to give the Massacre Day oration in 1773, he declined. He also declined to stand for re-election to the Assembly. "I am disengaged from public affairs," he confided to his diary. He was thirty seven years of age.[2]

Within a week, however, he was publishing in the newspapers articles defending the independence of the judiciary from control by the crown. In 1774 he accepted election to the Continental Congress, and, when hostilities broke out, he performed a service that won him the admiration of his colleagues by offering to turn over the seventeen thousand

[1] Catherine Drinker Bowen, *John Adams and the American Revolution*, Boston: Little, Brown, 1951, p. 358.
[2] *Life and Works of John Adams, op. cit.*, I:110–120; cf. Bowen, *op. cit.*, pp. 480–510.

Massachusetts soldiers to Congress and by proposing that the commander-in-chief be a Virginian, Colonel George Washington, in opposition to the ambitions of several New England generals. By these acts substantial progress was made toward converting the scattered skirmishes into a revolutionary war.

No one in the Congress felt a heavier sense of responsibility than did John Adams. "When fifty or sixty men have a constitution to form for a great empire," he wrote to his wife, "at the same time that they have a country of fifteen hundred miles in extent to fortify, millions to arm and train, a naval power to begin, an extensive commerce to regulate, numerous tribes of Indians to negotiate with, a standing army of twenty-seven thousand men to raise, pay, victual and officer, I shall really pity those fifty or sixty men."[3] In another mood, however, he could exercise both insight and patience: "America is a great, unwieldy body," he wrote. "Its progress must be slow. It is like a large fleet sailing under convoy. The fleetest sailors must wait for the dullest and slowest. Like a coach and six, the swiftest horses must be slackened, and the slowest quickened, that all may keep an even pace."[4]

In *The Reluctant Rebels: The Story of the Continental Congress, 1774–1789,* Lynn Montross, the author, quoted a letter from Thomas McKean to John Adams, written in later years, in which he said: "I do not recollect any *formal* speeches, such as are made in the British Parliament and our late Congresses, to have been made in the revolutionary Congress, though I was a member for eight years . . . . We had no time to hear such speeches; little for deliberation; action was the order of the day."

John Adams was wholeheartedly a part of the action. After doing all he could to insure unanimity in rebellion by turning over the New England troops to Virginian command, he proposed, on May 6, 1775, a resolution calling for "a government in every colony; a confederation of the whole; and treaties with foreign nations to acknowledge us a sovereign state."[5] For three days he supported this motion in debate, after which it was passed. Then, on June 7, 1776, in support of Richard Henry Lee, he seconded the motion that "these colonies are and by right ought to be free and independent." Naturally enough, he was appointed to a committee, headed by Thomas Jefferson, to draft a Declaration of Independence. And when Jefferson's draft was presented to the Congress, Adams carried so well the burden of defending it that

[3] John Adams, *Familiar Letters,* ed. C. F. Adams, New York: Houghton Mifflin, 1875, p. 85.
[4] Bowen, *op. cit.,* p. 523.
[5] *Journals of the Continental Congress,* Washington, D. C.: Government Printing Office, 1906, Vols. V–VI. Cf. *Familiar Letters, op. cit.,* p. 173.

Jefferson said: "He was the Colossus of that debate."[6] This was the sequence of events by which John Adams came to be known to his peers as "The Atlas of Independence"—bearing the cause forward to a large degree on his own shoulders.

As with Otis and Sam Adams, the virtual end of John Adams's career as an orator came long before the end of his life. His death was not to come until 1826—and then, fittingly, on the Fourth of July—by a remarkable coincidence on the same day as the death of Thomas Jefferson. The decades following the launching of independence were filled with honors for Adams: several ambassadorships, the vice-presidency, and the presidency. They were also marred by jealousies, hurt vanity, bitter quarrels with Hamilton and Jefferson, and widespread public denunciation that attacked even his appointment of John Marshall to be Chief Justice of the Supreme Court. Adams proved to be tactless and without skill as a political leader and saw the Federalist Party fall apart under his mismanagement. Moreover, the bright vision he entertained for the era of independence did not live up to his expectations. Even while the revolution was still in progress he became appalled by the self-seeking and irresponsible behavior of the states and the statesmen. "Unfaithfulness," he wrote his wife, "in public stations is deeply criminal. Neither profit, nor honor, nor applause is acquired by faithfulness. But I know by what. There is too much corruption, even in this infant age of our republic. Virtue is not in fashion. Vice is not infamous."[7]

The best speaking he ever did, perhaps, was in the Second Continental Congress, in defense of the Declaration of Independence. "He came out with a power of thought and expression that moved us from our seats,"[8] Jefferson years later recalled of this speech. At the time nobody took notes, and all, including the speaker himself, were too tired to recall what he said. Yet all the remainder of his life John Adams was to hear this speech referred to in terms of wonder and praise. Daniel Webster undertook a fictional recreation of it in his over-long and under-eloquent eulogy of Adams and Jefferson, delivered on August 2, 1826. There is authenticity, however, in the opening words Webster put in John Adams's mouth: "Sink or swim, live or die, survive or perish, I give my hand and my heart to this vote."[9] Whatever Adams did, he did without stint.

[6] *Papers of Thomas Jefferson*, ed. Julian P. Boyd, Princeton: Princeton University Press, 1950, I:299ff; Cf. Bowen, *op. cit.*, pp. 587–607.
[7] *Letters of John Adams*, ed. C. F. Adams, Boston; Little, Brown, 1841, pp. 166–167.
[8] Bowen, *op. cit.*, p. 596.
[9] Daniel Webster, "Adams and Jefferson," *The Life, Eulogy, and Great Orations of Daniel Webster*, Rochester, N. Y.: Haywood, 1854, p. 85.

Patrick Henry: Virginian or American? 📖

"RADICAL" AND "conservative" are useful terms only when arbitrarily defined. To most historians the radicals were those who supported the Declaration of Independence but opposed adoption of the Constitution; or those who trusted the generality of the people more than they did the aristocracy; or those who preferred unrestricted franchise to special privileges for property-holders; or those who were willing to venture upon new experiments in government rather than cling to precedent. The conservatives, in general, were the reverse. When all these bases of definition are applied, few among the revolutionists except Sam Adams and Tom Jefferson qualify as radicals.

The great Virginian agitator, Patrick Henry (1736–1799), whose eloquence aroused the South to side with New England, was conservative in that he knew of "no way to judge the future but by the past."[1] Yet in temperament, in manner, in disdain for established authority, in his faith in localized government controlled by the mass of the people, Henry belonged to the radical group. Just as Hamilton, Franklin, John Adams, and Washington trusted government only when it was centralized, directed primarily by men of wealth and education, and subject to the veto of a strong executive, so did Otis, Sam Adams, and Patrick Henry trust it most when its power was limited by the votes and muskets of "the people." Hamilton's dismissal of democracy as "a frail and worthless fabric"[2] contrasts meaningfully with Henry's distrust of "the contemptible minority."[3] Above all, however, the distinction that is most trustworthy is one of manner: of violent emotionalism contrasted with the suave appeal to reason. Just as Sam Adams depended primarily upon populist violence, so did Patrick Henry depend primarily upon popular feelings.

Patrick Henry had the temperament and something of the appearance of a frontiersman—tall, gangling, stooped, with a wide mouth, strong nose, high forehead, and a bush of brick-red hair. But he was born of an old and respected Virginia family, grew up on the outskirts of Richmond, and became sufficiently well educated to hold his own in

---

[1] William Wirt Henry, *Patrick Henry: Life, Correspondence, and Speeches*, New York: Scribner's, 1891, I:262.
[2] Alexander Hamilton, *Works*, ed. H. C. Lodge, New York: Putnam's, 1904, X:445. Cf. Merrill D. Peterson, *The Jefferson Image in the American Mind*, New York: Oxford University Press, 1960, p. 156.
[3] Ernest J. Wrage and Barnett Baskerville, *American Forum*, New York: Harper, 1960, Henry's speech in Virginia Ratification Convention, June 5, 1788, p. 13.

the thrust and parry of debate with such men as Madison, Mason, and the Randolphs, who delighted in bringing current problems to the test of both ancient and modern historical comparisons, sometimes in considerable detail.[4] Thomas Jefferson (who early took a dislike to Henry) called him "a man of little knowledge of any sort," and added scathingly, "He read nothing and had no books."[5] Actually, Henry attended a meager public school only until he was ten, studied under his father's guidance until he was fifteen, and for the rest depended largely upon a mind that was quick, perceptive, and eager to learn.

He was not only intelligent but had the right temperament for forensic duelling. He loved argument—and in the right way; for he would rather listen than talk, and he made a practice of analyzing, testing, and questioning the arguments he heard. Then, with a sharp understanding of what his coadjutors believed and felt, and of how their minds worked, he was ready to drive home and nail down his own conclusions. Both his parents loved to entertain and to stimulate their guests to thoughtful talk on the issues of the day. As a boy, Patrick sat silently in the background and filtered the ideas of the many visitors through his questioning mind. When he was sixteen his father set him up in the grocery business, and Patrick promptly converted his store into a discussion club. If the loungers were talkative, he listened; if silent, he goaded them with questions and challenges. Tradition has it that one day, as he sprawled on a sack of salt listening to a lively debate, a customer asked for salt, and Patrick impatiently replied, "Just sold the last peck." Naturally, the store failed. He tried farming, but his house and furniture burned and he suffered from the drought of the bad crop year of 1758.[6]

In 1759, married, without money or a home, and a failure in both business and farming, he borrowed a copy of *Coke Upon Littleton* and spent the next month or six weeks in the study of law. He came up for his bar examination before John Randolph, Sr., of Roanoke, who questioned and challenged him on imaginary cases for "several hours," then concluded: "You defend your opinions well, sir, but now to the law and the testimony . . . . Behold the force of natural reasons: you have never seen these books, nor this principle of the law; yet you are right and I am wrong . . . Mr. Henry, if your industry be only half equal to your genius, I augur that you will do well, and become an ornament and an honor to your profession."[7] By the end of 1763,

---

[4] The best-rounded account of Henry's speaking is Louis A. Mallory, "Patrick Henry," in Brigance, ed., *History and Criticism, op. cit.*, II:580–602.

[5] Quoted by George Ticknor Curtis, *Life of Daniel Webster*, New York: Appleton, 1870, I:585.

[6] George Morgan, *The True Patrick Henry*, Philadelphia: Lippincott, 1907, Chapters II and III and *passim*.

[7] *Ibid.*, p. 47.

Henry's fee-book contained records of 1185 cases he had defended—as compared to 504 conducted by Thomas Jefferson in his first four years of practice.[8] The red-haired Demosthenes of Hanover County had at last found his profession.

In that year, 1763, he moved dramatically onto a wider stage. The occasion was a trial that became famous as "The Parsons Case." In 1755 the House of Burgesses had enacted a law providing that salaries, including those to the Church of England clergymen, should henceforth be paid not in tobacco, but in cash, at the rate of two pennies per pound. The poor crop of 1758 resulted in an increase in the price of tobacco, but the Burgesses re-enacted the Two-penny law. The clergy were far from being the only ones who thereby suffered in effect a salary reduction, but their complaints were the loudest. In a sense, the dispute was between the aristocratic office-holders and the taxpaying public. On April 1, 1762, the Rev. James Maury brought suit against the collectors of Louisa County, demanding annual salaries for the clergy of £400 (then the market value of the sixteen thousand pounds of tobacco they were supposed to get) rather than the £133 6s. 8d. they were being paid under the Two-penny Act. On November 5, 1763, the case was heard and the verdict was given to Rev. Maury. On December 1, the case was again brought before a jury to determine whether the plaintiffs were entitled to damages for past losses of salary—and Patrick Henry was engaged to argue the case for the defendants.

On the morning of the trial, Hanover Courthouse was filled with complaisant clergymen and apprehensive townsmen. On the bench as presiding justice sat Colonel John Henry, Patrick's father. Peter Lyons was the courtly and graceful lawyer for the plaintiffs; his opening statement set forth the plain facts that the King had "disallowed" the Two-penny Act, that the court had already found for his client, and that damages should be allocated in the sum of £288, which would be the precise amount Rev. Maury would have received had he been paid in tobacco at the market price. Lyons sat down amidst murmurs of satisfaction from the clergy.

Patrick Henry arose awkwardly, hesitating for a few moments while he struggled to find words that would not come. His father sank down in his seat in shame, while the spectators felt sorry for the young barrister who evidently realized his case was hopeless. Then Patrick's mind began feeding words to his tongue, and strange words they were: that the King's duty was to his people, that he had no right to disallow a bill passed by the Burgesses. Lyons leaped to his feet to protest: "The gentleman has spoken treason!" "Treason, treason," echoed the clergy-

[8] *Ibid.*, pp. 49–50.

men. Patrick paused and turned toward the ministers. He straightened himself to his full height, his countenance glowed, and his voice became vibrant with emotion. Then he unleashed a torrent of eloquence denouncing the preachers whose dedication should be to serve God and their poor parishioners, but whose main concern was to fatten upon their own privileges. Aghast, the twenty clergymen present arose as a body and filed out of the courtroom in dignified rejection of this blasphemy. Patrick turned back to the jury. The time had come, he told them, to lift the burden of bondage from the backs of the people. Their duty, it was true, was to find for the plaintiff—but let him have merely a single farthing. Abruptly he concluded, his plea having lasted for one hour. Lyons spoke again, trying to shake the jurors from the spell; but when the twelve men returned to the box after a very brief consideration, their award to Rev. Maury was just what Patrick Henry had asked—one penny. This speech was, as the historian Charles Campbell said, "the commencement of the Revolution in Virginia."[9] As for its general effects, from that time forth when the people wished to praise an attorney they would say: "He is almost equal to Patrick Henry when he pleaded against the parsons."[10] The next year he was elected to the House of Burgesses as the member from Louisa County.

The members of the House numbered 116—dominated by an aristocratic minority that included George Washington, four Lees, two Pendletons, two Randolphs, and the great George Wythe. Patrick Henry sat in the House that year only nine days. On his third day a bill was introduced to borrow £240,000, mostly to pay debts owed to members of the great families so well represented in the Burgesses. Patrick rose to denounce the bill as favoritism and defeated it by rallying the county representation, leaving the aristocrats in a compact minority against him. It was a bold beginning. His next step was taken when a motion was made for the House to go into a Committee of the Whole to consider the Stamp Tax, which was to become effective on November 1, 1765. Henry then introduced a series of resolutions, culminating in the declaration that the Burgesses "have the only and sole exclusive right and power to lay taxes and impositions upon the inhabitants of this Colony."[11] Henry arose to speak; Thomas Jefferson, then a student at William and Mary College, was standing in the door of the lobby and "heard the splendid display of Mr. Henry's talents as a popular orator. . . . He appeared to me to speak as Homer wrote."[12]

[9] *Ibid.*, pp. 51–74; Wirt, *op. cit.*, 37–49; Mallory, *op. cit.*, I:583–586.
[10] Henry, *op. cit.*, I:46.
[11] Morgan, *op. cit.*, p. 94.
[12] *Ibid.*, p. 96.

In reply, the resolutions were opposed by a succession of the most notable men in the assembly: Randolph, Bland, Pendleton, Wythe, and others. Then Patrick Henry arose again, this time to pour forth eloquence that was, in the words of a witness, "beyond all power of description."[13] The text of his speech was not preserved, but many members remembered his great climax: "Tarquin and Caesar each had his Brutus, Charles the First his Cromwell, and George the Third—." He paused, while from the Speaker and many members came the cry, "Treason! Treason." Without haste and with great dignity, Henry concluded: "—may profit from their example! If this be treason, make the most of it."[14] The resolution was adopted by a vote of twenty to nineteen. Peyton Randolph, the Speaker, exclaimed: "By God, I would have given five hundred guineas for a single vote"[15]—for then he could have cast the deciding ballot against the resolution.

When Patrick Henry's papers were examined after his death, there was found among them a copy of the resolutions, with this note written upon the back of them:

> They formed the first opposition to the Stamp Act . . . . I had been for the first time elected a Burgess a few days before, was young, inexperienced, unacquainted with the forms of the House . . . I determined to venture, alone, unadvised, unassisted . . . Many threats were uttered and much abuse cast on me by the party for submission. After a long and warm contest the resolutions passed . . . The alarm spread throughout America with astonishing quickness, and the Ministerial party were overwhelmed. The great point of resistance to British taxation was universally established in the colonies. This brought on the war . . . . Reader! whoever thou art, remember this, and in thy sphere practice virtue thyself, and encourage it in others.[16]

Henry's estimate of the effect of his resolutions was just. William Robinson, the Royal Commissary for Virginia, wrote: "He blazed out in a violent speech; he is spreading treason."[17] The historian Bancroft concluded: "This is the way the fire began; Virginia rang the alarm-bell for the continent."[18] Eight Colonies adopted resolutions modeled on those Patrick Henry had introduced. More importantly, the reception accorded the resolutions in other Colonies won over the Virginia aristocrats to the cause of revolution; Henry exulted in praise from unexpected quarters: Jefferson, Edmund Randolph, Washington, Hugh

[13] *Ibid.*, p. 97, quoting Judge Paul Carrington, who heard the speech.
[14] *Ibid.*, pp. 92–98.
[15] *Ibid.*, p. 98; Wirt, *op. cit.*, 74–85.
[16] Henry, *op. cit.*, I:81–82.
[17] Morgan, *op. cit.*, p. 102.
[18] *Ibid.*, p. 103.

Blair Grigsby. From this time, "Mr. Henry became the idol of the people of Virginia."[19]

It was nine years later, when Patrick Henry was thirty eight and a continental celebrity, that he next exerted decisive leadership. Attending the First Continental Congress, when members recoiled from the step of banding their Colonies together against English oppression, Henry steeled their courage: "Government is dissolved," he thundered. "Fleets and armies and the present state of things show that government is dissolved. Where are your landmarks, your boundaries of Colonies? We are in a state of nature, sir . . . . The distinctions between Virginians, Pennsylvanians, New Yorkers, and New Englanders, are no more. I am not a Virginian, but an American."[20]

Back in Virginia, Patrick Henry pushed forward the cause of independence with speed and zeal. A revolutionary Convention was convened at Richmond, in the small St. John's Church, set on a hilltop in the midst of the city. There, on March 23, 1775, the third day of the meeting, Henry arose and offered to amend a harmless resolution of friendship addressed to the people of Jamaica by tacking onto it a motion "That this colony be immediately put into a posture of defense." Just a few hours previously in the British House of Commons, Edmund Burke was on his feet making a five-hour plea for "Conciliation with the Colonies." The mood of the Burgesses was more sympathetic to Burke than to Henry. Henry's motion was unexpected and several members rose at once to denounce it as being premature. The room was crowded, the atmosphere tense. One hundred twenty delegates occupied all the seats, with a few spectators near the door and others crowded outside the windows. Throughout the Colonies there was as yet little talk of war with England, though much of "resistance" in defense of "rights." The first speakers against Henry's resolution appealed for patience while further efforts were being made to preserve peaceful relations and secure justice.

Notes on Henry's speech in reply were taken carefully by Judge John Tyler, who sent them to William Wirt. Complete authenticity is too much to expect, but several who heard the speech testified that the version Wirt published closely approximated what the orator said.[21] The speech is probably the best known in American history, except for Lincoln's remarks at Gettysburg. It repays careful analysis. The opening remarks were conciliatory, as Henry praised the "patriotism, as well as

---

[19] *Ibid.*, p. 111.
[20] *Ibid.*, pp. 165–166.
[21] Wirt, *op. cit.*, pp. 134–142; Morgan, *op. cit.*, 183–198, adds fullness of description with first-hand accounts by several auditors.

the abilities," of his opponents, and promised to speak "freely and without reserve." Quickly he stressed the importance of the issue: "nothing less than freedom or slavery." At such a time the duty to seek and speak truth was paramount. Then he confronted the doubts he felt about him: "Mr. President, it is natural to man to indulge in the illusions of hope." Nevertheless, "I am willing to know the whole truth." He laid down the basis for his argument: "I have but one lamp by which my feet are guided; and that is the lamp of experience. I know of no way of judging of the future but by the past." He reviewed the past ten years: "We have petitioned; we have remonstrated; we have supplicated; we have prostrated ourselves before the throne . . . . Our petitions have been slighted; our remonstrances have produced additional violence and insult; our supplications have been disregarded; and we have been spurned, with contempt, from the foot of the throne." The issue, he argued, could not be evaded: "If we wish to be free . . . we must fight! I repeat it, sir, we must fight! An appeal to arms and to the God of Hosts is all that is left to us!"

With his point made, he turned to a rebuttal of the fears and qualifications probably felt by every man present. "They tell us, sir, that we are weak—unable to cope with so formidable an adversary. But when shall we be stronger? . . . . Shall we acquire the means of effectual resistance by lying supinely on our backs, and hugging the delusive phantom of hope, until our enemies shall have bound us hand and foot?" Then came his magnificent peroration:

> Besides, sir, we have no election. If we were base enough to desire it, it is now too late to retire from the contest. There is no retreat but in submission and slavery. Our chains are forged. Their clanking may be heard on the plains of Boston. The war is inevitable. And let it come! I repeat it, sir; let it come!
> It is in vain, sir, to extenuate the matter. Gentlemen may cry peace, peace—but there is no peace. The war is actually begun! The next gale that sweeps from the north will bring to our ears the clash of resounding arms! Our brethren are already in the field! Why stand we idle here? What is it that gentlemen wish? What would they have? Is life so dear, or peace so sweet, as to be purchased at the price of chains and slavery? Forbid it, Almighty God! I know not what course others may take, but as for me, give me liberty, or give me death!

The effect of the speech was mesmeric. A Baptist clergyman who heard it has given what seems to be the best account: "The tendons of his neck stood out white and rigid, like whipcords. His voice rose louder and louder, until the walls of the building and all within them seemed to shake and rock in its tremendous vibrations. Finally his pale face and glaring eyes became terrible to look upon. Men leaned forward in their seats with their heads strained forward, their faces pale and their eyes glaring like the speaker's . . . . When he sat down, I felt sick with excitement. Every eye yet gazed entranced on Henry. It seemed as if a word from him would have led to any wild explosion of violence. Men looked beside themselves."[22]

There was no applause; only silence. No reply; just the vote, as the resolution was adopted viva voce. The Revolution was launched.

After a brief and humiliating experience as Colonel of a militia regiment (in which he was out-maneuvered by political enemies), Henry attended the Virginia Convention, which convened May 6, 1776, to ratify the Declaration of Independence. Here, his speaking followed the customary pattern: at first cautious and halting, then building up to a tremendous crescendo of bold appeal. As Edmund Randolph reports: "His eloquence unlocked the secret springs of the human heart, robbed danger of its terror, and broke the keystone of royal power."[23] Next, the Convention turned to drafting "the first written Constitution of a free state in the annals of the world."[24] In a series of debates that lasted from June 12 to 28, Patrick Henry fought successfully (with the aid of George Mason) for a Bill of Rights and for a powerful executive. Against the opposition of the aristocracy, he was elected the first Governor, by a vote of sixty to forty six. He was elected to the governorship a total of seven times. For the next ten years he served either as executive or as legislative leader of the government of Virginia.

In 1788 commences the final chapter in Patrick Henry's public career: his fight against ratification by Virginia of the United States Constitution. The basis of his opposition has been well summarized by his biographer George Morgan in an analogous anecdote: "Mr. Speaker," said a member of the British Parliament, "I hear a lion roaring in the lobby. Shall we shut the door against him, sir, or shall we let him in to see if we are able to turn him out again;"[25] Henry had no wish to see the lion of federal power turned loose in Virginia. He had been the chief figure in the Virginia government under the Articles of Confederation; it was but natural that his defensive instincts should lead him to denounce the inference that this government had finally proved itself wholly ineffectual. During the course of the Ratification Convention, Patrick Henry fought as he never had before. The odds were strongly against him.[26] The Constitution was supported by Washington (who did not attend

22 Morgan, *op. cit.*, p. 193.
23 *Ibid.*, p. 259.
24 *Ibid.*, pp. 267–268.
25 *Ibid.*, p. 327.
26 Wrage and Baskerville, *op. cit.*, pp. 3–6.

the Convention), Madison, John Marshall and Edmund Randolph. A majority of fifty votes for ratification was forecast when the Convention convened on June 2. Eight States had already ratified and New Hampshire was confidently expected to do so (as it did on June 21), thus insuring that the Constitution would be placed in effect. Only Virginia and New York were doubtful—but, of course, as two of the greatest states, their adherence was essential. Henry entered the contest determined to win, with only George Mason as a dependable ally in the debate.

During the twenty three days of meetings, Henry spoke every day but five and as many as five times on one day and eight times on another.[27] One speech lasted as long as seven hours. One-fourth of the entire stenographic report is devoted to his speeches. David Robertson, with an assistant short-hand writer, took down the proceedings, but admitted that he could not keep apace with the "tremendous outpourings" of Patrick Henry. The printed texts obviously are marred by some omissions and paraphrasing; yet they give a dependable record of Henry's views and ample illustration of his forceful style. The feat was a mammoth test of endurance and of mental agility.

Henry's chief fear concerning the Constitution was that it would destroy the power of the States and result in a centralized government, far removed from the interests of and barricaded from control by the people. Next, he feared the executive would be too strong for his power to be checked, pointing out that the executive would be commander-in-chief of the army and navy, that he had wide power of appointment, and that he could be successively re-elected for life. His solution was for Virginia to withhold concurrence, remaining out of the Union while watching to see whether it would succeed. Meanwhile, Virginia would pay its due portion of taxes and supply its quota of men for the armed forces, thus "cooperating" with the federal government while remaining out of it. Never in all his life did Henry fight harder for victory. As he said, in concluding his June 5 address: "I have, I fear, fatigued the committee; yet I have not said the one hundred thousandth part of what I have on my mind."[28] When the vote was taken, the Constitution was ratified by eighty nine to seventy nine.

For a time Henry was tempted to move out to the frontier to get away from government, and he did join with land speculators in purchasing fifteen million acres of land in unsettled parts of Georgia. He refused election to the United States Senate, rejected offers by Wash-

---

[27] Jonathan Elliot, *Debates in the Several State Conventions*, Four Vols., Washington, D.C.: published for editor under sanction of Congress, 1836, III:35–598.
[28] Wrage and Baskerville, *op. cit.*, p. 22.

ington to make him Minister to Spain or to France, Secretary of State, or Chief Justice of the Supreme Court. He also declined efforts to make him Vice President and even declined offers of votes in the Electoral College for the presidency. Instead, he returned for a while to the practice of law, in which he was richly compensated, and accepted renewed election to the governorship. In 1799, in response to a personal appeal from George Washington, Patrick Henry let his name be entered as a candidate for the House of Representatives. On the first Monday of March, he undertook to speak at Charlotte, being so weak that he had to be lifted to the platform. John Miller, a student of Hampden-Sidney College, was present and left this description of the event:

> He was very infirm, ... arose with difficulty, and stood, somewhat bowed with age and weakness. His face was almost colorless . . . . his voice was somewhat cracked and tremulous. But in a few moments a wonderful transformation of the whole man occurred, as he warmed with his theme. He stood erect; his eyes beamed with a light that was almost supernatural; . . . his voice rang clear and melodious . . .[29]

Thus, to the very last, Henry was his typical self: slow to start, suddenly transforming to a rushing stream of wonderful eloquence. His theme is one of very special interest, in view both of his own record and of the southern views that were soon thereafter to emerge. Virginia, he declared, had taken the dangerous course of trying to nullify acts of the Federal Government: a course that would lead to civil war. He concluded: "United we stand, divided we fall. Let us not split into factions which must destroy that union upon which our existence hangs."[30] The report of this last talk is a paraphrase only; but to Dr. Rice, an observer, his "look and gesture" gave to his words "an energy on my mind unequalled by anything I have ever witnessed." At the conclusion of the speech, he was carried to an adjacent room to rest. Dr. Rice declaimed: "The sun has set in all its glory." In the April election, John Randolph of Roanoke was chosen for the seat in Congress, but Henry was given the consolation of election to the State Legislature. He never again left his home at Red Hill, where he died on June 6, 1799 at the age of sixty three.

[29] Morgan, *op. cit.*, p. 421.
[30] *Ibid.*, p. 423.

III

THE GREAT DEBATES
THAT FORGED OUR NATION
1788 ‑ 1850

Framing the Constitution

DECLARING INDEPENDENCE required courage; it was an act of rebellious intolerance. The establishment of the forms and powers of the new government required astuteness and a tolerant willingness to find workable compromises among conflicting views. Fortunately the agitators who fomented the revolution matured with passing years and increasing responsibilities. They became, or were succeeded by, constructive statesmen with the wisdom to put together an instrument of government which Gladstone called "the most wonderful work ever struck off at a given time by the brain and purpose of man."[1] It is also a tribute to the ability of strong minds to work together harmoniously in a process of group thinking. For the American Constitution was not devised by experts and then sold to the Philadelphia Convention by skillful argumentation and persuasion. Instead, it was hammered out from initial uncertainty through genuine discussion and honest debate.

The decision to call a convention "for the sole and express purpose of revising the Articles of Confederation"[2] was instigated primarily by George Washington. As Burton J. Hendrick wrote in his study of the Constitution: "No man had done so much to bring America to this final act of cooperation as the quiet but forceful gentleman who, two years previously, had retired to his Potomac home, seeking, as his only reward for his public services, a peaceful old age."[3] As commander-in-chief, Washington had suffered for seven years from the futilities of the toothless Confederation. Moreover, his eight trips through the West and his campaigns through New England and the Middle States had made him better acquainted with the whole country than was any other American.

[1] William E. Gladstone, "Kin Beyond the Sea," *North American Review*, I (Sept., 1878):185.
[2] Arthur Taylor Prescott, *Drafting the Federal Constitution*, Baton Rouge: Louisiana State University Press, 1941, p. 11. Cf. also, F. Rodell, *Fifty-five Men*, New York: Telegraph Press, 1936.
[3] Burton J. Hendrick, *Bulwark of the Republic*, Boston: Little, Brown, 1938, p. 12.

As early as December 20, 1776, in an official letter to the President of Congress, he had urged the need for a tighter union; and he re-emphasized this same view in his farewell talks at Princeton in August, 1783, and to the Congress in December of that year. Then Washington commenced quietly to prepare the way for what eventuated as the Annapolis Convention of September, 1786, convened to discuss trade relations "and other important matters."

Only nine States appointed delegates to Annapolis, and only five of the delegations arrived. They were unable to agree on trade regulations, and would have adjourned with nothing accomplished, except that Alexander Hamilton persuaded them to issue a call for another convention to revise the Articles of Confederation. Then, back in the New York Legislature, on February 18, 1787, Hamilton urged support for such revision. "If these States are not united under a Federal Government," he argued, "they will infallibly have wars with each other, and their divisions will subject them to all the mischiefs of foreign influence and intrigue . . . . And wars with each other would lead to opposite alliances with foreign powers and plunge us all into the labyrinths of European politics."[4] Against the opposition of Governor George Clinton and his majority in the Legislature, Hamilton won his plea for appointment of a delegation; but his own influence on it was curbed by appointment of Yates and Lansing, two ardent antifederalists.

The reluctance of New York was typical of widespread scepticism or indifference. Twelve States (with Rhode Island abstaining) appointed a total of seventy four delegates, of whom fifty five eventually arrived at Philadelphia. The opening date, May 14, found only a handful present and it was not until May 25 that the presence of a quorum could be secured. During these discouraging days George Washington met daily with the delegates who were present and tried to keep their resolution firm. In his funeral oration on Washington, Gouverneur Morris recalled one of these meetings: "He [Washington] was collected within himself. His countenance had more than usual solemnity. His eye was fixed, and seemed to look into futurity. 'It is' (said he) 'too probable that no plan we propose will be adopted. Perhaps another dreadful conflict is to be sustained. If to please the people, we offer what we ourselves disapprove, how can we afterwards defend our work? Let us raise a standard to which the wise and honest can repair. The event is in the hand of God.' "[5]

[4] Marion Miller, *Great Debates in American History*, New York: Current Literature Pub. Co., 1913, I:283.
[5] Gouverneur Morris, *An Oration Upon the Death of George Washington*, December 31, 1799, New York: John Furman, 1800.

The delegates who were gradually assembling had little reason to hope for success. As the North Carolina delegation wrote home to their Governor, "An union of sovereign states," which is what they were trying to achieve, "is a circumstance that has not occurred in the history of man."[6] Thirty nine of the delegates had served in the Congress of the Confederation and so were familiar with its futilities. Although Benjamin Franklin was eighty one, most of them were young: James Madison, Edmund Randolph, Hamilton, Morris, and Rufus King in their thirties; James Wilson, John Rutledge, and Oliver Ellsworth in their forties; several still in their twenties. Roger Sherman of Connecticut, sixty six, was known as the author of a cannily shrewd aphorism: "When you are in the minority, talk; when you are in a majority, vote."[7] George Mason was praised by Madison as having "the greatest talents for debate of any man he had ever seen or heard speak."[8] Washington, after being elected chairman, spoke only to accept the office, and then, when the Convention finally adjourned, to express his thanks to the members.

The ideas with which the delegates arrived were so divergent as to make agreement seem unlikely. Paterson, of New Jersey, set forth a plan that would insure equality of power to all the States, regardless of their size. Randolph, of Virginia, presented a plan, largely drawn by Madison, that was designed to give the preponderance of power to the larger States. Hamilton offered a plan to center power in a President, Senate, and Judges who would all be elected for life. The enormity of these differences had to be viewed against the experience of jealous contentions among the States.

In order to safeguard the opportunity for undisturbed discussion, the delegates agreed to bar "strangers" from the meetings, to keep all discussions confidential, and to maintain no record of the proceedings. James Madison, fortunately, violated the last injunction and kept careful notes of the debates, which, after his death, were published by Congressional authorization.

The first formal session was held May 25, 1787, on a gloomy and rainy Friday morning. Washington was made chairman and the delegations presented credentials emphasizing the independent sovereignty of their States. The delegates clearly specified that no more could be undertaken than to amend the Articles of Confederation. On the following Monday the first decisive action was taken—to safeguard conditions that would lead to discussion and collective thinking rather than to divisive debate.

[6] Marion Miller, *op. cit.*, I:284.
[7] Hendrick, *op. cit.*, p. 79.
[8] Max Farrand, *The Framing of the Constitution of the United States*, New Haven: Yale University Press, 1913, p. 281.

A motion by George Wythe providing for a roll-call vote on each proposal as it was presented was voted down after George Mason objected that "such a record of the opinions of members would be an obstacle to the change of them on conviction."[9] On Tuesday Edmund Randolph read the fifteen resolutions constituting the "Virginia plan" for a federal government; and Hamilton suggested that the essential point was to insure a federal government rather than a league of sovereign States. A crucial decision was reached not to debate and vote on specific details of any proposal, but to deal with the problem generally under the relaxed rules of a "committee of the whole." The final groundwork for the proceedings was laid on Wednesday, when the delegates directly confronted the question of whether to organize a new government that could "compel every part to do its duty,"[10] in the words of Gouverneur Morris; and that, as George Mason urged, could "directly operate on individuals."[11] By a bare majority of five State delegations it was resolved "that it is the opinion of this Committee that a national government ought to be established consisting of a supreme Legislative, Judiciary, and Executive."[12] The way was thus cleared for genuine group consideration of the nature of a new Constitution. The fact that they were violating the instructions under which they had assembled was tacitly ignored.

From May 30 until September 17, when the great document was finally adopted and signed, the delegates pursued a schedule of meeting from 10 A.M. until 3 P.M. five days a week. Hamilton proposed a plan calling for a virtual elected monarchy, supporting it with an eloquent speech that was heard with respectful attention but to which no one bothered to make a reply. Paterson of New Jersey presented another plan designed to preserve a veto power for the small States. The Virginia plan, however, was made the basis for discussion. Slowly feeling their way, and generally in a spirit of conciliation rather than attack, the delegates suggested and considered amendment after amendment, seeking what they hoped would be lastingly expedient compromises. Gouverneur Morris, young, wealthy, aristocratic, and impetuous, was the most frequent speaker, often more a barrier than an aid to joint thinking. Nevertheless, he played a major role as the chief draftsman for the Convention, whipping the final agreements into the text of the Constitution, with the aid of Hamilton, Madison, and Rufus King. With more sobriety, James Wilson of Pennsylvania, Charles Pinckney of South Carolina, and James Madison represented the calmness of mind

[9] *Madison's Papers*, Mobile: Allston Mygatt, 1824, II:724.
[10] Carl Van Doren, *The Great Rehearsal*, New York: Viking Press, 1948, p. 33.
[11] *Ibid.*
[12] Marion Miller, *op. cit.*, I:295.

and the legalistic knowledge and methodology that encouraged systematic exploration of ideas. Of the eighty four articles finally knit together into the completed document, Madison suggested thirty one or thirty two and Pinckney thirty four.

A tremendous step forward was agreement on a compromise whereby the States would be equally represented in the Senate but the population itself would be represented in the House. The definition of "population" proved to be troublesome until it was resolved that three-fifths of the slaves should be counted in the apportionment of representatives. A fundamental decision was reached that all powers not explicitly delegated to the federal government should be reserved to the several States. An effort was made to distribute essential functions among the executive, legislative, and judicial branches so that their powers would be balanced. On other points (as to how, for example, the President should be elected) the phraseology was deliberately vague; delegates freely confessed that they had no precedent to guide them and were unable to view the future with clear confidence.[13]

Finally, a draft was completed—and on every side there was a hollow fear of its inadequacies. No member of the Constitutional Convention considered that their work was "the most wonderful ever struck off at a given time by the brain and purpose of man." Madison, for one, was deeply disappointed that the Constitution did not grant federal power for the veto of acts by the State legislatures. There was scarcely a man present who did not object to some provision or wish for inclusion of one that had been omitted. The discussion drew to a close; but the vital step of adoption had yet to be taken.

It was at this point that Benjamin Franklin, then eighty two, and "the greatest philosopher of the present age,"[14] played his vital role. During the long discussions he had remained silent, although he wrote a long speech, read for him by James Wilson, opposing any payment of salary for the presidency. Now a critical juncture arrived, when the influence of Franklin was desperately needed. On September 15, a Saturday, Edmund Randolph, who had presented the plan which became the basis for a final document, lost his nerve and moved that the draft be submitted to special State conventions for consideration and amendment, after which a second Constitutional Convention could be called to consider and try to reconcile all differences. Such other influential members as Mason, Pinckney, and Elbridge Gerry of Massachusetts also spoke strongly against adoption of the Constitution as it then stood.

[13] This summation is based on the accounts by Van Doren, Hendrick, Prescott, and Miller, *op. cit.*
[14] Prescott, *op. cit.*, p. 28.

The debate continued until six o'clock, without recess for rest, food, or drink. Then, almost incredibly, a vote was taken on adoption of the Constitution and was carried. The meeting adjourned until Monday, when delegates would reconvene to sign the document.

On Sunday, Franklin called the Pennsylvania delegates to his home, to counsel with them concerning a speech he had prepared in an effort to stem the wave of doubt and to seek unanimity in the signing. When the meeting convened Monday morning, Franklin arose with his speech in his hand, which he then passed to James Wilson to be read for him. The sentiments were typical of his lifelong policy of conciliation:

> I agree to this Constitution with all its faults (he said), if they are such; because I think a general government necessary for us, and there is no form of government but what may be a blessing to the people if well administered; and believe further that this is likely to be well administered for a course of years and can only end in despotism, as other forms have done before it, when the people shall have become so corrupt as to need despotic government, being incapable of any other . . . . Thus I consent, sir, to this Constitution because I expect no better, and because I am not sure that it is not the best. The opinions I have had of its errors, I sacrifice to the public good.[15]

As the members trooped forward to affix their signatures to the embossed copy of the Constitution, Franklin gazed at the sun painted on the back of the presiding officer's chair and remarked: "I have often and often in the course of the Session and the vicissitudes of my hopes and fears as to its issue, looked at that Sun behind the President without being able to tell whether it was rising or setting: But now at length I have the happiness to know that it is a rising and not a setting Sun."[16]

Adoption was by consensus, all but three members present being willing to sign the document. The fearfulness of the majority, however, was well expressed by Edmund Randolph, who said: "our chief danger arises from the democratic parts."[17] They had done their best to guard carefully against popular rule. The President was to be elected indirectly by an Electoral College, the Senate by State legislatures. Voting in all but three States was restricted to property owners, and in those three to taxpayers. In Connecticut a further requirement was "maturity in years, quiet and peaceable behavior, and a civil conversation." Undue concentration of power, it was hoped, would be checkmated by divisions within the Federal Government and between the national and State govern-

[15] Madison Papers, *op. cit.*, pp. 1596–97.
[16] *Ibid.*, p. 1624.
[17] Cf. Max Farrand, *The Records of the Federal Convention*, New Haven: Yale University Press, 1911, III:123–128 and 307–310.

ments. Even so, many feared the presidency was too powerful, being in effect, as Mason claimed, "an elective monarchy."[18] With all their misgivings, the delegates had the one major consolation that the Constitution could not go into effect until after it should be ratified by at least nine States.

The Ratification Conventions

PROMPTLY AFTER adjournment of the Philadelphia Convention, Delaware, New Jersey, and Georgia held conventions that unanimously ratified the Constitution. Connecticut and Pennsylvania shortly followed suit by substantial majorities—although in the latter State the opposition was bitter. James Wilson, leading the fight in Philadelphia for ratification, had to admit that it had been constituted "almost without precedent or guide" and that in essence it was a compromise of "peculiar delicacy . . . . I mean that of drawing a proper line between the national government and the governments of the several States."[1] In Massachusetts, the great lawyer Rufus King and a plain farmer, Jonathan Smith, led a fight that resulted in ratification by the slender vote of 187 to 168, obtained only after the delegates made clear their demand for a series of subsequent amendments.[2] Maryland and South Carolina ratified the document during the Spring, and in June, New Hampshire (where approval was sure) and the crucial States of Virginia and New York held their conventions. Meanwhile, North Carolina and Rhode Island rejected the Constitution (finally to ratify in 1789 and 1790).

The most significant debates were those in Virginia and New York. Technically, their concurrence was not necessary, since New Hampshire's vote tallied the ninth State required to put the Constitution into effect. It was unthinkable, however, that the new nation could possibly succeed without the key States of Virginia and New York. In both States the opposition was substantial and was ably led, in Virginia, as we have seen, by Patrick Henry, the State's greatest orator and most notable statesman. In New York the struggle involved not only the Constitution but also the touchier problem of control over the State's politics. Moreover, while a majority of the delegates who assembled at Rich-

[18] Van Doren, *op. cit.*, p. 61.
[1] Jonathan Elliot, *Debates in Several State Conventions*, Washington, 1836, II:399.
[2] John Fiske, *The Critical Period of American History, 1783–1789*, Boston: Houghton Mifflin, 1893, presents a good summation both of the Constitutional Convention, pp. 230–305, and of the several ratification conventions, pp. 306–345, with an especially good account of the critical debates in the Massachusetts convention, pp. 316–331.

mond were pro-Constitution (backed by the tremendous prestige of George Washington), at Albany the opposition was in a two-to-one majority and was strengthened in its stand by the powerful influence of the State's most influential politician, Governor George Clinton.

In Virginia, James Madison, as chief spokesman for ratification, tried to avoid a direct clash with Patrick Henry, who was in the very height of his fame. Madison's appeal was to "calm and rational investigation," to deciding the question "on its own merits solely." To him the most urgent problem was not to safeguard individual liberty but to enforce cooperation among the States. Only a strong government could operate with efficiency. "The principal question is whether it [should] be a federal or consolidated government." On this question he concealed his own disappointment that the Constitution was less "consolidated" than he wished; and he admitted that the proposed instrument was "mixed . . . . in a manner unprecedented." He also admitted that the proposed government was too complicated to be readily understood, and he could not bring himself to forecast with assurance that it would be successful. But he knew confederation had failed and he felt sure that without a strong central power to raise taxes and direct defense, the nation would be open to foreign conquest.[3]

Edmund Randolph rose on June 6 to help in the defense: "We are told the report of dangers is false. The cry of peace, sir, is false; say peace when there is peace; it is but a sudden calm. The tempest growls over you—look around—wheresoever you look you see danger."[4] Patrick Henry must have smiled at this rather feeble paraphrase of his great speech in 1776 (which Randolph had opposed); but he kept up the attack on his own chosen ground: "At present we have our liberties and our privileges in our own hands. Let us not relinquish them." Then he concluded: "I look on that paper as the most fatal plan that could possibly be conceived to enslave a free people."[5] Finally, on June 24, as a vote impended which Henry knew he must lose, he launched one last widespread attack, listing a series of evils the Constitution might introduce, and ended with an appeal which would become in the next generation the principal concern of his region: "May they not pronounce all slaves free . . . ? The paper speaks to the point. They have the power in clear, unequivocal terms, and will clearly and certainly exercise it. As much as I deplore slavery, I see that providence forbids its abolition."[6] The old warrior was done. He had won thirty or forty votes with his eloquence; but by a margin of ten the Constitution was ratified.

[3] Elliot, *op. cit.*, III:108–117 and 143–151.
[4] *Ibid.*, III:90–108.
[5] *Ibid.*, III:72–89.
[6] *Ibid.*, III:531–598.

Meanwhile, at Albany, Alexander Hamilton faced an even more formidable opposition. In New York, George Clinton controlled the State political machine with its power of patronage; in fighting the Constitution Clinton was fighting for positions for himself and for the great majority of the delegates in the ratification convention. Moreover, in the person of Melancthon Smith he had a champion who was not only an able debater but a man admired for his integrity. Hamilton, confronted by an apparently unbeatable majority, had three hopes: first, that he could delay a vote until news might come of Virginia's ratification; second, that Smith's very intelligence and integrity might leave him open to argument; and third, that the manifest failure of the Confederation might make a change of government acceptable.[7]

When the New York Convention opened on June 17, Smith made a powerful attack against the Constititution and for the retention of the old system under which New York was prospering. Hamilton, the next day, gave a hard-hitting reply, sharply argumentative in tone and freely stigmatizing Smith's arguments as "ridiculous," for "nothing could be more false." Arguing that a uniform system of taxation was required, he pointed out that "Pennsylvania and New York are the only States which have perfectly discharged their federal duties." The next day he again took up almost alone the burden of defense: "We have erred through excess of caution . . . . Our counsels have been destitute of consistency and stability . . . . We have now found a cure." By June 24 he was beating down attempts to undermine the Constitution by amendments—such as one to grant the State Legislatures power to recall U.S. Senators at will: "The amendment will render the Senator a slave to all the capricious humors among the people."

The following day Hamilton shifted to a more conciliatory tone: "There is even a certain degree of truth in the reasonings of both sides." Then he made his strongest appeal: "There are two objects in forming systems of government—safety for the people, and energy in the administration . . . It is the happiest posssible mode of conciliating these two objects, to institute one branch peculiarly endowed with sensibility, another with knowledge and firmness." News arrived that New Hampshire had ratified, thus ensuring that the Constitution would go into effect, and Hamilton spoke on June 27 with new assurance. He defended the right of Congress to levy taxes and reviewed again the checks-and-balances safeguards. "The purse is lodged in one branch and the sword in another." Then with an appeal to high-minded patriotism, he urged:

[7] The basis of Hamilton's arguments had already been presented in careful detail in *The Federalist Papers*, of which he was the principal author, with the help of James Madison and John Jay. A handy edition is the Mentor edition, New American Library, with a helpful introduction by Clinton Rossiter, 1961.

". . . it is high time to dismiss our prejudices and banish declamation." Almost worn out, Hamilton waited for news from Virginia. Meanwhile he held the floor, trying once more to quiet the fears that the State government would lose its importance. "We love our families more than our neighbors: we love our neighbors more than our countrymen in general. The human affections, like the solar heat, lose their intensity as they depart from the centre . . . On these principles the attachment of the individual will be first and forever secured by the State government."[8]

One more major effort was made by the antifederalists—a proposal that New York ratify with the proviso that it might afterwards withdraw provided it became dissatisfied with the Constitution. By this time Madison had arrived from Richmond, with word of the Virginia decision. He advised Hamilton to make bold and strong the point that once a State entered the Union there would never be any legal means by which it could secede. Melancthon Smith nodded agreement; the Constitution could not provide the means for its own destruction. Hamilton sank back in his seat, exhausted but content. Clinton's majority melted away and New York assured the stability of the new government with its ratification of the Constitution, on July 26, by a final vote of thirty to twenty seven.[9]

Giving Form to Government

RATIFICATION OF the Constitution was followed by unanimous election of Washington as the first President. The new Government was launched, but many problems remained to be solved. What would be the role of the cabinet? The President had to have the "consent" of the Senate to appoint cabinet members, ambassadors, and other major officials; did he also need Senatorial consent to dismiss them? The question was decided in the negative, not to be raised again until impeachment proceedings were brought against Lincoln's successor, Andrew Johnson. What should be the role of the Senate? Washington conceived of it as an "advisory council" subservient to the presidency, and only the stubborn pride of members of the first Senate succeeded in

[8] Elliot, *op. cit.*, II:209–388. An excellent account of Hamilton as a speaker is Bower Aly, "Alexander Hamilton," in Marie K. Hochmuth, ed., *A History and Criticism of American Public Address* (completing the two vol. work edited by Brigance, *op. cit.*), New York: Longmans, Green, 1955, III:24–51.
[9] Cf. Clarence E. Miner, *The Ratification of the Federal Constitution by the State of New York*, New York: Columbia University Press, 1921, pp. 97–120.

converting that body into a coequal legislative arm.[1] What should be
the role of the Supreme Court? The first Chief Justice, John Jay,
thought of the Court primarily as a board of judicial review and it was
not until John Marshall held the office that the right of the Supreme
Court to quasi-legislative power—that of declaring Congressional acts
unconstitutional—was established. What should be the role of the President: a powerful executive or merely an administrator of policies
adopted by the legislature? Should the President be largely a ceremonial
Head of State, perhaps entitled "His Mightiness" and treated with a
non-partisan courtesy that in effect debarred him from exercising political power? Should the legislature be divided into "factions," or would
the country best be served by a single party system? Was the Senate or
the House the major source of legislative power? What should be the
foreign policy of the fledgling government? All these questions were subject to sharp debate and all had to be settled before the "Constitution"
ceased to be a piece of paper and became the framework of government.

Every session of the Congress was historic, but the first major issue
came to a head in Washington's second term. It took the form of a
debate centered in the House of Representatives on Jay's Treaty with
Great Britain; it involved almost all the questions indicated in the preceding paragraph.

From 1788 to 1791, England and the United States discontinued diplomatic relations because of dissatisfaction on both sides with failures to
observe the provisions of the peace treaty which ended the Revolutionary War. England refused to pay compensation, as was promised,
for slaves taken from the colonists during the war. England also failed to
withdraw from the forts in the Northwest and seemed determined to
retain all the territory west of the Mississippi and north of the Ohio
River. Moreover, England continued to encourage the hostility of the
Indian tribes to western settlement. The Americans, meantime, refused
to fulfill promises to compensate Tories for property seized from them;
and the intent to capture Canada at the first opportunity was freely
discussed. It was at this juncture that England, on November 6, 1793
(hard pressed in its war with France), issued an Order in Council for
the capture of all ships carrying goods to or from the French Colonies—
a trade that engaged several hundred American ships. The French Government complicated the situation by sending Citizen Genêt with instructions to organize American sentiment for a war against Great Britain.

[1] This struggle is well depicted in William Maclay, *Sketches of Debate in the First
Senate of the United States, in 1789–90–91*, ed. George W. Harris, Harrisburg,
Pa.: Lane S. Hart, 1880, in which he recorded: "What avowed and repeated attempts have I seen to place the President above the powers stipulated for him by the
constitution" (p. 110).

Jefferson rallied pro-French sympathizers to form an agrarian, anti-English "Republican Party," while John Adams, Alexander Hamilton, and Washington maintained the Federalists in a program that was pro-English, pro-industrial, pro-commercial, and to that extent anti-agrarian. Feeling against both England and France was heightened, with the West and South combining against the commercial and industrial New England and Middle States. When Lord Dorchester, England's Governor in Canada, reportedly encouraged Indian attacks against our western settlements with a promise that England would soon be at war against the United States, Hamilton urged Washington that "one more experiment of negotiation ought to precede actual war."[2] Jay was sent to London to try the experiment.

In December, 1794, Jay secured English signature on a treaty that pledged England to evacuate some of the Northwest Territory forts, to pay some compensation for losses inflicted on our shipping, and to continue the existing commercial treaty. There was no bar in the new treaty to continued impressment of American sailors, no indemnity for the slaves taken away, no prohibition of continued British fortifications south of the Great Lakes, and no check on inciting of Indian attacks. In general, New England favored the treaty (for the sake of continued trade), but one prominent Boston Federalist wrote on his walls: "Damn John Jay! Damn every one that won't damn John Jay! Damn every one that won't put lights in his windows and sit up all night damning John Jay!"[3] The newly emergent Republican Party was infuriated with what it considered Jay's betrayal of American interests. The Federalist majority in the Senate, however, promptly ratified the treaty and after some delay Washington proclaimed it in effect as of February 29, 1796.

It was then that the role of the House of Representatives became a crucial issue. In the course of March and April, thirty two speeches were made, comprising in effect two separate debates. From March 7 to 24, the debate dealt with the right of the House to review the instructions given by the President to his Ambassador, John Jay. This debate ended with a vote of fifty seven to thirty five, demanding that Washington submit the instructions for scrutiny by the House. Washington refused, on the ground that this constituted infringement by the legislative on the executive functions. Despite the majority vote, the fight was really won by Washington; and the principle he stated has ever since been upheld in practice.

The second debate, lasting from the middle to the end of April, dealt

[2] John Church Hamilton, *History of the Republic*, in *The Writings of Alexander Hamilton*, New York: Appleton, 1857–1864, V:544–554.
[3] Frank Monaghan, *John Jay*, New York: Bobbs-Merrill, 1935, p. 399.

with the question of whether it was the right of the House to participate in the making of treaties. James Madison, William B. Giles, Albert Gallatin, and James Hillhouse all made speeches insisting that the House could not vote the $90,000 required to put the treaty into effect without considering the merit of the treaty itself. Fisher Ames, who lay ill in Boston, had himself carried to the House, where he made a tremendous speech upholding the theory that the President and the Senate were alone responsible for treaty-making, and that the House had no choice except to concur in what they did.[4] The appropriation was adopted—and the Constitutional question decided—by the narrow margin of fifty one to forty eight. Washington, a few months later, declined election to a third term and retired with a warning against "foreign entanglements," in which he carefully avoided any specific consideration of the problems then existing.

Another and perhaps more important result of the debate was that two political parties emerged. What the founding fathers had feared as "factionalism" actually became the greatest source of strength in our democracy, insuring that henceforth there would always be a popular contest between conflicting candidates and programs, and that the voters, accordingly, would be able to make a choice—not merely to ratify at the polls what had already been decided by political managers.

The forms and structure of the new government were by now established. Its standing in the international community, however, was yet to be tested. This question was to be soon decided in the first of our foreign wars—the War of 1812.

Henry Clay's War

IN THE opinion of Josiah Quincy, as recorded by his son, "Henry Clay was the man whose influence and power more than any other produced the war of 1812."[1] Quincy was a partisan, prejudiced Federalist, bitter with disappointment because the political landslide of 1811 had swept nearly half the members of the Eleventh Congress from their seats and brought in a bevy of new young Republicans, popularly called "War Hawks," who were determined to end the peaceful pressures exerted by

[4] The speeches by Madison, Giles, Gallatin, and Ames in the debate on the Jay Treaty are included in E. B. Williston, *Eloquence of the United States*, Middletown, Conn.: E. and H. Clark, 1827, I:332–463.
[1] Edmund Quincy, *The Life of Josiah Quincy*, Boston: Ticknor and Fields, 1867, p. 255.

Jefferson and Madison in foreign affairs and launch the United States into a war of aggrandizement. The charge that Quincy made was hurled against a man whose final reputation was won as "the great pacificator." Yet at this time, in the hot impatience of his youth, Henry Clay was beyond doubt the prime mover in shifting the United States from a troubled neutrality on the sidelines of the Napoleonic War to a declaration of hostilities against Great Britain. He had already announced the keynote of his policy in a speech delivered to the Senate on December 28, 1810: "Is the time never to arrive when we may manage our affairs without the fear of insulting his Britannic Majesty? Is the rod of British power to be forever suspended over our heads?"[2]

The election of 1811 turned over the legislative government to a group of young men all born after 1776, with the Federalists being reduced to seven members out of thirty four in the Senate and to thirty seven out of 142 in the House. Henry Clay, already famous from triumphs won in the law courts and legislature of Kentucky, was elected, at the age of thirty four, Speaker of the House on the first day he entered into it. His lieutenants were also in their thirties: John C. Calhoun, Langdon Cheves, and William Lowndes of South Carolina; Felix Grundy of Tennessee; Peter B. Porter of New York; and Richard Johnson of Kentucky. The new British Minister, Augustus J. Foster, pleasure-loving but astute, who was promoted from his former post of secretary to the British Embassy in Washington, sent to the Foreign Office in London his estimate that the House of Representatives still contained "too many low and uneducated Individuals who are too ignorant to have any opinion of their own." Nevertheless, his forecast was that hope for peace might benefit from a "considerable accession . . . of men of talents and respectability."[3] Foster was unduly hopeful, for Clay opened the new session with the declaration that "I consider war with G. Britain as inevitable."[4] To effectuate it, he appointed his War Hawks as chairmen of the key committees.

In a sense, the issue was settled with the election results in 1811. Yet the new Congress launched itself heatedly into debate. Representative George Poindexter of Mississippi wrote home on December 12, 1811, that "Words, words, words appear still to be the rage. I am so much disgusted with the repetition of our wrongs and the windy storm which is sped from Capitol Hill to Canada, Novescotia, and even to Halifax, that I am sick to loathing of the most eloquent attempt to present them

[2] Bernard Mayo, *Henry Clay: Spokesman of the New West*, Boston: Houghton Mifflin, 1937, pp. 366–367.
[3] "Foster to Wellesley, December 21, 1811," cited by Mayo, *ibid.*, p. 404.
[4] "Clay to Rodney, Aug. 17, 1811," Rodney Mss., cited by Mayo, *ibid.*, p. 391.

in a new dress to the imagination."[5] Chief spokesman for the opposition to war was John Randolph of Virginia, a veteran of great ability, who was to be defeated for re-election in 1813 because of his stand. Clay, meanwhile, could muster an army of orators; yet he often stepped down from the elevated impartiality of the Speaker's desk to lead the parade of eloquence.

On January 2, in the debate on a resolution presented by Porter for the Select Committee on Foreign Relations, calling for a great increase in military preparedness, Clay spoke for two hours, with an impassioned fervor that aroused even the jaded members of the House. Clearly he pointed to the real cause for war—the need to establish the international prestige of the new nation. Britain was harassing their coasts and shipping, he said, "not to distress an enemy but to destroy a rival . . . . She sickens at your prosperity, and beholds, in your growth—your sails spread on every ocean, and your numerous seamen—the foundations of a power which, at no distant day, is to make her tremble for her naval superiority." Appeasement, he argued, would be fruitless. "For, sir, the career of encroachment is never arrested by submission." America must either "bow the neck to royal insolence" or exhibit "manly resistance." Referring with scorn to the Federalist demands for delay and further negotiation, he demanded: "When the burglar is at our door, shall we bravely sally forth and repel his felonious entrance, or meanly skulk within the walls of the castle?" Then he turned to a theme dear to his western constituents. Canada, he estimated, could be conquered and annexed within a year, with a force of twenty-five thousand men. The Indian confederation led by Tecumseh could be defeated only if their supplies of English guns could be cut off. The timorous were asking, "What are we to gain by war?" But the real question, Clay asserted, was, "What are we not to lose by peace?—Commerce, character, a nation's best treasure, honor."[6]

The best commentary on the war, perhaps, is the retort made in Moscow by the Russian Emperor Alexander I to John Quincy Adams, when Adams attempted to justify an American incursion that sought to seize Western Florida from Spain. "Everybody is getting a little bigger nowadays," his majesty observed.[7] Clay and his War Hawks saw no reason why the United States should be left out.

The only significant Congressional opposition to Mr. Clay's war came from John Randolph of Roanoke, or "Jack Randle," as he was nick-

[5] "Poindexter to Mead, Dec. 12, 1811," Poindexter Mss., cited by Mayo, *ibid.*, p. 430.
[6] Mayo, *ibid.*, p. 431.
[7] *Memoirs of John Quincy Adams*, ed. C. F. Adams, Philadelphia: Lippincott, 1877, II:260–262.

named—a conservative of a wildly radical temperament, perhaps the strangest mixture of oddities ever to become prominent in American political life. Randolph was one of Virginia's blue-blooded aristocrats: well-educated, widely read, with a mind sensitive to culture and interested in ideas. He was also an extreme individualist, who could scarcely abide agreement, let alone disagreement, with his views. He quarrelled with Thomas Jefferson and with most of the other influential leaders of his party and State. He fought several duels (including one over the pronunciation of a word) and seldom sought to curb the violence of his feelings or actions. When, for example, a fellow Virginian Representative, Willis Alston, made some comments at the dinner table that Randolph considered disparaging, he threw a glass of wine in Alston's face, then smashed the glass over his head. Six years later, as the two were leaving the legislative chamber, Randolph overheard Alston use the word "puppy," and assumed it was meant to apply to him. A few minutes later, as they met on the staircase, Randolph beat Alston soundly with his cane.

The chief weapon Randolph depended upon, however, was his tongue; and with it he made himself a master of the House of Representatives from 1800 until 1811. With a savagery that seemed at times almost insane, he poured fury and sarcasm on all who opposed him. At the same time, his superior mind, vast range of knowledge, quickness of thought, and analytical shrewdness assured him a predominance in debate that none could challenge. None, that is, until Henry Clay won election to Congress. Even then, Randolph won additional renown by coining for Clay a classic of vituperation, calling him: "this being, so brilliant yet so corrupt, which, like a rotten mackerel by moonlight, shines and stinks."[8]

In the debate on Porter's resolution calling for immediate armament, Randolph delivered the principal speech of opposition. The report, he stormed, was a call to "immediate war—a war not of defense, but of conquest, of aggrandizement, of ambition—a war," he continued, "foreign to the interests of this country, to the interests of humanity itself." Then, pointing to Clay, who sat secure with his War Hawk majority, Randolph cried: "There is a fatality, Sir, attending plenitude of power. Soon or late some mania seizes upon its possessors; they fall from the dizzy height, through the giddiness of their own heads . . . . Sir, you may raise this army, you may build up this vast structure of patronage, this mighty apparatus of favoritism; but . . . you sign your political death warrant."

Turning then toward the war party members from his own section,

[8] Henry Adams, *John Randolph*, Boston: Houghton Mifflin, 1910, p. 286.

Randolph went on: "I am not surprised at the war-spirit which is mani-festing itself in the gentlemen from the South." The prices of cotton and of tobacco, he conceded had fallen "to nothing," while the price of the imports they must buy had multiplied three and four times. But war would help no one, he warned, except a few speculators. Meanwhile, a war against England would introduce the "infernal doctrine" of French Revolutionary equality among the slaves. Already, he charged, "Men, dead to the operation of moral causes, have taken away from the poor slave his habits of loyalty and obedience to his master." Pointing squarely at the coterie of New Englanders, he went on: "You have de-prived him of all moral restraint; you have tempted him to eat of the tree of knowledge, just enough to perfect him in wickedness; you have opened his eyes to his nakedness; you have armed his nature against the hand that has fed, that has clothed him; that has cherished him in sick-ness; that hand which, before he became a pupil of your school, he had been accustomed to press with respectful affection."

That the British had committed "outrages and injuries" against American shipping, Randolph admitted, "I can never palliate, much less defend." But the French, he said, would do as much or worse if they had the power. Then, without attempting either to summarize what he had stated or to present any real alternative to war, he said he felt "my memory clouded, my intellect stupified, my strength and spirits ex-hausted," and abruptly sat down.[9] Calhoun, who replied to him, brushed aside "the whole of his speech as recommending patient and resigned submission as the best remedy."[10]

A few days later, refreshed but not reconciled, Randolph was on his feet again, warning that Clay's war policy "points to the mansions of eternal misery and torture—as a flaming beacon warning us of that vor-tex which we may not approach but with certain destruction." Urging that the South had no interest in allying itself with the West against New England for the sake of accomplishing a war from which it could not benefit, he demanded of his colleagues: "Are you willing for the sake of annexing Canada to the Northern States to submit to that ever-growing system of taxation which sends the European laborer supper-less to bed, to maintain by the sweat of your brow armies at whose hands you are to receive a future master?"[11] He was whistling against a wind whose force he could not stop.

[9] Marion Miller, *op. cit.*, II:153–161; *Annals of the Congress of the United States*, 12th Congress, 1st session, 1811-1812, Washington: Gales and Seaton, 1853, pp. 422–455.
[10] Miller, *op. cit.*, II:170.
[11] Cf. Hugh A. Garland, *The Life of Randolph*, New York: Appleton, 1850; Gerald White Johnson, *Randolph of Roanoke*, New York: Minton, Balch, 1929; Russell Kirk, *Randolph of Roanoke*, Chicago: University of Chicago Press, 1951.

The New Englanders whom Randolph excoriated for their opposition to slavery were his best and indeed only allies in resisting the surge toward war. In the Congress the voice of New England was scarcely heard (Daniel Webster was not elected until 1813). But at Hartford, on December 15, 1814, delegates from Massachusetts, Connecticut, and Rhode Island gathered to discuss secession from the Union. Restraint, however, overruled resentment. The convention adjourned in January with a resolution that denounced the war but concluded: "to attempt upon every abuse of power to change the Constitution would be to perpetuate the evils of revolution."[12]

Henry Clay, whose war it mainly was, lived to see two of its military heroes—Harrison, who triumphed over Tecumseh at Tippecanoe, and Andrew Jackson, the hero of New Orleans—defeat him for the presidency. The causes of the war which Madison soberly outlined in his war message were ignored in the peace negotiations, which were centered around John Quincy Adams's demand for a return to the *status quo ante bellum*. Finally, although the United States gained nothing tangible from the war, some historians assert that it was one of the most successful wars the nation ever fought; it did, after all, win for us a grudging but genuine recognition in Europe as a truly independent nation with power enough to demand respect.[13]

The Missouri Controversy

THE CONTROVERSY over Missouri, which dominated both sessions of the Sixteenth Congress, was notable not for any outstanding single speeches but for its bringing into focus the issue that was to dominate American life through the next generation. This sharp clarification of the degree of irreconcilability between North and South on the subject of slavery led Thomas Jefferson to describe the debate as a "fire-bell in the night,"[1] signalling an inevitable dissolution of the Union. Once the issue had been sharply and dramatically phrased, there was, he feared,

[12] Miller, *op. cit.*, Vol. V, Chapter I, discusses the Hartford Convention with definitive quotations from the principal speeches: Commager, *Documents, op. cit.*, presents the "Report and Resolutions of the Hartford Convention, January 4, 1815," I:209–211.
[13] Cf. the account by a noted English historian, George Dangerfield, *The Era of Good Feelings*, London: Methuen, 1953, Part I, "The Charterhouse of Ghent: 1814," pp. 3–91, in which he concludes: "the Americans fought for their chance to grow up" (p. 90).
[1] *The Writings of Thomas Jefferson*, ed. A. L. Bergh, Washington: Jefferson Memorial Assoc., 1907, XV:294.

no escaping its consequences: "We have the wolf by the ears, and we can neither safely hold him, nor safely let him go."[2] Henry Clay was sufficiently impressed by the danger to assume the role of "The Great Pacificator," which he was thenceforth to maintain throughout his life. John Randolph confronted the dilemma of the South frankly when he said that if all his other misfortunes should be combined they could not outweigh his single misfortune of being a slaveholder; yet he used all his oratorical and parliamentary skill to prevent the restriction of slavery in Missouri.

The debate commenced December 8, 1819, and did not end until February 26, 1821. In the "first debate," during the first session of the Congress, the arguments largely concerned two amendments to the bill to admit Missouri as a State: the first, presented by James Tallmadge, Jr., of New York, to prohibit slavery in Missouri—which lost; and the second, offered by Jessie B. Thomas, of Illinois (a slaveowner), to prohibit slavery from all the territories north of 36° 30'—which won. In the "second debate," during the second session, Northern sentiments were directly challenged by a provision in the Missouri Constitution, which Congress was asked to approve, forever prohibiting the entrance of free Negroes into the State. Clay engineered a compromise whereby the offensive provision was retained in the Constitution but the Missouri Legislature promised never to enact laws to implement it. Clay's compromise established a basis for knitting together a majority vote. But the futility of patch-work types of compromise is illuminated by the fact that in 1825, and then again in 1847, the immigration of free colored persons into Missouri "under any pretext" was explicitly prohibited.

The existence of sectional divisiveness had been dramatized as early as 1754, when the Albany plan for colonial union was rejected by the Massachusetts General Court because of "the great sway which the Southern Colonies . . . would have in all the determinations of the Grand Council."[3] In 1776 Thomas Jefferson wrote the abolition of slavery into the Declaration of Independence and it was amended out by the Continental Congress because unity against the British seemed more important then than humanitarian reform. The invention of the cotton gin, followed by the Louisiana Purchase, which opened up the rich lower Mississippi basin to cotton culture, combined to make slavery so profitable that it could not easily be abandoned. As early as 1786, in North Carolina, "a Dissolution of the Union was publicly and openly spoke of as a thing that would and ought to happen because the North-

[2] *Ibid.*
[3] Cf. R. C. Newhold, *The Albany Congress and Plan of Union*, New York: Vantage Press, 1955, pp. 141–155.

ern States were injurious to the Southern."[4] In the discussion during the Philadelphia Constitutional Convention, Rufus King had sadly noted that "the question of a difference in interests did not lie where it had hitherto been discussed, between the great and small States; but between the southern and eastern."[5] During the first two decades of the Republic "disunion" was largely a Southern theme; then, from 1800 to 1820, with Democrats largely controlling Congress and Virginians in exclusive occupancy of the White House, New England Federalists were the secessionists. In 1812, during the Congressional debate on the admission of Louisiana as a State, Josiah Quincy of Massachusetts pontificated: "If this bill passes, it is my deliberate opinion that it is virtually a dissolution of this Union; that it will free the States from their moral obligation; and, as it is the right of all, so it will be the duty of some, definitely to prepare for a separation, amicably if they can, violently if they must."[6]

Meanwhile, in 1820 there were more free Negroes in the South than in the North, more abolitionist societies south of the Mason-Dixon line than north of it. John Tyler of South Carolina aroused no dissent from his constituents when he called slavery a "dark cloud," nor did Robert Reid of Georgia when he likened it to a cancer. Economically and socially the South was bound to the slave system, but it did not pretend to like it. The Missouri controversy, however, signalled the start of a new era.

There was no great effort on either side to be conciliatory. When Tallmadge introduced his amendment to prohibit slavery from Missouri, he said: "If blood is necessary to extinguish any fire which I have assisted to kindle, I can assure gentlemen, while I regret the necessity, I shall not forebear to contribute my mite."[7] John Randolph retorted for the slaveholders: "God has given us the Missouri and the devil shall not take it from us."[8]

The *Annals of Congress* for these two sessions do not make exciting reading; yet into this controversy was introduced practically every argument that was to be used on the slavery and sectional issues for the next thirty years. Senator Nathaniel Macon, of North Carolina, introduced two themes: that white labor could not compete with free black labor,

[4] Edmund C. Burnett, *Letters of Members of the Continental Congress*, Washington, D.C.: Carnegie Institution of Washington, 1921–1936, VIII:533.
[5] *The Life and Correspondence of Rufus King*, ed. C. R. King, New York: Putnam's, 1894–1900, I:241.
[6] *Annals of Congress*, 14th Congress, 3rd session, p. 525. Cf. Susan Dixon, *History of the Missouri Compromise and Slavery in America*, Cincinnati: R. Clark, 1903, p. 40.
[7] *Annals of Congress*, 15th Congress, 2nd session, pp. 1203–04. Cf. Glover Moore, *The Missouri Controversy*, Lexington: University of Kentucky Press, 1953, p. 51.
[8] *Daily Advertiser*, Boston, Feb. 5, 1820.

so that "There is no place for free blacks in the United States"; and that slavery is no evil but a positive good. "Go home with me," he said invitingly, "or with some other southern member, and witness the meeting between the slaves and the owner, and see the glad faces and the hearty shaking of hands. The owner can make more free in conversation with his slave, and be more easy in his company, than the rich man where there is no slave, with the white hireling that drives his carriage."[9] Senator William Smith of South Carolina followed with a speech, on January 26, 1820, in which he not only agreed that slavery was good for both whites and blacks but asserted it was irreligious to question it, since "Christ himself gave a sanction to slavery."[10] Senator Rufus King, the 1816 candidate of the Federalists for the presidency, presented two long speeches in which he declared that slavery was contrary to natural law and hinted that he felt degraded to sit in a chamber with slaveowners. Senator William Pinckney, on February 15, used "the machinery of syllogism,"[11] presaging the methods of Calhoun, to prove that the Constitution protected slavery. King proposed to the Southerners that they accept the prohibition of slavery north of 36° 30′ on the curious ground that there never could be more than one state carved from the Northwest Territory, since most of the area was "a prairie, resembling the Steppes of Tartary, without wood or water excepting the great River and its few branches."[12]

In the House, Congressman Charles Pinckney declared that Negroes were "*created* with less intellectual powers than the whites,"[13] a declaration that his listeners accepted as a foregone conclusion. William Lowndes, of South Carolina, one of the War Hawks of 1812, now near his death, mourned "the Union verging to dissolution; and his own condition, verging to the grave."[14] Thomas Cobb of Georgia charged that antislavery speakers "were kindling a fire which all the waters of the ocean could not extinguish. It could be extinguished only in blood."[15] Said Benjamin Hardin of Kentucky, "Gentlemen think that if Missouri falls she will fall alone; but, sir, I will go with her, and so will her sister states, who have blood and treasure."[16] Charles Pinckney decided that the slaves were happy and "the man or men who would at-

[9] *Annals of Congress,* 16th Congress, 1st session, pp. 173–226.
[10] *Ibid.,* pp. 266–275.
[11] *Ibid.,* pp. 397–407.
[12] *The Life and Correspondence of Rufus King, op. cit.,* VI:289.
[13] *Annals of Congress,* 16th Congress, 1st session, p. 1136.
[14] *Abridgement of the Debates of Congress,* ed. Thomas Hart Benton, New York: Appleton, 1858, VII:12n.
[15] *Annals of Congress,* 15th Congress, 2nd session, pp. 1436–38. Cf. Moore, *op. cit.,* p. 59.
[16] Moore, *op. cit.,* p. 151.

tempt to give them their freedom would be their greatest enemies."[17] Henry Clay worrisomely pointed out that threats of disunion and civil war had become commonplace. Felix Walker, from Buncombe County in North Carolina, introduced a lasting phrase into the language when he resisted the calls of a weary House for adjournment by saying his constituents expected him to make their views known and he would "make a speech for Buncombe."[18] In the Electoral College in 1820, during the course of this Congressional brawl, James Monroe was re-elected with the vote of every State in the Union, thus curiously leading historians to label this period "the Era of Good Feelings."

The question of slavery was not "put to rest" by the compromise. In 1824 a second Adams entered the White House, by way of the only presidential election ever having to be decided by a vote of the House of Representatives. Within a decade of the Missouri debates, abolitionism arose as a system of organized political evangelism. Meanwhile, another issue intervened: the tariff.

The Tariff—Breeder of Sectionalism

THE COLONIAL demand of "No taxation without representation" became converted shortly to the even happier slogan of "No taxation." Under the Jeffersonian theory that *that government is best which governs least*,[1] and with the sales of western lands bringing in such limited funds as were needed, taxes were not a serious issue in the early years of the Republic. On July 4, 1789, with a war debt to be paid, the first national tariff in our history was enacted after little debate. In the wake of Alexander Hamilton's 1791 "Report on Manufactures," the Congress added a modest internal revenue tax on whiskey. At this, Congressman Jackson, of Georgia, arose to denounce it as "odious, unequal, unpopular, and oppressive, more particularly in the Southern States . . . as the citizens of those States have . . . no breweries or orchards to furnish a substitute for spiritous liquors; hence they become a necessary article."[2] When the farmers of western Pennsylvania staged a "Whiskey Rebel-

[17] *Annals of Congress*, 16th Congress, 1st session, pp. 132–325.
[18] Moore, *op. cit.*, p. 92.
[1] *The Inaugural Addresses of the Presidents of the United States*, Washington: Government Printing House, 1952 et seq., pp. 11–14. The "sum of good government," Jefferson defined as "a wise and frugal Government, which shall restrain men from injuring one another, shall leave them otherwise free to regulate their own pursuits of industry and improvement, and shall not take from the mouth of labor the bread it has earned" (p. 13).
[2] Marion Miller, *op. cit.*, XII:9.

lion," the tax plan of "drinking down the national debt,"[3] as Congressman Livermore of New Hampshire called it, was abandoned. Jefferson, in his second inaugural address, boasted that his administration had abolished all taxation except the tariff.

After the War of 1812, the combination of a national debt and the depressed condition of manufacturers convinced Congressmen from all sections that new tariff revenue and protection were needed. Calhoun drafted a tariff law that both Webster and Clay supported. Scattered and ineffectual opposition was voiced by Thomas Telfair of Georgia, who warned against making prices "dear to the consumer . . . merely that the manufacturer may derive a profit,"[4] and by John Randolph, who saw the good of the public being sacrificed for the "mushroom interest"[5] of inefficient manufacturers. Calhoun, interestingly enough, argued for the tariff on the grounds that it would be a "new and most powerful cement"[6] for joining together all sections of the union in a common interest.

In 1824, in a bid for the presidency, Henry Clay concocted an "American System" comprising an extensive system of roads and other internal improvements which were to be paid for by higher tariff revenues. In a careful speech begun on March 31, Clay argued that his dual-purpose system would benefit equally the North, West, and South. "With me," he said, "it is a fundamental axiom, it is interwoven with all my opinions, that the great interests of the country are united and inseparable."[7] The West and South would get the transportation arteries they needed; the Eastern laborers would gain protection against the cheap labor of Europe. Webster, mindful of the manufacturing and commercial interests of New England, praised the revenue features of the tariff. Calhoun, then Secretary of War and maneuvering for the vice-presidential nomination as his own shortest route to the presidency, had no need to make his views known; but he personally selected for the Senate young Robert Hayne, who opposed the tariff on the ground that it would injure the South by raising the prices of what it must buy.

It was four years later that the sectional issue became paramount when a new bill, denounced as "The Tariff of Abominations," was introduced. It was the first tariff bill to be drawn to serve intricate and complicated political interests—primarily the desires of Pennsylvania, Ohio, and New York manufacturers. Congressman Claiborne, of Vir-

[3] *Ibid.*, XII:11.
[4] *Ibid.*, XII:27.
[5] *Ibid.*, XII:31.
[6] *Ibid.*, XII:35.
[7] *The Life and Speeches of the Hon. Henry Clay*, ed. D. Mallory, Hartford: S. Andrus, 1853, I:496–539 and II:5–56.

ginia, warmly denied any "necessity for the Government to resort to a hot-bed system of legislation, to force into premature existence a number of sickly manufacturing establishments."[8] George McDuffie, of South Carolina, sought to unite Northern and Southern laborers and farmers by arguing that they had a common interest in keeping down prices of manufactured articles. Daniel Turner, wistfully recalling the Jeffersonian ideal of government, argued that "The True American system consists in the Government not interfering in matters which are calculated alone to promote the interests of comparatively few individuals."[9] John Randolph declaimed that "the bill, if it had its true name, should be called a bill to rob and plunder nearly one-half of the Union, for the sake of the residue."[10] With a pointed jab at his old enemy, Henry Clay, he concluded: "The bill referred to manufactures of no sort or kind, but the manufacture of a President of the United States."[11]

In still another session, during the tariff debate of 1831–32, Clay again fought for the system on which his presidential hopes rested, arguing that the then prosperous condition of the nation was proof of the advantages of a high tariff. John Tyler sharply retorted: "How comes it now about that, while the South is impoverished, the North has suddenly become so rich?"[12] He summarized the view of the South with a literal analogy based on the relations of four individuals: a Southern planter, an English manufacturer, and two Northern manufacturers. In a free market, so long as the Southerner could sell his cotton to the Englishman and buy textiles in return, neither could suffer, for their prices would rise and fall concurrently. But the two Northern manufacturers, unable to compete with the Englishman in a free market, used their preponderance of votes over their one Southern colleague to distort the market balance with tariff duties imposed on textile imports. "I demand of all candid men," Tyler concluded, "to say whether the power thus exerted is not selfish, despotic, and unjust."[13]

Rufus Choate, of Massachusetts, then entered the debate, and promptly illustrated his weakness as a politician, however great his abilities at the bar or in ceremonial orations. He admitted that "the system operates with a local and partial severity upon the planting States." Then he went on to argue that the "interests, pursuits, and opinions" of the two sections were "conflicting, almost irreconcilable." With an ap-

[8] Miller, *op. cit.*, XII:50.
[9] *Ibid.*, XII:57.
[10] *Ibid.*, XII:58.
[11] *Ibid.*
[12] *Ibid.*, XII:62.
[13] *Ibid.*, XII:64.

peal to "expediency," he proposed that legislation must serve "the greatest good of the greatest number"—that is, the more populous North. "What if there be some excitement of feeling," he asked suavely, "some harsh words, and some lowering looks between the brethren of this wide household? All these things must be, and may very safely be. They are only part of the price! how inadequate the price—which every nation pays for greatness and liberty."[14] Clayton of Georgia and Lewis of Alabama both answered him, reminding the Senate that the South had fought for the Union and had willingly borne more than its share of burdens in payment of the national debt. They recalled the promise that the tariff was introduced as a temporary measure to help Northern manufacturing get a start. Now the South demanded an end to the system that required a bounty from southerners for the benefit of Northern manufacturers. The debate was taking an ominous tone.

Rufus Choate had disingenuously pinpointed the essential fact: the North could outvote the South. Calhoun ceased maneuvering for the presidency, after Jackson's re-election postponed his hopes for at least another quadrennium, and organized a Nullification Convention in Charleston which threatened to prevent collection of tariff duties by force of arms. In the Senate, on February 15 and 16, 1833, Calhoun presented his doctrine of "concurrent majorities." Refining upon the analogy John Tyler had devised, Calhoun showed that in a community of five men, three could always outvote the other two. When the community is enlarged to twenty four (then the number of States) thirteen could always outvote eleven. He denied that majority government is just, pointing out that it could always be tyrannical against the rights of the minority. He argued for a new Constitution based upon "two absolute majorities combined."[15]

As a logical instrument, Calhoun's argument was unshakable; and Webster, who rose to reply to it, did not attempt refutation. Instead, he simply brushed it aside, saying he would not debate the merits of a fanciful Constitution that did not exist but would remain true to the real Constitution which was actually in effect. Then Clay, with his peculiar genius for postponing issues that could not under the circumstances be solved, proposed a new tariff that substantially lowered the most objectionable duties. With its passage South Carolina lost the need to quarrel with the federal government, and the threat of nullification was dropped.

John Davis of Massachusetts, in a fruitless plea against the tariff re-

---

[14] *Ibid.*, XII:67.
[15] *The Works of John C. Calhoun*, ed. R. Crallé, New York: Appleton, 1853, II:225.

ductions, introduced for the first time into the debate the question that would not bear examination: why the South had not developed an industrial capacity comparable to that of the North. His words were discreet, but no member of the Congress could misunderstand his meaning. "I do object to compromise . . . ," he said, "to appease the unnatural and unfounded discontent of the South; *a discontent, I fear, which has deeper root than the tariff, and will continue when that is forgotten*."[16] The tariff came up for lengthy debate again in 1846; but the arguments were half-hearted. By this time sectionalism had become far too emotional an issue to be discussed in economic terms. As Congressman Davis hinted, the differences between North and South became increasingly sharp while the tariff, at least for the time, was all but forgotten.

The Webster-Hayne Debate on Nullification

JUST BEFORE Christmas of 1829, Senator Samuel Foot of Connecticut, mannerly and astute, introduced a bill to abolish the office of Surveyor-General and bring the sale of western lands virtually to a halt. There were real issues involved: control of the diffusion of the limited population, safeguarding the labor force of the industrial East, taxation policies, relations with the Indians, the policies to govern construction and control of highways and railways. Thomas Hart Benton, the chief exponent of western settlement, arose on January 18, 1830, to commence a speech that lasted two days. He attacked the Foot resolution in a generally conciliatory manner; but he denounced New England for attempting to bottle up its supply of cheap labor and pleaded for continuing development of the West. Then he introduced a very different theme, suggesting that revenue from the sale of the lands be given to the States rather than the Federal treasury, since "the very life of our system is the independence of the States," and "there is no evil more to be deprecated than the consolidation of this Government."[1] Senator Robert Y. Hayne, from South Carolina, also spoke against the resolution. Hayne was forty years old, an eight-year veteran of the Senate and former attorney general of his State. He was intelligent, widely read, and polit-

[16] Miller, op. cit., XII:71.
[1] Cf. Norman W. Mattis, "Thomas Hart Benton," in Nichols, ed., *History and Criticism, op. cit.*, III:52–96 and W. S. Howell and H. Hopewell, "Daniel Webster," in Brigance, ed., *ibid.*, II:692–711. Text of speech in *Register of Debates in Congress*, 21st Congress, 1st session, pp. 22–27.

ically astute. Benton, evaluating Hayne in his memoirs, placed him among the solid statesmen: "He had a copious and ready elocution flowing at will in a strong and ready current and rich in the material which constitutes argument . . . . There was nothing holiday or empty about him—no lying in to be delivered of a speech of phrases."[2] Neither Benton nor Hayne said anything inflammatory about Foot's resolution; but Daniel Webster was looking for an opportunity to destroy the political appeal of the South before it could lure the Jacksonian Democrats into a lasting alliance.

In a scathing speech deliberately designed to anger Hayne, Webster attributed to him the anti-Yankee sentiments Benton had expressed and promised to "vindicate" Massachusetts "from charges and imputations on her public character and conduct, which he knew to be undeserved and unfounded."[3] Then he nailed down the issue he was determined to make the focal point of the debate: "The tendency of all these ideas and sentiments is obviously to bring the Union into discussion, as a mere question of present and temporary expediency . . . . The Union is to be preserved, while it suits local and temporary purpose to preserve it . . . . I deprecate and deplore this tone of thinking and acting."[4]

In this reply, Webster was not only deliberately provocative and cannily inaccurate, he was also guilefully careless, leaving himself apparently wide open to factual rebuttal. The temptation was greater than Hayne could resist.

On January 21 and 25, Hayne held the Senate floor with a brilliant and seemingly devastating reply to the innuendoes and inaccuracies Webster had used as bait. Referring to Webster's error in attributing to himself views that had been expressed by Benton, Hayne almost, but not quite, perceived the nature of the plot: "When I find a gentleman of mature age and experience . . . declining the contest offered from the West, and making war upon the unoffending South, I must believe—I am bound to believe—he has some object in view that he has not ventured to disclose."[5] If Hayne smelled a trap, however, he disdained to avoid it. For four hours he lavished scorn on New England, recalling that nullification was a child born of the Hartford Convention of 1814. He reminded the Senate that Webster had opposed the tariffs of 1820 and 1824 on the grounds that such an impost was unconstitutional. He concluded by arguing that if the Federal Government itself were the only judge of the limits of its own power, "the States are at once

2 Thomas Hart Benton, *Thirty Years' View*, New York: Appleton, 1856, II:186.
3 *Writings and Speeches of Daniel Webster*, National Edition, *op. cit.*, V:269.
4 Miller, *op. cit.*, V:40.
5 *Register of Debates in Congress*, ed. Gales and Seaton, Washington, 1830, VI:43.

reduced to mere petty corporations, and the people are entirely at your mercy."[6]

The following day Webster rose to make the reply which most surely supports his fame as America's greatest orator—a speech for which, as he later said, "I have been preparing all my life."[7] Public expectation was at its highest pitch, and the Senate chamber was crowded with Senators, Congressmen, and visiting men and women of fashion and influence. "The very stairways were dark with men who hung to one another like bees in a swarm," a journalist noted; "persons once in could not get out or change their positions."[8]

As was his custom, Webster spoke with great deliberation—only about ninety words a minute—and with the self-conscious majesty of a spokesman who stood above partisanship to represent the whole nation. Like a giant pestered but not disturbed by pigmies, he pretended the irrelevancies of the debate were not of his own making, and he grandly called for a reading of the Foot resolution to bring the debate back to its proper topic. Then he proceeded without a qualm to shift it once more to the ground he had chosen: the nature of the Union.

The mode of his detour was to refer to Hayne's attack upon Massachusetts and defense of South Carolina, concerning which Webster assumed high ground. "When I shall be found, sir, in my place, here in the Senate or elsewhere, to sneer at public merit because it happened to spring up beyond the little limits of my own State or neighborhood," he intoned, "may my tongue cleave to the roof of my mouth!" He went on: "I shall enter on no encomiums of Massachusetts; she needs none. There she is; behold her, and judge for yourselves. There is her history; the world knows it by heart . . . . Boston, and Concord, and Lexington, and Bunker Hill . . . . And, sir, where American liberty raised its infant voice, and where its youth was nurtured and sustained, there it still lives

---

[6] Miller, *op. cit.*, V:46.

[7] Peter Harvey, *Reminiscences and Anecdotes of Daniel Webster*, Boston: Little, Brown, 1878, supplies the origin of this widely-circulated remark. Actually, Webster referred not to generalized but to very specific acts of preparation, concluding: "In other words, if he had tried to make a speech to fit my notes, he could not have hit it better. No man is inspired with the occasion; I never was" (p. 152; cf. pp. 149–153). An excellent account of the background and progress of the debate is in Sydney George Fisher, *The True Daniel Webster*, Philadelphia: Lippincott, 1911, Chapter X, pp. 233–280. Some immediate preparation Webster did make; for, as Smucker reports, "He was heard by a friend to laugh to himself after returning home at the conclusion of Mr. Hayne's speech; and being asked the subject of his mirth, he replied that he was then thinking of the admirable way in which Colonel Hayne's quotation about Banquo's ghost could be turned against himself." Samuel M. Smucker, *The Life, Speeches, and Memorials of Daniel Webster*, Chicago: Belford, Clarke, 1859, Part I:84.

[8] Miller, *op. cit.*, V:37; Webster himself could barely struggle to his seat according to Smucker, *op. cit.*, p. 85.

. . . and it will fall at last, if fall it must, amid the proudest monuments of its own glory, and on the very spot of its origin."[9]

He felt, so he said, a "most grave and important duty . . . to state and to defend what I conceive to be the true principles of the Constitution under which we are here assembled. I understand the honorable gentleman from South Carolina to maintain that it is a right of the State legislatures . . . to annul an act of the general Government which it deems plainly and palpably unconstitutional. This is the sum of what I understand from him to be the South Carolina doctrine . . . . I propose to consider it and to compare it with the Constitution." Webster then spoke of revolution, inducing Hayne to interrupt with the declaration that he never intended revolution but merely had asserted the right of "interposition" by a State to block the operation within its boundaries of an unconstitutional law. Webster nodded with satisfaction. "If the gentleman had intended no more than to assert the right of revolution, for justifiable cause, he would have said only what all agree to. But I cannot conceive that there can be a middle course between submission to the laws . . . and open resistance, which is revolution or rebellion . . . . I do not admit that, under the Constitution and in conformity with it, there is any mode in which a State Government, as a member of the Union, can interfere and stop the progress of the general Government by force of her own laws under any circumstances whatsoever."[10] Here was Webster's point. He proceeded to prove it with logic and historical interpretation.

"It is, sir, the people's Constitution, the people's Government; made for the people; made by the people; and answerable to the people . . . . The general Government and the State governments derive their authority from the same source." Webster then turned to Hayne's charge that New Englanders in 1798 had denounced the Embargo Law as unconstitutional, concluding that "the people were not bound to obey it." This, Webster asserted, "was perfectly constitutional language." He explained: "There was heat, and there was anger"—but there was never a claim of the right of nullification by a State. Violation of law by individuals is vastly different from repudiation of law by governments claiming to be sovereign. "Sir, the very chief end, the main design, for which the whole Constitution was framed and adopted, was to establish a Government that should not be obliged to act through State agency or depend on State opinion and State discretion. The people had had quite enough of that kind of Government under the confederacy . . . . Con-

9 *Ibid.*, V:46–48.
10 *Ibid.*, V:48–51.

gress could only recommend; their acts were not of binding force till the States had adopted and sanctioned them. Are we in that condition still? . . . Sir, if we are, then vain will be our attempt to maintain the Constitution under which we sit." Relentlessly he drove his point home. "Gentlemen may say that, in an extreme case, the people might protect themselves, without the aid of the State governments. Such a case warrants revolution . . . . A nullifying act of a State legislature cannot alter the case nor make resistance any more lawful."[11]

Short of revolution, Webster went on, there lies the right to amend the Constitution. There is also provision for frequent elections, so that the people may control the nature of enacted laws. Thirdly, there is always the avenue of appeal to the Supreme Court if power is wrongly exercised. But, beyond this, the people have "at no time, in no way, directly or indirectly, authorized any State legislature to construe or interpret their high instrument of government."[12]

Some five hours had elapsed since Webster had commenced. In the tightly packed chamber, the muscles of the immobilized listeners were numbed and cramped. Webster gave a last glance at the five pages of notes which he had prepared as a brief outline for his argument, then launched into his conclusion, which became one of the most quoted passages in world oratory: "I have not accustomed myself to hang over the precipice of disunion, to see whether, with my short sight, I can fathom the depth of the abyss below . . . . When my eyes shall be turned to behold, for the last time, the sun in heaven, may I not see him shining on the broken and dishonored fragments of a once glorious Union; on States dissevered, discordant, belligerent; on a land rent with civil feuds, or drenched, it may be, in fraternal blood! Let their last feeble and lingering glance, rather, behold the gorgeous ensign of the Republic . . . blazing on all its ample folds . . . that sentiment dear to every true American heart—Liberty and Union, now and forever, one and inseparable!"[13]

Slowly, majestically, Webster took his seat. A Southern member approached him cordially and remarked, "Mr. Webster, I think you had better die now, and rest your fame on that speech."[14] Hayne, standing nearby, interjected, "You ought not to die: a man who can make such speeches as that ought never to die."[15] Webster himself, writing in April to his friend William Plumer, said, "I am willing to confess that,

[11] *Ibid.*, V:51–60.
[12] *Ibid.*, V:64–65.
[13] *Ibid.*, V:66.
[14] Harvey, *op. cit.*, p. 153; Allen L. Benson, *Daniel Webster*, New York: Cosmopolitan Book Club, 1929, p. 189.
[15] Harvey, *op. cit.*, p. 153.

having the occasion thus forced upon me, I did the best I could, under its pressure."[16] Shortly the speech was widely circulated in print, as a pamphlet and in newspapers, being more widely read than any other address in the history of the nation. There was nothing Hayne could do to stem its effect. But he tried.

The afternoon was far gone, and the crowd began streaming out of the Senate chamber. Hayne might have waited until the next day, letting the effect cool. Instead he replied at once, seeking through conciliation to blunt the powerful force of Webster's eloquence. "I said nothing which could be tortured into an attack on the East," he insisted gently. Then he reviewed the historical record, showing it was the States who made and ratified the Constitution. He concluded: "Sir, it is because South Carolina loves the Union and would preserve it forever that she is opposing now, while there is hope, those usurpations of the Federal Government which, once established, will sooner or later tear this Union into fragments."[17]

The star performers had played their roles. But the debate on Foot's resolution continued through the rest of January, February, and March. Then other subjects were taken up, but in mid-May the resolution was tabled, on a motion by Webster. Considering the dynamics of politics, it is likely that the most influential speech in the lengthy debate was an undistinguished legalistic argument delivered by Senator Edward Livingston of Louisiana. Livingston's defense of the primacy of the Constitution over the State governments was heard with very special attentiveness, for he spoke as a personal representative of President Andrew Jackson.[18] The South was thus given positive notice that its views would find no support from "Old Hickory." Calhoun made a last desperate effort to entrap Jackson into support for the Southern interpretation by inviting him to a Jefferson Day dinner at which twenty five toasts were presented to States rights. Jackson listened impassively, then arose and grimly lifted his own glass with a toast to the "Federal Union: it must and shall be preserved."[19] It had become clearly evident that

[16] *Writings and Speeches of Daniel Webster, op. cit.,* IV:196.
[17] Miller, *op. cit.,* V:66–73.
[18] Arthur Schlesinger, Jr., in his *The Age of Jackson,* Chapter V, fell into a curious error in interpreting the shifts of power and politics at this period. "The great party leader was no longer the eloquent parliamentary orator," he wrote, "but the popular hero, capable of bidding directly for the confidence of the masses." This concept fitted his hero Jackson very well, but Schlesinger's very effort to prove his point indicated its weakness: "The two greatest orators of the day, Webster and Clay, were almost invariably on the losing side." This is manifest nonsense; whether they were right or wrong, they were generally on the winning wide—and they received ample credit for helping their side win.
[19] *Theodore Jervey, Robert Y. Hayne and His Times,* New York: Macmillan, 1909, p. 299.

the Union could not be argued into dissolution. The next available expedient was to seek more Southern votes in the Senate through creation of additional slave States. This was another phase of the same general debate.

📖 *The Long Debate on Expansion*

DESPITE THE general futility of the Continental Congress, before its dissolution after thirteen years it enacted one of the most influential bills ever voted into law by an American legislature. This was the Ordinance of 1787, debated and adopted during the same summer in which the Constitutional Convention was providing for the demise of the Congress.

In 1784, in a momentous decision, the States ceded their western lands to the central government. By 1787 there was urgent need for some plan for settlement and development of this huge domain. For one thing, the national treasury was bare and funds were needed from sale of the land. Moreover, swarms of discharged and unpaid Revolutionary War veterans were unemployed and were demanding some remuneration and a chance to earn a livelihood. A group of New Englanders formed a company called the Ohio Associates and commenced a survey of suitable homesites in the Northwest Territory. They engaged a master propagandist and lobbyist, the Reverend Manasseh Cutler, who "speedily proved that the tongue of the preacher" could be used to good political effect.[1] There was money to be made from speculation in the western lands, he pointed out, but not until some arrangement could be made for the government and protection of the settlers. The plea was quickly effective. On July 13, the eighteen delegates representing eight States, who were present, cast seventeen affirmative votes.

Within its own broad sphere, the Ordinance was fully as influential upon later American history as was the Constitution itself. It provided a means by which the new nation could expand, with the new States having the same rights as the old. Its principal provisions were: (1) that a territorial governor was to be appointed by and be responsible to the Federal Government; (2) that new States, not fewer than three nor more than five, should be formed out of the Northwest Territory: (3) that no new State could be admitted to the Union until its Constitution should

[1] Edmund Cody Burnett, *The Continental Congress*, New York: Macmillan, 1941, p. 683; Walter Havighurst, *Wilderness for Sale: The Story of the First Western Land Rush*, New York: Hastings House, 1956, pp. 136–137.

be approved by the Congress; (4) that no State once admitted to the Union could ever thereafter secede from it; (5) that the Federal Government guaranteed to the residents in the territory equal voting rights and equal protection of the law; (6) that rights similar to those incorporated in the first ten amendments to the federal Constitution were assured to the inhabitants; (7) that establishment of free public schools should be "encouraged"; and (8) that slavery was prohibited in the area.

Daniel Webster later observed that, "I doubt whether one single law of any law-giver, ancient or modern, has produced effects of more distinct, marked, and lasting character than the Ordinance of 1787."[2] It became law "without the least color of constitutional authority," as Madison pointed out, for it never was submitted to the States for ratification, as the Articles of Confederation required. But neither was its legality ever formally challenged. Here was a solid declaration of the sovereignty of the central government. The right of secession was denied. The power of Congress was affirmed to define the limits of State rule and specifically to exclude slavery.

Despite its importance, the Ordinance was adopted without extensive debate and apparently with little comprehension of its significance. The reason probably was that it dealt not with the rights and privileges of existing States but with an unpeopled and largely unknown wilderness domain. Besides, the attention of the nation was quickly shifted from the Continental Congress and its enactments to the debates on the ratification of the federal Constitution.

Sporadically, during the next two or three generations, some attention was given to the question of the rights of the aborigines whose lands were being occupied. The debates in the treaty negotiations with the Indians comprise a chapter of our history as yet little investigated. The prevailing attitude was generally much like that expressed by John Quincy Adams, in a speech he delivered at Boston in 1802:

> There are moralists who have questioned the right of the Europeans to intrude upon the possessions of the aboriginals in any case, and under any limitations whatsoever. But have they maturely considered the whole subject? The Indian right of possession itself stands, with regard to the greatest part of the country, upon a questionable foundation. Their cultivated fields; their constructed habitations; a space of ample sufficiency for their subsistence, and whatever they had annexed to themselves by personal labor, was undoubtedly by the law of nature theirs. But what is the right of a huntsman to the forest of a thousand miles over which he has accidentally ranged in quest of prey? Shall the liberal bounties of Providence to the race of man be monopolized by one of

2 *Writings and Speeches, op. cit.,* V:263.

ten thousand for whom they were created? Shall the exuberant bosom of the common mother, amply adequate to the nourishment of millions, be claimed exclusively by a few hundreds of her offspring?[3]

Many answers were made by Indian spokesmen, one of the most poignant being a statement made by Chief Joseph, of the Nez Percés, when he was finally brought to surrender in the Wallowa country of the State of Washington, in October, 1877:

> Tell General Howard I know his heart. What he told me before I have in my heart. I am tired of fighting. Our chiefs are killed. Looking Glass is dead. Toohoolhoolzote is dead. The old men are all dead. It is the young men who say yes or no. He who led the young men is dead. It is cold and we have no blankets. The little children are freezing to death. My people, some of them, have run away to the hills, and have no blankets, no food; no one knows where they are—perhaps freezing to death. I want to have time to look for my children and see how many I can find. Maybe I shall find them among the dead. Hear me, my chiefs. I am tired; my heart is sick and sad. From where the sun now stands, I will fight no more forever.[4]

Until 1890, when the Census Bureau officially recorded that there was no longer a frontier, territorial expansionism lay close to the heart of every major American issue. It was a major cause of the War of 1812, as we have seen, and of the Mexican War. Numerous religious denominations were organized partially in response to new problems and needs of the expanding West. Multiple reform movements were launched in part through the restless individualism and optimism inspired by the opportunities offered by new land. Rivalry for control of the new territories and States marked the relations of North and South, of bankers and agrarians, of radical demagogues and conservative financiers. Meanwhile, specific occasions for the oratory of expansionism were the Mexican War, the Wilmot Proviso, and the Compromise of 1850.

Until John C. Calhoun became enthralled with the idea of maintaining a balance of numbers in the Senate, expansionism was a national rather than a sectional sentiment. It was a Virginian, John Floyd, who, during the eighteen-twenties, made the most persistent demands for American occupation of the Oregon territory, where slavery was impractical. It was during the Congressional debate on one of Floyd's bills, in

---

[3] John Quincy Adams, "An Address to the Members of the Charitable Fire Association of Boston, May 28, 1802," Massachusetts Historical Society *Collections*, VIII:105–110.

[4] Alvin M. Josephy, *The Patriot Chiefs*, New York: Viking Press, 1961, pp. 339–340. A fine study of an Indian orator who spoke eloquently for the rights of his people is Frank W. Merritt, "Teedyuscung—Speaker for the Delawares," in *Today's Speech*, III (Nov., 1955):14–18.

1823, that Francis Baylies of Massachusetts gave cogent expression to the theme of Manifest Destiny: "Gentlemen are talking of natural boundaries," he said. "Sir, our natural boundary is the Pacific Ocean. The swelling tide of our population must roll on until that mighty ocean interposes its waters, and limits our territorial empire."[5] During the presidential campaign of 1844, widespread popular demand for the whole of the Pacific Northwest was stereotyped by "Foghorn Bill" Allen of Ohio, chairman of the Senate Committee on Foreign Relations, in the phrase, "Fifty-four forty or fight." It was upon the question of the admission of Texas as a slave State, and the subsequent war with Mexico, that expansionism definitely became a sectional issue.

The chief contemporary critic of our war against Mexico was Senator Thomas Corwin of Ohio (1794–1865). Corwin won fame as a youth in his own state for his legal abilities and for his wonderfully effective irony and humor in stump speeches. In 1822, newly elected to the Ohio Legislature, he led a successful fight for abolishment of the whipping post as a means of public punishment. His fellow legislators measured his abilities as they listened to his fluent flood of scorn: "When the traveller shall inquire of you the use of that post . . . . [you] must tell him the truth; and you may inform him that it is a deity that is worshipped by the seven hundred thousand inhabitants of Ohio; that his peculiar attributes and qualities are a love of money and a thirst insatiable for human blood."[6] Although there had been little interest in the problem when Corwin introduced it, and though public whipping was then taken for granted, Corwin's persuasion swept the legislature into repeal of the law.

Five feet ten inches in height and broadly built, Corwin, like Webster, was both massive and very dark—"the blackest white man in the United States."[7] In the United States Congress, to which he was elected in 1831, he spoke seldom, making only six speeches during his nine years in the House. "I am very reluctant at any time," he explained, "to lift up my voice in this Babel of confused voices."[8] In his last year in the House, on February 14, 1840, he delivered a memorably scorching denunciation of the hapless General Crary, who had dared to criticize the Whig's presidential candidate, William Henry Harrison. "This House, Mr. Speaker," Corwin said, "knows that I am not given much to babbling here; yes sir, you all know that like Balaam's ass, I never speak here until I am kicked into it." Then he turned his atten-

[5] *Debates in Congress*, ed. Gales and Seaton, Washington, 1855, III:682–683.
[6] Josiah Morrow, ed., *Life and Speeches of Thomas Corwin*, Cincinnati: W. H. Anderson, 1896, p. 142.
[7] *Ibid.*, p. 83.
[8] *Ibid.*, p. 224.

tion to General Crary, who, "mounted on his crop-eared, bushy-tailed mare," was fit only to lead parades until the threat of rain forced him to seek refuge under a shed where he drew his sword and slashed a watermelon in twain. Then "our brave militia general and his forces, from the skulls of melons thus vanquished, in copious draughts of whisky, assuage the heroic fire of their souls, after the bloody scenes of a parade-day."[9]

Corwin returned then to the practice of law, but in 1845 he was elected to the Senate. On February 11, 1847, he cast the only vote in the Senate against the continuance of war with Mexico and delivered the most eloquent anti-war speech ever addressed to a war-time American audience. "How is it," Corwin demanded, "that a peaceful and peace loving people, happy beyond the common lot of man, busy in every laudable pursuit of life, have been forced to turn suddenly from these and plunge into the misery, the vice and crime . . . of war? The answer can only be, it was by the act and will of the President *alone* . . . . I trust we shall abandon the idea, the heathen, barbarian notion, that our true national glory is to be won or retained by military prowess or skill in the art of destroying life . . . . It is idle, Mr. President, to suppose that the Mexican people would not feel as deeply for the dismemberment and disgrace of their country as you would for the dismemberment of this Union of ours . . . . With twenty millions of people, you have about one thousand millions of acres of land . . . . But the Senator from Michigan [Lewis Cass] says we will be two hundred millions in a few years, and we want room. If I were a Mexican, I would tell you, 'Have you not room in your own country to bury your dead men? If you come into mine, we will greet you with bloody hands, and welcome you to hospitable graves.' " Then Corwin turned to the effects of success in the war upon the United States, pointing out that any territory taken from Mexico would have to be brought into the Union either as free soil or as slave—on which issue "the North and South are brought into collision on a point where neither will yield." The solution he offered was negotiated peace on the basis of the *status quo ante bellum.* "Let us call home our armies . . . let us wash Mexican blood from our hands."[10] The speech won applause, even from the war party, but expansionism was not to be stopped.

The domestic consequences were just what Corwin described. Already, in 1846, Senator David Wilmot, of Pennsylvania, had introduced his "Proviso," barring slavery from any territory that should be taken from Mexico; whereupon Calhoun had leaped to his feet with a cry of indignation. "The South like the North had fought to win the war," he

[9] *Ibid.*, 262.
[10] *Ibid.*, 277–314.

snapped; "now the South must not be cheated of its share of the spoils." President Polk confided to his diary: "The slavery question is assuming a fearful and most important aspect."[11]

Polk's concern was amply justified by the tone of the Congressional debates, as may be illustrated by a few selections from the debate in the House on December 3, 1849. The speakers were Richard K. Meade of Virginia, Robert Toombs and Alexander H. Stephens of Georgia, and William T. Colcock of South Carolina. Their words reflect the concern of the South over the Wilmot Proviso and indicate how close the nation was by that time to Civil War:

> *Meade:* If the North generally, whose big prosperity is the result of unrestricted intercourse with the South, refuse the terms we prescribe, let us talk no more about the blessings of Union.

> *Toombs:* I do not hesitate to avow before this House, and the country, and in the presence of the living God, that if by your legislation you seek to drive us from the Territories of California and New Mexico, purchased by the common blood and treasure of the whole people, and to abolish slavery in this district, thereby attempting to fix a national degradation upon half the States of this confederacy, *I am for disunion,* and, if my physical courage be equal to the maintenance of my convictions of right and duty, I will devote all I am and all I have on earth to its consummation.

> *Stephens:* I concur in every word uttered by my colleague, and, furthermore, I declare that, from the moment a concerted attack, made by the North upon the rights of the South, is an accomplished fact, the Union is thereby dissolved.

> *Colcock:* As soon as the abolition of slavery in the District of Columbia is resolved upon, or the Wilmot Proviso is passed, that moment I am for the dissolution of the Union.[12]

The worst fears of the Southerners were assuaged by the election of Howell Cobb of Georgia as Speaker of the House, in a close vote, on December 22. The Wilmot Proviso, however, was still on the agenda; and the South continued its threats. On January 22, 1850, Thomas L. Clingman, of North Carolina, warned angrily: "Attempt to trample upon us and we part company." The South had contributed proportionately twice as much as had the North, he claimed, for the winning of the war; yet the North "will not permit us to have the smallest portion of that territory." He concluded, "Why, Sir, this is the most impudent proposition that was ever maintained by any respectable body of

[11] Herbert Agar, *The Price of Union,* Boston: Houghton Mifflin, 1950, p. 322.
[12] Miller, *op. cit.,* IV:181.

men!"[13] Despite all the warnings of civil war, the Wilmot Proviso was adopted by the House—though it failed to win Senate approval. The North won a partial legislative decision; but the recriminations of the South sent a wave of foreboding through the nation.

One who was roused to try to quiet the dispute was the aged, ill, and weary Henry Clay, who had retired from public life to spend the remainder of his days at his Lexington, Kentucky, estate. In one of the most selfless acts in American history, Clay had himself re-elected to the Senate by the Kentucky legislature and undertook the thankless task of trying to patch together one last compromise by which the destruction of the Union might be averted. Back in Washington, on the 21st of January, 1850, on an evening when cold and wind shook his frail body, and hacked with a cough that made speaking difficult, Clay drove in his carriage to Webster's quarters to make a difficult request. The two had long been rivals for control of the Whig Party and for election as its candidate to the presidency. Webster still was ambitious for the White House; yet Clay came to ask him to join in a massive effort to conciliate the South—a move certain to lose support for him in New England. For several hours the two old men sat talking, drinking, planning, and reminiscing together. Webster gave his hand to Clay in support of the measures that, collectively, came to be known as "The Compromise of 1850." The sop to the North was the admission of California as a free State and abolition of the slave trade in the District of Columbia. For the South, there was offered continuance of slavery in the federal district, organization of the New Mexico and Utah Territories without reference to slavery, and stringent enforcement by federal agents of the Fugitive Slave Law. The South would be the major gainer; but since it was the more vociferous in its complaints it was more in need of being mollified.

After Clay introduced his bills on January 29, he supported them with two of his best and most appealing speeches. He begged the North to recognize the South's fears and yield to its pride; and he warned the South that secession would mean war: "furious, bloody, implacable, exterminating war." "This Union is my country," Clay said proudly; "the thirty States are my country; Kentucky is my country [but] if my own State should raise the banner of disunion, I would go against her . . . much as I love her."[14]

The debate lasted for months and drew into its devouring maw all the

[13] *Ibid.*, IV:182.
[14] *The Works of Henry Clay*, ed. Calvin Colton, New York: Putnam's, 1904, IX:397–398.

great men in the Congress. Thomas Hart Benton spoke for the compromises, thereby angering his Missouri constituents so much that he lost his seat in the Senate. William Henry Seward, a "Conscience Whig"—as distinguished from the "Cotton Whigs," who voted with the South because of profits made on the New York Cotton Exchange—supported the bills that favored the North and opposed those that favored the South. He thus helped to dramatize the point that the South had to choose between abolitionism and secession, and thus also made more difficult his own path to the presidency. Coming close to identifying himself with the Constitution-burning Garrisonian abolitionists, Seward appealed to "a higher law than the Constitution,"[15] and declared that on matters of morality and freedom "No human laws are of any validity, if contrary to this . . . law of nature . . . dictated by God himself . . . binding over all the globe."[16] Two of the principal Southern orators, Stephens and Toombs, threw their influence in support of Clay's compromise measures. No other debate in our history has brought together such an array of talents or more directly affected the careers of so many notable men. But the two greatest speakers—both, like Clay, near their death—were John Caldwell Calhoun and Daniel Webster. Their great efforts, both designed to save the Union which they both loved, were delivered on March 4 and March 7.

Calhoun had spoken often in favor of nullification and frequently had hinted at and even threatened secession. Yet no cause was dearer to his heart than the Union—provided only that the South's "peculiar institution" could be safeguarded within it. What he saw more clearly than his contemporaries was that in essence the South was a separate nation, and that it could be kept in the Union only if its separate identity were recognized and protected. He was determined to make one last fight. When he was brought into the Senate, wrapped in a heavy black cloak, the pallor of death was on his face; he indeed was to die twenty six days later. Twice during the preceding year he had fainted in public—once at the feet of Senator Douglas on a Washington street, once in the Senate chamber. Most days he lay in bed, suffering from a heart condition, so weak he could not even hold a pen. Yet his mind was as luminous as ever. Somehow he prepared a lengthy and closely reasoned speech—a speech that had to be read for him to the Senate by James Mason of Virginia, while he sat impassively listening to it, warmly wrapped against the March wind that blew in through an open window.

---

[15] *The Works of William H. Seward*, ed. G. E. Baker, New York: Redfield, 1853, I:74.
[16] Discussed by Herbert Agar, *op. cit.*, p. 332.

Throughout the reading Calhoun sat wracked in pain, "like a disembodied spirit . . . his head unwaveringly erect, his rugged features as white and motionless as if sculptured in marble."[17]

The opening words of the speech struck squarely toward the theme: "I have . . . believed from the first that the agitation of slavery would . . . end in disunion." The reason was that "the equilibrium between the two sections, as it stood when the Constitution was ratified," had been upset. From the Ordinance of 1787 to the Wilmot Proviso, the South had been deprived of its just share of the national lands. The tariff had taken "hundreds of millions of dollars" from the South for the benefit of Northern industrialists. Meanwhile, the Federal Government, through systematic concentration of powers once exercised by the States, had become "as despotic in its tendency as any absolute Government that ever existed."[18] As for remedies, the South had no concessions to make; all it demanded was an equal share, for slavery, in all the public lands and an amendment to the Constitution which would insure for the South an effective veto over any actions desired by the North. These were things the North must grant. As for himself, he had fulfilled his responsibility in setting forth what could and should be done. The old warrior was through.

A few days later, as Calhoun lay on his deathbed, he told Senator Mason: "The Union is doomed to dissolution . . . within twelve years. The probability is that it will explode in a presidential election."[19] His prophecy could scarcely have been more accurate. But three days after Calhoun's address to the Senate, Daniel Webster rose to make his own last great effort to save the Union that all knew was deeply threatened.

Calhoun, in the course of his speech, had declared that the Union could not be saved by eulogies. "The cry of 'Union, Union, the glorious Union!' can no more prevent disunion," Calhoun had said, "than the cry of 'Health, Health, glorious Health!' on the part of the physician can save a patient lying dangerously ill."[20]

But Webster, better than the South Carolinian, understood that patriotism is itself a healing salve which can remedy many an ill. To the Senate he said: "I wish to speak today not as a Massachusetts man, nor as a Northern man, but as an American."[21] He spoke slowly on, hour after hour, pouring forth conciliatory appreciation of Southern as well as of Northern patriotism, reminding his hearers of many great issues which the country had faced united. As he spoke of the Ordinance of

---

[17] Margaret L. Coit, *John C. Calhoun*, Boston: Houghton Mifflin, 1950, p. 491.
[18] Miller, *op. cit.*, V:195–198.
[19] Arthur Styron, *The Cast Iron Man*, New York: Longmans, Green, 1935, p. 355.
[20] Miller, *op. cit.*, V:200.
[21] *Ibid.*, V:204.

1787, which the South had made possible by its generous gifts of western lands to the central government, he paused and said with deep feeling, "An honorable member, whose health does not allow him to be here today . . ." To one side, near the entrance to the presiding officer's chambers, a pale, black-draped man clambered painfully to his feet and announced in a hollow voice, "The Senator from South Carolina is in his place."

Tears came into Webster's eyes as he greeted his old friend and opponent with a glance across the crowded chamber. He went on: "Sir, the honorable member from South Carolina thought he saw in certain operations of the Government . . . what accounts for the more rapid growth of the North than the South." Webster strained to be conciliatory. "It may be so." But, he pointed out gently, the Federal Government had purchased Louisiana, won Florida from Spain, and had taken Texas into the Union—all slave territory. As for the territories in the Southwest, geography and climate, not law, prohibited slavery in them. If he had his own way, Webster added, "I would put in no Wilmot Proviso for the purpose of a taunt or a reproach." Then he defended the Fugitive Slave Law, and declared he would disregard any instructions he might receive from his own State to interfere with slavery in areas where it was defended by the Constitution. He went further, saying that abolitionism was itself the chief cause of friction between the sections. "Sir," he said with a cumbersome attempt at winsome humor, "the extremists of both parts of this country are violent; they mistake loud and violent talk for eloquence and reason. They think that he who talks loudest reasons the best. . . . In truth, sir, I must say that, in my opinion, the vernacular tongue of the country has become greatly vitiated, depraved and corrupted by the style of our congressional debates."[22]

Webster had done his best to mollify the South. But he could not forget the challenge that confronted the nation. His eyes burned, as they always did when he spoke with deep emotion. "I hear with pain and anguish and distress the word secession . . . . Secession! Peaceable secession! Sir, your eyes and mine are never destined to see that miracle. . . . Who is so foolish—I beg everybody's pardon—as to expect to see any such thing?"[23] He spoke of the many practical difficulties: the common ownership of public lands and buildings, the indivisibility of the armed forces. Then he paused. "Sir, I am ashamed to pursue this line of remark. I dislike it—I have an utter disgust for it . . . . Gentlemen are not serious when they talk of secession . . . [Instead] of groping with

[22] *Ibid.*, V:210–215.
[23] *Ibid.*, V:217.

those ideas so full of all that is horrid and horrible, let us come out into the light of day; let us enjoy the fresh air of liberty and union; . . . let us not be pigmies in a case that calls for men."[24]

Webster had concluded his greatest effort. It won him a torrent of abuse in Massachusetts and throughout the North. Ralph Waldo Emerson said publicly of him that "Mr. Webster is a man who lives by his memory . . . . All the drops of his blood have eyes that look downward."[25] Whittier wrote a poem, *Ichabod*, denouncing him. Theodore Parker castigated "The giant intellect and rotten heart"[26] of Daniel Webster. James Russell Lowell described him as "a statesman who had communicated no impulse to any of the great ideas of the century."[27] It was a high price to pay for devotion to duty.

The debate on the compromise bills continued all through the Spring, and the Summer, and into the Fall. At length they were adopted—not all together, to signal a North-South agreement, as Clay had hoped; not promptly and with a conciliatory fervor—but slowly, grudgingly, amidst complaints, charges, and countercharges. The substance Clay sought was won, the spirit was not.

With this session of Congress the essential debate on expansion was ended. With the adoption of legislation establishing territorial governments in Oregon and in the Southwest, the present continental limits of the United States (Alaska excepted) were established. What remained was the admission of the remaining territories as States. Soon this question came to a head on the issue of Kansas and Nebraska. By this time the institution of slavery was nakedly and unavoidably the central focus of national concern. However much the legislators tried to avoid this issue which defied compromise, it refused, like Banquo's ghost, to remain at rest.

[24] *Ibid.*, V:219.
[25] James E. Cabot, *A Memoir of Ralph Waldo Emerson*, Boston: Houghton Mifflin, 1887, II:581.
[26] Cited by Gamaliel Bradford, "Daniel Webster," in *As God Made Them*, Boston: Houghton Mifflin, 1929, p. 9.
[27] Cited by Parrington, *Main Currents, op. cit.*, II:315.

IV

INDIVIDUALISM IN THE FABRIC
OF DEMOCRACY
1820—1860

The One Among the Many

ALEXIS DE TOCQUEVILLE, who had a sharp eye for the flaws in American society, wrote that "The very essence of democratic government consists in the absolute sovereignty of the majority; for there is nothing in democratic states which is capable of resisting it." The "right of the people" he held to be "an impious and detestable maxim," and he believed that "the main evil of the present democratic institutions of the United States" did not arise "from their weakness, but from their irresistible strength." Then he added: "I attribute the small number of distinguished men in political life to the ever-increasing despotism of the majority in the United States."[1] The year was 1835.

One is tempted to interrupt the observations of the twenty six year old critic with a catalogue of some of the names of the "distinguished men in political life" at that time. But perhaps it is better to hear him out: "In that immense crowd which throngs the avenues to power in the United States," he went on, "I found very few men who displayed that manly candor and masculine independence of opinion which frequently distinguished the Americans in former times, and which constitutes the leading feature in distinguished characters wheresoever they may be found. It seems, at first sight, as if all the minds of the Americans were formed upon one model, so accurately do they follow the same route."[2]

This seems a fair resumé of de Tocqueville's judgments. He pursues his inquiry through four books and ends substantially as he began, concluding that our form of democratic society seeks primarily to keep the people "in perpetual childhood: . . . to spare them all the care of thinking and all the trouble of living."[3]

[1] Alexis de Tocqueville, Democracy in America, New York: Knopf, 1945, I:254, 259, 260, 266. (Written in 1831–32.)
[2] Ibid., I:266–267.
[3] Ibid., II:392.

107

If de Tocqueville's brilliance was cabined by his youth and the brevity of his stay in America, his conclusions nevertheless are not strikingly different from those of the Englishman James Bryce, whose summary of "The True Faults of American Democracy," in his *The American Commonwealth*, repays meditative consideration:

> What are the consequences which we may expect to follow from these characteristics of democracy and these conditions under which it is forced to work?
>
> Firstly, a certain commonness of mind and tone, a want of dignity and elevation in and about the conduct of public affairs, an insensibility to the nobler aspects and finer responsibilities of national life.
>
> Secondly, a certain apathy among the luxurious classes and fastidious minds, who find themselves of no more account than the ordinary voter, and are disgusted by the superficial vulgarities of public life.
>
> Thirdly, a want of knowledge, tact, and judgment in the details of legislation, as well as in administration, with an inadequate recognition of the difficulty of these kinds of work, and of the worth of special experience and skill in dealing with them. Because it is incompetent, the multitude will not feel its incompetence, and will not seek or defer to the counsels of those who possess the requisite capacity.
>
> Fourthly, laxity in the management of public business. The persons entrusted with such business being only average men, thinking themselves and thought of by others as average men, with a deficient sense of their high responsibilities, may succumb to the temptations which the control of legislation and the public funds present, where persons of a more enlarged view and with more of a social reputation to support would remain incorruptible. To repress such derelictions of duty is every citizen's duty, but for that reason it is in large communities apt to be neglected. Thus the very causes which implant the mischief favour its growth.[4]

If the aim were to assemble foreign criticisms with the intent to demolish them, such sweeping denunciations as those published by Charles Dickens and Frances Trollope would offer fair game.[5] But the commentaries by the Frenchman and the Englishman are too substantial to be either ignored or refuted. Democracy does have weaknesses, and these are of such a nature that they tend to become magnified in the speeches of our public men.

It can scarcely be accidental that so many of the greatest Americans did not attain to the presidency, while so many mediocrities have done

[4] James Bryce, *The American Commonwealth*, New York: Macmillan, 1927, II:632–633.
[5] For such a compilation see Commager, *America in Perspective*, New York: Random House, 1927.

so. It is not insignificant that the political concept of "availability" for public office includes, among other things, the lack of a forthright position on controversial issues, with the result that one or another large block of votes would be lost. Successful speakers in a democracy are to a large degree *spokesmen* for the public or a considerable portion of it, rather than *leaders or critics* of its views or conduct. A fundamental requirement of public address designed for a general audience is that it be adapted to the interests, the needs, and the understanding of the largest possible proportion of potential listeners. This results, of course, in limitations upon the choice of topics, the kinds of subject matter, and the degree of profundity or of refinement of analysis. All these factors tend toward the reduction of the level of discourse to the least common denominator—or at least to the receptive qualities of the average mind. What is left for the speaker is the fabrication of verbal pyrotechnics, a brilliance of style, an attractiveness of diction, and a compelling vigor and variety of voice and manner. There is always the danger that the man who "stands well and booms well" will have more influence than the man who knows or who understands. Such dangers and such criticisms should never be lightly brushed aside.

Specifically, however, it is one thing to conclude that the nature of American democracy tends to debase the quality of our public discourse. It is quite another to determine whether the presumed result flows from the assumed cause. This problem is illuminated by a consideration of three orators of great ability, each markedly individualistic, each highly successful, and each, perhaps because of this very individualism, just missing the ultimate level of socially-approved achievement.

John Quincy Adams, Ralph Waldo Emerson, and Thomas Hart Benton had little in common except an unusual emphasis upon their own independence. Adams surely limited his own effectiveness as President by his unwillingness to reward partisan regularity through expedient use of patronage. Emerson was enthralled by his vision of "the infinitude of the private man," advising: "Trust thyself; every heart vibrates to that iron string." Benton, although a Southerner and a Democrat, refused to follow any pattern set by anyone except himself.

Each man, then, resembled a pinnacle rising in splendid solitude. Adams and Benton thereby suffered more than they need have and achieved less than they might have. Emerson remained largely aloof from the main currents of events, describing himself as an observer rather than a doer. But each of them, in his own way, both taught and exemplified the high virtues of individualism. This was their common bond—the fact that none of them could easily be bound.

〓 *The Old Man Eloquent*

FROM INFANCY John Quincy Adams associated mainly with adults, and especially with his parents, John and Abigail, whose pride, patriotism, and devotion to principle helped shape his personality in an exterior coldness that cloaked a core of lava-hot emotionalism. From earliest childhood his mind displayed qualities of calculating shrewdness and purposive addiction to long-range goals. All these qualities, which persisted throughout his eighty years, are displayed in a remarkable letter he wrote to his father on June 2, 1777, six weeks before his tenth birthday. "Dear Sir," the letter began:

> I love to receive letters very well much better than I love to write them. I make but a poor figure at composition, my head is much too fickle, my thoughts are running after bird's eggs, play and trifles till I get vexed with myself. I have but just entered the 3d volume of Smollett, tho' I had designed to have got it half through by this time. I have determined this week to be more diligent, as Mr. Thaxter will be absent at Court, and I Cannot pursue my other Studies. I have set myself a Stent and determine to read the 3d Volume Half out. If I can but keep my resolution I will write again at the end of the week and give a better account of myself. I wish, Sir, you would give me some instructions with regard to my time, and advise me how to proportion my Studies and my Play, in writing, and I will keep them by me and endeavor to follow them. I am, dear Sir, with a present determination of growing better, Your son,
>
> John Quincy Adams
>
> P. S. Sir, if you will be so good as to favor me with a Blank book, I will transcribe the most remarkable occurrences I met with in my reading, which will serve to fix them on my mind.[1]

From his parents the boy learned to love liberty and respect individualism. As the son of the man who had dared to defend the perpetrators of the "Boston Massacre," he was bred to courage and independence of mind. The pressure upon him to mature rapidly was relentless. He was taken abroad by his father at the age of eleven, and, as John wrote to Abigail, "He behaves like a man."[2] At fourteen he went to Russia as secretary to the American Minister. When he was twenty, he graduated from Harvard, two years after his admission, second in his

---

[1] *The Selected Writings of John and John Quincy Adams*, ed. Adrienne Koch and William Peden, New York: Knopf, 1946, p. 225.
[2] *Familiar Letters, op. cit.*, p. 327.

class; and he gave a Commencement Oration on citizenship that was deemed important enough to be published in Philadelphia and to be the subject of considerable public controversy. Three years later he commenced the practice of law, in which he experienced his first failure, being unable during the first four years to meet his expenses out of his earnings. More interested in public service than in private gain, he deluged the newspapers with letters attacking Tom Paine and Thomas Jefferson, and with arguments, during the Jay Treaty debates, for American neutrality. President Washington returned him to public life with an appointment as Minister to the Dutch Republic. From this time on he was never long out of office.

History presents few examples of a man less fitted to attain high reputation as an orator. Adams was unprepossessing in appearance: five feet seven inches tall, stockily built and soon plump, prematurely bald, so watery-eyed that he seemed to weep, and with a right hand that by middle age was palsied, perhaps by too much writing. His voice was shrill, high-pitched, and querulous. By temperament he was seclusive, with few friends and even fewer social graces. A compulsive worker, he was at his books from early morning until late at night, mastering six or seven foreign languages, along with mountains of facts. His vanity and suspiciousness kept him in a constant state of jealousy and fear of being underrated. What compensated for these grievous faults were his largeness of mind, his quickness of perception—which helped make him a great debater—his patriotic devotion, and his driving ambition to excel. Among all his voluminous self-revelatory diary entries, the one for May 16, 1792, seems best to depict his essential nature: "I am not satisfied with the manner in which I employ my time. *It is calculated to keep me forever fixed in that state of useless and disgraceful insignificance, which has been my lot for some years past.*"[3]

His lifelong habit of self-praise and dispraise is illustrated by his confession that if only his intellectual powers were greater, his diary would be, "next to the Holy Scriptures, the most precious and valuable book ever written by human hands."[4] How little he appreciated the actual superiority of his mind is shown by an 1804 entry in his diary:

> On this occasion, as on almost every other, I felt most sensibly my deficiency as an extemporaneous speaker. In tracing this deficiency to its source, I find it arising from a cause that is irreparable. No efforts, no application on my part, can ever remove it. It is slowness of comprehension—an incapacity to grasp the whole compass of a subject in the mind

---

[3] Bennett Champ Clark, *John Quincy Adams*, Boston: Little, Brown, 1932, p. 39.
[4] Quoted from Henry Adams, *The Degradation of the Democratic Dogma*, by Dangerfield, *Era of Good Feeling, op. cit.*, p. 9.

at once with such an arrangement as leaves a proper impression of the details and incapacity to form ideas properly precise and definite with the rapidity necessary to give them uninterrupted utterance. My manner, therefore, is slow, hesitating, and often confused. Sometimes, from inability to furnish the words to finish a thought commenced, I begin a sentence with propriety and end it with nonsense.[5]

Actually, although he delivered many set orations, it is solely as a debater and extemporaneous speaker that he is entitled to remembrance as a public speaker. In this, as in much else, his demands on himself were unreasonably high as well as realistically productive.

His long life was crowded with public services of many kinds. At every stage there was the paradoxical mixture of high success mingled with self-criticism and fear of rejection by his associates. In lectures delivered on Friday mornings at Harvard, from 1806 to 1809, he outlined an Aristotelian system of rhetoric which depends for success upon a sound adaptation to the audience; but it was precisely in this element of conciliatory adjustment that he was weakest. In the Senate he proved his courage and patriotism by supporting Jefferson, whom he earlier had attacked, though in so doing he enraged his constituents to the point where his resignation was required a year before his term ended. When he served as Minister to Russia (1809–1813), he labored assiduously to create friendly relations; yet he was described by an English visitor to St. Petersburg as "Of all men . . . the most doggedly and systematically repulsive."[6] When he headed the American delegation to Ghent, to negotiate the treaty ending the War of 1812, he antagonized his fellow delegates; but, far better than they, he understood how to reap advantages from Castlereagh's eagerness to leave for the Congress of Vienna and from the widespread European condemnation of the British burning of Washington.

As Secretary of State in Monroe's cabinet, Adams proved his real greatness and first mastered the difficult art of extemporaneous debate. In 1819, when Andrew Jackson made an unauthorized attack against the Spaniards in Florida, Adams succeeded, during four days of sharp debate within the the cabinet, in preventing a censure of Jackson. Then, during negotiations for the cession of Florida to the United States, he used his debating skill again, this time against no less an antagonist than John Caldwell Calhoun, to prevent a declaration that the United States would never annex Texas. During this same period Adams was holding at bay a series of eloquent demands by Henry Clay that the United States champion the newly independent republics of South America;

[5] Quoted by Clark, *op. cit.*, p. 93.
[6] Dangerfield, *The Era of Good Feelings, op. cit.*, p. 7.

and that, meanwhile, we should claim and occupy Cuba. He also became the father of the Monroe Doctrine, which he persuaded President Monroe to issue, against the advice of both Jefferson and Madison—and against British demands that it be accompanied by a statement excluding the United States from intervention in Europe. By this time his skill as a debater was unquestioned even by himself.

In a dual sense, Adams was not a popular President. He was the last of our chief executives to be elected not by popular vote but (largely) by State legislatures; and, in the opinion of George Dangerfield, author of *The Era of Good Feelings*, "There are few examples of political mismanagement more instructive than the presidency of John Quincy Adams, unless it be that of his father, John Adams."[7] His attempts to secure legislative justice for the Indians, and his projected vast program of public works, were impeded by unnecessary warfare with his own party. The astute Thurlow Weed, who worked hard in New York State for Adams's election, and was brushed aside for his pains, commented regretfully that "Mr. Adams during his administration failed to cherish, strengthen, or even recognize the party to which he owed his election; nor, so far as I am informed, with the great power he possessed did he make a single influential friend."[8] After his defeat by Jackson, he refused to ride with the new President to the inaugural (recalling the same behavior of his father toward Jefferson), and retired to "perfect solitude,"[9] deserted even by his old manservant, Antoine. He left the leadership of the new National-Republic (later Whig) party to Henry Clay.

Two years later a new and more glorious era in his life commenced. He was offered support for election to the House of Representatives, and accepted nomination on the twofold condition that he would never canvass for votes and that, if elected, he would always speak and vote precisely as he pleased. He was elected in 1830, to serve until his death eighteen years later—the only ex-President ever to serve in the House and one of the most eloquent and able Representatives in our history.

After 1830, when the abolitionists commenced their incessant campaign, and when the tariff was becoming inextricably a sectional issue, there were few significant national questions that did not directly or indirectly involve slavery. John Quincy Adams chose a front position in the battle lines. Particularly during the period from December 16, 1835, to the end of 1837, in the debates on the receiving of antislavery peti-

[7] *Ibid.*
[8] *The Life of Thurlow Weed*, ed. H. A. Weed, Boston: Houghton Mifflin, 1883, I:178ff.
[9] Clark, *op. cit.*, pp. 275–279.

tions by Congress, he was both the storm center and the principal speaker. The discussion ran the gamut of personal abuse and sectional bitterness, resulting in, among other things, the first formal threat of Southern secession. Repelling comradeship and disdaining political alliances, Adams waged and to some extent won the long-drawn battle.

The struggle commenced when Congressman Henry L. Pinckney, of South Carolina, introduced a resolution (soon tagged as the "gag rule") declaring that the House should henceforth refuse to discuss or consider any petitions relating to slavery. Adams entered the discussion quietly, suggesting the only way to discourage debate on the slave question would be to receive the petitions and then refer them to a committee— in which case, "you will never hear of them afterward."[10] But if it should be ordered that petitions must be filed away without so much as notice of their receipt, "Sir, you will have discussion . . . . discussion upon the merits of slavery . . . . The speeches of my colleagues, probably of myself, will be incendiary." He paused and, as was his wont, looked around the chamber with his hands raised in a questioning posture. "Will you introduce a resolution that members of this House shall not speak a word in derogation of the sublime merits of slavery?" His voice grew more shrill, his eyes more watery, his bald head agleam with the perspiration of strong feelings—a typical picture of Adams in the midst of an eloquent tirade. "What will be the consequences then? You suppress the right of petition; you suppress the freedom of speech; the freedom of the press and the freedom of religion; for, in the minds of many worthy, honest, and honorable men—fanatics if you please so to call them—this is a religious question, in which they act under what they believe to be a sense of duty to their God."[11]

The brilliant Waddy Thompson, also from South Carolina, seized upon Adams's expression. "Who is it at the North that we are to conciliate?" he demanded. "The fanatics? Fanatics, did I say, Sir? Never before was so vile a band dignified with that name. They are murderers, foul murderers, accessories before the fact, and they know it, of murder, robbery, rape, infanticide."[12] Pinckney rose again, this time to try to calm the debate, declaring that abolitionism was so unpopular among the public in the North that if the Congress refused to discuss it the agitation would soon die away. Two months were consumed in the debate before the vote was taken, on February 12. Adams sat grimly in his seat, refusing to vote, with the explanation that "I hold the resolution to be a direct violation of the Constitution of the United States, the rules

[10] Miller, *op. cit.*, IV:105.
[11] *Ibid.*, IV:105–106.
[12] *Ibid.*, IV:107.

of this House, and the rights of my constituents."[13] By a vote of 117 to 68 the "gag rule" was made effective. It was the first and only time in the history of the Congress that a subject of public interest was voted to be undiscussible. Adams had no intention of obeying it.

A year later, on February 6, 1837, he arose innocently with a paper in his hand which he said appeared to be a petition signed by twenty two persons who described themselves as slaves. He did not know whether it was proper to file such a paper with the Clerk of the House and he disarmingly asked the Speaker, John White, of Kentucky, for a ruling. Amidst a storm of cries of "Expel him! Expel him!" from outraged Southerners, White decided to ask the House for its decision. Thus was unleashed the very debate that was to have been prevented by the gag rule. Waddy Thompson finally got the floor, in competition with practically the whole of the Southern membership, and referred sourly to the protection Adams presumably expected from being an ex-President and from his advanced age. "The sanctuary of age is not lightly to be violated," he said; "but when the sanctuary is used to throw poisoned arrows, it ceases to be sacred." Then he demanded, "Does that gentleman know that there are laws in all the slave States, and here, for the punishment of those who incite insurrection?" He then introduced a resolution of censure against Adams for "gross disrespect to this House."[14]

Adams was demure in his response. "I did not present the petition. I asked the Speaker whether he considered such a paper . . . should be laid on the table."[15] The uproar continued, making mincemeat of the gag rule. Adams rose again. The petition, he explained, did not ask for the abolition of slavery, as the speakers supposed; on the contrary, it was a petition in defense of slavery. His explanation merely inflamed the opposition, as Adams no doubt intended. "Is it a light thing," Thompson demanded, "for the amusement of others, to irritate almost to madness, the whole delegation from the slave States?"[16] Whatever the petition contained, said Francis Pickens, of South Carolina, "It broke down the principle that the slave could be known only through his master."[17] Dixon Lewis, whom Adams called "the man mountain from Alabama," then declared that "by extending to slaves a privilege only belonging to freemen," Adams's presentation of the petition "directly invites the slave population to insurrection."[18]

Once again Adams secured the floor. "Petition, Sir," he said, "is a

---

[13] *Ibid.*, IV:104.
[14] Clark, *op. cit.*, p. 369.
[15] Miller, *op. cit.*, IV:112.
[16] Clark, *op. cit.*, p. 371.
[17] Miller, *op. cit.*, p. 113.
[18] Clark, *op. cit.*, p. 370.

right belonging to every human creature . . . . Will you put the right of petitioning, of craving for help and mercy and protection, on the footing of political privileges? It is an idea which has not even been entertained by the utmost extreme of human despotism . . . . That would be a sad day, Sir, in my opinion, when a vote should pass that this House would not receive a petition from slaves!" After another barrage of denunciation, Adams let loose his most inflammatory rejoinder. He "had heard," he said, and "was inclined to believe" that "there existed great resemblances in the South between the progeny of the colored people and the white man who claimed the possession of them!" The *Journal* indicated "great agitation in the House."[19]

Adams then assumed a tone of deep seriousness: "I should deem it to be the heaviest calamity which has ever befallen me in the course of a life checkered with many vicissitudes if a vote of censure from this House should pass upon my name or upon any action of mine in this House . . . . Has not the honor of this House been among the first and dearest sentiments of my heart? I have reverenced this House as the representatives of the whole people of this Union . . . . And now am I to be brought to the bar for a contempt of this House, for doing that which was done in the most respectful manner which it was possible to devise? For asking a question of the Speaker? . . . But if a majority of this House shall be found to pass censure on me, be it so; and if I have an enemy, let him know he has triumphed; for a worse calamity could not befall me on earth." He squared himself then in the aisle and concluded in the famous Adams spirit of independence: "I disclaim not one particle of what I have done; not a single word of what I have said do I unsay; nay, I am ready to do and say the same again tomorrow."[20]

The vote was taken: for censure, 92; against, 105. A group of Southern Congressmen met to consider a resolution "that the Union be dissolved." They decided against presenting it. But the gag rule was renewed—to persist until Adams won his fight against it in 1844.

Meanwhile, his loneliness and isolation in the House continued. In a debate instigated by President Jackson's request for payment of five million dollars owed to France, Adams staunchly came to the defense of his old enemy in the White House, even though in order to do so he had to attack two idols of Massachusetts—Edward Everett and Daniel Webster—and to accuse the whole Whig party of treason. After one of his most eloquent speeches Adams was supported by the unanimous vote of the House. In the interim he was besieged with petitions, many from abolitionists and many sent with mischievous intent by his enemies.

[19] Miller, *op. cit.*, IV:118, 119, 120.
[20] *Ibid.*, IV:122–123.

Among the latter were petitions asking that all free Negroes be deported, that the Union be dissolved, that Adams be deposed from his position as Chairman of the Foreign Affairs Committee on the ground that he was insane.[21] With equal nonchalance Adams faithfully transmitted them all to the Clerk.

Every one of his eighteen years in the House was marked by turmoil. As his biographer Clark says of him in this period: "He was utterly to be dreaded in debate. His great experience, his intimate lifetime familiarity with all phases of our governmental affairs, and the utterly ruthless ferocity of his invective, all combined to make him an awesome antagonist. He gloried in his almost infinite capacity for exasperating his opponents. Scarcely a member of the House but sooner or later felt the lash of his sarcasm, and he was as ready to flay those who usually acted with him as those who were his habitual opponents." In his diary Adams complained that he "walks between burning plowshares," for "both the ruling political parties are watching with intense anxiety for some overt act by me to set the whole pack of their hireling presses upon me."[22] With his lifelong capacity for self-pity, he wrote: ". . . upon the verge of my seventy-fourth birthday, with a shaking hand, a darkening eye, a drowsy brain, and with all my faculties dropping from me one by one, as the teeth are dropping from my head—what can I do for the cause of God and man?" His answer, however, was clear: "Yet my conscience presses me on; let me but die upon the breach."[23]

Adams's last great fight came in 1842, on yet another motion to censure him. After a three-day effort to get the floor, interrupted by calls to order, appeals from the Chair, and general tumult, he finally got permission on January 25 to present a petition from forty six citizens of Haverhill, Massachusetts, asking Congress to dissolve the Union. Then, beset by angry outcries, he moved reference of the petition to a Committee which would be charged to show reasons why it ought not to be granted. Theodore G. Weld, the Ohio abolitionist, sat in the gallery listening gleefully to the debate, and described Adams's speaking in a letter to his wife: "Old Nestor lifted up his voice like a trumpet, till slaveholding, slavetrading, and slavebreeding absolutely quailed and howled under his dissecting knife . . . . A perfect uproar like Babel would burst forth every two or three minutes as Mr. A. with his bold surgery would smite his cleaver into the very bone."[24]

[21] Clark, *op. cit.*, p. 342.

[22] *Ibid.*, p. 376.

[23] *Ibid.*

[24] Gilbert H. Barnes and Dwight D. Dumond, eds., *Letters of Theodore Dwight Weld, Angelina Grimké Weld and Sarah Grimké, 1842–1844*, New York: Appleton-Century, 1934, II:899–900; cf. also 909–911.

For two weeks the debate raged on, with Adams constantly subject to an enfillade of scathing abuse. The chief speaker against him was Thomas Marshall, of Kentucky, nephew of the great Chief Justice, and famous for his "splendid eloquence." In attacking Adams, Marshall was at his best.[25] With scorn for the very mention of disunion, he said: "Coming from any quarter, it was sacrilege; coming from the quarter it did, it assumed a political importance that it would not otherwise possess. He, Sir, from whom the proposition was made to pull down the temple of Liberty, was once its high priest and ministered at its altar. It was no obscure hand and no obscure name that was connected with this procedure. That name had gone abroad, connected with all that was bright and glorious in our country's history."[26] Marshall then called on the whole nation, North and South, to unite in punishing the monstrous conduct of the ex-President. Adams arose, shaking with palsy and his rheumy eyes streaming tears, but with his head high and his voice firm, to insist that in the name of the Declaration of Independence every citizen had the right to "alter, to change, to destroy, the Government if it became oppressive to him."[27]

During the two-week course of the debate, as he was leaving his home one morning, his wife fainted from strain and weakness. Adams looked at her, looked at his watch, then turned away to hurry to his seat in time for the opening of the day's session, leaving her to be cared for by the maid. In his diary he noted: "she soon recovered . . ." It was in this circumstance that he heard himself denounced in the debate for "deserting the early friends of his father, and trampling upon the ashes of the dead." Adams listened to what he called the "whole cargo of filthy invective," then retorted: "I am still in the power of the majority. If they say they will try me, they must try me. If they say they will punish me, they must punish me. If they say that, in grace and mercy, they will spare me expulsion, I disdain and cast their mercy away; and I ask them if they will come to such a trial and expel me. I defy them."[28] He proceeded to a vitriolic attack upon Marshall and concluded that the House had no right to be both his accuser and his judge.

As the debate continued, public opinion rallied to support Adams. The newspapers highlighted the point the House ignored: that Adams did not approve of the petition but merely of the right of citizens to present it. The motion of censure was tabled by a vote of 106 to 93. In

---

[25] Marshall deserves more study as a speaker than he has received. Cf. *Speeches and Writings of Hon. Thomas F. Marshall,* ed. W. L. Barre, Cincinnati: Applegate, 1858.
[26] *Ibid.,* p. 145.
[27] Clark, op. cit., p. 399.
[28] *Ibid.,* pp. 400–402.

his diary Adams noted that he had left Marshall "sprawling in his own compost."[29] Marshall agreed that he had taken a licking. A few days later, when some of his associates asked him to take the lead in another matter, he retorted: "Not I! You left me to fight the lion alone; you can skin your skunks yourselves!"[30]

During the stormy session of 1844–45, Adams opposed the moves toward war with Mexico but was willing, if necessary, to fight England for the whole of the Pacific Northwest. Then, in November of 1846, he suffered a stroke which kept him bed-ridden for three months. As soon as he could he returned to Washington and faithfully attended all the meetings of the House; but his days of conflict were ended. Old hostilities were so far suspended that his return was greeted by a spontaneous standing ovation in the Congress. On February 21, 1848, he tried to rise to speak against the award of medals to generals who had served in the war against Mexico; but he could not get to his feet and toppled over in a faint. Two days later he died, murmuring at the end: "This is the last of earth, I am content."[31] Eulogies were delivered in every part of the nation, with the theme perhaps best expressed by Senator Benton, who said: "Punctual to every duty, death found him at his post of duty; and where else could it have found him at any stage of his career, for the fifty years of his illustrious public life."[32]

The Sage of Concord

ON GRADUATION day in the Spring of 1854, in the yard at Harvard College, young Moncure Daniel Conway fell into step beside Ralph Waldo Emerson and engaged him in conversation. "He then told me," Conway later recalled, "that after graduation his ambition had been to fill a chair of rhetoric. I was startled by this, and he said that there was not sufficient training in the art of putting things, this being the secret of eloquence."[1]

In keeping with the desires of his parents, Emerson himself had gone to Harvard—where he was weak in Greek, hated mathematics, and did so poorly in the rote memorization that then passed for education that he graduated 30th in a class of 59. His only collegiate distinction was to place seventh in a poll to elect the class poet. Yet even while he was

[29] *Ibid.*, p. 406.
[30] *Ibid.*, p. 407.
[31] *Ibid.*, p. 418.
[32] Thomas Hart Benton, *Thirty Years' View, op. cit.*, II:709.
[1] Moncure Daniel Conway, *Autobiography*, Boston: Houghton Mifflin, 1904, I:183.

berating himself and being condemned by his schoolmasters for poor scholarship, he was driving himself with a frenzy of eagerness through the complete works of more than a score of the world's greatest writers. In his unheated room off Harvard Square, he used to snuggle under the blankets and read Plato far into the night—so that, as he confessed, he always associated the Socratic dialogues with the smell of wool. In his twentieth year, as he approached graduation, deprived of the social pleasures of college life, friendless, forced to earn his meals by waiting on table, generally cold, and always in poor health, he confessed to the private pages of his journal a "foolish ambition to be valued" and "a goading sense of emptiness and wasted capacity."[2] He also noted the "apathy" or "indolence" which kept him standing at the foot of the stairway his companions were climbing to success.

At this time, on April 18, 1824, he wrote a thoughtful passage in his diary headed simply "Myself." "I deliberately dedicate my time, my talents, and my hopes to the Church," he wrote. Preaching, rather than law, was his suitable vocation because "I have, or had, a strong imagination" and "My reasoning faculty is proportionately weak." He was concerned, however, about "a signal defect of character which neutralizes in great part the just influence my talents ought to have." This weakness he could not readily define, but he was clear that "its fruits are a sore uneasiness in the company of most men and women, a frigid fear of offending and jealousy of disrespect, an inability to lead and an unwillingness to follow the current conversation, which contrive to make me second with all those among whom chiefly I wish to be first." He felt encouraged to expect he might overcome this shyness because of his "passionate love for the strains of eloquence."[3]

Five years later he became minister of the Second Church, Unitarian, in Boston. He remained in this pulpit only three years, until, in September, 1832, he decided that he could no longer administer the Lord's Supper as a Communion service and offered his resignation.[4] The congregation urged him to take several weeks to reconsider, then reluctantly voted thirty to twenty four to accept his decision. The problem, of course, was more involved than the administration of a particular sacrament. Emerson's was a mind insistent upon roaming free, and a minister, as he pointed out, was a "retained attorney." Moreover, in withdrawing from the Church, it never occurred to him to feel that he was

[2] *The Heart of Emerson's Journals*, ed. Bliss Perry, Boston: Houghton Mifflin, 1926, May 13, 1823, p. 10.
[3] *Ibid.*, pp. 17–23.
[4] Ralph Waldo Emerson, *Works*, edited by Edward Waldo Emerson, New York: Wise, 1929, XI:3–25. "It is my desire, in the office of a Christian minister," he said in closing, "to do nothing which I cannot do with my whole heart." *Ibid.*, p. 24.

deserting his vocation; for, as he said, his study was his pulpit. In essence he remained a preacher till his death.

From 1826, when Emerson was "approbated to preach," until 1832, he preached approximately nine hundred times, apparently using some 170 different sermons. As was the custom in New England in that period, he often exchanged pulpits with other preachers. One sermon, "On Showing Piety at Home," he delivered twenty seven times. Over fifty were presented more than once in his own church, at intervals of a year. Some fifteen or sixteen were delivered several times to various congregations. In preparing a sermon, Emerson recorded that he typically selected a topic Friday night, making a choice among five or six potential subjects. Saturday he devoted to the writing of the sermon. In one of his sermons, in 1830, he explained his choice of topics: "I do not think it necessary to say to you, Do not worship idols. . . . Do not kill; do not commit adultery; . . . but I do think it important to say, Love the Lord thy God . . . Love thy neighbor as thyself. Do not bear false witness; Be temperate; Pray; Give."[5]

Critics customarily have contrasted Emerson's sermons unfavorably with his later writings. In any event, Emerson the speaker was justly foreshadowed in his ministry. He spoke slowly, then and later, at a rate of about one hundred words a minute. He then and always read his speeches from a complete manuscript—regretting all the while his inability to speak extemporaneously. In manner, his delivery was sedate and relatively unvaried; whatever effect he was to achieve had to be from the content and style, not from the delivery.

But there was one aspect of his speaking that showed a particularly keen rhetorical insight: his sense of the audience. The passage just quoted, explaining his choice of topics, is revelatory; Emerson always meant to say what an audience needed to hear, not what he needed to express. Moreover, he was particularly perceptive concerning the nature of audiences. In his first lecture on "Eloquence," which he delivered in February, 1847, before the Boston Mercantile Library Association, he declares his awareness that within any group of people there are numerous potential audiences; the speaker must aim toward bringing into communion whichever of these he wishes to address:

> The audience is a constant meter of the orator. There are many audiences in every public assembly, each one of which rules in turn. If anything comic and coarse is spoken, you shall see the emergence of the boys and rowdies, so loud and vivacious that you might think the house was filled with them. If new topics are started, graver and higher, these

---

5 Herbert A. Wichelns, "Ralph Waldo Emerson," in Brigance, ed., *History and Criticism, op. cit.,* II:506–507, and 501–525.

roisterers recede; a more chaste and wise attention takes place. You would think the boys slept, and that the men have any degree of profoundness. If the speaker utter a noble sentiment, the attention deepens, a new and highest audience now listens, and the audiences of the fun and of facts and of the understanding are all silenced and awed. There is also something excellent in every audience, —the capacity of virtue. They are ready to be beatified. They know so much more than the orator, — and are so just! There is a tablet there for every line he can inscribe, though he should mount to the highest levels. Humble persons are conscious of new illumination; narrow brows expand with enlarged affections; —delicate spirits, long unknown to themselves, masked and muffled in coarsest fortunes, who now hear their own native language for the first time, and leap to hear it. But all these several audiences, each above each, which successively appear to greet the variety of style and topic, are really composed out of the same persons; nay, sometimes the same individual will take an active part in them all, in turn.[6]

Twenty years later, in his second lecture on "Eloquence," first presented in Chicago in 1867, Emerson carried his conception of the speaker's relation to his listeners one stage further. Now he not only must select those qualities within his hearers he wants to communicate with; he also "must ever stand with forward foot, in the attitude of advancing. His speech must be just ahead of the assembly, ahead of the whole human race, or it is superfluous." The speaker, in short, "gains his victory by prophecy." His listeners are "interested like so many children" because "he surprises them with his tidings, with his better knowledge, with his larger view, his steady gaze at the new and future event whereof they had not thought." The whole compass of oratory is comprised within the relation of speaker to listener, for "Eloquence is *the power to translate a truth into language perfectly intelligible to the person to whom you speak.*"[7]

The question of whether, or to what extent, Emerson belongs to the field of American oratory (though he is known in the schools as an essayist) is easily answered. In the first place, he devoted his life to lecturing. This was the way he earned his living; but it was more than a means of livelihood, it was his *vocation* in the spiritual sense. And in the second place, time after time, whatever the subject of his discourse, he found it appropriate to pay genuine homage to the virtues of eloquence or else to interject some explanation of what eloquence truly is. A few examples will indicate the breadth and depth of his concern:

The Progress of Culture, delivered as the Phi Beta Kappa oration at Harvard, July 18, 1867:

---

[6] Ralph Waldo Emerson, *Works, op. cit.,* VII:66–67.
[7] *Ibid.,* VIII:115, 116, 117, 130.

If [a man] can converse better than any other, he rules the minds of men wherever he goes; if he has imagination, he intoxicates men . . . . Eloquence a hundred times has turned the scale of war and peace at will.[8]

Society and Solitude, first delivered at Boston, during the series of 1836–37:

All conversation is a magnetic experiment. I know that my friend can talk eloquently; you know that he cannot articulate a sentence: we have seen him in different company.[9]

Art, delivered at Boston in December, 1836; revised for the lecture series in Boston presented in April, 1861:

Eloquence, as far as it is a fine art, is modified how much by the material organization of the orator, the tone of the voice, the physical strength, the play of the eye and countenance . . . . In eloquence, the great triumphs of the art are when the orator is lifted above himself; when consciously he makes himself the mere tongue of the occasion and the hour, and says what cannot but be said . . . . The individual mind became for the moment the vent of the mind of humanity.[10]

Clubs, first delivered at Freeman Place Chapel, Boston, in the Spring of 1859:

He that can define, he that can answer a question so as to admit of no further answer, is the best man . . . . Conversation is the Olympic games whither every superior gift resorts to assert and approve itself.[11]

Poetry and Imagination is a lecture that grew in successive presentations, in 1841, 1847, 1848, 1854, 1861, and, in its present form, as two lectures presented at Chickering Hall, Cambridge, in April, 1872:

. . . [A] good symbol is the best argument, and is a missionary to persuade thousands . . . . There is no more welcome gift to men than a new symbol. That satiates, transports, converts them . . . . It is a rule in eloquence, that the moment the orator loses command of his audience, the audience commands him.[12]

Social Aims, the second lecture of a series on "American Life" delivered to the Parker fraternity, Harvard, in December, 1864:

Speech is power: speech is to persuade, to convert, to compel. It is to bring another out of his bad sense into your good sense. . . . Don't say things. What you *are* stands over you the while, and thunders so that I cannot hear what you say to the contrary. . . . Stay at home in your mind. Don't recite other people's opinions.[13]

[8] *Ibid.*, VIII:217, 218.
[9] *Ibid.*, VII:13.
[10] *Ibid.*, VII:44, 49, 50.
[11] *Ibid.*, VII:235, 241.
[12] *Ibid.*, VIII:13, 14, 30.
[13] *Ibid.*, VIII:92, 96, 99.

The purpose here is not to provide an anthology but to illustrate two points: first, that Emerson could scarcely speak of any topic whatsoever without finding a reason in it to refer to the power, or to the source of the effectiveness, of eloquent speech; and, second, that the celebrated "essays" of Emerson were largely lectures, revised again and again for different audiences and finally revised yet another time for publication.

Emerson's respect for public and private discourse was often stated. In his first lecture on "Eloquence," he declared that "the truly eloquent man is a sane man with power to communicate his sanity."[14] It was a theme to which he often recurred. There is no doubt that he considered it the business of his life to develop "a mind equal to any exigency,"[15] with the aim of teaching, inspiring, and converting listeners to his own view of the good life. Beyond this, the lecture platform quite simply was his means of livelihood. As his son, Edward Waldo Emerson, wrote: "Mr. Emerson derived little income from his books, and lecturing was his main resource."[16] He added: "to one who heard Emerson lecture, the printed essays recall the spoken word and the speaker's presence. They were all thus first tested on the average American audience in town and country."[17]

As a speaker Emerson was definitely deficient in platform arts. Yet James Russell Lowell gave testimony, in an article for the *Nation*, that

> I have heard some great speakers, and some accomplished orators, but never any that so moved and persuaded men as he. There is a kind of undertone in that rich baritone of his that sweeps our minds from their foothold into deep waters with a drift we cannot and would not resist. And how artfully (for Emerson is a long-studied artist in these things) does the deliberate utterance, that seems waiting for the first word, seem to admit us partners in the labor of thought, and make us feel as if the glance of humor were a sudden suggestion; as if the perfect phrase lying written there on the desk were as unexpected to him as to us![18]

The death of Emerson's wife in 1832, shortly before his resignation from the ministry, left him an income from her estate of some $1200 a year, money enough for him to live as he wished. His real vocation commenced in November of the following year, when he acepted an invitation from the Boston Society of Natural History, and presented his first general lecture, under the title, "On the Uses of Natural History." Early in 1834 he spoke before the Boston Mechanics' Institute, on

14 *Ibid.*, VII:91.
15 *Ibid.*, VII:76.
16 *Ibid.*, VII:340.
17 *Ibid.*, VII:341.
18 *Ibid.*, VII:342.

"Water," and gave other lectures on his travels in Italy. He was gradually getting used to the platform, and finding the experience simultaneously appealing and painful. To Nathaniel Hawthorne he promised: "Henceforth I design not to utter any speech, poem, or book that is not entirely and peculiarly my work."[19] To his diary he confessed: "Dear God that sleepest in man, I have served my apprenticeship of bows and blushes, of fears and references, of excessive admiration."[20] Stage fright was so real a bogeyman for him that in 1859, in his lecture on "Courage," he links the bravery of advancing into the cannon's mouth with the bravery of standing before an audience to deliver a speech.

In 1835 he delivered ten lectures on English literature, besides others on Michaelangelo, Luther, Milton, Fox, Burke, and the 200th anniversary of the founding of Concord. In 1836 and 1837 there were further series of lectures, all reasonably well attended. The fees he received ranged from $5 or $10 per lecture to $320 in 1842 for a series of eight lectures. As the years passed, Emerson began to make annual lecture tours through the West, where his fees were higher—$75 or more. But it should not be thought that Emerson belonged to the class of lecturers-for-hire. His concentration always was upon having something to say and upon saying what he thought he should, not what he felt would draw more profitable audiences.[21] His most notable speeches were not on the lecture platform and were not given for fees.

What lecturing meant to him is clearly indicated in his journal. On October 18, 1839, he wrote: "For the past five years I have read each winter a course of lectures in Boston, and each was my creed and confession of faith." Then he adds that it is his awareness of "the concatenation of errors called *society* to which I still consent" that makes lecturing a duty, even though he objects to this form of exerting influence. "So I submit to sell tickets again."[22] In an even more revealing passage, on September 19, 1837, he recorded: "On the 29th August, I received a letter from the Salem Lyceum, signed I. F. Worcester, requesting me to lecture before the institution next winter, and adding, 'The subject is, of course, discretionary with yourself, provided no allusions are made to religious controversy, or other exciting topics upon which the public mind is honestly divided!' I replied, on the same day, to Mr. W. by quoting these words, and adding, 'I am really sorry that any person in

[19] *Heart of Journals, op. cit.,* p. 88.
[20] Cited by Phillips Russell, *Emerson: The Wisest American,* New York: Blue Ribbon Books, 1929, p. 114.
[21] On Dec. 23, 1834, he wrote in his journal: "What must be said in a Lyceum? . . . . not what they will expect to hear, but what is fit for me to say." *Heart of Journals, op. cit.,* p. 89.
[22] *Ibid.,* p. 147.

Salem should think me capable of accepting an invitation so incumbered.' "23

This was the period in his life when Emerson made the two greatest of his speeches which are remembered specifically as speeches: "The American Scholar" and "The Divinity School Address."

The Panic of 1837 closed banks, caused the United States to suspend species payments, and impressed even Emerson, in the isolation of his closed universe of thought, with the "loud cracks in the social edifice." Unemployment, bankruptcies, and stagnation became for the first time serious problems on the American scene. To his diary Emerson confided: "Young men have no hope. Adults stand like day-laborers idle in the streets. . . . Let me begin anew; let me teach the finite to know its master."24 Then came an invitation to speak, on August 31, 1837, before the annual meeting of the Phi Beta Kappa Society, in Cambridge. On July 29 he recorded some thoughts for his speech; by August 18 he was able to state his theme as a "hope to arouse young men at Cambridge to a worthier view of . . . the Scholar's function. . . . To arouse the intellect; to keep it erect and sound; to keep admiration in the hearts of the people; to keep the eye upon its spiritual aims."25 James Russell Lowell, writing of this speech thirty years later, recalled that the hall was crowded, even in the aisles, with even the windows packed with listeners; and he recalled, too, that there was "a grim silence of foregone dissent."26 In the midst of economic disaster, the Harvard students apparently were not prone to applaud scholastic sentiments delivered by a recluse.

The result surprised everyone. What the audience heard was a plea that they be more than "meek young men in libraries," that they trust themselves, that they never quit their "belief that a popgun is a popgun, though the ancient and honorable of the earth affirm it to be the crack of doom." Emerson agreed with their severest criticisms of the scene into which they would soon graduate: "There is no work for any but the decorous and the complaisant." He did not advise them to surrender to the conformist demands. Quite to the contrary. "We will walk on our own feet; we will work with our own hands; we will speak our own minds."27 Youth responded as it normally does when it hears defiance boldly uttered. Oliver Wendell Holmes declared that "Nothing like it had been heard in the halls of Harvard since Samuel Adams supported

23 *Ibid.*, p. 114.
24 *Journals of Ralph Waldo Emerson*, ed. E. W. Emerson and W. E. Forbes, Boston: Houghton Mifflin, 1910, IV:242.
25 *Heart of Journals, op. cit.*, p. 113.
26 *Works* of Emerson, *op. cit.*, I:415.
27 *Ibid.*, I:89, 102, 114, 115.

the affirmative of the question, 'Whether it be lawful to trust the chief magistrate, if the commonwealth cannot otherwise be preserved.' . . . No listener ever forgot that address . . ."[28]

The senior class of Harvard's Divinity School was sufficiently impressed to invite him to deliver its commencement address. Emerson knew what he wanted to say. In his diary, on March 14, 1838, he wrote: "There is no better subject for effective writing than the clergy. I ought to sit and think, and then write a discourse to the American clergy, showing them the ugliness and unprofitableness of theology and churches at this day, and the glory and sweetness of the moral nature out of whose pale they are almost wholly shut."[29] The Divinity School Address was delivered July 15—with exceedingly diverse results. The faculty took great pains publicly to renounce and dissociate themselves from it, and it was another thirty years before Harvard found any occasion to invite him back. The students loved it, however, and the scholarly Dr. William Ellery Channing thought it "an entirely justifiable and needed criticism."[30]

Emerson's principal aim was to establish the fact and the significance of the immediacy of God. "If a man is at heart just, then in so far is he God," he said. "Whilst a man seeks good ends, he is strong by the whole strength of nature." He pursued the theme: "That which shows God in me, fortifies me. That which shows God out of me, makes me a wart and a wen." This understanding, he believed, is violated by "vulgar preaching" which "dwells with noxious exaggeration about the person of Jesus," as though only one created being ever partook of the divine nature. Because of the theological view of human depravity, "man is ashamed of himself; he skulks and sneaks through the world, to be tolerated, to be pitied, and scarcely in a thousand years does any man dare to be wise and good." Instead of stressing the vast difference that separates man from his Creator, Emerson asserted, "It is the office of a true teacher to show us that God is, not was; that He speaketh, not spake." Then he gave his charge to the graduating class: ". . . go alone . . . . cast behind you all conformity . . . . study the grand strokes of rectitude . . . . resist for truth's sake . . . . let us do what we can to rekindle the smouldering, nigh quenched fire on the altar."[31]

Emerson, in the usual sense, was devoid of the skills of the orator. But his message of warm, self-confident individualism was clothed in the

---

[28] *Ibid.*, I:415.
[29] *Ibid.*, I:420–421.
[30] *Ibid.*, I:423. Moncure Daniel Conway, in his *Autobiography, op. cit.*, I:166–167, relates a remarkable incident indicating that Emerson went to the Harvard dormitories in the early 1850's and conducted private lecture-discussions in the rooms of students who were interested in liberal religion.
[31] *Works, op. cit.*, I:122, 124, 130, 132, 142, 144, 145, 146, 148, 149.

magic raiment of dramatic phrases; and he spoke from his heart to the hearts of all who would come to hear. James A. Garfield was speaking for many when he "dated his first real intellectual life from the hour when he sat under the high pulpit in the old parish church at Williamstown and was dazed by the new vision Emerson opened before him."[32] This new vision was impressive even to those, probably a majority of his listeners, who but dimly understood it. Many must have felt as moved as Emerson's housemaid, who asked permission to leave the dishes unwashed so that she might go to the town hall to hear him lecture. When Mrs. Emerson asked in surprise if the maid could understand what Mr. Emerson was talking about, she replied, "No, I don't, but I like to hear him stand up there and talk as though he weren't a bit better than anyone else." The principal impact of his speaking was to make his hearers feel that they themselves were better than they had dared to believe. "Trust yourself," he insisted; "every heart vibrates to that iron string." There is, he urged, an "infinitude of the private man."

There was, as Robert Green Ingersoll observed, "a baked bean side"[33] of practicality to Ralph Waldo Emerson. However eloquent or impressive a man might be, Emerson warned, "There is always the previous question: how came you on that side."[34] He advised his hearers that "The truly eloquent man is a sane man with power to communicate his sanity."[35] On his annual lecture trips, which extended three times across the Mississippi and once out to California, Emerson liked to travel in the railway coaches so that he could talk to farmers and laborers. In Boston he went down to the wharves to listen to the speech of sailors and even admired the earthiness of their profanity. His advice to youthful orators was to study the vocabulary and rhythm of everyday conversation.

The passage of the compromise bills in 1850, and especially the Fugitive Slave Law, aroused Emerson politically as nothing had done before. During the next decade he gave vent to his feelings in speeches denouncing the capture of runaway slaves, the hanging of John Brown, the emancipation of slavery in the West Indies, and the assault upon Senator Sumner. In these and other "practical" addresses, Emerson sounded less the philosopher and more the political agitator. "America," he proclaimed, "is another word for opportunity."[36] The "conspiracy of slav-

---

[32] Theodore Clark Smith, *The Life and Letters of James A. Garfield*, New Haven: Yale University Press, 1925, I:76.
[33] *The Letters of Robert G. Ingersoll*, ed., E. I. Wakefield, New York: Philosophical Library, 1951, p. 405.
[34] *Works, op. cit.*, VIII:131.
[35] *Ibid.*, VII:91.
[36] *Ibid.*, XI:299.

ery," he declared, is not an institution; "I call it a destitution."[37] These speeches helped to satisfy his need to identify himself with the forward thrust of social improvement; but his greatness on the platform belongs to an earlier period. He was near the end. James Russell Lowell summed him up best of all: "A Greek head on right Yankee shoulders."[38]

The Magnificent Missourian 📖

THOMAS HART BENTON was the most effective spokesman for the West. Yet if he had to be judged only by the ability to utter memorable sentences, or by the power to enthrall an audience, he would remain submerged amid the group of eloquent men who crowded Congress in the great period of decision between 1820 and 1850. Throughout his lifetime he seldom surpassed the assessment of his oratorical ability made in 1817 by a St. Louis schoolmaster, Timothy Flint: "He is astute, laboured, florid, rather sophomorical to use our word, but a man of strong sense."[1] Benton never outgrew his habit of verbosity, his legalistic over-documentation, or his occasional bursts of temper tantrums. His speeches fail to compare in beauty of language, compact strength of reasoning, or terse memorability with the best speaking of Webster, Clay, or Lincoln. Yet he reached the highland of fame and influence while contesting against the greatest array of debating talent ever assembled in a legislative body.[2]

Benton's merit appears most clearly when it is recalled that he was the first man ever to serve thirty years in the United States Senate; that his political astuteness kept him in a position of central influence during all the complex changes of party alignment during that time; that his foresight into economic, ecological, and political trends was superior to that of any of his compeers; that he was wise enough to find a course of moderation between North and South extremism which offered the best, if not the only, means of preventing civil war; and that his integrity impelled him to pursue what he felt to be the right even at the cost of his reputation and his prized seat in the Senate. All these characteristics

---

37 *Ibid.*, XI:297.
38 James Russell Lowell, in his satiric poem "A Fable for Critics," in which he also said of Emerson: "All admire, and yet scarcely six converts he's got/ To I don't (nor they either) exactly know what."
1 Elbert B. Smith, *The Magnificent Missourian*, New York: Lippincott, 1958, p. 56.
2 Norman W. Mattis, "Thomas Hart Benton," in Nichols, ed., *History and Criticism*, *op. cit.*, pp. 52–96, thought Benton an "unlikely candidate for canonization in the anthologies," but insisted that his "merits were great and his weaknesses superficial" (p. 94).

(even if granted) may seem to relate more to Benton the statesman than to Benton the orator. There is more to be said about his career, however: whether or not individual speeches win admiration when considered for anthologies of enduring eloquence, the fact is that in his own laborious fashion he had an unrivalled knack of setting forth positions in a way that won for them the maximum of support. He was a master not of tact but of tactics, not of elegance but of enlightened expediency, not of style but of acutely intellectual realism. Only Seward equalled him in his grasp of the realities of politics; only Clay surpassed him in his sure perception of the workable compromise; only Webster matched the grandeur of his vision for America—with the significant difference that Webster's principal emphasis was on the magnificent foundation from which Americanism arose, while Benton's was more towards America's future development.

Maturing in the border states of Tennessee and Missouri, with his vision ever directed to the expanding West, Benton exercised with skill and scruple his conviction that mutual forebearance would eliminate sectional strife and that the fledgling United States could place its hope and its policies in a destiny of unquenchable expansion. He won the respect of his colleagues both by the consistency and the realism of his views and by the enormous industry with which he made his mind the master of the subjects his interest encompassed. Besides, his personality was always more exciting, more dramatic, more immediately interesting, and more lastingly appealing than the words he endlessly uttered. Thomas Hart Benton was an orator in spite of his speeches—a living exemplar of the theory that oratory is more than the verbal text; it is, in the end, man speaking. His dynamic personality did much to shape the course of events during one of the most crucial generations of American history.

Benton's life commenced in failure. He was born in 1782, and six years later his father died. In due course he entered the University of North Carolina, where he made a name as a debater in the literary societies but was expelled for stealing money from several fellow students. Mrs. Benton then moved her family to Tennessee to escape the shadow of this disgrace, rearing her family in debt and hoping for eventual income from her late husband's large investment in unsettled lands. Benton became a successful lawyer and won election to the State Senate on the strength of his attacks against the cumbersome judicial system. Then came the War of 1812 and Benton strove valiantly to make a name for himself as a Colonel of Militia. Through misunderstandings generated by jealous rivals, he was represented to General Andrew Jackson as a glory-seeking incompetent and was kept remote from battle. As a result, on September 4, 1813, when he and Jackson met unexpectedly in a Nashville hotel lobby, both men drew pistols and Jackson's left shoulder was shattered. Benton was thereafter continually beset by bullies who tried to force him into a duel to revenge the wounding of Tennessee's popular hero. In 1815 he fled to St. Louis, once more to start life anew after an irremediable failure.

Missouri was a goldmine of disputed land claims, following the expulsion of the French and Spaniards; Benton mastered both the French language and French law, with which knowledge he soon became a flourishing success. Then, in 1817, he made what he always thought to be the worst mistake of his life. As a result of a trifling exchange of words following a court case, he hounded Charles Lucas, the opposing attorney, until he forced him into a duel. In the first fight, at a distance of thirty feet, Lucas was wounded. Benton refused to let the matter drop, and engineered another encounter at ten feet. Lucas was killed. Benton was soon overcome by remorse, and during the remainder of his life he managed to evade duels, though many efforts were made to force him to fight. Until the last ten years of his life, he even curbed his quick-blazing temper; when it finally again burst from control, he paid for it with his career.

In 1818 he became editor of the St. Louis *Enquirer*, and wrote daily editorials demanding federal funds for roads and development of trade with the Orient via the Missouri and Columbia rivers. With these editorials came fame, and with this fame he was able, in 1820, to win by one vote election to the United States Senate. Arriving in Washington in the fall of 1821, he found Missouri statehood still being debated, and used a six-week interlude before he could take his oath as a Senator to learn Spanish and study Spanish law, literature, and history. In terms of later usefulness, this six-week span was one of the most fruitful of his life. On December 6, 1821, at the age of thirty eight, he took the Senate seat which he was to hold with distinction until, in March, 1851, defeated and broken in health, he cleaned out his desk and morosely returned to Missouri.

Within a few weeks after his induction into the Senate, Benton began an out-pouring of speeches that clarified policies he had long meditated upon and which he followed consistently the rest of his life. His fellow Senators admired his candor and the weight of evidence he presented, but despite the vigor of his delivery they found the length tiresome. On March 22 and again on April 25 of 1822 he spoke at great length on the urgent need for development of the Northwest, urging support for the American Fur Company as a counter to England's Hudson Bay Company. The goal he pictured was a rich trade with the

Orient that would equal "the wealth of merchants whose opulence is yet seen in the ruins of Alexandria and Palmyra." When Senator Dickerson of New Jersey countered contemptuously that, "Thank heavens, that country does not admit of a white population," Benton replied, in a tone "cold enough to chill one's blood," that: "Within a century from this day, a population greater than that of the present United States, will exist on the west side of the Rocky Mountains . . . . Within a century the population of the whole will be one hundred and sixty millions . . . . Upon the people of Eastern Asia, the establishment of a civilized power upon the opposite coast of America, could not fail to produce great and wonderful events."[3] On January 25, 1825, he made another great speech, arguing for a federal road from St. Louis to New Mexico, both for the development of trade and to secure American influence in an area that would provide gold and silver to strengthen our currency.

Meanwhile, on April 28, 1824, he introduced his famous "graduation plan"[4] for selling the western lands—a plan for which he fought until it was finally adopted in substance in 1854. The Federal Government then owned 1.9 billion acres of unsettled lands, which became a focus of the struggle between the East and the West. Webster and the Whigs generally wished to curb the sales, partly in order to keep cheap labor penned up to supply the coastal industries. Benton argued that the greatest value the United States could get from the land was to encourage its settlement, thus enhancing the prosperity of the nation. His graduation plan called for a reduction of the price of the land by twenty five cents per acre each year until the price should be down to twenty five cents—then to give away free whatever remained. As he said in 1826: "I contend that the Earth is the gift of God to man. *I go for donations!*"[5]

Intermixed with the argument on land policy was the running debate on the tariff.[6] Henry Clay, Kentuckian though he was, allied himself with Webster and the remnants of the Federalist party, then reconstituted as the Whigs, to introduce his "American System" of tariff laws in 1824. In 1828, partly to drum up a political issue on which he hoped he might defeat Jackson for the presidency, Clay introduced new tariff provisions that came to be known as "The Tariff of Abominations." The Clay thesis was compounded partly of protectionism—to keep com-

---

[3] Smith, *op. cit.*, pp. 83–85.
[4] William Nisbet Chambers, *Old Bullion Benton: Senator from the New West,* Boston: Little, Brown, 1956, pp. 134–136; Smith, *op. cit.*, p. 88.
[5] Smith, *op. cit.*, pp. 88–89.
[6] In the opinion of Theodore Roosevelt, "There has never been a time when there was more rabid, objectless, and unscrupulous display of partisanship." P. 57 of his *Thomas H. Benton,* Boston, Houghton Mifflin, 1899.

peting European goods from the market—and partly to secure revenue enough to build western roads without internal taxes. Calhoun led the South in opposition and Benton marshalled the counterattack of the Northern and Western Democrats.

In the 1830 debate on Senator Foot's resolution to restrict sale of the western lands Benton declared that "That manufacturer wants poor people to do the work for smaller wages; these poor people wish to go to the West to get land."[7] Now as a substitute for revenues from land sales Clay was proposing what Benton called "a most complex scheme of injustice, which taxes the South to injure the West, to pauperize the poor of the North."[8] Instead, Benton leaped a hundred years in advance of his time to propose (in 1830) a reciprocal tariff system. His speech was too long, too detailed, and the idea too new to win serious attention. In the 1828 debate Benton indulged in one of his ponderous attempts at humor, which he often tried, frequently to the irritation of his opponents, proposing a tariff on molasses to discourage the making of rum: "whiskey was the healthiest . . . as men were known who had been drunk upon it for forty or fifty years, while rum finished its victims in eight or ten."[9] Clay got the substance of the tariff he desired, thereby winning the support of Eastern industrialists; but Benton was content with his own results, which were in the form of votes for the Democratic Party from the masses who agreed with him that they were being bilked while the manufacturers were being protected.

Another interwoven economic theme dear to Benton's heart was his attack on the charter of the United States Bank. Nicholas Biddle, the director, had become a veritable Czar of the financial community. During the years 1831–32 he greatly expanded the loans on western lands; when a bad crop year resulted in inability to pay off mortgages, the Bank started foreclosing. In February, 1831, Benton introduced a bill against rechartering the Bank, making a long and fierce speech, in which he argued that "It tends to aggravate the inequality of fortunes; to make the rich richer, and the poor poorer."[10] With a large Whig majority in Congress in 1832, Clay tried to force a quick vote on the charter, but

[7] Smith, *op. cit.*, p. 109. At this time Benton was described by a Congressman from New York as follows: "Fine portly figure—rather aldermanic—neither tall nor short—sandy hair—large whiskers—a narrow, retiring forehead—a grey eye, that can glance like lightning—full face—regular features—a mouth well formed—tongue quick and voluble—altogether a handsome and a great man. His delivery is very accurate and distinct—his words flow sensibly and fluently—always in a soft, winning tone—except when his indignation is excited, for then the very d——l himself (my readers will pardon the expression) could not speak and look more terrible." Chambers, *op. cit.*, pp. 161–162.
[8] Smith, *op. cit.*, p. 109.
[9] *Ibid.*, p. 97.
[10] *Ibid.*, p. 122. Roosevelt devoted an entire chapter of his brief biography to Benton's championing of Jackson on the Bank question: *op. cit.*, pp. 102–127.

Benton managed to delay it for six months, meanwhile pouring out speeches which had an appreciable effect in bringing public pressure to bear on wavering members of Congress.[11] "All the flourishing cities of the West," Benton cried, "are mortgaged to the monied power. They may be devoured by it at any moment. They are in the jaws of the monster! A lump of butter in the mouth of a dog! One gulp, one swallow, and all is gone!"[12] When the vote was taken in the Congress, Clay won—but lost precious votes needed to override Jackson's veto. And in the presidential election of 1832 the people overwhelmed Clay and returned Jackson with a huge majority.

The winter of 1833–34 brought a panic, indubitably caused by restrictions on the Bank's power to extend credit, and Clay engineered a Senate vote of censure against Jackson (on March 28, 1834). Benton at once introduced an "Expunging Resolution," to wipe this vote from the Senate records. Support for Benton's move increased in 1835, as prosperity boomed and the national Treasury bulged with surplus funds. Finally, in January, 1837, as Jackson's second term neared its end, Benton won the expunging fight. To Jackson's enemies this assault upon the official record of the Senate was a crime akin to tearing a page from the log of a ship at sea. Webster called it a "ruthless violation"; it reminded Calhoun of the crimes of Caligula and Nero; and Clay denounced Benton's move as "a foul deed which, like the blood-stained hands of the guilty Macbeth, all the ocean's waters will never wash out."[13] Benton, gay with victory, exchanged a few more insults with Clay then escorted him home and put him to bed.

On the question of slavery Calhoun expected every Southerner to stand firm against the North. Benton, in the course of the 1830 debate on Foot's resolution, spelled out his own policy—one from which he never diverged: Slavery, he felt, was eventually doomed, for "a certain density of population and difficulty of subsistence, makes it cheaper to hire a man than to own him; cheaper to pay for the work he does and hear no more of him, than to be burthened with his support from the cradle to the grave." As to remedies, "I beseech and implore" the people of the North "to leave this whole business to ourselves . . . they must know that the wearer of the shoe knows best where it pinches and is most concerned to get it off."[14]

The Benton-Calhoun dispute became most bitter over the Oregon

---

[11] Roosevelt considered Benton "no match" for Webster "either as a thinker or as a speaker; but with the real leader of the Whig party, Henry Clay, he never had much cause to fear comparison" (*op. cit.*, p. 116).
[12] Smith, *op. cit.*, p. 127; Chambers, *op. cit.*, pp. 171–205.
[13] Smith, *op. cit.*, p. 164.
[14] *Ibid.*, p. 111.

and Texas questions. Benton, as we have seen, was an ardent advocate of northwestern development. He was also in favor of Texan independence and ultimate admission to the Union. But he was keenly aware of the need to maintain the friendship of Mexico. It was in the Democratic nominating convention of 1844, in Baltimore, that the issue boiled to its climax. Calhoun, determined to block the nomination of Van Buren (who was Benton's candidate), managed to impose a rule requiring a two-thirds majority for nomination; as a result, the prize went to a "dark horse," James K. Polk. Meanwhile, as Secretary of War in Zachary Taylor's cabinet, Calhoun was maneuvering to force a war with Mexico upon the specious ground that England was intriguing for control of Texas. The Democratic platform called for annexation of Texas and extension of the Oregon boundary northward to Alaska, with the slogan, "Fifty-four forty or fight!" Benton opposed both these planks, favoring the forty-ninth parallel as the northern boundary for Oregon. Nevertheless, he campaigned for Polk and became the new President's closest adviser. By the time of Polk's inauguration, war with Mexico was all but inevitable; Benton still tried to prevent it, but after the declaration of war, he gave his utmost efforts to passage of every bill needed to win it. He also served Polk as an informal director of psychological warfare, urging him to avoid any anti-Catholic measures and to do all he could to set peon against Mexican landowner.[15] In June of 1846 Benton secured passage through the Senate of a bill accepting the forty-ninth parallel as Oregon's northern boundary, and in talks with the British Ambassador won England's concurrence.[16]

In February, 1847, while Calhoun opposed measures to strengthen the war effort, arguing for a "masterly inactivity," Benton jumped to his feet, declaring that Calhoun was "wrong in 1819, in giving away Texas—wrong in 1836, in his sudden hot haste to get her back—wrong in all his machinations for bringing on the Texas question in 1844—wrong in breaking up the peace negotiations between Mexico and Texas—wrong in secretly sending the army and navy to fight Mexico while we were at peace with her . . . . —wrong in offering Mexico . . . ten millions of dollars to hush up the war which he had created—wrong now in refusing Mr. Polk three millions to aid in getting out of the war which he made . . ."[17] Then Benton still further angered Calhoun (and alienated many of his Missouri constituents) by supporting the Wilmot Proviso, which barred slavery from all territory won from Mexico. Benton's political difficulties mounted when he broke with Presi-

---

[15] *Ibid.*, pp. 214–215.
[16] Chambers, *op. cit.*, pp. 294–300.
[17] Smith, *op. cit.*, p. 221.

dent Polk after the President upheld a military charge of insubordination against Benton's cherished son-in-law, the explorer-politician, John C. Frémont.

The end of the Mexican War confronted the country squarely with the issue of what should be done about the extension of slavery. Clay returned to the Senate to propose his famous compromise measures and engaged Webster to support them. Calhoun mustered his last strength to rise from his deathbed in an attack against any restrictions upon the slavocracy. Benton, on May 9, 1849, roared into the fight with an irritability reminiscent of his youth: "I do not admit a dissolution of the Union to be a remedy, to be prescribed by statesmen, for the diseases of the body politic, any more than I admit death, or suicide, to be a remedy to be prescribed by physicians for diseases of the natural body."[18] A few days later he gave another of his lengthy diatribes, concluding: "A Senator for thirty years, I cannot degrade the Senate by engaging in slavery and disunion discussions. Silence such debate is my prayer; and if that cannot be done, I silence myself."[19]

The silencing was imminent, coming from the opposition his stand had aroused in Missouri (aggravated by the ambitions of politicians held down for a generation by his ascendancy). Announcing, "I shall crush my enemies as an elephant crushes piss-ants under his tread," Benton set off on a furious campaign trip through Missouri. His mood and his manner are indicated by a comment he made after hearing boos while he addressed a crowd in Platte City: "God damn Platte City—God damn it, I wouldn't make another speech there to save it from the fate of Sodom and Gomorrah." Warned that Stephen A. Douglas was coming into the State to campaign against him, Benton jeered: "Douglas can never be President, sir. His legs are too short, sir. His coat, like a cow's tail, hangs too near the ground, sir." In a major speech at St. Louis, heralding the projecting building of a transcontinental railroad, Benton briefly resumed the mantle of statesmanship: "Let us rise to the grandeur of the occasion. Let us complete the grand design of Columbus by putting Europe and Asia into communication . . . . through the heart of our country . . . . Let us now rise above everything sectional, local, personal."[20] When the votes were counted for the State Legislature, Benton's followers were in a minority and he knew his days in the Senate were numbered.

[18] *Ibid.*, p. 247; cf. Chambers, *op. cit.*, pp. 357–368.
[19] Smith, *op. cit.*, p. 249.
[20] *Ibid.*, pp. 250, 252, 254, 255. During this whirlwind campaign, Benton spoke of his Senatorial career already in the past tense; and he told an audience in Jefferson City that "I despise the bubble popularity that is won without merit and lost without crime." Chambers, *op. cit.*, p. 372.

Back in Washington, Benton put aside his ancient enmity for Clay and fought hard for the Compromise of 1850. Southerners attacked him with unreasoning rage, and Senator Henry Foote (who had fought four duels) poured insults upon him, seeking to force a fight. Finally, on the Senate floor, Foote pulled a pistol from his pocket and brandished it at Benton, whereupon the Missourian squared himself in the aisle, shouting, "I have no pistols! Let him fire! Stand out of the way! Let the assassin fire!"[21] Foote was disarmed, and to avoid a Senate censure he made a half-hearted apology. The violence of the debate continued and on another occasion Benton addressed the chair, saying: "I do not quarrel, sir; but sometimes I fight, sir; and when I fight, sir, a funeral follows, sir."[22] It was a stormy end to his public career. In April, the Compromise was adopted. In the following January, after forty ballots, the Missouri Legislature by a bare majority returned Thomas Hart Benton to private life.

Benton was sixty eight and many of his comrades had already passed away; but the old warrior was not through. While out of office he commenced his valuable book, *A Thirty Years' View*. When the publisher asked how many copies should be printed, Benton is supposed to have replied: "How many Americans can read?" The first volume had an advance sale of 65,000 copies. The manuscript for the second volume, and all his notes, were burned—but Benton doggedly went to work rewriting it, completing the task in May, 1856. Meanwhile, he ran for the Congress; and in December, 1853, he won after a furious and peculiar campaign, in which he told a St. Louis crowd: "What is a seat in Congress to me? . . . What is my occupation? . . . gathering the bones of the dead—a mother—a sister—two sons—a grandchild—planting cypress over assembled graves, and marking the spot where I, and those who are dear to me, are soon to be laid."[23] He returned to Washington to do furious battle against Stephen A. Douglas's repudiation of the 1850 compromise in the proposed Kansas-Nebraska bill. "Is all Clay's labor to be buried with him?" Benton demanded. To Benton, Douglas's doctrine of popular sovereignty was based on "untrue, contradictory, suicidal, and preposterous reasoning." The result of its passage could only be the destruction of "all confidence between the North and the South, and arraying one-half the Union against the other in deadly hostility."[24] This fight he lost. He turned, then, to an old topic, the settlement of the West, but with a new twist. For the only time in his life he entered a plea for fair treatment for the Indians, urging the appointment

[21] Chambers, *op. cit.*, p. 361.
[22] Smith, *op. cit.*, p. 139.
[23] *Ibid.*, pp. 288–289.
[24] *Ibid.*, pp. 296–297.

of knowledgeable men as Indian agents, "to settle, with all possible gentleness, these calamitous Indian wars, of which our own dreadful misconduct has been too much the cause."[25] In the election of 1856 he lost his Congressional seat but helped elect Buchanan, who, he promised, would administer the Constitution fairly and would "give to all its compromises full and free sway."[26]

In his seventy-seventh year, on the morning of April 10, 1858, he called his nurse to put her ear against his chest, telling her, "I shall not trouble you much longer . . . . that is the death rattle."[27] Like the others of his generation, he was passing from the scene that was soon to illustrate the truth of what Abraham Lincoln, on June 16 of the year of Benton's death, was telling the Republican Convention in Springfield, Illinois: "A house divided against itself cannot stand." Perhaps this eventual division reflected a kind of failure. But none could deny to Benton the consolation with which he closed the final volume of his *Thirty Years' View*: ". . . the knowledge of the fact that he has labored in his day and generation, to preserve and perpetuate the blessings of that Union and self-government which wise and good men gave us."[28]

[25] Smith, *op. cit.,* p. 308; Roosevelt, *op. cit.,* pp. 52, 152–154, 307–308.
[26] Smith, *op. cit.,* p. 315. A curious phase of the political maneuvering, in which President Polk offered to Benton a commission as lieutenant general, so he could outrank Generals Taylor and Scott, and thereby, presumably, win votes away from them for Buchanan, is related by Philip Klein, *President James Buchanan: A Biography,* University Park: Pennsylvania State University Press, 1962, p. 187.
[27] Smith, *op. cit.,* p. 324.
[28] Thomas Hart Benton, *Thirty Years' View, op. cit.,* II:788.

V

THE GREAT TRIAD:
WEBSTER, CALHOUN, AND CLAY
1812⌣1852

The Three Orators in Perspective

As WE have seen in Chapter III, Daniel Webster, John Caldwell Calhoun, and Henry Clay were leading figures in the discussions of most of the great national issues between 1812 and 1850. Many have considered them "the three who by the test of popular fame are counted the greatest American orators."[1] They were also party leaders who bore primary responsibility for the development of policies and of the lines of argument which formed the substance for many other speakers who followed where they led.[2] Different as they were from one another in method, mood, manner, and in many of their political ideas, they nevertheless are inseparably linked in the history of their time. For many years they sat together in the Senate. For an even longer period public reactions and party platforms were deeply influenced by what they said.[3] They entered upon the national political scene at very nearly the same time and they departed from it virtually together. All three were statesmen of a wide range of abilities, interests, and influence; yet all three were primarily public speakers—skilled in what Emerson called "the art of putting things." All could have said what Clay did say, in his late years, to a class of law students: "It is to this practice of the art of all arts that I am indebted for the primary and leading impulses that stimulated my progress and have shaped and moulded my entire destiny."[4]

[1] George Philip Krapp, *The English Language in America*, New York: Century, 1925, I:311.
[2] Richard Hofstadter, *The American Political Tradition*, New York: Random House, Vintage Books, 1954, phrased much the same idea with a different emphasis: "Where the founding fathers dreamed of and planned for a long-term future, the generation of Webster, Clay, and Calhoun was busily absorbed with a profitable present" (p. vi). He thought that of the three Calhoun "showed the most striking mind" and that the problem he dealt with, "that of defending a minority interest in a democracy, offered the toughest challenge to fresh thinking" (p. 68).
[3] Cf. Claude G. Bowers, *The Party Battles of the Jackson Period*, Boston: Houghton Mifflin, 1922, *passim*.
[4] Quoted by E. G. Parker, "Henry Clay as an Orator," *Putnam's Monthly Magazine*, III (1854):499.

Each in his own way was loyal to, spoke for, and was representative of his own section. Henry Clay early came to be known as "Harry of the West."[5] He was flamboyant, assertive, warm-hearted and shrewd, with a zest for neighborly accommodation of differences and grandiose dreams of imperialism. Of Webster, Senator George F. Hoar justly said, "We cannot think of Massachusetts without him"—though he quickly added with equal justice, "We cannot think of America without him."[6] He was a compact of idealistic patriotism and hard-headed conservatism, with a gift for seeing and stating self-interest as though it were a covenant with divinity. Calhoun sought his college education at Yale, and became closely identified with Texas and the great Southwest, yet he was Southern and South Carolinian to the core:[7] proud, rationalistic, unyielding, and gallant, with a gift for defending sectionalism in nationalistic terms. Yet each of the three was also a sincere and effective nationalist, with reverence for the Constitution and a patriotic devotion to the Union. Each long dominated a large political following with broad public appeal; yet none was able to achieve the presidency, which was the goal of all their ambitions. Each was patriotically selfless; yet each utilized politics in a manner to advance his own personal interests. Each devoted great intellectual abilities to analysis of the central issues of slavery, economics, and federalism—and each reached a different conclusion concerning methods, although they largely agreed on goals.

In their manner of speaking they represented three widely differing modes, illustrative of the broad range of the art of oral eloquence. Calhoun specialized in logical, rapier-like analysis, though he supported his rationalized conclusions with a floodtide of urgent emotionalism which could be countered only by striking at its vulnerable premises. Webster developed intellectualized generalizations which he interwove into the emotional currents of the American public's traditional loyalties. His is the impressiveness of sweeping sentiments phrased in rhythmic rotundity. Clay so naturally imbued conversational commonsense with the mood and the view of the moment that his manifest good will and desire for a practical solution made calm and analytical consideration of consequences seem inconsequential. Whatever we look for in oratory, except humor—and Webster even displays occasional flashes of that— one or the other of them demonstrated.

Webster was constantly in demand as a speaker, although he spoke

---

[5] Bernard Mayo, *Henry Clay: Spokesman of the New West, op. cit.,* p. 44.
[6] *The Proceedings of the Webster Centennial,* ed. Ernest Martin Hopkins, Hanover, N. H.: Dartmouth College, 1901, p. 272.
[7] Parrington rather rudely observed that Calhoun was "the master political mind of the South, an uncrowned king who carried his native Carolina in his pocket like a rotten borough" (*op. cit.,* II:69).

well only when aroused by his sense of the importance of the occasion. Calhoun reserved his speaking for situations and issues that could be shaped specifically to his cardinal purposes. Clay had a pragmatic propensity for whittling away verbally at whatever topic showed promise of producing some kind of desirable results. Students of speech find them collectively to illuminate the wide range of rhetorical effectiveness. Students of history find them representative of the divergent greatness of New England, the South, and the West, as these three sections converged in a crucial struggle to try to shape the United States into a pattern consonant with their regional interests. For anyone valuing the infinitude of resourcefulness of the human spirit, their careers and personalities are dramatic examples of both the greatness and the limitations of able individualism.

Webster began as a defender of New England sectionalism against the combined South and West, which, being a majority, called their position nationalism. He became a nationalist by interpreting basic Massachusetts doctrine as American federalism. Calhoun commenced as a nationalist and clung to that role until events defined the destiny of his section as an irreconcilable minority—after which he strove to establish the South Carolina doctrine as the essential prerequisite to constitutional union. Clay used all the guile of a Western medicine man to represent diversity as characteristic of the federal principle. Each was devoted both to his region and to the nation. Each feared the inevitability of a catastrophic civil conflict and sought vainly but hopefully to avert it with remedies that proved to be either impractical or inadequate.

All three were bedeviled by personal ambition which each interpreted to himself as sacrificial statesmanship. No other three men in American history ever wanted more urgently to be President. To this end they devoted their enormous talents. Their failure was on such a scale of grandeur that it almost seemed success—except to themselves. The America of their day was proud of them; and later generations have cherished their memories while learning from them the damaging effects of interpreting self-esteem and regional bias as national goals. If they were heroes with feet of clay, the colossal size of their stature compensates for the weakness of some of their foundation premises. Living in an age when agrarianism was crumbling before the onrush of industrialism, they spoke (as do most spokesmen for decaying systems) on behalf of measures designed to postpone what in the end prove to be irresistible trends. The enlightened morality nurtured by universal education and the heightened productivity born of the new machines combined to help doom both Southern slavery and Northern property privileges. The new lands of the West became a prize valued by North and South as each sought to expand its relative wealth and political power; and since the West needed both the waterways of the South and the markets of the North, it sought to appease and reconcile the two older sections.

Clay emerged as a fire-eater in his youth because the West then needed access to the Mississippi and protection from Canada; and he later became a compromiser because compromises offered the solutions his region needed as conditions for further growth. Calhoun remained a nationalist as long as Southern domination of the presidency and equality of power in the Congress protected the "peculiar institution" of slavery; and he fathered the idea of regional autonomy when self-determination proved to be the only bulwark upon which the South could depend. Webster commenced as a regionalist because the welfare of New England commercialism was more closely aligned to foreign markets than to its sister States; and he became a nationalist when a dependable coalition of Northern and Western votes assured the continuance of protective tariffs and the development of conditions conducive to domestic trade. If Calhoun was an aristocrat, Webster an oligarch, and Clay a democrat,[8] this was not so much a cause of their policies as a reflection of influences operative upon them.

The careers of these three demonstrate that the East, South, and West were all capable in different ways of producing greatness. They also demonstrate that the greatness was limited by regional influences too deep to be eradicated except as they were reshaped by war. That the war was postponed beyond their lifespan was owing in part at least to the sincerity of their efforts and their willingness to endorse almost any expedient rather than risk destruction of the Union.[9] The fact that the best they could achieve was postponement rather then prevention of the war indicates their inability to discover fundamental solutions. Great as they indubitably were, they were doomed to grapple with partial measures and to advocate inadequate programs. Every human actor must play a role in which the script is drafted by destiny and in which he himself can make only minor revisions in the part he must play and the speeches he must deliver. Webster, Calhoun, and Clay made such revisions as they could and spoke their lines with great skill. But the play of which they were a part was decreed to be a tragedy.

[8] The classification was first suggested by Parrington, *op. cit.*, II:69–82, 142–144, and 304–316.
[9] Lord Bryce, who underestimated their determination to pay whatever price was demanded to fend off civil war, was appalled by the expediency and characterized their era as one of "intellectual emptiness" and "even moral shortcomings." *Reflections on American Institutions*, ed. H. S. Commager, Greenwich, Conn.: Premier Americana Series, 1961, pp. 95–96.

Daniel Webster: Lion of the North 📖

"No MAN could be as great as Daniel Webster looks," an Englishman is supposed to have exclaimed upon seeing him in his prime. Many who knew him well thought his greatness as an orator was virtually superhuman. The sober and hard-headed publisher, George Ticknor, after hearing Webster deliver his Plymouth Oration on December 22, 1820, went to his room and wrote: "I was never so excited by public speaking before in my life. Three or four times I thought my temples would burst with the gush of blood . . . . When I came out I was almost afraid to come near him. It seemed to me as if he was like a mount that might not be touched and that burned with fire. I was beside myself, and am so still."[1] Thirty years later, the Unitarian Minister Moncure Daniel Conway heard Webster give a casual twenty-minute talk to the Senate, and reported: " . . . the Senate listened breathlessly. He stood there like some time-darkened minster-tower. He was an institution."[2] As early as 1818, when Webster at age of thirty six was presenting his plea in the Dartmouth College case before the Supreme Court, Professor Chauncey A. Goodrich, of Yale, who won fame with his volume on *Select British Eloquence*, described the scene during the closing moments of the speech:

> The courtroom during these two or three minutes presented an extraordinary spectacle. Chief Justice Marshall, with his tall and gaunt figure bent over as if to catch the slightest whisper, the deep furrows of his cheek expanded with emotion and his eyes suffused with tears; Mr. Justice Washington at his side, with his small and emaciated frame, and countenance more like marble than I ever saw on any other human being, —leaning forward with an eager, troubled look; and the remainder of the court at the two extremities, pressing, as it were, to a single point, while the audience below were wrapping themselves round in closer folds beneath the bench, to catch each look and every movement of the speaker's face . . .[3]

This was the Webster who impressed two generations on both sides of the Atlantic.

It was this same Webster, however, who inspired the waspish John Quincy Adams to write in his *Diary* of "the gigantic intellect, the envi-

[1] Henry Cabot Lodge, *Daniel Webster*, Boston: Houghton Mifflin, 1911, p. 118.
[2] Moncure Daniel Conway, *Autobiography: Memories and Experiences*, Boston: Houghton Mifflin, 1904, I:81.
[3] Lodge, *op. cit.*, p. 90.

ous temper, the ravenous ambition, and the rotten heart of Daniel Webster."[4] The judgment was as unfair as were the similar comments by Theodore Parker, Emerson, and other abolitionists who were angered by Webster's defense of the Fugitive Slave Law.

Withal, though, Webster himself is a convincing source of evidence that his life was dominated by ambition and distraught by fears of personal failure. His close friend William Plumer described an evening with him in 1822, during which "He broke out into the most passionate aspirations after glory. Without it life, he said, was not worth possessing. The petty struggles of the day were without interest to him, except as they might furnish the opportunity for doing or saying something that would be remembered in after time." In a fit of dejection, Webster told Plumer, "I have done absolutely nothing. At thirty Alexander had conquered the world; and I am forty." When Plumer smiled, Webster went on, "You laugh at me, Plumer! Your quiet way of looking at things may be best, after all; but I have sometimes such glorious dreams! And sometimes, too, I half believe that they will one day wake into glorious realities."[5] The great dream of Webster was the presidency, and his failure to attain it was a canker that ate into the vitals of his fame. In 1852, loaded with honors but beset by frustrations, Webster told his son, "I have given my life to law and politics. Law is uncertain and politics are utterly vain."[6] A few months later, on his deathbed, in a final wistful reaching out for lasting glory, he whispered: "Have I—wife, son, doctor, friends, are you all here?—have I on this occasion said anything unworthy of Daniel Webster?"[7] The springs of his personal motivation are not in doubt: he wanted desperately to achieve greatly and to achieve in a manner that would be noted and win fame. The presidency would have insured fulfilment of his desires. Oratory was a natural route to the goal he sought.

From July 4, 1800, when he delivered the Independence Day address at Dartmouth College, as an eighteen year old student, until his death fifty two years later, public speaking was for Daniel Webster the focal center of his life, thought, and the influence he sought to exert. He habitually viewed the world of ideas and action in terms of what could and should be said about it to appropriate groups of listeners. He trained himself in the skills that shaped his conception of great speaking: vocabulary, memory, impressive action, style. He gave great care to

---

[4] Bennett Champ Clark, *John Quincy Adams, op. cit.,* p. 343.
[5] William Plumer, "Reminiscences," in *The Writings and Speeches of Daniel Webster,* New York: J. F. Taylor, National Edition, 1903, XVII:560.
[6] Lodge, *op. cit.,* p. 346.
[7] Allan L. Benson, *Daniel Webster,* New York: Cosmopolitan Book Co., 1929, p. 399.

the composition of his speeches, telling the reporter Henry J. Raymond (who was amazed by his ability to speak extensively and meticulously without using any notes): "It is my memory. I can prepare a speech, revise and correct it in my memory, then deliver the corrected speech exactly as finished."[8] He read through Noah Webster's dictionary three times and studied the speeches of the Earl of Chatham and Edmund Burke; the debates of the Ratification Conventions and the Congress; Whately's *Elements of Rhetoric*; Harrington's *Oceana* (for economic theory); and the history of the United States. His mind seemed more capacious and penetrating than it was because, as his biographer Henry Cabot Lodge properly reports, "he read carefully, meditated on what he read, and retained it so that on any subject he was able to tell all he knew to the best advantage, and was careful never to go beyond his depth."[9] His physical equipment for public address was better than average. He stood five feet ten inches in height, with his weight gradually increasing to an eventual two hundred pounds; and his voice was deep, vibrant, though without great variety. He carried himself always with assured dignity, and his dark hair, cavernously deep eyes, deliberately slow utterance, and carefully calculated gestures added together to make a superbly impressive figure. More than any other American political orator, he took care to preserve and edit his speeches for publication, with the result that more than five hundred of his addresses (ranging upward to from three to five hours in length) are included in the eighteen-volume National Edition of his works. To Webster a speech was an opportunity for bringing to bear upon the largest possible audience a message addressed to fundamental issues and delivered in terms of all that he knew, felt, and believed.

His great speaking covered a span of more than three decades and achieved genuine greatness in a variety of modes: courtroom forensics, legislative debate, campaign persuasion, commemorative oratory. His greatest courtroom addresses were the defense of the charter of Dartmouth College before the Supreme Court, on March 10, 1818, and his speech for the prosecution in the charge against John Francis Knapp for the murder of Captain Joseph White, delivered before the court and jury at Salem, Massachusetts, on April 6, 1830. His greatest commemorative speeches were his address on the First Settlement of New England, at Plymouth, on December 22, 1820; the address at the laying of the cornerstone of the Bunker Hill Monument, at Charlestown, Massa-

---

[8] Chauncey M. Depew, *Memories of Eighty Years, op. cit.*, p. 22.
[9] Lodge, *op. cit.*, p. 17, citing this as Webster's opinion of himself. The general biographical details are drawn largely from Claude Moore Fuess, *Daniel Webster*, Two Vols., Boston: Little, Brown, 1930; and George Ticknor Curtis, *Life of Daniel Webster*, Two Vols., New York: Appleton, 1872.

chusetts, on June 17, 1825; and his eulogy in commemoration of John Adams and Thomas Jefferson, in Faneuil Hall, Boston, on August 2, 1826. In international relations his greatest speeches were on the revolution in Greece, in the House of Representatives, January 19, 1824; on the Panama Mission, also in the House, on April 14, 1826; on the Objects of the Mexican War, in the Senate, on March 23, 1848; and, also in the Senate, his defense of the Webster-Ashburton Treaty, on April 6–7, 1846. His greatest legislative addresses, chiefly on the nature of our constitutional government and in support of the federal union, include an exposition of his views of representative government in the Massachusetts Constitutional Revision Convention, December 15, 1820; his reply to Robert Hayne, in the Senate, on January 26–27, 1830; his debate with John C. Calhoun in the Senate, on February 16, 1833; and his speech in the Senate, on March 7, 1850, in support of the compromise bills. His principal campaign addresses include his speech before the National Republican Convention at Worcester, Massachusetts, on October 12, 1832; his speech in Niblo's Saloon, New York, on March 15, 1837; his speech at a mass meeting at Saratoga, New York, on August 12, 1840; and his speech at Buffalo, on May 22, 1851.

The texts of Webster's speeches are printed not precisely as they were delivered, but as he edited them. Howell and Hudson, in their excellent study of Webster in the Brigance *History and Criticism of American Public Address,* discuss in some detail the considerable variations between the stenographic report and the printed version of Webster's speech in Niblo's Saloon. Edwin P. Whipple, in the introduction to his selection of Webster's speeches, quotes a discussion between Webster and Henry J. Raymond, the New York *Times* reporter, when Raymond showed Webster a transcription of one of his speeches. "Did I use that phrase?" Webster asked. "I hope not. At any rate, substitute for it this more accurate definition." Again: "That word does not express my meaning. Wait a moment and I will give you a better one. That sentence is slovenly—that image is imperfect and confused. I believe, my young friend, that you have a remarkable power of reporting what I say; but, if I said that, and that, and that, it must have been owing to the fact that I caught, in the hurry of the moment, such expressions as I could command at the moment; and you see they do not accurately represent the idea that was in my mind."[10] Webster ordinarily gave great care to the preparation, even to the memorization, of his chief addresses, in order that they might fit the precise situation of his audience; but when the

[10] Edwin P. Whipple, *The Great Speeches and Orations of Daniel Webster,* Boston: Little, Brown, 1897, p. xxiv.

speeches were printed, Webster took care to revise them for the enlarged audience, including posterity, that would see them in print. It was thus that he sought to deal with the problem posed by the English parliamentary orator, Charles James Fox, who said: "Did the speech read well? Then it was not a good speech." Webster tried very consciously to reach two different audiences with what he had to say: his immediate listeners and his eventual readers.

Stylistically, Webster's greatest virtues were clarity of analysis and exposition, and a grandeur or elevation of sentiments deriving from a phrasing that sought to enshrine the noblest feelings of his audience. As a youth, his style was pretentious, with a self-conscious effort to be impressive. Whipple illustrates this tendency from a letter Webster wrote in February, 1800, to a close friend: "In my melancholy moments I presage the most dire calamities. I already see in my imagination the times when the banner of civil war shall be unfurled; when Discord's hydra form shall set up her hideous yell, and from her hundred mouths shall howl destruction through our empire; and when American blood shall be made to flow in rivers by American swords! But propitious Heaven prevent such dreadful calamaties!"[11] Jeremiah Mason, who contested with Webster in the law courts, worked hard to cure Webster of such florid rhetoric and to teach him to talk to a court as though he were a thirteenth juryman, seriously considering the significance of the facts and the law. By the time of his appeal for Dartmouth College, Webster had learned to secure his greatest effects with the simplicity of understatement: "It is, sir, as I have said, a small college. And yet there are those who love it."

He learned to search for his style in the conversation of intelligent men, for, as he told Charles Sumner: "Their minds, in conversation, come into intimate contact with my own mind; and I absorb certain secrets of their power, whatever may be its quality, which I could not have detected in their works. Converse, *converse*, CONVERSE with living men, face to face, and mind to mind—that is one of the best sources of knowledge."[12] It also proved to be a sound guide to a style that was exalted but simple. In his second Bunker Hill address, for example, he condemned Spain's oppression of its South American colonies in a passage that penetrated into the minds of his listeners with clarity and force, one that did not smother them with impressive but inexact verbalisms: "Spain," he said, "stooped on South America like a vulture on its prey. Every thing was force. Territories were acquired by fire and

[11] *Ibid.*, p. xix.
[12] *Ibid.*, p. xxv.

sword. Cities were destroyed by fire and sword. Hundreds of thousands of human beings fell by fire and sword. Even conversion to Christianity was attempted by fire and sword."[13]

One of the greatest of Webster's stylistic virtues was the clarity with which he could discriminate precise meanings and imbue them with force through cumulative repetition. An instance of this quality occurs in his debate with Calhoun, in which Webster denied that the Constitution is a mere compact between the States, which any State might at its own will abrogate. "Secession," Webster declared, "as a revolutionary right, is intelligible; as a right to be proclaimed in the midst of civil commotions, and asserted at the head of armies, I can understand it. But as a practical right, existing under the Constitution, and in conformity with its provisions, it seems to me nothing but a plain absurdity; for it supposes resistance to government, under the authority of government itself; it supposes dismemberment, without violating the principles of union; it supposes opposition to law, without crime; it supposes the total overthrow of government, without revolution."[14]

One further factor of Webster's style deserves emphasis. This is his sincerity and honesty. He did not indulge in the common political practice of trying to blacken the reputation of his opponents in order to lessen respect for their views. He did not shun consideration of facts which appeared to render his position unsound. Calhoun, on his deathbed, paid high tribute to this character in Webster's life and speaking. "Mr. Webster has as high a standard of truth as any statesman I have met in debate," he told a visitor. "Convince him, and he cannot reply; he is silenced; he cannot look truth in the face and oppose it by argument."[15]

Oratory, in his view, was a high art which, more than any other, unites the people in a common conception of their traditions, their ideals, and their destiny. As he said in the introduction of his speech celebrating the two hundredth anniversary of the landing of the Pilgrims:

> It is a noble faculty of our nature which enables us to connect our thoughts, our sympathies and our happiness with what is distant in place or time; and, looking before and after, to hold communion at once with our ancestors and our posterity. Human and mortal though we are, we are nevertheless not mere insulated beings, without relation to the past or the future. Neither the point of time, nor the spot of earth, in which we physically live, bounds our rational and intellectual enjoyments. We live in the past by a knowledge of its history; and in the future, by hope

[13] Writings and Speeches, op. cit., I:273.
[14] Ibid., VI:211.
[15] Whipple, op. cit., p. xliii; cf. also, Plumer, op. cit., p. 219.

and anticipation. By ascending to an association with our ancestors, by contemplating their example and studying their character; by partaking their sentiments, and imbibing their spirit; by accompanying them in their toils, by sympathizing in their sufferings, and rejoicing in their successes and their triumphs; we seem to belong to their age, and to mingle our existence with theirs.[16]

Three decades later, speaking to a large audience at Buffalo, on May 22, 1851, he again indicated his theory of public address: that it must be fitted precisely to the circumstances of the moment and yet must transcend these factors to aim toward universality of import. "I know to whom I am speaking," he said. "I know for whom I am speaking . . . . I know where I am, under what responsibility I speak, and before whom I appear; and I have no desire that any word I shall say this day shall be withholden from you, or your children, or your neighbors, or the whole world; for I speak before you and before my country, and, if it be not too solemn to say so, before the great Author of all things."[17] Webster's sense of his own greatness was an asset to him precisely because he viewed it in terms of responsibility to clarify and magnify the historic significance of great themes.

With his view of the responsible role of the orator, he composed his ceremonial speeches with care. William Mathews, the University of Chicago professor who wrote *Oratory and Orators*, quotes an anecdote related by Starr King, who accompanied Webster on a fishing trip before his First Bunker Hill Oration. The story illustrates the deliberateness with which Webster composed his speech, keeping it always in his mind even during his recreation. "He would pull out a lusty specimen," King reported, "shouting, 'venerable men, you have come down to us from a former generation. Heaven has bounteously lengthened out your lives, that you might behold this joyous day.' He would unhook them into his basket, declaiming. 'You are gathered to your fathers, and live only to your country in her grateful remembrance and your own bright example.' In his boat, fishing for a cod, he composed or rehearsed the passage in it on Lafayette, when he hooked a very large cod, and, as he pulled his nose above water, exclaimed, 'Welcome! all hail! and thrice welcome, citizen of two hemispheres.' "[18] Despite this habit of careful preparation—or, in part, because of it—he was able in Congressional debate to speak impromptu with a pattern of organization and a felicity

[16] *Writings and Speeches, op. cit.,* I:181.
[17] *Ibid.,* IV:243. In his eulogy of Adams and Jefferson he said: "True eloquence does not consist in speech . . . . It comes, if it comes at all, like the outbreaking of a fountain from the earth, or the bursting forth of volcanic fires, with spontaneous original native force." Quoted by Fisher, *The True Daniel Webster*, Philadelphia: Lippincott, 1911, p. 216.
[18] William Mathews, *Oratory and Orators*, Chicago: Griggs, 1891, p. 285n.

of phrasing that far transcended extemporaneous style. When amazement was expressed at the lucidity, depth, and comprehensiveness of his Reply to Hayne, in 1830, Webster replied, "Gentlemen, I have been preparing that speech all my life."[19] All his life was, indeed, concentrated upon the preparation for and the utterance of considered sentiments on the themes of his choice.

The sentiments and the themes to which he devoted his life were capacious but connected, inclusive but homogeneous. He was little concerned with the philosophy of ultimate meanings. His religious views are adequately indicated in his declaration that "Whatever makes men good Christians, makes them good citizens."[20] He was unattracted to basic principles which might serve as an impetus to reshaping society. He had a lifelong attraction to agriculture, and he was a proud champion of the kind of education which inculcates an understanding of and admiration for established traditions. In his view, the American Constitution is a dependable bulwark protecting individual liberties and national greatness; accordingly, after 1814 he devoted his life to its defense.

Because of such views, Webster has commonly been described as a conservative. Ralph Waldo Emerson, who generally regarded Webster as the great orator of the age, unfortunately gave impetus to an interpretation of Webster as a doctrinaire spokesman for wealth and privilege. Emerson, like the other abolitionists, was hurt and angered by Webster's defense of the Fugitive Slave Law in his March 7 speech on the 1850 compromise bills; impelled by these feelings, he wrote: "Mr. Webster is a man who lives by his memory, a man of the past . . . . He believes, in so many words, that government exists for the protection of property . . . . What he finds already written, he will defend. Lucky that so much had got well written when he came. For he had no faith in the power of self-government."[21] The fact that Webster regularly received an annual retainer from the Bank of the United States, that he

---

[19] This is the usual phrasing of what Webster is supposed to have said. A very particularized account is given by Webster's friend Peter Harvey, in his *Reminiscences and Anecdotes of Daniel Webster*, Boston: Little, Brown, 1878, pp. 149–152. Webster explained to Harvey that on several earlier occasions he had carefully prepared portions of the materials he used in the debate with Hayne. Then Webster added: "I was already posted, and had only to take down my notes and refresh my memory. In other words, if he had tried to make a speech to fit my notes, he could not have hit it better. No man is inspired with the occasion; I never was." Fisher in *The True Daniel Webster*, *op. cit.*, p. 261, relates that Webster took with him to the Senate chamber five pages of notes but had little use for them: for, "All I had ever known," Webster said, "seemed to be floating before me."
[20] Lodge declares that "Webster took both his politics and his religion from his father, and does not appear to have questioned either" (*op. cit.*, p. 42).
[21] Ralph Waldo Emerson, *Works*, *op. cit.*, XI:203–204. Emerson nevertheless thought Webster the greatest orator of the time; cf. *ibid.*, VII:369 and XI:202 and 221.

loved good living, and that he chose to associate with and to defend men of wealth, all give support to this interpretation. There is every reason, however, to consider him a moderate who valued the past for the guidance it can provide as we advance into the future, and who considered that wealth must be protected, distributed, and regulated in a manner that ensures stability while encouraging the broadening of individual welfare.

Webster's most urgent plea for special privileges for wealth was made in his December 15, 1820, speech before a convention met to revise the constitution of Massachusetts. He argued for a bicameral legislature, with the members of the House to be "chosen in proportion to the number of inhabitants in each district," and for the Senators to be elected "in proportion to the taxable property in each district." His reasoning was that which the English philosopher Harrington had presented in the *Oceana*—that society is best preserved when there is a balance of interests: "as far as the object of society is the protection of something in which the members possess unequal shares, it is just that the weight of each person in the common councils should bear a relation and proportion to his interests."[22] The problem of saying precisely what he meant was not well solved in this speech; he returned to it a week later, in his December 22 address at Plymouth, where he amplified his views:

> A republican form of government rests not more on political constitutions than on those laws which regulate the descent and transmission of property. . . . The freest government could not exist, would not be long acceptable, if the tendency of the laws were to create a rapid accumulation of property in few hands, and to render the great mass of the population dependent and penniless. . . . It would seem, then, to be the part of political wisdom to found government on property; and to establish such distribution of property, by the laws which regulate its transmission and alienation, as to interest the great majority of society in the support of the government.[23]

It is manifestly a misreading of his views to cite the phrase, "to found government on property," and to overlook the care with which he insists that government must regulate inheritance and prevent the rapid accumulation of property, in order that ownership should always be widespread. To protect property is one thing; to ensure stability of democracy by securing to all the right and the opportunity to share in its ownership casts quite a different light upon his economic theory.

In a speech at Pittsburgh, in 1833, Webster went still further and

22 *Writings and Speeches, op. cit.,* V:8–25.
23 *Ibid.,* I:211, 214, 215.

called for government regulation "for the encouragement and protection of . . . the whole chain of human occupation and employment," for this "touches the means of living and the comfort of all."[24] The year before his death, speaking to a businessmen's group in Albany, he insisted that American greatness had been achieved primarily by federal regulation of interstate commerce. In the Senate, in July, 1832, he forecast that Jackson's veto of the National Bank bill "will depreciate the value of every man's property from the Atlantic States to the capital of Missouri. Its effects will be felt in the price of lands, the great and leading article of Western property, in the price of crops, in the products of labor, in the repression of enterprise, and in embarrassment to every kind of business and occupation."[25] Jackson's veto message was a strong statement of his intent to champion the people against the Eastern financial interests—which, to Webster, meant that "It manifestly seeks to inflame the poor against the rich; it wantonly attacks whole classes of the people, for the purposes of turning against them the prejudices and the resentments of other classes."[26] It is easy, considering only the words uttered by Jackson and by Webster, to maintain that the former was a defender of the masses, the latter of the privileged classes. But the events precipitated by (or at least that followed) the veto occurred much as Webster forecast, and the veto no doubt was partly responsible for the disastrous Panic of 1837.

In the broad perspective of Webster's views on government, it is apparent that (like many other men long in public life) he shifted from a youthful sectionalism to a mature nationalism. It is also true that his shift of views corresponded in the main with the interests of his constituents. He was against the tariff while New England was predominately commercial; and when, in the early 1820's, New England became a manufacturing area, he in turn became a spokesman for high tariffs. Similarly, in his early speeches he presented some of the most eloquent passages in our history in denunciation of slavery; after he began to campaign for the presidency, he softened the charges that would alienate large blocks of voters. Fundamentally he was, throughout his life, a staunch supporter of the Constitution as a document derived from the popular will and superior to the States; but as he saw the gathering forces of conflict threatening civil war, he sought by every available means to help shore up the limited sovereignty which allowed the Southern States to protect their "peculiar institution."

[24] *Ibid.*, II:141.
[25] *Ibid.*, VI:152.
[26] *Ibid.*, VI:180.

The principles, the style, and the political strategy of Webster all become manifest in a review of his statements about slavery. During the Missouri controversy, he stated flatly that "We have a strong feeling of the injustice of any toleration of slavery."[27] In his 1820 Plymouth Address he spoke feelingly against the slave trade:

> I hear the sound of the hammer. I see the smoke of the furnaces where the manacles and fetters are still forged for human limbs. I see the visages of those who, by stealth and at midnight, labor in this work of hell—foul and dark as may become the artifices of such instruments of misery and torture. Let that spot be purified or let it cease to be New England. Let it be purified, or let it be set aside from the Christian world; let it be put out of the circle of human sympathies and human regards, and let civilized men henceforth have no communion with it.[28]

By 1830 he was able to assure the Senate, in his debate with Hayne, that "There is not and never has been a disposition in the North to interfere with these interests of the South." Seven years later, in his Niblo Garden address, Webster took the same ground Lincoln was later to take: "I frankly avow my entire unwillingness to do anything that shall extend the slavery of the African race on this continent . . . . I regard slavery itself as a great moral, political, and social evil . . . [But] we have slavery already amongst us. The Constitution found it in the Union, it recognized it, and gave it solemn guarantees. To the full extent of the guarantees we are all bound in honor, in justice, and by the Constitution."[29] He voted, however, for the receiving of antislavery petitions by the Congress and he warned that any attempt to restrain antislavery agitation by the abolitionists would cause the Union itself to "be endangered by the explosion which might follow."[30]

It was in 1850, when Clay appealed to him to support the compromise measures they both hoped might avert civil war, that Webster incurred the wrath of his constituents by hedging on the question of admitting additional slave States and by defending the Fugitive Slave Law. He arose to speak with a full sense of the dangers and difficulties he personally confronted. "I have a duty to perform, and I mean to perform it with fidelity," he said evenly. "I speak today for the preservation of the Union."[31] Concerning the refusal of certain Northern communities to return escaped slaves to their masters, he declared that "I say the South has been injured in this respect, and has a right to com-

27 *Ibid.*, XV:72.
28 *Ibid.*, I:221–222.
29 *Ibid.*, II:206.
30 *Ibid.*, II:207.
31 Miller, *Great Debates, op. cit.*, IV:205.

plain." Concerning the abolitionist societies, "I do not think them use-ful. I think their operations for the last twenty years have produced nothing good or valuable." Then he proceeded to the main point of his speech—that the separation of the nation into two separate federations, slave and free, was an utter impossibility. He concluded, typically, with an urgent, emotional appeal for unity and constructive, forward-looking hopefulness:

> And now, Mr. President, instead of speaking of the possibility or utility of secession, instead of dwelling in those caverns of darkness, instead of groping with those ideas so full of all that is horrid and horrible, let us come out into the light of day; let us enjoy the fresh air of Liberty and Union; let us cherish those hopes which belong to us; let us devote ourselves to those great objects that are fit for our con-sideration and our action; . . . let us not be pygmies in a case that calls for men.[32]

The effort was one of the greatest Webster ever made, in the greatest cause of his time. And it failed. It failed to win the support of his own constituents, failed to unite the opinion of the North, failed to appeal to the South, and failed to provide a solution that could "bind up the nation's wounds." The basic persuasive technique that Webster used was of a type often highly praised: that of giving the language to one side (the South) while attempting to give the substance to the other side (the North). Perhaps the basic cause of the failure was that there was too little substance to give. What Webster, together with Clay, had to offer was comparable to what Hitler offered the democracies at Munich: saying, in effect, "we have the power to dominate, but do not mean to use it." The North as a whole was unwilling to temper its political power to confine and eventually even to eliminate slavery; and the South was fearful of remaining in a Union in which it was fore-doomed to political inequality. These were attitudes, based on realities, which Webster and Clay could not alter. With all his artistry, and from a depth of sincere patriotism, Webster sought to bridge the widening gulf with exalted sentiments drawn from the common heritage of the entire nation. But there is always a point at which words themselves, no matter how well phrased, do not suffice. Statesmanship could not materialize a solution that was unavailable. Oratory could not reshape an ugly reality into appealing form. There are limits even to the great art in which Webster superbly excelled. Two and a half years later he was dead. But there is poignancy and truth in his last recorded words: "I still live."[33]

[32] *Ibid.*, IV:219.
[33] S. M. Smucker, *Life, Speeches, and Memorials of Daniel Webster, op. cit.*, p. 153.

John Caldwell Calhoun: Prophet of the South 🔖

WHEN CALHOUN was a young man he felt the impulse, common to youth, to express his pulsating emotions in verse. According to a story widely told in South Carolina, he pondered for a time over a sheet of blank paper, then wrote a beginning: "Whereas . . ."[1] Beyond this he was unable to proceed. Wisely, he tore up the sheet and recognized that whatever else he might be, he definitely was not poetic. The incident sharply etches the nature of his limitations. But the qualities of his strength are far less quickly catalogued.

No American orator better illustrates Aristotle's faith that man is a rational creature.[2] Intellect, courage, and a burning loyalty to duty as he saw it were Calhoun's cardinal characteristics. He has been called "the cast-iron man";[3] like Oliver Cromwell, he was a Puritan in armor—every inch a soldier, although his weapons were ideas and words. It was part of his tragedy that he was spokesman for a region and a system that were doomed to minority status; and that he was born in a time that impelled him to spend his life in defense of an institution that was both obsolescent and morally wrong. The defense of slavery is not a theme out of which to construct greatness. Nevertheless, confronted as he was with this duty to his State and his class, Calhoun converted it into a philosophical defense of the right of a minority to coexist independently with an antagonistic majority. This problem, which was paramount with the *ante bellum* South, has again become crucial in an age which finds the world united but hardly unified.

More than any other orator since the founding fathers, unless it be Abraham Lincoln, Calhoun possessed an encompassing mind that necessarily interpreted immediate issues in terms of their ultimate effects. The result of his concentration upon root causes and long range effects gave to his speeches an appearance of cold logic that ignores the driving power of his intense feeling, a feeling which impelled him to dedicate

---

[1] Cited by Richard Hofstadter, *op. cit.*, p. 73, as "a traditional gibe." The presumed incident is not mentioned by Margaret L. Coit in her *John C. Calhoun, op. cit.*, nor by Arthur Styron, *The Cast Iron Man: John C. Calhoun and American Democracy, op. cit.* The story nevertheless exemplifies a *truth* of typicality: it is Calhoun in essence.

[2] Calhoun might have profited if he had studied the injunction of the great sophisticate of his later years, Henry Adams, who wrote: "distrust above all other traps the trap of logic." *The Education of Henry Adams*, New York: Book League of America, 1928, p. 429.

[3] The term was originally applied to him by Harriet Martineau in *Retrospect of Western Travel*, I:243–246.

his life to a personal conception of duty.[4] Conscience, in the career of Calhoun, played fully as central a role as did mind.

Henry Clay did not understand him, as is very evident in the description he concocted of Calhoun as "tall, careworn, with furrowed brow, haggard and intensely gazing, looking as if he were dissecting the last abstraction which [had] sprung from metaphysician's brain, and muttering to himself in half-uttered tones, 'This is indeed a real crisis.' "[5] John Quincy Adams understood him better, and in his diary he described him (in 1818) as "above all sectional and factional prejudices more than any other statesman of the Union with whom I have ever acted."[6] Calhoun may very well have understood himself best of all. "Whether it be too great confidence in my own opinion I cannot say," he once wrote, "but what I think I see, I see with so much apparent clearness as not to leave me a choice to pursue any other course, which has always given me the impression that I acted with the force of destiny."[7]

Stern as he seemed in the fierce conflict of debate, Calhoun was an unusually kind man, who never became too great to be interested in helping young men. Often in his later years he invited fledgling Congressmen, regardless of their views, to his quarters, to advise them on how to win effectiveness for their programs. Many repaid him with lasting gratitude and friendship. The young abolitionist Congressman John Wentworth was convinced that "If he could but talk with every man, he would have the whole United States on his side."[8] The antislavery newsman John Dyer found him "so morally clean and spiritually pure . . . that it was a pleasure to have one's soul close to his soul . . . as fresh and bracing as a breeze from the prairie, the ocean, or the mountain."[9] To young Albert Rhett of Charleston, Calhoun's intellect seemed "a more wonderful creation than any mountain on earth."[10] Such tributes were given by many, including Calhoun himself. On February 10, 1844, he wrote to Duff Green a rather remarkable testament: "In looking back I see nothing to regret, and little to correct."[11]

[4] "I hold the duties of life to be greater than life itself," said Calhoun at the end of his career, when he confronted both death and failure. Coit, op. cit., p. 504.
[5] Hofstadter, op. cit., p. 74. Clay's taunting of Calhoun continued all through January and February, 1838, in the fight over the National Bank. Cf. Coit, op. cit., pp. 338–341.
[6] The Diary of John Quincy Adams, ed. Allan Nevins, New York: Scribner's, 1951, p. 265.
[7] William Meigs, The Life of John Caldwell Calhoun, New York: Neale Pub. Co., 1917, II:98. Cf. also, Coit, op. cit., pp. 334–335 and 341.
[8] John Wentworth, Congressional Reminiscences, Chicago: Fergus Printing Co., pp. 33–35. Cf. also, Coit, op. cit., p. 343.
[9] Coit, op. cit., p. 462.
[10] Ibid., p. 464.
[11] John C. Calhoun, Correspondence of John C. Calhoun, ed. J. Franklin Jameson, Washington: Annual Report of the American Historical Assoc., 1899–1900.

His life was of moderate length, from 1782 to 1850. His career as an orator of genuine distinction was considerable: from 1812 until his death. His ideas were dominant as the "policy line" of the South from about 1830 to 1860, when force was substituted for argument. His *Disquisition on Government* was the most important American book on political theory published in the nineteenth century. It dealt with the theme that democracy results in despotism unless each class or community within the political group has the power to protect its own interests. His theory of "the concurrent majority" was denounced by post-Civil War historians who interpreted it as a rationalistic defense of slavocracy; but it is in effect the guiding principle of the United Nations. History has ironically produced a justification for the special pleading which Calhoun elevated into a philosophy.

No one has surpassed the summary by which Ulrich Bonnell Phillips, in his sketch on Calhoun in the *Dictionary of American Biography*, identified the principal forensic devices with which the South Carolina orator fought to maintain the rights of his section within the federal Union. "His devices were manifold: to suppress agitation; to praise the slave-holding system; to promote Southern prosperity and expansion; to procure a Western alliance; to frame a fresh plan of government by concurrent majorities; to form a Southern bloc; to warn the North of the dangers of Southern desperation; to appeal to Northern magnanimity as indispensable for saving the Union." These were his lines of argument.

As for his persuasive methods in seeking to win adherence through these arguments, John T. Morse, Jr., editor of The American Statesmen Series, summarized a catalog of logic-chopping severities, in his introduction to the two-volume biography by Hermann von Holst, which represents the view commonly presented of Calhoun as a depersonalized intellect. It would appear from his description that Calhoun sought to operate upon an audience with arguments as tools, much as a surgeon in a sterile operating room works upon an anesthetized patient. "The rigidity of his logic," Morse wrote, "the straightforwardness with which he made the journey from his premises to his conclusions, equally without mercy and without fear, took the place of brilliant oratory and personal charm. Of course he established his premises to suit himself, and he established them with infinite care, skill, and accuracy, for he was a far-sighted logician; but, having once settled them, he allowed nothing to tempt him aside from the road of argument which led onward from his starting point; whithersoever that road led him he followed it inexorably; he was always loyal to logic."[12] Herbert L. Curry concluded his study of Calhoun's speaking by saying: "Almost every known logical

[12] H. Von Holst, *John C. Calhoun*, Boston: Houghton Mifflin, 1899, pp. v–vi.

device may be found in Calhoun's speeches," resulting in "speeches characterized by dry intellectuality."[13] Richard Hofstadter concluded his brilliant essay entitled "John C. Calhoun: The Marx of the Master Class" by charging that Calhoun tended "to see things that other men never dreamt of and to deny what was under his nose"; and thought that "His weakness was to be inhumanly schematic and logical."[14] But testimony of this sort, while impressively general, is not unanimous. Margaret L. Coit, in her prize-winning biography of Calhoun, depicts him as warm-hearted, emotional, sensitive, and all his life swept toward his goals on currents of strong feeling—as might be expected of a man whose father was a Donegal Irishman, with the first name of Patrick.

Calhoun himself fancied his role to be that of the logician and the philosopher—and to play these roles upon a plane of exalted ability. In the Senate, on February 15, 1833, in reply to Senator Clayton of Delaware, who had accused him of "metaphysical reasoning," Calhoun not only described his conception of his own method but also illustrated his penchant for interpreting an immediate question in terms of universal and immutable laws:

If by metaphysics he means that scholastic refinement which makes distinction without difference, no one can hold it in more utter contempt than I do; but if, on the contrary, he means the power of analysis and combination—that power which reduces the most complex idea into its elements, which traces causes to their first principle, and, by the power of generalization and combination, unites the whole in one harmonious system—then, so far from deserving contempt, it is the highest attribute of the human mind. It is the power which raises man above the brute—which distinguishes his faculties from mere sagacity, which he holds in common with inferior animals. It is this power which has raised the astronomer from being a mere gazer at the stars to the high intellectual eminence of a Newton or a Laplace, and astronomy itself from a mere observation of insulated facts into that noble science which displays to our admiration the system of the universe. And shall this high power of the mind, which has effected such wonders when directed to the laws which control the material world, be forever prohibited, under a senseless cry of metaphysics, from being applied to the high purposes of political science and legislation? I hold them to be subject to laws as fixed as matter itself, and to be as fit a subject for the application of the highest intellectual power. Denunciation may, indeed, fall upon the philosophical inquirer into these first principles, as it did upon Galileo and Bacon, when they first unfolded the great discoveries which have immortalized their names; but the time will come when truth will prevail in spite of prejudice and denunciation, and when

[13] In Brigance, ed., *History and Criticism, op. cit.,* II:660, 661.
[14] Hofstadter, *op. cit.,* pp. 91, 92.

politics and legislation will be considered as much a science as astonomy and chemistry.[15]

There is in this passage a great deal of what made Calhoun a great debater: a political philosopher who could establish and win adherence to a policy line for the Democrats of the South, and a rationalist who could make it appear that any attack against the sectional interest of his region was in fact a renunciation of ultimate truth. There is no slightest hint of derogation of Clayton—yet the effect is to depict the Delaware Senator as an intellectual pigmy clawing futilely amidst ideas he lacks the capacity to understand. When passages such as this were delivered in a tone of inevitable finality, disdainful of argumentative reinforcement, there were few opponents who were able or sufficiently bold to reply.

Yet the picture of Calhoun as a logician has been overdrawn. Few public men were driven more fiercely than he to fight, by any available means, for both the appearance and the substance of justice—for the dignity, the honor, the repute, the privileges which he felt were due to his State and his region. When Senator Grundy of Tennessee spoke of Jackson's "Force Bill" as a "measure of peace," in the debate on February 20, 1833, Calhoun responded with a surge of emotionalism: "Yes, such a peace as the wolf gives to the lamb—the kite to the dove! Such a peace as Russia gives to Poland, or death to its victim! A peace by extinguishing the political existence of the State, by awing her into an abandonment of the exercise of every power which constitutes her a sovereign community. It is to South Carolina a question of self-preservation; and I proclaim it that should this bill pass, and an attempt be made to enforce it, it will be resisted at every hazard—even that of death itself. Death is not the greatest calamity: there are others still more terrible to the free and the brave, among which may be placed the loss of liberty and honour."[16] One function of emotion is to give propulsive force to ideas; and all his life Calhoun recognized the value of dramatizing the manifest urgency of what he had to say. Clay, it may be recalled, in his burlesque of Calhoun, selected explicitly this factor of emotional exhortation: "This is indeed a crisis."

Calhoun's career as a public speaker commenced at Yale, when, in 1803, he was elected to the Alpha chapter of Phi Beta Kappa—a social fraternity with such high scholastic standards that it soon became an honorary. In July and then again in December of that year he took part in the debates within the fraternity on the questions: "Is government

[15] John S. Jenkins, *The Life of John Caldwell Calhoun*, Auburn: James Alden, 1858, pp. 277–278.
[16] Styron, *op. cit.*, pp. 199–200.

founded on the Social Compact?" and "Is language of Divine Origin?" During the following years as a lawyer and (from 1807 to 1817) as a legislator, he spoke frequently, gradually overcoming an initial stammer and awkwardness of manner and learning to phrase ideas not only clearly but also imaginatively. Then he served for sixteen years as Secretary of War (1817–1825) and as Vice President (1825–1832), during which time his public speaking was infrequent and largely ceremonial. His return to the Senate threw him into the midst of a forensic conflict that seldom calmed during the remainder of his life.

In the election of 1832 Jackson defeated Clay for the presidency by an Electoral College majority of 219 to 49. The campaign had been fought largely on the issue of Jackson's veto of the renewal of the charter of the Bank of the United States—which veto Jackson successfully represented as a defense of the poor against the cupidity, of the rich. Economic welfare was the issue of the day and, next to the Bank, it focused on the tariff. The tariff had been amended in July, reducing the rates in a compromise which Clay hoped would remove the issue from controversy. Calhoun resigned from the vice-presidency to accept a seat in the Senate, where it would be his role to face down the wrath of the President and the overwhelming majority who supported the dominance of federal law. South Carolina was inflamed, and in November, after Jackson's election, Calhoun called a Nullification Convention at Charleston and issued a proclamation declaring that the tariff would be inoperative in the state after February 1, 1833. Jackson announced that "If a single drop of blood is shed in defiance of the laws of the United States I will hang the first man I lay hands on engaged in such treasonable conduct upon the first tree I can reach."[17] Few doubted that he meant Calhoun. When Calhoun arrived in Washington on January 4 and took his seat in the Senate, the galleries thronged with people expecting a dramatic confrontation. A friend hurried to Calhoun's side to warn him he would be assassinated; another told him he was to be arrested. In the talk of Washington Calhoun was likened to Benedict Arnold and Aaron Burr.

For ten days Calhoun sat quietly, letting the tension mount. Then he introduced a series of resolutions asserting the basic sovereignty of the States. These were remanded to committee without debate. The next scene in the drama opened February 12, when Clay introduced a new tariff bill designed to side-step the impasse by eliminating the tariffs South Carolina had threatened to nullify. Meanwhile, Congressman Robert Letcher of Tennessee, a friend of both Jackson and Calhoun, burst into Calhoun's quarters at midnight, arousing him from bed to say

[17] Amos Kendall, Autobiography, ed. William Stickney, Boston: Lee and Shepard, 1872, p. 631.

he had just come from the White House, where Old Hickory had exclaimed that if South Carolina's resistance continued, "he would try Calhoun for treason, and if convicted, would hang him as high as Haman."[18]

This was the situation when, on February 16, Calhoun arose in the Senate to deliver a carefully staged speech.[19] First he pushed away all the chairs from the space between the Senate chamber and the lobby, providing a space which he used during his speech for rapid pacing back and forth. Then he briefly hurried through a history of tariff legislation, which, he said, had been initiated to pay the national debt, but which was soon politically "so arranged as to be, in fact, bounties on the one side and taxation on the other."[20] In consequence, South Carolina had been "compelled to choose between absolute acquiescence in a ruinous system of oppression, or a resort to her reserved powers." He went on to state the heart of the South Carolina Doctrine: that "the right of resistance to the unconstitutional acts of Congress belongs to the State." Drawing toward his conclusion, he declared, "Disguise it as you may, the controversy is one between power and liberty." And he went on to assert that the circumstances of the South "are almost identically the same" as those which led the Colonies to revolt against Great Britain.

The next day, still holding the floor, Calhoun resumed: "the great question at issue is, whether ours is a federal or a consolidated system of government." He knew, he said, that in the popular view "the very beau ideal of a perfect government is the government of a majority." But "no government of the kind . . . has ever endured for a single generation." Nor should it; for "The view which considers the community as an unit, and all its parts as having a similar interest, is radically erroneous." He next argued from the analogy of a small community, wherein the less numerous group must have a right of self-protection against the more numerous. Then, for the first time, his feelings hurried him into extremism. "The constitution has gradually become a dead letter," he charged. There has been a "growth of faction, corruption, anarchy, and, if not despotism itself, its near approach." The federal government has become "a mere instrument of taking money from one portion of the community, to be given to another." This was a "system of plunder" which could only be "opposed by power." At this point, having drawn close to the brink of rebellion, he drew back. What he sought, he said, was the "ascendancy of the constitution." This could only be accom-

[18] Coit., *op. cit.*, p. 245.
[19] Described *ibid.*, based on accounts in the *United States Telegraph*, Washington, Feb. 15 and 16, 1833. The paper was edited by Calhoun's friend, Duff Green.
[20] The text of this and Calhoun's other extant speeches are in *Works of John C. Calhoun*, ed. Richard K. Crallé, Six Vols., New York: Appleton, 1853–1855.

plished by a restoration of the ability of the States to protect the powers which were reserved to them. The "tendency to conflict," he pointed out, clearly was "between the southern and other sections." He repeated a theme from his address of the preceding day—that the conflict was between "power and liberty," and called for a guaranteed balance of power between the North and the South. Then, abruptly, without bothering to epitomize his reasoning in a conclusion, he called the opponents of his ideas "political prostitutes," and sat down.

Webster, in reply, denounced the "original error" of describing the Constitution as "nothing but a compact between sovereign States." He ridiculed Calhoun's account of how the States "acceded" to the Constitution, pointing out that the "natural converse of accession is secession." The States, Webster, pointed out, did not accede to the Constitution; they ratified it. "The language actually employed," he went on, "is, adopt, ratify, ordain, establish." The right of each State to adjudge which federal laws it would obey "strikes a deadly blow at the vital principle of the whole Union." Then Webster struck at Calhoun the blow which hurt most:

> Does not the gentleman perceive, Sir, how his argument against majorities might here be retorted upon him? Does he not see how cogently he might be asked, whether it be the character of nullification to practice what it preaches? Look to South Carolina, at the present moment. How far are the rights of minorities there respected? I confess, Sir, I have not known, in peaceable times, the power of the majority carried with a higher hand, or upheld with more relentless disregard of the rights, feelings, and principles of the minority . . .[21]

The aged and now nearly insane John Randolph, who favored an independent Southern Confederacy embracing all the area south of Ohio, and including Cuba, listened to the debate from the galleries and believed Calhoun had won. "Webster is dead!" he exclaimed. "I saw him dying an hour ago."[22] The general opinion was quite to the contrary. "A total failure" is what the Richmond *Enquirer* called Calhoun's speech.[23] President Jackson rejoiced: "Many people believe Calhoun to be demented . . . . Webster handled him like a child." Webster himself wrote to a friend: "He cannot, I am convinced, make a coherent . . . argumentative speech."

Ten days later Calhoun made another speech in which he defended the "compact theory" of the Constitution with arguments drawn primarily from his interpretations of some of Webster's own contentions. Then the Senate turned its attention to Clay's compromise tariff bills,

[21] *Writings and Speeches of Webster, op. cit.,* VI:221.
[22] Styron, *op. cit.,* p. 199.
[23] Coit, *op. cit.,* p. 252 for this and following two quotations.

and Calhoun gratefully voted for them. The Senate adjourned on March 3, and Calhoun hastened to Columbia, South Carolina, where the Nullification Convention was to reassemble on March 11. The journey lasted for eight days, during which Calhoun had to sit on his luggage, with no stops night or day except for hasty gulps of food while horses were being changed. His health already bad, he arrived in Columbia bone-weary, with clothes mud-spattered, his face white and drawn, and did not even stop to wash up, but dashed to the Convention hall. When he arrived, a young radical, Robert Barnwell Rhett, was on the rostrum shouting for secession and the establishment of a Southern Confederacy. Calhoun did not attempt to make a speech, but slowly, painfully, made his way from one delegate to another, pleading for patience and sanity. The tariff revisions, he pointed out, had removed the very complaints against which they were raging. The delegates listened and the next day repealed the Nullification Act and adjourned. Calhoun went home, but not to rest. "The struggle . . ." he wrote, "has only just commenced."[24]

The next years were deeply troubled not only for Calhoun but for the American body politic. Abolitionism commenced an organized assault upon the public conscience. Jackson completed his second term and was succeeded by the able but not popular Martin Van Buren. The Panic of 1837 caused nationwide fear and distress. That fall Van Buren called a special session of Congress to request a law that would substitute a Sub-Treasury system for the United States Bank and its branches. Even though this seemed a step toward the "consolidation" of federal power, Calhoun believed it to be wise and both spoke and voted for it. His support is what made the difference and resulted in adoption of the new law—though he exaggerated more than a bit in a letter to his daughter, when he wrote: "I held the fate of the country, by the confession of all, in my hand, and had to determine in what direction I should turn events hereafter."[25]

Henry Clay was both outraged and enraged. He had had Van Buren reeling and, with the votes of Calhoun's followers, could have destroyed the effectiveness of his administration. During January and February, 1838, Clay time after time attacked Calhoun with unleashed fury. To him the States rights advocate had proved a "turncoat." Calhoun's efforts to explain his position Clay dismissed as "metaphysical subtleties," illustrative of "too much genius and too little commonsense." Calhoun held his peace until March 10, when he made a masterful rejoinder, calmly dignified and cuttingly sarcastic. With careful precision he reviewed his own legislative history on the Bank issue to show he had

[24] *Ibid.*, pp. 256–258.
[25] *Ibid.*, p. 338.

been consistent. As for the charge that his mind was characterized by "powers of analysis and generalization," he could not reply in kind, for "The absence of these higher qualities is conspicuous throughout the whole course of the Senator's public life." Clay retorted with a scathing reminder that his compromise tariff bill of 1833 had saved Calhoun from an impossible situation. "Calhoun bridled," as his biographer described the situation. "He shot Clay a look of hatred, so defiant, so wild, that to one observer, writing years afterward, it seemed as vivid as yesterday." Then Calhoun declared that the tariff bills were "necessary to save the Senator politically. Events had placed him flat on his back." In effect, Calhoun claimed, Clay's sponsorship of the tariff compromise was a political expedient for his own benefit, which was given importance by the situation Calhoun had created in South Carolina. "I was his master," Calhoun said coldly. "I repeat it, Sir, I was his master . . . . He went to my school. He learned from me."

Clay leaped from his seat and lunged toward Calhoun, while members fell back out of his way. Then he drew back again a pace from the gaunt and rigid figure of the South Carolinian and shook his finger under his nose. "He, my master!" Clay exclaimed, again stepping backward. "He, my master!" Still pointing, he drew further back, then flung his arms down in a gesture of contempt. "He, my master! Sir, I would not own him as a slave!"[26]

For the next decade, Calhoun's participation in the national debates was considerably reduced. During a brief term as Secretary of State, he connived to get Texas admitted to the Union. Then, back in the Senate in 1846, he fought desperately to prevent war with Mexico. There must be no war, he urged, over a "mere border brawl." No war, he argued, could be declared—as this one had been—by the President; such a power rested solely with the Congress. As for President Polk's reasons for the war, set forth in his message to the Congress: "Sooner than vote for that lying preamble, I would plunge a dagger through my heart." Calhoun's reasons for opposing the war were simple. Texas, already in the Union, was good slave territory. Any further land that might be taken from Mexico would be unfit for slavery—yet as a matter of principle the South could never admit to its being free. The only way to avoid a dangerous and damaging sectional struggle was to avoid acquiring additional southwestern lands. The introduction into the Senate of the Wilmot Proviso, explicitly barring slavery from the territories taken from Mexico, justified his fears. Once again he returned to the forensic battle, not because he wished to but because he must. The North must be prevented from gaining a preponderance of political power. "The day

[26] *Ibid.*, pp. 340–341.

the balance between the two sections is destroyed," he told the Senate on February 19, 1847, "is a day . . . not far removed from revolution, anarchy, and Civil War."[27]

Now Calhoun found himself pushed to the necessity of defending slavery as a "positive good." A quarter of a century earlier he had stood on the ground that "I am no panegyrist of slavery. It is an unnatural state, a dark cloud which obscures half the lustre of our free institutions. But . . . would it be fair, would it be manly, would it be generous, would it be just, to offer contumely and contempt to the unfortunate man who wears a cancer in his bosom because he will not submit to cautery at the hazard of his existence?"[28] By 1836, during the initial excitement over the presentation of petitions on slavery in the House of Representatives, Calhoun "trembled, not for the South, but for the Union" as he saw "the black question, like a portentous cloud . . . gathering and darkening"—the trouble, of course, being caused not by the inherent injustice of the slave system but by "incendiaries and agitators."[29] And by 1849 he was aligned with the extremists in arguing that "the two races cannot live together in peace, or harmony, or to their mutual advantage, except in their present relation." He was insisting that a slavocracy is the most "stable basis for free institutions." He was ridiculing Thomas Jefferson's "false view" that men unqualified to exercise freedom were "fully entitled" to it. He was rejecting the claim of the Declaration of Independence that "All men are created free and equal." "Men are not born," said Calhoun. "Infants are born . . . . While infants they are incapable of freedom." He dug himself deeper and deeper into the dilemma that he must renounce the very principles upon which the Union was based in his effort to prevent it from breaking apart.

As the forces gathered in the Senate for the great debate on the compromise measures of 1850, personalities became almost as significant as principles. Daniel Webster made a futile effort to salve the bitter feud between Missouri's Thomas Hart Benton and Calhoun. Benton, however, would have none of it. "Webster," he said, "don't you mention that to me . . . . I won't be reconciled to Calhoun—I won't, Sir . . . . I won't have anything to do with him . . . . My mind is made up, Sir . . . . Anybody else, but not Calhoun. He is a humbug, and I won't do it, Sir."[30] The divisive issues were both too sharp and too basic to admit of genial reconciliation. Calhoun himself uttered very similar sentiments in his last remarks in the Senate, in March, 1850. His final great argu-

[27] *Works of Calhoun, op. cit.,* IV:343.
[28] Styron, *op. cit.,* p. 120 [1825].
[29] Cited by Chambers, *Old Bullion Benton, op. cit.,* p. 214.
[30] Coit, *op. cit.,* p. 498.

ment in behalf of the principle of concurrent majorities had been read for him by Senator James Mason, of Virginia, and Calhoun had dragged himself back to his quarters and to his bed. Then he heard that the fiery young Whig from Mississippi, Samuel A. Foote, was attacking him and painfully he made his way back to the Senate chamber, assisted to his seat by two Senators. For more than an hour he listened to Foote's harangue, while other Senators whispered "Shame! Shame!" in an effort to quiet the Mississippian. Then Calhoun heard the term "Disunionist" applied to himself, and with aching slowness he struggled to his feet.

"I am not," he said simply. Then he went on: "I will not be on good terms with those who wish to cut my throat. The honorable Senator [Seward] from New York justifies Northern treachery. I am not the man to hold social intercourse with such as these." Foote agreed that Calhoun should not go that far in an effort at reconciliation. "I recognize them as Senators," Calhoun resumed, "say good morning and shake hands with them, but that is the extent of my intercourse with those who I think are endangering the Union."[31]

This word, *Union*, was the last he was to utter in the Senate chamber. On the morning of Sunday, March 31, he died, making one final effort to speak. His last thoughts were for the nation and the troubles that beset it. From either the clarity or the cloudiness of approaching death, whichever it may have been, he said shortly before the end to his son: "If I had my health and my strength to give one hour in the Senate, I could do more for my country than at any previous time in my life."[32] Both Clay and Webster joined the many Senators who pronounced eulogies on Calhoun. Benton refused to do so. But at the close of the service in the Senate chamber, Benton claimed the last word: "He is not dead, Sir; he is not dead. There may be no vitality in his body. But there's plenty in his doctrines."[33] The principle of *nullification*, a century later to be renamed *interposition*, could not so easily be laid to rest.

Henry Clay: Gamecock of the West

HENRY CLAY was Abraham Lincoln's "beau ideal of a statesman."[1] To John C. Calhoun he seemed in his latter years "a bad man, an im-

[31] *Ibid.*, pp. 501–502. Styron, *op. cit.*, pp. 353–354, got the wrong Foote in his mouth.
[32] Quoted by James Hammond in his eulogy of Calhoun, Coit, *op. cit.*, p. 509.
[33] Oliver Dyer, *Great Senators of the United States*, New York: R. Bonner's Sons, 1889, p. 213.
[1] In 1858, in Southern Illinois, where Clay's memory was held in affectionate regard, Lincoln made the comment during his debates with Douglas. Sandburg, *Lincoln: The Prairie Years*, *op. cit.*, p. 407.

postor, a creator of wicked schemes. I wouldn't speak to him, but by God! I love him."[2] The Whig Party, which he founded, twice refused him the presidential nomination and three other times failed to get him elected to the presidency. His name was so definitely associated with most of the important legislation enacted during the forty years of his public life that, as A. C. McLaughlin wrote: "The recognition of the South American republics, the tariff, the bank, the public lands, the distribution of the surplus revenue, the slavery question in all its phases, expansion, and the Mexican War [and certainly the War of 1812] can scarce be studied better than in the story of his life."[3] No man yearned more than did Henry Clay to plow his name and his fame into the history of his nation. Although he spoke often and considered oratory "the art of all arts," he insisted that he had "neither time, taste, nor, perhaps, talents"[4] for mere ceremonial speaking; and Lincoln, in his eulogy on Clay, found that "He never spoke merely to be heard. He never delivered a Fourth-of-July oration, or a eulogy on an occasion like this."[5] And yet, for all his efforts and contributions, to the majority of critics he seemed to have missed greatness.

V. L. Parrington considered him "a brilliant opportunist . . . modifying his convictions with his environment."[6] The historian John T. Morse, Jr., concluded that Clay "contented himself always with steering the ship of state from day to day; he undertook to lay out no long voyage, no definite course in any direction."[7] Carl Schurz thought him "a very strong leader, but "not a safe guide," principally because of his "lack of accurate knowledge and studious thought."[8] Ernest Wrage conceded that "To men who live by fixed principles, Clay's policies smack of shifting, temporizing, and opportunism."[9]

Clay himself seemed sometimes to lend explicit credence to such criticisms. "Of all men upon earth am I the least attached to the productions of my own mind," he once told the Senate. "No man upon earth is more ready than I am to surrender anything which I have proposed and to accept in lieu of it anything which is better."[10] In his speech of April 8, 1850, near the end of his life, he said: "I go for honorable compromise whenever it can be made. Life itself is but a compromise between death and life, the struggle continuing throughout

[2] Joseph M. Rogers, *The True Henry Clay*, Philadelphia: Lippincott, 1905, p. 250.
[3] *Cambridge History of American Literature*, New York: Macmillan, 1918, II:87.
[4] Ernest J. Wrage, "Henry Clay," in Brigance, ed., *History and Criticism, op. cit.*, II:620.
[5] *The Collected Works of Abraham Lincoln*, ed. Ray P. Basler, New Brunswick, N. J.: Rutgers University Press, 1953, II:126.
[6] Parrington, *op. cit.*, II:142–143.
[7] Carl Schurz, *Henry Clay*, ed. John Morse, Boston: Houghton Mifflin, 1915, p. x.
[8] *Ibid.*, I:409.
[9] Wrage, *op. cit.*, II:623.
[10] *Life and Speeches of Henry Clay*, ed. D. Mallory, Hartford: S. Andrus, 1854, II:646.

our whole existence, until the great destroyer finally triumphs. All legislation, all government, all society is founded upon the principle of mutual concession, politeness, comity, courtesy; upon these everything is based. I bow to you today because you bow to me. Let him who elevates himself above humanity, above its weaknesses, its infirmities, its wants, its necessities, say, if he pleases, I never will compromise, but let no one who is not above the frailties of our common nature disdain compromise."[11]

As is not unusual among men, Clay saw himself in a light more favorable than that in which he often appeared to others. In a letter written during the presidential campaign of 1844, he said: "If any one desires to know the leading and paramount object of my public life, the preservation of this Union will furnish him the key."[12] Eleven years earlier, urging his bill to reduce the tariff and thereby side-step the impasse confronted by Calhoun and Jackson upon nullification, Clay said: "While we would vindicate the federal government, we are for peace, if possible, the Union and liberty. We want no war, above all, no civil war, no family strife. We want to see no sacked cities, no desolated fields, no smoking ruins, no streams of American blood shed by American arms." Then, in concluding his speech, Clay shook with emotion:

> I have been accused of ambition in presenting this measure. Ambition! Inordinate ambition! If I had thought of myself only, I should have never brought it forward. I know well the perils to which I expose myself; the risk of alienating grateful and valued friends, with but little prospect of making new ones . . . . Ambition! If I had listened to its soft and seducing whispers; if I had yielded myself to the dictates of a cold, calculating, and prudential policy, I would have stood still and unmoved. I might even have silently gazed upon the raging storm, enjoyed its loudest thunders, and left those who are charged with the care of the vessel of State, to conduct it as they could.

The political analysis was perfectly sound. Clay was far too shrewd in the ways of politics not to have realized that if Jackson had dispatched troops into South Carolina, the likelihood was that one or both of his chief political foes would have been driven from public life. His safest position, by any reckoning, was one of silent neutralism. Yet he had plunged directly into the center of the fray, attempting to establish an honorable basis of retreat for both his enemies. This much did he do in devotion to the Union.

Clay surveyed the House, while his tall, thin frame drew to its full

---

[11] *The Works of Henry Clay*, ed. Calvin Colton, New York: Henry Club Pub. Co., 1897, VI:412.
[12] Schurz, *op. cit.*, II:260.

height and his eyes flashed. His voice was often praised for its power to mirror every shade of feeling; now it dripped scorn:

> I have been hitherto often unjustly accused of ambition. Low, grovel-ling souls, who are utterly incapable of elevating themselves to the higher and nobler duties of pure patriotism—beings who, forever keeping their own selfish aims in view, decide all public measures by their presumed influence or their aggrandisement—judge me by the venal rule which they prescribe to themselves. I have given to the winds those false accusations, as I consign that which now impeaches my motives. I have no desire of office, not even the highest.

Swept on by the torrent of his feelings, Clay had gone too far. His quick mind must indeed have sensed the blunder into which he had betrayed himself; but with typical daring, he determined to magnify the impres-sion of the moment—to get out of the trap later by any means he might. After all, he had just been soundly defeated for the presidency for the second time; and it could even be good tactics to declare he no longer wanted it. In any event, he had committed himself and might as well make the most of it. He went on:

> The most exalted [office] is but a prison, in which the incarcerated incumbent daily receives his cold, heartless visitors, marks his weary hours, and is cut off from the practical enjoyment of all the blessings of genuine freedom. I am no candidate for any office in the gift of the people of these States, united or separated. I never wish, never expect to be. Pass this bill, tranquillize the country, restore confidence and affection in the Union, and I am willing to go home to Ashland and renounce public service forever. I shall there find in its groves, under its shades, on its lawns, amid my flocks and herds, in the bosom of my family, sincerity and truth, attachment and fidelity, and gratitude, which I have not always found in the walks of public life. Yes, I have ambition; but it is the ambition of being the humble instrument in the hands of Providence to reconcile a divided people; once more to revive concord and harmony in a distracted land—the pleasing ambition of contemplat-ing the glorious spectacle of a free, united, prosperous, and fraternal people![13]

His bill was passed; and, as he hoped, the members and the public refrained from taking seriously his expressed wish for retirement. From his first public appearance in Lexington, in 1798 (when he climbed on a wagon to mesmerize a vast outdoor throng with a torrential denuncia-tion of the Alien and Sedition Acts), until his last outpouring of elo-quence, in the 1850 debates (as when he retorted to Robert Barnwell Rhett's defiant threat of secession: "Sir, I denied the doctrine twenty

[13] *Works of Clay*, ed. Colton, op. cit., VII:566–567.

years ago. I deny it now. I will die denying it. There is no such principle."), Clay cast a spell of fascination upon his listeners. When a Jacksonian Democrat, who admitted to being no more than an agent for his masters, was reproved for being absent from the House except when votes were being taken, he replied: "I am willing to do my duty when I can, but I'm d—d if I can listen to Henry Clay speak and believe he is wrong."[14]

An intimate picture of the other Clay, the private man who seldom emerged into public view, was given by Henry A. Wise, after the 1840 Whig Convention in Harrisburg gave the nomination to Harrison rather than to Clay. The Clay majority had been outmaneuvered through adoption of a rule requiring unit-voting by States, rather than individual votes by each delegate. Clay had confidently counted upon being the standardbearer, in a year when a Whig victory was inevitable; and when a messenger brought news of the rule to the hotel room where he sat with his cronies, the bitterness of Clay's disappointment broke through his customary self-possession. "Such an exhibition we never witnessed before," Wise wrote, "and we pray never again to witness such an ebullition of passion, such a storm of desperation and curses. He rose from his chair, and walking backwards and forwards rapidly, lifting his feet like a horse string-halted in both legs, stamped his foot upon the floor, exclaiming, 'My friends are not worth the powder and shot it would take to kill them.' He mentioned the names of several, invoking upon them the most horrid imprecations, and then, turning to us, approached rapidly and stopped before us, with violent gestures and loud voice said, 'If there were two Henry Clays, one of them would make the other President of the United States.' "[15]

Henry Clay was born in Hanover County, Virginia, on April 12, 1777, where he enjoyed the enormous advantages of growing up in the homeland of Patrick Henry, of serving as an amanuensis for George Wythe, and of studying law under Robert Brooke. In this environment, "Oratory was esteemed the first attribute of superior minds, and was assiduously cultivated."[16] Clay set out to develop his own speaking ability—perhaps taking as his model the great Patrick Henry, whom he twice heard and ardently admired. He undertook the regular practice of reading aloud and of speaking. "These off-hand efforts were sometimes made

---

[14] Rogers, *op. cit.*, p. 286.
[15] Henry A. Wise, *Seven Decades of the Union*, Philadelphia: Lippincott, 1881, p. 171.
[16] W. H. Sparks, *Memories of Fifty Years*, Philadelphia, 1870, p. 22, quoted by Wrage, *op. cit.*, II:606. W. J. Cash, *The Mind of the South*, New York: Doubleday, Anchor Book, 1954, pp. 63–64, makes the same point. Clay himself, in a letter to Ninian Edwards, July 9, 1800, says that in Richmond he lived in an atmosphere of oratory, electioneering, speech-making, and legal debating. Mayo, *Henry Clay, op. cit.*, p. 22.

in a cornfield; at others in the forest; and not infrequently in some distant barn, with the horse and ox for my only auditors."[17] He also joined the Richmond debating society, where he sharpened his wits in contests with the young lawyer-politicians of the city. When he was ready to engage in the practice of law, he decided to settle in Lexington, Kentucky—no wild frontier town, but a flourishing city of 1600, with a college and library, proudly calling itself "The Philadelphia of Kentucky," and the "Athens of the West."[18] It was also a scene of such oratorical enthusiasm and emulation that Ben Hardin advised Daniel Webster: "Sir, if you will come and settle in Kentucky, and learn our mode of speaking, you will be an orator equal to any Greece or Rome ever produced"—to which Webster much later replied: "Would to God I had taken your advice."[19]

Land cases abounded, and so did trials indicting or defending violence. Money was to be made at the law, and Henry Clay rapidly became one of the best and best paid among the brilliant lawyers in the State. He joined the Junto debating club and shortly made a name for himself as a dazzling star amidst a large group of eloquent speakers. His future was extremely promising. Then, at twenty one, when he had been in Lexington scarcely a month, he deliberately risked his career by selecting as an antagonist the able and popular leader of Kentucky democracy, John Breckinridge. And he challenged him on the topic of all topics a young newcomer in Kentucky would find most difficult: an attack against slavery. Demanding a convention to revise Kentucky's Constitution specifically to outlaw slavery, Clay won his fight and the Convention was held. However, the cause of gradual emancipation for which Clay fought was lost and the State he was thenceforth to represent committed itself to the slavocracy. Clay himself became a slaveowner. But almost three decades later, speaking to the American Colonizing Society, on January 20, 1827, he expressed the view that he held consistently all his life:

> If I could be instrumental in eradicating this deepest stain from the character of our country, and removing all cause of reproach on account of it, by foreign nations—if I could only be instrumental in ridding of this foul blot that revered State that gave me birth, or that not less beloved State which kindly adopted me as her son, I would not exchange the proud satisfaction which I should enjoy for the honor of all the triumphs ever decreed to the most successful conqueror.[20]

[17] Wrage, *op. cit.*, II:607.
[18] Mayo, *op. cit.*, pp. 54–60.
[19] Lucius P. Little, *Ben Hardin: His Times and Contemporaries*, Louisville, 1887, p. 355.
[20] *Works of Clay*, ed. Colton, *op. cit.*, III:60ff.

Abolitionism, however, he despised, as a breeder of war; and the best solution he could think of was to protect slavery where it existed but to prevent its spread.

As a lawyer Clay proved beyond question that forensic ability may be a larger determining factor than justice in court cases.[21] Under Kentucky law, two laymen sat with the judge on the bench, thus insuring by deliberate design that neither legal technicalities nor legalistic evidence would have as much effect as skillful pleading. Clay defended a wide assortment of rascals; but none of his clients was ever hanged. In one of his famous cases, a Mrs. Doshey Phelps, with careful premeditation, shot her husband's sister to death—but Clay got her off with five years imprisonment on the then completely novel plea of "temporary delirium." In another, defending Abner Willis for what Mayo called "a peculiarly cold-blooded murder," Clay managed to get a split jury; then, when the prosecuting attorney moved for a new trial, Clay pretended to be outraged that his client's life should twice be placed in jeopardy for the same crime. After haranguing the bench to this effect with no success, Clay haughtily gathered his papers and strode from the courtroom, as though he were washing his hands of such flagrant injustice. The worried judge sent a messenger to bring Clay back, listened again to his argument, then set Willis free. On another occasion, Clay was tricked into defending a man who had stolen a bee-gum, or bee hive, by being assured the accused had witnesses establishing an alibi for him. At the trial there were no witnesses and the enraged Clay heard the judge hand down a verdict of guilty. His client seized him by the coat and cried loudly, "Mr. Clay! Mr. Clay! we've lost our case!" And Clay replied, just as loudly, "Yes, but by God, we've got our bee-gum!"[22] While serving briefly as prosecuting attorney, Clay secured the death penalty for a Negro slave of good repute who, in self-defense, killed his brutal overseer. The slave was hanged. Clay abruptly resigned and never again served as a criminal prosecutor.

Clay was said sometimes to appear in court wholly unprepared and to plan the defense while listening to the prosecutor's case. More typically, he worked hard, as he had to in dealing with the complicated land cases. But always he was alert to take maximum advantage of any opportunity his quick mind might perceive. While questioning one hostile witness about the financial dependability of his client, the witness began hesitantly, "He is *slow* . . . " "But *sure!*" Clay swiftly interjected. "Yes, Sir, slow and sure," the witness agreed, glad to be relieved of further ques-

---

[21] Mayo, *op. cit.*, Chapter III, "A Frontier Lawyer," pp. 87–114.
[22] *Ibid.*, pp. 107–108.

tioning.[23] Another time, as the trial was about to start, Clay demanded to be shown the warrant of arrest, and stood before the bench studying it for some time. Then he swung upon his client and said, "Go home, Sir." The man hesitated and Clay shouted sternly: "Go home!"; whereupon the accused ran from the courtroom, while neither the judge nor the sheriff ventured to interfere.[24] Amos Kendall, tutor to the Clay children, may have had Clay's jury speeches in mind when he presented as his formula for oratorical success the advice: "Drink whiskey and talk loud with the fullest confidence." Once a deafened farmer observed Clay presenting an address to the jury, then left the courtroom in an ecstasy of appreciative excitement. "I couldn't hear a word he said," the old man confessed; "but Lord, didn't he make the motions!" As a matter of fact, all his life Clay was to be praised again and again, often by critics of great discernment, for the refined expressiveness of his gestures and features.[25]

His quickness of wit and sure adaptation to his listeners were well illustrated in the Congressional election of 1816. Clay was by then already famous, as a result of his service in the State Legislature, the U.S. Senate, and the House of Representatives, where he was Speaker and had masterminded the plunge into the War of 1812. Not even his fame, however, was a sufficient shield for the grievous sin committed by the Congress in raising the pay of its members from $6 per day to $1500 for each session. The nation was scandalized and few members of the House won re-election. Clay, on the stump, asked his frontier listeners if they would throw away a good rifle because it misfired once. Amid the cries of "No, no, of course not," Clay calmly asked: "Have I ever flashed except on the Compensation bill?" He squeaked back in by a small majority.[26]

If Clay were no more than clever, to whatever exalted degree, he would be remembered, if at all, only as an exemplar of rhetorical skill. Without mitigating his faults, he was far more than this. He was one of the greatest Speakers the House has ever had[27]—and unlike other Speakers, he entered freely and often in the debates, for in that period the House did much of its business under the rules of the Committee of the Whole, with some other member in the chair. Besides sponsoring the War of 1812, Clay spoke solidly and with effect, through several

[23] *Ibid.*, p. 107.
[24] *Ibid.*, p. 108.
[25] Wrage, *op. cit.*, II:633.
[26] Rogers, *op. cit.*, p. 97.
[27] Neil MacNeil, *Forge of Democracy: The House of Representatives*, New York: David McKay, 1963, pp. 67–69 and *passim.*

decades, in support of the Bank of the United States, for tariff measures, and for a system of public works. He ably supported the new republics in Latin America and tried to win American support for the revolution in Greece. He devised compromise measures which postponed a collision between North and South in the controversy over Missouri, in the impasse created by South Carolina's Ordinance of Nullification, and in the debate on the disposition of the territories taken from Mexico. Among his greatest speeches are included his address on the Seminole War, on January 17, 1819; his address on American Industry, March 30 and 31, 1824; his address at Lexington, on the Mexican War, November 13, 1847; and the introductory defense of his omnibus bill in the Senate, February 6 and 7, 1850.

The Congressional debate on the Seminole War, lasting for three weeks in the House of Representatives, during January and February, 1819, and in which thirty one of the most outstanding members participated, merits more analysis than present space permits.[28] The circumstances are among the most interesting in our history. The question involved Spanish ownership of Florida, a situation which was represented to the public as a pistol pointed at the heart of the American republic; the problem of runaway, and vengeful, slaves; the policies and practice for dealing with the frontier Indians; and the burgeoning ambitions of a new generation of politicians and a new alignment of political parties.

In 1786 Thomas Jefferson had sought to crystallize into a national policy the sentiments that had guided William Penn in dealing with the Indians, when he wrote: "It may be regarded as certain that not a foot of land will ever be taken from the Indians without their consent. The sacredness of their rights is felt by all thinking persons in America as much as in Europe." The Indians in Florida were refugees from the Creek Nation, called Seminoles, a word that meant strangers or isolates. Also in Florida there dwelt in 1816 some 800 escaped Negro slaves, who held a well-armed English fort that had been abandoned after the War of 1812. In the summer of 1816 they captured an American sailor, tarred him, and burned him alive. In revenge, an American convoy attacked the fort and blew it up, killing the 344 inhabitants. Meanwhile, in skirmishes across the Florida-Georgia border, seven Americans and ten Seminoles were slain. The Spanish rulers in Florida were far too weak to enforce order. In Washington a lackadaisical negotiation was proceeding concerning the eventual transfer of Florida from Spain to the United States. At this juncture, President Monroe ordered General Andrew

[28] The circumstances are vividly portrayed by George Dangerfield, *The Era of Good Feelings, op. cit.,* pp. 122–136.

Jackson into Florida to chastise the offenders and prevent a recurrence of attacks against Americans. In a series of quick victories he defeated the Indians and Negroes, seized the Spanish posts at St. Marks, Pensacola, and Fort Barancas, and summarily hanged two Indian chiefs and two British traders who were living with them.

Following Jackson's triumphant return to American territory on May 30, public opinion hailed him for a heroic and patriotic deed little less notable than his 1815 victory at New Orleans. But official Washington waited nervously till it became evident that neither England nor Spain was inclined to demand redress for the indignities to their subjects and sovereignty. Very gingerly the House took cognizance of the affair through the medium of a motion to "disapprove the proceedings" in the hanging of the traders, Arbuthnot and Ambrister.

Clay, when he rose to open the debate, had to find some way of censoring Jackson's actions without offending the public which hailed him a hero. He had to review the circumstances without fanning the fuel of British and Spanish resentment, and without appearing to favor the cause of these foreign powers over that of his own official representatives. And he had to avoid the political pitfall of seeming to support President Monroe (whose instructions Jackson had exceeded), since he meant to develop a political party of his own in opposition to the Republicans. Aiming toward this last goal, he opened with an air of condescending kindness: "Rather than throw obstructions in the way of the President, I would precede him, and pick out those, if I could, which might jostle him in his progress; I would sympathize with him in his embarrassments, and commiserate with him in his misfortunes."[29] Here was safe ground upon which to champion Monroe against Jackson!

In dealing with General Jackson, Clay was carefully circumspect. He first pointed out that "no other censure is proposed against general Jackson himself, than what is merely consequential. His name even does not appear in any of the resolutions." He then argued at some length that the Indian forays against our people were in simple retaliation for the unjust and harsh treaty of Fort Jackson which had earlier been forced upon them—after which he added, "I am far from attributing to general Jackson any other than the very slight degree of blame that attaches to him as the negotiator of the treaty . . ." After this he excoriated Jackson (without using his name) for having first trapped the Indian chiefs by hoisting an English flag over a ship, to which the Indians went seeking refuge; and then for having them summarily hanged. There is no use, Clay said, to justify such an act with tales "about the tomahawk and scalping knife; about Indian enormities, and foreign miscreants and

[29] Rogers, op. cit., pp. 263–265.

incendiaries. I, too, hate them; from my very soul I abominate them. But I love my country, and its constitution; I love liberty and safety, and fear military despotism more, even, than I hate these monsters." Commenting then upon the hanging of the two Englishmen, Clay declared that the "evidence would show, particularly in the case of Arbuthnot, that the whole amount of his crime consisted in his trading, without the boundaries of the United States, with the Seminole Indians, in the accustomed commodities which form the subject of Indian trade." But even if the two men were guilty of having aided the Indians in their depredations against the Georgia settlers, Clay said, "every page of history, in all times, and the recollection of every member" provide evidence that alien enemies are not to be hanged without due trial. The precedents of history were all against such an action. "Yes, although Napoleon had desolated half Europe; although there was scarcely a power, however humble, that escaped the mighty grasp of his ambition; although in the course of his splendid career, he is charged with having committed the greatest atrocities, disgraceful to himself and to human nature, yet even his life has been spared." Clay then laid down a principle few of his auditors could fail to accept: "No man can be executed in this free country without two things being shown—first, that the law condemns him to death; and, secondly, that his death is pronounced by that tribunal which is authorized by the law to try him."

Clay continued with a detailed analysis of the events in Florida, to show the illegality and inhumanity of Jackson's course of action. He said Monroe had taken the right course in returning promptly to Spain the forts Jackson had seized. Then he asked how the republics of former years had lost their liberties. "If a Roman citizen had been asked, if he did not fear that the conqueror of Gaul might establish a throne upon the ruins of public liberty, he would have instantly repelled the unjust insinuation. Yet . . . Caesar passed the Rubicon . . ." "Beware how you give a fatal sanction," Clay warned, "in this infant period of our republic, scarcely yet two score years old, to military insubordination."[30] Clay won the debate but created enmities among the Jacksonians that repeatedly barred him from the presidency.

When Clay spoke to the House on March 30 and 31, 1824, choosing to discuss the growth and significance of American industry, in justification of his tariff measures, he was an active candidate for election that Fall to the presidency. He chose to occupy high ground—to demonstrate the thorough knowledge of the economy which he did possess, to show his comprehensive appreciation of the inter-relationship of agriculture, commerce, and industry, and to manifest a statesmanlike avoidance of

[30] *Works of Clay*, ed. Colton, *op. cit.*, III:60.

personalities. If the speech is not typical of Clay's usual style, it may be because its results did not encourage his continuance of this mode of discussion. In the November election he came in third, behind Jackson and Adams. Then, as the election was shifted to the House of Representatives, Clay gave his support to Adams, thereby insuring his election and also saddling Clay for the remainder of his life with the charge that he had entered into a "corrupt bargain" to trade his votes for the post of Secretary of State. He did indeed accept the cabinet appointment; and he never thereafter was able to escape the suspicion that he had sold his principles for the position that traditionally had led onward to the White House.

The speech which Clay delivered on November 13, 1847, to an "immense concourse of citizens" in Lexington, Kentucky, was his bid for re-entry into public life.[31] Even as early as 1824, Clay was referring to himself as "an old man." In 1842 he resigned from the Senate to recoup his fortunes through the practice of law. His defeat for the presidency in 1844 confirmed his feeling that he should lead a private life. But he was profoundly disturbed by Polk's maneuvering the nation into war with Mexico and even more so by the ominous dangers posed by annexation of Mexico's Southwest territories.

His introduction set the tone at once: "The day is dark and gloomy, unsettled and uncertain, like the condition of our country in regard to the unnatural war with Mexico . . . . I have come here with no purpose to attempt to make a fine speech, or any ambitious oratorical display. I have brought with me no rhetorical bouquets to throw into this assemblage."

He continued, nevertheless, in a tone of more than usual exalted eloquence. After a panegyric on the frightfulness of war, Clay examined the question of annexing considerable amounts of Mexican territory:

> Does any considerate man believe it possible that two such immense countries, with territories of nearly equal extent, with populations so incongruous, so different in race, in language, in religion, and in laws, could be blended together in one harmonious mass, and happily governed by one common authority? Murmurs, discontent, insurrection, rebellion, would inevitably ensue, until the incompatible parts would be broken asunder, and possibly, in the frightful struggle, our present glorious Union itself would be dissevered or dissolved . . . .
>
> We have already, in our glorious country, a vast and almost boundless territory. Beginning at the north, in the frozen regions of the British provinces, it reaches thousands of miles along the coasts of the Atlantic Ocean and the Mexican gulf, until it almost reaches the tropics. It extends to the Pacific ocean, borders on those great inland seas, the lakes,

[31] Rogers, *op. cit.*, pp. 198–199.

which separate us from the possessions of Great Britain, and it embraces the great father of rivers, from its uppermost source to the Balize, and the still longer Missouri, from its mouth to the gorges of the Rocky Mountains. It comprehends the greatest variety of the richest soils, capable of almost all the productions of the earth, except tea and coffee and the spices, and it includes every variety of climate, which the heart could wish or desire. We have more than ten thousand millions of acres of vast and unsettled lands, enough for the subsistence of ten or twenty times our present population. Ought we not to be satisfied with such a country?[32]

Clay proceeded, then, to speak of the evils of slavery which, having been introduced into the country, must now be endured; but by no means should it be extended into new areas. Then he introduced a series of resolutions calling for a conclusion of the war without territorial aggrandizement. His resolutions were adopted; and they also were applauded by Whigs throughout the East. Clay went to Washington, where he enjoyed a round of plaudits and receptions. In the Whig Convention the following year Clay's name was presented and on the first ballot he received ninety seven votes, as against one hundred and eleven for Zachary Taylor. The Convention yielded to the argument that Clay could not be elected, whereas a popular military hero of the war could scarcely fail, and on the fourth ballot Taylor was named the Whig candidate. Clay went back again to Lexington, this time, he felt sure, never again to return to public life. How and why he decided otherwise has already been discussed in Chapter III.

In his last fight, as always throughout his life, Clay gave to the forensic encounter everything he had. In the view of one able critic, he "sought to float the Compromise to success upon a sea of stately speeches." During the course of the Senate debate on his omnibus measures, he spoke in their behalf more than seventy times. Meanwhile, he was constant in his labors on and off the floor, drumming up support wherever and however he could. Yet there was some truth in an observation Stephen A. Douglas expressed in a private letter at the time, that "if Mr. Clay's name had not been associated with the bills they would have passed long ago. The Administration were jealous of him and hated him and some Democrats were weak enough to fear that the success of his bill would make him President." No man can be a perennial, or at least a quadrennial, candidate for the presidency all his life without suffering some adverse political consequences. Nevertheless, it was the simple truth Douglas uttered when he concluded: "But let it always be said of Old Hal that he fought a glorious and patriotic battle."

[32] *Works of Clay*, ed. Colton, *op. cit.*, III:60ff.

In summing up Clay's career as an orator, there is doubtless truth in Ernest Wrage's conclusion that because of his gambling, irregular relations with women, and apparent political opportunism, "there were thousands who voted against Clay on grounds of his moral delinquency."[33] Nevertheless, in the eulogies that were delivered upon his death by his colleagues in Congress, there is much more than the usual degree of personal affection and also of high admiration and respect. There was more than formalism, and more of truth than is usually found in commentaries on the newly dead, in the summation pronounced by Senator John C. Breckinridge, of Kentucky:

> As a leader in a deliberative body, Mr. Clay had no equal in America. In him, intellect, person, eloquence, and courage united to form a character fit to command. He fired with his own enthusiasm, and controlled by his amazing will, individuals and masses. No reverse could crush his spirit, nor defeat reduce him to despair. Equally erect and dauntless in prosperity and adversity, when successful he moved to the accomplishment of his purposes with severe resolution; when defeated, he rallied his broken bands around him, and from his eagle-eye shot along their ranks the contagion of his own courage. Destined for a leader, he everywhere asserted his destiny. In his long and eventful life, he came in contact with men of all ranks and professions, but he never felt that he was in the presence of a man superior to himself. In the assemblies of the people, at the bar, in the Senate—everywhere within the circle of his personal presence, he assumed and maintained a position of preëminence.[34]

In the long perspective of history Clay's eminence has declined, primarily because his principal aims were, one way or another, determined so decisively that they ceased to be a cause of continuing discussion. He precipitated the War of 1812, but its goals were not won. He fought hard for the tariff and for internal improvements, both of which shortly became commonplaces. He tried repeatedly for the presidency, without getting it. He contributed mightily to postponing the Civil War, but he could not prevent it. In contrast with Webster or Calhoun, he left little positive political philosophy. And he cared so little for post mortem fame that he disdained to prepare his speeches for the press, with the result that his words proved more fleeting than did those of his great compeers. There was a magic about Henry Clay, but it was evanescent.

[33] Wrage, *op. cit.*, II:612.
[34] Epes Sargent, *The Life and Public Services of Henry Clay, Down to 1848*, edited and completed by Horace Greeley, Philadelphia: Porter and Coates, 1852, pp. 394–395.

VI

SPOKESMEN FOR THE
OLD SOUTH
1830–1874

📖 *The South as a Permanent Minority*

SOUTHERN SPOKESMEN before the Civil War, as well as some of their successors, found pleasure in reiterating that the States below the Mason-Dixon line were doomed to perpetual political inequality and inequity. The case was often made by Dixie speakers, though perhaps never more cogently than by Calhoun in his Senate speech on February 16, 1833, in which he forecast that "Warfare, by legislation, would thus be commenced between the parties, with the same object, and not less hostile than that which is carried on between distinct and rival nations—the only distinction would be in the instruments and the mode. . . ."[1]

Northern speakers, meanwhile, were no less prone to charge that the South "blackmailed" the nation into giving it the preponderance of federal offices and in formulating pro-Southern national policies. Of the first twelve Presidents of the United States, eight were Southerners. The two judges, both Chief Justices, who did the most to establish and give direction to the power of the Supreme Court as the agency superior to both the legislative and executive branches in the interpretation of constitutional law were John Marshall and Roger Brooke Taney, both Southerners. The first eight Secretaries of State were Southerners; and the office of Attorney General was virtually a Southern preserve for more than the first half-century of the Republic. W. E. Dodd, in *The Cotton Kingdom*, interpreted the election of 1848 in this guise: "A population of two and a half millions in the lower South, with only a tenth of them directly connected with slavery, would guide a nation of twenty millions, nine tenths of whom were either outspoken or silent opponents of slavery and all it connoted."[2] Nevertheless, during the two decades preceding the Civil War, no responsible person, North or South, really doubted that the Southern position within the Union was one of weak-

[1] *Works of John C. Calhoun*, ed. Richard H. Crallé, op. cit., I:248–249.
[2] W. E. Dodd, *The Cotton Kingdom*, New Haven: Yale University Press, 1920, p. 123.

ness. It was in these circumstances that the orators of Dixie inevitably assumed their character as firebrands.

In the first place, they had to speak. In the second place, they had to address their appeals more directly than is usual to the patent self-interest of their hearers. They had to speak because, as W. G. Brown points out in *The Lower South in American History*, in their region, "it was the spoken word, not the printed page, that guided thought, aroused enthusiasm, made history. It is doubtful if there ever has been a society in which the orator counted for more than he did in the Cotton Kingdom." Then he added: "The man who wished to lead or to teach must be able to speak."[3] And what they spoke about was very nearly mandatory. As Henry Clay, an eminently reasonable man, and certainly far removed from being a Southern extremist, phrased their situation, in 1850: "The North is contending for a mere abstraction, while with the people of the South it is a principle involving their property . . . their prosperity and peace."[4] As a guide to what they should say, the Southern speakers not only were confronted with the fact of the ownership (in 1850) of 3,950,000 slaves—an extraordinary amount of wealth—but they also had in cherished memory the words of the Kentucky resolutions, adopted at Lexington in November, 1798: The Union of the States is a compact, by which "*each party has an equal right to judge for itself, as well of infractions as of the mode and measure of redress.*"[5] They had the need; they had the formula; they had their defined role to play. Defeat stalked their careers, as it did the "peculiar institution" of their section. Their voices were often strident as they warned of dangers they could foresee but could not prevent.

Yet amid their failures and their failings there is evident both an ability and a recurrent statesmanship which entitle them to respect as national personages rather than derogation as merely regional demagogues. In their careers is reflected one side of the most dramatic and gigantic conflict in the history of free democracy. The tragedy is that they were saddled with a cause of such moral perversion that they could win the verdict neither from the nation nor in the depths of their own hearts. Many have disputed whether slavery was the root cause of the Civil

[3] William G. Brown, *The Lower South in American History*, Gloucester, Mass.: Peter Smith, 1930, pp. 125, 127.
[4] Henry Clay, in the Senate, Feb. 5–6, 1850. On July 22, during the course of the long debate, he turned the coin over and said: "I call upon all the South. Sir, we have had hard words, bitter words, bitter thoughts, unpleasant feelings toward each other in the progress of this great measure. Let us forget them. Let us sacrifice those feelings. Let us go to the altar of our country and swear, as the oath was taken of old, that we will stand by her; that we will support her; that we will uphold her Constitution; that we will preserve her Union; and that we will pass this great, comprehensive, and healing system of measures . . ."
[5] Commager, *Documents of American History, op. cit.*, I:178–179.

War. No one can study the public speaking of the period without realizing that it was the most dramatic among the various tangled issues of the time in the impact it made upon the public imagination. Nor is there cause to doubt that it was a cancer which ate into the manhood of the very men who were its most ardent defenders.

⊞ The Georgia Triumvirate: Stephens, Toombs, and Cobb

PRE-WAR GEORGIA was a curious nest in which to nurture genius, though the results speak for themselves. Huge cotton plantations leached its red clay soil, each plantation with its stately-columned white mansion to house the aristocratic owners of scores or hundreds of slaves. On the poorer lands back from the seacoast small farmers scratched painful livings from patches of corn and potatoes, helped sometimes by underfed creatures whom they called "my nigras," and even more often by a scrawny team of mules. Neither the mansions nor the shanties had much access to schools; and the newspapers had small circulation. The general intellectual level is hinted at by a story of the period, in which a farmer and his son are represented as seeing a railway train for the first time. "Dad, what is that ar thing?" the boy asked; and the answer was: "I dunno, son, but I 'spect hit ar the tariff."[1] Out of this environment came a bevy of great men: John M. Berrien, who sat in Andrew Jackson's cabinet; Herschel V. Johnson, whom the Baltimore Convention of the Democratic Party named as Douglas's running mate for the presidency in 1860; Benjamin H. ("Our Ben") Hill, who fought against secession, for the Confederacy, and for sane reconstruction following the war; William L. Yancey, who won his dubious fame in Alabama; Lucius Q. C. Lamar, who left reluctantly to try his fortune in Mississippi; Henry Grady, eloquent editor of the Atlanta *Constitution*; and the three orators who are remembered as the Georgia Triumvirate: Alexander Hamilton Stephens, Robert Augustus Toombs, and Howell Cobb.

Georgia may have been lacking in education, social equality, culture, and prosperity; but few States could match either the vigor or the hardcore practicality of its politics. In 1788 Georgia was among the most ardent supporters of the federal Constitution. But in 1793, when a federal court awarded damages against the State to a citizen of South Caro-

---

[1] For a sound analysis of pre-war Georgian politics, see Horace Montgomery, *Cracker Parties*, Baton Rouge: Louisiana State University Press, 1950.

lina, the Governor threatened to hang any United States marshal who came into the State to try to enforce the decree—and none came. Two years later the State again quarrelled with the national government when its western lands were taken away to comprise the territory of Mississippi. More difficulty developed in 1828, when the Supreme Court decided that Georgia State law could not apply to the Cherokee Indians living on treaty-ceded reservations; but President Jackson backed the State in refusing to accept the decree. Right up to the eve of the Civil War, Georgia politics were State-centered, with few national or even regional ties of consequence. The Democrats, the Whigs, and the American or Know-Nothing parties outdid one another in championing States rights.

By the mid-1830's, when the triumvirate were entering politics, party allegiances were at least fuzzily coalescing; but interest centered on local personalities and cliques rather than on national problems and programs. Votes were won less by party labels than by personal appeal; and the chief means of reaching the farmers and small towners, who comprised over eighty percent of the population, was by stump speaking. Ambitious politicians spent their time on horseback or in buggies, travelling red-banked roads, ready whenever they saw a group or could assemble one to spit dust from their mouths and pour forth streams of extemporaneous oratory. Theirs was a whip-lash, homespun, rude and raucous school of eloquence; and somehow it produced astonishing results.[2]

Alexander Hamilton Stephens (or "Little Ellick," as he came to be known)[3] was born February 11, 1812, and was reared in poverty. His mother died when he was a month old, his father and step-mother when

[2] The importance attached to oratory in Georgian politics, with some indication of its style, may be inferred from a letter written by Stephens to his friend and mentor, Dr. Thomas Foster—cited by Henry Cleveland, *Alexander H. Stephens in Public and Private, with Letters and Speeches, Before, During, and Since the War*, Philadelphia: National Publishing Co., 1866, pp. 51–52: "I have, since I came here [to the Georgia Legislature], come to the conclusion that words are—if you please—moral instruments capable of effecting much, when properly applied and directed. And it is altogether useless, at any and all times to talk, without having in view some object to effect. In legislating *in* Georgia, it is waste of breath for a man to talk about Greece and Rome, Scipio and Hannibal, Tyre and Carthage, or any of that learned sort of lore. If any one indulges much in it, he is soon looked upon as a fool, speaking in an 'unknown tongue,' and very properly so too. Eloquence, true eloquence, is certainly in some degree an art; but in nothing more than fitting the matter to the time, place, and circumstances. The whole generation of our young orators, instead of reading Blair for rules, Scott and Addison for figures, and Byron and Shakespeare for quotations, had better be studying their subject, and thinking to whom they are going to present it, and how they will most probably gain attention, and produce conviction in the minds of those to whom it is presented. Success in producing conviction is the object of oratory."
[3] Sometimes spelled differently, as in E. Ramsay Richardson, *Little Aleck: A Life of Alexander H. Stephens*, New York: Grosset & Dunlap, 1932.

he was fourteen. The few months of random schooling he picked up were capped by a generous gift of funds for an education at Franklin College (later to become the University of Georgia), from which he graduated first in his class, with a notable record as a debater. He taught school for a year; but he hated it so much that, despite the offer of a munificent salary of $1500 a year, he left the schoolroom and turned, in 1833, to the study of law.

By almost any standards, except those of ambition and ability, he seemed unsuited for professional life. He was well over five feet in height, but with a maximum weight of ninety four pounds, scarecrow gaunt, cadaverous, scrawny, untidy, yellow-visaged, with feverishly intent black eyes and scraggly, unkempt chestnut hair.[4] His hypochondriac temperament, intensified by recurrent sick headaches, is reflected again and again in his diary and letters. Typical of many of his diary entries is one he wrote as he turned from teaching to the study of law, subsisting in the meantime on six dollars a week: "I believe I shall never be worth anything and the thought is death to my soul."[5] Then, more hopefully, he added: "Discussion and debate are my delight."

All his life he was to be called "boy," and "sonny," remaining painfully aware of his physical inadequacies. He never married and had few close friends—almost none except the mammoth Robert Toombs and his brilliant younger brother Linton. To his brother Linton he poured out letters filled with Chesterfieldian advice: study Shakespeare, "repudiating his vulgar obscenity"; "Cultivate female society—it tends wonderfully to refine the coarser feelings"; "Trust too much to no man"; "always look up—think of nothing but objects of the highest ambition." The letters mirror the man who wrote them: ambitious, wistfully eager, eaten by self-doubt. This was Stephens. And within his limitations he created great statesmanship and enduring eloquence.

His first public speech was a Fourth of July oration in 1833, in which he won polite applause by denying the right of nullification while insisting that every State had the right of secession. Elected to the State Legislature in 1836, he quickly made a reputation by rising from a sick-bed (which he was often to do, for he spent his life as a semi-invalid) to

---

[4] Stephens's height has often been underestimated. He himself, in an entry in his diary dated May 17, 1834, wrote: "My weight is 94 pounds, height 67 inches, and my whole appearance that of a boy of eighteen." Quoted by Myrta Lockett Avary, *Recollections of Alexander H. Stephens*, New York: Doubleday, Page, 1910. Reverend William Henry Millburn, the Chaplain of the House, described him as "a man of medium height, but when seated he looks like a boy, for his trunk is exceedingly short . . . . His arms and legs are very long." Millburn added, "His voice . . . is thin, high-pitched, and inclining to the falsetto." Quoted by Cleveland, *op. cit.*, pp. 31–32. Richardson, *op. cit.*, p. 18, thought "he measured five feet ten."
[5] The diary entries and letters are cited from R. M. Johnston and W. H. Browne, *Life of Alexander H. Stephens*, Philadelphia: Lippincott, rev., 1884.

speak on behalf of a ten-mile railroad, which was derisively dismissed by the majority as "The Big Snout." Stephens's speech was a carefully documented proof of the economic advantages of building the spur line. His speech was rewarded with an unusual burst of applause and by a vote of 100 to 54 in favor of the bill.[6] This success carried him to Congress in 1843, where he proved to be a very independent-minded Whig. Against his party's policies, he favored the annexation of Texas, but he supported the Whigs in denouncing the war with Mexico. "Fields of blood and carnage may make men brave and heroic," he said in his speech on June 16, 1846, "but seldom tend to make nations either good, virtuous, or great."[7] As the war continued Stephens spoke often, opposing any acquisition of territory from Mexico—primarily because disputes over whether slavery should be excluded from it would endanger the Union. His very personal hatred of President Polk (for what reason is not known) was expressed in continual attacks against him that were supercharged with emotionalism. Concerning one of them, delivered on February 2, 1848, Abraham Lincoln, then serving his single term in Congress, wrote to Herndon that "Mr. Stephens of Georgia, a little, slim, pale-faced consumptive man, with a voice like Logan's, has just concluded the very best speech of an hour's length I have ever heard. My old, withered, dry eyes are full of tears yet."[8]

In the running debates on the Wilmot Proviso, which continued for two years, Stephens declared he was not a defender of slavery "in the abstract," but he argued that the system was so deeply entrenched in Southern life that it must be maintained. By this time three billions of dollars were invested in slaves; and the plantation system proved incapable of evolving into an industrialized society. Sharply countering the generally rapid economic growth of the nation, fourteen of the twenty two counties that comprised Stephens's congressional district lost population during the years between 1840 and 1860. Besides these economic and demographic factors, the pride and prestige of the South was by now deeply involved in repelling the "aggression" of the North. All through the eastern tier of the older Southern States, the blight of slavery was taking an increasing toll. But since the "peculiar institution" could not be abandoned without a convulsion that would mean the final ruin of both the economic and the social systems, the worse conditions became, the more fiercely Southern spokesmen defended the *status quo*. With Stephens playing a prominent part in the Harrisburg Convention, the Southern Whigs outmaneuvered the Clay supporters to win

[6] Cleveland, *op. cit.*, pp. 52–54; Richardson, *op. cit.*, p. 73.
[7] The texts of this and Stephens's other speeches are in Cleveland, *op. cit.*
[8] Sandburg, *Lincoln: The Prairie Years, op. cit.*, p. 240.

the presidential nomination for Zachary Taylor, a planter and slave-owner. The ensuing campaign was embittered with personal feuding. As one notable instance, Stephens undertook to cane a muscular and bulky Democrat, Judge Francis Cone, who thereupon drew a knife, hurled Stephens to the ground, fell upon him, and slashed him again and again, while the "damned little *pigmy*," as Cone declared, continued to yell defiance.[9]

Stephens recovered in time to participate in the debates on the Compromise of 1850, during which he declared: "My Southern blood and feeling is up and I feel as if I am prepared to fight at all hazards and to the last extremity." When President Taylor refused to veto the Wilmot Proviso, Stephens threatened to lead a fight to impeach him, and he probably would have done so were it not for Taylor's death. As the congressional sentiment made it clear that slavery was to be effectively barred from the Southwestern territories, Stephens asserted that "the people before long will find this government is a humbug." Then he drew his ninety pounds up to his full height and in his squeaky voice concluded: "Whenever this Government is brought in hostile array against me and mine, I am for disunion—openly, boldly, and fearlessly, for revolution." Before the voting commenced on Clay's omnibus bill, Stephens left the Congress in disgust and returned home.

National politics were by this time in as uncertain a turmoil as were those in Georgia; and Stephens confessed to a great yearning to leave public life. Instead, he joined with Toombs and Cobb to form a new Unionist Party in Georgia.[10] In the presidential year of 1852 he worked for the nomination of Daniel Webster; and he cast his ballot for him even though Webster was not nominated and died before the election. During this period Stephens's letters are filled with self-castigation, and his public speeches became domineering and temperamental. "I am never wrong," he snapped in a debate with Congressman Campbell of Ohio. And to a great crowd in Augusta he declared: "I am afraid of nothing on earth, or above the earth, or under the earth, except to do wrong."

Aside from his own hypochondria, his chief problem was that he saw the Union breaking apart and he did not know what to do to prevent it. In the 1856 election he campaigned for Buchanan; and in the House he attacked Douglas's Kansas-Nebraska bill. So irascible had his temper become that he often was compared with John Randolph of Roanoke, the

---

[9] Richardson, *op. cit.*, pp. 118–120.
[10] The political relations of Stephens, Toombs, and Cobb are best traced through Ulrich B. Phillips, ed., *The Correspondence of Robert Toombs, Alexander H. Stephens, and Howell Cobb*, American Historical Assoc., Annual Report, Vol. II, 1911.

near-mad eccentric of the preceding generation. Always in the Congress his speeches commanded a fascinated attention, well-portrayed by a Southern woman who listened from the galleries and wrote: "That vast crowd of listening faces were turned toward a shrunken and attenuated figure, the shoulders contracted and turned in, the face dead and the color of ashes."[11] A fellow Congressman testified that "Members are afraid of him. They submit to him their measures and if he does not approve of them, it is no use to argue, he will oppose. If he approves and consents to take charge of a Bill you have to let him take his own course—he will not take any suggestions."[12] In 1859 he gave up the burden and retired from Congress.

During the next months, in the quietude of retirement, he was able to plumb the depths of his own troubled mind and to discover that his devotion to the Union was second only to his devotion to the South. After Lincoln's election, Stephens stood in the forefront of the tiny band trying to keep Georgia from joining the secession movement. On November 14, 1860, speaking by special invitation to the Georgia Legislature, he denied that Lincoln's election was a threat to the South.[13] He succeeded only in deferring action until a decision could be made by a special convention. When it was called, he made a last futile appeal for moderation, warning: "Revolutions are much easier started than controlled, and the men that begin them seldom end them."[14] He was heard with respect but he stood almost alone. His friends Toombs and Cobb were against him; and with a whoop of exultation, the famed rebel yell, the delegates voted Georgia out of the Union.

The difficulty that at this late date confronted the unionists of the South, Stephens and others, is well-illustrated in the situation of Zebulon B. Vance, Governor of North Carolina, who, in April, 1861, addressed a hostile crowd in Buncombe County, trying to stem the secessionist movement in that State. Years later, in 1886, in a speech in Boston, Vance recalled the circumstances as follows: "I was addressing a large and excited crowd, large numbers of whom were armed, and literally had my arm extended upward in pleading for the Union of the fathers, when the telegraphic news was announced of the firing on Fort Sumter and the President's call for seventy five thousand volunteers. When my hand came down from that impassioned gesticulation, it fell slowly and sadly by the side of a Secessionist. I immediately, with altered voice and manner, called upon the assembled multitude to volun-

[11] Quoted by Rudolph Von Abele, *Alexander H. Stephens*, New York: Knopf, 1946, p. 159.
[12] *Ibid.*, p. 168.
[13] Cleveland, *op. cit.*, pp. 694–713.
[14] Richardson, *op. cit.*, p. 195.

teer, not to fight against, but for South Carolina. I said, if war must come, I preferred to be with my own people."[15] Vance had every motive, of course, to rationalize his recollection of the event; but the fact that a great many Southerners were swept into the war against their real wishes is true enough.

It is also a fact that, contrary to the popular myth, the Confederacy was not an uninterrupted crusade, united in sacrifice and devotion, through a four-year period of breathlessly heroic devotion. The doctrine of States rights that sundered the federal Union proved just as difficult to reconcile with the centralized administrative power needed to mobilize Southern strength. Stephens, who served as Vice President of the Confederacy, considered Jefferson Davis a despot of limited ability and unlimited ambition; and he described the legislators in the Confederate Congress as "children in politics and statesmanship."[16] Procuring men to fill the fighting ranks proved as difficult for the South as it was for the North. In April, 1862, a conscription act was adopted and met with not only popular denunciation but also organized renunciation by the States. Benjamin Hill secured an invitation to address the Georgia Legislature on December 11, 1862, to defend the Davis administration and, particularly, to plead the necessity of supporting the conscription act:

> . . . Congress adopted every conceivable mode of getting volunteers. Even the humors of states and the caprices of individuals were all consulted. If men wished to come by tender through the States, there was the law. If directly, by offer to the President, there was the law. If as cavalry, artillery, infantry, or mixture of all, or even as independent partisans, there was the law. If they wished to volunteer for three, six, twelve months, for three years, for the war, or for any other time, there was the law. If they wished to enter the general service or be enlisted to defend a particular State, or county, or city, or town, or fireside, there was the law. If they wished to come in legions, or regiments, or battalions, or squadrons, or companies, or even singly—all alone and all ablaze with patriotism—there was the law precisely fitting the case, and made to fit the case. Come, —it matters not how, it matters not from where, it matters not with whom, it matters not for how long, come, come, and come quickly, and defend our invaded country—was, and is, and ever has been the earnest appeal of the Government—the President and the Congress—to all our people. Will any complaining far seeing assailant tell me what other form of tender or acceptance Congress could have adopted to encourage men to volunteer . . .[17]

[15] Burton J. Hendrick, *Statesmen of the Lost Cause*, New York: Knopf, 1946, p. 342.
[16] *Ibid.*, p. 419, and *passim*.
[17] Haywood J. Pearce, *Benjamin H. Hill: Secession and Reconstruction*, Chicago: University of Chicago Press, 1928, pp. 70–71.

After the war ended, Stephens was to live for another two decades, until March 3, 1883, and to achieve yet further greatness as author of a two-volume *Constitutional View of the Late War between the States,* and as a post-war member of Congress for nine years. During this period he spoke often, but with little of his old power and with little effect.[18] Ironically, the phrase for which he is best remembered was his worst political blunder. In 1861 he was led, by a perverse spirit of anger against the Northern abolitionists, to make a speech at Savannah in which he described slavery as "the cornerstone of the Confederacy."[19] The phrase spread like wildfire across Europe and many Southerners felt it defeated their chance for diplomatic recognition, thereby insuring their defeat. Truer to the spirit that manifested itself in the central tendency of Stephens's life is the sentiment he expressed in a Fourth of July oration, in 1875: "No one, however high, has any rightful power to wrong another, however low."

Robert Augustus Toombs, who became Stephens's closest friend as they "rode the circuit" together as young lawyers, was born to wealth and blessed with robust health and a handsome, if Falstaffian, physique.[20] His career closely parallelled that of Stephens, including service in the Georgia Legislature and, after 1844, in Congress. Like Stephens, he was a Unionist who fought for the rights of the South under the Constitution. Also like Stephens, he was profoundly alarmed by Northern insistence on keeping slavery out of the territories won from Mexico.

Unlike Stephens (except for the unfortunate "cornerstone" speech), Toombs defended slavery as a positive good. Indeed, Wrage and Baskerville selected him as the Southerner who gave the most cogent statement of the advantages of the system—to the Negroes, to the Southern whites as individuals, and to the social, political, and economic structure of Southern society. Toombs spelled out his views most fully in an ad-

[18] Cleveland, *op. cit.,* p. 102, quotes a vivid description, written by a Washington newsman, of Stephens speaking in 1855, at the height of his power: "True, there is no mark of extraordinary intellectuality in his countenance; but draw him out in debate, do anything to set at work the powerful intellectual battery within, and that poor, sickly, emaciated frame, which looks as if it must sink under the slightest physical exertion, at once grows instinct with a galvanic vitality which quickens every nerve with the energy of a new life, imparts to every feature a high, intellectual expression, makes the languid eyes glow like living coals, and diffuses a glow of reviving animation over the pallid countenance. . . . You cease to be annoyed by that voice that pierces the ear with its shrill and discordant tones, and the awkward gestures seem awkward no longer. . . . The intellectual power of the man seems to transfigure the outward appearance."
[19] Cleveland, *op. cit.,* pp. 717–729.
[20] Ulrich B. Phillips, *Life of Robert Toombs,* New York: Macmillan, 1913; and Pleasant A. Stovall, *Robert Toombs, Statesman, Speaker, Soldier, Sage,* New York: Cassell Pub. Co., 1892.

dress at Emory College, in Atlanta, on July 20, 1853. Then, with typical courage and forthrightness, he repeated the same speech, with embellishments, on January 24, 1856, in the heart of abolitionism, at Tremont Temple, in Boston.

Far from assuming an apologetic stance, Toombs asserted that: "In glancing over the civilized world, the eye rests not upon a single spot where all classes of society are so well content with their social system, or have greater reason to be so, than in the slaveholding States of the American Union." Then Toombs used the "cornerstone" term which Stephens was later to pick up—but in Toombs's view "the cornerstone of republican government" is the principle of "all individual rights as subordinate to the great interests of the whole society." Since he reasoned not from a premise of equal rights but of the utility of individuals to the needs of the State, Toombs found it easy to deduce that "the African is unfit to be intrusted with political power and incapable as a freeman of securing his own happiness or contributing to the public prosperity, and that whenever the two races co-exist a state of slavery is best for him and for society." Then he added: "This fact has had itself recognized in the most decisive manner throughout the Northern states. No town, or city, or state, encourages their immigration; many of them discourage it by political legislation." On the contrary, in the South, "The nature of the relation of master and slave begets kindnesses [and] imposes duties . . . which exist in no other relation of capital and labor." When he spoke in Boston he added another consideration— that, rightly or wrongly, the Negroes were in the South and had to be lived with somehow. "The question is not whether we could not be more prosperous and happy with these three and a half million slaves in Africa, and their places filled with an equal number of hardy, intelligent and enterprising citizens of the superior race; but it is simply whether, while we have them among us, we would be most prosperous with them in freedom or in bondage."[21]

A fair picture of Toombs as a speaker was given in a journalistic summary, in which he is evaluated along with other members of the State legislature:

> This member possesses high genius, thorough acquaintance with mankind, and is distinguished by physical and moral courage. Often eloquent, always sensible and convincing, he is a formidable adversary in debate. He is a bold, fluent, sarcastic speaker, ever ready, ever fortunate and clear in illustration. Frank and careless in his manner, he

[21] Ernest J. Wrage and Barnett Baskerville, *American Forum: Speeches on Historic Issues, 1788–1900*, New York: Harper, 1960, pp. 158–168.

appears to be wholly indifferent to rhetorical embellishment. With infinite tact and sagacity, with a commanding talent for the management of men, it is with himself to select his own rank among the rising men of the state.[22]

The paper noted with regret that Toombs had declined that year to be a candidate for Congress. In 1844 he sought the post eagerly and was elected.

For the first two years, Toombs listened much, spoke little, and sought to prove his devotion to the Union. To show his lack of sectional bias, he delivered a carefully drafted speech on January 12, 1846, in favor of taking Oregon from England, by war if that should be necessary. Then, in a letter to Governor Crawford, of Georgia, written on February 6, Toombs explained that he had taken this stand purely for political reasons, to undercut the Democratic claim to priority as an expansionist party. As for his real views, "The country is too large now, and I don't want a foot of Oregon or an acre of any other country, especially without 'niggers.' "[23] In the same letter he waved off any war with Mexico, saying, "Mr. Polk never dreamed of any other war than a war upon the Whigs." After war was proclaimed, Toombs took the orthodox Whig position of deprecating it but promising to "vote all necessary supplies and take all necessary measures."[24]

By 1848, the debate on the Wilmot Proviso forced Toombs to abandon his program of conciliation and his role as a nationalist. From this time on he spoke frankly and fervently as a sectional partisan. Speeches poured from the fullness of his feelings as the issue was debated in the House. On December 13, 1849, he swore "in the presence of the living God, that if by your legislation you seek to drive us from the territories of California and New Mexico, . . . I am for disunion."[25] On December 22 he spoke against a tumult of mingled opposition and applause, giving what Phillips, his biographer, calls "one of the finest examples of vigorous oratory to be found in forensic records."[26] On February 27, in a carefully prepared speech, he declared the time had come "to test the sufficiency of written constitutions to protect the rights of a minority against a majority of the people." He went on to say that Northern attacks on slavery were making the Southerners "aliens in our own government." Then he concluded: "When the argument is exhausted we

[22] The Milledgeville, Georgia, *Journal*, Dec. 31, 1839.
[23] Phillips, *op. cit.*, p. 68.
[24] *Ibid.*, p. 72.
[25] *Ibid.*, pp. 75–76.
[26] *Ibid.*, p. 77.

will stand by our arms."[27] By June 15 he was saying that if slavery were excluded from the territories, "it is then your government, not mine. Then I am its enemy . . . . Give us our just rights, and we are ready, as heretofore, to stand by the Union . . . . Refuse it and I, for one, will strike for Independence."[28]

Following adoption of the Compromise measures, Toombs was elected to the Senate. There he supported Douglas's program of "popular sovereignty," though he was outraged by the rejection of the Lecompton slave constitution for Kansas. During the campaign of 1856, he said: "The election of Frémont would be the end of the Union and ought to be. I am content that they own us when they conquer us, but not before."[29] Lincoln's election convinced him that "Black Republicanism" was about to crush the South, and he became a leader in the move for immediate secession.

During the war Toombs commenced as Secretary of State in the Confederate cabinet but was soon saying of Jefferson Davis in letters to his political friends that he "clothes his naked villainy with old odds and ends stolen from holy writ and seems a saint when he plays the devil."[30] By January, 1864, in a speech to his Georgia constituents, Toombs was calling openly and loudly for a "counter-revolution" against Davis, whose "despotism" was "daily pouring itself out upon the country." Said Toombs: "I am a revolutionist for liberty and I will be one till I get liberty. If the Yankees stand in the way I am their enemy. If domestic traitors stand in the way I am their enemy." Then, after comparing Davis with Charles I, James II, and Louis XVI, Toombs cried, "Better die than bear such oppression . . . . Save your country, your family; above all, save liberty. I address you as citizens, not as soldiers . . . . I look for no mutiny, unless it be necessary in defense of constitutional liberty."[31]

After the war, Toombs fled to Europe, but returned home in 1867 with full amnesty. He entered quietly upon the practice of law and meanwhile worked backstage in politics, often in alliance with some of his staunchest pre-war opponents, in an effort to win back control of the State from the "black and tan" citizens. In 1871, to a tumult of Georgian rejoicing, a Democratic Governor was again elected. In 1877 Toombs participated in a convention to revise the Georgia constitution,

[27] *Ibid.*, p. 78.
[28] *Ibid.*, pp. 81–82.
[29] Hendricks, *op. cit.*, p. 73, comments that Toombs suffered from the "fatal gift of epigram," yielding to the temptation to say what sounded bright and pungent, rather than searching for the precise statement of his exact views.
[30] *Ibid.*, p. 417.
[31] *Ibid.*, pp. 428–429.

making few speeches but exercising considerable influence. By the time of his death, on December 15, 1885, "the old ways" were once again fairly firmly re-established.

Howell Cobb, who lived from September 7, 1815 to October 9, 1868, was, like Toombs, a scion of Southern wealth and aristocracy.[32] He inherited a tradition of public service, and his influence was widened by his marriage to a Lamar. His entrance into the law came in 1836, where he associated closely with Stephens and Toombs. But, being a Democrat, and also being more addicted than they were to the sensual pleasures of life, this association did not ripen into close friendship. Three years of service as Solicitor-General in the western part of the State helped Cobb to develop a warm sympathy with the poor. He became an effective stump speaker and in 1842 won election to Congress.

In appearance, Cobb was a "fat, pussy, round-faced, jolly looking fellow."[33] He was short, squat, heavily bearded, with pig-like eyes and sensuous lips. In his manner of speaking he was ever the parliamentarian, courteous to his opponents, polished and debonair in manner. His views were so nationalistic that he proved the ideal Southerner for election as Speaker of the House in 1849, in a serious effort to pave the way for conciliation of the deeply split sectional dispute. Cobb favored the Compromise of 1850, utilizing both his influence in the House and speeches delivered to his constituents. With Stephens and Toombs, he helped organize the new Constitutional Union Party in Georgia, to stem disaffection. As the candidate of this party in 1851, he was elected Governor of Georgia, after a hot campaign, on an anti-secessionist platform. This won him appointment as Secretary of the Treasury in Buchanan's cabinet.

The election of Lincoln, however, caused Cobb to catapult himself into the secessionist cause. He was in the van among Georgian separatists; and when a convention was called at Montgomery to organize the Confederacy, Cobb was elected Chairman. Two dominant impressions that must have stood out in his mind were expressed by his younger brother in letters written from Montgomery: "The almost universal belief here is that we shall not have war"; and "I had the folly to believe that there was great patriotism in this movement. God help us! It looks now as if it was nothing but office seeking."[34] During the course of the

---

[32] Cf. Horace Montgomery, *Howell Cobb's Confederate Career*, Tuscaloosa, Ala.; Confederate Pub. Co., 1959; Joseph R. Lamar, *Men of Mark in Georgia*, 1911; and Zachary T. Johnson, *The Political Principles of Howell Cobb*, Nashville, Tenn.: George Peabody College, 1929.
[33] Huntsville, Alabama, *Southern Democrat*, Feb. 20, 1861.
[34] Cf. Hendricks, *op. cit.*, pp. 75–78 and 96–99.

war Cobb largely refrained from speaking, serving instead, without distinction, as a General in the field. However, in February and March, 1864, he made a two-month speaking tour on behalf of President Davis, urging that it would be folly to trust Lincoln and that the Southern people now could trust only in God, themselves, and Jefferson Davis.

At the war's end, Cobb proudly informed Union officials that he had not followed his State into secession; he had led and the State had followed him. He was arrested but was pardoned by President Johnson while en route to prison. He settled down quietly to the practice of law, re-entering public life only once again. On July 23, 1868, a Democratic mass meeting was held in Atlanta, and Cobb addressed it with more than his usual eloquence. "My friends," he cried, the Republicans "are our enemies . . . . Enemies they were in war, enemies they continue to be in peace. In war we drew the sword and bade them defiance; in peace we gather up the manhood of the South, and, raising the banner of constitutional liberty, and gathering around it the good men of the North as well as the South, we hurl into their teeth the same defiance, and bid them come on to the struggle."[35]

For Cobb, however, the conflict was over. On September 7 of that year he wrote his wife: "Today I enter my fifty-fourth year, a tolerably old man who has reached the summit of life's journey—and must soon begin its descent."[36] Thirty two days later he was dead.

📖 *The Father of Secession: Robert Barnwell Rhett*

DESPITE THE closeness of interests and similarity of character between Georgian and South Carolinian politics, there never was any cordial bond between the Georgia Triumvirate and the man who succeeded John C. Calhoun as the most prominent politician in pre-war South Carolina. The relative sobriety of the three Georgians was in sharp contrast to the fiery oratory of ferocious rebelliousness which earned for Robert Barnwell Rhett in his youth the title of "father of secession"— though he sank toward the end into a futility that won him Jefferson Davis's contemptuous label as "this little man." Nature itself conspired to mark Rhett with a brand of misfortune. His generally attractive features were marred by a persistent pimple that for years caused him to wear a patch on the side of his nose and that finally proved to be cancerous, requiring a series of operations which left him in his last fifteen

[35] Phillips, Toombs, *op. cit.*, p. 261.
[36] Montgomery, *op. cit.*, p. 132.

years "too hideous a spectacle," as he sadly described himself, "to be seen by any but those whose love and affection can overlook my diseased deformities."[1]

Rhett was born December 21, 1800, as Robert Barnwell Smith—and until he was thirty seven he was known by that name, or, more familiarly, as Bob Smith. Then, famous and determined upon retirement from politics, he took the name by which he is known in history, that of his mother's mother, who claimed descent from Sir Walter Rhett, of The Hague. His father was a well-to-do lawyer, who drained away resources won at the bar by incompetent efforts to become a rice-growing planter. The boy was given only a scanty education and at twenty one he commenced the practice of law, with few qualifications except an attractive personality. He was six feet tall, thin, with narrow hips and broad shoulders, and with a small but well-shaped head, a ruddy, close-shaven face, and a clear but not melodious voice. His temperament was volatile and generally gay; and his habits were meticulously pure, with "no vices great or small," as his son dutifully attested. He married well and was fortunate in a lifelong happiness in his home, always assured of the affectionate support of his wife, brothers, and children. It was a refuge of which he was much in need.

Young Rhett was elected to the South Carolina legislature in 1826, where his quick mind and tongue, backed by blazing courage, soon made him prominent. When the "Tariff of Abominations" was enacted in 1828, Calhoun sought to quiet Southern discontent in order to enhance his chances of national support for the presidency. Rhett would have none of this caution. In Calhoun's own city of Charleston, Rhett called a mass meeting of citizens on June 12 and with savage intentness blazed that there was no remedy for the South except to secede from the Union. "The day of open opposition to the pretended powers of the Constitution," he said, "cannot be far off; and it is that it may not go down in blood that we now call on you to resist."[2] In a series of direct and indirect negatives that illustrate his typical style, he presented a "Manifesto of Disunion," with this challenge: "If you are doubtful of yourselves, if you are not prepared to follow up your principles wherever they may lead, to their very last consequence—if you love life better than honor—prefer ease to perilous liberty and glory, awake not! stir not! Impotent resistance will add vengeance to your ruin. Live in smiling peace with your insatiable oppressors, and die with the noble conso-

[1] Cf. Laura A. White, *Robert Barnwell Rhett: Father of Secession*, New York: Century, 1931; and the files of the Charleston, S. C., *Mercury*, which Rhett edited, from 1820 to 1868.
[2] White, op. cit., p. 15.

lation that your submissive patience will survive triumphant your beggary and despair."[3]

Despite political pressure from the dominant Calhounites to quiet him, in the December session of the legislature Rhett again argued for the "glorious and inalienable right" of the people to throw off an oppressive government. Delay, he stormed, would invite "incumbent ruin," and the North would laugh at the "puny rage" of the betrayed and victimized Southerners. Still the Calhoun forces threatened political quarantine and ruin of his career unless he would cease to advocate secession and would accept the South Carolina Doctrine of Nullification as the effective remedy against Northern oppression. But Rhett refused to be intimidated even by the great John C. Calhoun himself. In a public address in 1830 he thundered: "Washington was a disunionist, Samuel Adams, Patrick Henry, Jefferson, Rutledge were all disunionists and traitors . . . . Shall we tremble at epithets?" In a Fourth of July oration that same year he declaimed that membership in the federal Union was nothing but "conditional allegiance"; and he cried in a ringing conclusion, "The Spirit of '76 is not dead in Carolina!"[4]

In 1833, as has appeared earlier, Clay's compromise tariff bill brought South Carolina back from the brink of nullification; but it failed to dim, let alone still, Rhett's insistent call for secession.[5] He admitted that South Carolina lacked the resources to constitute an independent nation all by itself; but he argued that its secession would force the other Southern States to follow suit. "Sir," he declared in the legislature, "if a Confederacy of the Southern States could be obtained, should we not deem it a happy termination—happy beyond expectation, of our long struggle for our rights against oppression?"[6] Slavery, he pointed out, would never be acceptable to the people of the North. "A people owning slaves are mad, or worse than mad, who do not hold their destinies in their own hands." In disgust, when the legislature withdrew the nullification ordinance, Rhett resigned his seat—a move made easier by his appointment as State Attorney General. In this office he continued his attack upon the Union. He ruled that it was "foully unconstitutional" to require South Carolinians who held federal office to take an oath to uphold and support the United States Constitution.

The next two decades were a time of comparative calm for Rhett. The power of Calhoun in the State was too great for him to oppose; and with bad grace he acceded to nullification and lawful resistance as the only available weapons against federal tyranny. His fortunes were ruined in the panic of 1837 and he found it necessary to devote his attention

[3] *Ibid.*, p. 15.
[4] *Ibid.*, pp. 20, 21.
[5] For Clay's opinions of Rhett, cf. Miller, *Great Debates, op. cit.*, IV:225, 252, 253.
[6] White, *op. cit.*, p. 27.

largely to the law. Through this he successfully rebuilt his wealth, after which he became, as his father had longed to be, a gentlemanly plantation owner. His one significant emergence into public life in this twenty-year period was a one-year stint in the United States Senate, at the time the 1850 compromise measures were being debated. Rhett opposed the compromise with all his force, arguing instead for a constitutional amendment that would provide a peaceful and legal means for the secession of States. Should such an amendment be adopted, he argued, the North would then check its course of "constant aggression" against the South; and the Union could be preserved. When this proposal was spurned even by his Southern colleagues, Rhett disgustedly resigned from the Senate. This resignation was thoroughly in accord with a demand he had made in 1848, when the Wilmot Proviso was near adoption, that every Southern legislator ought to "return home" from Washington, "should Abolition in any of its forms prevail in the legislation of Congress."[7]

For seven years after his resignation Rhett refrained from making a single public speech, though he continued actively at work by correspondence, consultation with other Southern politicians, and editorials in his newspaper, *The Charleston Mercury.* He failed to win election to the Senate in 1858. But in 1859 he re-emerged onto the public platform, with a stormy Fourth of July oration, on the theme that the South was in true fact a separate nation.[8] Whether or not Northern "aggression" was constitutional, he declared, was incidental. What did matter was that the interests and the destiny of the two sections lay in separate spheres.

The old Rhett was back; and his fire was to flame with its youthful fierceness for another seven years. But from this time on his career was marked by futility. He failed to win election as a delegate to the Charleston Democratic Convention of 1860. At the Richmond Southern Rights Convention he failed to win agreement for secession; though he argued that leaving the Union would, paradoxically, be the only means of preserving it—for "it would not, I am sure, require over two years to reconstruct a union with them on such terms as we shall think proper."[9] So great was his desperation that in this speech he deviated from his lifelong rule against attacking personalities and relayed the rumor that Lincoln's vice-presidential nominee, Hannibal Hamlin, was a mulatto.

The secession for which Rhett had pleaded so long was, after Lin-

[7] *Ibid.,* p. 99.
[8] This speech is analyzed in detail by H. Hardy Perritt, "Robert Barnwell Rhett's Speech, July 4, 1859," in J. Jeffrey Auer, ed., *Antislavery and Disunion, 1858–1861,* New York: Harper, 1963, pp. 98–107.
[9] White, *op. cit.,* pp. 166, 167.

coln's election, initiated by South Carolina. But the Confederacy proved a long series of disappointments to him. He ardently wanted to be President; and he particularly did not want to see Jefferson Davis, whom he considered to be overly-cautious, in that office. He desired a post in the cabinet, which he claimed as his simple right; but he could get it neither for himself nor for his second-choice nominee. In the Provisional Legislature at Montgomery, when the Confederate Constitution was being formulated, he failed time and again to win acceptance for provisions he thought essential. Instead, the new Constitution prohibited the slave trade—the revival of which had for years been Rhett's principal recipe for the return of Southern prosperity; and it provided for tariff duties—which were his chief basis of complaint against the Union. As a final blow, he failed even in his bid for election as a Confederate Senator. Throughout the war Rhett raged against Jefferson Davis; and in 1864 his son introduced into the South Carolina legislature a bill demanding a declaration of war by the State against the Confederacy.

Because he was not an office-holder, Rhett's violent views were forgiven and he was spared from Northern vengeance after the defeat. For two years he proved himself an "unreconstructed rebel" by strident attacks against congressional reconstruction policies, including a denunciation of the Fourteenth Amendment. Then, nearing seventy, and in need of repeated operations for the cancer on his face, he retired to New Orleans to write his own version of the history of the Confederacy, and to mellow in the role of a tender and playful grandfather. When he died on September 14, 1876, there were few to notice his passing. To the very end, however, he remained true to his convictions. *The War for Southern Independence*, he insisted in his manuscript history, was lost only because of the vast incompetence of Jefferson Davis. The cause was not yet beyond reach; for a renewed effort would be "certain of accomplishment if the Southern people will it."[10] And he closed his book, as he closed his life, with the stubborn insistence that "We must be separate as a people if we are to be free." His history was never published— remaining a final futile effort of a finally futile life.

Judah P. Benjamin: Defender of Privilege

IF ALEXANDER H. STEPHENS was the apostle of moderation with honor, and Robert B. Rhett was the father of secession, Judah P. Benja-

---

[10] *Ibid.*, p. 243.

min may be fairly denominated as a defender of privilege.[1] It was a role of which he need not have been and was not ashamed. Property and prerogative are worthy of defense; and Benjamin was a lawyer well-equipped by temperament and ability to speak for them. Jefferson Davis, on the basis of intimate experience, praised him for "the lucidity of his intellect, his systematic habits, and capacity for labor."[2] Benjamin was deserving of the tribute of the South; among the orators of the nation, he occupies an assured place.

A descendant of Spanish Jewry, Judah Benjamin, like Alexander Hamilton, was born in the West Indies, in 1811, and grew up in genteel poverty in North and South Carolina. After two years at Yale University, where he excelled in debate, he left under charges of having stolen from fellow students. At the age of seventeen he went to New Orleans—which was in a period of rapid growth: from 50,000 in 1830 to 100,000 in 1840—to study law. By the age of twenty one he was married to an empty-headed sixteen year old Catholic belle, who spent his money lavishly and always scorned him for his religion. Through sheer hard work and ability he became shortly the most successful commercial lawyer in the city. By 1845 he was sufficiently prominent in Whig politics to be sent as a delegate to the convention called to revise the 1812 Louisiana Constitution. The issue he fought for, unsuccessfully, was free public education, which was to be available to girls equally with boys. Although he was too far in advance of his colleagues to win his cause, he stated in the course of the debate a conciliatory theory of persuasion which describes fairly well what he always practiced: "How can anyone expect that he can induce those who differ with him to change their opinions, when he begins by telling them that he is impractically wedded to his own?"[3] This was a persuasive methodology which the Southern spokesmen much needed, but one which they were disinclined to follow.

In 1853 Benjamin moved onto the national stage, becoming in that year the second Jew ever to be elected to the United States Senate. The following year he won genuine fame by holding his own in a debate on the Kansas-Nebraska bill with the renowned Charles Sumner. President Franklin Pierce was impressed to the extent of offering him the distinction of becoming the first Jew ever to be named a Justice of the Supreme Court; but Benjamin, who had no intention of withdrawing from

[1] Cf. Robert Douthat Meade, *Judah P. Benjamin: Confederate Statesman*, New York: Oxford University Press, 1943; and Pierce Butler, *Judah P. Benjamin*, Philadelphia: Geo. W. Jacobs, 1906.
[2] Hendrick, *op. cit.*, p. 174.
[3] Meade, *op. cit.*, p. 53.

the increasingly grave struggle between the sections, declined the appointment.

The New Orleans *Delta*, which opposed Benjamin, mockingly described him in this period as having a "boyish figure and girlish face . . . gentle, innocent, ingenuous expression and manner . . . sweet and beautifully modulated voice." In another issue the paper admitted that he also possessed a "fine imagination, an exquisite taste, great power and discrimination, a keen, subtle logic, excellent memory, admirable talent of analysis . . ."[4] Senators in Washington found him sarcastic in debate but with a charm that won back in the cloakroom the friendship of men he had castigated on the floor. Varina Howell Davis, wife of the senator from Mississippi, was particularly taken by his voice—as, indeed, were all who heard him. "It seemed a silver thread," she wrote, "woven amidst the warp and woof of sounds which filled the drawing room; it was low, full, and soft; yet the timbre of it penetrated every ear like a silver trumpet. From the first sentence he uttered, whatever he said attracted and chained the attention of his audience."[5]

On May 2, 1856, in a notable speech on Kansas, Benjamin defended the thesis that the Constitution was a compact among the States, and warned: "Take away this league of love; convert it into a bond of distrust; of suspicion, or of hate; and the entire fabric which is held together by that cement will crumble to the earth, and rest scattered in dishonest fragments upon the ground."[6] During this speech he informed the Senate that he was leaving the broken and dissolving Whig Party to ally himself with the Democrats. The shifting partisan situation of the time made political footing slippery, and for a brief period it appeared that Benjamin might be washed into obscurity. In 1858 he abandoned his usual polite manner far enough to get into a sharp quarrel with Jefferson Davis, which would have ended in a duel but for a graceful apology made by the Mississippian. In the next election Benjamin was up for re-election and was barely returned to the Senate by a two-vote margin after some fifty ballots in the Louisiana legislature.

With delicate and mobile features, ebony black hair and beard, and with his wonderfully gentle and expressive voice, Benjamin sought in debate to entice, entangle, beguile, undermine, or refute his opponents so unostentatiously that they lost their cause without realizing quite how. In the courtroom, where it was his preference to have his cases tried by a judge alone, without a jury, this skill of gently unveiling essential weaknesses in the logic of opposing cases—almost incidentally, almost

[4] The *Delta* passages are cited by Meade, *op. cit.*, pp. 78, 79.
[5] Quoted by Meade, *ibid.*, p. 89.
[6] *Ibid.*, p. 100.

apologetically, as though he very much hoped not to offend or to suggest a fault in his opponent—won for him fame and fortune. In the rough and tumble debates of the Senate, where there was so much sensationalism that subtlety passed unnoticed, his method was less effective. Nevertheless, his delicate eloquence filled the galleries and won applause even from his opponents.

A typical example of his Senatorial speaking is the address he presented on March 11, 1858, where he sought to emphasize and particularize the Supreme Court's decision in the Dred Scott case, that Congress could not exclude slavery from the territories. For the most part his speech consisted of historical exposition rather than argument, with his presumptive interpretations so gently yet firmly interwoven into the fabric of the historic recital that his opponents could see his case being built, stage by stage, yet could scarcely find a place to grasp hold of an argumentative proposition which could be refuted. Then, in alluding to the fact that slavery, once universal in the thirteen Colonies, came to be excluded from those in the north, Benjamin indulged in the gentle but biting sarcasm which suddenly transmuted a polite and impersonal exposition into a searing attack. "Slavery was to be abolished after a certain time," he said "—just enough time to give their citizens convenient opportunity for selling the slaves to southern planters, putting the money in their pockets, and then sending to us here, on this floor, representatives who flaunt in robes of sanctimonious holiness; who make parade of a cheap philanthropy, exercised at our expense; and who say to all men: 'Look ye now, how holy, how pure we are; you are polluted from the touch of slavery; we are free from it.' "[7]

Like Henry Clay, Judah Benjamin fell under criticism because of his efforts to understand and at least verbally to accommodate his own position to that of the opponents of slavery. His biographer Pierce Butler admitted there was much evidence for the charge against Benjamin of self-seeking opportunism, though his own conclusion was to find him "steadfast in adherence to political principles and ideals."[8] Markedly unlike Rhett, his personal relationships, within his own home and amidst his associates, were far from satisfactory. For one thing, he never escaped feeling the sting of covert but continuing scorn because of his religion. It was not easy to be the first Jew in prominent political life. His home life was miserable, with a wife who was unfaithful, recklessly extravagant, and meanly contemptuous of his religion, yet who refused him a divorce. From such miseries he sought relief by inveterate gambling and gay living. Moreover, as a poor boy who rose to wealth and

[7] *Congressional Glove*, 1857–58, Part II, pp. 1065ff.
[8] Butler, *op. cit.*, p. 427.

always was barred from an assured social position, he chose his legal cases with an eye to being always on the winning side and especially on the side that paid the largest retaining fees.

On the question of slavery his views were orthodox for the South. True, to win a law case in 1847 he argued that a slave "is a human being. He has feeling and passions and intellect. His heart, like the white man's, swells with love, burns with jealousy, aches with sorrow, pines under restraint and discomfort, boils with revenge and ever cherishes the love for liberty."[9] Yet his conclusion in this speech, as throughout his career, was that for these very reasons it was necessary to use the utmost of police power to keep the Negro in subjection. Throughout his political life Benjamin was an ardent defender of the privileges of the Southern whites; but it was not until after the election of Lincoln that he reluctantly accepted secession as the only available remedy for the sectional difficulties.

His speech announcing his forthcoming resignation from the Senate was a graceful mixture of friendly sentiments and unyielding defiance. On December 31, 1860, after Louisiana had seceded, he spoke to a full floor and crowded galleries in the Senate chamber. "And now, Senators," he said, "within a few weeks we part to meet as Senators in one common council chamber of the nation no more forever." His musical voice thrilled through every portion of the crowded chamber, low yet penetrating, "like a silver thread" that hung and quivered in the air. Especially, it was said by those who heard it, the word "forever" seemed to hang tremulous in a breathless quiet, like an organ chord that gradually fades away. "We desire, we beseech you, let this parting be in peace." But, he went on, after a pause, gathering his force now, with the flaming power that in his speaking seemed all the greater because of his generally quiet tone, if war should be pronounced against the South, "you may carry desolation into our peaceful land, and with torch and fire you may set our cities in flames . . . but you never can subjugate us; you never can convert the free sons of the soil into vassals, paying tribute to your power; and you never, never can degrade them to the level of an inferior and servile race. Never! Never!" Spectators attested that his *never*, spoken in his sweet yet penetrating voice, without any emotional enhancement, swept through the chamber like the cold, flat voice of doom.[10] His speech, like those of the other departing Southerners, had all the greater effect because the North, without leadership from the White House, without a program, without a prophet to rally its spirits, could do no better than await the course of events as the months

[9] Meade, *op. cit.*, p. 62.
[10] *Ibid.*, pp. 152–154.

stretched ahead until a new President should be inaugurated and, perhaps, would tell them then what they should do. Benjamin, meanwhile,
back home in Louisiana, spoke on Washington's birthday to a huge
outdoor crowd in New Orleans, telling them that war "is not the un-
mixed evil which many consider it to be . . . . The fire sweeps over the
stubble . . . . Yet a little while and the spring rains descend . . ."[11]

When the Confederacy was organized, Jefferson Davis named Benjamin first as Attorney General, then as Acting Secretary of War, and
finally as Secretary of State. Especially in this last capacity he served
with distinction, being considered by many the ablest man in the cabinet. At the close of the war he escaped capture by the Union soldiers
only by hiding in the bushes while they searched his home. Then he fled
to England—probably, as was charged, taking with him some small
sums from the Confederate treasury. In England he once more proved
his transcendent abilities by winning admission to the British bar and by
spending the last twenty years of his life, in the midst of severe competition, as one of the ablest and most respected barristers in London.

Because of his severe restraint and lack of social warmth, he seemed
all his life to be acting as a retained attorney, serving where the fees
were greatest, with his head rather than with his heart. His English
acquaintances depicted him in these last two decades as always cheerful,
always speaking of "the amusing side of things"; bitter toward the
North only for the burning of his law library and the drinking of his
cellar of Madeira wines by the soldiers who occupied his home. Yet he
was admired by no less a statesman than Benjamin Disraeli. And he won
high success in three successive careers: as an American corporation lawyer; as a politic statesman in both the Union and the Confederacy; and
in the spirited competition of the British law courts. When the end
came he was ready: "I am tired of work and need repose."[12]

William Lowndes Yancey: Apostle of Disunion 🏛

NEXT ONLY to Rhett, William Lowndes Yancey, of Alabama, was the
leading spokesman in the South for secession. He was American in the
Southern style—descendant of a family of wealth and distinction that
landed in Virginia in 1642, and born, on August 10, 1814, the son of a

[11] *Ibid.*, p. 160.
[12] *Ibid.*, p. 376.

brilliant lawyer and a daughter of the famous Colonel William Bird.[1] His natal State was Georgia (what a nest of orators its red-clay soil nurtured!); but the Yanceys moved to South Carolina in 1817, where the father died at the early age of thirty two.

Yancey was educated as a young aristocrat, partly in South Carolina and partly in New England, where he attended Williams College and where he spent twelve formative years among the Yankees. He commenced his public career at the age of twenty, with a Fourth of July oration at Lodi, S.C., arousing the crowd's enthusiasm with his theme: "Where liberty is, there is my country." That same fall he brashly spoke out against Calhoun's leadership, in a speech at Greenville, saying: "We have great and insurmountable objections to having the doctrines of those Nullifiers crammed down our throats."[2] Then, perhaps not unwisely, he left the state, going west in 1836 to seek his fortune in the rich cotton lands of Alabama, where he settled on a rented estate near the town that was then the state capital, Cahawba. It was a prosperous region, settled by cultured graduates of Yale, the University of Virginia, and South Carolina College. Books were scarce and "Oratory and conversation supplied the wholesome friction of minds."[3] For three years Yancy pursued a life of plantation graces, content with a pleasant sociability that ignored public responsibilities. Then, in 1839, his life was vitally affected by a strange and tragic catastrophe. A quarrel between his overseer and the overseer of a neighboring plantation led to the poisoning of a spring, by which many of Yancey's slaves were killed and the remainder incapacitated. To recoup his finances, Yancey turned to the study of law—which precipitated him into politics.

His physical, mental, and social attainments were well suited to a public career. He was five feet ten inches tall, handsome, slender, well built, with deep blue eyes and a profusion of light brown hair. His features were pleasant and his manners gently courteous, without any tendency toward back-slapping affability. While he was still a small child, his mother used to tell him of his father's eloquence and had him spend hours practicing declamations, with particular attention to clarity of articulation and to physical poise. His temperament combined a lofty sense of duty with a self-confidence so manifest that it was often described as extreme egoism. In conversation he was reserved; but when he

---

[1] John Witherspoon DuBose, *The Life and Times of William Lowndes Yancey*, New York: Peter Smith, 1892 and 1942; Clarence P. Denman, *The Secession Movement in Alabama*, Montgomery, 1933; and Rexford S. Mitchell, "William L. Yancey," in Brigance, ed., *History and Criticism, op. cit.*, II:734–750.
[2] DuBose, *op. cit.*, p. 66.
[3] *Ibid.*, p. 79.

arose to make a speech the power of his mind and personality multiplied.

His political reputation commenced in 1840, through speeches he made on behalf of Van Buren. Then, as always, he spoke extemporaneously and few records remain of what he said. But the effect was noted by many, including Chief Justice Stone of the Alabama Supreme Court, who wrote: "I heard Mr. Yancey first in 1840. I thought then and I yet think he was the greatest orator I ever heard."[4] As a result of the plaudits he won in this campaign, he was elected the following year to the State legislature. There an observer declared, "I say confidentially, he was the most fascinating man I ever knew."[5] Two years later he sought and won election to the State Senate, "to represent the great mass of the people versus the aristocracy," according to his campaign claim. In 1844 he won election to Congress and became a nationally known spokesman for his regional interests.

The metamorphosis from the Yancey who, in 1834, had jeered at nullification was considerable. Like all the Southerner leaders, he spoke with respect of the Union and the Constitution, but always and only provided the interests of the South should be paramount. In the very opening days of the new session of Congress, on January 7, 1845, he won instant acclaim with a blistering speech demanding the annexation of Texas. The Baltimore *Sun* described the speech as "at once terribly severe in denunciation and satire and again overpoweringly cogent in argument and illustration." The Richmond *Enquirer*, assaying him as a regional champion, decided: " . . . if he be not paralyzed by the admiration he has already excited . . . he is destined to attain a very high distinction in the councils of the nation."[6] As a result of the "terribly severe denunciation" in this speech, he fought a gentlemanly duel with Congressman Thomas L. Clingman, of North Carolina, in which both men discretely fired into the air.

Throughout the next two years, Yancey spoke often and vigorously in Congress. He came to be known as "the Charles James Fox of America"; and to counteract this reputation for extemporaneous ingenuity, he deliberately worked to develop a power of clear analysis and a habit of carefully documenting his speeches. Often, however, he was on his feet in impromptu debate, meeting and matching the greatest of his contemporaries—matching wits with A. H. Stephens, J. Q. Adams, and New England abolitionists in the House, and aiming barbs toward

[4] *Ibid.*, p. 90.
[5] *Ibid.*, p. 104.
[6] *Ibid.*, p. 141.

Webster and Stephen A. Douglas in the Senate. Then, well begun on a congressional career of importance, he abruptly resigned at the conclusion of the session of 1846—because he disliked committee work and found many of the meetings of the House to be dull; because he preferred the money he could earn in law to the plaudits he won from the galleries; and above all because he became convinced that under the constitutional restrictions, the rights of the South could not be protected in Congress but must be attained through unremitting public pressure. Hence, he returned to Alabama to start a new career as a popular agitator. He became what many have considered the very prototype of the demagogue.

During the remainder of his life he remained out of office, but spoke year after year at scores of mass meetings, usually held out of doors. His name became a byword throughout the South and his flaming utterances were widely discussed. His was a triumph of personality rather than of reasoned discourse. Like his English counterpart, Fox, he scorned to write out his addresses and was content with the influence he could exert upon the 40,000 or 50,000 who heard him each year, with their word-of-mouth reports to their neighbors, and with the sketchy paraphrases that were widely published in the newspapers. Little remains from all his speaking except his reputation—and the fruits of his influence. Despite his seeming carelessness for his reputation, every speech was carefully prepared; and one source of his power was the outpouring of facts and ideas that seemed to erupt with limitless force from an endless supply. Yancey never spoke down to his audience but gave always of his best, with a passionate belief both in the soundness of his cause and in the patriotism and worth of his listeners.

It is a mistake to call him, as many have, a radical. In his early speaking he was both humanitarian and conservative. He argued for sound money and a stable economy. He also defended the rights of women. During his one year in the State legislature, he advocated a bill assuring to married women the right to retain ownership of their own property; and in a Jackson Monument address at Baltimore, on May 22, 1846, he chose a theme strange to the occasion: "The Rights and Wrongs of Woman." When the Mexican War, the dispute over the Wilmot Proviso, and the proffered compromise in 1850 swung his attention wholly to the problem of how to insure the rights of the South and the security of slavery, he did not follow a partisan course but hewed an intensely individualistic line.

In a blistering series of speeches in Alabama and other States, he denounced his own Democratic Party, to the outrage of his friends and the sacrifice of any prospect of future election to office. During the campaign of 1848, at a mass meeting in Montgomery, "Yancey took the stand," wrote an eyewitness, "and never have I witnessed such a display of arrogance and dictatorship . . . . I do not pretend to quote his words, but his speech was an outpouring of bitterness you would not expect from a Whig, delivered in his usual brilliant and vehement style. It was fine sport for the Whigs, and they came down in repeated and thunderous applause. I do not think he relished this, for he upbraided them and said they had no right to interfere in a family quarrel."[7] On July 13, 1850, at another Montgomery mass meeting, Yancey declared that "The South was approaching, if not already arrived at, a unanimous determination to uphold her Constitutional rights."[8] Despite Yancey's confidence in the rebelliousness of the populace, the people of Alabama were prone to accept the Compromise of 1850. His repeated assertions that secession was the only means of stopping the aggression by the North were rejected. Yancey abandoned the hustings in anger, and until he was once more aroused by the Kansas-Nebraska bill, he retired to the practice of law.

"Bleeding Kansas" brought him out again. At Columbus, Georgia, in 1855, he launched his renewed drive for secession, demanding: "Does not wisdom cry aloud to us to take care of ourselves?" His "only aim," he insisted, was to assure "the equality of the South in the Union or her independence out of it."[9] But the latter he was sure was the only practical alternative, for the differences between Northerners and Southerners were too basic to make a homogeneous union between them possible. "Those who occupy the one," he said, "are cool, calculating, enterprising, selfish, and grasping; the inhabitants of the other are ardent, brave and magnanimous, more disposed to give than to accumulate, to enjoy rather than to labor." To the State Democratic Convention in Montgomery, in January, 1860, he said: "You have heard passionate appeals to you not to dissolve the Union . . . . I appeal to a higher principle of your nature. I invoke that gallant and wise sentiment . . . that 'eternal vigilance is the price of liberty.' "[10]

Yancey went to the Democratic National Convention at Charleston determined to block the nomination of Stephen A. Douglas and to steer the platform away from any appearance of moderation. To accomplish these ends, he himself put on a sly and subtle guise of conciliation. Speaking on April 28, on the fifth night of the Convention, according to Lindsey S. Perkins, "Yancey's periods were elegant, majestic rivers winding over their flood plains . . . . Yancey was graceful, debonair, sure in

[7] *Ibid.*, pp. 225–226.
[8] *Ibid.*, p. 248.
[9] *Ibid.*, pp. 297–310.
[10] *Ibid.*, p. 445.

movement . . . . Yancey challenged with the melodious call of the gamecock." Suavely he insisted that he was "no disunionist . . . no disruptionist."[11] Then he catalogued the injustices heaped upon the South by the North and gently challenged the Convention not to sacrifice principles for the hope of success. His speech throughout the campaign was quoted by politicians of widely divergent views—to show that the slaveholders did not wish to break up the Union, or that they must do so. The Charleston Convention, at any rate, was indeed broken up. As it adjourned, unable to agree on a candidate, one of the delegates wrote: "What a season for Demagogues and Charlatans!"[12]

In mid-August of that year, campaigning for Breckenridge's election as President, Yancey proclaimed in Memphis that "The country, my friends, has for many years been alarmed for its fate under this government."[13] No one labored harder to intensify that alarm than did William Lowndes Yancey. His own description of his public career, given in a speech at Montgomery, in May, 1858, is a fair summary: "All my aims and objects are to cast before the people of the South as great a mass of wrongs committed on them, injuries and insults that have been done, as I possibly can. One thing will catch our eye here and determine our hearts; another thing elsewhere; all united may yet produce spirit enough to lead us forward, to call forth a Lexington, to fight a Bunker's Hill, to drive the foe from the city of our rights."[14] In his opinion "the Union had already been dissolved" after the House of Representatives approved the Wilmot Proviso. Even before that, however, he was asserting that the South had no recourse except to withdraw as a separate nation.

As to the nature of his oratory, there seems to be general agreement that, in the words of a newspaper correspondent, "It was all argument, but it was argument instinct with life and spirit. It was not only solid, it was shining—just as sparks ascend from the anvil under the blows of the skillful smith."[15] Another newsman, describing a speech Yancey made in 1858, likened it to "the burst of a hurricane . . . tearing, uprooting, demolishing, and scattering all in its path. Along its entire course was, and is, utter desolation. By the by, when the storm of Mr. Yancey's argument and invective did sometimes lull, a tinge of humor bordered the ferocious sarcasm, as a gleam of sunlight tints the edge of the thunder cloud with a soft violet hue."[16] Yancey himself left his own esti-

---

11 Lindsey S. Perkins, "The Democratic Conventions of 1860," in J. Jeffrey Auer, *Antislavery and Disunion, op. cit.,* pp. 187–188.
12 *Ibid.,* p. 191.
13 DuBose, *op. cit.,* p. 491.
14 *Ibid.,* p. 362.
15 *Ibid.,* pp. 405–406.
16 *Ibid.,* p. 351.

mate of the source of his power in a conversation he recorded, with a Whig neighbor who visited him while he was ill. Their talk inevitably ran to politics, and after a while the Whig declared: "Ah, Mr. Yancey, you can out-talk me!" Yancey snorted in reply: "Out-talk you! And what does that mean? Do I talk louder and longer than you? Do I talk faster? I have heard the phrase before, but never understood it. You mean, sir, to say that you cannot answer my argument."[17]

His views on slavery were that it was imposed on the South by the rapacity of New England slave traders; that it persisted in the South because there the "climate and economy" favored it; and that the slaves themselves were the happiest of laborers to be found anywhere. "These glorious sons of toil," he told a New York audience in Cooper Institute on October 10, during the 1860 campaign, "satisfied in their estate, living with their masters, multiply the prosperity of the civilized world and are the happiest people under the heavens, when your philosophers let them alone." As to the moral argument of the abolitionists, "My idea is, that the Government of the United States . . . is not a school of ethical theories . . . and that our morals are to be in no ways meddled with . . ."[18]

When the South's anticipated fears culminated in what Yancey called "the awful calamity" of Lincoln's election, the Alabamian joyously denounced as "treason" any opposition to immediate secession. The time had come, he felt, to reap the fruits of his long labors. The Confederacy sent him on a diplomatic mission to London, which proved unsuccessful. He then returned home to serve for two years in the Confederate Senate. There he was constantly embroiled in the quarrels that snarled its legislative processes, finally incurring a vote of censure from his colleagues. In general he supported President Davis, arguing that the war needs called for more, not less, executive power. His efforts now were aimed not for but against States rights, as he pleaded for submission by the nervously jealous State governments to the central authority. Speaking to the Confederate Congress on December 2, 1862, he expressed views that contrasted oddly with his earlier renunciation of the authority of Congress. Addressing himself to the public, outside the hall, he said: "If, upon a fair trial and due reflection, you do not deem your laws the best that could have been made, change your representatives and enact new laws; but review the conduct of your public agents as friends, not as enemies."[19] Had he defended the U. S. Congress in this manner to his constituents before 1861, the fever of secessionism might not have risen

17 *Ibid.*, p. 294.
18 *Ibid.*, pp. 499, 507.
19 *Ibid.*, pp. 674–675.

to the ignition point. As has so often happened to so many men, the holding of responsible office wrought a substantial change in his views. It is difficult to judge the quality of a shoe without trying it on. But now, in the midst of the war he had done much to precipitate, the old warrior was near the end. Shortly after the battle of Gettysburg, which has been called "the high tide of the Confederacy," Yancey died painfully of an internal infection. No less painfully, the cause to which he had given his life was also drawing toward its close.

Seargent Smith Prentiss and Lucius Q. C. Lamar

MISSISSIPPI, WHICH is not always considered the citadel of moderation and sweet reasonableness, nurtured two of the most generally attractive and constructive spokesmen for the Old South. Neither man was born in the State; but both deliberately chose it for their home and in it both found support for views that aligned them with Clay and Benton; though Southerners, both sought to stem the tide of sectional extremism.

Seargent Smith Prentiss was born September 30, 1808, in Portland, Maine.[1] Crippled in infancy,[2] probably by polio, his prospects seemed so bleak that when his father, away on a trip, erroneously heard that he had died, he wrote his wife that the death was a blessing. Smith hobbled on crutches from the time he was ten until he was eighteen, then walked with a cane for the remainder of his life, with his right leg greatly weakened. Because of his physical ailment he was the only child in a family of nine to be given a college education—attending Bowdoin, where he was a brilliant student, good debater, and friend of Longfellow, Hawthorne, and Franklin Pierce.

After graduation he migrated to Natchez, Mississippi, to look for a teaching position. He arrived with no friends, no prospects, and five dollars in his pockets. After registering at a hotel, he sent down to the desk to have a bottle of wine and a box of cigars sent up to his room—a gesture that took his last cent but that, as he said, "established his

---

[1] Dallas C. Dickey, *Seargent Smith Prentiss*, Baton Rouge: Louisiana State University Press, 1945.
[2] "Mr. Prentiss was small and lame, but his glorious head once seen made one forget that he had any infirmity. He lisped slightly, or rather had a soft pronunciation of his s, which gave a tender tone to his eloquent denunciation." Varina Howell Davis, *Jefferson Davis: Ex-President of the Confederate States of America, A Memoir*, New York: Belford, 1890, pp. 184–185. With a womanly feeling for character, Mrs. Davis also presents brief but telling sketches of J. Q. Adams, pp. 244–245; Benton, pp. 269–270; Calhoun, pp. 210, 275; and Webster, pp. 277–278.

credit."[3] He soon had a tutoring job that paid $300 a year, plus room and board, and also provided ample time for horseback riding and a chance to study law. Initially he disliked the South, finding that "Slavery is the great pest of this as well as the other Southern States."[4] As for the efficiency of slave labor: "Of course, things are done in a poor and slovenly manner." However, upon further observation, he came to believe that the Negroes were at least "as happy as their masters." He also came to the conclusion that slavery was the only tenable relationship between the two races. When he was admitted to the bar in Natchez, he cast his lot wholly and sincerely with the South.

Prentiss was never an extremist. Remaining out of politics, he did not have to pander to prejudice in the search for votes. The speaking that he did, outside the courtroom, where he prospered, was usually on ceremonial occasions. In his *Memoirs* he wrote: "It is said against me, that I have Northern feelings. Well, so I have; and Southern, and Eastern, and Western, and I trust that I shall ever, as a citizen of this Republic, have liberality enough to embrace within the scope of my feelings both its cardinal points and its cardinal interests."[5] On December 22, 1845, at New Orleans, he deliberately chose to speak in praise of New England, and with equal deliberation emphasized the values, neglected in the South, of universal public education. "The common village school is New England's fairest boast," he said. "True liberty is the child of knowledge; she pines away and dies in the arms of ignorance."[6] Prentiss is one of the few speakers in the South in this period who illustrates that the people had interests other than the sectional conflict. Again in New Orleans, on February 4, 1847, he spoke on the Irish potato famine, illustrating the gracefully ornate style which won him repute as an artist on the platform: "Famine, gaunt and ghastly famine, has seized a nation with its struggling grasp; and unhappy Ireland, in the sad woes of the present, forgets for a moment the gloomy history of the past."[7] At the age of forty two, on July 1, 1850, Prentiss passed away.

Lucius Quintus Cincinnatus Lamar,[8] far from being a self-made man, was born, on September 17, 1825, into impeccable aristocracy, numbering among his close relatives the presidents of Texas and Peru, and the president of the Bank of the Republic. Far from having to earn status,

[3] Dickey, *op. cit.*, p. 30.
[4] *Ibid.*, p. 41.
[5] *Ibid.*, p. 146.
[6] *Ibid.*, p. 295.
[7] *Ibid.*, p. 300.
[8] Cf. Edward Mayes, *Lucius Q. C. Lamar: His Life, Times, and Speeches*, Nashville: Barbee & Smith, Agents, 1896; and Wirt Armistead Cate: *Lucius Q. C. Lamar: Secession and Reunion*, Charlotte: University of North Carolina Press, 1935.

he was honored by two States, the Georgia of his birth and the Mississippi of his adoption, each of which elected him to Congress. In both states he won financial success as a lawyer and academic acclaim as a college professor. As a Professor at Emory College, in Atlanta, he married the daughter of President Augustus B. Longstreet; and at the University of Mississippi, in three different periods he was appointed a Professor of Mathematics and of Philosophy. His home life was notably happy and his habits were sedate, settled, and eminently respectable. Like Yancey and Benjamin, Lamar served the Confederacy during the war both at home and as a diplomat; then, unlike Benjamin, after the defeat he remained in the South, saying simply, "I shall stay with my people and share their fate."[9] Far from being ambitiously opportunistic, Lamar seemed always to flee from the demands and burdens of fame and public acclaim; yet time and again he surrendered his cherished life of scholarly seclusion in order to serve the needs of his section and his class. Eventually he was to make his greatest speech, at the deliberate risk of his reputation, in an effort to conciliate the North and reunite the bitterly divided nation. He was a man to whom fame justly belonged.

In every essential respect, Lamar's life represented the triumph of unruffled "correctness." His childhood home, a magnificent colonial mansion set amidst an estate of eleven hundred acres, contained one of the best libraries in the South; and it was presided over by parents who entertained wisely and guided him into intellectual interests and social graces. A neighbor of Joel Chandler Harris, he shared with the great storyteller an unquestioning view of the Negro as a quaint and childlike creature who enjoyed a gay and carefree life of safe inferiority. Reading the speeches of Calhoun and of the Georgia Triumvirate, young Lamar never doubted that the South was battling righteously against an evil Northern conspiracy that sought for selfish reasons to violate the constitutional rights of the Southern States.

Even in his early teens, in school and college, he excelled as a public speaker, with an unerring instinct for phrasing attractively what his listeners most strongly felt and believed. His equipment for oratory was more mental than physical, for his greatest gifts were a keenly analytical mind and an ability to state complex matters in appealingly simple terms. Late in his life, in 1873, these were precisely the qualities to which the usually unfriendly *Hernando Press* ascribed his success: "Mr. Lamar possesses, in an eminent degree, two qualities not often combined, and which, when they meet, must always produce a first-class

---

[9] Cate, *op. cit.*, p. 114.

orator: he has great beauty and power of expression, and a mind deeply philosophical and analytical."[10] Beyond this, he was below medium height, broadly built, with flowing brown hair and a fashionably full beard. His gestures were dignified and his appearance meticulously neat. He always dressed with great care—"my linen always pure white—my boots spotless and my coat and pants strangers either to lint or motes of dust," as he pointedly and primly reminded a young man who sought to learn from him the secret of success.

Lamar's first emergence into fame occurred when, as a twenty six year old Adjunct Professor of Mathematics at the University of Mississippi, he accepted the urgent request of Democratic politicians to engage in a public debate with the able Senator H. S. Foote, who had outraged his constituents by voting for the Compromise of 1850. Lamar demolished his veteran opponent by pillorying him for having violated the explicit instructions of the State legislature—an ironic beginning for a career that was to reach its own climax in just such a repudiation of instructions from the same source. The speech won statewide applause. But Lamar's reaction was: "I don't care about it . . . . When I deliver a speech that elicits applause and praise, my first thought of it is, what good will it do?"[11] He seemed too pure for politics; but the politicians didn't think so.

Ignoring the partisan efforts to propel him into public office, Lamar left Mississippi to return to Georgia, where his wife felt more at home. But scarcely had he arrived before he was elected to the Georgia legislature. There his first speech so paralyzed opposition, "even in the breast of the most bitter partisan," that "none ventured a reply." One member of the opposition, apparently in a state of awe, described him as "of over-endowed brain and nerve power . . . charged as if by a galvanic battery in all his physical and mental composition when called forth to make intellectual effort."[12] Once again an assured political career was thrust upon him; and once again he turned his back upon it—this time, in October, 1855, to return to Mississippi where he now decided to make his permanent home. Near Oxford he purchased a thousand-acre estate, to provide employment for his numerous slaves, and confided to a friend: "I do not look to be more than a village lawyer or a country gentleman. I have relinquished all my high hopes of imperishable fame; and I have lost much of the energy and animation of character which I had when with you."[13]

[10] *Ibid.*, p. 175.
[11] *Ibid.*, p. 42.
[12] *Ibid.*, p. 44.
[13] *Ibid.*, p. 50.

His hopes for a quiet life were bootless. Frequently he was invited to make speeches; and his skill in defending slavery was so urgently in demand that in 1857 the Democratic caucus nominated him for Congress. Several weeks after his arrival in Washington he delivered an "impetuous, scholarly, and defiant" attack against the Kansas-Nebraska bill, during which he asserted: "Any proposition which has for its object the advancement and progress of Southern institutions, by equitable means, will always commend itself to my cordial approval. Others may boast of their widely extended patriotism, and their enlarged and comprehensive love of this Union. With me, I confess that the promotion of Southern interests is second in importance only to the preservation of Southern honor."[14] He remained in Congress until the secession of Mississippi, frequently advocating the breakup of the Union as the only way to safeguard slavery—even though, more clearly than most, he saw the inevitable result. "Disunion," he admitted, "cannot take place quietly; the vast and complicated machinery of this government cannot be divided without general tumult and, it may be, ruin. When the sun of the Union sets, it will go down in blood."[15] In December, 1859, he told the Congress: "I am devoted to the Constitution . . . so long as this Republic is a great tolerant republic, throwing its arms around both sections of the country." However, when the Constitution "is violated, persistently violated, when its spirit is no longer observed upon this floor, I war upon your government, I am against it. I raise then the banner of secession, and I will fight under it as long as the blood flows and ebbs in my veins."[16]

While the war was being fought there was no time for oratory, nor even for statemanship, as Lamar told an audience at Montgomery, after the firing on Fort Sumter. For a time he served as a Lt. Col. in the infantry, then went on a diplomatic mission to France. In Paris he learned that the South could never win a place among free nations until after it freed the slaves; and he came home to argue fruitlessly for emancipation. After the war he taught for three years at the University of Mississippi, until it was taken over by carpetbaggers. Then for another three years he resumed the practice of law. During this interval Lamar endured with other Southern whites the spectacle of riot and ruin introduced from the North. He was outspokenly bitter about it, repeatedly describing President Grant as a tyrant and mourning the fate of the South under "the chill shadow of such a despotism." Increasingly he

[14] *Ibid.*, pp. 57–58.
[15] *Ibid.*, p. 59.
[16] *Ibid.*, p. 66.

worried lest "the Southern people will feel that death is better than life; and then despair and nemesis will rule the hour."[17]

In the slow and painful aftermath of the war, however, like the whole defeated white population of the South, he had somehow to find a way of coming to terms in his own mind with the new order. When friends hoped to secure his election to Congress in 1872, he confessed: "I have not yet learned to expand my sense of political duty" to the whole nation.[18] After he was in fact elected, he declared in a speech to the House of Representatives that "the South comprehends its own necessities, and wishes to be no longer the agitating and agitated pendulum of American politics."[19] Explaining to a friend his acceptance of election to the national legislature, Lamar wrote: "You may be assured of one thing: I am a patriot—that is, my heart beats with more fidelity to the interest and happiness of the American people, and to the principles of public and individual freedom, than it does to my own tranquility."[20]

Lamar found it difficult to submerge his uneasy sense of guilt at having brought to an end his own feud with the federal system. Again and again he had to explain how he could repudiate his pre-war record of unremitting resistance to the national authority. "If I could talk to you," he wrote to a former law partner, "I think I could show that I am consistent in *purpose* and *principle*, though I have changed my relative position as to men and measures. This is true patriotism and statesmanship in my opinion. Consistency in your *end* and *aim*; variety, change, and adaptability in the use of your means."[21] Both in meaning and even in terminology, this is perilously close to what the world, a couple of generations later, would be hearing from V. I. Lenin, as the "zig-zag theory" of Communist tactics. Lamar, however, meant it no more deeply than as a temporary salve to his own conscience. He was like a soldier who had surrendered, rationalizing that the fight would now have to be carried on by different means.

What he did feel, honestly and strongly, was that the South must accept unquestioningly the unalterable finality of the outcome of the

---

[17] History, dealing kindly with Lamar, has brushed lightly over his bitterness to emphasize his later spirit of reconciliation. Ben: Perley Poore, in *Perley's Reminiscences*, Philadelphia: Hubbard Bros., 1886, II:361–362, praises his "influence in molding public opinion at the South . . . as healthy as it had been powerful." Claude G. Bowers, in *The Tragic Era*, New York: Blue Ribbon Books, 1929, sentimentalized that "The gentle Lamar, depressed, is standing by the gate of his cottage at Oxford in the twilight, looking sadly across the solemn fields, watching his neighbors passing in the middle of the road for safety" (p. 368).
[18] Cate, *op. cit.*, p. 146.
[19] *Ibid.*, p. 149.
[20] *Ibid.*, p. 148.
[21] *Ibid.*, p. 152.

war—and must make the North realize that its acceptance was complete. Only on this basis could there be a reconciliation of the sections. For months Lamar meditated upon what he might be able to say that would help achieve this object. He recognized his opportunity on the unlikely occasion of the death of one of the South's bitterest enemies, Senator Charles Sumner, on March 11, 1874.

Lamar determined to join the eulogists of Sumner, and he picked March 28 as the date for his speech. In the interval he labored thoughtfully upon what he would say. "It is a very delicate subject, and it is very difficult to determine what *not* to say," he confessed to a friend.[22] To his wife he wrote, after the speech had been delivered: "I never in all my life opened my lips with a purpose more single to the interests of our Southern people."[23] Yet the purpose he sought to serve could be achieved only if the North felt he were speaking both to and for the whole nation. Above all, Lamar had to express conciliatory sentiments in such a vein that the South would accept and join in them. Otherwise a negative reaction in Dixie might undermine all he sought to achieve.

The eulogy opened with praise of Sumner's "instinctive love of freedom" and of his courage in championing the cause of the Negro.[24] But it soon shifted to the theme that "both sections should gather up the glories won by each section: not envious, but proud of each other, and regard them as a common heritage of American valor . . . . Bound to each other by a common constitution," he urged, "destined to live together under a common government, forming unitedly but a single member of the great family of nations, shall we not now at last endeavor to grow *toward* each other once more in heart, as we are already indissolubly linked to each other in fortunes?" He went on: "The South, prostrate, exhausted, drained of her lifeblood . . . accepts the bitter award of the bloody arbitrament without reservation . . . . The North, exultant in her triumph . . . still cherishes . . . a heart full of magnanimous emotions . . ." Then he concluded with a sentence he had "tried out" in private letters and in conversations, until he felt assured of its effect: "My countrymen! *know* one another, and you will *love* one another."[25]

The impact of the speech was enormous. It was reprinted in newspapers all through the nation; and it received unqualified praise, North and South. Typical was the editorial of the Springfield, Massachusetts, *Republican:* "When such a Southerner of the Southerners as Mr. La-

[22] *Ibid.,* p. 156.
[23] *Ibid.,* p. 5.
[24] *Ibid.,* pp. 1–7; 156–163.
[25] *Ibid.,* p. 2.

mar, of Mississippi, stands up in the House of Representatives to pronounce such a generous and tender eulogy upon Charles Sumner as this . . . it must begin to dawn upon even the most inveterate rebel haters in Congress, and the press, that the war is indeed over, and that universal amnesty is in order."[26] In Atlanta, the young editor of the *Constitution*, Henry Grady, gave lavish praise to the speech and studied it with such care that, twelve years later, he made it the model for an address of his own that was to be even more influential. Mississippi, far from misunderstanding or disapproving what Lamar intended, promptly rewarded him by electing him to the Senate.

Although in the years to come Lamar suffered a series of apoplectic strokes, he was to live for yet another two decades and to win many more honors, including the Interior post in Cleveland's cabinet and appointment to the United States Supreme Court. Meanwhile, his courage and skill in debate were to be tested in many more struggles: against the violent reconstructionists in Congress, in the Hayes-Tilden electoral battle, and especially on the inflationary "silver bill" sponsored by "Silver Dick" Bland of Missouri.

It was on this last occasion that Lamar, under explicit orders from the Mississippi Legislature to vote for the Bland bill, violated the instructions and voted as his conscience dictated "for sound money." When the Legislature demanded that its instructions be obeyed, Lamar refused with a courageously direct statement of his view of the function of a representative in a democracy: "Between these instructions and my convictions there is a great gulf. I cannot pass it . . . . Today I must be true or false, honest or cunning, faithful or unfaithful to my people. Even in this hour of their legislative displeasure and disapprobation I cannot vote as these resolutions direct. I cannot and will not shirk the responsibility which my position imposes. My duty, as I see it, I will do; and I will vote against this bill."[27] Once again national fame was won by his stand, with President F. A. P. Barnard of Columbia University writing to Lamar: "What an astonishing thing . . . that the truest friends to the Union are those who honestly tried once to get out of it."[28] Lamar was sharply criticized in Mississippi; but the State regarded him far too highly to cast him aside for his show of independence. Besides, his apostasy was the less serious since the Bland bill passed without his vote.

Lamar died on January 23, 1893, while serving on the Supreme Court. From his youth as a secessionist, he had lived to win enduring fame as

[26] *Ibid.*, pp. 3–4.
[27] *Ibid.*, p. 316.
[28] Mapes, *op. cit.*, p. 333.

an architect of reconciliation. As an orator he left few brilliant passages of memorable prose (with the notable exception of the Sumner eulogy); for he shone, rather, in the thrust and parry of impromptu debate, where the quickness of his mind and the clarity of his understanding had few equals. His own self-critique is just: "I cannot write a speech," he declared in 1871. "The pen is an extinguisher upon my mind and a torture to my nerves. I am the most habitual extemporaneous speaker that I have ever known. Whenever I get the opportunity I prepare my argument with great labor and thought . . . . But my friends all tell me that my offhand speeches are by far more vivid than my prepared efforts."[29]

Throughout his life, at many stages, on many topics, many who knew him would gladly have joined in the tribute paid him by Chief Justice Fuller of the U. S. Supreme Court: "His was the most suggestive mind that I ever knew, and not one of us but has drawn from its inexhaustible store."

📖 *Jefferson Davis: Confederate President*

FOR GENERATIONS after the Civil War, children everywhere except in the deep South were lustily singing, "We'll hang Jeff Davis to a sour apple tree." During and after the war he was not only hated in the North but was bitterly excoriated by many leaders in his own section. He and Abraham Lincoln were curiously alike during their presidential tenures in the snarling, snapping venom of the attacks made upon them. "We shall win our independence," Robert Toombs declared angrily, while the war went on, "but it will be in spite of him."[1] In American history his name has become synonymous with rebellion, as has that of Benedict Arnold with treason. Davis himself did little to mitigate the harshness of this judgment. He remained an unreconstructed rebel, saying two years after the surrender that "nations are not immortal, and their wickedness will surely be punished in this world"[2]—clearly meaning his audience to understand his reference was to the United States. In 1886, in a farewell tour through the South, when he received from his people praise that had been long deferred, he still proudly asserted:

[29] Cate, *op. cit.*, p. 163.
[1] Hendricks, *Statesmen of the Lost Cause, op. cit.*, p. 417.
[2] Robert McElroy, *Jefferson Davis: The Unreal and the Real*, New York: Harper, 1937, II:638. However, in a last speech in Mississippi City, just before his death, he said: "The past is dead; let it bury its dead, its hopes, its aspirations; before you lies the future." Elizabeth Cutting, *Jefferson Davis: Political Soldier*, New York: Dodd, Mead, 1930, p. 311.

"I am too old to fight again and God knows I don't want you to have the necessity of fighting again. However, if that necessity should arise, I know you will meet it as you always have discharged every duty you felt called upon to perform."[3] Not surprisingly, he bore until death the label of the "Great Rebel."[4] Yet he was peculiarly American; and with some small but significant shifts of circumstances his name might have ranked among our national heroes.

When he was born on June 3, 1808, in Kentucky, his parents named him in honor of the great Democrat who was then nearing the end of his second presidential term. The family was moderately poor; and the father, Sam Davis, was a true pioneer. A few years before Jefferson Davis's birth, the family had "gone West" from Georgia, and while the boy was still below school age they made other long, covered-wagon journeys through Indian-infested wilderness—first to Louisiana, then to Mississippi. When he was six, young Jeff was sent with another venturesome family on the long horseback trip to Kentucky (stopping en route for a visit with Andrew Jackson at The Hermitage), where Davis spent the next three years in a Catholic school. Then once again the boy returned to Mississippi, this time travelling in style down the great river, on a side-wheeler steamboat. This time he was sent to Lexington, to attend Transylvania College—where in his third year he was chosen Junior Class Orator.

History offers strange coincidences and is replete with accidents. Sam Davis was temperamentally much like Tom Lincoln, though somewhat more industrious and prosperous. Both families migrated restlessly under the spell of Western fever. It could easily have happened that the Lincoln family might have turned south to find a home, and that the Davises might have been drawn to the flourishing lands of Ohio (or Illinois). What did happen was that for a year—the first Jeff Davis spent in the Catholic school—the two sons of these families lived just thirty miles apart. They met in their young manhood, when Jefferson Davis, as a stiff young Second Lieutenant, fresh from West Point and proud in his uniform, administered the oath of allegiance to the United States to tall, shambling, awkward, un-uniformed Abraham Lincoln, who came as a Captain of Illinois volunteers to fight in the Black Hawk War. Lincoln did little in this conflict except to slap mosquitoes. Davis admired and sympathized with the Indians, yet he led his troops valiantly and skillfully against them.

---

[3] *Ibid.*, II:678.
[4] The other side of the story is told by his wife, Varina Howell Davis, in her *Memoir*, *op. cit.*, in which she says: "The era is closed, the cause sleeps, but the people survive, and revere the memory, and mourn him dead, whom, living, they delighted to honor" (I:1).

Chief Black Hawk was fighting for "minority rights" and he fought so well that, as Lt. Davis said, if he had been on the winning side his name would have been immortalized.[5] The genesis of the war was that the Indians refused to abide by a treaty they considered unjust. In 1804 General Harrison had purchased some fifty million acres of the best midwestern land from the chiefs of the Sac and Fox Indians, for the promise of a $1000 annuity to be distributed amongst them. Black Hawk was one of these chiefs; nevertheless, he and his people remained on the land, refusing to leave. For, as he explained, in a fruitless effort to renegotiate the treaty: "I touched goose quill to the treaty, not knowing . . . that by that act I gave away my village. My reason teaches me that land cannot be sold. The Great Spirit gave it to his children to live upon . . . . Nothing can be sold but such things as can be carried away."[6] Davis was dispirited by the duty of fighting and destroying an antagonist such as this. At this juncture he fell in love with the daughter of Zachary Taylor, who did not want her to marry into the military. For both these reasons Davis resigned his commission and settled twenty miles below Vicksburg on an estate of tangled brush appropriately named Briarfields, which was given him as a wedding present by his elder brother Joseph. Within three months Davis's bride was dead from "river fever." Davis threw himself into the work of building his plantation and of indoctrinating himself into the principles and views of this new way of life.

Throughout the remainder of his life, Davis's political views remained remarkably consistent. He believed that slaves were property and that under the law they should be regarded precisely like property of any other kind. He believed that the Constitution was a compact made by the States and that every State had the legal and moral right to withdraw from that compact at any time it wished. Since he could and did present these views with great skill, he became, after the death of Calhoun, the acknowledged leader in the Senate and in the nation of the Southern cause.[7]

Davis developed an extensive and prosperous plantation in the delta country at the very time when this area was illustrating the worst features of the slavocracy. The rich bottom lands bordering the great river were enormously productive of cotton. But first the land had to be cleared, and the field work had to be done in the summer heat and

---

[5] Significantly, Mrs. Davis, in her account of the Black Hawk War, presents an account decidedly sympathetic to the Indians. *Memoirs, op. cit.,* I:104–135.
[6] Alvin M. Josephy, Jr., *The Patriot Chiefs, A Chronicle of American Indian Leadership,* New York: Viking, 1961, p. 230.
[7] Another factor, mentioned by Allan Nevins, was that "Mississippians had an intense appreciation of good popular oratory." *The Ordeal of the Union,* New York: Scribner's, 1947, I:185.

humidity. Fever was endemic; and field hands were not expected to survive for more than a few years. Because of the continually expanding need, slaves were purchased from the soil-depleted Southeastern seaboard areas at the average rate of eighteen thousand a year between 1830 and 1860. Slave auctions were a commonplace in New Orleans and St. Louis. Families were separated; slave girls were sold as "breeders"; runaways had to be punished severely to discourage the temptation of flight. At no other time or place in American history did slavery so much resemble the callous cruelties of the old Roman galleys. Of all this Davis remained unaware.

He was certain that God had created the Negro inferior and that slavery was the only condition in which he could be secure and happy. Freedom would place him in direct competition with the whites, which would result in "harsh social restrictions and treatment." In a speech delivered on April 12, 1860, he declared that the "human" attributes of slaves were no more remarkable than the fact that Balaam's ass could speak. Ownership of such slaves, he insisted, "awakens whatever there is of kindness or of nobility of soul" in their owner—unless, he admitted candidly, he owns "such masses that the owner himself becomes ignorant of the individuals who compose it."[8]

Davis was a careful, systematic, and generally humanitarian master. For his 113 slaves he provided twenty eight cabins, comparable with the seventy six cabins his brother Joseph provided for his 355 slaves. The average annual food cost for slaves, besides the vegetables they grew, was $30 apiece. Davis guarded himself against carelessly mistreating his slaves by establishing a system under which they exercised considerable self-government, including a guarantee against punishment for any offense until after the slave was found guilty by a jury of his fellows. Even after the Civil War Davis was insisting that if "the whites are better off for the abolition of slavery," it was "an equally patent fact that the colored people are not."[9] During the Senate debates on the Compromise of 1850, Davis declared that "through the portals of slavery alone has the graceless son of Noah ever entered into the temple of civilization." Wherever one dips into his views on this subject, they are found to be consistent. His judgment may have distinguished itself by a peculiarly one-sided selection of evidence; but there is no reason to doubt that he was sincere in his belief that slavery was beneficial for the Negroes.

The most comprehensive statement of his views on the Constitution

[8] *Jefferson Davis: Constitutionalist*, ed. Dunbar Rowland, Jackson, Miss.: Dept. of Archives, 1923, IV:23ff; cf. McElroy, *op. cit.*, I:42.
[9] McElroy, *op. cit.*, I:44.

and on the nature of the sectional dispute was given in a series of speeches delivered in New England, the center of radical abolitionism, during the fall of 1858. Having served with distinction for four years as Secretary of War, Davis was now once again in the Senate, where his fame rivalled or surpassed that of Seward, Douglas, and Sumner. In August he was awarded an honorary LL.D. degree by Bowdoin College, in Brunswick, where Harriet Beecher Stowe was just receiving a letter from her sister Isabel that induced her to write *Uncle Tom's Cabin*. On the 24th of that month, to a Democratic Convention in Portland, he boldly attacked "geographical tests" of the Constitution. On September 29 he was back in Augusta, denouncing sectional partisanship. On October 11 he gave a widely acclaimed speech in Boston's Faneuil Hall, where he identified New England as the primary "asserter of democratic state rights doctrine."[10] All this was what his New England audiences wanted to hear. Then he turned to direct attack upon the abolitionists—still not an unpopular theme. Why, he demanded, "are you so agitated" about slavery? "With pharisaical pretension it is sometimes said it is a moral obligation to agitate . . . . Who gave them a right to decide that it is a sin? By what standard do they measure it? Not by the Constitution . . . . Not by the Bible; that justifies it. Not by the good of society; for if they go where it exists, they find that society recognizes it as good . . . . Is it in the cause of Christianity? It cannot be, for servitude is the only agency through which Christianity has reached that degraded race." The reaction of his listeners was generally favorable.

On his way home from New England, Davis spoke at the Palace Garden, in New York, where he denounced the claim of the abolitionists that hatred and fear were the brand marks of the relations between masters and slaves. "Our doors are unlocked at night," he pointed out; "we live among them with no more fear of them than of our cows and oxen. We lie down to sleep trusting to them for our own defense, and the bond between the master and the slave is as near as that which exists between capital and labor anywhere . . . . The delusion which has always excited my surprise the most is . . . the higher law doctrine . . . . The doctrine is now advanced to you only in relation to property of the Southern States . . . but it will react upon yourselves if you accept it. What security have you for your own safety if every man of vile temper, of low instincts, of base purpose, can find in his own heart a law higher than that which is the rule of society, the Constitution and the

---

[10] Ralph Richardson, "Jefferson Davis: Sectional Diplomat, 1858," in Auer, *op. cit.*, pp. 51–62. Mrs. Davis presented her own account of the New England tour in *Memoir*, *op. cit.*, I:584–643, which, she reports, left him "far more happy over the hope of a peaceable adjustment of the sectional dissonance" (I:641).

Bible?" Then, for the first time on his northern tour, he launched into a bitter tirade: "The higher law preachers should be tarred and feathered and whipped by those they have thus instigated. This, my friends, is what was called in the good old revolutionary times, Lynch Law. It is sometimes the very best law . . ."[11] His surface calm was beginning to break.

Flushed with the excitement generated by his favorable reception up North, Davis went home to deliver, on November 16, a report to the Mississippi Legislature. After denouncing Seward for a speech given at Rochester, New York, three weeks earlier, declaring there was an "irrepressible conflict" between slavery and freedom, Davis turned to a consideration of how the South could best confront its enemies. His proposed solution contrasts sensationally with his denunciation of sectionalism in his New England speeches. "I hold the separation from the Union by the State of Mississippi to be the last remedy—the final alternative. In the language of the venerated Calhoun, I consider the disruption of the Union as a great, though not the greatest, calamity." He then urged military preparedness, not to "precipitate upon us the trial of secession," but to "give to our conduct the character of earnestness of which mere paper declarations have somewhat deprived us." In conclusion he said that "if an Abolitionist be chosen President . . . I should deem it your duty to provide for your safety outside the Union."[12]

Davis considered himself a defender of strict constitutionalism. In a Senate speech on February 24, 1851, he had said, regarding the Fugitive Slave Law, "I deny the power of Massachusetts to nullify the law and remain in the Union, but I concede to her the right . . . to take the 'extreme medicine,' secession . . . . If she has resolved to cast off the obligation of the Constitution . . . then she is, of her own free will and sovereign act, virtually out of it. I, for one, will never give a dollar to coerce her back."[13] He was well aware, however, that the division of the nation was along sectional lines and that it was unlikely secession could be accomplished peacefully. On January 10, 1850, he warned that the South would defend slavery "even by civil war." In that same debate, on February 5, responding to remarks by Henry Clay, Davis declared that, "considering as I do the cold, calculating purpose of those who seek for sectional dominion, I see nothing short of conquest on the one side, or submission on the other." During all the years of the continuing debate, Davis remained true to sentiments he expressed on June 27, 1850: "God forbid that the day should ever come when to be true to

---

[11] *Jefferson Davis: Constitutionalist*, op. cit., III:332–339, especially, p. 338.
[12] *Ibid.*, III:339–361, especially, pp. 358–359.
[13] *Ibid.*, II:35–43.

my constituents is to be hostile to the Union."[14] Even so, the welfare of his constituency came first.

Loving both the Union and the rights of his own class and section, Davis did not retreat from the quandary but was ready with a solution, which he proposed on the day following Webster's famous Seventh of March speech.[15] In effect Davis felt, as did Lincoln, that slavery must be placed in "the course of ultimate extinction"—to borrow Lincoln's careful phraseology. But whereas Lincoln believed this could be accomplished only by confining slavery tightly within its existing territories, Davis was convinced that eventual emancipation could and would be accomplished only when slaves were so vastly scattered over a wide area that the ratio of owners to slaves would be equalized in all parts of the country. Then and only then would it be possible to reach agreement on a practical plan of emancipation that would be fair to all the owners of this kind of property.

His last extended speech to the Senate, presented on January 10, 1861, was received with respectful attention; for many felt the truth of his assertion that "I have striven unsuccessfully to avert the catastrophe which now impends over the country." The sober sense of responsibility which marks his career was mirrored in his words: "God knows the hearts of men will judge between you and us, at whose door lies the responsibility."[16] On January 21 it was known that Jefferson Davis would deliver his farewell to the Senate and as early as seven A.M. crowds were seeking admission to the galleries. His statement was brief and dignified: "In the presence of my God, I wish you well; and such, I am sure, is the feeling of the people whom I represent toward those whom you represent. It only remains for me to bid you a final farewell."[17] He remained in Washington for five days longer, hoping to be arrested, thereby to provide the South with a martyr to help rally its unified strength; then he started home.

On his way from Washington to the Convention called in Montgomery to inaugurate the Confederacy, Davis made some twenty five speeches that were so conciliatory in tone that Rhett complained: "Davis will exert all his powers to reunite the Confederacy to the Empire."[18] Despite a subsurface roiling of severe opposition, Davis was elected to the Presidency by a unanimous vote. In his inaugural address he stressed the desire for peace, reiterating the favorite Southern theme

[14] *Ibid.*, I:250–254 and 379.
[15] For a discussion of the circumstances from Davis's point of view, cf. McElroy, op. cit., II:131–147.
[16] *Constitutionalist*, V:1–35; especially, pp. 31, 25.
[17] *Ibid.*, V:44.
[18] McElroy, *op. cit.*, I:269.

that secession was clearly sanctioned under the Constitution. He sent a commission to Washington to negotiate peace "between the two governments." Nevertheless, he knew that war was inevitable and he labored, without great success, to weld the sovereign and highly individualistic Southern States into a sufficient harmony of action to make defensive war possible. As an orator his career was ended.

He lived on for a quarter-century after the war's end, dying on December 6, 1889, at the age of eighty one. At daylight of that day he awakened, looked up at his wife, and said: "I want to tell you I am not afraid to die."[19] Circumstances had made him the chief defender, after Calhoun, of the least defensible of American institutions. He never viewed slavery as immoral and never viewed the Union as perpetual. But he argued the cause in which he believed with logic and with dignity. No better description of Davis as a speaker has been preserved than that written by his second wife, Varina Howell Davis: " . . . no speech was ever written for delivery," she said. "Dates and names were jotted down on two or three inches of paper, and these sufficed. Mr. Davis's speeches never read as they were delivered; he spoke fast, and thoughts crowded each other closely; a certain magnetism of manner and the exceeding beauty and charm of his voice moved the multitude, and there were apparently no inattentive or indifferent listeners. He had one power that I have never seen excelled; while speaking, he took in the individuality of the crowd, and seeing doubt or a lack of coincidence with him in their faces, he answered the mental dissonance with arguments addressed to the case in their minds." She went on to say that he was a "parenthetical speaker, which was a defect in a written oration, but it did not, when uttered, impair the quality of his speeches, but rather added a charm . . . . At first his style was ornate . . . but it soon changed into a plain and stronger cast of what he considered to be, and doubtless was, the higher kind of oratory."[20]

Jefferson Davis left behind few words or few acts for which he himself ever felt remorse. Had he lived in a different place or at a different time he might well have been a happier and a greater man. As it was, he spoke for his own people; and he could not rise above them to see and to lead toward different horizons that were hidden from their view. He could not be a statesman but he tried.

[19] Mrs. Davis, *Memoir, op. cit.*, II:931.
[20] *Ibid.*, I:214–215.

VII

THE ANTISLAVERY
CRUSADE
1831‒1865

🕮 Prophets of Secular Salvation

HISTORIANS AND social critics have long been concerned with "why humanitarian reform appeared in America when it did."[1] Whatever the causes, the great surge of do-goodism was far from being confined to America. This was the era of the Reform Bill in England. All Europe was swept with a rising tide of nationalism and of democratic revolution. Perhaps it was the fruit of the progressivism discovered and preached by the French Encyclopedists in the eighteenth century. It surely was a political and social manifestation of the age of romanticism. It must have taken impetus in part from the shift away from supernatural religion toward ethical brotherhood, as celebrated in Leigh Hunt's poem, "Abou Ben Adhem." No doubt it was partly owing to the initial disruption of living conditions and of the communal sense of values that occurred when agrarianism was undermined by the uncontrolled factory system of the nascent Industrial Revolution. In America it was aided by the start of a cycle of financial strains that culminated in the frightening Panic of 1837. The sociologists appear to have a point in their contention that its leadership came from a group of young individuals from once-great families that were falling markedly toward mediocrity.[2]

Dates for such a social movement are tenuous.[3] During the Era of Good Feeling that followed the War of 1812, Americans set about

---

[1] David Donald, *Lincoln Reconsidered*, New York: Random House, Vintage Books, rev., 1961, p. 21. Particularly valuable on this subject are: Alice Felt Tyler, *Freedom's Ferment*, Minneapolis: University of Minnesota Press, 1944; Carl Russell Fish, *The Rise of the Common Man*, New York: Macmillan, 1937; Lawrence Lader, *The Bold Brahmins*, New York: Dutton, 1961; and Oscar Sherwin, *Prophet of Liberty: The Life and Times of Wendell Phillips*, New York: Bookman Associates, 1958; together with biographies and collected speeches of the orators discussed in this chapter.

[2] Donald, *op. cit.*, pp. 19–36.

[3] J. Bronowski and Bruce Mazlish, *The Western Intellectual Tradition: From Leonardo to Hegel*, New York: Harper, 1960, dates the beginnings of humanitarianism in the Renaissance. A review of values lost or threatened in the movement is presented by Irving Babbitt, *Rousseau and Romanticism*, New York: Houghton Mifflin, 1919.

demonstrating that a little prosperity is an intoxicating thing. President Monroe issued a doctrine warning Europe to keep hands off any part of the new world. Farmers and laborers elected Andrew Jackson as their very own president and exulted in their new sense of power. The intellectuals turned toward Thomas Hobbes, with his theory that men needed considerable government to civilize them, and began to re-examine the Lockian and Rousseauistic cult of natural rights.[4] Government, they were coming to feel, must take a far more active role in regulating affairs than Thomas Jefferson had believed. A heady quest for perfectionism unloosed a ferment of reform. Amidst a fresh conviction that the universe itself is run by moral law and that progress is to be earned by goodness and brotherly love—which in turn were to be enforced by the police power of the enlightened minority—a spirit of renovation swept the United States, making its windy way into every cranny of institutional and individual life. Communist communities, a newly revealed religion for Latter Day Saints, abolitionism, women's rights, antiwar enthusiasm, dietary reforms, crusades against tobacco, and prohibitionism all helped to give explicit form to the burgeoning determination to bring paradise down to earth, rather than to wait passively for "pie in in the sky" to be served up in an uncertain heaven. Within the churches the social gospel became exuberant, leading Theodore Parker, for example, to preach on the duties of milkmen, rules for fair merchandizing, and Christianizing influence of clean streets. So much had already been accomplished toward achieving the good life in the first generation after the Revolution that hopes bounded high for a Yankee Utopia.[5]

Ralph Waldo Emerson, in "The Chardon Street Convention," set the tone that has generally been followed by later critics of the eruption of philanthropic zeal. The Friends of Universal Reform assembled in November, 1840, he wrote, exhibited "a great deal of confusion, eccentricity, and freak." The assemblage, he went on, "attracted a great deal of public attention" consisting both "of abhorrence and merriment." Those who attended were "madmen, madwomen, men with beards, Dunkers, Muggletonians, Come-Outers, Groaners, Agrarians, Seventh-Day Baptists, Quakers, Abolitionists, Calvinists, Unitarians and

---

[4] Thomas Hobbes, in Chapter XIII of *Leviathan*, wrote that in a state of nature there are "no arts, no letters, no society, and, which is worst of all, continual fear and danger of violent death, and the life of man solitary, poor, nasty, brutish, and short." Rousseau, on the other hand, believed that man is better off when left to his natural condition. As he wrote in *Emile*, "God makes all things good; man meddles with them and they become evil."

[5] Among the many explanations of this Utopian upsurge, cf. R. L. Bruckberger, *Image of America*, New York: Viking Press, 1959; V. L. Parrington, *Main Currents of American Thought*, op. cit., Vol. II; and Merrill D. Peterson, *The Jefferson Image in the American Mind*, New York: Oxford University Press, 1960.

Philosophers . . . . The most daring innovators and the champions-until-death of the old cause sat side by side."[6] As this passage makes clear, the attitude of the populace was far from unanimous. The reform movement was a sensational annunciation of prophetic zeal by a small handful whose energies of expressiveness were so strong that they seized the nation's attention and held it for a generation, getting for their pains a mixed reaction of dread, delight, and dedication.

Most typical and most assertive of the reform movements was the revival of abolitionism. During the colonial period slavery had been taken for granted,[7] though it was attacked sporadically by such idealists as the Quaker John Woolman, who spoke against it in every Colony after 1743, and the Congregationalist Samuel Hopkins, who preached an influential sermon against it at Newport, Rhode Island, in 1770. The Founding Fathers deprecated slavery but scarcely beyond the point expressed in 1773 by Patrick Henry, when he wrote in a private letter that "I believe a time will come when an opportunity will be offered to abolish this lamentable evil," and added: "let us transmit to our descendants, together with our slaves, . . . an abhorrence of slavery."[8] The invention of the cotton gin by Eli Whitney in 1793, which enormously increased the profitableness of slavery, is commonly cited as the root cause for the decline of the Revolutionary era's interest in abolitionism. As we have seen, Henry Clay tried in 1798 to write gradual emancipation into the Kentucky Constitution; and in 1800 there were still more than 100 abolitionist societies in America, with four-fifths of their membership below the Mason–Dixon line.[9] During the next two decades abolitionism subsided, supposedly given an anesthetized death blow by the Missouri Compromise in 1820. John Quincy Adams, however, shared with his *Diary* the conviction that "the bargain between freedom and slavery contained in the Constitution of the United States is morally and politically vicious." His remedy was to split the Union into two nations. "If the Union must be dissolved, slavery is precisely the question upon which it ought to break."[10]

Meanwhile, grubbiness and idealism contended for supremacy. Fortunes were spawned in the black loam soil of the Mississippi, worked by the unfortunate blacks who were sold down the river. Adventurers

[6] Ralph Waldo Emerson, *Works*, op. cit., "The Chardon Street Convention," X:373–377.
[7] Clinton Rossiter, *The First American Revolution*, op. cit., p. 148.
[8] George Morgan, *The True Patrick Henry*, op. cit., pp. 246–248.
[9] Lader, op. cit., reported that in 1827 there were from 140 to 180 abolitionist societies, at least half of them in the South. Ten years later, "not one society remained in slave territory" (pp. 44–45).
[10] John Quincy Adams, *Diary*, ed. Allan Nevins, New York: Scribner's, 1951, p. 232.

rushed into Texas to stir up a war against Mexico; covetous eyes were directed toward Cuba and indeed the whole of Latin America. Another invention of Whitney's, the assembly line, gave tremendous impetus to industrialization. The "noble savage" of Rousseau's dream seemed fated to change into a grimy-faced day laborer, flanked by a sword-waving imperialist and a slaveowning landholder. As Emerson sadly noted, "Things are in the saddle and ride mankind." The possibilities for universal improvement were vast; but impediments of selfish materialism seemed to be increasing. From Europe came inspiring news of a new French Republic, of new suffrage laws in England, of the revolutionary oratory of O'Connell in Ireland, and from France and Germany a transcendental philosophy of brotherhood based on the moral identity of man with nature.[11] Nature is bountiful and beautiful; only man is vile.[12] But the vileness of man was only the failure of institutions to reflect the true goodness of the human heart. The stage was set for agitation and reformist zeal. Many Americans leaped to answer the call.

The New England Radicals: Garrison and Phillips

In 1831, with an initial list of twenty five subscribers, William Lloyd Garrison founded a weekly newspaper, *The Liberator*, announcing the mood of the reformers: "I *will be* as harsh as truth and as uncompromising as justice . . . . I will not retreat a single inch—and *I will be* heard."[1] The same theme was declared with equal exuberance, if in a soberer tone, by Emerson: "We are to revise the whole of our social structure, the State, the school, religion, marriage, trade, science, and explore their foundations in our own nature." For, after all, "What is man born for but to be a Reformer?"[2]

In all reasonableness this question could have been asked of William Lloyd Garrison.[3] Born December 10, 1805, in Newburyport, Massachu-

---

[11] Cf. E. J. Hobsbawm, *The Age of Revolution: Europe, 1789–1848*, London: Weidenfeld and Nicolson, 1962.

[12] The phrase was popularized in a missionary hymn by Reginald Heber (1783–1826).

[1] Commager, *Documents of American History, op. cit.,* I:278.

[2] Emerson, *Works, op. cit.,* I:248.

[3] Wendell Phillips Garrison and Francis Jackson Garrison, *William Lloyd Garrison,* Four Vols., New York: Houghton Mifflin, 1894; Russel B. Nye, *William Lloyd Garrison and the Humanitarian Reformers,* Boston: Little, Brown, 1955; Dwight L. Dumond, *Antislavery Origins of the Civil War in the United States,* Ann Arbor: University of Michigan Press, 1939; John J. Chapman, *William Lloyd Garrison,* Boston: Atlantic Monthly Press, 1921; and Oscar Sherwin, *Prophet of Liberty, op. cit.*

setts, the son of a heavy-drinking sea captain who deserted his wife and infant child, Garrison received little schooling; but his real education commenced when he was indentured at the age of fourteen to a printer and newspaper editor. Soon he was not only setting type but also writing editorials. The revolt of Greece against Turkey so stirred his martial spirit that he considered becoming a professional soldier. However, when his apprenticeship ended in 1826 he commenced the editorship of a series of short-lived newspapers, one of which, *The Philanthropist*, was the first publication in America to advocate the total prohibition of spiritous drink. In 1829 he joined Benjamin Lundy, at Baltimore, in the publication of *The Genius of Universal Emancipation*. The mild Lundy was appalled, however, when Garrison wrote so vitriolic an attack on a slave trader that he was found guilty of libel and jailed. Garrison's radicalism needed its own agency.

Actually, Garrison developed two mediums for the propagation of his views. His newspaper, *The Liberator* (with its masthead motto: "Our country is the world—our countrymen are mankind"), advocated abolition, pacifism, and prohibition, and assailed tobacco, freemasonry, capital punishment, and imprisonment for debt. Through this journal, which continued publication until the ratification of the thirteenth amendment, he established a niche for himself in the history of journalism. His other agency was the New England Antislavery Society, founded in January, 1832, and the American Antislavery Society, established in December, 1833. Through these organizations, which existed largely to sponsor abolitionist lectures, and through his own extensive speaking, he won a place in the oratory of agitation.

Garrison's views were so radical and his influence so great that 1831, the date when *The Liberator* first appeared, marks the start of a new era in America. Prior to that time abolitionism was respectable and widely popular. *Gradualism* and *irresponsibility* had been its basic characteristics. The theme was that slavery had been introduced into the country long ago, and the present generation had no responsibility for it. Freedom for the slaves was a good thing, but such an ideal would be chaotically disruptive of the socio-economic system. Only through some system of gradual emancipation could freedom be accomplished. This system could neither hurt the present owners nor help the present slaves, since the ideas presented usually recommended eventual freedom for all, or some, slaves who might be born after some future date. Finally, when the Negroes were freed, the next step would be to return them all to Africa, for which purpose a colony was established in Liberia, and societies were organized to raise money to pay their passage. Such a program made it easy for almost everyone to condemn slavery as an abstract system without, in fact, endangering either its existence or its extension. Garrison absolutely renounced this respectable and irreproachable way of dealing with slavery.

His themes were that slavery is evil; that those who were not against it were for it; that it must be fought to the death by any and every means available, here and now; that the churches were anti-religious because they sanctioned slavery; that the Constitution was "a covenant with death and a compact with hell" because it sanctioned slavery; and that the best solution short of war (which, as a pacifist, he opposed) was to break up the Union, form a free Northern nation, and from it as a base to do everything possible to assist as many slaves as possible in escaping from their Southern masters. He compounded this radical recipe still further by insisting that women must be accorded equal status with men and by even appointing some of them as lecturers to help propagate the cause.

The man who fought for this radical program was exceedingly sober in appearance, with a balding head and an abstracted, professorial air, dressing habitually in plain black clothing. He could scarcely see without his glasses and carried an ear-trumpet because of increasing deafness. His face, according to the English woman, Harriet Martineau, was "wholly expressive of purity, animation, and gentleness. I did not wonder at the citizen who, seeing a print of Garrison at a shop window without a name to it, went in and bought it, and framed it as the most saint-like of countenances . . . . Garrison has a good deal of a Quaker air; and his speech is deliberate like a Quaker's, but gentle as a woman's."[4] This was the man who launched a campaign of harsh and unremitting attack, which he continued for more than thirty years. In 1854, speaking at the Broadway Tabernacle, in New York, Garrison could say with all apparent sincerity, reviewing his long struggle, "I have avoided fanaticism on the one hand and folly on the other."[5] Few of his countrymen, however, agreed with him on either count. Because of his ideas and methods, and because of the public renunciation of both, Garrison spent his life, until after the Civil War, in an almost continual storm of violence. He often was jeered, stoned, hustled, and mobbed by crowds. But the most sensational occasion was on October 21, 1835, when he was dragged out a window and down a ladder from his office, and pulled through the streets with a rope around his waist—not by hoodlums, but by the most respectable people of Boston. Then he was jailed, allegedly for his own protection, but under a warrant charging

[4] Harriet Martineau, *The Martyr Age of the United States*, Boston: Weeks, Jordan & Co., 1839.
[5] Wrage and Baskerville, *American Forum, op. cit.*, p. 174.

that Garrison himself "did disturb and break the peace, and a riot did cause and make . . ."[6] After his release from jail, he was forced to leave Boston for his own safety. The real reason for the riot was stated in a paragraph from the Richmond *Whig*, which was approvingly reprinted by the Boston *Morning Post:* "The people of the North must go to hanging these fanatical wretches, if they would not lose the benefit of the Southern trade; and they *will* do it. They know too well which side their bread is buttered on, ever to give up these advantages."[7]

By 1835 Garrison had helped to establish sixty abolition societies; and the American Antislavery Society had an annual budget of $30,000. By 1837 the number of such societies grew to one thousand, and by 1838 to thirteen hundred, with 108,000 members.[8] Lecturers were hired at a weekly fee of $12, to pay their living and travelling expenses—and to replace their ripped and ruined clothing. With tireless zeal they commenced to jab at the American conscience. The audiences fought back, with jeers, stones, tar, and feathers. In 1835, the worst mob year, more than one hundred abolitionist lecturers were mobbed. In 1837 not a hall could be hired for the annual meeting of the Massachusetts Antislavery Society, which was forced finally to meet in the loft of a livery stable. Then, on November 7, 1837, a mob at Alton, Illinois, murdered an abolitionist editor, Elijah Lovejoy,[9] resulting in abolitionism's greatest triumph—the enlistment in its cause of the eloquent Boston aristocrat, Wendell Phillips. A second effect of the Lovejoy murder was to split the ranks of the abolitionist movement; for, as Garrison and his followers became more violent, more insistent that there was no political remedy for slavery, and that secession of the North was the only available solution, there arose in Ohio and New York a more moderate movement that advocated the election of antislavery candidates and the passage of antislavery laws. One result was the splitting of the American Antislavery Society, with some of its followers forming the American and Foreign Antislavery Society. Another result was the formation of the Liberty Party, which nominated James Birney, a Kentucky slaveholder, as its candidate for the presidency in 1840 and 1844—preparing the way for the Free Soil Party and then the Republican Party. But Wendell Phillips was not moved to moderation. He became fully as violent as Garrison himself and, as a speaker, was far more influential.

Wendell Phillips brought to abolitionism not only some of the best

[6] Lader, *op. cit.*, Chapter I, "Garrison's Bloody Year: 1835," pp. 13–29.
[7] *Ibid.*, p. 14.
[8] Sherwin, *op. cit.*, pp. 100–101; and Benjamin Quarles, "Sources of Abolitionist Income," *Mississippi Valley Historical Review*, XXXII (June, 1945):63ff.
[9] Henry Tanner, *The Martyrdom of Lovejoy*, Chicago: Fergus Printing Co., 1881; and Lader, *op. cit.*, pp. 71–85.

oratorical ability in American history but also the ultra-respectability of one of New England's most aristocratic family backgrounds.[10] He was born on November 29, 1811, into a family prominent in Boston since 1630. As the son in a family of ministers and lawyers, he early developed a love of speaking. When he was a small child, he use to arrange chairs in a semicircle and make speeches to them. He attended the famous Boston Latin School, where he was a superior student and won a prize for declaiming a Patrick Henry oration. He then went on to Harvard, where again he excelled in both scholarship and speaking—his first speech of record, in an organization called the Harvard Washington Corps, being an assault against the "untried theories" and "mad schemes" of those "advocates of reform" who neglected to follow the sane and safe paths marked out by "the wisdom of the ages."[11] His next stage was attendance at the Harvard Law School, from which he graduated with prospects of an assured success at the bar and in politics. Then he observed the 1835 mobbing of Garrison by the "best people of Boston," and was deeply disturbed. The following year he married Anne Terry Greene, a passionately idealistic invalid who, Phillips confessed, "made an out and out Abolitionist of me."[12] On June 4, 1837, at Lynn, before a local antislavery society, Phillips made his first abolitionist speech.

This was the background, the seedbed in which Phillips's sentiments were nurtured, when, at ten o'clock on the morning of December 8, 1837, he joined an excited crowd of five thousand that met in Faneuil Hall to hear a discussion of the murder of Lovejoy. William Ellery Channing presided, from a stand in the middle of the hall, surrounded by the audience, all standing and crowded closely and noisily together. Then James T. Austin, Attorney General of Massachusetts, presented a long, eloquent, and applauded speech in which he praised the rioters who had slain Lovejoy, likening them to the Boston patriots who had resisted British tyranny in 1776. Phillips had come expecting to make a speech, but whatever he had planned to say he discarded while he listened to Austin's effusion and the roar of approval that greeted it. He threw off his topcoat and started pushing his way through the crowd to the platform, saying to his wife, who tried to hold him back: "I am going to speak, if I can make myself heard." Heard he finally was, after a

---

[10] Wendell Phillips, *Speeches, Lectures, and Letters*, Boston: Lee and Shephard, rev., 1892; George E. Woodberry, *Wendell Phillips: The Faith of An American*, Boston: D. B. Updike, 1912; Oscar Sherwin, *Prophet of Liberty, op. cit.*; Richard Hofstadter, "Wendell Phillips: The Patrician as Agitator," in *The American Political Tradition*, New York: Random House, Vintage Books, 1960, pp. 137–163; and Willard Hayes Yeager, "Wendell Phillips," in Brigance, ed., *History and Criticism, op. cit.*, I:329–362.
[11] Sherwin, *op. cit.*, p. 30.
[12] *Ibid.*, p. 56.

series of attempts to shout him down. And he finally swung the crowd to his side, with a tremendous burst of applause, when he said: "Sir, when I heard the gentleman lay down principles which place the murderers of Alton side by side with Otis and Hancock, with Quincy and Adams, I thought those pictured lips [pointing to the portraits on the walls] would have broken into voice to rebuke the recreant American— the slanderer of the dead!"[13] That evening Maria Chapman visited the Phillipses and urged Wendell to cast his career to the winds and devote himself wholeheartedly to the cause of abolition. For a while he pleaded that he was too young, too inexperienced—that others, Webster, Everett, were better qualified;[14] then he succumbed and abolitionism had made its greatest convert to the cause of action.

Even so, he commenced gently. In 1838 he gave a very prim and proper lecture on "The Lost Arts," which he repeated for forty five years, reportedly more than two thousand times, donating part of the proceeds to the antislavery cause.[15] In June, 1840, he and his wife sailed for London, partly to help her regain her health, partly to attend the first World Antislavery Convention in London. Almost all the delegates were men, except for Anne Phillips, Maria Chapman, Lucretia Mott, and Elizabeth Cady Stanton, who had accompanied Phillips and Garrison from America. The Executive Committee rejected the credentials of the women, and suggested they sit behind the latticework screen in the gallery as spectators. Phillips took the rostrum: "When we have submitted to brickbats and the tar-tub and feathers in New England rather than yield to the custom prevalent there of not admitting colored brethren into our friendship, shall we yield to parallel custom or prejudice against women in Old England?"[16] By overwhelming vote the women were denied membership; and Phillips promptly added the women's rights movement to his program of reform.

Shortly he was adding other causes: advocacy of shorthand (or "phonography"), abolition of capital punishment, the rescue of religion from the church, the prohibition of liquor, integration of Negroes into white schools, housing projects for the poor, improvement of railway cars, development of recreation areas, promotion of boycotts against

[13] *Ibid.*, pp. 58–72. Yeager, *op. cit.*, who studied this speech in detail, reported that "Careful search has not revealed a single adverse comment" on it. I:338.
[14] George Lowell Austin, *Life and Times of Wendell Phillips*, Boston: Lee and Shephard, 1888, p. 86.
[15] In the opinion of Bronson Alcott, "More than any lecturer, unless it be Emerson, he has made the lecture a New England, if not an American, institution." Quoted by Katherine H. Porter, "The Development of the American Lyceum," unpublished thesis, University of Chicago, 1914, p. 34. Sherwin questions the oft-cited "2000 times" figure and also doubts that the lecture netted $150,000, as has often been claimed (*op. cit.*, p. 645).
[16] Austin, *op. cit.*, p. 98.

slave-produced goods, defense of Indians and of Chinese immigrants, the improvement of conditions of factory labor, and the growth of labor unions. Both in scope and in spirit he became the "complete reformer." How the public reacted was indicated in an editorial in the New York *Pilot*, which pointed out: "As a general thing whenever you find a free-soiler, you find an anti-hanging man, woman's rights man, an infidel frequently, bigoted Protestant always, a socialist, a red republican, a fanatical teetotaller, a believer in Mesmerism, Rochester rappings, and in every devil but the one who will catch him. You get in a rather dirty set, you perceive, when you join their ranks."[17] From the point of view of persuasive practicality the abolitionists might have done better to have limited their scope and to have sought success in one cause before undertaking the whole renovation of society. But it was characteristic of them all, and surely of Garrison and Phillips, not to try to be practical. They followed where conscience led; and their consciences were exceedingly dynamic.

Phillips's feelings mounted as the years passed; and his speaking reflected the turmoil of his convictions, the urgency of his need for results. Liberty, he told a Boston audience in Faneuil Hall, in October, 1842, "is chained down by the iron links of the United States Constitution . . . . The fault is in allowing such a Constitution to live an hour."[18] A few days later: "There is a Fourth of July, 1776, to men as well as to nations." Again: "As for Disunion, it must and will come . . . . It is written in the counsels of God." In 1848, appealing to the Judiciary Committee of the Massachusetts Legislature to support a bill calling for secession by the State, Phillips based his plea not on the constitutional right of a State to withdraw from the Union but on "the sacred right of Revolution." At an abolitionist meeting, he proclaimed: "We make no secret of our determination to tread the law and the Constitution under our feet." In 1850 he explained why his sentiments were radical and his language sensational: "The scholar may sit in his study, and take care that his language is not exaggerated; but the rude mass of men are not to be caught by balanced periods—they are caught by men whose words are half battles . . . . Rough instruments are used for rough work."

When a runaway slave named Thomas Sims was arrested in Boston under the Fugitive Slave Law, in April, 1851, Phillips spoke to an outdoor mass meeting, urging that Sims be liberated by force of arms. "It will be a damning disgrace," he thundered, "if such a man can be dragged back without every village on the route rising en masse to block

---

[17] Sherwin, *op. cit.*, p. 130.
[18] This and the following quotations are from Sherwin, *op. cit.*, pp. 138, 144, 175, 180, 181, 216, and 234.

the wheels of the government." Revolution became his preoccupation. In a carefully considered speech to the Massachusetts Antislavery Society, on January 28, 1852, he said: "No matter where you meet a dozen men pledged to a new idea—wherever you have met them, you have met the beginning of a revolution."[19] He warmed to his theme: "We may be crazy. Would to God he would make us all crazy enough to forget for one moment the cold deductions of intellect, and let these hearts of ours beat, beat, under the promptings of a common humanity!"

By April 12, 1852, he reached a new crescendo of violence. In a fury of denunciation against the enforcement of the Fugitive Slave Law, he declared to an abolitionist meeting: "I shall say to every slave, Strike now for Freedom . . . . I can imagine the scenes of blood through which a rebellious slave population must march to their rights. They are dreadful. And yet, I do not know that to an enlightened mind, a scene of civil war is any more sickening than the thought of a hundred and fifty years of slavery." The good people in the churches renounce such a program of liberation, he went on; but "the Christianity of this country is worth nothing, except as it is or can be made more capable of dealing with the question of slavery."[20]

How the small handful of abolitionists, despised and rejected in their own communities, could hope to bring the nation to support their program was the subject of an address by Phillips to the New England Antislavery Society on January 27, 1853. In the first place, what was needed was not fact and argument—not an appeal to the mind—but an arousal of feeling. "There are far more dead hearts to be quickened than confused intellects to be cleared up," he pointed out. As for the methods they should use: "We will gibbet the name of every apostate so black and so high that his children's children will blush to hear it. Yet we bear no malice . . . . In our necessity we seize this weapon in the slave's behalf."[21] The price they would have to pay was loss of respectability, loss of friends, loss of opportunities to earn a living, loss of all respect except self-respect. But, he thundered, let them "call us fanatics . . . what of that? We did not come into the world to keep ourselves clean . . . . We came into the world to give truth a little jog onward."[22]

The violence of language which Phillips advised and the expediency to which he admitted both attained to greater effect because of the quietness and restraint of his delivery. The most vitriolic of sentiments

[19] Phillips, *Speeches, op. cit.,* p. 36.
[20] *Ibid.,* pp. 85–86.
[21] *Ibid.,* pp. 107 and 115.
[22] *Liberator,* June 8, 1860.

he uttered in a tone of gentle assurance, as though he were sharing confidences with listeners who were already convinced. He always dressed like the aristocrat he was—in frock coat, restrained, dignified, polished. "He was the finest type of the cultured New Englander," wrote Depew, who heard him often. "Besides, he was one of the handsomest men I ever saw upon the platform, and in his inspired moments met one's imagined conceptions of a Greek god."[23] His voice was low and musical, his gestures unobtrusive. His own expressed ideal of oratory was "animated conversation." His best biographer, Oscar Sherwin, concluded that his "compelling power lies in the force of his ideas, in his simple, earnest, direct language." Then he added: "He is the orator of the colloquial."[24]

Phillips recorded his own formula: "The chief thing I aim at is to master my subject. Then I earnestly try to get the audience to think as I do."[25] He used no manuscript and no notes. Nevertheless, his speeches ordinarily were carefully prepared, written in advance, and largely memorized. Before a speech, he often was moody, distrustful of himself, reluctant to take the platform. Yet when he stepped before an audience he was roused to a keen pitch of excitement; and he was at his best when he met the strongest opposition. His physical courage was often tested, for he frequently was confronted by mobs. Once in New York when infuriated men cut a cord and rushed toward the platform threatening to hang him, Phillips quietly observed, "Oh, wait a minute till I tell you this story."[26]

Phillips's method of speaking helped make bombast ridiculous. Sherwin went further and claimed that "It taught the bar, the pulpit, the platform, the value of conversationalism in oratory."[27] A change in manner was indeed taking place at this time; but in the revolution of method Phillips did not stand alone. The oracular style could be effective only when orators could stand before the public in the guise of oracles.[28] By midcentury the American audience was maturing and becoming more impatient with pretentiousness, pomposity, and dogmatic assertiveness. The democracy dreamed of in 1776 and announced with

---

[23] Chauncey M. Depew, *My Memories of Eighty Years, op. cit.*, p. 313. Phillips's most cogent defense of his methods was given in a speech to the Massachusetts Antislavery Society, Jan. 27, 1853: "We have facts for those who think, arguments for those who reason." But, he went on, the number of such is few. For the remainder, he must use "harsh rebuke, indignant denunciation, scathing sarcasm, and pitiless ridicule." The justification was that "Our reckless course, our empty rant, our fanaticism, has made Abolitionists of some of the best and ablest men of the land." Phillips, *Speeches, op. cit.*, pp. 106, 109, and 135.
[24] Sherwin, *op. cit.*, pp. 295, 301.
[25] *Ibid.*, p. 296.
[26] *Ibid.*, p. 298.
[27] *Ibid.*, p. 303.
[28] Richard Weaver, *The Ethics of Rhetoric*, Chicago: Regnery, 1953, pp. 165–186.

the election of Andrew Jackson was gradually becoming increasingly real through the spread outward and upward of general education. People were more than ever willing to listen, but only when ideas were given them to ponder. For more people, listening to more speakers, the force of ideas came to be more influential than rhetorical emphasis—always, of course, with notable exceptions. Phillips himself gave the right explanation when he said: "The man who launches a sound argument, who sets on two feet a startling fact and bids it travel across the continent, is just as certain that in the end he will change the government, as if to destroy the Capitol he had placed gunpowder under the Senate chamber."[29] What he felt strongly is that facts never march forth by themselves; they must always be propelled by a force of powerful statement, and they must be aimed through a careful adaptation to the minds and feelings of the projected audience. He not only stressed the need for oratorical ability, he also illustrated it—better than most, in many ways, for many years.

The outbreak of the Civil War brought a sharp challenge to both Garrison and Phillips. Garrison abandoned both his pacifism and his desire to break up the Union by a secession of the Northern States; he plunged into efforts to help coerce the South. After the thirteenth amendment was ratified, he announced that his work as an abolitionist was closed, and turned his attention, much more quietly than before, to promoting free trade. By the time of his death in 1879, he was widely accepted in both the United States and Europe as a symbol of respectability. Not so Phillips. On January 20, 1861, he took the pulpit of Theodore Parker's church to preach a sermon praising Disunion. "Sacrifice anything to keep the slaveholding States in the Union?" he demanded. "God forbid! we will rather build a bridge of gold, and pay their toll over it . . ."[30] After the firing on Fort Sumter, Phillips joined in the general celebration of the war, declaring it meant the end of slavery. After the Emancipation Proclamation, however, Phillips did not, as did most of the abolitionists, abandon the fight for equal rights for the freedmen. In a speech to the Massachusetts Antislavery Society at the end of 1863, Phillips pointed out: "There stands the black man, naked, homeless; he does not own a handful of dust; he has no education; he has no roof to shelter him. You turn him out like a savage on the desert, to say to Europe, 'Behold our magnanimity!' "[31] In 1864 he strongly opposed the re-election of Lincoln, remarking to Senator Sumner: "We are paying thousands of lives and millions of dollars as penalty for having

[29] Phillips, *Speeches, op. cit.*, p. 45.
[30] *Ibid.*, p. 354.
[31] Sherwin, *op. cit.*, p. 488.

a timid, ignorant President all the more injurious because honest."[32] In May of 1865, at the annual meeting of the American Antislavery Society, Garrison moved that it be disbanded, on the grounds that its work was done. Phillips denounced the motion with his usual forcefulness, declaring that equality of the races was the real goal; "and I never shall leave the Negro until, so far as God gives me the power, I achieve it."[33] He lived on until February 2, 1884, fighting until the end for a variety of further reforms—but the story of these years belongs to another chapter.

The Tornado Out of Ohio: Theodore Weld

THE ORATORICAL career of Theodore Weld spanned only six years—although he lived through nine decades of the century, from November 23, 1803 to February 3, 1895.[1] For a time his influence blazed across the Near West (between the Ohio and Hudson rivers) like a searing flash of lightning: "logic on fire," as Lyman Beecher described him, "eloquent as an angel and powerful as thunder!"[2] The last image was not meant to be unkind. Thunder, of course, is an empty sound that reverberates only after the lightning has done its work. But Weld's oratory was lightning and thunder combined.

Weld was notably impatient of speech for the sake of speech: "buzz—hum, hum, buzz," he scornfully called it.[3] For a time his reputation in abolitionist circles was at least the equal of the repute accorded Garrison and Phillips. Yet he persistently refused to attend any of the national antislavery conventions, saying that he considered them merely scenes for empty ceremonialism and mutual admiration. Even so, he was very far from being a solo performer. His best work was that of organization, mapping out strategy, and recruiting, training, and directing the speaking of a total of some seventy abolitionist lecturers. In an unusual burst of generosity, Garrison once described Weld as "the central luminary around which they all revolved."[4] In fact, Weld consti-

---

[32] *Ibid.*, p. 491.
[33] *Ibid.*, p. 513.
[1] *Letters of Weld . . . Weld . . . and Grimké, op. cit.,*; Dumond, *Antislavery Origins of the Civil War, op. cit.*; and Benjamin P. Thomas, *Theodore Weld: Crusader for Freedom*, New Brunswick: Rutgers University Press, 1950
[2] Thomas, *op. cit.*, p. 101.
[3] *Ibid.*, p. 123.
[4] *Ibid.*, p. 120. Weld reciprocated this generous judgment in his eulogy on Garrison, when he said: "We cannot speak his name, but it is the highest praise that can be given him . . . The fact is, nothing that he has done can be spoken of that is not a eulogy." Quoted by Sherwin, *op. cit.*, p. 677.

tuted Garrison's principal opposition within the abolitionist crusade; and it was Weld's policies and methods that came at last to dominate the movement.

Theodore Weld was born in Connecticut, son of a puritanically strict but kindly Congregational minister. By the age of fourteen Theodore was managing a hundred-acre farm to save enough money to put him through Phillips Academy. There, however, his eyesight was ruined by overstudy, and he was told the only remedy was to remain for seven years in a darkened room. With innate self-assurance, Weld rejected this unacceptable remedy and undertook a bizarre remedial scheme of his own devising—to make a lecture tour, on the subject of Memory.

His father was dubious not only of the medical efficacy of the idea but also of the mere possibility that Theodore could succeed on the platform. Already the boy manifested the traits and the appearance that were to characterize his manhood. He himself, at a later date, found the ideal descriptive phrase: "I am a *Backwoodsman untamed*."[5] So he was: tall, shambling, with a dark, forbidding countenance that looked stern as judgment except when lighted by a rare smile. He wore unpressed, ill-fitting clothing, cared little for cleanliness, and never polished his shoes. As for his hair, he massaged it thoroughly with a stiff brush and left it uncombed, sticking out in all directions. He loved physical exercise and commenced each day with a four-mile run, interspersed with hops and jumps. He was careless of the reactions of other people, remaining silent in company, and was so self-contained that often he would sway back and forth like a pendulum, lost in his own thoughts. He was notably forgetful of names, even those of his own close acquaintances; and he was so absent-minded that he would hunt around the room for a pen that he held tightly clenched between his teeth. This was the youth who deliberately prescribed for himself a lecture tour to remedy his failing vision—and his was the mind that selected as the subject, memory control.

His only obvious assets were three: a marvellously rich and melodious voice, a superbly analytical mind, and a fierce ambition to make his influence felt. He carefully wrote out a lecture on mnemonics, memorized it, then threw the manuscript away and went to a neighboring town to "try out" his speaking prowess. When he came home with $20 as his fee and with praises ringing in his ears, he felt he was ready. His first lectures were in the nearby cities of Hartford and Litchfield. Then he swung across upstate New York. From there he went into Ohio, Pennsylvania, and Maryland. After that, he toured through the South.

[5] Thomas, *op. cit.*, p. 114.

It was three years before he returned home with his eyesight restored and with enormous confidence in his own powers.

The money earned on this tour enabled him to enter Hamilton College, where his arrogance richly earned him the dislike of the faculty and the administration. An aunt, trying to curb his intransigence, tricked him into attending a sermon by the evangelist Charles Grandison Finney. But Weld, far from being impressed, was outraged by Finney's unorthodox air of familiarity with God and by his personalized denunciations of the worldiness of the sinners sitting in front of him in the pews. The next day Weld was both entertaining and shocking a group of loungers with a satiric excoriation of Finney, when the evangelist strode up behind him. Weld, caught by surprise, reacted with defensive arrogance, pouring upon Finney such a flood of savage denunciations that reply was impossible. That evening, however, overcome by remorse, Weld went to Finney's home to beg his pardon. In the conversation of that evening and later, Weld became a convert to Finney's preaching that true religion best expresses itself in a benevolent heart.

At about this same time Weld became acquainted with a young English abolitionist, Charles Stuart, who urged him to devote his life to winning freedom for the slaves. Weld at first was indifferent. His own father had owned a few slaves; and during his Southern tour he saw nothing to shake his acceptance of slavery as the best and most natural relation between a superior and an inferior race. Besides, Weld already had causes enough to keep him occupied: temperance, strict observance of the Sabbath, and a program of enforced manual labor for all students. With talks on these subjects he was winning wide acclaim, often leaving his classes at Hamilton for weeks at a time to go on speaking tours. "If you don't take care," Finney warned him, "I fear you will be spoiled by an idea of your own importance."[6]

In 1832, Weld attached himself to Lane Seminary, in Cincinnati, where Lyman Beecher had just become president. Because of his demonstrated abilities and the fame he already had won, Weld was offered one of the four "cornerstone positions" on the faculty—that of Professor of Sacred Rhetoric and Oratory. With the strange trickle of modesty that occasionally licked its way out through his wall of arrogance, Weld declared that he yet had too much to learn to be a teacher and enrolled, instead, as a student.[7] He quickly proved to be as obstreperous and un-

[6] *Ibid.*, p. 23.
[7] Weld's friends thought him shy; but Weld himself realized his troubles stemmed from immoderate pride. "It is the great besetment of my soul," he thought, "the poisoned thorn that festers and corrodes. I am too proud to be ambitious, too proud to seek applause, too proud to tolerate it when lavished upon me—proud as Lucifer that I can and do scorn applause and spurn flattery." Quoted by Gilbert H. Barnes, *The Anti-Slavery Impulse, 1830–1844,* New York: Appleton-Century, 1933, p. 34.

disciplinable at Lane as he had been at Hamilton. He set about at once arousing the students to rebellion against the formalism of the seminary rules. He insisted that they must prove their religious sincerity by boarding with Negro families, attending Negro Church services, and speaking whenever they could on behalf of justice for the colored race. It was here, at this time, that Weld became an abolitionist.

Unlike Garrison and Phillips, Weld did not demand immediate abolition; nor did he regard gradualism as a sin. On the contrary, he confessed freely that he regarded the Negro as inferior; and he did not believe the colored people should suddenly be allowed to vote and to assume the full responsibilities of citizenship. Instead Weld advocated a national agreement on a plan for gradual emancipation, to be enacted into national laws, and to be accompanied by systematic education for Negroes during a transition period of white stewardship. In 1834 he organized at Lane a crucial series of debates on abolitionism, which lasted for eighteen evenings.[8] At the conclusion of the series, the students organized an abolition society. When the Lane Seminary trustees demanded that the students abandon their antislavery agitation and return quietly to their studies, Weld led a general exodus in which many of them followed him to Oberlin, there to join Charles Grandison Finney.

During the next four years Weld labored at the cause of Negro liberation with incredible energy and courage. In part his genius expressed itself in organization. He well understood that many voices were far better than one; and he set out to gain seventy recruits who would dedicate their lives to the abolitionist lecture platform. His most notable convert was James G. Birney, a slaveowning aristocrat of Kentucky, whom Weld enlisted in the cause and who stood twice, in 1840 and 1844, as the Liberty Party candidate for the presidency.[9]

If there were to be many speakers working together as a team, there must be a "policy line" for them to follow. Weld was horrified by the nihilism of Garrison and he abhorred the radicalism of burning the Constitution. Instead, he felt, the argument for freedom must be couched in reasonable terms, based on religion, economics, and humanitarianism. These were universal appeals that even Southerners could accept. The speakers' aim was to seek united support, rather than to widen and emphasize differences. To support such appeals there would need to be an arsenal of facts; and it was in the work of gathering data

---

[8] Thomas, op. cit., pp. 70–87.
[9] James G. Birney, *Letters of James Gillespie Birney, 1831–1857*, ed. Dwight L. Dumond, New York: Appleton-Century, 1938; and William Birney, *James G. Birney and His Times*, New York: Appleton, 1890.

that Weld particularly excelled.[10] With a fiercely persistent impatience, he tore his way through libraries, assembling masses of newspapers, gathering stories on slave auctions, on murdered slaves, on separated families, on enforced prostitution, and every other example he could find illustrating the evils of slavery. This material he published anonymously in books and pamphlets for the use of abolitionist speakers, refusing credit for his work, just as he refused office in any of the abolitionist societies. Still another problem that had to be solved was the selection of the "target audiences" the speakers should try to reach. Weld never doubted that these were in the small towns and country districts. Garrison and Phillips, he thought, were making a major mistake in concentrating on the cities and the large lecture halls. "Let the great cities *alone*," he pleaded. "They must be burned down by back fires."[11] As for himself, "My bearish proportions have never been licked into *city shape*, and are quite too uncombed and shaggy for 'Boston notions.' . . . A stump is my throne, my parish, my home, my element the *everydayisms* of plain common life."[12]

It was not enough for Weld to recruit scores of speakers, to arm them with multiple materials, to send them combing the countryside for audiences he selected, to which they should deliver appeals he had formulated, to support his policy of gradual abolition accomplished through the agency of constitutional legislation. In addition to being the prime organizer, policy formulator, and researcher, Weld also proved to be a veritable tornado as a lecturer.

Beginning in the fall, after the farmers had their crops in, Weld would start across Ohio and thence into New York and Pennsylvania. His method was to arrive unannounced in a small town and then to appeal to the minister to allow him to use the church for a lecture. Usually after his initial talk he would be refused permission to return. Then he would find an old barn, a warehouse, or even an open field he could use. But after his first appearance, an audience for subsequent lectures was assured. He would remain in a town for a week or ten days, pouring out whitehot lectures, each lasting about two hours, in which specific facts and ideas were welded together by illustrations into a rush of emotional fervor. Of one thing Weld was absolutely certain—that *no man could be lastingly converted by a single speech*. This lesson he had

---

[10] "I have never done half so much for Abolition as since I have stopped speaking," Weld wrote; quoted by Thomas, *op. cit.*, p. 131. The journalist Henry B. Stanton observed that "He will dig for a month with the patience of a Cornwall miner, into a dusty library for a rare fact to elucidate or fortify a new position." *Random Recollections*, New York: Harper, 1887, p. 46.

[11] Thomas, *op. cit.*, p. 110.

[12] *Ibid.*, p. 114.

learned from the evangelist Finney. He also felt that by staying in a single place for a dozen speeches he could create a solid core of support, however small, that would persist and spread. The success of his method is attested to by the fact that from 1834 to 1836, Ohio far surpassed Massachusetts in the number of antislavery societies founded, with New York next.

What an abolitionist speaker had to endure in propagating his cause is well illustrated in Weld's experiences. Night after night he was assailed by mobs who screeched, threw rotten eggs, stones, and clubs, and rushed the platform to force him off.[13] But all this Weld welcomed; for, as he assured his band of speakers, these very excesses of attack were essential to the arousal of public opinion in their behalf. Better martyrdom than indifference. Finally, in Troy, New York, he was severely injured and for the first time in his life was driven from the locality without being able to complete his planned sequence of lectures. By this time his voice was almost gone and his tremendous physique was near collapse.

For a time he accepted a position in the office of the American Antislavery Society, though he refused any title. Although he was supposed to be resting, he threw himself with greater zeal than ever into the gathering of information and wrote a book, *Slavery As It Is*, that later became a major source for Harriet Beecher Stowe's *Uncle Tom's Cabin*.[14] Also, with this interval off the platform to permit him time for reflective thought, he urged the abolitionists to ease off their attacks on slavery and, instead, to devote their efforts to elevating the position of the free Negroes.

The reason for the shift of emphasis in Weld's thinking is that he had gradually come to realize that slavery itself was not the crucial issue. The major question was not whether the Negro was enslaved but whether he was genetically and potentially the equal of the whites. If his basic equality could be established, slavery would crumble. If it could not, racial prejudice would make the lot of the Negro in freedom as degraded as it was under slavery. This conviction was inspired by conditions that Weld considered to be simple facts: that all through the North, as well as the South, the freed Negroes lived in enforced squalor

[13] Weld came to be known as "the most mobbed man in America." Sherwin, *op. cit.*, p. 81; and Lader, *op. cit.*, p. 76.
[14] Harriett Beecher Stowe's *A Key to Uncle Tom's Cabin* identified twenty one citations from Weld's *Slavery As It Is*. Weld got nothing for his book; Mrs. Stowe made ten percent royalty on some six and a half million copies of hers. Cf. Frank Luther Mott, *The Golden Multitudes*, New York: Macmillan, 1947, pp. 114–122. Money was always interesting to the Beechers. While Weld was at Lane Seminary, Lyman Beecher told him: "If you want to teach colored schools, I can fill your pockets with money, but if you will visit in colored families and walk with them in the streets, you will be overwhelmed." Lyman Beecher Stowe, *Saints, Sinners, and Beechers*, New York: Blue Ribbon Books, 1934, p. 59.

and amidst a denial of opportunities that made their lot often worse than that of the plantation slaves. Once again, this "policy line" of Weld's was vastly different from that of Garrison and Phillips. Moderation of the type he counselled became predominant in the abolitionism prevalent in the Middle Atlantic and Midwestern States.

In 1836 Weld gave what proved to be his last great speech—on the Fourth of July. By this time his voice had become little more than a hoarse whisper; and not until after the Civil War was he able to speak naturally again. Meantime he established an institute for the teaching of public speaking to abolitionist lecturers, as he sought to pour into his followers the vital power he once had possessed. His marriage to Angelina Grimké, the abolitionist from South Carolina, allied him to a spirit as ardent for reform as was his own. But from this time on his influence was to be derivative rather than direct. His ardor was forced to find outlet through the writing of a series of books and in teaching school. He lived on until almost all his old associates were dead; and his last years found him much mellowed in manner and in philosophy.

The history of oratory is not much enriched by the texts of his speeches, none of which are more than approximations of what he actually said. His speaking was all extempore; and he was far from being a master of style. Of Weld it surely must be said that the style was the man himself, that his eloquence consisted largely in the immediate influence of his burning personality. Yet during the six year span from 1830 to 1836 he accomplished as much on the platform as many a better known orator achieved in the course of decades. His life was an exemplification of a lesson that Lyman Beecher once taught to the seminarians at Lane: "Young gentlemen, don't stand before a looking-glass and make gestures. Pump yourself brim full of your subject till you can't hold another drop, and then knock out the bung and let nature caper."[15]

Spokesman for His Own Cause: Frederick Douglass

JOHN RANDOLPH of Roanoke, when he was besought by a young Northerner to name the greatest orator he had ever heard, snapped, "A slave, Sir. She was a mother, and her rostrum was the auction-block."[1] It was a way of saying that the conditions of slavery spoke for them-

[15] Stanton, *Random Recollections, op. cit.*, p. 46; Thomas, *op. cit.*, pp. 101–102.
[1] Samuel Eliot Morrison and Henry Steele Commager, *The Growth of the American Republic*, New York: Oxford University Press, 1942, I:539.

selves. Of course they did not. It was also a hint, at least, that the most effective spokesman for the Negro was the Negro himself. But there were many reasons why this could not be true: the poverty, ignorance, and lack of education of the colored people; the simple fact that almost all of them remained in bondage, far removed from any receptive audience; and the social prejudices which made unwelcome outcasts of even the freed Negroes who lived in areas where slavery itself was despised.[2]

The belief that the Negroes were genetically as well as culturally inferior was, as Abraham Lincoln said in a speech at Springfield, in 1850 "a universal feeling, whether well or ill founded . . . . We cannot then make them our equals."[3] A Negro orator was as much an anomaly as a high school student urging his opinions about current issues to a general community audience. The adults might (and often do) admire the youngster's skill and praise his accomplishments; but this is far from taking seriously the advice he has to offer. What is being judged is a performance rather than an assertion of leadership. Negroes (and, parenthetically, women) who sought to influence public opinion and policies in that time, through the influence of public speaking, were oddities to be observed and in some fashion perhaps even to be admired—but certainly not leaders to be followed. The wonder is not that there were few Negro orators but that there were any who attained to genuine distinction under such circumstances.[4] A few, however, did succeed, notably Charles Lennox Remond, Henry Highland Garnet, Samuel Ringgold Ward, and, by far the greatest of them all, Frederick Douglass.[5]

Frederick Douglass was born in Maryland in 1817—in what month he never knew—to a slavewoman whom he almost never saw (being reared instead by an elderly Negress who was too feeble for field work), with a father (probably a white man) who remained unknown. In 1825 he was sent to Baltimore to serve as a houseboy in the home of Hugh Auld, whose wife taught him to read from the Bible. Auld, finding them so

---

[2] Gunnar Myrdal, *An American Dilemma*, New York: Harper, 1944. For a study of problems confronting Negro spokesmen of today, cf. Daniel C. Thompson, *The Negro Leadership Class*, Englewood Cliffs, N. J.: Prentice-Hall, Spectrum Book, 1963.

[3] Carl Sandburg, *Lincoln: The Prairie Years*, op. cit., p. 315.

[4] Cf. Carter G. Woodson, *Negro Orators and Their Orations*, Washington, D.C.: Associated Publishers, 1925; and an anthology of recent Afro-American speeches, *Rhetoric of Racial Revolt*, ed., Roy L. Hill, Denver: Golden Bell Press, 1962.

[5] Frederick Douglass, *Life and Times*, Boston: De Wolfe, Fiske, rev., 1895; Philip S. Foner, *The Life and Writings of Frederick Douglass*, Four Vols., New York: International Publishers, 1950; Frederick May Holland, *Frederick Douglass: The Colored Orator*, New York: Funk, Wagnalls, rev., 1895; and Benjamin Quarles, *Frederick Douglass*, Washington, D.C.: Associated Publishers, 1948.

engaged one day, upbraided his wife severely, saying, "A boy who learns to read will be forever unfit to be a slave"—a comment that sank deeply into the youngster's mind. Shortly afterward, with the first pennies he earned, he bought his own first book, *The Columbian Orator*, a collection of declamations. When Douglass was fifteen Auld found him too rebellious to be a good slave and hired him out to Edward Covey, a professional slavebreaker, who worked him mercilessly in the fields and flogged him every week for six months. Finally the young slave, in desperation, knocked Covey down and soundly thrashed him, after which the overseer was afraid to flog him again. At the age of eighteen the youth attempted to escape and was loaded down with chains as a result. But when he was twenty, with papers of identification stolen from a sailor, Douglass boarded a train for New York and left forever a condition he later described as "perpetual unpaid toil; no marriage, no husband, no wife, no parent, no child; ignorance, brutality, licentiousness; whips, scourges, chains, auctions, jails and separations; and embodiment of all the woes the imagination can conceive."[6]

In New York he married Anna Murray, a free Negress of Baltimore, who had provided the money to make possible his escape. In search of work, the couple went to New Bedford, where the name Douglass was given him by a friend who had admired the hero of that name in Scott's *Lady of the Lake*. In August, 1841, he attended an abolitionist meeting in Nantucket, where he was induced to make an impromptu speech that turned out to consist of a few halting remarks. Garrison, who was present, magnified the importance of the occasion and leaped to his feet, crying, "Have we been listening to a man or a thing?" and then, with electric force, "Shall such a man be sent back to slavery from the soil of old Massachusetts?"[7] The abolitionists well realized, as John A. Collins put it, that "The public have itching ears to hear a colored man speak, particularly a slave."[8] Douglass had the classic story to tell: unknown parentage; a kindly mistress who taught him to read; a stern master, a brutal overseer who beat him mercilessly; an escape attempt that failed and another that succeeded; marriage to a free Negress who had plotted and aided in his flight to freedom. Moreover, as a voracious reader, and with the benefit of a first-rate intelligence, Douglass had acquired a vocabulary far beyond the ordinary and developed a keen ear

[6] *Bugle*, Aug. 11, 1849; cited by Quarles, *op. cit.*, p. 5. Douglass's years in slavery are vividly described by Shirley Graham in her novel, *There Was Once a Slave*, New York: Julian Messner, 1947, pp. 3–80.
[7] Sherwin, *op. cit.*, p. 85.
[8] Foner, *op. cit.*, I:46. Collins was Field Director for the Massachusetts Antislavery Society.

for speech rhythms and verbal combinations. With practice before abolitionist meetings he soon acquired poise and directness as a speaker and a courageously forthright manner of telling his story.

Douglass naturally associated himself with the Garrison-Phillips philosophy of violence, which led him to such utterances as: "Liberty must cut the throat of slavery or have its own cut by slavery";[9] and, to a state convention of the Republican Party, in Syracuse, "You are called Black Republicans. What right have you to that name? Among all the candidates you have selected or talked of, I haven't seen or heard a single black one."[10] Despite such verbal emotionalism, Douglass actually was extremely self-controlled. His manner was quiet, courteous, and correct, his diction distinctly superior. Indeed, so little did he resemble the stereotype of the fugitive slave that he felt impelled in 1845 to publish his autobiography. He was forced to flee to Europe, where he spent the next two years lecturing in the British Isles, to escape being arrested and returned to his lawful master. When funds were raised to purchase his freedom, he returned to America and continued his work as an agitator, both as a speaker and as editor of *Frederick Douglass's Paper*, published in Rochester, New York. After his return from England, he shifted allegiance from Garrison to the Weld-Birney faction of moderates who sought reform through legal action. When he openly renounced John Brown's raid on Harpers Ferry, he came under sharp criticism from many of his own earlier associates. Such criticism for what some felt to be a "self-serving moderation" continued during the years after the Civil War, during which Douglass held a succession of high governmental appointments, culminating in the post of Minister to Haiti. He died in Washington, D.C., on February 20, 1895, prosperous and popular amidst the capital's international social set.

The oratorical career of Frederick Douglass was important in four distinct categories: his speaking as an agent for the abolitionist societies; his lectures in England, Scotland, and Ireland; his speeches and organizational work in connection with the Negro Convention movement; and his participation in a variety of other reform movements. As a speaker, he was himself the strongest tangible exhibit that could be found. The influence of his person, quite aside from what he said or even how he said it, was well described by Wendell Phillips at a meeting in Faneuil Hall on May 31, 1849, when, following Douglass on the platform, he said:

> Fellow citizens, when such a man as Frederick Douglass tells you his story, the result of American prejudice—speaks the honest indignation

[9] *Radical Abolitionist*, July, 1856; cited by Quarles, *op. cit.*, p. 161.
[10] Syracuse *Daily Standard*, May 29, 1856.

of his race against his wrongs—when he tells you of your own conduct towards him—keep your hands by your sides. Hush those echoing plaudits of yours; keep silent. What right have you to applaud? What have you done to aid the slave to his liberty? . . . . Can he find shelter in any pulpit in Boston? How many? One, two, or three, alone. Do one of two things—confess that your hearts blush for the deeds your hands are not ashamed to do; or go, coin your plaudits into statutes . . .[11]

In many ways Douglass was superbly fitted for oratory. With a magnificent physique and a rich, dark coloring, he made an imposing appearance. His voice was a warm baritone of such tremendous power of "rolling thunder" that he could be heard, as was often necessary, above the roar of hostile crowds. He spoke without manuscript and sometimes without careful preparation, his words erupting into torrential streams of invective or denunciation. His vivid imagination and command of vocabulary were so effectively joined that, as one sympathetic listener, William J. Wilson, recorded, even when his subject matter wore thin, his "words came and arranged themselves so competely that they not only captivate, but often deceive us for ideas."[12] He gestured little and maintained his poise even under conditions of vicious verbal denunciation and mob violence. But always and chiefly, the greatest source of his eloquence lay in who and what he was. As James Russell Lowell wrote of him: "The very look and bearing of Douglass are an irresistible logic against the oppression of his race."[13]

Representative of his abolitionist lecturing was the "hundred conventions" tour, lasting six months in 1843, which took Douglass, Remond, and several white lecturers through New England, New York, Ohio, and Indiana. They spoke under all manner of conditions to whatever audiences they could assemble.[14] Sometimes Douglass sang abolitionist songs to assemble a crowd. Often he and his companions were booed and showered with rotten eggs, vegetables, and stones. Always he had to travel in "Jim Crow" style, sometimes in cattle cars filthy with manure. Finding places to stay or to eat was a constant problem. Cries of "Kill the nigger," "Whitewash him," "Get a white man," and all manner of profanity and vulgarities were the commonplace atmosphere into which he had to propel his speech. In Indiana he and his companion orator were knocked down and severely beaten, an experience that for years afterward "haunted his dreams." Under such circumstances what was said was of less moment than that he continued to speak at all.

[11] Sherwin, *op. cit.*, pp. 187–188.
[12] Quarles, *op. cit.*, p. 61. Wilson was a Negro and an abolitionist journalist.
[13] *The Pennsylvania Freeman*, Feb. 13, 1845.
[14] Quarles, *op. cit.*, pp. 29–33.

When an audience permitted him to develop the orderly sequence of his lecture, he normally spoke rather quietly, and with a moderation in choice of words that gave all the greater strength to his sentiments. A typical paragraph from an address he presented to a sympathetic audience in Rochester's Corinthian Hall on Sunday evening, December 8, 1850, will illustrate these characteristics of his style:

> The northern people have been long connected with slavery; they have been linked to a decaying corpse, which has destroyed the moral health. The union of the government; the union of the north and south, in the political parties; the union in the religious organizations of the land, have all served to deaden the moral sense of the northern people, and to impregnate them with sentiments and ideas forever in conflict with what as a nation we call *genius of American institutions.* Rightly viewed, this is an alarming fact, and ought to rally all that is pure, just, and holy in one determined effort to crush the monster of corruption, and to scatter "its guilty profits" to the winds. In a high moral sense, as well as in a national sense, the whole American people are responsible for slavery, and must share, in its guilt and shame, with the most obdurate men-stealers of the south.[15]

His experiences during a two-year lecture tour of Ireland, Scotland, and England, in 1845-47, were relatively, though far from completely, pleasant. It was a revelation for Douglass to be in a society without racial prejudice, where he could travel, sleep, eat, and visit without restrictions. Moreover, his autobiography was selling well in the British Isles, bringing him fame and even a small measure of prosperity. With typical insouciance, in Ireland he threw himself gayly into the fight for Irish freedom from England; and in Scotland he carelessly allowed himself to become a storm center in a local church controversy. Everywhere he went he spoke freely and frequently on behalf of temperance, and also for women's rights. Other topics, anything smacking of reform, also appealed to him from time to time. And recurrently, wherever he went, he spoke of the evils of slavery. In Ireland he gave over fifty lectures in four months. In Scotland, where he was for a time embarrassed by involvement in a dispute over the factionalism in the Presbyterian Church, he soon was so well received that he wrote, "Old Scotland boils like a pot." In England, which was rejoicing over its recent emancipation of its slaves in the West Indies, Douglass spent eleven months, speaking frequently to what his biographer Holland rather extravagantly calls "one long ovation."[16] It was not exactly unpopular, in that time, to denounce Americans to a British audience, and Douglass was not

[15] Foner, *op. cit.,* II:146.
[16] The tour is well described by Holland, *op. cit.,* Chapter V, "Beyond the Color Line," pp. 112–148.

sparing in his denunciation. To an audience in London, on May 22, 1846, he said: "While America is printing tracts and Bibles, sending missionaries abroad to convert the heathen, expending her money in various ways for the promotion of the Gospel in foreign lands, the slave not only lies forgotten, uncared for, but he is trampled under foot by the very Church of the land. What have we in America? Why, we have slavery made part of the religion of the land. Yes, the pulpit there stands up as the great defender of this cursed institution, as it is called. Ministers of religion come forward and torture the hallowed pages of inspired wisdom to sanction the bloody deed."[17]

In England Douglass often delivered (as part of a longer lecture) a parody of a sermon by a Southern slaveholder to his slaves, a parody which he had prepared and made part of his regular repertoire shortly after he became an abolitionist lecturer. The text for this pseudosermon was, "Servants, be obedient to your masters." Douglas represented the slaveholder as saying: "The Lord in His Providence sent pious souls over to Africa—dark, heathen, benighted Africa—to bring you to this Christian land, where you can sit beneath the droppings of the sanctuary and hear about Jesus!" Then he reverted to the obedience theme and related how a slave named Sam was whipped so hard he was disabled for three and a half weeks for sleeping when he was supposed to have been at work. "For only through the channel of obedience can happiness flow!"[18]

Douglass's greatest discovery in England was that prejudice against people of color is not universal amongst all white people. He developed a hope that in time it might be completely eradicated. And he returned home to devote more of his attention to the Negro Convention movement, an effort to unite Negro leaders and to urge the Negro people to follow their own promptings rather than to depend upon the leadership of sympathetic whites. Moreover, this movement directed its attention to the plight of the half-million free Negroes in America, as well as to that of the nearly four millions who were held in slavery. "Jim Crowism" was practiced wherever free Negroes lived. Strict segregation was enforced in all their activities; and accommodations for them, where they existed at all, were always substandard. In 1829 Ohio courts upheld the constitutionality of laws passed in 1804-07 that required every free Negro in the State either to post a $500 bond or to be deported immediately. Even in communities that professed a horror of slavery, the Negro himself was a manifestly unwelcome intruder.[19]

[17] *Ibid.*, pp. 130–131; Graham, *op. cit.*, pp. 150–152.
[18] *Ibid.*, pp. 93–94.
[19] Foner, *op. cit.*, II:19–38.

The Negro Convention movement had commenced in 1830, but was raised from dormancy in 1843, when Douglass and Henry H. Garnett aroused the convention in Buffalo with their spirted debate on the measures the Negroes should pursue to get their rights. Garnett urged violence, Douglas moral suasion. Four years later, however, at the annual convention, held in Troy, New York, Douglas was leading the activists. He called upon all Negroes to leave the pro-slavery churches, declaring that his right arm would wither before he would worship at their blood-stained altars. Since the annual conventions made no provision for continuous action or for organized efforts in the intervals between their meetings, Douglass attempted in 1849 to organize a National League of Colored People. This plan met with small favor and for the next several years, after the passage in 1850 of the Fugitive Slave Law, the Negroes feared to attend meetings, for if they were arrested they were considered to be escaped slaves unless they could prove the contrary. However, in July, 1853, 140 delegates from nine States gathered at Rochester, where Douglass drew up an "Address" that ever since has been a rallying point for the colored people of America. It demanded that "the doors of the school-house, the work-shop, the church, the college, shall be thrown open as freely to our children as to the children of other members of the community; . . . the white and black may stand upon an equal footing before the laws of the land; . . . colored men shall not be either by custom or enactment excluded from the jury-box; . . . the complete and unrestricted right of suffrage, which is essential even to the dignity of the white man, be extended to the Free Colored Man also"; and that all laws "flagrantly unjust to the man of color . . . ought to be repealed."[20] When Garrison and other abolitionists proposed to raise money for a college for young Negro men, Douglass at first opposed the idea on the ground that it was segregationist. Shortly, however, he swung to its support, for he found that unemployment was very high among uneducated Negroes. "We must find new methods of obtaining a livelihood, for the old ones are failing us very fast," he wrote in 1853. In 1857 the last of the Negro Conventions was held. The movement broke apart in factionalism, with disputes over the kinds of measures to be pursued, and many came to feel that the drive to end slavery should not be complicated by argumentation over the future status of Negroes who should be freed.

During the Civil War Douglass was among the first to demand that Negro troops be enlisted, and two of his own sons fought with the federal armies. Following the conclusion of the war Douglass spent some

[20] *Ibid.*, "The Claims of Our Common Cause," II:254–268.

two years as a popular lecturer, then devoted the remainder of his life to appointive offices—many of his own people feeling he had "sold out" for personal advantages. Unquestionably the Republican Party found him useful as a "showpiece" to demonstrate its regard for the Negro race. His crusade as a spokesman for racial equality was not again resumed.

Two Gentlemen from Massachusetts: Everett and Sumner

EDWARD EVERETT and Charles Sumner were significantly alike and also significantly different. Both were eminently and unquestionably prototypes of the New England gentlemen. The paternal ancestors of both arrived in Massachusetts in the 1630's. Both excelled at Harvard and then capped their educaton with extended tours of Europe. Both were tall, thin, distinguished in appearance, with great dignity of manner, restraint in gesture, and with clear, musical voices. A contemporary, E. L. Magoon, called Everett a "consummate master of rhetorical art";[1] and Carl Schurz, another contemporary, described Sumner's speeches as "vast and elaborately ornamented rhetorical structures, built after classic models."[2] Both excelled in literary and historical scholarship and delighted in embroidering their themes with a rich profusion of allusions and also with a consciously elaborate and ornate style. Both were extravagantly overvalued in their own day and have been undervalued in retrospect. Sumner sought to win fame by becoming one of the most violent exponents of a violent cause; and Everett just as consciously sought lasting fame by expressing with superb skill sentiments which everyone admired and from which none could dissent. Sumner was a master of irony, sarcasm, and all manner of vitriolic denunciation; Everett of the sirupy panegyric and the conciliatory platitude. Both were excessively vain, ambitious, industrious, and haunted by the fear of failure. Whatever they achieved they owed primarily to their skill in speech.

Edward Everett (April 11, 1794–January 15, 1865) lived through the nation's time of troubles but had very little to say about them, despite the fact that he occupied positions of high responsibility (Congressman, Governor of Massachusetts, Minister to England, President of Harvard, Secretary of State, and United States Senator) throughout most of his

[1] E. L. Magoon, "Edward Everett," in *Living Orators in America*, New York: Baker and Scribner, 1849, p. 65.
[2] Carl Schurz, *Charles Sumner*, ed., Arthur Reed Hogue, Urbana: University of Illinois Press, 1951, p. 60.

adult life.[3] At the age of eleven he joined a declamation and debating society, but derived little advantage from it, for, as he wrote later: "I wanted courage to make the first essay at improvement: and as our Master did not possess the art of speaking well himself, he could not impart it to others."[4] At Harvard he graduated with highest honors and then, still short of his nineteenth year, was elected minister of the Brattle Street Church, the largest and most fashionable in Boston. He memorized carefully-composed sermons and drew great crowds to hear them,[5] including the young Ralph Waldo Emerson, who idolized him and thought him the greatest American orator.[6] After fourteen months in the ministry, he accepted appointment as Professor of Greek Literature at Harvard, together with an advance of $5300, with which he made a two and a half year tour of Europe to expand his education. During the next seven years at Harvard he made his lecture room a notable experience for the young men who heard him.

On August 25, 1824, a few weeks before his election to Congress, he delivered to the Phi Beta Kappa Society an address which reads almost like a caricature of Everett's faults, yet which was received with tears and wild applause. In his opening words he declared himself "anxious" to be "the public organ of your sentiments" during the "short armistice" provided by "the academical holidays" from their "professional cares of life." His theme, he said, was "*the peculiar motives to intellectual exertion in America*," concerning which he thought "a few general answers may be attempted, that will probably be just and safe, only in proportion as they are vague and comprehensive." The three factors he discovered which stimulated intellectuality in America were political democracy, the large size of the country, and the rapid rate of growth of the population. His "happy vision" for America was one of "glory to crown its success," and, he concluded, "If this be false, may I never know the truth." All was beautifully expressed.[7]

[3] Paul Revere Frothingham, *Edward Everett: Orator and Statesman*, New York: Houghton Mifflin, 1925.

[4] *Ibid.*, p. 9.

[5] The only sermon from his ministry known to be printed and thus preserved was a funeral discourse preached on Oct. 14, 1814. Some indication of his pulpit style may appear even from a brief quotation: " 'Hark! From the tombs a doleful sound.' Sons of earth, he calls to you; daughters of pleasure, he calls to you; slaves of the world, he calls to you! Awful eloquence, persuasion of the grave! Shut not your hearts, your consciences to the sound."

[6] In a lecture presented in 1867 and published in October, 1883, Emerson likened Everett to "Pericles in Athens," and described "his radiant beauty of person, of a classic style, his heavy large eyes, marble lids . . . sculptured lips; a voice of such rich tones, such precise and perfect utterance, that, although slightly nasal, it was the most mellow and beautiful and correct of all the instruments of the time. The word that he spoke, in the manner in which he spoke it, became current and classical in New England." Emerson, *Works, op. cit.*, X:331.

[7] The text is in Edward Everett, *Orations and Speeches on Various Occasions*, Boston: American Stationers' Co., 1836, pp. 9–39.

E. L. Magoon, who shared the general conviction of his contemporaries that Everett was one of the great orators of all time, wrote that "The gentle order of imagination peculiar to Mr. Everett's mind, enables him to excel in picturesque description." This gift was well exhibited in a speech delivered at Plymouth Rock on December 22, 1824, in which the orator depicted the fearful ordeal of the Atlantic voyage by the Pilgrims in the *Mayflower*, "driven in fury before the raging tempest, on the high and giddy waves. The awful voice of the storm howls through the rigging. The laboring masts seem straining from their base;—the dismal sound of the pumps is heard;—the ship leaps, as it were, madly, from billow to billow; the ocean breaks, and settles with engulphing floods over the floating deck, and beats with deadening weight, against the staggered vessel." None was lost; none was hurt. But the troubles only multiplied after a safe landing had been accomplished. "Was it the winter's storm beating upon the houseless heads of the women and children; was it hard work and spare meals;—was it disease,—was it the tomahawk,—was it the deep malady of a blighted hope, a ruined enterprise, and a broken heart, aching in its last moments at the recollection of the loved and left beyond the sea; was it some, or all of these united, that hurried this forsaken company to their melancholy fate?" The outcome of all these hardships, however, as the orator triumphantly displayed, was not disaster but "a progress so steady, a growth so wonderful, a reality so important, a promise, yet to be fulfilled, so glorious."[8] The contemplation of such speeches as this led Magoon to conclude that: "Suppose a clear and gentle stream flowing through a cultivated glade, on a bed of the purest gravel; its bank generally smooth and level, with all rudeness concealed by tufts of flowers, fragrant shrubs, elegant trees, and trailing plants hanging over the clear waters . . . and in such a picture we have a fair type of Mr. Everett's mind."[9]

His first speech in Congress, delivered on March 9, 1825, was long and carefully prepared; yet his nervous excitement was such that he could not sleep the preceding night and arose that morning with a splitting headache. He commenced his speech by saying, "I rise to address the committee in a state of indisposition, under which I ought in prudence to be at home rather than on this floor." There must have been a temptation in some quarters to suggest that he might as well withdraw from the ordeal—for the question under discussion (a motion to amend the Constitution to obviate the possibility of the President being elected

---

[8] Magoon, *op. cit.*, p. 79. The oration from which the passage is quoted is contained in Everett's *Orations, op. cit.*, pp. 40–64; the portion cited is from the conclusion, on pp. 61–62.
[9] Magoon, *op. cit.*, p. 95.

by the House of Representatives) was not to be brought to a vote for another month. Nevertheless, he went on. The Constitution, he admitted was far from ideal, since it was put together by compromises. "Sir, I do not think it perfect; but it is good enough for me." Those who sought to change the Constitution he likened to the "poor deluded" reformers in England, "who, without leaders, without counsel, are following the phantom of reform through the dark paths of treason and assassination to the scaffold." Then, since the resolution which Everett was opposing had been introduced by Mr. McDuffie of South Carolina, he undertook to ameliorate the personal effects of his opposition to it by saying something agreeable about the South. What he did say constituted the only completely injudicious words in his public career and continued to haunt him throughout the remainder of his long life:

> The great relation of servitude, in some form or other, with greater or less departures from the theoretic equality of man, is inseparable from our nature. I know of no way by which the form of this servitude shall be fixed but political institution. Domestic slavery, though I confess not that form of servitude which seems to be most beneficent to the master—certainly not that which is most beneficent to the servant— is not, in my judgment, to be set down as an immoral and irreligious institution . . . . I know the condition of the working classes in other countries; I am intimately acquainted with it in some other countries, and I have no hesitation in saying that I believe the slaves in this country are better clothed and fed and less hardly worked than the peasantry of some of the most prosperous states on the Continent of Europe.[10]

The storm that descended upon Everett's head is a reminder that in that period, before the advent of Garrisonian abolitionism, slavery had few avowed defenders. Horace Binney, the noted Pennsylvania lawyer, wrote of Everett that "He has uttered a confession of faith on the subject of slavery that was gratuitous, not at all called for by the occasion, and will make him infinitely odious to many people who wished him well."[11] Within a few days Everett was attacked in Congress by Representatives Whipple, Hoffman, and Cambreling, the last of whom said that if "I had persuaded myself to adopt the political maxim so hostile to liberal institutions and the rights of mankind—I would have locked it up forever in the darkened chamber of my mind." The storm of criticism spread far across the nation and continued so long that fifty five years later Wendell Phillips was still using this gaffe of Everett's as a horrible example in his Phi Beta Kappa address on "The Scholar in a Republic." Everett bravely wrote to his sister: "I anticipated the conse-

[10] Frothingham, *op. cit.*, pp. 100–106.
[11] *Ibid.*, p. 106.

quences of what I said and am ready to meet them."[12] But thereafter he carefully avoided becoming involved in any phase of the slavery and broader sectional disputes, and in general steered a circuitous rhetorical course around and away from controversies.

His longtime friend George A. Hillard commented after Everett's death on this aspect of his career: "If it be said that his discourses are not marked by originality of construction, or philosophical depth of thought, it may be replied that had they been so, they would have been less attractive to his hearers." And this, Hillard implied, was Everett's standard of judgment in deciding what he should say. "Praise was ever cordial to him, and more necessary than to most men who had achieved such high and assured distinction . . . . He never appeared in public without a slight flutter of apprehension lest he should fall short of that standard he had created for himself."[13] His biographer Frothingham agreed that "he was singularly sensitive to criticism, censure, and attack. He had an inborn dislike for controversy, and the hurly-burly of the House was not to his taste."[14] After five terms in Congress, he refused to stand for re-election, explaining to his wife, "I do no good here; I sacrifice my happiness; neglect my duty to my family, and get not even thanks for my reward."[15]

Everett was promptly elected Governor of Massachusetts, and in his inaugural address, January 13, 1836, he called for a "conciliatory forebearance" on the subject of slavery, that would "abstain from a discussion, which, by exasperating the master, can have no other effect than to render more oppressive the condition of the slave."[16] Everett was successively re-elected for four one-year terms—during which his greatest contribution was establishment of the system of normal schools to prepare teachers—then was defeated for a fifth term. Daniel Webster, then Secretary of State, appointed him Minister to England. Shortly, President Tyler conceived the idea of sending a special mission to China and wished Everett to undertake it. He offered him a salary of $9000, plus an equal amount for expenses, and a frigate to conduct him there. Everett declined the appointment "chiefly on the grounds that there was no certainty the Mission would be received, and secondly, that the appropriation was inadequate."[17] In 1845 his appointment in England terminated and immediately upon his return home he was elected President of Harvard, a post he gladly resigned after a stint of three years. In 1852

[12] *Ibid.*, p. 108.
[13] *A Memorial of Edward Everett from the City of Boston*, Boston: Printed by Order of the City Council, 1865, pp. 138–139 and 139–140.
[14] Frothingham, *op. cit.*, p. 121.
[15] *Ibid.*, p. 124.
[16] *Ibid.*, p. 132.
[17] *Ibid.*, p. 232.

he accepted appointment from President Fillmore to succeed Webster as Secretary of State; and in the change of administration that brought Franklin Pierce into the White House four months later, Everett was elected to join Charles Sumner in representing Massachusetts in the Senate.

On February 8, 1854, as Everett noted in his diary, he spoke about an hour and a half on the Kansas-Nebraska bill to a crowded Senate chamber and "received the congratulations of the Senators from every part of the country and every shade of opinion from the most ultra free-soil to the most ultra pro-slavery." The tone of the speech was well described by Everett himself in its conclusion. Concerning "slavery—that terrible question," Everett pointed out that he had uttered "no other words on that subject than those of moderation, conciliation, and harmony between the two great sections of the country."[18] So distasteful did he find the "agitation on the slavery question" in the Senate debates that, in 1855, he resigned his seat, confessing that the turbulence of public life was too demanding for him to endure. For the next ten years he appeared before the public only as an orator; and in this role he was thought to have few if any peers.

His most famous address was on George Washington, first delivered on February 22, 1856, and afterwards repeated to various other audiences. The oration for which his name is best remembered, however, is a speech that historians and critics make a point to forget: Everett's address at Gettysburg, on November 19, 1863, when Abraham Lincoln was also, belatedly, asked to offer "a few appropriate remarks." The one speech lasted two hours, the other two minutes; and Everett's greatest notoriety is as an exemplar of wordy emptiness on an occasion rendered notable by the sublime cogency of the Lincolnian classic. Everett, in fact, was one of the few who instantly recognized the greatness of Lincoln's remarks; and Lincoln, replying to his note of congratulations, justly said: "In our respective parts yesterday you could not have been excused to make a short address, nor I a long one."[19]

The seventeen Governors who composed the committee that arranged for the dedication of the national cemetery at Gettysburg unanimously agreed upon Everett as their choice for speaker of the day. When he could not accept a date in October—on the grounds that this would not give him sufficient time to prepare—they obligingly postponed the date a month (even though this involved a serious risk of encountering bad weather for an occasion that would assemble scores of thousands

[18] *Ibid.*, p. 348.
[19] *Ibid.*, p. 458.

of people in the out-of-doors). Everett undertook to prepare an address worthy of both the occasion and his reputation. The most significant portion of Everett's long speech was its plea for a reconciliation between the North and South. After he pointed out, with numerous examples, that "all history teaches" that feuds within nations are transitory, he made his point explicit: "The bonds that unite us as one people—a substantial community of origin, language, belief, and law—these bonds of union are a perennial force and energy, while the causes of alienation are imaginary, factitious, and transient. The heart of people North and South is for Union . . . . The weary masses of the people are yearning to see the dear old flag again floating upon their Capitols."[20] The sentiments in retrospect may seem commonplace; at the time, not even Lincoln himself was prepared to go so far as to declare that the North and South were in fact "one community," regardless of the fierceness of their war.

Concerning this address, Everett wrote in his diary: "I omitted a good deal of what I had written, but [it] was nevertheless two hours long. Parts of the address were poorly memorized, several long paragraphs condensed, several thoughts occurred at the moment, as happens generally."[21] Much earlier, on July 4, 1855, he had also confided to his journal that his method was to prepare long and carefully, to write out his speeches, to memorize them, and then to extemporize, with the prepared text as his point of departure. Of that Fourth of July address, as of his speeches in general, he reported: "But a very few of the sentences were spoken exactly as written; one third [were] left out; not by omission entirely, but in some parts by an extemporized abridgement."[22] To Edward Everett public speaking was above all an art—not a weapon with which to bludgeon down opposition and to be judged, therefore, solely by its effects, but an artistic composition to be evaluated by such standards as unity, coherence, emphasis, beauty, and appropriateness. His own principal functions as a speaker were suggested in a eulogy by Henry Chapin: "He was the eloquent expositor of the past, the beautiful delineator of the present, but he was not the bold prophet of the future."[23]

Charles Sumner (January 6, 1811–March 11, 1874) started life much as did Everett, but in early maturity became one of the boldest of the

[20] *Ibid.*, p. 457.
[21] *Ibid.*
[22] *Ibid.*, p. 396.
[23] *A Memorial, op. cit.*, pp. 266–267.

bold prophetic advocates of change.[24] More than for most people his life seemed to be impelled forward by a series of crucial accidents; still he was able to guide the drift by his largeness of intellect, industry, and essential kindliness of spirit. Partly because of an attack upon him in 1856 by Preston Brooks—and of the nature of the speech by Sumner, which precipitated the attack—he is remembered as a violent man. He is also stigmatized for vanity and egoism, the impression being bolstered by such contemporary comments as one from Thaddeus Stevens, who, during the Civil War period, knew him as well as one self-centered man can know another: "I go neck and neck with Sumner a long way, but we differ essentially in one particular. The god of my idolatry is my country. The god of his idolatry is Charles Sumner." Many agreed with Stevens; for what Sumner believed he advocated impetuously, wholeheartedly, with small respect for the appropriateness of the occasion or the predilections of his hearers. The greatness of his speaking lay in the fact that he said what he felt had to be said, regardless of how it would be heard.

Sumner was sent to the Boston Public School, then to Harvard, and on to the Harvard Law School, primarily because his father (who had had no intention of educating him) improved his financial circumstances at just the right time. As a student Sumner did well in languages, literature, and history, but had to bluff his way through mathematics and science. He grew up in a home in which his father was openly hostile, his mother unable to express her affection, and the nine children were more rivals than friends. Nevertheless, Sumner somehow developed such loquacity that his schoolboy nickname was "Chatterbox," and he also made an unusually large number of genuinely intimate friendships. After a few months of practicing law, Sumner borrowed $3000 and set off for Europe, like Everett, to expand his education. During the next three years, in England, France, Italy, and Germany, he won immediate and cordial entrance into the highest social circles, establishing lifetime friendships with many of the most notable political and literary leaders, so that, for the remainder of his life, he was the best known American in European political circles and also the American who best understood European politics.

Back in America, Sumner did not find the law particularly congenial and his office became an informal club for genteel reformers. He became attracted to the cause of prison reform, to education, and to peace. He

[24] Of the several early biographies of Sumner, the most useful is Edward L. Pierce, *Memoir and Letters of Charles Sumner*, Four Vols., Boston: Roberts Bros., 1877. The best book on Sumner is David Donald, *Charles Sumner and the Coming of the Civil War*, New York: Knopf, 1960. In Brigance, ed., *History and Criticism, op. cit.*, the study on "Charles Sumner" is by R. Élaine Pagel and Carl Dallinger, II:751–776.

did not speak in public (except at meetings of The Peace Society and the Boston Prison Discipline Society) but he became so well known through his social contacts that in 1845 Boston's Mayor and City Council invited Sumner to give the Fourth of July oration—an honor carefully reserved for youngish men who showed indubitable promise of rising to eminence. At first Sumner "peremptorily refused," and even after he was persuaded to undertake the speech he did not commence its preparation until mid-June. It was difficult for him to envision himself as a public speaker; yet with this speech he projected himself more than was wise into the forefront of attention not only in his homeland but also in Europe. The title he selected was "The True Grandeur of Nations," and his theme was that "In our age there can be no peace that is not honorable; there can be no war that is not dishonorable."[25]

The occasion had been carefully planned to do full honor to the great role Boston had played in the American Revolution. A parade wound through flag-draped streets from City Hall to Tremont Temple, where two thousand people crowded in to hear the speaker. A choir of two hundred school girls sat on the stage, to sing the national anthem. Army and Navy officers and Massachusetts Militiamen sat resplendent in their uniforms in the section immediately before the speaker. The meeting opened with an impressive reading of the Declaration of Independence. Then Sumner arose, meticulously dressed in a long-tailed blue coat, with a white waistcoat and white trousers, and proceeded at once to denounce the projected annexation of Texas and to ridicule the popular slogan "Fifty-four forty or fight!" as "a presumptuous assertion of a disputed claim to a worthless territory." For two hours, speaking largely from memory, Sumner plunged on, describing war as a "monstrous and impious usage" that "wasted lands, ruined and famished cities, and slaughtered armies." The causes of war, he declared, included "a selfish and exaggerated *love of country*." "Our country, be she *right or wrong*," declaimed Sumner, was "a sentiment dethroning God and enthroning the Devil." As for professional soldiers, he said, looking down at them massed before him, in their padded coats "smeared with gold," they were incompetent even to put down a street riot. The commanding officer had to restrain the militia from walking out. West Point, the orator continued, was a "seminary of idleness and vice." Military training was "farcical and humiliating." The Navy, he said, would prove "unavailing" for "defense against any serious attack." The "true golden age" would arrive, he thought, when war for any purpose was re-

[25] Cf. Donald, *op. cit.*, pp. 106–117. Charles Sumner, *The True Grandeur of Nations*, Boston: J. H. Eastburn, 1845; reprinted in David J. Brewer, ed., *The World's Best Orations*, Chicago: Fred P. Kaiser, 1923, IX:317–328.

nounced. But how universal peace could be achieved, Sumner did not explain—except to assert: "*Believe* that you can do it, and you can do it."

There was nothing in the speech that was new—except the rhetorical patterning of the historical allusions and the eloquent phrasing. The ideas Sumner took were from his friends and mentors, William Ladd, founder of the Peace Society, and William Ellery Channing, the Unitarian minister whose pulpit was Sumner's principal intellectual guide. Neither then nor later did Sumner deserve credit for any special originality of thinking. If the speech had been delivered in a church or at a peace society meeting, it would have attracted little attention. The sensational feature of it was the time and place of its delivery; it was a speech that, as Edwin P. Whipple, the Boston essayist and critic, judiciously observed, won widespread notoriety precisely because it "was studiously framed so as to be utterly inappropriate to the occasion."[26] Samuel Eliot, the treasurer of Harvard, thought that for the hope of "the applause of thousands of excited and enthusiastic persons . . . the young man has cut his own throat."[27] In a sense he had; for it was Sumner's life's ambition to be named Professor of International Law at the Harvard Law School, and largely because of this speech this opportunity was decisively lost. For several years Sumner continued to pursue the theme of pacifism except in cases of absolute necessity of self-defense. Then, in 1849, he delivered another speech on "The War System of the Commonwealth of Nations," this time within the safe confines of the American Peace Society, in which he advocated establishment of a Congress of Nations as a substitute for war. After that he seldom referred to the topic again and in 1861 he was a staunch supporter of war to preserve the Union.

The years 1844 and 1845 were crucial for Sumner. Unable to fall in love[28] and troubled by a deep-seated melancholia, he was becoming so increasingly indrawn that his friends deliberately undertook to interest him in programs of reform and in politics. The widespread discussion of his "True Grandeur of Nations" precipitated him into politics and for several years he engaged in the struggle between the "Conscience Whigs" and the "Cotton Whigs," the latter linked by Sumner to the slaveholders with the stinging phrase, "the lords of the loom and lords of the lash." Finally he emerged in 1848 as an unsuccessful Free-Soil candidate for Congress. In undertaking to support abolitionism, how-

[26] Donald, *op. cit.*, p. 117.
[27] *Ibid.*, p. 112.
[28] In 1866 Sumner married a widow from whom he quickly separated. His biographers pass over the incident with barest mention. Not so the gossipy Ben: Perly Poore, who described it all in his *Reminiscences*, *op. cit.*, II:199–200.

ever, Sumner rejected the Constitution-burning approach of Garrison and Phillips. In his view "the Constitution of the United States does not recognize man as *property*."[29] Slavery, he declared, rested upon local laws and should be eradicated by seeking to change those laws. On this platform he sought election in 1851 to the Senate, and was finally chosen, on the 26th ballot in the State Legislature, by a majority of one out of the 385 votes cast.[30] It was far from being a public mandate of confidence; and, on his part, Sumner asserted that the result "will find me *an absolutely independent man*, without any pledge or promise."[31]

Shortly after arriving in Washington, Sumner wrote, "I am sick at heart with what I find here."[32] Thomas Hart Benton, who had just been defeated for re-election, told him that you "have come to the Senate too late. All the great issues and all the great men were gone. There was nothing left but snarling over slavery, and no chance whatever for a career."[33] Sumner was one of only three Free-Soilers in the Senate, Salmon P. Chase and John P. Hale being the others. He settled down to being a good Senator, never absent from his seat while the Senate was in session, and working in his rooms every night from nine until midnight. His maiden speech was an elegant eulogy of the Hungarian patriot, Louis Kossuth, which offended no one and which everyone applauded.[34] In this and in his other speeches, Sumner took great care, writing out what he would say and memorizing it. From Professor Edward T. Channing, at Harvard, he had learned that a speech should have an exordium, narration, partition, proof, refutation, and peroration—and almost always he tried to follow this classic pattern. To Horace Mann, in 1850, he wrote: "Let your points be clear; and the arrangement careful—divided, and subdivided. These resting places help the understanding of a long document." His sentences were architectonic rather than conversational, his vocabulary deliberately classic, avoiding both neologisms and technical terms. He scorned the use of humor and disingenuously likened his own speaking to the Book of Revelation. Standing six feet two inches tall and weighing, in maturity, 185 pounds, he spoke in a deeply sonorous voice and used gestures that

---

[29] In "his first political speech," on a dark and stormy evening in early November, 1845, Sumner pleaded with the Whigs to oppose the annexation of Texas. "Let us wash our hands of this great guilt," he cried. "God forbid that the blood which spurts from the lacerated, quivering flesh of the slave should soil the hem of the white garments of Massachusetts." Donald, *op. cit.*, p. 140.
[30] *Ibid.*, p. 202.
[31] *Ibid.*, p. 195.
[32] *Ibid.*, p. 206.
[33] *Ibid.*, p. 208.
[34] *Ibid.*, p. 211. Shortly Sumner made another speech, opposing a federal land grant for the building of a railroad in Iowa, which the *Atlas* called "uninteresting and heavy . . . unsound and visionary"; and which Sumner himself thought "the most important speech for the West uttered in Congress for 10 years." *Ibid.*, p. 213.

were strong rather than graceful, appearing, as the poet Longfellow said, "like a cannoneer . . . ramming down cartridges."[35]

For seven months Sumner sat in the Senate saying little in general and nothing at all about the Fugitive Slave Law in particular, which his followers had sent him to Washington to oppose. Bostonian liberals fumed and complained, while Sumner insisted that he had a speech written out and memorized and only awaited an opportunity to deliver it. Finally, on August 26, 1852, his chance came when an amendment to pay the expenses of federal law enforcement officials was offered to an appropriations bill. The speech, which came to be known by the title under which it was published, "Freedom National; Slavery Sectional,"[36] was a carefully meditated attempt to dissociate abolitionism from radicalism and to win conservatives to its support. In the speech he set forth the principles from which he never afterward departed: that the federal government stood for what was *right*, for *freedom*, for *equality*. In respect to slavery, which the founding fathers abominated, the nation had not grown but had shrunk in character. The Constitution neither accepted nor rejected slavery; but no one could "be so absurd as to imagine, infer, suppose, conjecture, surmise, fancy, guess or presume that Slavery can have any sanction in words which do not plainly and unequivocally declare it." Trying to turn the tables on the Southerners' favorite argument that the Constitution was only a "compact between the States," Sumner declared the Fugitive Slave Act was such a compact and that no State was bound to enforce it against its will.

The speech ran on, replete with classical allusions and quotations, for three and a half hours; the galleries crowded with ladies representing the height of Washington society, the floor with Representatives squeezed in among the Senators. Sumner's principal point was that slavery would die out if it received no support except from local and State laws. To the white South he threw the sop of his admission "that a race, degraded for long generations under the iron heel of bondage" could not expect "at once all the political duties of an American citizen." But inferiority should not be a cause for mistreatment. He concluded his speech to a swelling of applause for his final sentences: "Beware of the groans of the wounded souls. Oppress not to the utmost a single heart; for a solitary sigh has power to overset a whole world." When the vote was taken on Sumner's motion to repeal the Fugitive Slave Law, it received only four votes. But the speech rendered his position safe in Massachusetts.

---

[35] *Ibid.*, pp. 213–218. Longfellow remained one of Sumner's most unrestrained admirers.

[36] The text is in Sumner's *Works*, Statesman Edition, Fifteen Vols., Boston: Lee and Shephard, 1900, III:95–196.

"Now," Theodore Parker wrote to him, "you have done yourself Justice and put yourself out of reach of attack from friend or foe."

In the campaign of 1854, Massachusetts was swept by the new Know-Nothing Party, based on renunciation of Catholics and immigrants; Sumner was cowed into silent acquiescence with its program, but, in a spirit of frustration and humiliation, he left home on a long trip through the South and West. On this trip he observed numerous examples of the mistreatment of slaves and returned to Washington aboil with moral indignation and general irritability. The Garrisonians were by now complaining that he loved the Union more than he hated slavery, making him "as bad as Webster." Nothing either in his personal situation or in the affairs of the nation accorded with his sense of decorum, dignity, or righteousness. To stay in office he had to beg support from politicians whom he detested; and those reformers who should be his allies were his bitterest critics. It was in this spirit that he wrote a speech, the "Crime against Kansas," which he found opportunity to deliver on May 19–20, 1856.[37] Chiefly because of its aftermath, it is the address for which he is best remembered.

For two months he worked on the manuscript, which in print runs to 112 pages. He sprinkled it copiously with many classical quotations and carefully worked out the cadences of the sentences. When it was concluded he memorized it thoroughly so that he would have no need to refer to his notes, then practiced delivering it to Senator William Henry Seward. Finally he gave it to the congressional printer so that it might be set in type. Then he was ready for his audience. The word that he was to speak at one o'clock on May 19 was spread about, and when the time came the chamber was completely packed. "No such scene has been witnessed in that body since the days of Webster," wrote the correspondent for the New York *Post*. From the opening remarks, in which Sumner promised to display the proslavery crime against Kansas "without a single rag, or fig-leaf, to cover its vileness," until he finished three hours later, the crowded chamber was hushed in stillness. On the following day Sumner delivered the second part of his speech—the possible remedies for the crime—then launched into a carefully rehearsed attack against Senators Douglas, Butler, and Mason, the first two having already been scourged by him the preceding day. Douglas, in the rear of the Senate, muttered, "That damn fool will get himself killed by some other damn fool." Edward Everett, who heard the speech, thought that "from a man of character of any party I have never seen anything so

[37] Donald, *op. cit.*, devotes a splendid chapter to this speech, pp. 278–311. Pagel and Dallinger felt that "It does not seem that he intended to be malicious," but noted as "a rather obvious criticism . . . his lack of subtlety." *Op. cit.*, II:760, 762.

offensive." Sumner well knew what he was about. Before making the speech he wrote to a friend: "I shall pronounce the most thorough philippic ever uttered in a legislative body." He had a great deal of spleen to work out of his system. The speech has few equals in its chosen realm of vicious denunciation.

Actually, much of the speech, in keeping with Sumner's abilities and habits of mind, was a carefully organized restatement of familiar arguments against Douglas's Kansas-Nebraska bill, against the "compact" theory of the Constitution, against the behavior of the slave States, and in favor of strict restrictions upon the extension of slave territory. But the whole was deliberately placed within a framework of the most severe denunciation that a man of Sumner's purity of language could concoct. Whether to please his abolitionist friends or to so madden the South that it would commit an act the North could no longer tolerate, Sumner launched a guerrilla type of verbal warfare.

He commenced by describing the Lecompton Constitution ("a Tyrannical Usurpation") as "the rape of a virgin Territory, compelling it to the hateful embrace of Slavery." He proceeded: "There, sir, stands the criminal, all unmasked before you—heartless, grasping, and tyrannical . . . . the slave power of our Republic." This power he then likened to a serpent, adding, "the creature, whose paws are fastened upon Kansas, whatever it may seem to be, . . . in its loathsome folds, is now coiled about the whole land." He then directed his attention to one of the gentler and more popular of the Southern Senators, Andrew P. Butler, of South Carolina, who was absent, likening him to Don Quixote, with Stephen A. Douglas as his squire, Sancho Panza. The South Carolinian, Sumner sneered, "has read many books of chivalry, and believes himself a chivalrous knight, with sentiments of honor and courage. Of course he has chosen a mistress to whom he has made his vows, and who, though ugly to others, is always lovely to him; though polluted in the sight of the world, is chaste in his sight—I mean the harlot, Slavery . . ." Still later, in heartless reference to Butler's partial labial paralysis, Sumner said that "with incoherent phrases," he "discharged the loose expectoration of his speech . . . nor was there any possible deviation from truth which he did not make . . . . He shows an incapacity of accuracy . . . . He cannot open his mouth, but out there flies a blunder." At the end of this three-hour philippic, Sumner piously concluded: "in the name of the Heavenly Father, whose service is perfect Freedom, I make this last appeal."

The next day Senator Douglas commented to the Senate on Sumner's speech: "He seems to get up a speech as in Yankee land they get up a bedquilt. They take all the old calico dresses of various colors, that have been in the house from the days of their grandmothers, and invite the young ladies of the neighborhood in the afternoon, and the young men to meet them at a dance in the evening. They cut up these pieces of old dresses and make pretty figures, and boast what beautiful ornamental work they have made, although there was not a new piece of material in the whole quilt." Then Douglas asked: "Is it his object to provoke some of us to kick him as we would a dog in the street, that he may get sympathy upon the just chastisement?" Senator Mason, of Virginia, who was also an object of Sumner's attack, commented that Sumner had taken cowardly advantage of the absence of Senator Butler to attack him. But this was not the case, Douglas retorted. "I think the speech was written and practiced, and the gestures fixed; and, if that part had been stricken out the Senator would not have known how to repeat the speech."[38] Sumner was stung by the element of truth in this aspersion and undertook one of his rare extemporaneous replies: "No person with the upright form of man can be allowed, without violation to all decency, to switch out from his tongue the offensive stench of offensive personality. Sir, that is not a proper weapon of debate, at least, on this floor. The noisome, squat, and nameless animal, to which I now refer, is not a proper model for an American Senator."[39] Douglas refused to reply, saying, I "will not imitate you, sir"; and the Senate adjourned.

A week later the poet Longfellow wrote Sumner: "Your speech is the greatest voice on the greatest subject that has been uttered."[40] By this time Sumner was in the hospital and needed comfort. For on Thursday, May 22, Representative Preston S. Brooks, of South Carolina, a moderate who had been criticized in his home State for preferring national to sectional interests, went to the Senate chamber, waited until 12:45, after the adjournment for the day, then walked over to Sumner's desk, where the orator sat franking copies of his speech. Brooks spoke to him, struck him lightly with the small end of his cane, then, as Sumner rose and threw out his arm in protection, commenced to beat him on the head. Some thirty blows were struck before Sumner fell unconscious in the aisle. "Towards the last he bellowed like a calf," Brooks commented. "I wore my cane out completely but saved the Head which is gold."

The reaction was what Sumner might have hoped: Brooks was expelled from the House. But he was promptly re-elected and returned. Meetings of sympathy for Sumner were held in virtually every Northern city. The assault occurred at almost the identical time as a Southern raid

---

[38] Alexander Johnston and James Albert Woodburn, eds., *American Eloquence,* Four Vols., New York: Putnam's, 1896, III:112, 113, 114–115.
[39] *Ibid.,* p. 19.
[40] Donald, *op. cit.,* p. 288. The description of the beating and its aftermath is based on Donald's account, *op. cit.,* pp. 289–311.

upon the free-soil town of Lawrence, Kansas, supplying the Republicans with a dual slogan: "Bleeding Sumner," and "Bleeding Kansas." Sumner was re-elec'ed to his Senate seat, receiving all but twelve of the 345 votes cast. He took a three year vacation from the Senate to regain his health, his empty seat speaking more eloquently than he could have done. When he finally returned to his duties, John Brown's Raid was the center of interest, but Sumner refrained from discussing it, explaining to friends, "Not, indeed, that I hesitate to judge the act; but how can I refuse my admiration to many things in the man?"[41] In 1860 he supported Seward for the Republican nomination, thinking Lincoln too moderate and that he had "very little acquaintance with Government." Finally, on June 4, 1860, to support the admission of Kansas as a free State, Sumner appeared in the Senate for an evening meeting, in full evening dress, with white gloves, to deliver a four-hour speech that was published under the title, "The Barbarism of Slavery."

Sumner commenced this renewal of his oratorical career by saying: "I have no personal griefs to utter . . . . I have no personal wrongs to avenge." He did not tax his strength by memorizing this speech, but read its 35,000 words, including all the elaborate tables of statistics from the closely printed galley proofs he held in his hand.[42] To make up, perhaps, for the inadequacies of the delivery, he employed particularly strong language. A slave society, he declared, was not a civilization. "Barbarous in origin; barbarous in its law; barbarous in all its pretensions; barbarous in the instruments it employs; barbarous in consequences; barbarous in spirit; barbarous wherever it shows itself, Slavery must breed Barbarians." A Southern Negro, he said, could be "marked like a hog, branded like a mule, yoked like an ox, maimed like a cur, and constantly beaten like a brute," while the "whole race is delivered over to prostitution and concubinage, without the protection of any law." He referred to the story of six thousand skulls of infants supposedly taken from a fishpond near a nunnery, during Europe's period of Catholic supremacy; then he added that "Under the law of Slavery, infants, the offspring of masters . . . are not thrown into a fishpond . . . . They are sold." Then, examining the charge that the Negro is an inferior breed, he declared that if so "it is the unquestionable duty of a Christian Civilization to lift it from its degradation, not by bludgeon and the chain . . . but by a generous charity." He concluded with an appeal for a federal law to guarantee "impartial Freedom without distinction of color or race." Senator James Chesnut of South Carolina commented briefly that Sumner was "the incarnation of malice, mendacity, and coward-

---

[41] *Ibid.*, p. 351.
[42] The circumstances are described by Donald, *op. cit.*, pp. 353–357.

ice"; and Sumner arose to say he would reprint these comments as an appendix to his speech, to help prove his contention that Southerners were barbarians. The debate closed.

Southern newspapers, as expected, denounced the speech. But so did the Republican newspapers in the North; for they felt it essential to dissociate the Party from this kind of violence at a time when votes were to be won. The Springfield *Republican* summed up a very widespread reaction: "We do not think Charles Sumner a statesman and we doubt if he ever can become one, or has any bent in that direction." Sumner took note of the criticism in a letter to Elizur Wright: "Perhaps I deserve it. At all events, I have labored for the truth, and I accept the consequences." He added, however: "*That* speech will yet be adopted by the Republican Party." Within weeks a reaction set in. The Republican Congressional Campaign Committee decided to circulate the speech as a campaign document; and Sumner found himself in great demand as a campaign speaker. When Lincoln was elected, and the Southern States began to secede, a new phase began in the career of Charles Sumner. Teamed with Congressman Thaddeus Stevens of Pennsylvania, he became a co-architect of a vindictive settlement to be foisted upon the South. But his career in oratory was virtually at an end.

VIII

PRACTICAL POLITICS AND THE HIGHER LAW: DOUGLAS, SEWARD, AND LINCOLN 1850⌐1865

▥ Giants in Conflict

OF WEBSTER, Clay, and Calhoun it may always be said that they held war at bay until after their time. Not so for their successors. Whatever the virtues of the second great triumvirate—William Henry Seward, Stephen Arnold Douglas, and Abraham Lincoln—they did not succeed in the task to which they dedicated their lives; indeed the Civil War was, in the words of Douglas's biographer "the great failure in the history of the United States."[1] Lincoln, of course, is credited with the greater statesmanship, for under his presidency the Union was preserved and the slaves were freed. But this was an achievement of the statesman, not of the orator; for after his inauguration Lincoln virtually retired from the platform. In his day it was not considered a major function of the presidency to guide public opinion. "In my present position," Lincoln explained in 1862, "it is hardly proper for me to make speeches."[2] Douglas tried hardest to devise programs for the guidance of the nation through its shoals of troubles. Lincoln followed the conservative course of clinging to an established past; and Seward sought to walk the tightrope between the abolitionists, who almost captured him, and the conservatives, who wrung their hands but hoped for the best.

On the whole it was a period of observation, of commentary, of attaching blame, of avoiding responsibility, of watchful waiting, of fear and anxiety, of hapless drift. It is almost enough to remind ourselves that Franklin Pierce and James Buchanan were the Presidents during most of this time. Allan Nevins concluded that "The nation has never seen a period in which so little was done to solve the exigent problems."[3] Talking about the problems provided a more available channel

[1] Gerald M. Capers, Stephen A. Douglas: Defender of the Union, Boston: Little, Brown, 1959, p. ix.
[2] David Donald, Lincoln Reconsidered, op. cit., p. 59.
[3] Allan Nevins, Ordeal of the Union, New York: Scribner's, 1947, I:158.

for the surging tumult of seething emotions than the uncertainty of indeterminate actions. "Great emphasis was placed on oratorical art," wrote Nevins. In the Congress, "apt retorts were eagerly applauded; and the members were eager critics of debating skill."[4]

A lack of centrality of purpose was everywhere apparent. The Church was splitting apart into contrasting and contesting denominations. The Lyceum, which was intellectually challenging in the prior decade, faded away. In politics the uncertainties were accentuated. The Whig Party was falling apart and died listlessly early in the decade. A Free-Soil Party had arisen with a bold slogan: "Free soil, free speech, free labor, and free men!"; but it made one unsuccessful presidential nomination, then collapsed. The Democratic Party split into Northern and Southern wings. A new Republican Party emerged with a candidate in 1856, and in 1860 won its first presidential election—with fewer than two million votes out of the 4.7 million total.

It was a time of questing and questioning. The issues of slavery and of State versus Federal authority, both divisive along sectional lines, aroused passionately partisan loyalties; but emotional intensity is not a suitable substitute for practical programs. Such "revisionist" historians as Avery O. Craven and James G. Randall insist that the Civil War could have been avoided were it not for the ineptness of the "blundering generation" of the 1850's.[5] Such a "re-revisionist" as David Donald believes the fault lay less in a lack of leadership than in the social character of the nation at that date: ill-disciplined, without binding traditions, unstable from too rapid growth, drunk from the heady brew of too much democracy.[6] The prime sophisticate, Henry Adams, who lived through the period, excused his own passivity by explaining that "he never got to the point of playing the game at all; he lost himself in the study of it, watching the errors of the players." To him the outbreak of the war was no surprise, since "man from the beginning had found his chief amusement in bloodshed."[7] The ultimate irony is that excepting the radicals who represented small minorities on either side, the major spokesmen insisted that the only acceptable solution was the maintenance of a *status quo* which both sides repeatedly declared to be unsatisfactory.

[4] *Ibid.*, I:268–269.
[5] Avery Craven, *The Coming of the Civil War*, New York: Scribner's, 1942, and *The Repressible Conflict*, Baton Rouge: Louisiana State University Press, 1938; and James G. Randall, *The Civil War and Reconstruction*, Boston: Heath, rev., 1961, and *Lincoln the President: Springfield to Gettysburg*, New York: Dodd Mead, 1945.
[6] Donald, *op. cit.*, Chapter XI, "An Excess of Democracy: The American Civil War and the Social Process," pp. 209–235.
[7] *The Education of Henry Adams: An Autobiography*, New York: Book League of America, 1928, pp. 4, 128.

If we are searching for speakers who are seers, this decade does not disclose them. Many eloquent words were spun from fine minds inspired by good intentions. But in the main expediency bulked larger than principle; and the solutions proposed seldom went further than mere postponement, or pleas for mutual forebearance. But granting the circumstances in which these men lived, what more could be demanded of them? By and large they were estimated rightly by those who heard what they had to say. The popular craving for oratory was not solely a confession of incapacity or insecurity on the part of the listeners. In part it was a recognition that when no solution is available, there is value simply in talk. When no one knows what to do, it is rather pointless to blame the speakers for sharing the general deficiency. At least they maintained, for as long as they could, a stream of words as a counterfoil to war. So long as the dialogue between North and South could be maintained, war was prospect, not reality. The great speakers of this decade were not supermen; but they were far more than mere papier-maché silhouettes. The leadership they provided was the best the nation under those circumstances could produce.

Stephen A. Douglas: Apostle of Popular Sovereignty

FRIENDS AND opponents alike called Stephen Arnold Douglas "the little giant." He stood only five feet two inches tall;[1] but unlike "Little Ellick" Stephens, Douglas was muscular, broadly built, heavy set, thoroughly masculine—and Douglas accepted the shortness of his stature with an easy equanimity. When he was Chief Justice of the Illinois Supreme Court, he would on occasion leave the bench to sit playfully on the lap of a lawyer or spectator, well realizing that to make fun of his own puniness was the best defense against ridicule. His energy was so great that he was described as a "steam engine in britches." His voice held a "peculiar fascination," swelling with a "deep, vibrant energy." Without effort or strain, his voice reached with equal effectiveness listeners at a distance or close by.[2] His articulation was precise; and the

[1] Douglas's height was reported by Capers, *op. cit.*, p. 7, as five feet, when he was twenty years old. George Fort Milton described him as being five feet four inches tall, *The Eve of Conflict: Stephen A. Douglas and the Needless War*, Boston: Houghton Mifflin, 1934, p. 2. The *Encyclopaedia Britannica* depicted him as "conspicuously small, being hardly five feet in height." 1954 ed., VII:555A. Carl Schurz, who saw him often, called him "a man of low stature," *Reminiscences*, *op. cit.*, II:30.
[2] Cf. Milton, *op. cit.*, p. 3.

authority of his tone mirrored his own assurance that he was truly a giant in intellect, in strength of character, and in ability to sway the opinions and inspire the loyalty of both masses and individuals. He dressed meticulously though not fussily, wore his hair long and in a defiantly high wave, and altogether was a man of fascinatingly magnetic personality. Although he rose from poverty on the strength of his own ambition and abilities, Douglas always carried himself with the grace and assurance of a born patrician. His career, as viewed in historical perspective, was a charade of superficial success and fundamental failure; but none among his contemporaries thought to treat him with either pity or ridicule, for the stamp of greatness was upon him, easily to be seen.

Born April 23, 1813, in Vermont, Douglas moved with his mother to upstate New York in 1830, where he attended the Canandaigua Academy, winning prizes as a debater and studying law in his spare moments. At the age of nineteen he left home for the West, supposedly promising to stop by ten years later when he would be returning to a seat in Congress. He arrived in Illinois with seventy five cents in his pocket and earned his living teaching school until he could win admittance to the bar. Almost at once he made a name for himself with a series of speeches supporting Andrew Jackson, and was propelled into the forefront of the rapidly growing Democratic Party in Illinois.[3] In 1836 he was elected to the State Legislature and within four years he became successively Secretary of State for Illinois and a Justice of the Illinois Supreme Court. In 1843, just a few months behind the schedule he set for himself when he bade farewell to his mother, he was elected to Congress. Three years later he was sent to the Senate, where he remained until his death on June 7, 1861. A few hours before his death he painfully uttered a last message to be given to his sons: "Tell them to obey the laws and support the Constitution."[4] This was his own estimate of the central significance of his career.

Life in Illinois was easy for Douglas and robustly successful. Aside from his rapid rise in law and politics, he invested wisely in Chicago real estate and acquired wealth without much effort. In 1847, when he married a charming girl from North Carolina, he had both the resources and the strength of will to refuse politely a dowry of a plantation and slaves worth at least $100,000.

As his sphere of activities became nationwide, however, his difficulties began to accumulate. He was immediately projected into the complexities of the sectional issues, being named chairman of the important

[3] Capers, *op. cit.*, p. 16.
[4] Milton, *op. cit.*, pp. 568–569.

committee on territories. The position was right for him, for he was all his life passionately committed to expanding the national domain. One of his first acts in Congress was to bring in a bill providing statehood for Texas, and he followed this by demanding annexation of the whole of the Oregon Territory, echoing the slogan, "Fifty-four forty or fight!" He denied the right of England to hold so much as "one acre on the Northwest coast of America." Then, in a burst of unrestrained ebullience, he grandiloquently laid claim to all the American possessions of England, Russia, and Mexico: "I would blot out the lines of the map which now mark our national boundaries on this continent, and make the area of liberty as broad as the continent itself."[5] He was ardent in his support of Polk's policies in the Mexican War and equally ardent in joining Calhoun's attacks upon the Wilmot Proviso. In 1847 his imagination was caught by Lewis Cass's proposal of the doctrine of popular sovereignty—the principle that only the inhabitants of the territories had the power to endorse or prohibit slavery in the constitutions they would propose when they applied to the Congress for admission as States.

In all this there was a unity of principle. From his youth to his death, Douglas looked for a solution to the North-South impasse on the growing influence of the West.[6] "There is a power in this nation," he told the Senate in 1850, "greater than either the North or the South—a growing, increasing, swelling power, that will be able to speak the law to this nation, and to execute the law as spoken. That power is the country known as the great West—the Valley of the Mississippi, one and indivisible from the Gulf to the Great Lakes . . . . There, Sir, is the hope of this nation—the resting place of the power that is not only to control, but to save, the Union."[7] Lincoln was finally won to the same point of view and made it a central theme in his December 1, 1862, address to Congress on the State of the Union.

On the dismal and dangerous subject of slavery, Douglas tried hard to find and hold a middle ground, one which was defined in terms of legality, not morality. In private he could pronounce slavery "a curse beyond computation to both white and black"; but in the same conversation he renounced abolitionism as "false morality and worse policy."[8] In the 1848 debate on the Wilmot Proviso, Douglas charged the rancorous Foote of Mississippi with "wild and reckless fanaticism." But in a debate with Calhoun he pleaded, "We stand up for all your Constitutional rights, in which we will protect you to the last." Then he pointed

[5] For Douglas's speech entitled, "An Ocean Bound Republic," see Appendix, *Congressional Globe*, 28th Congress, 2nd Session, pp. 65–66.
[6] Milton, *op. cit.*, Chapters II, III, and VII.
[7] Henry Nash Smith, *Virgin Land*, New York: Vintage Books, 1957, pp. 186–187.
[8] Capers, *op. cit.*, p. 98.

out that each section must decide for itself between slavery and freedom: "if slavery be a blessing, it is your blessing; if it be a curse, it is your curse; enjoy it—on you rests all the responsibility!"[9] In Douglas's view, since slavery was sanctioned by constitutional law, the question was how the nation might live with it, not how to get rid of it. On December 23, 1851, in consideration of Clay's compromise bills, Douglas feelingly assured the Senate that he was "resolved never to make another speech upon the slavery question in the Houses of Congress." Both for the sake of his own career and for the welfare of the nation, this was a consummation he devoutly wished; but the slave issue would not down.

How to keep the sectional rivalry from splitting the Union was his chief concern. During the Compromise debates, in 1850, he hammered away at the notion that one section could dictate to another. "If the people of California want slavery, they have a right to it," he insisted, "and if they do not want it, it should not be forced upon them . . . . Why, Sir, the principle of self-government is that each community shall settle this question for itself."[10] Impatiently he swept aside the view that national legislation could provide a solution. It had been neither the Ordinance of 1787 nor the Missouri Compromise, he declared, that had kept slavery out of the Northwest, but "the laws of nature, of climate and production." He pleaded with the South to give up its fight to maintain an "equilibrium of power" in the Senate; for, he forecast, Delaware, Maryland, Virginia, Kentucky, and probably North Carolina and Tennessee as well, would eventually adopt plans for gradual emancipation. Moreover, seventeen new States would someday be carved out of western territory that was unsuitable to slavery. No equality of votes in the Senate could be maintained. The only safeguard for the deep South, and thus for the integrity of the Union, lay in the principle of popular sovereignty—the inherent right of local self-rule.

This was the argument Douglas used as the central theme of his career. Back home in Chicago, on October 23, 1850, speaking to an angry mass meeting of 4000, in which a carefully assembled group of fugitive slaves was featured, Douglas boldly defended his Senate vote for the Fugitive Slave Act. Refusal to enforce it, he said, would be "naked, unmitigated nullification." With a persuasive skill that won the hostile audience over to his side, he concluded: "We cannot expect our brethren of the other States to remain faithful to the compact and permit us to be faithless."[11] This was courage; and, right or wrong, it was a policy

[9] *Ibid.*, pp. 43–44.
[10] Milton, *op. cit.*, p. 59.
[11] *Ibid.*, p. 81.

he defended consistently, regardless of the storms that beat against him. Illinois understood his worth; and in 1852 he was returned to the Senate by a vote of seventy five to twenty.

It was in 1853 that Douglas finally managed to make "popular sovereignty" the focus of national attention—and thereby insured the defeat of his greatest ambition. Congress was debating a land grant to finance construction of the Pacific Railroad. Thomas Hart Benton wanted it to run through St. Louis, Douglas through Chicago. Both men had personal as well as political axes to grind, for the effect upon the value of their real estate holdings would be enormous. But both men were also sincerely concerned with the effect a coast-to-coast railway would have in binding the country together. A problem that remained to be solved was that of providing some form of organized government for the territories through which the rail line would run. For this purpose, Douglas attached a "caboose" to the railway bill, providing for organization of the Nebraska Territory.

In a March 10 speech on the railway bill he recalled his 1846 fling with Manifest Destiny and remarked: "I am content for the present with the territory we have. I do not wish to annex any portion of Mexico now. I did not wish to annex any part of Central America then, nor do I at this time." [12] His immediate problem was to squirm away from his reputation as a fanatical imperialist, a reputation which had resulted in the politically damaging nickname of "Little Napoleon." Attention had to be concentrated on what should be done with the great land areas the nation already possessed. But whenever and however this issue was faced, the North-South rivalry resulted in an impasse. Douglas's amendment was tabled in a strictly sectional vote.

On January 4, 1854, he tried again, introducing a separate Kansas-Nebraska bill and supporting it with a major speech. These new States, his bill provided, "shall be received into the Union with or without slavery, as their constitutions may prescribe at the time of their admission." He interpreted the Compromise of 1850 as meaning that "Congress is invested with no rightful authority to legislate upon the subject of slavery in the Territories." Then he went busily to work among his colleagues, drumming up votes. The South, he was assured by Dixon of Kentucky, would not vote for the bill unless it contained an explicit repudiation of the Missouri Compromise. Douglas hesitated for several days, then inserted this provision in his bill, though "I know it will raise

---

[12] At this time Douglas was concentrating his efforts upon securing legislation that would make Chicago the railway hub of the nation; and he did not want any Southwestern territory that might cause a shift of the railway line southward to a St. Louis junction (for which Thomas Hart Benton was fighting).

a hell of a storm." Benton watched the outraged reaction of the North and remarked sardonically, "Douglas has committed political suicide."[13] The Little Giant did his best to be a lively corpse.

With the tremendous energy that amazed his colleagues, he worked day and night to win support for his bill through intensive lobbying, incessant letter-writing, and a continual outpouring of speeches in the Senate. In a long speech on January 30, he detailed why he thought nature had excluded slavery from the Northwest Territories, so that legislation to that effect was irrelevant. On March 3 he restated his popular sovereignty solution in terms designed to win the broadest possible support: "the people shall be left free to regulate their domestic concerns in their own way." Then he shrewdly observed that the North had no right to claim any proprietary interest in the Missouri Compromise since in the 1820 vote twenty of the twenty four Northern Senators had voted *against* the bill. At the close of this deba'e Douglas won his case; the Senate adopted his bill by the overwhelming vote of thirty seven to fourteen, the House by the narrower margin of 113 to 100.

Douglas was overjoyed and exuberantly set about trying to win full political advantage from his victory. "The speeches were nothing," he asserted, well aware that no one could detract from his credit for them. What he had done behind the scenes was what he wanted the Democratic president-makers to understand and appreciate. "It was marshalling and directing of men, and guarding from attacks, and with a ceaseless vigilance preventing surprises."[14] He savoured to the full his moment of triumph. But as the news spread across the country, the reaction was somberly foreboding. Out in Illinois Abraham Lincoln discussed the import of the measure far into the night with his friend Judge T. Lyle Dickey; then, the next morning, pronounced the verdict that was to match him against Douglas in crucial combat: "I tell you, Dickey, this nation cannot exist half slave and half free."[15]

Repercussions from the victory came quickly and violently. Politicians confront their greatest dangers when the public knows where they stand. Opinions from all extremes promptly focused their opposition upon Douglas's Nebraska bill. Hurrying home in August to mend fences, Douglas wryly confessed, "I could travel from Boston to Chicago by the light of my own effigy. All along the Western Reserve of Ohio I could find my effigy upon every tree we passed." That September, attempting to calm a jeering crowd in Chicago, Douglas had the rare experience of complete defeat. For four full hours he stood on the

[13] Milton, *op. cit.*, pp. 114, 118.
[14] *Ibid.*, p. 142.
[15] *Ibid.*, p. 143.

platform attempting to be heard, while waves of jeers, cat-calls, pounding of tin cans, and stamping of feet drowned him out. At last, pulling his watch out and noting it was past midnight, he shouted above the clamor: "It is now Sunday morning. I'll go to Church and you may go to hell!"[16]

Douglas's courage was admirable; but his political prospects were dimmed. Franklin Pierce aimed toward re-election in 1856 and thought he had Douglas's support. Douglas, meanwhile, was shrewdly exploring every possible channel of support for his own candidacy. Since the Democratic Party was the only viable political organization in the country that year, few doubted that nomination by it was tantamount to election. The Whigs had dissolved into a fantastic array of splinter groups. A nascent Republican Party was striving to unite antislavery sentiment while remaining untainted by abolitionism. Prohibitionists organized a tremendous drive that achieved antiliquor legislation in Maine, Vermont, Michigan, Wisconsin, Connecticut, and New York. In Illinois, too, the prohibitionists were building strength. Meanwhile, anti-immigration sentiment gave rise to a swarm of reactionary clubs. Principal among them was the Order of the Star-Spangled Banner, which aimed its shafts against the Irish Catholics who had been swarming into America ever since the potato famine of 1846. This remarkable organization operated as a secret fraternity, with secret grip, pass-word, ritual, and an oath never to vote for a Catholic or a foreigner. Because of its secrecy, members answered all questions about it with an "I know nothing," for which reason it soon came to be called the Know-Nothing Party. Like its strange antecedent of a quarter-century earlier, the Anti-Masonic Party, Know-Nothingism swept to a series of quick victories, winning the governorships of New Hampshire, Connecticut and Rhode Island in 1855. Douglas was alarmed by the violation of democracy and the threat to political stability posed by both Know-Nothingism and prohibition. On July 4, 1854, in an oration delivered in Independence Hall, he coupled a defense of his Kansas-Nebraska bill with a bold frontal attack on both these popular-isms.

All through September and October he stumped Illinois, inadvertently precipitating the first, now almost-forgotten, Lincoln-Douglas debates. Everywhere he appeared Douglas was challenged to debate his opposition. But he refused, declaring he was confronted by Whigs at one spot, Know-Nothings at another, Republicans elsewhere. "The people came here to hear me," he declared proudly, "and I want to talk to them."[17]

[16] *Ibid.*, pp. 175–176.
[17] *Ibid.*, p. 179.

Lincoln was among the opponents who followed hot on Douglas's trail, making sure he was answered on each day after he spoke. Lincoln's first major bid for national attention was made at Springfield, on October 4, when he answered a speech Douglas had given the previous evening. Douglas sat glowering on the platform as Lincoln mounted the rostrum, in shirt sleeves, with no collar or tie, dressed in ill-fitting trousers. But if his appearance was uncouth, his speech was carefully prepared. He used an address he had "tried out" at Winchester on August 26, afterwards repeating it for weeks, polishing it, buttressing the arguments, and giving his stories point. Instead of popular sovereignty, the old guarantees of the Missouri Compromise should be restored. The local option principle that Douglas advocated meant, in reality, unleashed competitiveness: "The South flushed with triumph and tempted to excess; the North, betrayed as they believe, brooding on wrong and burning for revenge. One side will provoke, the other resent. The one will taunt, the other defy." Lincoln spoke slowly, almost casually, the speech lasting for three hours. His talk sounded, as Sandburg described it, "as if he and another man were driving in a buggy across the prairie, exchanging their thoughts." The Douglas line, Lincoln urged, was leading from bad to worse: "Little by little, but steadily as man's march to the grave, we have been giving up the old for the new faith." The "greed-chase to make profit of the negro" was "fatally violating the noblest political system the world ever saw."[18]

After Lincoln finished, Douglas jumped up to answer him and, as his supporters fondly believed, "flayed his opponent alive."[19] This direct confrontation was followed on October 16 with another debate at Peoria, where Douglas spoke in the afternoon and Lincoln in the evening. There Douglas described "the integrity of this political Union as worth more to humanity than the whole black race." Neither in eloquence nor in political philosophy was Lincoln at this time a match for Douglas. But he and the nation took note that Douglas was being pushed into a position that undermined his Northern support.

The next year, as Pierce's troubles accumulated, Douglas whiffed success for his presidential aspirations. Strenuously he campaigned through Illinois, Indiana, and Kentucky, attacking "abolitionism, Know-Noth-

[18] Sandburg, *Lincoln: Prairie Years, op. cit.,* pp. 314–318.
[19] Herndon, Lincoln's admiring partner, thought that Douglas was "the grand master of human passions and rules the crowd with an iron rule." Cited by Milton, *op. cit.,* p. 182. For an estimate of Herndon's reliability, cf. Donald, *Lincoln's Herndon, op. cit.,* pp. 346–351. A vivid contemporary account of the vigor of Douglas's speaking (in 1846) was penned by John Quincy Adams, in his diary: "In the midst of his roaring, to save himself from choking, he stript off and cast away his cravat, unbottoned his waistcoat, and had the air and aspect of a half naked pugilist." Cited by Sandburg, *Lincoln: Prairie Years, op. cit.,* p. 221.

ingism, and all the other-isms." That fall Know-Nothings were defeated in elections across the nation. Happily Douglas wrote to Howell Cobb: "The torrent of fanaticism has been rolled back almost everywhere." His personal affairs, however, were not going well. His wife died in 1853 and, without her care, exhausted by his constant labors, his health began to fail and he commenced to drink heavily. In the fall of 1855 his voice failed and he had to undergo three operations on his throat, at the very time the nomination for 1856 was being decided.

In the Cincinnati Convention, Douglas suffered the mortification of seeing the prize go to James Buchanan, whom he considered a pompous nonentity.[20] Nevertheless, as a good party man, he worked zealously for Buchanan's election. He urged the "Black Republicans" to "stand unafraid for their platform . . . . Let us have a fair, bold fight before the people, and then let the verdict be pronounced."[21] The Republicans took up the challenge. In particular, Charles Sumner, far from retreating, flung defiance at the popular sovereignty advocates, calling Douglas "the squire of Slavery, its very Sancho Panza—ready to do all its humiliating offices." It was a time of inflamed feelings. The Republican nomination of John C. Frémont, on a "Free Soil, Free Men" platform, aroused the South to new threats of secession. If Frémont were elected, said Forsyth of Alabama, "the South ought not to submit and will not submit"; and Mason of Virginia said the only course would be "immediate, absolute, eternal separation." Even Frémont's fond father-in-law, Thomas Hart Benton, wanted the Pathfinder to withdraw from the contest, warning, "We are treading upon a volcano that is liable at any moment to burst forth and overwhelm the nation."[22]

Disasters mounted for Douglas. In Kansas, subsidized immigration from North and South was making the territory a bloody battlefield. At Lecompton a proslavery constitution was adopted by a concourse of Missourians who came into the territory to vote for it, then returned to their homes. For Douglas this presented the supreme test. He had staked his career on popular sovereignty, and the fruits were now garnered. Courageously he turned his back on the harvest, denouncing the Lecompton constitution as a fraud and demanding a new vote by actual Kansans. Buchanan, wooed by the South, made support of the Lecompton constitution a test of party loyalty and tried to read Douglas out of the party.

Then, in March, 1857, came the crowning blow—a decision by the

[20] Philip Klein, President James Buchanan, State College: Pennsylvania State University Press, 1962, pp. 254–255.
[21] Capers, op. cit., p. 136.
[22] Klein presents a somewhat different version, thus indicating that the anecdote was in general circulation, op. cit., p. 256.

Supreme Court in the case of Dred Scott, a slave who had appealed for his liberty on the grounds that his master had taken him into the free territory of Minnesota. Chief Justice Roger Taney read the majority decision, that "the right of property in a slave is distinctly and expressly affirmed in the Constitution," and that the Missouri Compromise which prohibited slavery in the northern tier of States "is not warranted by the Constitution, and is therefore void."[23] By this blow the whole fabric of popular sovereignty seemed demolished; a territory could indeed vote itself slave, but no vote could keep it free. Douglas was confronted with a dilemma that threatened his political ruin—to renounce his principle of local option or to renounce the authority of the Supreme Court. Lincoln took careful note and began to recast his thinking in terms of the Senatorial election that would be held the following year in Illinois. The issue came to a head in the 1858 Lincoln-Douglas debates.

Although Douglas is remembered chiefly for his Kansas-Nebraska Bill and his debates with Lincoln, his career was marked even more fundamentally by his ardent Americanism and his imperialistic vision of national expansion. By his contemporaries he was viewed as a very great man who somehow never achieved his potential. He attracted attention even when he missed admiration.

When he first appeared in the Senate in 1844, the vitriolic old John Quincy Adams noted that he "raved out his hour in abusive invective, his face convulsed, his gesticulation frantic."[24] All his life Douglas was active as a windmill in a storm while speaking; and often the violence of his action was fully matched by the violence of his words. His very sincerity sounded demagogic, as in a speech in 1853, when he said: "It is our destiny to have Cuba, and it is folly to debate the question . . . . The same is true of Central America and of Mexico."[25] After secession commenced, in 1861, Douglas pleaded for mutual recognition of the independence of North and South as two separate nations, arguing that otherwise there would be civil war; and "Whether the war last one year, seven years, or thirty years, the result must be the same.[26]

His Americanism, unfortunately marred by jingoism, appeared ex-

---

[23] Vincent C. Hopkins, S.J., *The Dred Scott Case*, New York: Fordham University Press, 1951, p. 204.

[24] *Diary of John Quincy Adams*, ed. Allan Nevins, *op. cit.*, p. 566.

[25] Douglas repeated these same sentiments five years later; cf. New Orleans *True Delta*, Dec. 8, 1858.

[26] Milton, *op. cit.*, pp. 540–541. It should be noted that Douglas suggested a duality of unions, joined in a strong commercial pact, only as a reluctant last resort, after the Crittenden and Douglas compromises had been rejected and when nothing less than recognition of the Southern Confederacy could prevent war. Are we, he asked, "prepared in our hearts for war with our own brethren and kindred? I confess I am not." Capers, *op. cit.*, p. 218.

plicitly in his March 10, 1853 speech concerning the Clayton-Bulwer treaty, in which he said:

> Europe is antiquated, decrepit, tottering on the brink of dissolution. When you visit her, the objects which enlist your highest admiration are the relics of past greatness; the broken columns erected to departed power. It is one vast graveyard, where you find here a tomb indicating the burial of the arts; there a monument marking the spot where liberty expired; another to the memory of a great man whose place has never been filled . . . . Here everything is fresh, blooming, expanding, and advancing . . . . Sir, the statesman who would shape the policy of America by European models, has failed to perceive the antagonism which exists in the relative position, history, institutions—in every thing pertaining to the Old and New Worlds.[27]

In his last speech to the Senate, on January 3, 1861, Douglas revealed to the full his strength and his weakness: his astuteness in politics, and his impatience with moralistic principles. "We are told that secession is wrong," he said, "and that South Carolina had no right to secede. I agree that it is wrong, unlawful, unconstitutional, criminal. In my opinion South Carolina had no right to secede; *but she has done it* . . . . *In my opinion, war is disunion, certain, inevitable, irrevocable.* I am for peace to save the Union."[28] To save, that is, whatever shreds of Union were left.

But on March 4 another voice was heard from the portico of the Capitol, as Abraham Lincoln warned the seceding States: "You have no oath registered in heaven to destroy the government, while I shall have the most solemn one to 'preserve, protect, and defend it.' " Had Douglas achieved his own ambition to stand where Lincoln stood, he might have seen his duty in the same light. In any event, after the firing on Fort Sumter, he loyally set out on a tour of the country to support Lincoln's war policies. It was near the commencement of that tour, in Chicago, that he died. Few would want to revise history to put Douglas in Lincoln's place. But despite his limitations, there is no reason to accept his own judgment that "My life is a failure, a flat failure."[29] The boy who left upstate New York in 1822 to seek his fortune in the West accomplished much. His failures were largely due to the nature of the time in which he lived.

---

[27] Capers, *op. cit.*, p. 75, thinks he spoke with "tongue in cheek."
[28] Milton, *op. cit.*, pp. 531, 532.
[29] Carl Sandburg, Lincoln's greatest admirer, considered Douglas "the nearest to any man in Congress to filling the shoes of Clay, Calhoun, or Webster as an orator and parliamentary whip," adding that "he was the most daring and forthright personal political force that had held the American stage since Andrew Jackson." *Lincoln: Prairie Years, op. cit.*, p. 310.

William Henry Seward: On the Verge of Greatness 〔U〕

THE IMAGE of William Henry Seward emerges with startling clarity; there is here little of the ambiguity that shrouds most of the complex orators who spoke to and for the sectional disputants. Seward's appearance, manner, temperament, policies, his mode and mood of speaking, all seem fixed in time and type. Unquestionably this fixity indicates his lack of capacity for growth. Yet the corollary is equally true: his maturity arrived early.

Seward was forty eight before he stepped forth upon the national stage by winning a seat in the Senate. But he brought to Washington qualities that seemed already developed in his youth. Like Douglas, he remains a tragic figure who reached only the threshold of greatness. He was intelligent, high-principled, honest, and humane. If he appeared to be adroit rather than profound, this was partly because of his unruffled equanimity, his unfailing urbanity, and the gentility which masked and blunted the fierce turmoil of his intense emotions. In an age of unrestrained crusaders, he somehow impressed his associates as a calculating opportunist. His uncompromising libertarian convictions enraged the Southern slaveholders while his careful prudence disappointed the Northern reformers. Few politicians matched his astuteness in sensing the direction of popular feeling; yet none in his time suffered so much irremediable damage from the statement of fundamental truths. The greatness of his vision was matched by his skill in making words say what he meant. Strangely, it was by his very skill in composition that he was undone—by this and also by the very urbanity which kept his attention fixed on the surface level of communication rather than on the inexpressible turmoil seething beneath and behind the verbal expression.[1]

His two immortalized phrases—"the higher law" and "the irrepressible conflict"—caused him to be daubed in lurid denunciations as an irresponsible demagogue. Yet his whole career was marked by a rather professorial restraint. In appearance, he was below medium height, slender, meticulously garbed, with reddish hair that turned brown before it became grey, small blue eyes that seemed dreamy when they were not shrewdly alight, a rounded hook nose, beardless thin cheeks, and an abstractedly nervous manner. He was and seemed shy, much preferring

[1] Frederic Bancroft, *The Life of William H. Seward*, New York: Harpers, 1900, I:189.

writing to speaking and solitude to company. He was happiest in his study and at his desk, where he often would sit writing continuously for as long as twenty-four hours at a time. His ability to master an audience developed slowly and late. As a youth he belonged to several debate societies, where he listened rather than spoke. In early manhood he sedulously attended political meetings, where he was almost invariably and revealingly pressed into service as secretary. His most revelatory personal utterances are imbedded in his outpouring of letters to his wife and to his political mentor, Thurlow Weed.[2]

When he emerged into oratory, it was through the medium of speeches carefully written out and memorized for delivery. He had neither talent nor taste for extemporaneous debate. He could be witty, but he avoided risking the loss of friends for the sake of a jest; he had skill in enshrining truths in trenchant anecdotes, yet his taste ran rather to abstract generalizations. In his youth he suffered from a catarrhal infection that left his voice permanently husky and toneless. Galusha A. Grow, the "father of the Homestead Act," thought his speaking manner perfunctory and seemingly indifferent.[3] Charles A. Dana, describing his Senate speaking, said: "He stood up and talked as though he were engaged in conversation, and the effect was always great. It gave the impression of a man deliberating 'out loud' with himself."[4] W. C. Wilkinson, who became Professor of Rhetoric at the University of Chicago, described the delivery of the "Irrepressible Conflict" speech, which he heard, in similar terms: "Altogether it was quite as if a self-absorbed man, in a tense state of moral and mental excitement, had got a couple of thousand of us closeted alone with him there, and was thinking aloud to us."[5]

Carl Schurz, who first heard him in 1854, called him "A quiet little man . . . whose elocution was a dull sound, scarcely distinct, and never sounding a resonant note of challenge or defiance. But he made upon me, as well as upon others, the impression of a man who controlled hidden, occult powers which he could bring into play if he would." Then he added the point that mattered most: "He would compress into a single sentence, a single word, the whole issue of a controversy; and those words became inscriptions on our banners, the passwords of our

[2] Frederick W. Seward, *Seward at Washington as Senator and Secretary of State: A Memoir of His Life with Selections from His Letters, 1846–1861,* New York: Derby and Miller, Three Vols., 1891.
[3] Bancroft, *op. cit.,* I:190–191.
[4] *Ibid.,* I:191.
[5] *Ibid.* Horace Greeley, however, who knew Seward better than any of these enthusiasts, reached an opposite conclusion about him: "Seward has and always must have a policy; a policy is just what we don't want. We want manliness." Conway, *Autobiography, op. cit.,* I:331.

combatants."[6] Typically Seward spoke as he thought, with a deep sense of the flow of history, placing his subject in the context of the long past and the unfolding future. Like Woodrow Wilson, he seemed a professor of politics. Like Robert Taft, he was the intellectual mentor of his party. Like Franklin D. Roosevelt, he was a master politician who sensed what the people would think before they knew it themselves. But he was too much the politician to be the statesman; too careful to permit himself to take the daring plunge; and his very skill in words tripped him up short of the presidential goal he craved.

Seward was born on May 16, 1801, in the small village of Florida, New York, on the Hudson River. His father was a doctor whose sternness led all four of his sons to revolt and leave home in their teens. Because William was small, frail, shy, and studious, he was the only one of the six children in the family to be given an education. His desire was to roam the woods, but his father's discipline and his own sense of duty kept him confined through childhood to his studies from five in the morning until nine at night. At the age of fifteen he entered Union College, Schenectady, as a sophomore. Here he was unpopular with his fellow students because he studied too hard and refused to join in their pranks against the staff. He was unpopular with his teachers because he disliked their system of teaching, which stressed discipline rather than stimulation and consisted principally of set lessons to be memorized verbatim. He was unhappy because the parsimony of his father kept him ill-dressed; and to match the appearance of his associates he ran up tailor bills which his father refused to pay.

On New Year's Day, 1819, he slipped secretly away from school and took a coastal steamer down to Georgia, where he arrived with eighteen cents in his pockets. He found himself 1000 miles from home, without friends, and in an alien society. Happily he quickly secured a job as a teacher, at a salary of $800 a year, with room and board to be provided at an annual cost of $100. The Georgian scene impressed him favorably. Slavery as he observed it was not to him at that time objectionable. His father had owned a few slaves and the Negroes he saw seemed generally well treated. He was, however, homesick; and when his father ordered him to return he quietly obeyed. Back at Union he spoke up in defense of the "hospitable and chivalrous character of the South." Foreswearing popularity for achievement, he buried himself in study and graduated at the top of his class, giving a commencement oration on "The Integrity of the American Union." For another year and a half he studied law in New York City, where he helped to organize "The Forum," a debating

[6] Schurz, *Reminiscences, op. cit.*

society for young law students, but in which he seldom spoke. In October, 1822, he was admitted to the bar and settled in Auburn—a place he selected in part because it was, next to Utica, the largest city in New York west of Albany, and in part because it was the home of a demure young lady named Frances Miller. Seward entered into partnership with her father and shortly paid his longstanding tailor bills. Two years later he married Miss Miller, who encouraged his work in the unsensational organizational activities of politics.

Despite his lack of fondness for public speaking, it was politics, not the law, which soon became Seward's chief interest. True, he continued the practice of law with considerable success for many years. But, as he said only half-humorously in 1844: "I fear, I abhor, detest, despise, and loathe litigation."[7] When possible he settled cases by compromise, out of court. Shortly after his fiftieth year he had attained sufficient prosperity so that he felt able to "quit [his] professional labors, and . . . be at peace."[8] The following year he commented quite sincerely in a Senate debate, "I do not pretend to be a lawyer."[9] Yet his profession brought him substantial wealth and at least a modicum of fame.

His most famous case was his defense, in 1846, of William Freeman, a feeble-minded Negro who broke into a farmhouse and stabbed four people to death, and wounded several others who lived to testify against him. Seward defended on the ground that Freeman's idiocy rendered him non-accountable; and he made a plea to the jury so eloquent that Sumner declared it "worth more for fame than the whole forensic life of Choate."[10] It remains the most eloquent speech Seward ever delivered. Public opinion was strongly aroused against Freeman and Seward was courageous in risking political punishment for undertaking his defense. Freeman could pay him neither with money nor gratitude, for his mind was a blank. "I plead not for a murderer," Seward told the court. "My dog caresses me with fondness if I will but smile on him," he went on. "My horse recognizes me when I fill his manger. But what reward, what gratitude, what sympathy and affection can I expect here? There the prisoner sits . . . . He laughs while I am pleading his griefs. He laughs when the attorney-general's bolts would seem to rive his heart. He will laugh when you declare him guilty . . . . Follow him to the scaffold.

[7] Bancroft, *op. cit.*, I:171.
[8] *Ibid.*, I:174.
[9] This must be interpreted in terms of Seward's confession in his autobiography: "It has been my habit always to distrust my capacity and qualifications for every new enterprise." *Autobiography of William H. Seward*, ed. Frederick W. Seward, New York: Appleton, 1877, p. 30.
[10] Bancroft, *op. cit.*, I:180. The tribute takes added force in view of the fact that Sumner "had an instinctive distrust of Seward." Conway, *Autobiography, op. cit.*, I:208.

The executioner cannot disturb the calmness of this idiot. He will laugh in the agony of death . . . . That chaotic smile is the external derangement which signifies that the strings of the harp are disordered and broken . . . . If you are bent on rejecting the testimony of those who know, by experience and science, the deep affliction of the prisoner, beware how you misinterpret the handwriting of the Almighty."[11]

For nine hours Seward pleaded the case in the preliminary hearing; then he spoke again at length in the trial. When Freeman was found guilty and was sentenced to be hanged, Seward pleaded in vain for a gubernatorial pardon. Then he appealed to the State Supreme Court for a retrial; but a few months later Freeman died in his cell. A postmortem examination of his brain proved his mental incapacity. Seward had risked much—but not without reward. The public reaction was well summarized by Salmon P. Chase, who declared the trial had proved him to be "one of the very first public men of our country."[12]

It was not, however, as a trial lawyer that Seward became financially independent. Early in his career he became the legal agent for a land company that owned three and a half million acres of New York land, most of it mortgaged to farmers. In this work, and in settling the disputes over land titles, which were often in a state of chaotic ambiguity, Seward earned a substantial income. The labor, however, was distasteful; for in every case some family lost what his employers gained. It is small wonder that Seward found the drama of politics much more to his liking.

The political scene at that time was unusually exciting. The Federalist Party was disrupted. The Republican (then re-forming as the Democratic) Party was opposed by various splinter groups. Most notable among these was the Anti-Masonic Party, which had a brief but sensational existence. An apostate Mason named Henry Morgan boasted of writing a book that exposed the secrets of the order; and, in an effort to prevent its publication, he was kidnapped by a gang of Masons. Morgan disappeared and was presumed to have been murdered. Feeling ran high and soon took shape as a political movement. Seward was nominated for Congress by the Anti-Masons in 1828, but withdrew. The following year he served as a delegate to the State Anti-Masonic Convention; and in 1830 he won election on this ticket to the State Senate.

The Senate comprised only thirty two members, and the quietly conversational tenor of the debates suited Seward's temperament well. Disingenuously, he wrote his wife: "I shall, from the force of constitu-

---

[11] *The Works of William H. Seward*, ed. George E. Baker, New York: Redfield, 1853, I:414.
[12] Bancroft, *op. cit.*, I:180.

tional bias, be found always mingling in the controversies which agitate the country. Enthusiasm for the right and ambition for personal distinction are passions of which I cannot divest myself."[13] In Albany, as editor of the *Evening Journal*, was a political genius, Thurlow Weed, one of the earliest and greatest of the backstage "political bosses."[14] Weed spotted in Seward a man who could serve his purposes well, and the two spent most evenings in affectionate conversation, knitting a partnership that was to raise Seward close to the top. As a third member of the group, another young journalist, Horace Greeley, became junior partner in the combine.[15] Weed was to plot the strategy, Greeley, later as editor of the New York *Tribune*, to defend it in the press, and Seward to carry it to the people.

In 1834 Seward made a bid for prominence in the Senate, opposing a bill to instruct New York's United States Senators how to vote. In this year the opponents of the Democratic Party began calling themselves "Whigs," as an indirect means of accusing the dominant party members of being Tories. By the Whigs Seward was nominated for the Governorship but suffered defeat in the fall election under the castigation of being "a man of small abilities, little experience, and no consistency."[16] Seward himself described the reaction of his friends and neighbors to his nomination, with a wry humor that blunted but did not conceal the hurt:

> The scene which occurred at the American Hotel in Auburn on the return of our local delegates was infinitely amusing. My political friends received them with complaints and reproaches, saying: "You promised to oppose Seward for Lieutenant-Governor, and here you have let him be nominated for Governor! The nomination is a disgrace to the State, and will be the ruin of the party!" Mr. Jacobs, the orator of the delegation, attempted to reason with him:
>
> "Why, gentlemen, it is very easy for you, who have stayed at home, to say all this. But, if you had been where we were, you would have found that we had nothing to do with making the candidate, and we did all we could to prevent it. The people from the other parts of the State wouldn't hear of anybody else."
>
> "We don't believe it," they replied; "they could have found a more proper man in every other county in the State."

[13] *Autobiography of Seward*, op. cit., p. 231.
[14] Cf. *The Autobiography of Thurlow Weed*, ed. Harriet A. Weed, Boston: Houghton Mifflin, 1883; and Glyndon G. Van Deusen, *Thurlow Weed: Wizard of the Lobby*, Boston: Little, Brown, 1947.
[15] Cf. *The Autobiography of Horace Greeley, or Recollections of a Busy Life*, New York: E. B. Treat, 1872; and William Harlan Hale, *Horace Greeley: Voice of the People*, New York: Harper, 1950.
[16] *Albany Argus*, Oct. 31, 1834; Bancroft, op. cit., 1:55.

"Well, gentlemen," replied the orator, preserving his good-humor, "I have known Mr. Seward long, and thought him a bright and smart young man, but I never supposed he was a great man; but, when I came to Utica, I found that everybody inquired of me about him, and spoke of him as if he was the greatest man in the State."

"Well," replied they, "the State must be in a strange condition if Seward is among its greatest men."

"Gentlemen," answered the delegate, "I have learned one thing by going to Utica, and that is, that a great man never lives at home!"[17]

Seward left politics for a time, not without public encouragement to do so, noting that the Whigs could not win power "until there is a time of popular convulsion, when suffering will make men feel, and because they feel, think!"[18] The panic of 1837 offered such a chance; and to a Whig Convention in Auburn, Seward said: "The change has come. We no longer warn the people against impending evils and apprehended danger. The evils are here."[19]

The next year Seward was elected Governor of New York, in which position he served for two terms. Antislavery agitation was coming to dominate politics; but Seward fully endorsed the view of Thurlow Weed that slavery was "too fearful, and too mighty in all its bearings and consequences, to be recklessly mixed up in our partisan conflicts."[20] Seward tried hard to avoid embroilment. When the State Legislature considered a bill to declare free any slaves brought into the State and kept there for longer than nine months, Seward opposed it on the ground that it would be "an act of inhospitality" toward the Southerners. In 1842, however, his sense of justice led him to defend a projected law to require a jury trial before any fugitive slave could be returned to servitude: "I cannot believe," he said, "that a being of human substance, form, and image—endowed with the faculties, propensities, and passions common to our race, and having the same ultimate destiny, can . . . be converted into a chattel or a thing . . . . I do not believe that can be stolen which is not and cannot be property."[21] By this stand he committed himself irrevocably to the position which came to dominate his career. Southerners had been deeply irritated by the abolitionist

[17] *Autobiography of Seward, op. cit.*, pp. 158–159.
[18] *Ibid.*, p. 258.
[19] *Ibid.*, p. 340.
[20] Bancroft, *op. cit.*, I:101–107; Van Deusen, *op. cit.*, p. 357. The feeling of the New England abolitionists that slavery was vastly too vile an evil to be an object of political controversy was vividly portrayed by New Hampshire's Senator John P. Hale when he said: "You cannot steer an iceberg through the tropics. The warm sun will shine on it and melt it; the rains will fall on it and melt it; the winds will beat on it and melt it." Conway, *Autobiography, op. cit.*, I:209.
[21] Bancroft, *op. cit.*, I:104. A different though similar wording is in *Works of Seward*, ed. Baker, *op. cit.*, II:434.

campaigning. But in this speech of Seward's they found something far more alarming. Here were not the verbal meanderings of irresponsible reformists who were rejected by all respectable Northerners. Here, rather, was an official declaration by the Governor of the North's largest State. Seward became, accordingly, the chief target of their wrath, just as he also became the principal prize the abolitionists sought to win as a solid convert to their cause.

In letters to his wife and in correspondence with Theodore Parker and other abolitionists, Seward indicated the dilemma that confronted him. He had come to despise slavery as being basically inhumane; but as an ambitious politician he wanted nothing so much as to remain free from the contaminating stain of this controversy. Meanwhile, much as he liked politics, he found the Governorship largely disappointing. There were 1500 appointive offices to be filled, and Weed's assiduity in nominating partisan worthies prevented Seward from appointing "sound and patriotic" candidates. The expenses of official living soon ate away the fifty or sixty thousand dollars he had accumulated from his law practice and left him so deeply in debt that his friends counselled bankruptcy proceedings. Such a course he disdained; nevertheless, he could not enjoy "wearing out old clothes, burning tallow candles, smoking a pipe instead of cigars, economizing fuel." In 1844 his second term ended and he returned to Auburn to rebuild his law practice and pay his debts.

This did not mean an abandonment of politics. Seward campaigned very actively that fall on behalf of Henry Clay's candidacy for the presidency. He opposed the annexation of Texas, urging that, "Whatever else may happen, let us be spared from subjugation to an aristocracy of wealth consisting of human bones, sinews, and veins—consisting of the bodies and souls of our countrymen!" To the pleas of the abolitionists that he join the Liberty Party, he replied that he felt he could do far more good for the cause by working with the Whigs. Pulled in one direction by the Garrisonian abolitionists and in another by the Weld-Birney legalists, Seward's sympathies were with the latter. "I shall stand on the ground I now occupy," he said, "always demanding the abolition of slavery in America by political argument and suffrage, and by the constitutional action of all the public authorities."[22]

By 1848 he had made his position clear in a succession of speeches. He stood for suffrage and equality for the free Negroes in the Northern

[22] All through 1845–46 Seward's letters deal often with the theme that "The political situation is becoming infinitely complex." In pursuit of the political influence he yearned to exercise, he argued his way through Virginia on one trip and through the Midwest on another, speaking much both in private and in public, always trying to present the image of a man definitely but never defiantly opposed to slavery. Cf. *Autobiography of Seward*, op. cit., pp. 738–809.

States; against the admission to the Union of any more slave States; for abolition of slavery in the District of Columbia; and for an "inquiry" into the domestic slave trade carried on among the Southern States. In a major speech in Cleveland during the campaign of 1848 he tried to hew out a line midway between abolitionism and complacency: "Much can be done," he said. "Whenever the public mind shall will the abolition of slavery, the way will open for it."[23] After the election the Whigs once more commanded a majority of the New York Legislature; and Seward was elected, by a majority of four to one, to the United States Senate. Now, at last, at the age of forty eight, he was moving into the center of the national scene. It was a time when the nation was searching for fresh leadership, and Seward quickly emerged into the limelight.

With Zachary Taylor inaugurated as the first Whig President, a great housecleaning of federal offices was in order, and Seward and Weed set to work to take New York's federal patronage away from Vice President Millard Fillmore.[24] The task was scarcely to Seward's liking, but he did it well. Jocosely he remarked that the whole population seemed divided into two classes: those joining the gold rush to California, and those joining the rush for offices in Washington. The victory over Fillmore, however, suddenly became Pyrrhic when Taylor died in July, 1850, and the Vice President from Buffalo moved into the White House. Everything Seward had done to cement an alliance with Taylor by taking patronage away from Fillmore now boomeranged. His own hope for the presidency could not now be advanced by internal political maneuvering but would depend on winning broad public support. To his credit, however, he did not seek popularity by being innocuously platitudinous. Instead he took the risky course of joining openly with the abolitionists. In the debate on the 1850 Compromise, he met in competition the greatest array of Senatorial talent ever assembled in the chamber at one time. Yet he rose among them into notice and notoriety. For several weeks he listened to a parade of speeches, the majority representing the Southern point of view: by Clay, Calhoun, Douglas, various southerners, and then, on March 7, Daniel Webster. Finally, on March 11, Seward arose to assume the role of the outstanding spokesman for the Northern viewpoint.

In a carefully considered speech he attacked the proposition that the admission of California as a free state should be balanced by guarantees favoring the South. "I am opposed to any such compromise, in any and all the forms in which it has been proposed," he declared. "I think all

[23] *Works of Seward, op. cit.*, III:301, 302.
[24] For a report on New York politics of the period from Fillmore's point of view, see Robert J. Rayback, *Millard Fillmore: Biography of a President*, Buffalo: H. Stewart (for Buffalo Historical Society), 1959.

legislative compromises, which are not absolutely necessary, radically wrong and essentially vicious." Young Donn Piatt heard Seward at about this time and left a vivid description of him as a speaker in the Senate:

> We had about exhausted the list of celebrities when a slender, hook-nosed, gray-eyed, homely man rose to address the Senate from the outer circle of the chamber. His voice was harsh and unpleasant, and his manner extremely angular and awkward. I made a move to leave, when my friend from the House caught me by the arm and said, "Don't go, that is Seward of New York." I had no particular interest in Seward of New York, but fortunately obeyed my friend. I at once observed that he commanded the attention of the Senate. One and all ceased reading, writing, and conversation, and turned toward the speaker. I saw Douglas look with interest, and Clay with an expression of contempt. From these, however, I turned to regard the orator. For a few moments he stood by his desk, whirling a pair of glasses in his hand, and then stepped back and leaned upon the railing immediately in the rear of his seat. He clasped his arm about the pillar, and with the other hand grasping the rail, half braced and half leaning, held his awkward position throughout nearly the entire hour of his speech. He had not spoken ten minutes before a startling proposition sent a sensation, expressed in a murmur and a motion, over the entire Senate. I soon lost all sense of his awkward pose and harsh voice in the subject-matter of his discourse, it was so original, startling, quaint, and, at times, truly eloquent. In common with the listening Senate I sat spell-bound, and when he ended amid a general murmur of disapprobation, I could scarcely realize that he had occupied an hour and a quarter.[25]

Sweeping aside Clay's careful plan for a "package deal," Seward insisted that there was no correlation between the admission of California and enforcement of the fugitive slave law or the abolition of the slave trade in the District of Columbia. All such measures should be considered separately, on their merits. He attacked Calhoun's "concurrent majority" theme as an attempt to convert the government into an alliance. With an ironic reversal of the position he had taken, while Governor, that the North should be "hospitable" to Southerners who brought slaves with them on their northern travels, he declared, "Your constitution and laws convert hospitality to the refugee from the most degrading oppression on earth into a crime, but all mankind except you esteem that hospitality a virtue." As for the fugitive slave laws: "Armed power could not enforce them, because there is no public conscience to sustain them." Then he made his climactic point. Slavery was pro-

[25] Donn Piatt, *Memories of the Men Who Saved the Union*, New York: Frank F. Lovell, 1887, pp. 132–133.

tected where it already existed, but when it came to considering its extension into new territories: "There is a higher law than the Constitution . . . . Sir, wherever I find a law of God, or a law of nature disregarded or in danger of being disregarded, there I shall vote to reaffirm it with all the sanction of the civil authority."[26]

For three hours the speech continued, often monotonous in delivery, without any noticeable reactions from its listeners. But in retrospect, few of the great orations that marked the debate had an effect equal to Seward's appeal to "a higher law," or to the careful reasoning with which he went on to consider "the fearful issue whether the Union shall stand, and slavery . . . be removed . . . or whether the Union shall be dissolved and civil wars ensue." Valiantly he strove for judicious balance. "We hear on one side demands—absurd, indeed, but yet unceasing—for an immediate and unconditional abolition of slavery," he said. Countering this, others say that "slavery has always existed, and, for aught they know or can do, it must always exist."

Then he defined his own stand:

> Here, then, is the point of my separation from both of these parties. I feel assured that slavery must give way, and will give way, to the salutary instructions of economy, and to the ripening influences of humanity; that emancipation is inevitable, and is near; that it may be hastened or hindered; and that whether it shall be peaceful or violent depends upon the question whether it is hastened or hindered . . . . But I will adopt none but lawful, constitutional, and peaceful means to secure even that end; and none such can I or will I forego. Nor do I know any important or responsible political body that proposes to do more than this. No free State claims to extend its legislation into a slave State. None claims that Congress shall usurp power to abolish slavery in the slave States. None claim that any violent, unconstitutional, or unlawful measures shall be embraced.[27]

The speech was reasoned, calm, and expressive of the simple faith that slavery if left alone would be (to use Lincoln's later phrase) "in the course of ultimate extinction." The philosophy, indeed, was thoroughly Lincolnian. But whereas the Illinois backwoodsman would show skill in masking the essential point under the unexciting phrase, "gradual extinction," Seward, to his later agonized regret, employed the highly quotable phrase: "a higher law."[28] Both the South and the abolitionists set gleefully to work to prove that Seward had joined Garrison and Phillips in renouncing the Constitution. Storms of denunciation beat upon

---

[26] *Works of Seward*, op. cit., I:65, 66, 74, 80.
[27] *Ibid.*, 1:86, 87.
[28] Piatt reports that Seward told him, "It was an imprudent speech and I ought to have been more careful" (*op. cit.*, p. 136).

Seward, together with exaggerated paraphrases of his remarks by the abolitionists. Weed wrote urgently to Seward, pleading with him to re-state his position in a more conciliatory manner; but Seward manfully replied: "With the single exception of the argument in poor Freeman's case, it is the only speech I ever made that contains nothing that I could afford to strike out or qualify."[29] Far from retreating, Seward continued his drift toward outright abolitionism. By May, 1854, it surprised no one to hear him say in the Senate: "Come on then, gentlemen of the slave States! Since there is no escaping your challenge, I accept it in behalf of the cause of freedom. We will engage in competition for the virgin soil of Kansas, and God give the victory to the side which is stronger in numbers, as it is in the right."[30] Such talk won the praise of Sumner—but the voting public was far from abolitionist. In February, 1855, Seward "barely escaped political annihilation," winning re-election to the Senate by eighty seven votes out of 157.

That fall Seward was confronted with the choice of joining the newly formed Republican Party, remaining with the dissolving Whigs, or try-ing to patch together another middle-of-the-road coalition. In a speech to a mass meeting of equally troubled political hangers-on in Albany, in November, Seward chose Republicanism, saying: "The heart of the country is fixed on higher, nobler things. Do not distrust it."[31] Eighteen months later the same choice confronted Abraham Lincoln, when a group of Republicans met in Bloomington, Illinois, to organize their new party. Lincoln, called on for a speech, set a safe course: "We must not promise what we ought not, lest we be called on to perform what we cannot."[32] This was advice Seward could have used. He never learned the political value of avoiding commitment. Perhaps it is true, as many have charged, that he was impelled less by idealism than by ambition. Undoubtedly he very much wanted the presidential nomination in 1856,[33] and he might have had it except for the venom of one old

---

[29] *Seward at Washington,* op. cit., II:129.
[30] Bancroft, op. cit., I:360.
[31] *Works of Seward,* op. cit., IV:225ff.
[32] Sandburg, *Lincoln: Prairie Years,* op. cit., p. 324.
[33] Klein believes Seward avoided nomination because he "did not want to risk the defeat which he anticipated" (op. cit., p. 256). Hale reports (rightly) that Greeley worked behind Seward's back to deny him the nomination (Greeley, op. cit., p. 193). In the "Seward-Weed Papers," at the Rush-Reese Library, University of Rochester, there is considerable unpublished correspondence on this subject. In-cluded is a letter from Robert P. Toms of Detroit, dated June 10, 1856, which expresses dismay that "your friends" are working for other candidates. Another un-signed and undated letter reads: "I spent two or three days at the Philadelphia convention and tried very hard to secure the nomination of the Governor. The convention itself was ripe for it and could it have been left to itself would have nominated him, and it was with much difficulty that Weed, Schoolcraft, Morgan (from Cayuga Co.), Greeley and a few others prevented it." Bancroft believed that Seward wanted the nomination and that Weed worked to block it—but he adds that Seward could not have had it in any event since the new party needed a colorless candidate without a record that could be attacked (op. cit., I:410–421).

friend and the caution of another. Horace Greeley, who nursed a long-smoldering grudge because Seward had not helped him into political office, swung the *Tribune* and his personal influence with abolitionists against Seward; and Thurlow Weed, with a canny sense of political trends, maneuvered behind Seward's back to throw the nomination to Frémont, who was slated as a "sacrificial lamb," thus saving the more valuable 1860 nomination for Seward.

Seward felt betrayed by both men and sourly resented what seemed to him the ingratitude of his party in New York. As a result, he determined to "sit out" at Auburn the 1858 State campaign. Late in October, however, he was convinced by friends that if he did not support the party that fall, he would have little backing for the nomination two years later. Grudgingly, then, he consented to make five speeches in upstate cities. One of them, on October 25, 1858, was given in Rochester.[34] There was little advance publicity and Seward intended nothing more than a routine speech to an audience of already-convinced Republicans, who needed no more than ritualistic reassurance. He reviewed the history of slavery in America, covering the old familiar ground, and then, with his uncanny and unfortunate skill as a phrase-maker, he quite unintentionally ignited the passions of the nation. There had gradually evolved, he said, "an irrepressible conflict between opposing and enduring forces, and it means that the United States must and will, sooner or later, become entirely a slaveholding nation or entirely a free-labor nation." Unemotionally, almost perfunctorily, he minced on through his memorized speech to its conclusion: "I know, and you know, that a revolution has begun . . . . The people of the United States have been . . . gathering together the forces . . . to confound and overthrow, by one decisive blow, the betrayers of the Constitution and freedom forever."[35] The speech meant little either to Seward or his listeners. The two Rochester newspapers ignored it, and the country would have known nothing of it—except that, two days later, Seward bethought himself of his usual practice to send the manuscript copies of his speeches to Albany for publication in Thurlow Weed's *Evening Journal.* Thereby was launched the ruination of his career, smashed by a phrase the South and the anti-abolitionist North emblazoned into a slogan of defiance: *the irrepressible conflict!*

Greeley reprinted the speech from the *Evening Journal,* and Southern newspapers commenced printing a misleading paraphrase of a single paragraph which a Mississippi editor falsely attributed to Seward, representing him as calling for an "irrepressible conflict" to wipe out slav-

---

[34] For a detailed study of this speech see Robert T. Oliver, "William H. Seward on the 'Irrepressible Conflict,' " in Auer, *Antislavery and Disunion, op. cit.,* pp. 29–50.
[35] The text is in *Works of Seward, op. cit.,* IV:289–302.

ery. Sensing that nothing could save him but silence, Seward went to Europe. The storm continued and was fanned to catastrophic proportions by John Brown's raid at Harpers Ferry. Back in the Senate, in February, 1860, Seward tried to repair the damage with a very mild speech, in which he quietly insisted that "we do not seek to force, or even to intrude, our system on you." Free labor and slavery, he said, are "divided between us by unmistakable boundaries . . . . Each must be maintained in order that the whole may be preserved." Then, in a truly touching appeal for recognition of his tolerant policy of noninterference, he ended: "We have never been more patient and never loved the representatives of other sections more than now."[36]

Words once launched, however, cannot be recalled. When the presidential nominating convention was held in Chicago, Seward suffered the final humiliation of seeing the prize snatched from him by an awkward backwoodsman from Illinois, a man whom he felt was indubitably and by far his intellectual, moral, and political inferior. After the election, when he was given the sop of appointment as Secretary of State, and when he was rebuked for "disappointing" an applicant for a patronage job, he burst out: "You talk of disappointment to a man who has been denied the rightful leadership of his party!"[37] After Lincoln's inauguration, Seward sought to do his duty by writing the President a memorandum artlessly offering to bear the real burdens of governing the country. Lincoln replied with a curt note: "If this must be done, I must do it."[38] Thereafter Seward comported himself with complete loyalty. While many in the North assailed Lincoln's delay in emancipating the slaves, Seward defended his caution, saying that emancipation should be "borne on the bayonets of an advancing army, not dragged in the dust behind the retreating one."[39] To promise freedom for the slaves in the midst of military disasters, he said, would be like "a cry for help—the government stretching forth her hands to Ethiopia, instead of Ethiopia stretching forth her hands to the government." Lincoln found Seward a tower of strength. There is no oddity nor accident in the fact that the assassins of Lincoln in 1865 sought also to kill Seward (and succeeded in stabbing him nearly to death); the two men had indeed stood for the same cause.

[36] Henry B. Stanton, reporter for the New York Tribune, was shown a copy of the speech before delivery and understood that Seward intended it "to remove all obstacles to his nomination to the presidency at Chicago." Random Recollections, op. cit., pp. 212–213.
[37] Edward Everett Hale, Jr., William H. Seward, Philadelphia: Geo. W. Jacobs, 1910.
[38] Sandburg, Lincoln: Prairie Years, op. cit., p. 223.
[39] Lincoln appreciatively cited this support by Seward when defending his delay in issuing the Emancipation Proclamation. Bancroft, op. cit., II:334.

History has given Seward less than his due. In regard to the sectional dispute, he and Lincoln occupied almost identical positions. Just as Lincoln insisted that slavery was morally wrong, so did Seward. In a speech on February 17, 1854, he declared to the Senate: "The slavery agitation you deprecate so much is an eternal struggle between conservatism and progress, between truth and error, between right and wrong."[40] Just as Lincoln believed that preservation of the Union was more important than abolition of slavery, so did Seward dismiss the possibility of dissolving the Union. "Commercial interests bind the slave States and the free States together in links of gold," he insisted. "Either party will submit to the ascendancy of the other rather than yield the commercial advantages of this Union." Soothingly he assured a partisan audience of Republicans, at Buffalo in 1855, that threat of disunion was no more than a Southern bluff. As for the great mass of the Southern people, "I never knew a disloyal man among them." Like Lincoln, Seward often asserted his faith that eventually slavery would be eradicated simply through prevention of its spread to new areas. Like Lincoln, Seward was generally friendly and amiable in debate. When he made his first speech in the Senate, he promised: "I shall never assail the motives of any member of this body. I shall never defend myself against any imputation of motives made against me."[41] Never was this promise broken. Despite the storminess of the political scene, Seward remained on cordial terms with all his Senatorial colleagues, however strongly he and they disagreed. Finally, Seward's addiction to making full use of patronage as a political instrument was also an attribute shared by Lincoln.

In education, in urbane sophistication, and in breadth of knowledge and interests, Seward was unquestionably the superior. Far from limiting his attention to the slavery question, Seward's concern for the welfare of the nation was as broad as were its problems. He was consistently in favor of both immigration from Europe and emigration to the West, in both cases "to cover the earth with population as fast as possible, and to distribute the wealth acquired as broadly as possible."[42] In contrast with Douglas's scorn for Europe, Seward, in one of his most eloquent speeches, on April 27, 1852, urged additional federal aid for the merchant marine, so that the Atlantic ocean may be "reduced to a ferry."[43] When the Atlantic cable was laid in 1858, Seward assured a gathering at Auburn that this event marked the start of a world community. All

[40] Appendix to the *Congressional Globe*, 33rd Congress, 1st Session, Washington, D.C., XXXI:155.
[41] There seems no reason to believe Seward ever consciously departed from the high ideal of unselfish political conduct he expressed in a letter to his wife dated Nov. 24, 1833, included in *Autobiography of Seward*, op. cit., I:232.
[42] *Works of Seward*, op. cit., I:289–296.
[43] *Ibid.*, I:222–235.

through his political career he supported internal improvements, to strengthen the nation both economically and militarily. In an 1860 speech at St. Paul he forecast that Alaska, Canada, and Latin America would one day be coequal parts of the United States; and in 1867 he forestalled future grief by purchasing Alaska from Russia. By the time of his death, on October 10, 1872, he could confidently assume that his constructive position in American history was safely assured.

History, however, has been less than kind to his memory. In part this is because his personality was too cool, too abstract, too remote, too self-possessed. In part it is because he sought for himself the presidential nomination that went to Abraham Lincoln. In part Seward destroyed himself by his own literary flair for compressing issues into phrases. He led the political fight for too long and he led it too well. When the final battle came, he was in the foremost rank and thereby was cut down.

The Quality of Abraham Lincoln: Artistry and Heart

No ONE has better described the Lincoln everyone knows than the brilliant young German immigrant Carl Schurz, who first saw him in 1856: "I must confess that I was somewhat startled by his appearance," Schurz wrote many years later.

> On his head he wore a somewhat battered "stovepipe" hat. His neck emerged, long and sinewy, from a white collar turned down over a thin black necktie. His lank, ungainly body was clad in a rusty black dress coat with sleeves that should have been longer; but his arms appeared so long that the sleeves of a "store" coat could hardly be expected to cover them all the way down to the wrists. His black trousers, too, permitted a very full view of his large feet. On his left arm he carried a gray woolen shawl, which evidently served him for an overcoat in chilly weather. His right he had kept free for handshaking, of which there was no end until everybody in the car seemed to be satisfied. I had seen, in Washington and in the West, several public men of rough appearance; but none whose looks seemed quite so uncouth, not to say grotesque, as Lincoln's.[1]

Many observers were to speak of his crudeness. Lincoln became the living embodiment of the "log cabin president," the man who rose to prominence and power from amidst the common people. In part, of course, his greatness lay in the very fact that he represented so well the

---

[1] *Reminiscences of Carl Schurz*, New York: McClure, 1909, II:90.

rough and uncultivated mass of our frontier society. With this in mind it is fruitful once again to view the scene as it appeared to young Schurz, freshly arrived from his experiences in the social and political life of Europe. At first Schurz was shocked by what he saw of American democracy: "the most contradictory tendencies and antagonistic movements openly at work, side by side, or against one another, enlightenment and stupid bigotry, good citizenship and lawlessness, benevolent and open-handed public spirit and subserviency to party despotism and to predominant public opinion—all this is bewildering confusion." Then Schurz found the key: "in a condition of freedom, man manifests himself, not as he ought to be, but as he is, with all his bad as well as his good qualities, instincts, and impulses: with all his attributes of strength as well as all his weaknesses: that this, therefore, is not an ideal state, but simply a state in which the forces of good have a free field as against the forces of evil." The men who rose to leadership, he noted, were "representative" of the people, "in average ability, character, culture, and manners."[2]

Only to a degree was Schurz right: American democracy had indeed to reflect the crudities of the average man. But his vision did not penetrate far enough. Crudity was represented by millions. What was needed for leadership—what was above all required for the greatness of Lincoln—was identification with the people (as Shurz observed) plus other qualities that far transcended the characteristics of the mass. The real secret of Lincoln lies not in the grotesqueries that marked his appearance, but in the qualities of mind and spirit that slowly ripened into a late maturity until they could find expression in such utterly matchless passages as the closing paragraphs of his first and second inaugural addresses. To these superb utterances must be added a small selection of scarcely inferior statements: several of his letters, the whole text of both inaugurals, the Gettysburg Address, the "House Divided" speech, and the careful reasoning that elevated his debates with Douglas and his speech at Cooper Union. All these speeches, except the one at Gettysburg and the second inaugural, were presented within a span of two years; but no other speaker, however lengthy his career, has surpassed them. Even more impressive, however, than the words that remain was the impress of the personality that slowly, finally, made itself felt in a time and among a people that responded reluctantly but surely to what he truly was. Lord Charnwood, the Englishman, one of Lincoln's greatest biographers, put the matter aright: "it is not to be thought that he was ordinarily what could be called eloquent; some of his speeches are

2 *Ibid.,* II:16.

commonplace enough . . . . But the greatest gift of the orator he did possess; the personality behind the words was felt."[3]

Despite his late emergence into greatness, the essential qualities of Lincoln were evident in his youth: the curiosity supported by industry that made him a student in a community that lacked both schools and any tradition of scholastic inquiry; the self-confident independence of mind that made it possible for him to pursue his intellectual interests within a family and in a society that were markedly anti-intellectual; the habit of holding his mind fixed upon a particular subject until he exhausted its possibilities, rather than ranging rapidly and superficially from one topic to another; the capacity to be genuinely and intimately a part of the social group while simultaneously remaining constant to his own understanding and his own ideal. Furthermore, even though his great speaking lay far in the future, Lincoln mastered or intuitively possessed, even in his youth, the art of saying what he most truly meant in terms that most surely corresponded with the fundamental traits of the audience and the situation. Sensitive responsiveness to the nuances of reaction among his listeners he may have mastered through interminable practice as an oral story-teller; but the gift of being equally true to his own vision of reality must have come from an innate integrity, from a secure sense of confidence. He was fortunate in both his mother, Nancy Hanks, and his stepmother, Sarah Bush. Both saw in their dreamy-eyed, awkward son a greater spirit than that in their indolently good-natured husband, Tom; and, successively, they quietly accepted him as he was and taught him to accept himself as the ultimate standard by which to judge his own acts and thoughts. Only from an unquestioning confidence in self could come the honest humility that never found need for proud assertiveness,[4] yet which did provide strength to stand where his mind and conscience told him his destiny lay.

From these roots there grew the two-fold paradox that marked the peculiar genius of Abraham Lincoln. The first was an intertwining of what John Hay, his wartime secretary, called his "intellectual arrogance" and his genuine humility, such as that which marked his first campaign speech, in 1832 for the State Legislature: "I presume you all know who I am—I am humble Abraham Lincoln . . . . If elected I shall be thankful; if not, it will be all the same." Here was the first paradox: self-assurance manifesting itself as modesty, for it required support neither

[3] Godfrey Rathbone Benson, Lord Charnwood, *Abraham Lincoln*, New York: Pocket Books, 1939, p. 146; cf., "The Principles and the Oratory of Lincoln," *ibid.*, pp. 131–147.
[4] H. B. Stanton, *op. cit.*, p. 232, reports that when Lincoln heard he had been called a fool by Secretary of War Edwin M. Stanton he replied, "Then I must be a fool, for Stanton is generally right."

from his associates nor from "measurable" success. And the second paradox was akin to the first: an integrity of dedication to the right, so far as he could understand it, allied to a shrewd and penetrating responsiveness to the ego-needs of his fellows. It was the latter quality that made Lincoln an astute politician, and the former which raised him to the forefront of statesmanship. He respected himself too thoroughly to compromise his own principles; and he respected his fellowmen too unquestioningly to think of asking them to sacrifice their own. Nowhere did Lincoln express this two-fold aspect of his character better than in an otherwise unexciting speech to the Washingtonian Temperance Society of Springfield, on February 22, 1842, when he told his audience of reformed drunkards how to win a convert—one at a time, an individual appealing to an individual:

> . . . assume to dictate to his judgment, or to command his action, or to mark him as one to be shunned and despised, and he will retreat within himself, close all the avenues to his head and heart; and though your cause be naked truth itself, transformed to the heaviest lance, harder than steel, and sharper than steel can be made, and though you throw it with more than Herculean force and precision, you shall no more be able to pierce him, than to penetrate the hard shell of a tortoise with a rye straw.
>
> Such is man, and so must he be understood by those who would lead him, even to his own best interest.[5]

Better than any other, this passage contains a key to Lincoln's career. It explains the cautious conservatism of his politics which separated him so markedly from the arrant reformist zeal and crusading righteousness of Phillips, Sumner, Douglas, and Seward. "Men must be taught as if you taught them not." New ideas must be presented with an awareness that they are not really new but are already present in the better impulses and the fundamental if inert understanding of those whose thought and actions are to be reformed. Here was the real "intellectual arrogance" that Hay sensed: the consciousness of being a spokesman for the right, combined with the deeply humble faith that respect for the right is implanted in every human being. Here was the revolutionary capacity to remake society, combined with the conservative realization that the path to the future must be a projection of existing realities.

Whether Lincoln's early life was success or failure is a question that can be answered either way, depending on the standards used. He failed in business and he never became wealthy, as Douglas did, nor a truly outstanding lawyer. He was always personally popular with those who

---

[5] Basler, *Works of Lincoln*, op. cit., I:273.

knew him, and he was a leader among the Whigs of Illinois by his thirtieth birthday. In any event, he remained largely content to enjoy a pleasant popularity within a limited circle of acquaintances until 1854, in his forty-fifth year, when the passage of the Kansas-Nebraska Act "aroused him as he had never been before," as he wrote in one of his autobiographical fragments. In August of that year he commenced a new series of speeches, which led up to a four-hour shirtsleeve exposition at Springfield, on October 4, of his basic theme that slavery's "ultimate extinction" was certain because it was morally wrong and that it could be accomplished under the Constitution simply by preventing its extension into any new areas. This was very nearly the whole of his philosophy concerning slavery and in the many speeches that followed he had little more to do than to render it clear, emphatic, and emotionally compelling.

At this date, however, he was far from sure as to the channel his efforts should follow. In politics he was a party man who knew and adhered to the rules. Throughout early manhood he had idolized Henry Clay and worked as a loyal Whig. By 1854 it was apparent the Whig Party was dying; and on the very October 4 of Lincoln's marathon speech at Springfield, a new party calling itself Republican met in the town to organize. Lincoln was unsure whether or not to commit himself to it and slipped out of town to avoid having to make a decision.[6] In February, 1855, Lincoln stood through nine ballots as a Whig candidate for election to the United States Senate and came within five votes of election. A year later, on Washington's birthday, with a Republican elected Speaker of the House of Representatives, and a Republican candidate sure to be nominated for the presidency, Lincoln threw in his fortunes with the new party. At Bloomington, on May 29, he made a speech on its behalf so impassioned that the reporters threw away their pencils to listen, leaving behind no recorded text.[7] During the campaign he made over fifty speeches, and in Illinois the Republican vote almost equaled that given to Buchanan, the Democrat. Then, just after Buchanan's inauguration, the Supreme Court delivered the decision on Dred Scott that appeared to destroy completely the Republican Party's program of prohibiting the spread of slavery into the territories. Lincoln was a politician attached to an unstable party that had just had its platform declared illegal.

In June of 1858, this Republican Party offered to nominate Lincoln as its candidate for the United States Senate, and he set to work carefully

[6] Paul M. Angle, *Created Equal? The Complete Lincoln-Douglas Debates of 1858*, Chicago: University of Chicago Press, 1958, p. xi.
[7] *Ibid.*, p. xvi. This is known as "The Lost Speech."

to prepare a speech which, for the first time in his life, he would read from the manuscript.[8] His law-partner, William Herndon, twenty seven years later recalled that he spent "off and on about one month" writing it. "If a good idea struck him, if a forcible one, he pencilled [it] down on a small piece of paper and put it in his hat." When Lincoln "had finished the speech by putting piece to piece and note to note" he read it to Herndon, who told him, "Lincoln, deliver and publish your speech just as you have written it; it will make you President of the United States."[9] Lincoln also read the prepared draft to a dozen political friends, in a gathering at the State Library, and was warned that "it was a fool utterance," especially the first paragraph.[10] Lincoln followed his own judgment and opened his speech with the declaration that " 'A house divided against itself cannot stand.' I believe this government cannot endure permanently half slave and half free. I do not expect the Union to be dissolved—I do not expect the house to fall—but I do expect it will cease to be divided. It will become all one thing or all the other." There was nothing here the newspapers could pick up to whip into a storm, as, that same fall, they would do with Seward's "irrepressible conflict" phrase. The remainder of his speech Lincoln devoted to an argumentative exposition of the idea that a "conspiracy" directed by Presidents Pierce and Buchanan, Senator Douglas, and Justice Roger Taney was attempting to implant slavery in every State of the nation. He ended the speech with the common political tactic of prophecying victory at the polls. Herndon's account concludes: "Lincoln had a million of curses from his foolish friends about this speech."[11] The Convention that heard it was not particularly enthusiastic but unanimously gave him its nomination.

By nature Lincoln was moderate, seeking always a gradual path of peaceful and unostentatious evolution from one stage to another. As early as 1836 he had announced: "I go for admitting all whites to the right of suffrage (by no means excluding females)";[12] but he did not join the movement for women's suffrage. He was a teetotaler and an occasional speaker at temperance societies; but he did not join the prohibitionists, who were rampant in the early fifties. He declared publicly for the first time in his speech of October 4, 1854, that he hated slavery "because of the monstrous injustice" of the system; but he insisted he could not blame the Southern whites for maintaining a system they inherited; and he confessed, "If all earthly power were given me, I

---

[8] Sandburg, *Lincoln: Prairie Years,* op. cit., p. 376.
[9] Emanuel Hertz, *The Hidden Lincoln,* New York: Blue Ribbon Books, 1940, p. 97.
[10] Donald, *Lincoln's Herndon,* op. cit., pp. 118–119.
[11] Hertz, op. cit., p. 98.
[12] Basler, *Works of Lincoln,* op. cit., I:48.

should not know what to do as to the existing institution."[13] To free
the slaves and send them all to Liberia would be "manifestly impossible." But—"What next? Free them, and make them politically and socially our equals? *My own feelings will not admit to this.*"[14] As for the
economic problems of the new industrialism, with uncontrolled competition and unprotected factory labor, Lincoln's observation, in 1859, was
that "Republicans are for both the man and the dollar, but in case of
conflict the man before the dollar."[15]

Nowhere did Lincoln's careful conservatism emerge more unmistakably than in his attitude toward the relation of the races. Paul Angle
thought that the inferior social status of free Negroes "tortured Lincoln's conscience."[16] If so, he suffered in private. At Charleston, in debate with Douglas, he said, "I as much as any other man am in favor of
having the superior position assigned to the white race."[17] Most revealing is the fact that Lincoln stated as well as it ever has been done the
ridiculousness of trying to prove any one race inferior to another—but
that he never chose to make this statement public. Among his unpublished papers was found this fragment, presumably written in 1854:

> If A can prove, however conclusively, that he may of right enslave
> B, why may not B snatch the same argument and prove equally that he
> may enslave A? You say A is white and B is black. It is color, then; the
> lighter having the right to enslave the darker? Take care. By this rule
> you are to be slave to the first man you meet with a fairer skin than your
> own. You do not mean color exactly? You mean the whites are in-
> tellectually superiors of the blacks, and therefore have the right to
> enslave them? Take care again. By this rule you are to be slave to the
> first man you meet with an intellect superior to your own. But, you say,
> it is a question of interest, and if you make it your interest you have
> the right to enslave another. Very well. And if he can make it his
> interest he has the right to enslave you.[18]

In his debates with Douglas he tried to hew out a middle position
between abolitionism and the extension of slavery. Even though he
failed in his goal of getting into the Senate, he did attract enough interest among the Eastern Republicans so that he received an invitation in
the fall of 1859 to take part that winter in the lecture series sponsored
by Henry Ward Beecher's Plymouth Church, for a fee of $200. Lincoln

[13] *Ibid.*, II:240–247.
[14] *Ibid.*, II:247ff. Basler presents the text of the speech delivered at Peoria, Oct. 15,
which he calls "much the same speech" as the Springfield address of Oct. 4.
[15] *Ibid.*, II:247ff.
[16] Angle, *Created Equal?*, *op. cit.*, p. xxix.
[17] *Ibid.*, p. 235.
[18] T. Harry Williams, ed., *Selected Writings and Speeches of Abraham Lincoln*,
Chicago: Packard and Co., 1943, p. 30.

accepted—in part because he wanted to have a talk with his son Robert, a student at Phillips-Exeter Academy, in New Hampshire, who had just failed in fifteen of the sixteen examinations required for entrance into Harvard. Subsequently the locale for the speech was changed to The Cooper Institute, a lecture hall fitted with 2000 revolving chairs upholstered in red leather, but with the auditorium broken up by a series of pillars that stood between the speaker and some of his auditors. For Lincoln's lecture an entrance fee of twenty-five cents was charged. The meeting was well advertised and the hall was filled, although Lincoln was not highly regarded in the East and was not mentioned in the *Twenty-One Prominent Candidates for the Presidency in 1860* nor in *Our Living Representative Men, Prepared for Presidential Purposes*— the former published before The Cooper Union Address, the latter after it. Richard McCormick, a member of the committee in charge of the speech, who entertained Lincoln for two or three days before the lecture was given, recorded that Lincoln's own highest hope was that he might get the vice-presidential nomination, to run with Seward.[19]

According to Herndon, Lincoln never worked as hard in preparing any other speech as he did for this one.[20] The committee in charge also worked hard to make the occasion a success; and, although the night of the lecture was cold and slushy, an audience of 1500 gathered, mostly men, described as "the pick and flower of New York." William Cullen Bryant was chosen as chairman, and gave Lincoln a brief but gracious introduction. Then the orator stepped forward. "His dress that night," wrote Charles C. Nott, who had invited Lincoln, "was the most unbecoming that a fiend's ingenuity could have devised for a tall, gaunt man—a black frock coat, ill-setting and too short for him in the body, skirt and arms—a rolling collar, low-down, disclosing his long, thin, shrivelled throat, uncovered and exposed." Amidst cheers, however, Lincoln walked to the lectern, with his speech written on blue foolscap paper, and commenced: "Mr. *Cheerman*." As the shrill voice uttered this Westernism, a member of the audience muttered: "Old fellow, you won't do. It's all very well for the Wild West but this will never go down in New York."[21] Lincoln himself was "for once in his life" embarrassed and ill at ease as he contrasted the disarray of his own clothing to the meticulous neatness of the others on the platform.[22] But as his speech unfolded, Lincoln not only regained control of himself but also won such enthusiasm from his listeners that time after time they leaped

[19] Andrew A. Freeman, *Abraham Lincoln Goes to New York*, New York: Coward-McCann, 1960, p. 72.
[20] *Herndon's Life of Lincoln*, ed. Angle, *op. cit.*, pp. 359–360.
[21] Freeman, *op. cit.*, pp. 75–83.
[22] *Herndon's Life of Lincoln*, *op. cit.*, pp. 360–361.

to their feet, "yelling like wild Indians." McCormick said afterwards, "I think I never saw an audience more thoroughly carried away by an orator." Horace Greeley hustled Lincoln over to the *Tribune* office to read proof on the speech, so that it could appear in the next morning's edition. The New York Central Railroad president, who heard the speech, offered Lincoln a retainer of $10,000 a year to represent his company. Invitations for more speeches in New England came pouring in. Two months and twenty three days after the Cooper Union address, Lincoln was nominated for the presidency.

The style of the speech was neither eloquent nor exciting. It commenced casually but with precise directness: "The facts with which I shall deal this evening are mainly old and familiar; nor is there anything new in the general use I shall make of them." He took as his text a sentence from a recent speech by Senator Douglas: "Our fathers, when they framed the Government under which we live, understood this question just as well, and even better, than we do now." Then he launched into a lengthy, carefully detailed exposition of historical facts which demonstrated that the great majority of the Founding Fathers believed slavery to be wrong and that it would shortly be abolished. Lincoln concluded, then, by pinpointing what he considered the essential matter: that the enslavement of one human being by another is morally wrong. This, not legalism, was the real issue, he said, between North and South. "If it is right, we cannot justly object to its nationality—its universality; if it is wrong, they cannot justly insist upon its extension—its enlargement."[23] Then he added that "necessity" required the Republican Party to acquiesce in the continuance of slavery, but nothing should be done to permit its extension.

This same spirit of moderation dominated Lincoln's first inaugural address—a closely-knit argument for seeking a solution to sectional problems within the framework of democratic government.[24] "Why should there not be a patient confidence in the ultimate justice of the people?" Lincoln pleaded. "Is there any better or equal hope in the world?" Even as he spoke for conciliation, however, he knew the die was already cast; secession was no longer a threat but had become a reality.[25] Nothing he could say could prevent the tragedy of civil war; but

[23] Basler, *Works of Lincoln, op. cit.,* III:549.
[24] For a detailed study of this speech see Marie Hochmuth Nichols, "Lincoln's First Inaugural Address," in Auer, *Antislavery and Disunion, op. cit.,* pp. 392–414.
[25] The dates on which secession was actually voted in the various state conventions are: Dec. 17, 1860: South Carolina—unanimous; Jan. 9, 1861: Mississippi—84 to 15; Jan. 10, 1861: Florida—62 to 7; Jan. 11, 1861: Alabama—61 to 39; Jan. 19, 1861: Georgia—208 to 130; Jan. 25, 1861: Louisiana—113 to 17; Feb. 1, 1861: Texas—166 to 7. In Texas one of the most colorful, if minor, American orators, Sam Houston, who was then Governor, refused to recognize the secession conven-

at least he could enshrine for the centuries his awful sense of the need-lessness of the catastrophe. His feelings culminated in the magnificent conclusion (which he revised from a draft offered by Seward) :

> I am loath to close. We are not enemies, but friends. We must not be enemies. Though passion may have strained, it must not break our bonds of affection. The mystic chords of memory, stretching from every battlefield and patriot grave to every living heart and hearthstone all over this broad land, will yet swell the chorus of the Union when again touched, as surely they will be, by the better angels of our nature.[26]

During the war Lincoln sought always for a victory that would render reconciliation easier, not harder. He delayed the Emancipation Proclamation until it was clearly inevitable. On the battlefield of Gettysburg, where the tide of battle turned irrevocably against the South, he stated the aims of his administration in the broadest possible terms: "that government of the people, by the people, and for the people, shall not perish from the earth." As the war drew to its close, he ended his Second Inaugural with a heartfelt plea for complete restoration of political and spiritual unity: "With malice toward none, with charity for all, with firmness in the right as God gives us to see the right, let us strive on to finish the work we are in, to bind up the nation's wounds, to care for him who shall have borne the battle and for his widow and his orphan, to do all which may achieve and cherish a just and lasting peace, among ourselves and with all nations." In a spirit compact at once of simple goodness and of adroit political understanding, he asked the Marine Band at the victory celebration to play "Dixie," thus initiating the sentiment that the North and the South shared together the feelings of both sides. In his last public address, on April 11, 1865, he appealed for acceptance of the proposed constitution for Louisiana, as a basis for Southern Reconstruction, admitting that it did not incorporate as much justice for the freed slaves as the North would wish, but urging that it went as far as the Southern whites were then able to go. "Now if we reject and spurn them, we do our utmost to disorganize and disperse them . . . . Concede that the new government of Louisiana is only to what it should be as the egg is to the fowl, we shall sooner have the fowl by hatching the egg than by smashing it."[27]

---

tion; and when, on March 4, the State Legislature confirmed the vote of secession, he refused to sign the act or to take the oath of allegiance to the Confederacy. Cf. Marquis James, *The Raven: A Biography of Sam Houston*, New York: Blue Ribbon Books, 1929, pp. 404–412. Houston's speech renouncing secession is in Dudley G. Wooten, ed., *A Comprehensive History of Texas*, Dallas, 1898, II:126.
[26] The two versions are in Robert T. Oliver, *Training for Effective Speech*, New York: Cordon, 1939, pp. 234–235.
[27] Basler, *Works of Lincoln, op. cit.*, VIII:404.

We shall sooner have the fowl by hatching the egg than by smashing it. Here is the essential Lincoln: move slowly, wait patiently, be content so long as the germ of the right course is being nurtured and will eventually emerge. Believe in the good sense and right intentions of those whom you oppose. Understand their problems and be willing to help them to find the right goal according to their own choice of the way. But when the course of events veers from the path that leads toward a right decision, then, "In your hands, my dissatisfied fellow countrymen, and not in mine, is the momentous issue of civil war."[28]

Abraham Lincoln won the presidency by proving, in his address at Cooper Union, that his moderation, rooted historically in the traditions of our nation, made him "available." Skillfully he avoided the extremist labels that barred Seward from the cherished prize. He avoided the controversy that Douglas relished. But behind the artful dodging was the far greater and more essential fact of impregnable concentration on the only ultimate goal he found acceptable: the achievement of a solution for the nation that would accord with the fundamental moral sense of the people. "With firmness in the right," said Lincoln, asserting the integrity of a man who would not deviate from his own vision of truth; "as God gives us to see the right," he added, in humble recognition of the fact that truth is not easily discerned. When the bullet of John Wilkes Booth brought his life to a close, the nation, North and South, mourned the loss of a leader whose compassionate greatness was never more needed than for the trial of reconstruction. What he really was—a combination of simplicity and adroitness, an intermingling of high idealism with shrewd political canniness—is well revealed in the famous debates with Douglas in 1858.

Strategy in the Great Debate

LINCOLN AND DOUGLAS knew one another from top to bottom. They liked, admired, and respected one another both as men and as astute and patriotic politicians.[1] Both were trained in law and skilled in the rough and tumble tactics of frontier stump speaking. Both realized that the importance of the 1858 campaign was not alone the election to the

28 *Ibid.*, IV:271.
1 At Beardstown, Illinois, August 12, 1858, Lincoln himself said with no more than a cordial degree of exaggeration that "He and I are about the best friends in the world, and when we get together he would no more think of fighting me than of fighting his wife." Paul M. Angle, *The Lincoln Reader*, New Brunswick: Rutgers University Press, 1947, p. 234.

Senate but the shaping of issues and perhaps the determination of candidates for the 1860 presidential race. From years of criss-crossing the state of Illinois on the legal circuit and on the political hustings, they knew their audience in great detail, and they were well known personally as well as by reputation to their hearers. The frequently asserted notion that Douglas was trapped into debating against a Lincoln whose qualities were unknown to him is utterly ridiculous.[2] Both men wanted to debate. The issues were as momentous as the nation had ever faced: what was to be done about slavery and what could be done to stop the obvious drift toward civil war. The two protagonists went into battle primed to fight hard and knowing they both would have the struggle of their lives.

The pair made an odd contrast. But nothing was able to conceal the fact that each man had an unusually acute mind, that each was shrewd in politics, learned in American history, and adapted by nature and experience to the thrust and parry of platform persuasion.

The campaign started with Lincoln's speech at Springfield on June 16, 1858, accepting the Republican Senatorial nomination. During the next four and a half months, each man made at least sixty speeches. This meant sleepless nights and grindingly hard days as they scoured the State for votes from the clay-soil farms of the proslavery southern tier of counties on up through the rich prairie lands and industrial, antislavery northern districts. But the formal debates, launched by the challenge Lincoln issued on July 24, were seven: at Ottawa, August 21, with an audience of twelve thousand, mostly pro-Lincoln, where they spoke for three hours under a hot sun; at Freeport, on August 27, where 15,000, mostly Republicans, stood for three hours in a cool drizzle; at Jonesboro, on September 15, where fourteen hundred Douglas Democrats gathered; at Charleston, on September 18, where a hotly pro-Lincoln crowd of twelve thousand whooped it up in a carnival spirit; at Galesburg, October 7, where another Republican audience of twelve thousand was dispirited by raw, damp cold and a piercing wind; at Quincy, on October 13, where the auditors were largely Douglas men from across the river in Missouri; and finally at Alton, on October 15, where the six thousand dirt-poor farmers were mostly Democrats.[3]

At Ottawa, Douglas commenced with a promise of sober reasonableness: "I desire to address myself to your judgment, your understanding and your conscience, and not to your passions or your enthusiasm." Lin-

---

[2] Douglas is reported to have said of Lincoln in 1858, before the debates: "I shall have my hands full. Lincoln is the strong man of his party, the best stump speaker in the West." Sandburg, *Lincoln: Prairie Years*, op. cit., p. 385.

[3] Angle, *Created Equal?*, op. cit., "Introduction," pp. v–xxx; Sandburg, *Lincoln: Prairie Years*, op. cit., pp. 392–412.

coln was equally disarming: "I hope to deal in all things fairly, with Judge Douglas, and with the people of the State, in this contest . . . . If I have brought forth anything not a fact, if he will point it out, it will not even ruffle me to take it back." From this point on, however, both men settled down to fight as politicians for acclaim, publicity, and votes.[4] Douglas did his utmost to identify Lincoln with abolitionism (though he knew this was unjust) and Lincoln tried to trap Douglas with an ingenious dilemma.

Douglas, Lincoln insisted, must either renounce the Supreme Court decision in the Dred Scott case (which declared it illegal for voters to prohibit slavery in the territories) or else he must renounce his own program for popular sovereignty. If he did the first, he would be rejecting an essential part of the Constitution and ingredient of American democracy; if he did the latter he would be admitting that for more than four years he had fought for a national policy that was both impractical and illegal. In either case, Douglas would be digging his own political grave. It was then with considerable satisfaction that Lincoln sprang this trap, during the second debate, at Freeport—and repeated it afterward in speech after speech, trying to nail Douglas's political hide to the wall. Douglas responded by trying to show that the dilemma was false: that there was in reality a third alternative Lincoln had ignored. The facts of history and geography, he said, proved that regardless of whatever the Supreme Court might decide, slavery was suited only to the cotton and tobacco culture, only to the agricultural South, and only to people who were traditionally habituated to it. The law might *permit* slavery in Northern States, but the fact was the people would reject it. "If the people want slavery they will have it, and if they do not want it you cannot force it upon them."[5]

Douglas tried to turn the tables by confronting Lincoln with the reversal of his own dilemma: did Lincoln choose to advise the people to renounce the decision of the Supreme Court? If so he was really standing for anarchy and was aligning himself with "all the little Abolition orators who go around and lecture in the basements of schools and churches."[6] But if Lincoln rejected this horn of the dilemma and chose to adhere to the Court's decision, then he must either support popular sovereignty or accept the alternative of extension of slavery into every territory even when the people did not want it.

Lincoln's reply was that the decision on Dred Scott was unworthy of

[4] Angle, *Lincoln Reader, op. cit.,* p. 250; Marvin Bauer, "Methods of Persuasion Used by Lincoln and Douglas," *Quarterly Journal of Speech,* XIII(Feb., 1927): 29–39.
[5] Angle, *Created Equal? op. cit.,* p. 58.
[6] *Ibid.,* p. 111.

public acceptance because it clearly was the result of a conspiracy among outgoing President Pierce, incoming President Buchanan, Douglas, and Justice Taney. In any event, Lincoln contended, the choice Douglas offered was no choice at all, for the legal fact was that if the Supreme Court decision were not overturned, perhaps by a constitutional amendment, the extension of slavery to every section of the nation was inevitable. His own position, Lincoln made clear, was that slavery was an evil—something he could not get Douglas to admit. "The real issue," Lincoln asserted, "is the sentiment on the part of one class that looks upon the institution of slavery *as a wrong*, and of another class that *does not* look upon it as wrong." Lincoln's solution was to place slavery "in the course of ultimate extinction," perhaps in a hundred years, by preventing its spread to new territories.

Douglas tried hard to represent Lincoln as an advocate of Negro equality with the white man, but Lincoln stubbornly refused to be pushed into this position. Said Douglas: "I am opposed to negro citizenship in any and every form. I believe this government was made on the white basis." However, Douglas added, "humanity and Christianity both require that the negro shall have and enjoy every right, every privilege, and every immunity consistent with the safety of society."[7] Lincoln rejoined: "I, as well as Judge Douglas, am in favor of the race to which I belong having the superior position. I have never said anything to the contrary, but I hold that notwithstanding all this, there is no reason in the world why the negro is not entitled to all natural rights enumerated in the Declaration of Independence."[8] In a speech at Edwardsville, which was part of the campaign, although not in one of the formal debates, Lincoln explained his view that injustice to the Negro weakened justice itself, for everyone:

> When by all these means you have succeeded in dehumanizing the negro; when you have put him down and made it impossible for him to be but as the beasts of the field; when you have extinguished his soul, and placed him where the ray of hope is blown out in darkness that broods over the damned, are you quite sure the demon you have roused will not turn and rend you? . . . Familiarize yourself with the chains of bondage, and you are preparing your own limbs to wear them.[9]

Defending himself against the charge that the Republican Party, and he explicitly, were abolitionist, Lincoln declared: "I have no purpose

[7] *Ibid.*, pp. 294, 295.
[8] *Ibid.*, p. 117. However, Anthony Hillbruner has sought to show that Lincoln believed in *eventual* equality for the Negroes, in "The Lincoln-Douglas Debates: A Study in Equality," *The Lincoln Herald*, 62(Spring, 1960):3–12.
[9] Basler, *Works of Lincoln, op. cit.*, III:95.

directly or indirectly to interfere with slavery in the States where it exists. I believe I have no lawful right to do so, and I have no inclination to do so."[10] Then, to avoid the stigma of being labelled a "Negro lover," Lincoln made clear that his opposition to the spread of slavery was fundamentally intended as the championship of white labor: "I am still in favor of our new territories being in such a condition that white men may find a home."[11] His listeners well understood and appreciated the view that white men could not compete equally with freed Negroes.

Both the arguments and the argumentative methods in the debates have been almost endlessly analyzed and evaluated. Neither man sought to encompass in his speeches the broad range of interests and issues confronting the country; on the contrary, even on the issue of sectionalism, the effort by both was not to place the subject in its historic perspective, but narrowly to thrust and parry, seeking crowd-pleasing drama and forensic advantage. In the critical view of James G. Randall, "The debate was a spectacle, a drama, an exhibition, almost a sporting event . . . not an effort to work out a formula of agreement."[12] Marvin Bauer found that both speakers indulged freely in *ad hominem* arguments.[13] Earl G. Wiley thought Lincoln lost the slug-fest because he "lacked the stomach" for demagoguery, and Wiley quoted from Machiavelli's *The Prince* a formula which, he said, proved more applicable to Douglas's speaking than to Lincoln's: "Of this, however, I am well persuaded, that it is better to be impetuous than cautious. For fortune is a woman who to be kept under must be beaten and roughly handled and we see that she suffers herself to be more readily mastered by those who so treat her than by those who are more timid in their approach."[14] Harry V. Jaffa wrote a book to express his view that Lincoln won the debate, to the extent of destroying Douglas as an acceptable compromise candidate for 1860, and thereby precipitated an avoidable war.[15]

Albert J. Beveridge, in his biography of Lincoln, wrote that "Solely on their merits, the debates themselves deserve little notice."[16] George Fort Milton, the best biographer of Douglas, wrote that, "Judged as

---

[10] Angle, *Created Equal?, op. cit.,* p. 117.
[11] On August 27, 1856, Lincoln phrased the same idea to an audience at Kalamazoo, Michigan: "Have we no interest in the free territories of the United States— that they should be kept open for the homes of free white people?" T. Harry Williams, *Selected Writings and Speeches of Abraham Lincoln, op. cit.,* p. 49. Lincoln's views on the relations of the races are well summarized by Sandburg, *Lincoln: Prairie Years, op. cit.,* pp. 313–317.
[12] Quoted in Angle, *Lincoln Reader, op. cit.,* p. 250.
[13] Bauer, *op. cit., passim.*
[14] Earl G. Wiley, "A Footnote on the Lincoln-Douglas Debates," *Quarterly Journal of Speech,* XVIII(April, 1932):224.
[15] Harry V. Jaffa, *Crisis of the House Divided: An Interpretation of the Issues in the Lincoln-Douglas Debates,* New York: Doubleday, 1959.
[16] Albert J. Beveridge, *Abraham Lincoln,* Boston: Houghton Mifflin, 1928, II:635.

debates, they do not measure up to their reputation. On neither side did the dialectic compare with that in the debates between Webster, Hayne, and Calhoun."[17] Earl Wiley, a rhetorician who specialized in the study of Lincoln, pointed out that Lincoln failed to demonstrate debating skill in pursuing either the cardinal issue or weaknesses in Douglas's case.[18] Lord Charnwood believed that in these debates "Lincoln had performed what, apart from results, was a work of intellectual merit beyond the compass of any American statesman since Hamilton"[19]; and even judging by results, the fight Lincoln made resulted, Charnwood thought, in preventing the Republican Party from falling apart, as happened to so many new parties in that era.

Whatever the argumentative merit may have been, the campaign was decided in large part by factors having nothing to do with the stump speaking. Thousands of new Irish immigrants who had fled from the potato famine settled in Illinois as supporters of the Democratic Party. William Henry Seward and his powerful eastern organization wanted to eliminate Lincoln from competition for the Republican nomination by having him defeated for the Senate; and leading eastern Whigs and Republicans wrote to friends in Illinois arguing that since Douglas was quarrelling with Buchanan, he, rather than Lincoln, deserved their support. Douglas, meanwhile, was handicapped by his quarrel with Buchanan, which diffused the strength of his own party following, and by bad health. He was, however, aided by the principal national newspapers, which backed Douglas on the ground that his compromise position might prevent a civil war. In the election, Lincoln's candidates for the State Legislature won a popular majority by some four thousand votes, though Douglas men won a majority of the legislative seats and thereby assured his return to the Senate. When the results were in, Lincoln remarked that he felt like a boy who had stubbed his toe: "It hurts too much to laugh, and I am too big to cry."[20]

Rhetoricians find a principal interest in the debates because this was the first occasion on which news correspondents travelled with candidates to report their views and to write personality sketches about them and their audiences; and this was also the first time a series of speeches was reported stenographically.[21] The debates are also interesting as a compendium of the arguments used by moderates on both sides of the sectional struggle. But, most significantly of all, they introduced Lincoln

[17] Milton, *op. cit.*, p. 315.
[18] Wiley, *op. cit.*, p. 223.
[19] Charnwood, *op. cit.*, p. 161.
[20] Sandburg, *Lincoln: Prairie Years*, *op. cit.*, p. 412, and Milton, *op. cit.*, p. 351, give variant versions.
[21] Angle, *Created Equal?*, *op cit.*, pp. xxiv-xxv.

to the national audience, with a program around which the Republican Party could rally. This, more than political maneuvering, is why Lincoln was nominated at Chicago, in 1860. Seward could not shake off the impression that he was a radical; and Lincoln managed to convince the plurality which he required to get into the White House that he was safe. Speculative historians might even reason that the debates made Lincoln President—which made secession of Southern States inevitable—which made civil war inescapable. How different would events have been had Douglas been elected President in 1860, or Seward? The "ifs" are far more numerous than the "whereases." So it must ever be.

IX

RESTRICTION, RECONSTRUCTION AND RECONCILIATION
1865﹀1886

Confronting the Problems of Peace 📖

ON MONDAY, April 3, 1865, the news that Richmond had fallen set the nation's capital agog with excitement. "Oratory burst spontaneously from the steps of public buildings and hotels."[1] In the park before the War Department offices the dour Secretary Edwin M. Stanton spoke to a packed multitude, asking God "to teach us how to be humble in the midst of triumph." In the South there had been a last flurry of oratory before the war's end, as speakers tried to stem the tide of defeat. On March 11, "the last speech made by any Southern man in behalf of the Confederacy" was delivered by Benjamin H. Hill at La Grange, Georgia. Fight on, he pleaded, for defeat would mean: "1. That the freed Negro must have this country to inhabit. 2. That he must be furnished with lands to cultivate, and with means to cultivate them. 3. That he must have civil rights, civil and political power and social equality with us. 4. That he must have power to protect himself in all these rights." Faced with so dismal a prospect, Hill called for renewed zeal. "Oh dastardly is the cowardice of that trooper who lingers from the battle now; hopelessly suicidal is that avarice which can withhold its offerings now; and hateful, hateful far beyond the darkest thought of the traitor's mind is that ambition which cannot forget its personal griefs and personal schemings and cease to divide our people now."[2]

When Lee surrendered his sword to Grant at Appomattox, the Southern people cared little to listen to the forlorn leaders of the lost cause; but in the North the men who stood in the public eye had to step forward and utter definite words. Ready or not, their audience was waiting and they must speak on cue. The tailor from Tennessee, newly inducted as Lincoln's successor, spoke words he would soon regret: "Treason is a crime and crime must be punished. Treason must be made

---

[1] Margaret Leech, *Reveille in Washington, 1860–1865,* New York: Harper, 1941, p. 378.
[2] Benjamin H. Hill, Jr., *Senator Benjamin H. Hill of Georgia: His Life, Writings, and Speeches,* Atlanta: H. C. Hudgins, 1891, pp. 279–280.

infamous and traitors must be impoverished."[3] In a similar vein but with a different emphasis, Wendell Phillips announced his view: "The whites of the South are our enemies. If the Union is ever reconstructed, it must be reconstructed from the blacks."[4] Thaddeus Stevens told his fellow citizens at Lancaster, just three days before Lincoln's assassination, that he favored seizing from those who took part in the rebellion "every foot of ground they pretend to own."[5] Charles Sumner was advocating suffrage for the Negroes "incessantly in the streets, in clubs, at dinner-tables."[6] In Concord the quiet philosopher, Ralph Waldo Emerson, confided to his Journal: " 'Tis far the best that the rebels be pounded into a peace."[7] Georges Clemenceau, a young French correspondent whose fame was to belong to another greater and later war, wrote: "When the war ended, the North was concerned not to let itself be tricked out of what it had spent so much trouble and perseverance to win."[8]

With the end of the war new interests, new influences, new personalities, and a new style came to dominate the American scene. A Golden Age of Oratory was ended; an Age of Tinsel came to take its place. From Patrick Henry to Abraham Lincoln, the speakers strode into the forum of Congress, the pulpit, or the lecture hall with an air of greatness. Even those who were demagogic appealed to sweeping principles which they represented as illimitable truths. When they indulged in personalities, it was with an Olympian disdain. They regarded themselves and their adversaries as great men; and they viewed the sweep of American history in epic proportions. Their speeches were replete with comparative references to the civilizations and empires of Greece and Rome. The Almighty and His purposes for the nation were their frequent theme. The vast extent of the continent was much in their thoughts; and their words reflected a self-conscious awareness that they were spokesmen for destiny. Like actors in a tragic drama that surged to its denouement at Appomattox, they spoke their lines with magisterial grandeur. Fittingly the drama reached both its climax and its close in the war. Most of the heroic figures of the sectional struggle were obliterated before, or during, or shortly after the holocaust. A few readjusted their careers to push on into the new era.

But the times were changed and the tragic drama of the irrepressible

---

[3] New York *World*, April 29, 1856.
[4] Sherwin, *Prophet of Liberty, op. cit.*, p. 537.
[5] Lancaster, Penna., *Intelligencer*, March 21, 1867.
[6] Claude G. Bowers, *The Tragic Era*, New York: Blue Ribbon Books, 1920, p. 15.
[7] *Journals of Ralph Waldo Emerson*, ed. E. W. Emerson and W. E. Forbes, Boston: Houghton Mifflin, 1914, X:93.
[8] Georges Clemenceau, *American Reconstruction, 1865–1870*, New York: Dial Press, 1928, p. 296.

conflict was superseded by a loosely-knit series of relatively minor problem plays. The great orators of the first half-century were succeeded by skilled actors who seldom mouthed their lines or muffed their gestures. The new age was one of skill, not sagacity, of proficiency rather than prophecy, often with profit looming more importantly than patriotism. When greatness re-emerged, in the idealism of William Jennings Bryan, the crusading zeal of Theodore Roosevelt, and the utopian intellectualism of Woodrow Wilson, it was most often directed against the greed and the selfishness which they found implanted in American life—a form of verbal surgery designed to restore the moral health of the nation. This, of course, was not the whole story of our post-Civil War platform speaking. But it was the hallmark of the main currents of the political talk.

Union and liberty were replaced as dominant themes by quarrels over the distribution of property and the allocation of power. Speakers all too prone to follow where the interest of their audience led were discussing new kinds of questions. How were the Southern States to be reconstructed? What if any punishment should be meted out to the wartime profiteers? What new taxes could be legislated to pay off the monumental four and a half billion dollar debt contracted by the Government to wage the war? Was it right to permit the burgeoning of multi-million dollar private fortunes? How could the freed Negroes, the industrial workers, the women, and the farmers respectively get their just shares of privileges and prosperity? How could the economy be protected against cheap foreign goods and cheap foreign labor? What role should the United States play amidst the immature republics of Latin America? How could we compete with Europe for the tantalizing, potentially profitable markets that were beginning to move world interest toward the Orient? And along with the questions there were new ideas to be discussed: the assault upon the old religious certainties by the methods and the hypotheses of the new science; the social changes induced by increased mobility and speed of communication; depersonalization of employment relations in the new manufacturing corporations; the impetus of universal and vocationalized education.

Many of these problems were rooted well before the Civil War, but were diverted from public attention by concentration on the twin issues of sectionalism and manifest destiny. The problems of westward expansion were not ended by the war; but passage of the Homestead Act, building of the railroads, and virtual elimination of hostile Indian tribes greatly changed the nature of the influences exerted by the frontier upon the American mind. The crusade to strike the fetters from the slave was followed by nagging dispute concerning how to live with him as a neighbor. The mood and the manner of American life underwent significant change. Heroism was succeeded by heroics. Opportunism and cleverness came to be accepted. Speakers such as Roscoe Conkling, James G. Blaine, Benjamin Harrison, Robert Ingersoll, Chauncey Depew, Henry Grady, Russell Conwell, Phillips Brooks, Dwight L. Moody, and Bourke Cockran aroused admiration, sometimes affection, even hatred, but they could scarcely generate awe.

An age of greatness was closed. Artisans of the spoken word were heard instead of artists. Whereas the great pre-war issues demanded and dominated public attention, in the post-war era politicians were able to select and to fabricate campaign slogans, which they called issues, in terms of their presumed vote-winning potential. Of course there was much that was tawdry and tinsel in the first half of the nineteenth century. But the hard-cider campaigning, and the Anti-Masonic, and Star-Spangled, and Know-Nothing absurdities had done little more than magnify the greatness into which they obtruded. In the decades between 1865 and 1900, genuine grandeur either of heart or mind seldom manifested itself. It was a time when little men looked big.

The Victors: Thaddeus Stevens and Company

THADDEUS STEVENS was one of the strangest and least typical of American orators. In 1835, at the age of forty three, he made one of the few speeches in all history that indubitably, and through the power of its eloquence alone, shifted enough votes in a legislative assembly to effect the enactment of a genuinely significant piece of legislation. Then, in 1858, at the age of sixty six, he started on the career for which he is best remembered. This phase of his life culminated in speeches advocating harsh reconstruction measures; in his whiplash mastery of the House of Representatives during and immediately after the Civil War; and in his leadership of the effort to impeach President Andrew Johnson.

Born April 4, 1792, into a poor family in the Green Mountain country of Vermont, Stevens was afflicted with a club foot and with childhood ill-health. His father was a drunkard who wandered off one day and never came home; and his mother was intensely if not fanatically religious. His childhood associates mocked and mimicked his hobbling gait and drove him into a solitude from which he never emerged.[1]

[1] Richard N. Current, *Old Thad Stevens: A Story of Ambition*, Madison: University of Wisconsin Press, 1942, pp. 4–5; Fawn W. Brodie, *Thaddeus Stevens: Scourge of the South*, New York: Norton, 1959, p. 25.

Somehow he got to and through Dartmouth, where he was once expelled, and finally graduated without honors, castigating those classmates who were elected to Phi Beta Kappa as "fawning parasites." Then he "read law" and left Vermont for Pennsylvania, where he became well-to-do through sharp real estate practices, and established a reputation as a successful trial lawyer by defending, with a plea of insanity, the perpetrator of a peculiarly brutal murder.[2] He never married but lived all his mature life, quietly and unobtrusively, with a mulatto woman, Lydia Smith, who also served as his housekeeper and hostess.[3]

In appearance and manner Stevens was moodily and dourly impressive. He was described in a eulogy by his friend Senator James S. Morrill as having "more the stony features of authority than sweetness."[4] He was just over six feet tall, gaunt-thin, and with a perpetually stern countenance crowned by a wig of thick hair, sometimes brown, sometimes black. Despite his lameness he was physically strong and active—although in the period of his greatest national notoriety, during the impeachment trial, he was so crippled with arthritis that he had to be carried to the sessions in a chair. His manner of speaking is sharply depicted in an unfriendly newspaper story that hopefully proclaimed his decline: "That wrathful voice had lost its mastery, that severe satire its power, and that extended forefinger its omnipotence."[5] Charles Sumner thought that "Nobody said more in fewer words or gave language a sharper bite. Speech was with him a cat-o'-nine tails and woe to the victim on whom the terrible lash descended."[6] Carl Schurz noted his "hollow voice devoid of music . . . his face long and pallid . . . beetling brows overhanging keen eyes of uncertain color . . . the underlip defiantly protruding . . . a certain absolutism of opinion with contemptuous scorn for adverse argument."[7] He was known for a kind of wit illustrated by a dual apology he made to Lincoln for having accused Simon Cameron, the Secretary of War, of being a thief. When Lincoln challenged his view that Cameron would steal, Stevens admitted, "Well, I don't think he would steal a red-hot stove." Lincoln thought the apology worth repeating and told Cameron of it. Cameron thought the retraction no improvement over the original charge and demanded that

---

[2] Samuel W. McCall, *Thaddeus Stevens*, Boston: Houghton Mifflin, 1899, pp. 24–26; Current, *op. cit.*, pp. 9–12; Alphonse B. Miller, *Thaddeus Stevens*, New York: Harper, 1939, p. 31; Elsie Singmaster, *I Speak for Thad Stevens*, Boston: Houghton Mifflin, 1947, pp. 99–119.
[3] Miller, *op. cit.*, pp. 11–13; Current, *op. cit.*, pp. 289–290; Bowers, *op. cit.*, pp. 81–83.
[4] Bowers, *op. cit.*, p. 66.
[5] New York *Herald*, Feb. 8, 1866.
[6] Brodie, *op. cit.*, p. 269; *Congressional Globe*, for Dec. 18, 1869, 40th Congress, 3rd Session, pp. 203–204.
[7] Schurz, *Reminiscences*, *op. cit.*, III:214.

Stevens go to Lincoln and again apologize. Stevens did as requested, saying to Lincoln, "I believe I told you he would not steal a red-hot stove. I now take that back."[8] There is no record that Cameron sought any further apology.

His first and perhaps principal rise to greatness came in 1835, when, as a member of the Pennsylvania House of Representatives, he saved the State's system of free public education. A law providing for tax-supported, tuition-free schools had been adopted by the 1834 legislature; but it was ignored by more than half the school districts of the State, and in the ensuing election the voters returned a large majority of legislators who were pledged to its repeal. Promptly the Senate replaced the law with another providing free schools only for the poor, with only eight dissenting votes. In the House a count showed a majority of thirty against the universal free school system. Petititions poured into Harrisburg demanding repeal of the free school law; and newspapers urged the legislators to accept the verdict of the public. Stevens was absent from the city until after the Senate vote, and returned just as the House members were about to whoop through their concurrence. When he announced that he would support the existing law, the House chamber was packed with Representatives, Senators, and visitors, eager to hear whether he could think of anything to say. Unfortunately, there was no stenographic reporting at that time, and no copy of the speech was taken down—though a fabricated text for it was later put together and received wide circulation. But there is no question as to the effect upon its hearers. The House immediately after he sat down reaffirmed its support of the existing law by a two-thirds majority; and, even more impressive, the Senators who heard him rushed back to their chamber and reversed their own previous action of nullifying the law.[9] "No one questioned that Stevens's eloquence was responsible for this about-face," wrote the historian Richard N. Current.[10] Stevens himself, at the end of his life, commented that it was this success which saved his entire career from being a failure.[11] As for what he said, the arguments today seem scarcely worth repeating: that the public profits from free schools as much as from free jails; that well-educated children are of more benefit to the community than well-fattened hogs; and that educating the poor enhances the welfare of all. What was characteristic of Stevens's oratory was that the words he spoke were driven home to the listeners with such a fury of intensity that it was hard to fend off acceptance of

[8] Bowers, *op. cit.*, p. 76; Brodie, *op. cit.*, pp. 144–145.
[9] Brodie, *op. cit.*, pp. 59–62; Singmaster, *op. cit*, pp. 181–192; McCall, *op. cit.*, pp. 34–35.
[10] Current, *op. cit.*, p. 23.
[11] *Ibid.*, p. 317.

his conclusion. Both the style and the sentiments may be indicated in a brief passage that is probably close to what he actually said: "Hereditary distinctions of rank are sufficiently odious; but that which is founded upon poverty is infinitely more so. Such a law should be entitled 'An Act for Branding and Marking the Poor.' "[12]

Stevens became active in politics as he opposed Jacksonian democracy and advocated Anti-Masonry. In 1848 he was elected to Congress as a Free-Soil Whig, where he heard Daniel Webster's Seventh of March speech and commented on it, "Damn him, I could cut his heart out." Stevens himself opposed Clay's compromise bills in speeches in which he promised to leave the "filth and the slime" of personal abuse to others. Then he went on: "There is, in the natural world, a little, spotted, contemptible animal, which is armed by nature with a foetid, volatile, penetrating virus which so pollutes whoever attacks it, as to make him offensive to himself and all around him for a long time. Nothing, sir, no insults shall provoke me to crush so filthy a beast."[13]

Then Stevens proceeded to the heart of his deepest belief: that all men are, and of right ought to be, free and equal. He had listened, as he said, to many pious declarations that the slave was a happy creature, blessed by the paternal solicitude of his master, "contented, happy, fat and sleek." Then his gift for satire found vent: "If it will save the Union, let these gentlemen introduce a 'compromise' by which these races may change conditions; by which the oppressed master may slide into that happy state where he can stretch his sleek limbs on the sunny ground without fear of deranging his toilet; where he will have no care for tomorrow; another will be bound to find him meat and drink, food and raiment, and provide for the infirmities of old age." With withering scorn, he concluded: "Let not the white man despair on account of the misfortune of his color."[14]

After two terms in Congress, Stevens withdrew, with the feeling that at the age of sixty he no longer cared for the tense kind of debating that filled the Capitol. Besides, his legal services were much in demand and he planned to spend the rest of his life earning money rather than fame. However, in 1858 he felt sufficiently eager to work for a protective tariff and for more restrictions on slavery; and also sufficiently angry with his Lancastrian neighbor, James Buchanan—who, he declared, "is dead of lockjaw"—because Buchanan refused to debate or discuss the issues, so that he once more ran for a seat in Congress. He had helped organize

[12] McCall, *op. cit.*, p. 41.
[13] Miller, *op. cit.*, p. 96. This speech was delivered June 10, 1850; the "filth and slime" speech on Feb. 20, 1850.
[14] *Ibid.*, pp. 96–97. Cf. Singmaster, *op. cit.*, pp. 290–299.

the Pennsylvania Republican Party; he ran, however, not as a Republican but as a candidate of the "People." He won three-fourths of the votes in his county and returned to the House of Representatives to find the Republican Party only six votes short of a majority. In the campaign two years later he worked hard for Lincoln's election and then was mortified that the reward of a place in the cabinet went to his enemy Simon Cameron rather than to himself. But Stevens made the best of his present position. Shortly, in the words of gossipy Ben: Perley Poore, he "was the despotic ruler of the House."[15] Without any position of special influence, he browbeat and terrorized members into disciplined action with savage personal attacks that reminded old-timers of John Randolph. By use of such tactics he whipped through legislation for high taxes and for conscription, closely supporting Lincoln's program. After Johnson became President, Stevens still further strengthened his position by assuming the key post of chairman of the Appropriations Committee. Then he made himself a cardinal power in shaping and administering reconstruction policies by establishment of a fifteen-member Joint Legislative Committee which would have the sole power to pass on the credentials of Southerners elected to the Senate or to the House. With this weapon Stevens was set to veto whatever reconstruction plans he might not like. The program he demanded included permanent disfranchisement of the leading rebels and forfeiture of their property; guaranteed protection of the rights of Southern Negroes and loyal whites; reduction of the Southern States to territorial status; and eventual Negro suffrage. He threw down the gauntlet most decisively in a major speech at Lancaster, on September 7, 1865, when he said: "The whole fabric of Southern society *must* be changed, and it never can be done if this opportunity is lost."[16]

Stevens was in close accord with Senator Sumner, who was bearing the chief torch in the Senate for immediate Negro suffrage and for condign punishment of the Southern whites. But Stevens and Sumner were too headstrong to work long together and by January of the next year Sumner was denouncing Stevens in a four-hour speech in the Senate. Stevens, enraged, formulated a Freedman's Bill that was deliberately phrased to keep the South in bondage rather than to restore the Union with guarantees of Negro equality—which was Sumner's aim. Johnson vetoed the bill; then, on Washington's birthday, he made a bitter speech on the north portico of the White House, naming Stevens, Sumner, and Wendell Phillips as "being opposed to the fundamental

[15] Ben: Perley Poore, *Perley's Reminiscences, op. cit.,* II:101.
[16] Current, *op. cit.,* pp. 214–217.

principles of this Government and as now laboring to destroy them."[17] Phillips, indeed, was heart and soul with Stevens's aim of remaking Southern society. "Better a renewal of the war than a surrender of the Negro to the control of his old master," he proclaimed in the summer of 1866.[18] But like Sumner, he wished to accomplish this not by bayonet rule of the South but by constitutional amendment. Furthermore, quite unlike Stevens, Phillips renounced the Republican Party, crying that, "The soul is dead. It announces to the world that it waits."[19] Moreover, Phillips now felt that the essential battle for the Negro was won and gave his principal attention for the remainder of his life to labor reform, temperance, and women's rights.[20] Stevens, in effect, was left to carry the banner alone for his view that the South was a "conquered province," and that "The conqueror rules; the conquered is ruled."[21] Restoration of the Southern States, he said, "is too lenient for my hard heart. Not only to 1870, but to 18,070, every rebel who shed the blood of loyal men should be prevented from exercising any power in this Government. Gentlemen here have said you must not humiliate these people. Why not? Do they not deserve humiliation?"[22]

The tragic drama of Stevens's life then entered upon the final scene. On February 24, 1868, at 4:30 p.m., Stevens arose from a couch on which he had been lying all day, entered the House chamber, "and, supported by his friends, made his way to a position near the Speaker's desk." *Harper's Weekly* described the scene: "A death-like silence reigned through the House. Members approached the speaker and gazed up in his face as he spoke . . . . This speech will probably be the last great effort of Mr. Stevens, as he is very weak and aged; and has been warned of an early end to his earthly career." The flat, harsh voice rasped out its demand that Andrew Johnson be impeached:

> When the so-called Confederate States of America were conquered, the government and final disposition of the conquered country belonged to Congress alone. Neither the President nor the judiciary had any right to interfere except so far as necessary to control it by military rule until the sovereign power . . . had provided for its civil administration. Yet Andrew Johnson, with unblushing hardihood, undertook to rule them by his power alone . . . . In my judgment, his conduct was a high-handed usurpation of power which ought long ago to have brought him to impeachment.[23]

[17] Bowers, *op. cit.*, p. 104.
[18] Sherwin, *op. cit.*, p. 547.
[19] *Ibid.*, p. 580.
[20] *Ibid.*, pp. 574–604.
[21] Singmaster, *op. cit.*, pp. 412–421.
[22] Miller, *op. cit.*, p. 267.
[23] *Ibid.*, pp. 343–345.

The time was long past when Stevens encountered any opposition from his own party in the House. By a vote of 126–47, with every Republican concurring, the resolution to bring impeachment proceedings was adopted. Without delay, on the very next day, Stevens went to the Senate to make formal announcement of the vote and to demand that the trial commence.

When, during the trial, it came Stevens's turn to speak on April 27, he was suffering from extreme exhaustion. "His voice was almost gone," an observer recorded, "and there is a strange huskiness about it, startlingly suggestive of the rattle in the throat of a dying man." Too feeble to stand, he read the first part of his speech, then handed the text to Ben Butler, who finished it for him. Three weeks later the vote was taken and Johnson escaped by the margin of a single vote: thirty five for impeachment, nineteen against. "There has been great, manifold, deep damnation," said Stevens sourly, hinting the result had been influenced by corruption. On July 7, he presented renewed articles of impeachment. But before any action could be secured, at midnight on August 13, he passed away.[24]

It was out in Illinois that the truest judgment was passed upon him— by Samuel Bowles, writing in the Springfield *Republican* for August 12, 1868: "When the hour came, the man was ready—not with broad views, wise doctrines, good taste, faultless manners, or exemplary morals—but resolute, shrewd, unsparing; willing to use friend or foe, careless of both, possessed with his cause and that alone, and equal to every occasion."

As for Charles Sumner, the last chapter of his life was failure—and in this failure he rose to his tallest stature as a man. In the interests of achieving reconciliation between North and South, he introduced a bill in the Senate to end the practice of printing the names of battles on the Army's regimental flags; for, he said, "It is contrary to the usages of civilized nations to perpetuate the memory of civil war." The legislature of Massachusetts greeted this suggestion with a vote of censure for what it called "an insult to the loyal soldiery of the nation." At about the same time, Sumner opposed an order from General Grant for the removal of John Lothrop Motley as Minister to England and also opposed Grant's attempt to annex Santo Domingo. For these offences Sumner was deposed from the chairmanship of the Senate Foreign Relations Committee and was widely denounced as a traitor to his own party. Not to be outdone, however, he retorted angrily that "Among the foremost purposes ought to be the downfall of this odious, insulting, degrading,

24 *Ibid.*, pp. 331–363.

aide-de-campish, incapable dictatorship."[25] For a man who was accused of being "exclusively occupied with himself and his own greatness,"[26] it was no small thing to court public disgrace at the end of his life by defending a friend, opposing seizure of a helpless country, and attempting reconciliation with a defeated foe. Sumner died better than he lived.

Andrew Johnson: Frontiersman from the Middle Border

IN STUDYING the oratory of Andrew Johnson, three different approaches may fruitfully be considered. In the first place he was an individual, with his own traits, limitations, and convictions. Secondly, he represented the difficult median position of the border States—definitely Southern in commitment to slavery and States rights, definitely Northern in determination to maintain the Union above all other considerations. Thirdly, he was a product of the frontier and in a frontier society he formed his personality and his manner of speaking.

As a man he was earthily strong. One of his critics may have been right in saying: "He possessed neither a first-rate mind nor a first-rate personality."[1] Even Johnson's friendliest biographer thought him an "obstinate, narrow-minded defender of lost causes," and "one who was so tactless that he often threw obstacles in his own way and ran against snags that might have been avoided."[2] Yet he was also "the most democratic of Presidents"[3]—not excepting Jefferson and Jackson—with an unquestioning concern for people as individuals, without regard for their education, social status, or political influence. He held his beliefs with a savage tenacity, putting them into the strongest words or acts that flashed into his crudely simple mind. It could well be said of Andrew Johnson that he was a bull in a china shop—if we keep in mind that the bull simply acts as his nature directs and that he surely was not in the china shop of his own volition.

Born December 29, 1808, the son of a poor tailor in Raleigh, South Carolina, Johnson grew up in poverty, without education, rough in

[25] Sherwin, *op. cit.*, pp. 605–608.
[26] Gamaliel Bradford, "Charles Sumner," *Yale Review*, V(April–July, 1916):552.
[1] Miller, *Thaddeus Stevens, op. cit.*, p. 210.
[2] Robert W. Winston, *Andrew Johnson: Plebian and Patriot*, New York: Holt, 1928, p. xiv.
[3] *Ibid.*, p. xiv. Samuel Eliot Morrison and Henry Steel Commager declared that "No truer democrat ever occupied the presidential chair." *Growth of the American Republic*, New York: Oxford University Press, 1937, II:34. However, Johnson was not considered worthy of even passing mention by Merrill D. Peterson in his *The Jefferson Image in the American Mind, op. cit.*

manner, violent in temper, yet, somehow, with ambition nurtured by a high self-esteem. At sixteen he walked to eastern Tennessee; then, liking what he found, he walked back again to Raleigh to get his mother and her brood of children. At nineteen he added further to his responsibilities by marrying Eliza McArdle, who taught him to write and cipher. He was some five feet nine inches in height, broad-shouldered and muscular, with a wealth of black hair, deep-set, piercing eyes, and a bearing that was grave, decorous, and dignified.[4] Despite his limitations of background and education, he had a tailor's eye for dress and was always neatly attired in a suitable and unostentatiously stylish fashion. The outer man, in short, was far more sedate than the turbulent impetuosity of his speech would suggest.

In Greeneville he established his tailor shop, under favorable circumstances that insured its prosperity. This was the time and the part of Tennessee in which Davy Crockett lived, whose fame rests in part on 'possum and bear hunts and fights with the Indians. In sober fact during Johnson's early period in the State, the bulk of the area was filled with game and dominated by Indian tribes. However, around Greeneville were many farms, averaging about one hundred acres, devoted chiefly to growing tobacco, but with diversified crops as well. The farmers were well-to-do, independent, and mostly did their own work, although a few slaves were domiciled on larger places. Johnson attended regularly the debating societies of Greeneville College and Tusculum Academy. Although at first he seemed "a very timid speaker, afraid of his own voice,"[5] he persisted in his own speaking till he gained both confidence and fluency. Finding this the best means of self-education, he founded yet another debating society, and employed a boy to read aloud to him and his employees in the shop the great orations of Burke, Chatham, Fox, and Erskine.

In 1835, at the age of twenty seven, prospering in business, popular among the intellectuals who frequented the debating societies, and inspired by the example of his fellow-Tennesseean Andrew Jackson, young Johnson arose in a public meeting, slapped his hands together, and nominated himself for the State Legislature. He campaigned with carefully prepared, fact-crammed speeches, chiefly on the theme that "there are no good laws but such as repeal other laws," and was elected. In the Legislature he ridiculed a bill to raise taxes to finance a system of macadamized roads and opposed a subsidy for a railroad, saying: "Why, it would frighten horses, put the owners of public vehicles out of business,

[4] Winston, op. cit., p. 99.
[5] Lloyd P. Stryker, *Andrew Johnson: A Study in Courage*, New York: Macmillan, 1936.

break up inns and taverns and be a monopoly generally."[6] In order to best the Whig speakers, who generally represented the well-educated upper class, in debate, Johnson read widely and filled scrap books with clippings and quotations on the major issues of the time. Meanwhile, he haunted the back hills, becoming acquainted and identified with the mountain people, who were poor, coarse, and homespun. The kind of language they liked to hear, he liked to talk. He learned to intersperse his factual recitals with exaggerations, homilies, and personalities, and to deliver his talks with finger-stabbing emphasis. No less than Davy Crockett was he a frontiersman, while also being himself.

In 1842, with experience in both houses of the State Legislature, and with a prospering tailor shop that no longer needed his direct supervision, Johnson announced himself a candidate for Congress. When the Democratic leadership indicated he was not their choice, he whipped them in line by promising to run anyway as an independent, thereby splitting the vote so that a Whig would get in. After the nomination was reluctantly given to him, the conservative Democrats sought to turn the tables by supporting his Whig opponent. Despite spirited opposition in successive campaigns by the redoubtable "Fighting Parson" W. G. Brownlow and others, Johnson served five years in the Congress, then became Governor, Senator, Governor again, then Vice President, President, and, finally, won another term as Senator. As a stump-speaker, he was the best Tennessee had, and one of the best the country has produced. He was indubitably crude, but he talked with a flailing directness the people liked to hear.

In Washington his modest quarters were crammed with books, and when he was not studying he would sit in the Senate listening to Clay, Webster, Calhoun, and Benton. In the House, he opposed John Quincy Adams on the petitions issue and declared that "if slavery must go by blood and war, let it come," winning from the crusty Sage the rare compliment that he was "possessed of great native ability."[7] In his first speeches he tried to develop an "Eastern style," as indicated in his support of the bill admitting Texas to the Union: "Uncle Sam with the Stars and Stripes in his right hand was seen approaching in the distance, and, as he drew near the hymeneal altar, Texas, the interesting young virgin of the South, was seen leaning on his arm, the ring of 'Annexation' on her finger; and the vows are said. Uncle Sam and Texas sit down to the marriage feast."[8]

However, his native manner soon reasserted itself, as did his inde-

[6] Winston, *op. cit.*, p. 32.
[7] John Quincy Adams, *Diary, op. cit.*, XII:240.
[8] Winston, *op. cit.*, p. 47.

pendence of spirit. Increasingly he found himself drawn into opposition to his Southern colleagues. In one debate, replying to a charge by Bayly of Virginia that he was an "ally" of the abolitionists, Johnson stormed: "The gentleman's scowls and threats have no terrors for me. He may go and show his slaves how choleric he is, and make his bondsmen tremble."[9] On another occasion, he rejected a Southern jibe at Northern intelligence by saying, "Why, in Pennsylvania only one person out of 122 is illiterate and unable to read and write, whereas in North Carolina one person out of four is illiterate."[10] Once he accused Jefferson Davis of belonging to "an illegitimate, swaggering, bastard, scrub aristocracy."[11] Always he opposed expenditures, most of which he thought "exhorbitant," arguing that the ideal country would have "a poor government but a rich people."[12] Perhaps his speeches displayed "sometimes a want of the usual niceties and proprieties of debate"[13]; but he was learning his own method, which was to research every topic thoroughly, make free use of facts, pinpoint the conclusion he wished to establish, and buttress his argument with frequent repetitions. His voice was rich and full-bodied and his volume had been developed to reach the outer edges of crowds gathered in the out-of-doors.

In the 1852 campaign for the Governorship, he engaged in a series of sixty debates with his Know-Nothing opponent, Meredith P. Gentry, "the best natural orator in Congress." His reckless courage was well illustrated in the first of these debates, at Murfreesboro, a Know-Nothing stronghold, where he was warned that he would be assassinated while he spoke. He pulled out a pistol as he mounted the platform, laid it on the table before him, and invited the would-be assassin to step forward and engage in a duel. Then in an unusually violent speech he denounced this anti-Catholic, anti-immigration, "America first" party in these terms: "Show me a Know-Nothing and I will show you a loathsome reptile, on whose neck every honest man should put his foot."[14] When he added, "Why, such a gang are little better than John A. Murrell's clan of outlaws," the audience, packed with Johnson's opponents, became "pale with rage and still as death." Cries of "It's a lie—it's a lie," rang out, and the clicking of hostile pistols could clearly be heard. Johnson paused, looked scornfully around, and continued his speech. Afterwards a committee of Democratic politicians called on him to insist that he conduct a safer and saner campaign, but Johnson snapped, "I will

[9] *Ibid.*, p. 49.
[10] *Ibid.*
[11] *Ibid.*, p. 50.
[12] *Ibid.*, p. 53.
[13] *Ibid.*, p. 56.
[14] *Ibid.*, pp. 70–72.

make that same speech tomorrow if it blows the Democratic Party to hell."[15] Such talk was typical of the man: sensible and moderate in principle, violent and without a shred of tact in manner.

In the campaign of 1856 Johnson supported Buchanan and made clear his stand on the great issues of slavery and secession: favoring the former and rejecting the latter. "Slavery exists," he thundered to the Nashville Convention. "It is black in the South, and white in the North, and it will continue to exist." As for States rights: "My own opinion is that the South has been engaged in compromises, as they are termed, long enough . . . . Our rights have all been compromised away. It is now time to stop."[16]

When he arrived in the Senate, however, he was equally repelled by the timidity of Buchanan and the secessionist sentiments of the Southern extremists. During the next crucial years he tried hard to define for himself the same position Lincoln was hewing out: defense of the constitutional rights of all the States; eventual emancipation of "the sable sons of Africa . . . from bondage to freedom;" and preservation of the territories as "free land for free labor."[17] Johnson's principal labor in the Congress was in behalf of the Homestead Act, which Lincoln was finally to sign into law. In 1858, debating the admission of Minnesota, he denied that "this government has the power to go inside a sovereign State and prescribe the qualifications of her voters at the ballot box." After the inflammatory raid by John Brown at Harpers Ferry, Johnson was the only Southern Senator to plead for moderation: "Because we cannot get our constitutional rights, I do not intend to be one of those who will violate the Constitution . . . . I intend to place myself on the Constitution, which I have sworn to support, and to stand there and battle for all its guarantees." In the 1860 campaign he worked hard for the election of Breckenridge; but after Lincoln won, he pleaded with the South to forebear secession and to keep their representatives in the Senate, where Lincoln "could not form his cabinet . . . he could not even appoint a first-class postmaster," without their concurrence.[18]

Buchanan's indecisiveness made the position of moderation hard to maintain. On December 4, 1860, Buchanan averred that South Carolina's grievances justified her secession, although under the Constitution no State had a right to secede nor did the Federal Government have the right to prevent secession.[19] The die was cast for war when, on De-

[15] Greeneville *Sun*, Feb. 23, 1911.
[16] Andrew Johnson, *Political Issues of the Day*, July 15, 1856, pamphlet, in Tennessee State Library.
[17] Winston, *op. cit.*, p. 135.
[18] *Ibid.*, pp. 164–167.
[19] Klein, *President James Buchanan, op. cit.*, pp. 361–363.

cember 14, the Southern Senators and Congressmen issued an *Address to the People of the South*, in which they said: "All hope of relief in the Union is extinguished. The honor, safety and independence of the Southern people require the organization of a Southern Confederacy." Senator Crittenden of Kentucky proposed a series of compromise measures which were rejected by a vote of twenty (all Republicans) to nineteen (all Democrats).[20]

On December 18 Johnson commenced a two-day speech which, in the view of A. H. Stephens of Georgia, was "the most masterly effort ever delivered by man on earth." Johnson's proposal was to "equalize" the power of North and South: by prescribing that either the President or Vice President must always be a Southerner; by apportioning half the membership of the Supreme Court to the South; and by having U.S. Senators elected directly by the people. To his Southern colleagues Johnson said: "If this doctrine of secession is carried out upon the mere whim of the State, this government is at an end." He further argued that "The continuance of slavery depends upon the preservation of the Union"—a cue Stephens picked up and incorporated in his subsequent speech to the Legislature of Georgia. Speaking for his own constituents, Johnson said: "We do not intend that you shall drive us out of this house that was reared by the hands of our fathers." He agreed with Buchanan's view that the Federal Government had no power to coerce a State; but he said it could and should enforce its laws "upon individuals within the limits of each State."[21] The speech won no votes in the Senate; but an admirer declared it made Johnson the most popular man in the North except for Lincoln; and Alexander H. Stephens rendered the more sober judgment that it dissuaded the border States from seceding.

In a last desperate effort to undo the secession that was already occurring, delegates from most of the States met informally at a convention in the Willard Hotel in Washington, still working for a compromise solution.[22] And, as all these pleas failed, on March 2, 1861, Johnson issued his own personal declaration of war against the secessionists: "Were I the President of the United States . . . I would have them arrested and tried for treason; and if convicted, by the Eternal God, I would see that they suffer the penalty of the law at the hands of

[20] Commager, *Documents of American History*, op. cit., I:369–371. Cf. Walter Ray Fisher, "An Analysis of the Arguments in the Senate Debate on the Crittenden Compromise Resolutions, 1860–61," unpublished Ph.D. thesis, University of Iowa, 1960.
[21] Frank Moore, *Life and Speeches of Andrew Johnson*, Boston, 1865.
[22] Robert Gray Gunderson, *Old Gentlemen's Convention: The Washington Peace Conference of 1861*, Madison: University of Wisconsin Press, 1961.

the executioner."[23] Then, with his habitual bravado, he set out for Tennessee via Virginia—saved en route from being lynched by a protective screen of Southern troops operating under Jefferson Davis's orders. Back home Johnson was cheered by his mountaineer followers, but he had to be hustled out of the State to save him from more lynch mobs. On March 2, 1862, he yielded to Lincoln's plea to resign his Senate seat and become Military Governor of Tennessee, to clear it of secessionists and keep it loyal.

This is the record that led Lincoln to select Johnson as his running mate in 1864, when he was desperately in need of every vote he could get. In this campaign Lincoln laid down his policy that since secession was illegal every Southern State would be qualified to resume its role in the national government as soon as one-tenth of its voters concurred in a suitable State Constitution; and he promised amnesty to every Confederate who laid down his arms. Johnson heartily concurred. But the Congressional Radicals, led by Thaddeus Stevens, were quietly resolving "to suppress by arms armed rebellion, and leave political reorganization to Congress."

To these formidable opponents, Andrew Johnson delivered himself bound and powerless. The travesty of his inauguration as Vice President has been often described. Suffering from illness, he tried to strengthen himself with whiskey; and under the combined influences of weakness and over-stimulation, in the Senate chamber, before taking his oath of office, he delivered "a rambling and strange harangue," in which he awkwardly expressed the mingling of humiliation and pride he had for so long felt as a border plebeian among men so greatly his superiors in education and gentility. To the Senators and Supreme Court members he cried, "[you] are but the creatures of the American people." To the assembled foreign diplomats he expressed scorn for "all your fine feathers and gewgaws." As for himself, "Humble as I am, plebeian as I may be deemed . . . I, though a plebeian boy, am authorized by the principles of the government under which I live to feel proudly conscious that I am a man, and grave dignitaries are but men." He concluded with a gratuitous challenge to Stevens and his Radical majority: "It is the doctrine of the Federal Constitution that no State can go out of this Union; and moreover, Congress cannot reject a State from this Union." Lincoln sat with his head bowed in humiliation; and as the assemblage arose to go out for the inaugural ceremony he whispered to the marshall, "Do not let Johnson speak outside."[24] Thus was the stage

---

[23] Winston, *op. cit.*, pp. 178–187. This speech led the New York *Times*, on March 4, 1861, to call Johnson "the greatest man of the age."
[24] Stryker, *op. cit.*, pp. 166–168; Winston, *op. cit.*, pp. 264–265.

set for the great battle over Reconstruction between Andrew Johnson and Thaddeus Stevens.

At ten o'clock on the morning of April 15 Johnson took the oath of office as President in his chambers and made a brief speech, hoping that the nation, "in passing through its present perils," would become "more permanent and enduring than heretofore." That very afternoon, as he knew, the Radicals were caucasing to decide on their own policies. In an effort to forestall a break with them, Johnson hastened on April 21 to define a position he hoped they would be unable to oppose: "Treason must be made odious . . . . traitors must be punished and impoverished, their social power must be destroyed . . . . I say, as to the leaders, punishment. I also say leniency, conciliation and amnesty to the thousands whom they have misled and deceived."[25] The Radicals moved slowly, cautiously; but by mid-October the storm was rising. Wendell Phillips exclaimed in Boston: "Andy Johnson may not be a traitor, but he is an enemy."[26] Thaddeus Stevens got from the Congress approval for his Joint Committee on Reconstruction. Then, with the power firmly in his hands, he sat back to await the struggle.

Open warfare commenced in February, 1866, when Johnson vetoed the Freedmen's Bill, which was designed to protect the rights of Negroes in the South. Unquestionably they needed protection. With "ineffable folly" several Southern States in 1865 adopted "black codes" designed to maintain slavery in effect even if it were lost in form.[27] Mississippi decreed that every Negro under eighteen must be apprenticed, preferably to his former owner; that all unemployed Negroes should be classed as vagrants and would have to work for whatever white man paid their fines; that no Negro could own any property except within an incorporated town; that no Negro could quit his job before his work contract expired; that no Negro could carry or possess arms; that every Negro must pay an annual poll tax or work for the man who paid it for him. Louisiana provided that if any Negro workman should feign illness, double the amount of his wages for time lost should be deducted. Alabama defined as a vagrant any Negro unemployed and any who were impudent or stubborn or who loitered while at work; it fixed the fine for vagrancy at $50 and decreed that a Negro must work for six months for any white man who paid his fine. South Carolina enforced apprenticeship, and denied to any Negro the right to be a shopkeeper, merchant, artisan, or skilled workman except after payment of an annual license of from $10 to $100. It also defined the workday for Negro field hands as

---

[25] Sherwin, *op. cit.*, p. 509.
[26] *National Antislavery Standard*, October 28, 1865.
[27] Commager, *Documents of American History*, *op. cit.*, II:2–7.

from sunrise to sunset, with the proviso that all chores such as care of animals and preparation of food must be done before or after the period of regular labor. Laws such as these naturally aroused resentment in the North; but Johnson viewed the Freedmen's Bill as an infringement on States rights and hence rejected it. Thaddeus Stevens retorted with a speech in the House on March 10 in which he called the President "an insolent drunken brute, in comparison with whom even Caligula's horse was respectable."[28]

In the 1866 elections Johnson carried his case for executive power to the people in a "swing round the circle," wherein he planned to deliver in successive cities a carefully written and moderate speech. But he was induced by hecklers to throw it aside and indulge in wild impromptu denunciations of the "enemies of the South." When the votes were tallied in November, the Radicals had a majority of 143 to 49 in the House and 42 to 11 in the Senate. Stevens convulsed the House with a madcap victory speech in which he said, "I was a Conservative in the last session of this Congress, but I mean to be a Radical henceforth." In January, when the new members took their seats, the House authorized committee investigation to determine whether Johnson had connived in Lincoln's assassination. Then the Congress adopted a "Tenure of Office" act, making it illegal for the President to dismiss Senate-approved officers without consent, and a law subjecting the South to virtual military government. Johnson reacted by summarily dismissing Edwin M. Stanton, Secretary of War, who long had been working openly with the Radicals in their efforts to embarrass and destroy him. On Monday, February 24, the House voted impeachment charges; but to make it appear that this patriotic act was performed on Washington's birthday the official clock in the House chamber was stopped so the vote was recorded in the *Journal* as February 22.

The impeachment trial opened in the Senate on March 4, with Chief Justice Salmon P. Chase presiding and with the indictment brought upon eleven articles. Proceedings were postponed till March 30 to grant time requested by the defense attorneys. "Butcher Ben" Butler opened for the prosecution, charging that in the "swing round the circle" the crudities of Johnson's speaking had lowered the dignity of the presidential office. Benjamin Curtis, opening for the defense on April 9, attempted to narrow the debate to the legal issues and insisted that Johnson could rightfully dismiss Stanton because the Secretary was a Lincoln appointee. Other speeches of attack and defense were heard from

[28] Howard Kennedy Beale, *The Critical Year*, New York: Harcourt Brace, 1930, p. 371.

George S. Boutwell, Thomas Nelson, and William Groesback. Then the stars appeared for the closing arguments. Thaddeus Stevens pinpointed the real issue—that "the great crime of Andrew Johnson" was "to set up his own will against that of the law-making power." William Evarts then spoke for the defense in a speech enlivened with wit and satire. The concluding plea for Johnson was a burst of eloquence by Henry Stanberry, who said: if "your votes have been canvassed and the doom of the President is sealed, then let the judgment not be pronounced in this Senate chamber . . . where he fought the good fight for the Union and the Constitution . . . . Seek out rather the darkest and gloomiest chamber in the subterranean recesses of this Capitol, where the cheerful light of day never enters. There erect the altar and immolate the victim."[29]

"Conviction almost a Certainty," headlined the New York *Tribune* on April 22. At the African Methodist Episcopal Church General Conference, meeting in Washington, the Reverend Sampson Jones was reported to have prayed that "de Lord would stiffen wid de grace of fortitude de doubtful backbone of de wavering Senators, and dat Andrew Johnson, de demented Moses of Tennessee, would be removed by de sanctimonious voice of de Senate to where de wicked cease from troublin' and de weary am at rest." The impeachment failed by a single vote, with Republican Edmund Ross of Kansas the key factor in swinging the scales to acquittal.[30]

Seven years later, after several attempts, following an attack of cholera that almost killed him and left him shaken in health, Johnson won a kind of final exoneration in being again elected to the Senate, after a blistering campaign that took him into every part of the State. His margin of victory in the legislature was just one vote, achieved on the fifty-fourth ballot. On March 22, 1875, he made a last speech in the Senate, denouncing the "gigantic fraud" of military rule of the South. Then he went home, to die on July 31.

As an individual he was crude, rough, honest, and direct. As a frontiersman, he was loud, boisterous, personal in attack, exaggerated in statement, tactless, bombastic, and given to impromptu and impetuous outbursts. As a representative of the border, he veered and tacked backward and forward between the positions represented by North and South, generally favoring the former on legal issues and the latter in emotionalized loyalties.

[29] David Miller DeWitt, *Impeachment and Trial of Andrew Johnson*, New York: Macmillan, 1903.
[30] John Fitzgerald Kennedy, *Profiles in Courage*, New York: Harper, 1956, pp. 126–151.

Revenge, Reaction, and Reform: Harrison, Conkling, and Ingersoll

IF THE impeachment trial of Andrew Johnson was a dramatic anti-climax to the sectional struggle, the bitterness nevertheless lingered on. Opportunistic Republican politicians did their best to squeeze the last drop of advantage out of the military conflict with "bloody shirt" campaigning. Public office came to seem less a sacred trust to champion human freedom, or the integrity of the Union, or States rights. More and more political power became a prize measurable in dollars: redeemable in patronage, in differential taxation, and in class legislation. Politics came to be defined as the science of compromise and unwavering adherence to principle to be denounced as stubborn lack of realism. Pandering for votes emerged out of the shadows into respectability. Political oratory came increasingly to emphasize "giving the people what they want."[1]

Yet, unsavory as the combination was, genuine expertness in the operation of large-scale democracy also developed. The tight little aristocracy envisioned by the makers of the Constitution evolved into a universal-suffrage, representative, popular government. Liberty became of less moment than equality. Liberalism departed from its Jeffersonian base to favor big government that would be strong enough to control big business. A new reform movement arose that foreswore the "perfectionism" of the 1830's and fought instead for practical advantages for women, factory workers, and the consuming public. A new professionalism of the platform emerged, with "word wizardry" practiced by such men as Robert Green Ingersoll, Chauncey Depew, and Russell Conwell, and with lecturing, like politics, becoming big business. Such professional politicians as Roscoe Conkling, James G. Blaine, and Benjamin Harrison became dominant figures on the American scene.

Benjamin Harrison is less important in the history of American oratory as an individual than as the exemplar of a type. In outward appear-

---

[1] What the people wanted as their presidential candidate came to be stereotyped in terms of comfortable mediocrity, in the opinion of a historian who specialized in the analysis of campaign biographies. The "ideal" candidate of this period was described as follows: "As he sits before the hearth of his own unpretentious home awaiting the verdict of the people, one sees a plain, simple man of modest means, surrounded by a dutiful wife and adoring children; a man of practical good sense and boundless energy, a man of deep but unostentatious piety, of impeccable moral character, and of sturdy republican virtue." William Burlie Brown, *The People's Choice: The Presidential Image in the Campaign Biography*, Baton Rouge: Louisiana State University Press, 1960, p. 145.

ance he was the acme of ultra-respectability: descendant of a signer of the Declaration of Independence, grandson of a President, a Hoosier lawyer, always neat of garb, carefully groomed, bearded, courteous, comfortably corpulent, restrained in gesture, with a voice that was strong and resonant, given to an extemporaneous flow of grammatical and clear but not particularly vivid speech.[2] Beneath the respectable surface boiled a mixture of rancor and personal ambition, vented through shrewd skill in exploiting the revenge motive as a means of winning votes.

He was far from being alone in this genre of political oratory. The "bloody shirt" was dominant in national campaigning from 1866 through 1880, and often appeared even after that.[3] The classic statement of the theme was spoken in Harrison's own Indianapolis, on September 21, 1876, and although Harrison was in the audience rather than on the platform, he could take credit for having prepared the way for it. It was Robert Ingersoll's frank, friendly face and generously outflung arms that lent support to the musical cadence of the voice that said:

> Every State that seceded from the Union was a Democratic State. Every ordinance of Secession that was drawn was drawn by a Democrat. Every man that endeavored to tear the old flag from the heaven it enriches was a Democrat . . . . Every man that shot down Union soldiers was a Democrat . . . . The man that assassinated Abraham Lincoln was a Democrat. Every man that raised bloodhounds to pursue human beings was a Democrat. Every man that clutched from shrinking, shuddering, crouching mothers the babes from their breasts, and sold them into slavery was a Democrat . . . . Every man that tried to spread smallpox and yellow fever in the North . . . was a Democrat. Soldiers, every scar, every arm that is missing, every limb that is gone, is the souvenir of a Democrat . . . . Yes, the question is, "Shall the solid South, a unified South, unified by assassination and murder, a South solidified by the shotgun—shall the solid South with the aid of a divided North control this great and splendid country?"[4]

Harrison never produced so scintillating a passage. But it was not from want of trying. On June 16, 1865, speaking at a reception in Indianapolis for returning veterans, he said with significant emphasis: "We mean to be felt in politics as well as business."[5] Harrison was

[2] Harry J. Sievers, *Benjamin Harrison*, I: *Hoosier Warrior*, and II: *Hoosier Statesman*, New York: University Publishers, 1959; and Charles Hedges, ed., *Speeches of Benjamin Harrison*, New York: United States Book Co., 1892.
[3] Stanley C. Hirshson, *Farewell to the Bloody Shirt*, Bloomington: Indiana University Press, 1962; and Paul H. Buck, *The Road to Reunion, 1865–1900*, Boston: Little, Brown, 1937.
[4] *The Works of Robert G. Ingersoll*, New York: Dresden Pub. Co., 1909–1911, Thirteen Vols., IX:157ff.
[5] Sievers, *op. cit.*, I:315.

bitter and in this speech he made no effort to conceal the fact. As a Brigadier General he had led his troops through campaigns in which twenty percent were killed and an equal number wounded. He came home to find that many who escaped participation in the war had become rich through profiteering. The homesteads of many veterans had been seized through mortgage foreclosures "by hardhearted grasping men." Even worse villains were the Southerners, "mean, impudent, and devilish," as he called them in a speech on August 12, who "if they can, will sneak in upon you while you sleep, and steal away the fruits of this bloody contest."[6] Quickly, then, he made his point: the identification of the Democratic Party with secession and treason. "Now when we are rejoicing in victory," he urged, "tell them that this is not their day." If Hoosier Democrats pretend to be loyal members of the community, "don't believe them. They would rather you had been buried beneath four feet of rebel soil." Then he spelled out the theme he was to make his principal bid for political power: "Keep them and their Northern allies out of power. If you don't, they will steal away, in the halls of Congress, the fruits won from them at the glistening point of the bayonet."[7]

These two speeches helped establish Harrison as a leading spokesman for the veterans associations—a role he continued to play assiduously all the rest of his life. In the fall of 1867 he campaigned steadily, branding Democratic policies as "treasonable schemes." Then he concentrated on the practice of law, quickly emerging into the forefront of the profession. In 1872 he failed in a bid for the gubernatorial nomination, although he delighted the Republican Convention with a speech identifying the Ku Klux Klan midnight raiders as "barbarian Democrats." At this time he was described as "a quiet, undemonstrative man," who walked with "an erect military bearing, head high," and who "often passed friends on the street without seeing them."[8] In 1876, drafted at the last moment as candidate for Governor, he said of the Democratic opposition: "Is it not a shame that these fellows, coming right out of the rebel Congresses and blood-stained rebel armies, should go into a political convention and proclaim themselves custodians of the nation's honor?"[9] As the campaign continued through September, he told his audiences: "For one, I accept the banner of the bloody shirt. I am willing to take as our ensign the tattered, worn-out, old gray shirt, worn by some gallant Union hero, stained with his blood as he gave his life for his country . . . . When they purge their party of the leprosy of seces-

6 *Ibid.*, II:13.
7 *Ibid.*, II:14.
8 *Ibid.*, II:63.
9 *Ibid.*, II:114.

sion . . . we will bury the 'bloody shirt' in the grave of the honored corpse who wore it, and not before."[10] Again: "I would rather march by your side on the dusty road under the dear flag of our Union and wear the old army shirt stained with drops of blood, than to do service under the black banner of treason."[11]

The voters of Indiana demanded both more and less than he was giving them. In the private polling booths Harrison was defeated by 6000 votes—in the same election in which Tilden became the first Democrat after the war to win a popular majority, although he failed of election in the politically controlled Electoral College.

In 1878, on June 5, Harrison sought to broaden his appeal through emphasis on sound money and support for big business, saying: "Capital is a timid bird, and seeks close shelter in times when the elements are disturbed."[12] Finally, in 1881, after fifteen years of effort, he won his first major election: to the United States Senate. Then he reverted wholeheartedly to his major theme. Speaking in the Des Moines Opera House on September 21, 1883, he noted that he had been accused of "bloody-shirtism," and declared: "Yes, the bloody shirt again! I have seen thousands of them on the field of battle wet with the blood of loyal men—and I would a thousand times rather march under the bloody shirt, stained with the life-blood of a Union soldier, than to march under the black flag of treason or the white flag of cowardly compromise."[13] A year later, in Chicago, he was urging: ". . . for the sake of the old Flag, for the sake of those brave boys that we put to everlasting sleep in their narrow beds in the South, I beg of you to give the vote of Indiana to the men who stood by the country."[14] Again, in the campaign against Cleveland, now at last with himself as the Republican nominee for President, he told another Chicago audience twenty three years after Appomattox: "We took the ship of state when there was treachery at the helm, when there was mutiny on the deck, when the ship was among the rocks"—that is to say, during Cleveland's first term—"and we put loyalty at the helm."[15]

From July 7 to October 25, Harrison waged a "front-porch campaign," remaining at home to give over eighty extemporaneous talks to crowds of visitors totalling some 300,000. Occasionally he discussed economics, aligning himself with big business and demanding a high tariff. "It is quite as illogical to despise a man because he is rich as because he

[10] *Ibid.*, II:117.
[11] *Ibid.*
[12] *Ibid.*, II:154.
[13] *Ibid.*, II:231.
[14] *Ibid.*, II:259.
[15] Hedges, *op. cit.*, p. 20.

is poor," he said.[16] But once again he shifted easily from economics to the intriguing theme of the Civil War. "My countrymen, it is no time now to use an apothecary's scales to weigh the rewards of the men who saved the country."[17] Cleveland won a plurality of ninety thousand votes; but Harrison carried the Electoral College 233 to 168.

His final success in achieving his ambition marked the end of his career in oratory. As he said in a farewell address to friends in Indianapolis, as he left for his inauguration: "There is a great sense of loneliness in the discharge of high public duties. The moment of decision is one of isolation."[18] The enemy of the South now had become the President of all the people. He served without distinction; but at least he performed his functions quietly. The era of the bloody shirt finally came to a close.

Politics, meanwhile, washed into public prominence three New Yorkers, Thurlow Weed, Richard Croker, and Roscoe Conkling, who each won dubious distinction by making political bossism a distinctive feature of American democracy. Of the three, Conkling was the only with the oratorical power to carry his own banner into the forefront of the political battles.[19] Born October 30, 1829, son of a prominent judge in Utica, Conkling began serious speechmaking by the age of eighteen, often indulging in four-hour addresses as he whipped up enthusiasm for Seward's Whigs. He was a tall, handsome man, standing six feet three inches, with wavy reddish blond hair and a full red beard. He spoke slowly and meticulously, delivering carefully memorized speeches. Far from being a back-slapper, he was solitary, vain, suspicious, disliked people who smoked, and "seemed to consider all men who differed with him as enemies of the human race."[20] His political success derived from his tremendous ability to sway audiences, which he demonstrated on the platform and at the bar, and in an infinite capacity for hard work. His political views were narrowly nationalistic, conservative, and jingoistic.

He favored a high tariff because, as he said in 1852, "America cannot, and, for one, I trust God she will never, sink so low in wretchedness that she can compete unaided in cheapness of products with the pauper labor of England."[21] In his view, American slavery was "one of the blackest and bloodiest pictures in the book of modern times," yet in

[16] Sievers, *op. cit.*, II:379–380.
[17] Hedges, *op. cit.*, p. 71.
[18] *Ibid.*, p. 191.
[19] "Behind these titular leaders [the Presidents of the Reconstruction era] were the real rulers . . . . At the head of the ranks of those who really ran the country were great bosses like Conkling . . ." Morison and Commager, *Growth of the American Republic*, *op. cit.*, II:216. Cf. Max Lerner, *America as a Civilization*, *op. cit.*, p. 313.
[20] Donald Barr Chidsey, *The Gentleman from New York: A Life of Roscoe Conkling*, New Haven: Yale University Press, 1935, p. 6.
[21] *Ibid.*, pp. 9–10.

comparison with English wage slavery, it "is as much to be preferred as the Christian religion is preferable to the dark idolatry of chance."[22] In 1866, while in the House of Representatives, he aligned himself with Thaddeus Stevens and took up with gusto the theme of the bloody shirt. "Are you ready," he asked "after staggering through four years of agony, to fool away and give away for nothing all you have struggled for the moment you have it in your grasp?" Better "that the cripples should have time to limp back to their homes, that the inky cloak should begin to disappear before the authors of our woes come back into the presence of their surviving victims."[23] In 1872, on August 20, speaking to a veterans meeting in Utica, he thundered: "The worst elements of the Rebellion, which failed in war, now creep and prowl in the stealthy path of politics."[24]

With good family connections, a wonderfully attractive physique, and a vastly superior intellect which was narrowly concentrated on personal success, Conkling sprang as a youth into instant prominence. Six months before his twenty-first birthday he won election as District Attorney. From the age of sixteen he was prominent in Whig, then in Republican, conventions—always seizing the spotlight with bold and calculatingly practical speeches. His single-mindedness was amazing. For hours upon end he studied the orations of Chatham, Burke, Pitt, Fox, Erskine, Grattan, and Mansfield, and he learned by heart long passages from the Bible, Shakespeare, Milton, and Macaulay. He strengthened his political position by marrying the sister of the powerful Governor of New York, Horatio Seymour. And he established a reputation for cold and remorseless political management, never forgiving an adverse vote, never failing to mete out carefully measured rewards for support. Without a shred of humor, or softness, or sentiment, he won advancement through ability and by inspiring fear of reprisal among those who might oppose him. In 1857, at the age of twenty eight, he was handpicked in a smoke-filled room for election to Congress. There he allied himself with the Radical Republicans but maintained an aloof independence. In 1861, trying to avoid the war, he voted for the Crittenden Compromise; for, as he said in a speech on January 30, "War is no longer a question of personal valor or individual prowess; but a mere question of money—a question of who can throw the most projectiles, who can indulge in the most iron and lead."[25]

[22] Alfred R. Conkling, The Life and Letters of Roscoe Conkling: Orator, Statesman, Advocate, New York: Charles L. Webster Co., 1889, p. 30.
[23] From a speech at Utica, in Conkling, op. cit., p. 277.
[24] Hirshson, Farewell to the Bloody Shirt, op. cit., cf. Bowers, Tragic Era, op. cit., pp. 388–389.
[25] Chidsey, op. cit., p. 27.

On April 24, 1866, a savage encounter occurred between Conkling and James G. Blaine, dramatizing a personal conflict that eventually kept Blaine out of the White House. Blaine made the mistake of underestimating Conkling and ridiculed him for his "turkey gobbler strut." Then the Maine politician rushed on to say that Conkling compared to the late Senator Winter Davis as "Hyperion to a satyr, Thersites to Hercules, mud to marble, dunghill to diamond, a singed cat to a Bengal tiger, a whining puppy to a roaring lion."[26] Conkling said little in reply, but years later he was revenged in being able to weigh the scales against Blaine's election as President.

When General Grant became President, Roscoe Conkling, the calculating politician, was his choice as chief dispenser of federal patronage. For eight years Conkling was the most powerful political figure in America. Then came 1880, and Conkling determined to try to break the tradition against a third term. Blaine was the opposing candidate for the nomination, and Conkling was selected to place Grant's name in nomination. His speech was a meticulously moulded eulogy, so replete with emotionalism that "men babbled and gibbered about it for years afterward."[27] "Standing on the highest eminence of human distinction," Conkling said, "modest, firm, simple and self-poised . . . the name of Grant will glitter a bright and imperishable star in the diadem of the republic when those who have tried to tarnish the name have moldered in forgotten graves and their epitaphs have vanished utterly."[28] The speech resulted in a wild outburst of enthusiasm—but it shifted few if any votes. Blaine was blocked, but so was Grant; and what Conkling contemptuously called "the angle-worm nomination" finally went to James A. Garfield, who was not even a candidate but had come to the convention as manager for General John Sherman. In an attempt to mollify Conkling, the vice-presidential nomination was given to a New Yorker, Chester A. Arthur—and Conkling promptly set about rebuilding his political alliance by going on a fishing trip with Arthur.

During the campaign Conkling spoke little and late, damning Garfield with faint praise. Now that his patronage control was ending, he proved to have few friends and little influence; and his chosen nominee for the Senate from New York was defeated by Chauncey Depew.[29] A

[26] *Ibid.*, p. 91. Chidsey devotes two chapters (pp. 72–92) to this quarrel; Conkling, *op. cit.*, passes it by without mention. Biography, it appears, is what the biographers make of it.
[27] Chidsey, *op. cit.*, p. 287. Conkling presents the full text of the speech, *op. cit.*, pp. 596–600, together with several encomiums on it, pp. 600–603.
[28] Conkling, *op. cit.*, pp. 597–598.
[29] Defeat by Depew—one of the several men Conkling especially hated—was a grievous blow. Depew summed up his opinion of Conkling as follows: "Roscoe Conkling was created by nature for a great career. That he missed it was entirely his

great outpouring of public illwill against Conkling was unleashed when the assassin of President Garfield was found to have in his pocket a copy of an editorial denouncing Garfield for alleged unfair treatment of Conkling. Editorials and thousands of threatening letters accused Conkling of having plotted the murder of Garfield. Chester Arthur drew away from Conkling and the political prize of patronage-dispenser was denied him.

The end of his career was at hand. In July, 1885, when Conkling's friend, Oliver P. Morton, died, Conkling delivered a eulogy in the Senate chamber, saying: "Death is nature's supreme abhorrence. The dark valley, with its weird and solemn shadows . . . is still the ground which man shudders to approach. The grim portals and the narrow house seem in the lapse of centuries to have gained rather than lost in impressive and foreboding horror."[30] Less than a year later, on April 17, the "grim portals" opened for Roscoe Conkling. Colonel Robert Ingersoll spoke his epitaph: "He would not turn aside to avoid a foe—to greet or gain a friend . . . . He had the pose of the great statues—the pride and bearing of the intellectual Greek, of the conquering Roman, and he stood in the wide free air, as though within his veins there flowed the blood of a hundred kings . . . . Proudly he entered the darkness, or the dawn, that we call death."[31]

It cannot be without significance that Ingersoll delivered so overcharged a eulogy of such a man as Roscoe Conkling; nor that he established another record for extravagant praise in his nomination for the presidency of such a run-of-the-mill politician as James G. Blaine; nor that he could and did say of William Jennings Bryan that "His brain is an insane asylum without a keeper"[32]—and of Samuel J. Tilden that "He never gave birth to an elevated, noble sentiment in his life. He is a kind of legal spider, watching in a web of technicalities for victims. He is a compound of cunning and heartlessness—of beak and claw and fang."[33] It is alongside such verbal irresponsibilities as these that we should place his equally sensational commentaries on orthodox religion, such as: "This dogma of hell is the infinite of savagery—the dream of

---

own fault. Physically he was the handsomest man of his time. His mental equipment nearly approached genius. He was industrious to a degree. His oratorical gifts were of the highest order, and he was a debater of rare power and resources. But his intolerable egotism deprived him of vision necessary for supreme leadership. With all his oratorical power and his talent in debate, he made little impression upon the country and none upon posterity." Depew, *My Memories of Eighty Years, op. cit.,* p. 79.

[30] Chidsey, *op. cit.,* p. 379.
[31] Ingersoll, *Works, op. cit.,* XIII:437ff.
[32] *Ibid.,* IX:575.
[33] *Ibid.,* IX:114.

insane revenge. It makes God a wild beast, an infinite hyena. It makes Christ as merciless as the fangs of a viper."[34] For another example, consider this passage from an 1882 lecture on "Talmagian Theology," which Ingersoll's most judicious biographer considers "Ingersoll at his best."[35] Commenting on the eminently respectable De Witt Talmage, in a three-hour lecture that kept its New York audience "alternating between shouts of laughter and bursts of applause," the orator said:

> Some ministers think he has more gesticulation than grace. Some call him a pious pantaloon, a Christian clown, but such remarks, I think, are born of envy. He is the only Presbyterian minister in the United States that can draw an audience . . . . He believes in a literal resurrection of the dead, that we shall see countless bones flying through the air . . . . I am charged, too, with saying that the sun was not made till the fourth day, whereas, according to the Bible, vegetation began on the third day, before there was any light. But Mr. Talmage says there was light without the sun. They got light, he says, from the crystallization of rocks. A nice thing to raise a corn crop by! There may have been volcanoes, he says. How'd you like to farm it, and depend on volcanic glare to raise a crop? That's what they call religious science . . .[36]

More than any other American orator, more even than Edward Everett, Robert Green Ingersoll seems in retrospect to have been a necromancer whose forte was the weaving of spells with words. In his command of language and in the mesmeric effects he produced upon audiences he has to be accounted a great orator. Yet his ultimate reputation seems ephemeral and somewhat comparable to that of his contemporary, the great showman, P. T. Barnum. This is not to say that Ingersoll was a fakir. Rather, he enjoyed word wizardry for its own sake. He was an artist who revelled in his own art.

The encomiums he won from distinguished contemporaries have seldom been surpassed for unrestrained admiration. Walt Whitman exclaimed: "That is a grand brow: and the face—look at the face—see the mouth; it is the head, the face, the poise, of a noble human being. America don't know how proud she ought to be of Ingersoll."[37] To

---

[34] Quoted by Wayland Maxfield Parrish and Alfred Dwight Huston, "Robert G. Ingersoll," in Brigance, ed., History and Criticism, op. cit., I:377. More typical, of course, of what Ingersoll meant to say about Christianity is this, from his lecture on "Skulls": "Orthodoxy is the night of the past, full of the darkness of superstition, and heresy is the eternal coming day, the light of which strikes the grand foreheads of the intellectual pioneers of the world." Printed in Mistakes of Ingersoll and His Answers, ed. J. B. McClure, Chicago: Rhodes and McClure, 1879, II:108.
[35] Orvin Larson, American Infidel: Robert G. Ingersoll, New York: Citadel Press, 1962, p. 171.
[36] Ibid., p. 172.
[37] Horace Traubel, With Walt Whitman in Camden, New York: Appleton, 1908, I:37.

Chauncey Depew he was "one of the greatest intellects of the century."[38] Henry Ward Beecher thought him "the most brilliant speaker of the English tongue of all men on this globe."[39] Mark Twain, too, was attracted principally by Ingersoll's verbal brilliance, calling his 1879 after-dinner eulogy of General Grant "the supremest combination of English words that was ever put together since the world began."[40] To Professors Wayland Maxfield Parrish and Alfred Dwight Huston it appeared that "For more than twenty years Robert G. Ingersoll stood in the top rank of American speakers as lecturer, lawyer, political campaigner, and speaker of occasional addresses."[41] His reputation stretched far beyond the magnitude of his worth.

Aside from and transcending politics, the law, and all other topics, Ingersoll was known in his own time and remembered in ours chiefly for his lifelong campaign to liberate the minds of his countrymen from the superstitions and fears that were then generally associated with religion. The home in which he grew up was devout. A regular parishioner of the Reverend John Ingersoll, the orator's father and a Congregational minister, said of him in 1836, when Robert Green was just three years old, that "He made salvation seem so plain, so easy, I wanted to take it to my heart without delay."[42] His mother Mary believed implicitly every word of the Old and New Testaments and almost as devoutly in the sermons of Jonathan Edwards.[43] Ingersoll's own recollection of his youthful home religious influence was dismal. Concerning his father, he said that "he had one misfortune and that was his religion. He believed the Bible, and in the shadow of that frightful book he passed his life."[44] His remembrance of Sunday observance was: "Nobody said a pleasant word; nobody laughed; nobody smiled; the child that looked the sickest was regarded as the most pious. That night you could not even crack hickory nuts."[45] The church to him was a bleak and cheerless place, for "It was thought to be a kind of sin to be comfortable while you were thanking God."[46] All his life he recalled an illustration heard in his youth of how long sinners would roast in hell:

---

[38] Quoted in Ingersoll, *Works, op. cit.*, XI:505. Elsewhere Depew calls him "one of the greatest orators of his generation." *My Memories of Eighty Years, op. cit.*, p. 319.
[39] Quoted by I. Newton Baker, *An Intimate View of Robert G. Ingersoll*, New York: C. P. Farrell, 1920, p. 34.
[40] Twain's best tribute to Ingersoll, in anecdotal form, too long to quote, in *The Autobiography of Mark Twain*, ed. Charles Neider, New York: Harper, 1959, pp. 243–244.
[41] Parrish and Huston, *op. cit.*, I:363.
[42] Cameron Rogers, *Colonel Bob Ingersoll*, New York: Doubleday, Page, 1927, p. 10.
[43] *Ibid.*, p. 4.
[44] *Ibid.*, p. 108.
[45] Ingersoll, *Works, op. cit.*, I:377.
[46] *Ibid.*

Suppose that once in a billion years a bird should come from some far-distant planet, and carry off in its little bill a grain of sand, a time would finally come when the last atom composing this earth would be carried away; and when this last atom was taken, it would not even be sun-up in hell.[47]

Early impressions are difficult to erase and as late as 1865, in a speech to the 86th Regiment, Ingersoll was still addressing "the Infinite" and giving thanks for "the spires of our churches," which still "point to the skies."[48] Even later, in a eulogy spoken at the grave of a child, he said, "I wish I could take from every grave its fear." And in the funeral service he conducted for his favorite brother he needed for himself the religious solace he tried to deny to others. "We strive in vain to look beyond the heights," he said, " . . . but in the night of death hope sees a star, and listening love can hear the rustle of a wing."[49]

However, in 1869 he tentatively tried out an anticlerical lecture, "Humboldt," and when it went well he prepared another on "Thomas Paine," then, more confidently, a bold series on "The Gods," "Individuality," "Heretics and Heresies," "Skulls," "Hell," and "Some Mistakes of Moses." The sincerity of Ingersoll's conviction that the mind of man must be liberated from the awful fear of hell is unquestionable. As an orator, however, he was a craftsman rather than a seer or a prophet. It is noteworthy that he is the first great speaker after Emerson and Phillips to prepare lectures which he "used" to fulfill a planned series of paid engagements. His attitude toward the business of lecturing is illuminated by an incident in 1895, when his fame was unshakably established so that any audience would listen to him on his own terms. Before going to Indianapolis to fill a lecture date on March 28, he had his agent distribute six hundred ballots to representative citizens to determine which of his lecture topics was the most popular. The results were: "About the Holy Bible," 270 votes; "Shakespeare," 65; "The Gods," 55.[50] To a man of Ingersoll's courageously independent spirit, "give 'em what they want" would not seem to be an applicable governing principle; but it had become a mark of the times.

To Newton Baker, an ardent admirer, "He was not a phrase-tinker or a word-carpenter." Yet Baker disingenuously added: "No matter what the theme, his tongue responded to his thought in instant and perfect epigram, illustration, simile, or metaphor."[51] Two principal influences in shaping his style of thought and expression were Shakespeare and

[47] Larson, *op. cit.*, p. 19.
[48] C. H. Cramer, *Royal Bob: The Life of Robert G. Ingersoll*, Indianapolis: Bobbs-Merrill, 1952, p. 72.
[49] Ingersoll, *Works*, *op. cit.*, XII:390–391.
[50] Larson, *op. cit.*, p. 250.
[51] Baker, *op. cit.*, p. 48.

Robert Burns. Of Burns, "The first man to let up a curtain in my mind," he said in a Lotos Club speech in 1895:

> Burns, you know, is a little valley, not very wide, but full of sunshine; a little stream runs down it making music over the rocks, and children play upon the banks; narrow roads overrun with vines, covered with blossoms, happy children, the hum of bees, and little birds pour out their hearts and enrich the air. That is Burns.[52]

And of Shakespeare: "Other writers are like a garden diligently planted and watered, but Shakespeare is a forest where the oaks and elms toss their branches to the storm, where the pine towers."[53] Such passages, and there are many in his lectures, show a pictorial imagination; but they contribute less to an understanding of the subject than to the admiration felt for the felicity of the phrasing.

Perhaps his famous ironic commentary on Napoleon indeed depicted the essence of a judgment, however embroidered with conscious decoration:

> I thought of the orphans and widows he had made—of the tears that had been shed for his glory, and of the only woman who ever loved him, pushed from his heart by the cold hand of ambition. And I said I would rather have been a French peasant and worn wooden shoes. I would rather have lived in a hut with a vine growing over the door, and the grapes growing purple in the kisses of the autumn sun. I would rather have been that poor peasant with my loving wife by my side, knitting as the day died out of the sky—with my children upon my knees and their arms about me—I would rather have been that man and gone down to the tongueless silence of the dreamless dust, than to have been that imperial impersonation of force and murder, known as "Napoleon the Great."[54]

Much this same imagery was re-used in a mood of ridicule, in his last political speech, delivered October 29, 1896, to try to distract public attention from William Jennings Bryan's campaign demands for reform of the currency. To an audience in New York's Carnegie Music Hall he said:

> Here is a man buys a little piece of linen for twenty-five cents, he buys a few paints for fifteen cents, and a few brushes, and he paints a picture; just a little one: a picture, maybe, of a cottage with a dear old woman, white hair, serene forehead and satisfied eyes; at the corner a few hollyhocks in bloom—maybe a tree in blossom, and as you listen you seem to hear the songs of birds—the hum of bees, and your child-

---

[52] Cramer, *op. cit.*, pp. 28–29.
[53] Ingersoll, *Works*, *op. cit.*, XII:172.
[54] From "Skulls," in McClure, *Mistakes of Ingersoll*, *op. cit.*, II:121–122.

hood all comes back to you as you look . . . . Genius has done its work. And the little picture is worth five, ten, maybe fifty thousand dollars.[55]

His point seemed to be that politicians like Bryan should forget about the grubby subject of monetary reform and let the public center its attention upon the creative genius of nostalgic artists. It is evident, too, that he revelled in the admiration of listeners who gaped at his incredible ability to spin out pictorial imagery with seemingly endless and effortless ease.

Ingersoll was less a man of affairs who used speech to help him accomplish his aims than he was a speaker *sui generis*, a man who made a profession and (in its literal sense) a vocation of the platform. His official biographer pointed out that over a span of forty three years he lectured in "every town and city of any considerable size and importance" in the nation, plus many in Canada—except that, somehow, he missed North Carolina, Mississippi, the Indian Territory, and Oklahoma.[56] For this lecture career, he wrote out and memorized thirty lectures, which he presented again and again. He was a successful lawyer, yet his opinion of this career was that "I must make some money and get out of the law business."[57] Both his dedication and his skill are indicated in the account Larson gives of his preparation of the speech that propelled him into national fame, his nomination of Blaine. Ingersoll went to bed in his Indianapolis hotel room about midnight the night before his speech, having been reminded by his brother that the speech would be important and that he must prepare it. About three a.m., he awakened, got up and wrote out the speech on a large piece of brown wrapping paper, then calmly went back to sleep.

As for his power over an audience, few speakers have exceeded it. Concerning his nomination of Blaine, a newspaper said: "Words can do but meagre justice to the wizard power of this extraordinary man. He swayed and moved and impelled and restrained and worked, in all ways, with the mass before him, as if he possessed some key to the innermost mechanism that moves the human heart, and when he finished, his fine, frank face as calm as when he began, the overwrought thousands sank back in an exhaustion of unspeakable wonder and delight."[58]

As a rhetorician, he depended less upon reason or fact than on the sheer wizardry of words. Fighting against the rise of Populism, in October, 1893, he said: "Ah, there is no charity like business. Business gives

[55] Ingersoll, *Works, op. cit.,* IX:561.
[56] Ingersoll, *Works, op. cit.,* XIII:532.
[57] Cramer, *op. cit.,* p. 221.
[58] Chicago *Times,* June 16, 1876, quoted by Rogers, *op. cit.,* p. 204.

work to labor's countless hands; business wipes the tears from the eyes of widows and orphans; business dimples with joy the cheek of sorrow; business puts a roof above the heads of the homeless; business covers the land with happy homes."[59] In another retort to the Populists, he asked: "Why should we envy the rich? They never drank any colder water than I have . . . . They never saw any more glorious sunsets . . . . They never had any better weather in June."[60]

Ridicule was his frequent weapon, as when he quipped that the churches of Baptists needed no roof, and said their denominational slogan should be: "The wetter the better."[61] During his series of debates with DeWitt Talmage, when Talmage declared Ingersoll might have won the Governorship of Illinois if he were not an infidel, Ingersoll twisted the phraseology to represent Talmage as saying he should have concealed the fact of his infidelity; and then he developed the theme that the pulpits and the pews of the churches were filled with such hypocrites as Talmage assertedly wanted him to be. When a religious weekly charged that his only son went insane from reading cheap novels and died in an insane asylum, Ingersoll replied:

1. My only son was not a great novel reader;
2. He did not go insane;
3. He was not sent to an asylum;
4. He did not die; and
5. I never had a son![62]

Kittredge called his style "utterly unique" and believed that, "Should one of his marvellous pages, separated from its context, be found in the sands of Sahara, its author would be instantly recognizable."[63] James Redpath, perhaps recalling the ancient distinction between Asian and Attic style, called Ingersoll's "an Oriental style of rhetoric." Both the best and the worst of the Ingersollian style can be found in almost any of his lectures, for he apparently never sensed the difference between granite strength and tinselled decoration. In the "Mistakes of Moses," for example he said: "the sun wooed with amorous kiss the waves of the sea, and . . . their vaporous sighs changed to tears and fell again as rain." And in that same lecture he also said: "I want it so that every minister will be not a parrot, not an owl sitting upon a dead limb of the tree of knowledge and hooting the hoots that have been hooted for eighteen hundred years." In it he posed the challenge: "Are we to get to

[59] Ingersoll, *Works, op. cit.,* IX:562–563.
[60] Cramer, *op. cit.,* p. 248.
[61] *Ibid.,* p.153.
[62] *Ibid.,* pp. 72–73 and 158.
[63] Quoted by Parrish and Huston, *op. cit.,* I:381.

Heaven by creed or by deed? That is the question. Shall we reason, or shall we simply believe?" And he concluded that lecture with sentiments and in a style upon which his claim as a great speaker most surely rests: "One world at a time is my doctrine . . . . I cannot help God; I cannot injure God. I can help people; I can injure people. Consequently humanity is the only real religion."[64]

Spokesmen for Stability: Grady, Washington, and Depew

WHILE THE Ku Klux Klansmen rode by night to herd the Negroes back from their carpetbagging alliance to a renewed subservience, and while a new breed of businessmen (with such names as John Jacob Aster, Jay Gould, Andrew Carnegie, J. Pierpont Morgan, and John D. Rockefeller) learned to skim the kettle of economic growth into the thick cream of personal multi-million dollar fortunes, spokesmen were needed who could rationalize contentment-with-things-as-they-are. Three speakers representing three different groups, each with his own style but all with much the same social function, were Henry Grady, editor of the moderately liberal Atlanta *Constitution*, Booker T. Washington, "Principal" of Tuskegee Institute (because "President" was too pretentious a title for a Negro), and the prince of after-dinner speakers, Senator, and president of the New York Central Railway, Chauncey Depew. Their collective motto could well have been: "We're all in the same boat; why rock it?"

Marvin G. Bauer's study of Henry W. Grady's oratory,[1] leaning upon Raymond B. Nixon's biography,[2] highlights the essential facts: that he was nationally known as a speaker only from 1886, when he was thirty six, until his death three years later; that he gave only eight speeches of real consequence, and that only two of them attracted much interest outside the South; and that his principal aim was to dissipate Northern hostility toward the Southern whites without sacrificing the new system of racial hierarchy that was devised to mitigate the influence of emancipation. In essence his message was: "We Southerners understand our Negroes and if you Yankees will leave us alone we'll get along with them just fine."

[64] Ingersoll, "The Mistakes of Moses," in McClure, op. cit., pp. 97–118.
[1] Marvin G. Bauer, "Henry Grady," in Brigance, ed., *History and Criticism*, op. cit., I:387–406.
[2] Raymond Blalock Nixon, *Henry W. Grady: Spokesman of the New South*, New York: Knopf, 1943.

As an editor and voracious reader, and with a keenly analytical mind, Grady understood the currents that were sweeping through the post-war society and possessed the skill to adapt his arguments and manner to the predilections of the leadership class that the Southern whites had to mollify. The new businessmen, with their eyes on Dixieland markets, were as eager as were the aspiring aristocrats of the new order in the Old South to achieve an armistice that would serve their common needs. The ultra-conservative New England Society of New York invited him to become one of a half-dozen speakers for the annual banquet they would hold on December 22, 1886. It was not an election year; Grover Cleveland had just started his first term as the first post-war Democratic President; the "bloody shirt" was too threadbare to be serviceable any longer; and it seemed a good time for the three hundred top-flight financiers and business leaders who composed the audience to consider a reconciliation with the Southern post-war generation. Grady had very thoughtfully studied L. Q. C. Lamar's eulogy of Charles Sumner, delivered twelve years earlier. He had studied, too, the career and speeches of Benjamin Hill, who, had he not died that Spring, would have been the more logical choice for the New York address. Grady determined to speak on the *new* South, which he meant to define in terms acceptable to both his own class and his audience. His success was heralded the next morning in the New York *Times*: "No oration of any recent occasion has aroused such enthusiasm in this city."

Despite the favorableness of the basic situation, the immediate circumstances challenged all the speaker's tact and skill. Never before had this Society listened to a Southern speaker; and its established habits of baiting the South and basking in its own glory were not to be abandoned. Among the speakers who preceded Grady, Ingersoll's familiar antagonist DeWitt Talmage presented a glossy and glorified description of the heroic return home from the battlefields of the union soldiers. Then General William Tecumseh Sherman got up and related anecdotes belittling the Southern people, after which the audience rose and sang lustily, "Marching through Georgia." Then Grady was introduced. "When I found myself on my feet," he said later, "every nerve in my body was strung as tight as a fiddle-string, and all tingling. I knew then that I had a message for that assemblage, and as soon as I opened my mouth it came rushing out."[3]

With a lengthy introduction that comprised nearly half the entire speech, Grady carefully laid a basis in good-fellowship and sentiment for

[3] Joel Chandler Harris, *Henry W. Grady: His Life and Speeches*, New York: Cassell Pub. Co., 1890, pp. 15–16.

the development of his theme—which he stated in his opening words, as a quotation from Benjamin Hill: "There was a South of slavery and secession—that South is dead. There is a South of union and freedom—that South, thank God, is living, breathing, growing every hour." Breaking new ground into the unfamiliar domain of the humorous after-dinner speech, Grady launched quickly into a couple of broad, almost slapstick jokes, guaranteed to produce roars of laughter, as indeed they did. Then, quickly, he reminded his listeners that in colonial America there had been a Virginian Cavalier as well as a New England Puritan; and that while the Puritan "forbade men to kiss their wives on Sunday, the Cavalier was courting everything in sight." Both, however, were "lost in the storm of the first Revolution." Then he made his first reference to the unfriendly speeches that had preceded his, and that an oblique one. Dr. Talmage, he reminded them, had said the typical American was yet to come—but "Let me tell you that he has already come . . . Abraham Lincoln." Having established an invulnerable base from which to disagree with his critics, he ventured a step further: in speaking on the "New" South, he was "in no sense disparaging the Old." Identifying himself with all who cherish "the home of my childhood," he felt ready to take the major leap—to point out that the return home of the Union soldiers, "with proud and victorious tread," as described by Talmage, was paralleled by the "footsore Confederate soldier" who "turned his face southward . . . . ragged, half-starved, heavy-hearted, enfeebled by want and wounds . . . lifting his tear-stained and pallid face for the last time to the graves that dot the old Virginia hills." Once home, "He finds his house in ruins, his farm devastated, his slaves free, his stock killed, his barns empty, his trade destroyed, his money worthless; his social system, *feudal in its magnificence* [italics added], swept away; his people without law or legal status, his comrades slain, and the burden of others heavy on his shoulders." Then, fearing lest he may have gone too far, he backstepped into humor, telling of Bill Arp, who "killed as many of them as they did of me, and now I am going to work." And, when that won "laughter and applause," he went on with another anecdote of the returned Johnny Reb who determined to "kiss my wife and raise a crop, and if the Yankees fool with me any more I will whip 'em again."

With "renewed applause" from that quip filling the room, Grady then took the boldest plunge yet—referring to the hero of the banquet, General Sherman, "who is considered an able man in our hearts, though some people think he is a kind of careless man about fire"; and while this brought not laughter but a sudden catch of breath, he added quickly that "from the ashes he left us . . . somehow or other we have caught the sunshine in the bricks and mortar of our homes . . . and have builded therein not one ignoble prejudice or memory"—and this brought applause.

From this point he launched into the development of his theme. To his dubious claim, "We have planted the schoolhouse on the hilltop and made it free to white and black," he quickly added the note that appealed directly to the commercial interests of his listeners: "We have sowed towns and cities in the place of theories and put business above politics." In a sheer masterpiece of humorous identification with parts of his audience's ideas and rejection of the rest, he said: "We have let economy take root and spread among us as rank as the crabgrass which sprang from Sherman's cavalry camps, until we are ready to lay odds on the Georgia Yankee, as he manufactures relics of the battlefield in a one-story shanty and squeezes pure olive oil out of his cotton-seed, against any down-easter that ever swapped wooden nutmegs for flannel sausages in the valleys of Vermont." In the wake of "loud and continuous laughter," he pledged the "upbuilding of the prostrate and bleeding South, misguided perhaps, but beautiful in her suffering, and honest, brave and generous always."

He next proceeded to the most delicate question: "what of the Negro?" In essence he claimed precisely the same ground as that held a generation earlier by those who pictured slavery as "a positive good." "No section shows a more prosperous laboring population than the Negroes of the South," he said; "none in fuller sympathy with the employing and land-owning class." Then he admitted quickly that slavery was an evil, but added that the New Englanders, who sold their slaves to the Southerners, were "not to be praised for knowing a paying thing when they saw it." Stubbornly he laid down the proposition that was the dearest orthodox doctrine of the Southern whites: "The relations of the Southern people with the Negro are close and cordial." Even in the statement of the claim, the distinction is clearly made that the Negroes are not *Southern people.* As for how the Negro should be treated, that "should be left to those with whom his lot is cast."

Regarding the goals and aims of the New South, "We fought hard enough to know that we were whipped, and in perfect frankness accepted as final the arbitrament of the sword to which we had appealed." The New South, "stirred with the breath of a new life . . . , upright, full-statured, and equal" accepts the fact that it had been set upon the right path "because in the inscrutable wisdom of God her honest purpose was crossed and her brave armies were beaten." Every battleground of the war is a reminder not of treason on one side and loyalty on the other, as Harrison was trumpeting, but "of the matchless valor of American hearts and the deathless glory of American arms."

In a short, almost abrupt conclusion, he asked whether New England would "permit the prejudices of war to remain in the hearts of the conquerors, when it had died in the hearts of the conquered?" Amidst "tumultuous cheering and cries of 'No! No!'" he ended by quoting Webster's plea to "clasp hands" and Milton's description of how even Satan wanted those who had disagreed—actually those who had rebelled—to "march all one way."[4]

The time was ripe for a message of reconciliation, the audience was right for it; the speaker was a young man who had grown up after the war's end; and, although the occasion was fraught with difficulties, the audience was ready to respond to the speaker's skillful progression along the route of humor, sentiment, dubious or downright deceitful claims, and flattery, to his depiction of the war as a sort of brotherly competition within which were tested and exemplified all the noblest attributes of genuine Americanism. Chauncey Depew, who heard it, testified that "The effect was electric, and beyond almost any that have ever occurred in New York or anywhere, and Grady sprang into international fame."[5]

Rich with fame from the success of this speech, Grady went about the South, during the next three years, primarily pleading for political unity so that it might defend its position in the Congress.[6] Then he went to Boston, to discuss in the city of Garrison, Phillips, and Sumner, "The Race Problem." In a long and rather soberly argumentative speech he maintained that the South was dealing with a difficult problem by the best methods available and must be left free from outside interference. On this trip he contracted pneumonia, from which, on December 23, 1889, waiting for Christmas, he died.

The principal spokesman of the era from the other South was Booker T. Washington, educator and founder of Tuskegee Institute. Although he claimed (as have many speakers) to like action better than words,[7] during more than thirty years of speaking he delivered perhaps as many as four thousand talks, an average of between two and three a week. One of his principal aims was to raise money for his school; another was to advise his fellow Negroes to seek satisfaction from earning money and respect through hard work; still another was that the Negro wanted lit-

[4] Harris, *op. cit.*, pp.83–93.
[5] Depew, *My Memories of Eighty Years, op. cit.*, p. 381.
[6] Bauer, *op. cit.*, I:395.
[7] Booker T. Washington, *Up from Slavery*, New York: Bantam Books, 1956, based on 1900 edition, p. 140. Cf. Karl Wallace, "Booker T. Washington," in Brigance, ed., *History and Criticism, op. cit.*, I:407.

tle beyond the right to work and grow toward a larger competence: "It is more important that we be prepared for voting than that we vote, more important that we be prepared to hold office than that we hold office."[8] In developing these themes, Washington always kept in mind that, considering his subject matter, there were three major audiences in America: the Northern whites, the Southern whites, and the Negroes His lifelong aim was to deliver a single message, in a relatively similar manner, that would be equally acceptable to all three. He prided himself that he never said anything in the North that he would not repeat in the South, nor anything to a black audience that he would not say to white listeners.[9]

After a decade of such speaking, Washington was invited, in 1893, to speak "for five minutes" to two thousand Northern and Southern whites in Atlanta, at an international conference of religious workers. What he had to say concerning the relation of the races was so satisfactory that two years later he was asked to be one of the speakers at the opening of the Atlanta Cotton States and International Exposition, on September 18, 1895. The occasion was important: "the first time in the entire history of the Negro that a member of my race had been asked to speak from the same platform with white Southern men and women."[10] He was very conscious of the risk his hosts were taking, for "by one sentence I could have blasted, in a large degree, the success of the Exposition."[11] With great care Washington worked out a speech, which he read to various Negroes and sent for criticism to a number of Northern and Southern whites.[12] Finally, with a carefully prepared text memorized, he arose before a segregated audience, to the sound of "considerable cheering, especially from the coloured people."[13]

He wasted no time and took no risks in his opening. His first words were: "One-third of the population of the South is of the Negro race." Then he quickly allayed fears by adding that "in no way have the value and manhood of the American Negro been more fittingly and generously recognized than by the managers of this magnificent Exposition." He proceeded to lay the basis for his theme with a story of mariners lost at sea who pleaded with a passing vessel for water and received back word to "Drop down your buckets where you are." Dying of thirst as they had been, their ship was actually floating on the pure, sweet water

[8] *Selected Speeches of Booker T. Washington*, ed. E. D. Washington, Garden City, N. Y.: Doubleday, 1932, p. 76.
[9] *Up from Slavery*, op. cit., p. 141.
[10] *Ibid.*, p. 148.
[11] *Ibid.*, p.149.
[12] Wallace, op. cit., I:417.
[13] *Up from Slavery*, op. cit., p. 153.

of the mouth of the Amazon River. Washington's application of this story was direct and immediate. Both the Southern whites and the Negroes should "drop down their buckets where they were," learning to live together to their mutual advantage. And how? "In all things that are purely social we can be as separate as the fingers, yet one as the hand in all things essential to mutual progress." This was what has come to be known as "the Atlanta Compromise." To avoid any doubt, Washington elaborated: "The wisest among my race understand that the agitation of questions of social equality is the extremest folly . . . . The opportunity to earn a dollar in a factory just now is worth infinitely more than the opportunity to spend a dollar in an opera-house."[14]

In his autobiography, *Up from Slavery*, Washington acknowledged the supreme importance of this speech by including the complete text in his brief book. He followed it by writing that "Governor Bullock rushed across the platform and took me by the hand." Then he quoted various encomiums on the speech, among them an editorial by Clark Howell in the Atlanta *Constitution:* "I do not exaggerate when I say that Professor Booker T. Washington's address yesterday was one of the most notable speeches, both as to character and as to the warmth of its reception, ever delivered to a Southern audience. The address was a revelation. The whole speech is a platform upon which blacks and whites can stand with full justice to each other." As for the Negro reaction, at that date it was mute. But in 1903 W. E. B. DuBois represented general Negro sentiment when he wrote: "His doctrine has tended to make the whites, North and South, shift the burden of the Negro problem to the Negro's shoulders and stand aside as critical and rather pessimistic spectators." This and Washington's other speeches, Du Bois went on, "belittles the emasculating effects of caste distinctions, and opposes the higher training and ambition of our brighter minds . . ."[15] Washington's own feeling on the matter was unequivocal: "I have come to the conclusion that these prejudices are something that it does not pay to disturb."[16] In one of his last speeches, delivered in August, 1915, before the National Negro Business League, which he had founded, he said: "No matter how poor you are, how black you are, or how obscure your present work and position, I want each one to remember that there is a chance for him, and the more difficulties he has to overcome the greater will be his success."[17]

[14] *Selected Speeches of Washington*, op. cit., pp. 31–36.
[15] W. E. B. Du Bois, *The Souls of Black Folk*, Greenwich, Conn.: Fawcett Pub. Co., Premier Americana, based on 1903 edition, pp. 53, 54.
[16] Emmett J. Scott and Lyman Beecher Stowe, *Booker T. Washington: Builder of a Civilization*, Garden City, N. Y.: Doubleday, Page, 1917, p. 124.
[17] *Ibid.*, p. 191.

At Tuskegee Institute, the principal monument to his lifework, there is erected a more than life-size statue of Booker T. Washington, with this inscription on its base: "No man can drag me down low enough to make me hate him."

Chauncey Mitchell Depew (April 23, 1834–April 5, 1928) left twelve published volumes of his speeches and two volumes of autobiography.[18] He was remarkably successful in both business and politics, and his eminence is dramatized in the fact that he actually refused President Harrison's offer to appoint him Secretary of State. What he is best remembered for is his graceful and pleasant after-dinner speeches. He himself regarded both them and the genre highly. "I have been making after-dinner speeches for sixty years to all sorts and conditions of people, and on almost every conceivable subject," he wrote. He pointed out that this type of speaking originated in England, where it proved its worth in providing a social and noncontroversial occasion for the insinuation of ideas that could not be frankly avowed in parliamentary debate.[19]

Depew was a master of the art of pleasing. When addressing an Irish banquet, he was a descendant from the Old Sod; when speaking to Netherlanders, his ancestors came from Holland. He was a Republican who ran for the office of Lieutenant-Governor of New York as a Democrat. In his speeches he aimed sallies of humorous irony all around and close to, but never at, his listeners. His favorite themes were the bounties and benefits of business—"the genius of trade making the wilderness a garden"—and the comfortableness of tolerance: "You see coming from the church of the Catholic, from the synagogue of the Jew, from the meeting-house of the Episcopalian, the Methodist, the Baptist, the Presbyterian, or the Unitarian, the people who, while worshipping according to their own ideas, recognize the right of all men to follow the dictates of their own consciences."[20] Both his style and his trend of ideas are well illustrated in one of his several speeches to the New England Society of New York, on December 22, 1879:

> My friend, Mr. Curtis, has eloquently stated, in the beginning of his address, the Dutchman's idea of the old Puritan. He has stated, at the close of his address, the modern opinion of the old Puritan. He was an uncomfortable man to live with, but two hundred years off a grand historic figure. If any one of you, gentlemen, was compelled to leave this festive board, and go back two hundred years and live with your ancestor

[18] Chauncey M. Depew, *One Hundred Years of American Commerce*, New York: D. O. Haynes, 1895; and *My Memories of Eighty Years, op. cit.*
[19] Depew, *My Memories of Eighty Years, op. cit.*, p. 378.
[20] The date for this speech was Jan. 10, 1890.

of that day, eat his fare, drink his drink, and listen to his talk, what a time there would be, my countrymen! Before the Puritan was fitted to accomplish the work he did, with all the great opportunities that were in him, it was necessary that he should spend two years in Leyden and learn from the Dutch the important lesson of religious toleration, and the other fundamental lesson, that a common school education lies at the foundation of all civil and religious liberty. If the Dutchman had conquered Boston, it would have been a misfortune to this land, and to the world. It would have been like Diedrich Knickerbocker wrestling with an electric battery.

But when the Yankee conquered New York, his union with the Dutch formed those sterling elements which have made the Republic what it is. Yankee ideas prevailed in this land . . . . Yankee ideas conquered again in that historic meeting when Lee gave up his sword to Grant. And when, in the disturbance of credit and industry which followed, the twin heresies Expansion and Repudiation stalked abroad, Yankee ideas conquered again . . . in the funding of our national debt at four percent, and the restoration of the national credit, which has given an impulse to our prosperity and industry that can neither be stayed nor stopped.

Depew's principal function was the creation and preservation of good will; and in this function he has seldom been equalled. He was a representative of the business community who realized the need to keep the public sympathy and support for the aims and methods of his class. "Success" was the only goal he thought worthy of pursuit; and in his "best of all possible worlds" he did not pause to contemplate the failures and the failings of the society of which he was a part. His speeches read like romantic novels: everything sunny and bright.

X

THE EXPANDING INFLUENCE
OF THE PULPIT
1800–1920

〽️ The Growth of Denominations

WITH THE exception of schoolteaching, the most frequent and perhaps the most influential public speaking in America has been in the pulpit. This was undoubtedly true in the period of the New England theocracy; and the pulpit expanded its interests to exercise a very diversified range of influence during the formative years of the new nation. William Warren Sweet estimates that at the end of the colonial period not more than five percent of all Americans were regular churchgoers. By 1850 some sixteen percent of the population were church members. Not until well into the twentieth century were as many as half of all Americans listed on church rolls—with many members always lax in Sunday attendance.[1]

Much of the speaking has been narrowly doctrinaire; most of it has been repetitively patternized. The words flowing from many pulpits have been designed to soothe, to repeat, and to sustain beliefs and feelings established and taken for granted. There is substantial evidence supporting the charge that religion is the opiate of the masses. But there is also much evidence to the exact contrary. Portions of the vast outflow of sermons have exercised a tremendously stimulative effect upon American life. Both the form and the content of preaching have changed to conform to changing social patterns. But the sermons have done more than merely record changes that were brought about by education,

---

[1] For this section, free use has been made of William Warren Sweet's *Religion in the Development of American Culture*, New York: Scribner's, rev., 1952, which is valuable for its excellent annotations and bibliography as well as for its perceptive text; and of the same author's *The Story of Religion in America*, New York: Harper, 1939. Concise summaries of the status of religion in America during and after the Revolution are in J. Franklin Jameson, *The American Revolution Considered as a Social Movement*, Boston: Beacon Press, 1956, pp. 83–100; and in Clinton Rossiter, *The First American Revolution*, New York: Harcourt, Brace, 1956, pp. 65–99. Also useful has been William L. Sperry, *Religion in America*, New York: Macmillan, 1946; and the *Yearbook of the American Churches*, published annually by the National Council of Churches of America.

prosperity, expanding power, and a growing cosmopolitan urbanity. Many preachers have been in the front line of progress, battling either to advance or to retard new ideas and attitudes. The church by its nature may be more conservative than revolutionary,[2] but in our history it has sometimes proved a dynamic force.

One evidence of its dynamism is the great increase in numbers of denominations. First the Revolution and then the Constitution (Article VI, and first amendment) unloosed the bonds that had restricted religious practices in the Colonies. No longer was any church either tax-supported or forbidden. The existence of 250 separate denominations with an aggregate membership of sixty three percent of the population in 1960,[3] demonstrates both freedom of choice and the significance of the church as a social institution. This significance was asserted by General Benjamin Lincoln in a letter to George Washington, on the eve of the Massachusetts convention called to ratify the Constitution. "It is fortunate for us that the clergy are pretty generally with us," he wrote. "They have in this state a very great influence over the people."[4] The extent of the influence was demonstrated by what happened after the new Federal Government ended the ties between church and state and permitted the free development of the religious impulse.

During the colonial period Congregationalism had dominated New England and Presbyterianism spread through the Middle Colonies and into the South—wherever the Scotch-Irish went. By 1775 there were 656 Congregational and 543 Presbyterian churches in America. Their ministers were generally accounted the superior men in their communities. Of the 1586 Congregational ministers who served New England churches during the colonial period, all but seventy nine were college graduates. The Presbyterian preachers, too, were mostly college-educated, though large numbers of them attended "Log Colleges," private lectures given at home by outstanding ministers. As the Revolution began, there were only 170 Presbyterian ministers, most of whom served two or even three churches simultaneously.

The Baptists claim Roger Williams as the founder of their faith in the New World; but the real beginning was in 1654, when Henry Dun-

[2] Adolf Harnack, *Outlines of the History of Dogma*, trans., E. K. Mitchell, Boston: Beacon Press, 1957, based on 1893 edition. Harnack believes that "the bishops asserted the stability of the Church at the expense of its Christianity" (p. 106).

[3] *Yearbook of the American Churches*, 1961.

[4] This is one of many letters from General Lincoln to Washington, included in *The Writings of George Washington*, ed., John C. Fitzpatrick, Thirty Nine Vols., Washington, D.C.: U.S. Gov't. Printing Office, 1944. W. E. Woodward, *George Washington: The Image and the Man*, Greenwich, Conn.: Fawcett Pub. Co., Premier Book, 1956, takes care to make clear that Washington was not a religious man (pp. 90–92).

ster resigned the presidency of Harvard with the statement of a five-point set of beliefs renouncing infant baptism. The first Baptist church in Massachusetts was founded in 1663 and the first Baptist Association was organized in Philadelphia in 1707. Prior to the Revolution only some twoscore Baptist churches were conducting services in the Colonies; and during the decade of persecution preceding Bunker Hill over thirty of their ministers were "honored with the dungeon." The sentiment of the Calvinists was well stated by a New England minister when he said: "All familists, Antinomians, Anabaptists, and other Enthusiasts shall have free liberty to keep away from us." After the Revolution the Baptists grew rapidly. By 1790 they had a membership of 65,000 in 688 churches, with 710 ordained ministers and many other licensed preachers. The principal appeal of the Baptists was to rural dwellers and their greatest strength lay in their use of "farmer-preachers." A typical example was John Taylor, who moved from Virginia to Kentucky, becoming wealthy as a farmer and land-investor while also preaching every Sunday and helping to establish ten Baptist churches. As Theodore Roosevelt wrote in *Winning of the West:* "The Baptist preachers lived and worked exactly as their flocks . . . . they cleared the ground, split rails, planted corn, and raised hogs on equal terms with their parishioners."[5] Scorning all education except familiarity with the Bible, they exploited their identification with the people and rapidly emerged as the most numerous Protestant denomination in America: twice the size of the Methodists, their nearest competitors, by 1950.

Methodism was a late arrival in the Colonies. The first two officially sanctioned Methodist ministers arrived in 1769, with two more in 1771—one of the latter being Francis Asbury, who set the pattern of circuit riding that was to build the strength of Methodism in the expanding West. Asbury, his biographer notes, "rented no house, hired no lodgings, made no arrangement to board anywhere, but simply set out upon the Long Road, and was travelling forty-five years later when Death caught up with him."[6] Along with Asbury the most famous of the circuit riders was Peter Cartwright, Lincoln's opponent in the Congressional election of 1846, whose *Autobiography* is a minor classic of Americana. Unlettered and sometimes uncouth, but aflame with tireless zeal, Cartwright and his fellow home missionaries rode horseback from settlement to settlement and indeed from cabin to cabin, preaching wherever they could find an audience. More respectable but no less as-

[5] *The Works of Theodore Roosevelt,* National Edition, Twenty Vols., New York: Scribner's, 1926, VIII:258, 454.
[6] Ezra S. Tipple, *Francis Asbury: The Prophet of the Long Road,* New York: Methodist Book Concern, 1906, pp. 158–159.

siduous was Bishop Matthew Simpson, who was chosen to preach Lincoln's funeral sermon.[7] Another notable Methodist pulpiteer who pointed away from ruralism toward identification with the powerful and the rich was Bishop Charles Henry Fowler. Largely as a rural church, with its ministers educated in "Brush College," Methodism by 1844 claimed 7730 pastors and 3988 circuit riders; then, broadening its appeal to the city dwellers it continued its growth to hold rank as the second largest denomination.

In 1800 originated, in Kentucky, the great Camp Meetings which served as the evangelical instrument of the early nineteenth century. A camp ground was prepared for a fall meeting, with seats for several thousand persons, surrounded by a brush fence inside which farmers pitched tents and engaged in a week-long series of worship services.[8] This first meeting was held by the Presbyterians, who were encouraged to repeat the experiment the next year. The 1801 meeting, however, was so drunken and disorderly that the Presbyterians withdrew from the field. The Methodists took up the idea; and by 1811 Bishop Asbury noted in his *Journal* that at least four hundred such meetings were held. By 1820 the number had grown to over a thousand. The meetings were always held after the harvest was gathered and partook of the nature of harvest festivals. Gangs of rowdies enjoyed the sport of trying to break up the meetings with whips, dogs, and gunfire; but the Methodists countered by establishing armed guards around the camps and appointing young boys as "runners" to chase away dogs and hogs. A camp meeting day commenced at dawn, with the blowing of bugles to call the people to prayer. At 10:00 a.m. and 3:00 p.m., and again in the evening, two- and three-hour sermons were delivered by ministers speaking in relays and as teams, with some preaching while others presided over the "mourners bench." Critics jeered at the "holy laughing," the jerks, jumping, and barking of the excited worshippers; and Abraham Lincoln indelicately suggested that "more souls were made than saved" at these camp meetings. On their part, the ministers sought to induce a spirit of quiet if intense worship and thousands of converts were registered every fall.

A much smaller but always influential denomination was the Unitarian. Joseph Priestley, the famous English scientist of this faith, came to Pennsylvania in 1794; but it was not until 1815 that the liberal wing

[7] Robert D. Clark, *The Life of Matthew Simpson*, New York: Macmillan, 1956, p. 246.
[8] Charles A. Johnson, *The Frontier Camp Meeting*, Dallas: Southern Methodist University Press, 1955, presents a sympathetic account. More sceptical is Bernard A. Weisberger, *They Gathered at the River*, Boston: Little, Brown, 1958. Cf. particularly his Chapter II, "Walking and Leaping and Praising God," pp. 20–50. Both books have good bibliographies.

of the Congregational Church of New England consented to assume the name Unitarian. During the period 1820–25, the American Unitarian Association was formed with 125 churches, one hundred of them in Massachusetts. When Lyman Beecher arrived in Boston in 1826 to crusade for reforms in the Presbyterian church, he noted with dismay that all the literary men, all the trustees and professors of Harvard, all men of wealth and fashion, and all the judges were Unitarian.[9] His fears exaggerated the facts; but it is true that the Unitarian rationalism appealed to the intellectuals, especially as it was expounded by William Ellery Channing, Ralph Waldo Emerson, and Theodore Parker. The companion denomination, Universalism (in 1960 united with Unitarianism), was established by John Murray in 1779 and developed by his successor Hosea Ballou. Theologically, the Unitarians believed man was too good to be damned; the Universalists that God was too good to damn mankind. Socially the appeal of Unitarianism was to the educated urban minority, of Universalism to the rural and lower middle class.

Roman Catholics comprised another minority of significance. The first Colony to insist upon religious liberty was Maryland, founded by Lord Baltimore as a refuge for English Catholics. Even in Maryland, however, and notably in the other Colonies, Catholics were unwelcome. During the early national period Catholics were almost the only Christian group to suffer continuous political attack. Antagonism of the Know-Nothing Party was enhanced by the efforts of Bishop Hughes (in 1823–40) to secure tax support for Catholic schools in New York, and by the large influx of Catholic immigration, which catapulted the membership of the Church from 600,000 in 1831 to 4.5 million in 1860. By mid-twentieth century, Catholics comprised one-quarter of all church members in America.

Anti-English feeling kept the Episcopal Church in "suspended animation and feeble growth" during the Revolution and until after the War of 1812. The "dis-establishment" of the church left the ministers with the unaccustomed problem of persuading parishioners to make voluntary contributions for their salaries. The urbanity of the Episcopalians unfitted them for expansion into the frontier; and it was not until 1818, when Philander Chase called the first Episcopal Convention in Ohio, with an attendance of eleven persons, that a small movement commenced in the Midwest. In the East, Bishops Alexander V. Griswold in New England, John Henry Hobart in New York, and Richard Channing Moore in Virginia did the most to rescue the church from the obloquy of its Toryism and to commence its national growth.

[9] Weisberger, *op. cit.*, p. 79.

Another denomination that rose from small beginnings to widespread membership was the Church of the Disciples, later renamed the Church of Christ. It was founded in 1809 by Thomas Campbell and raised to influence by his great preacher-son, Alexander Campbell.[10] Until 1832 Campbell preached as a Baptist, but on that date the Disciples emerged as a separate denomination, based on literal acceptance of the Scriptures, with the slogan: "Where the Bible speaks, we speak; where it is silent, we are silent." The second great Disciple preacher was Benjamin Franklin,[11] who did much to make the church a national institution—by 1960 the fourth largest denomination in America.

The Germanic settlers in America brought with them their Lutheranism; and Henry Melchior Muhlenberg, arriving in 1742, did most to establish its strength. Despite their large numbers, the Lutherans restricted their influence by long-continued use of the German language and by other "Old World" characteristics. The Americanization of the Lutherans was largely the work of Samuel S. Smucker, founder of Gettysburg College. The Mennonites, the Dunkers, the German Reformed Church, and the Society of Friends (Quakers) were other notable components of the growing religious community. The Seventh Day Adventist Church was founded by William Miller, who, in 1831, announced that Scriptures predicted the end of the world for sometime during the year commencing on March 21, 1843. He was invited to expound his message in many of the leading evangelical pulpits; and a tremendous wave of excitement spread around the country. The failure of the prophecy seemed not to discourage Miller's followers, and the denomination was formally organized in 1861.

In 1830 Joseph Smith launched a notably different church, the Latter Day Saints, or Mormons, based upon new scriptures which he asserted were delivered to him by the Angel Moroni, and which he said were written in the "reformed Egyptian tongue" on plates of gold. He did not show these plates to anyone but dictated their translation from behind a curtain.[12] The Mormons moved in 1840–44 to Nauvoo, Illinois, where they were well received until, in 1843, Brigham Young announced the doctrine of polygamy. The idea was far from new, for it had been espoused since 1836 by John Humphrey Noyes, in his "Bible Community" at Putney, Vermont; and from 1847 to 1879 Noyes continued to advocate his system of "complex marriage" at his Oneida

---

[10] See Earl Irvin West, The Search for the Ancient Order, Vol. I: 1849–1865, Nashville, Tenn.: Gospel Advocate Co., 1949.

[11] Ottis Castleberry, They Heard Him Gladly: A Critical Study of Benjamin Franklin's Preaching, n.p., Old Paths Publishing Co., 1963.

[12] "Origin of the Book of Mormon," in The Book of Mormon, Salt Lake City: Church of Jesus Christ of Latter Day Saints, 1950.

Community, in New York. Nevertheless, outraged Illinoisans attacked the Mormons at Nauvoo, murdered Joseph Smith, and induced Brigham Young to lead his followers on the epic trek that ended on the site of Salt Lake City.[13] So zealously has this religion been spread that in 1950 it numbered almost a million adherents and its stronghold, Utah, is the only State in which the majority of the residents belong to a single church.

Aside from the diversification of the church into multiple denominations, still further North-South splits within the major churches arose over the issue of slavery. In 1794 an interdenominational convention in Philadelphia, with as many Southern as Northern delegates, agreed that slavery was Unchristian and should be ended. National conventions of Methodists in 1796, of Baptists in 1789, and of Presbyterians in 1787 and 1818 approved resolutions condemning slavery. Between 1820 and 1830, the churches abandoned abolitionism and instead some of them advocated colonization of freed Negroes in Africa. After 1830, Northern churches generally ignored the question of slavery; whereas the Southern attitude was well stated in 1833 by Dr. Furman of South Carolina, who asserted that "the right of holding slaves is clearly established in the Holy Scriptures both by precept and example." Schisms within the denominations were unavoidable. The Baptist Church divided in 1844; the Southern Methodists seceded in 1845; the Southern Presbyterians formed their separate Synod in 1853. Both North and South, the truncated denominations rose to the challenge of their loss of united membership by increased evangelism.

📖 Theological Theorists: Beecher, Channing, and Parker

AMERICAN PREACHERS have been necessarily concerned with the nature of doctrinal truth and means by which it may be explored. Notable in this discussion were Lyman Beecher, William Ellery Channing, and Theodore Parker. The first sought his sanction in scripture, the second in reason, and the third in social need.

Lyman Beecher, who was born in Connecticut on October 12, 1775 and lived to the age of eighty five, was called by Theodore Parker "the father of more brains than any other man in America," his progeny in-

[13] Ray B. West, Jr., *Kingdom of the Saints: The Story of Brigham Young and the Mormons*, New York: Viking, 1957.

cluding Henry Ward Beecher, Edward Beecher, Harriet Beecher Stowe, and Catherine Beecher.[1] He would merit considerable attention even if he had died childless, for he possessed intelligence, courage, an attractive personality, and great skill in persuasion. True to his Connecticut heritage, he was Presbyterian with a difference. He accepted the dogma of predestination but sought to reconcile it with his views of God's love, of the redemptive power of the crucifixion, and of the freedom of man's will. His solution was a painfully contorted view that although God had indeed preordained who was to be saved and who must suffer eternal damnation, yet the voluntary choice of whether to live righteously or in sin coincided with this "supreme discretion or good pleasure of God."[2] By such a means he sought to maintain the absolute sovereignty of God while also insisting upon the free and responsible will of individuals; and he sought also to reconcile his sense of God's all-encompassing love with the notion that an all-powerful God punishes His helpless creatures.

The inherent contradictions within this theology proved insupportable. Beecher sought to solve (or evade) his problem in two ways. First, he left his Boston church to accept the presidency of the Lane Theological Seminary in Cincinnati, where he would administer and teach but need not preach. Second, he dissociated himself from the doctrine of predestination so that he might give greater emphasis to the saving power of God's love—thereby bringing upon himself, in 1835, a trial for heresy.[3] Beecher was acquitted, but the conservatives among the Presbyterians harried him with criticism and attacks throughout his remaining years. Presbyterianism, in this period, was undergoing a difficult period of transition. Union Theological Seminary was founded (1836) as a center of liberalism, whereupon the Princeton University Seminary became more conservative. In the struggle that ensued, the General Assembly of the Church expelled 533 churches, with a membership of over 100,000. Predestination and inescapable hellfire died hard. Lyman Beecher was among their effective opponents. It never occurred to him, however, to search for any other religious instruction than that which he found in the Bible. When his son Edward published a book, *The Conflict of the Ages*, seeking to find a broader basis for religious liberalism, Lyman remarked to him: "Edward, you've destroyed the Calvinistic

[1] Their collective story is told in Lyman Beecher Stowe, *Saints, Sinners and Beechers*, New York: Blue Ribbon Books, 1934; and in Constance Mayfield Rourke, *Trumpets of Jubilee*, New York, Harcourt, Brace, 1927, pp. 1–237.
[2] Lyman Beecher, "The Faith Once Delivered to the Saints," preached at Worcester, Mass., Oct. 15, 1823; in Ernest J. Wrage and Barnett Baskerville, *American Forum*, New York: Harper, 1960, pp. 99–113.
[3] Paxton Hibben, *Henry Ward Beecher*, New York: Press of the Reader's Club, 1942, pp. 53–54.

barns, but I hope you don't delude yourself that the animals are going into your little theological hencoop!"[4] Of his greater son, Henry Ward Beecher, who was even more liberal in his outlook, he declared: "Thought I could preach 'til I heard Henry."[5]

Beset by theological disputes, Lyman Beecher was equally unfortunate in his choice of position in the assault upon slavery. "Were it in my power to put an end to slavery immediately I would do it, but it is not," he said. When abolitionism became a fever among his students at Lane Seminary, chiefly because of the ardor of Theodore Weld, Beecher attempted to calm the storm. "I regard the whole abolition movement, under its most influential leaders, with its distinctive maxims and modes of feeling, and also the whole temper, principles, and action of the South in the justification of slavery as signal instances of infatuation permitted by Heaven for purposes of national retribution," he declared in 1838. In his view, "God never raised up such men as Garrison." The mid-position he sought to maintain was one that kept him under continual attack from both sides.[6]

Lyman Beecher's life, like his preaching, was a strange mixture of practicality and idealism. As a student at Yale he earned his expenses by selling grog and wine to fellow students; later he became a founder of the temperance movement. By means of a powerful sermon preached after Hamilton's fatal duel with Burr, Beecher was influential in putting an end to duelling. Unlike many of the great preachers, he devoted much of his time to pastoral calls; yet he was so introspective that often he would walk home and leave his horse where he had visited. He loved fishing so much that he would indulge in the sport on his way to church, once shoving the fish he caught into the pockets of his coat, where it remained until his wife brushed the garment for the following Sunday. To insure adequate exercise, he had a load of sand delivered into his basement, where he would tirelessly shovel it back and forth from one side to the other. In the pulpit, he blazed his messages to his congregation with fiery intensity; yet he was unable to drive his meaning home with local or personalized illustrations. Once he wrote on the margin of his sermon notes: "Shout loudly; have little to say." His name and fame became great in the America of his day; yet because his confusion was greater than his understanding of the theology with which he struggled, he is remembered today less for himself than because of his paternity.

A contemporary and direct opponent of Lyman Beecher was the learned and intellectual but colorless Boston Unitarian, William Ellery

---

[4] Lyman Beecher Stowe, *op. cit.*, p. 70.
[5] *Ibid.*
[6] *Autobiography of Lyman Beecher*, ed. Charles Beecher, Two Vols., New York: Harper, 1865.

Channing. Channing preferred the quiet of his study to the boisterous work of either evangelism or religious controversy. Nevertheless, in 1819, he was induced by his colleagues, because of his manifest superiority, to undertake the task of defining the meaning of the Unitarian faith—no mean job, since the denomination abjured creed and dogma. Channing accepted the challenge to deliver the ordination sermon for Jared Sparks at Baltimore, on May 5 of that year, deliberately preparing a sermon that was intended for wide circulation in print. The sermon consisted of two parts, the first explaining how Unitarians seek religious truth, the second outlining what kind of truth they find. The discussion is notably restrained and conciliatory, despite the explosive nature of its conclusions, for Channing's whole purpose was to quiet controversy rather than to inspire it.[7]

He made clear that the Unitarians regarded the Bible, as did all the orthodox of that day, as the literal exposition of God's will. "Whatever doctrines seem to us to be clearly taught in the Scriptures, we receive without reserve or exception." However, he went on, Unitarians, like other Christians, are selective in their reading of the Bible. "Our religion, we believe, lies chiefly in the New Testament . . . . Jesus Christ is the only master of Christians, and whatever he taught . . . we regard as of divine authority." Beyond this, he said, Unitarians insist that "the Bible is a book written for men, in the language of men, and that its meaning is to be sought in the same manner as that of other books." Indeed, since the Bible is written in figurative style, employs many obscurities, and is a compilation of books written by many men over a period of many hundreds of years, it requires more selective and critical interpretation than does any other important book. "From a variety of possible interpretations, we select that which accords with the nature of the subject" and we "distrust every interpretation which, after deliberate attention, seems repugnant to any established truth. We reason about the Bible precisely as civilians do about the constitution under which we live."

Having unfolded the method of reason and comparative analysis, Channing then proceeded to "state some of the views which we derive from that sacred book." The first was "the doctrine of God's unity . . . . We object to the doctrine of the Trinity . . . . With Jesus, we worship the Father, as the only living and true God." Second, "we believe in the unity of Jesus Christ." The doctrine that "makes Jesus Christ two beings" is a "corruption of Christianity, alike repugnant to

---

[7] The circumstances are described by Arthur W. Brown, *Always Young for Liberty*, Syracuse: Syracuse University Press, 1956, Chapter 10, "Baltimore Pentecost," pp. 125–137 The text of the address is in *Works of William E. Channing, D.D.*, Boston: American Unitarian Assoc., 1885, pp. 367–384.

common sense and the general strain of the Scriptures . . . . To denominate him one person, one being, and yet to suppose him made up of two minds, infinitely different from each other, is to abuse and confound language." Third, "We believe in the *moral perfection of God* . . . . We conceive that Christians have generally leaned towards a very injurious view of the Supreme Being . . . . To give our views of God in one word, we believe in his Parental character . . . . We look upon this world as a place of education, in which he is training men . . . for union with himself." The doctrines of original sin, predestination, and infant damnation are, he said, "false and dishonorable views of God."

Fourth, concerning the mission of Jesus, "we believe that he was sent by the Father to effect a moral or spiritual deliverance of mankind"—in short, to help men accomplish a change in themselves which will make them worthy of salvation. This was a major shift from the general orthodox view that Jesus was offered up by God as a substitute sacrifice "to appease God's wrath" concerning the incurable sinfulness of mankind. Finally, "We believe that all virtue has its foundation in the moral nature of man . . . . We think that much which is called piety is worthless . . . . We cannot sacrifice our reason to the reputation for zeal . . . . We read with astonishment and horror the history of the church . . . . An enemy to every religion, if asked to describe a Christian, would, with some show of reason, depict him as . . . arrogating all excellence to his own sect and all saving power to his own creed, sheltering under the name of pious zeal the love of domination, the conceit of infallibility, and the spirit of intolerance, and trampling on men's rights under the pretence of saving their souls." He closed with the hope that "the conspiracy of ages against the liberty of Christians may be brought to an end."

Channing lived from April 8, 1780 to October 2, 1842. His published works reveal a mind deeply studious and hospitably open to culture and enlightenment and a spirit dedicated to the liberation and just treatment of all men, regardless of their color, class, or creed. In a commemorative sermon, Theodore Parker said of him: "since Washington, no man has died amongst us whose real influence was so wide, and so beneficent, both abroad and at home . . . . He did not see all the truth that will be seen in the next century. He did what was better, he helped men to see somewhat of truth in this . . ."[8]

Theodore Parker, born at Lexington on August 24, 1810, and grandson of the leader of the Minutemen who fought there in 1775, lived less

[8] Brown, *op. cit.*, p. 244.

than fifty years, until May 10, 1860. Moreover, it was not until May 19, 1841, when he preached his famous sermon on "The Transient and the Permanent in Christianity" that his religious views fully matured. Nevertheless, in a relatively short space of time, he made an enormous impact upon America and the western world. More than two decades after his death, in 1883, the Lord Chief Justice of England, John Duke Coleridge, was applauded in Boston for calling him "perhaps one of your highest and greatest souls."[9] And James Russell Lowell, speaking in England the following year, paid tribute to Parker for teaching that "Democracy meant not 'I'm as good as you are,' but 'You're as good as I am.'"[10] From Parker's July 4, 1858 sermon, Abraham Lincoln underlined a sentence which he stored away in his memory for later use: "Democracy is Direct Self-government, over all the people, for all the people, by all the people."[11] F. B. Sanborn thought him "a shadowy figure in the vast drama of national regeneration."[12] Wendell Phillips praised him not for "his unmatched pulpit talent" but because he avoided "Oriental metaphysics" and instead preached about "the whole encyclopedia of morals—social questions, sanitary matters, slavery, temperance, labor, the condition of women, the nature of the Government, responsibility to law, the right of a majority, and how far a minority may yield, marriage, health,—the entire list."[13] One of Parker's sermons was on "The Temptations of Milkmen." Another was on "Clean Streets." He drew the substance for his preaching not from a study of the Bible nor of other books (although he was a voracious reader with a remarkably retentive memory) but from looking around him to see what needed to be set aright.

Parker matured slowly. He was twenty six when he graduated from theological seminary, and his experimental sermons were criticized so harshly that he was reduced to tears. His first regular charge was at West Roxbury, where he remained for nine years. "I determined to preach nothing as religion which I had not experienced inwardly and made my own," he declared. While at West Roxbury he preached 766 times, but prepared only 362 sermons, each one completely written out and read to his congregation. As was customary, he frequently exchanged pulpits with other ministers. One sermon he delivered twenty five times, others ten or twelve times.[14] Meanwhile, his intellect was

[9] Thomas B. Reed, *Modern Eloquence*, Philadelphia: John D. Morris, 1900, Nine Vols., I:256.
[10] *Ibid.*, VIII:797.
[11] Donald Davis, *Lincoln's Herndon*, op. cit., p. 128.
[12] Quoted by Emanuel Hertz, *The Hidden Lincoln*, op. cit., p. 10.
[13] Sherwin, *Prophet of Liberty*, op. cit., pp. 410–411.
[14] John W. Chadwick, *Theodore Parker: Preacher and Reformer*, Boston: Houghton Mifflin, 1901, pp. 62–63.

growing. At the age of twelve he had bought his first book, a Latin dictionary, with money earned picking huckleberries. Steadily he bought more books—and read them—until his personal library numbered thirteen thousand volumes, perhaps the largest in Boston.[15] But as his mind grew through study of other men's ideas, he gradually became more independent in the development and advocacy of his own. Much that he heard and read about religion seemed to him to be sheer traditionalism, tinged even with hypocrisy. "Alas for that man who consents to think one thing in his closet," he wrote in his journal, "and preach another in his pulpit!"[16]

By 1840 his reputation as a heretic was spreading and he began to find it hard to find ministers who would exchange pulpits with him. "I have the reputation of washing down my dinner with nice old sulphuric acid and delighting to spear men with a jest and to quarrel with all sorts of people," he wrote in bitter jest.[17] Then, on May 19, 1841, he preached a crucial sermon: "The Transient and Permanent in Christianity." The theme simply was that Christianity possesses so much merit that it can stand without the support of miracles. More specifically, it did not need to lean upon the claim of having a divine founder. "If it could be proved that Jesus of Nazareth had never lived, still Christianity would stand firm and fear no evil." In his view Jesus was the greatest man who ever lived—and just a man. "Measure him by the world's greatest sons— how poor they are! Try him by the best of men—how little and low they appear! Exalt him as much as we may, we shall yet, perhaps, come short of the mark. But still was he not our brother, the son of man, as we are; the Son of God, like ourselves?" Parker himself did not consider this a good sermon, and a trusted friend called it the worst he had written.[18] It was in fact loosely organized and repetitive, with the style flat in parts and overly decorative in others. Yet the sensation it created was enormous—far more so than the response two decades earlier to Channing's equally revolutionary challenge to orthodoxy. The difference lay primarily in the contrast between the two men. Whereas Channing avoided controversy, Parker sought it. Parker was so eager to implant his ideas

---

[15] *Ibid.*, p. 17.
[16] *Ibid.*, pp. 94–95.
[17] Henry Steele Commager, *Theodore Parker: Yankee Crusader*, Boston: Beacon Press, 1936, pp. 291–292. Much this same picture of Parker is presented by Roy C. McCall, "Theodore Parker," in Brigance, ed., *History and Criticism, op. cit.*, I:238–264; John Weiss, *The Life and Correspondence of Theodore Parker*, Two Vols., London: Longmans, Green, 1863; and O. B. Frothingham, *Theodore Parker: A Biography*, Boston: J. R. Osgood, 1874.
[18] Chadwick, *op. cit.*, p. 96. For this and the other extant sermons, see *The Works of Theodore Parker*, Centenary Edition, Boston: American Unitarian Association, Fifteen Vols., 1907–1910.

that he exaggerated, repeated, and sought means of shocking his way into his listeners' minds. In another sermon shortly after this one, he asserted: "There is but one Religion, as one Ocean; though we call it Faith in our church and Infidelity out of our church."[19]

In July, 1843, after two years of ceaseless criticism and ostracism by his fellow ministers, he told his West Roxbury congregation that "If I could not find a place in a church, then I meant to take it in a hall, in a schoolhouse, or a barn, under the open sky, wherever a word could be spoken and heard."[20] He left, then, for a year's recuperative travel in Europe; and when he returned he did indeed transfer his preaching into a hall—the Melodeon in Boston, a huge building that was poorly heated in the winter, hot in the summer, dirty, and used for vaudeville-type entertainments during the week. He insisted upon a small salary and refused to have a collection taken up. Here he gave his first sermon on January 22, 1845, and in November a group of devoted followers organized the Twenty-Eighth Congregational Society to sponsor and support his ministry. He remained in Melodeon until November 21, 1852, when, under the same auspices, he shifted to Boston's Music Hall, which seated 2700 people and, under his ministry, often had an additional three hundred standees.

Parker was far from being oratorical in appearance or manner. He stood five feet eight inches, was early bald, and by the age of forty had a full snow-white beard. His features were plain, his gestures few and graceless, and he read all his sermons. A laborer who had been brought to hear him exclaimed in surprise, "Is that Theodore Parker? You told me he was a remarkable man; but I understood every word he said." The principal sources of his power were that he thought independently, he said what he thought, and he personalized his messages so that they penetrated to every hearer.

His first antislavery sermon was preached January 31, 1841, but it was not until he was roused by the Mexican War that he devoted major attention to this problem. On February 4, 1847, lecturing in Faneuil Hall, he thundered: "This is a war for slavery, a mean and infamous war; an aristocratic war, a war against the best interests of mankind. If God please, we will die a thousand times, but never draw blade in this wicked war." Six months later he was even more emphatic: "If you take all the theft, all the assaults, all the cases of arson, ever committed in time of peace in the United States since the settlement of Jamestown in 1608 [sic], and add to them all the murders, they will not amount to

[19] Commager, *op. cit.*, p. 82.
[20] Chadwick, *op. cit.*, p. 130.

half the wrongs committed in the war for the plunder of Mexico."[21] This was bold enough to fit into the Garrisonian pattern, but since New England was Whiggish and the Whigs were against the war, it was far from being reckless.

Far braver were his sermons on the ordinary activities of the day, such as his installation sermon at Melodeon Hall. Under the title, "The True Idea of the Christian Church," he said: "We expect the sins of commerce to be winked at in the streets; the sins of the state to be applauded on election day and in a Congress, or on the Fourth of July . . . . If there be a public sin in the land, if a lie invade the state, it is for the church to give the alarm; it is here that it may war on lies and sins; the more widely they are believed in and practised, the more are they deadly, the more to be opposed."[22] This cue he followed up with a widely-discussed "Sermon on Merchants" in which he declared: "The bad merchant still lives. He cheats in his trade; sometimes against the law, commonly with it. His truth is never wholly true nor his lie wholly false. He overreaches the ignorant; makes hard bargains with them in their trouble . . ." And so on, and on, and on, taking care to make it clear that he meant specifically the merchants of Boston, though many of them had pledged the funds which made it possible for him to enjoy the luxury of foreswearing a collection.

Perhaps the greatest, and surely the most noted, of all Parker's sermons was his excoriation of Webster. He wrote it at white heat, twice the length of his usual sermons, and carried the bulky manuscript into the pulpit. "Of all my public trials, this is my most trying day," he commenced. Webster had outraged the abolitionists by his Seventh of March speech; yet he was the hero of New England and the idol of many. In the sermon Parker paid him high compliments for his innate greatness, but he made clear it was greatness of the intellect, not of morality. "His life has been one long vacillation," Parker charged. The climax of his denunciation was the passage: "No living man has done so much to debauch the conscience of the nation, to debauch the press, the pulpit, the forum, and the bar. There is no Higher Law, quoth he, and how much of the pulpit, the press, the forum, and the bar denies its God. He poisoned the moral wells of society with his lower law, and men's consciences died of the murrain of beasts, which came because they drank there at." Julia Ward Howe, author of "The Battle Hymn of the Republic," listened enraptured, then, hurrying home late for dinner, cried, "Do not scold me. I have just heard the greatest speech I shall

[21] *Ibid.*, p. 238. The sermon was preached June 25, 1848.
[22] Commager, *op. cit.*, pp. 225–231.

ever hear." But Parker went moodily home and that night wrote in his journal: "A sad and dreadful day."[23]

There came a Sunday when the congregation gathered but Parker did not appear. Instead he sent a note saying he had meant to preach on the uses of religion and urging the congregation not to forget to give to the poor. Choking with consumption, he went to Italy, where he died in Florence, unhappy and discontent. He was not unaware that there had arrived "the period of the lowest ebb tide of vitality in the history of American Christianity." Chief Justice Marshall feared that the church was "too far gone ever to be revived." Emerson had had to leave the church in an endeavor to find religion. And when another great period of preaching commenced, it was concerned less with theology than with sociology. The new preachers were more influenced by Parker than he was able to discern. The path he had marked became the one to be chiefly trod: not authority, not even reason, but social need became the principal theme and motive power of the resurgent pulpits.

The Shakespeare of the Pulpit: Henry Ward Beecher

By GENERAL agreement Henry Ward Beecher is accounted the greatest American preacher since Edwards and Whitefield. Lionel Crocker, who devoted many years to the study of Beecher's rhetoric, concludes that "Beecher will be remembered as one of the greatest preachers produced in America, if not in the world."[1] Crocker then quoted the judgment of another fine preacher, S. Parkes Cadman, who said: "I place him at the summit of the sacred oratory of the last two hundred years."[2] Still a greater minister, Phillips Brooks, called him simply "the greatest preacher in America."[3] The Christian minister Edgar DeWitt Jones said that he made his pulpit "a throne of spiritual and political power";[4] and the agnostic Robert Ingersoll testified that "I

---

[23] "Mr. Webster stamped his foot, and broke through into the great hollow of practical atheism," Parker mourned. "There was a twist in Faneuil Hall, and the doors could not open wide enough for Liberty to regain her ancient cradle." *Works, op. cit.,* VII:338. The account of the speech and its reception is based on Commager, *op. cit.,* pp. 223–231.
[1] Lionel Crocker, "Henry Ward Beecher," in Brigance, ed., *History and Criticism, op. cit.,* I:272.
[2] S. Parkes Cadman, *Ambassadors of God,* New York: Macmillan, 1920, p. 80.
[3] Alexander V. G. Allen, *Life and Letters of Phillips Brooks,* New York: Dutton, 1901, III:229.
[4] Edgar DeWitt Jones, *Lords of Speech,* Chicago: Willett, Clark, 1937, p. 135.

think Mr. Beecher has liberalized the English-speaking people of the world."[5] Sinclair Lewis called him "a combination of St. Augustine, Barnum, and John Barrymore."[6] Paxton Hibben, his most critical biographer, thought he did not exercise notable leadership in the great social, political, and religious changes taking place in his time, but that he was their effective "barometer and record." "More than any other man he was their voice." His chief significance, to Hibben, lay in his representative character. "He was not in advance of his day, but precisely abreast of his day."[7] From his sermons we see evidence of his development (and that of the America of his generation) from "the provincial, self-opinionated, ignorant and intolerant . . . flint-like faith of the Puritans" to "an apostle of evolution, an advocate of women's suffrage and the higher education of women, a clergyman who attended the theater and who drank his wine or beer when he felt like it."[8]

In 1869 a newspaper estimated that Beecher's "influence on religious thought was greater than that of all the theological seminaries put together."[9] This was an exaggeration. But the friendly Lyman Abbott sought to confirm it when he wrote in the *Christian Union*: "He has rendered his generation many and great services—moral, political, social, theological; but his greatest service is in this, that he has taught the Puritan Church that God is love."[10] Harry Emerson Fosdick, paying tribute to Beecher's theological influence, quoted from him a statement that could almost as well have been lifted out of a lecture by Ingersoll. "To tell me that back of Christ there is a God, who for unnumbered centuries has gone on creating men and sweeping them like dead flies—nay, like living ones—into hell, is to ask me to worship a being so much worse than the conception of any mediaeval devil as can be imagined; but I will not worship the devil, though he should come dressed in royal robes and sit on the throne of Jehovah."[11]

The great pulpit orator and creative theological thinker who is praised in these encomiums was, as a child, so clumsily awkward and unclear in his speech that an aunt said of him: "When Henry is sent to me with a message, I always make him say it three times. The first time I have no manner of an idea, than if he spoke Choctaw; the second, I catch now

---

[5] Rogers, *Colonel Bob Ingersoll*, op. cit., p. 245.
[6] Hibben, *Henry Ward Beecher*, op. cit., p. vii.
[7] *Ibid.*, pp. xiii, xiv.
[8] *Ibid.*, p. xiv.
[9] *Patriotic Addresses . . . by Henry Ward Beecher*, ed. John R. Howard, New York: Fords, Howard, & Hulbert, 1887, p. 157.
[10] *Ibid.*, p. 158.
[11] Harry Emerson Fosdick, *The Power to See It Through*, New York: Harper, 1935, p. 64.

and then a word; by the third time I begin to understand."[12] He improved his articulation by going out into the woods and practicing the vowel sounds.[13] Meanwhile he suffered the agonizing terror of believing himself damned by a God who was incapable of mercy,[14] and just in the period of his life when he most needed comradeship to help him find himself and build confidence, he was sent to a female academy run by his sister Catherine, where he was the only boy among forty girls. He still spoke "as if he had pudding in his mouth," and he had neither interest nor apparent aptitude for study. It was here in his second year, however, that his mind was awakened. The crucial influence was exerted by John F. Lovell, who came to the academy as instructor in elocution. Lovell was author of a very bad book on speech and insisted that the path to eloquence led through the thorny byways of interminable drill in articulation, vocal phrasing, and use of set gestures. Nevertheless, his influence was both great and helpful, for he taught Beecher that he must have something to say and should learn to say it in a way that would influence his fellow beings. Late in his life Beecher told an audience in London how much the practice of oratory meant to him: "I fed on the privilege of making men hear things, because I was a public speaker. I glorified in my gifts, not because they brought praise, for they brought the other thing continually; but men would come and would hear, and I rejoiced in it."[15] Hibben put the same idea in unkinder terms when he said Beecher never escaped from the theatrical performance of Henry Ward Beecher played by Henry Ward Beecher.[16] Forced into the ministry without any consideration for his own preferences, Beecher resisted the pressure by sheer mental lethargy, until during his otherwise undistinguished years at Amherst he discovered the joy of public speaking.[17] Even so, in revolt against the family discipline that was shaping his career, he sought audiences away from the school and neglected his assigned roles in the Athenian debating society at Amherst. Along with skill in speech he was also achieving independence of mind.

To Beecher, all the remainder of his life, public speaking came very close to being the center of his heart's idolatry. What he believed did, of

[12] Lyman Beecher Stowe, *Saints, Sinners and Beechers*, op. cit., p. 236. Cf. Hibben, op. cit., p. 17.
[13] Crocker, op. cit., I:280.
[14] Hibben, op. cit., p. 19.
[15] *Patriotic Addresses*, op. cit., p. 68.
[16] Hibben, op. cit., p. 18.
[17] Constance Mayfield Rourke, *Trumpets of Jubilee*, op. cit., pp. 153–154. See also, Henry Ward Beecher, *Yale Lectures on Preaching*, New York: J. B. Ford, 1872, p. 143.

course, matter greatly to him; but his approach to propositions was in terms of considering how to present them effectively to listeners. In his first series of lectures to the divinity students at Yale, he told them that "what the preacher wants is the power of having something that is worth saying, and then the power of saying it. He is to hold the light up so that a blind man cannot help feeling that it is falling on his orbs. He needs to put the truth in such a way that if a man were asleep it would wake him up; and if he were dead, it would give him resurrection for the hour." Inevitably his concern was with the power to exert influence through speaking. "You know how beautifully some men write," he told the divinity students, "and how poorly they deliver; how well they prepare their materials, and yet their materials when prepared are of no force whatever. They are beautiful arrows,—arrows of silver; golden-tipped are they, and winged with the feathers of the very bird of paradise. But there is no bow to draw the arrows to the head and shoot them strongly home, and so they all fall out of the sheath down in front of the pulpit or platform."[18] Time and again he reverted to the theme: "One's message to his hearers should be so delivered as to bring his personality to bear upon them."[19] The process of speaking itself intrigued him. "At times," he said, "there are no gestures comparable to the simple stature of the man himself." As for the voice, it "is the bell of the soul, or the iron and crashing of the anvil. It is a magician's wand, full of incantation and witchery; or it is a scepter in a king's hand, and sways men with imperial authority."[20]

When, in Brooklyn, Beecher was able to plan the construction of a new church according to his own design, he renounced the traditional pulpit in favor of a platform that extended well out into the congregation. To the architect he said: "I want the audience to surround me, so that they will come up on every side, and behind me, so that I shall be in the centre of the crowd, and have the people surge all about me."[21] Some ministers might find "audience" and "crowd" less indicative of their meaning than "parishioners" and "worshippers." But Beecher, while maintaining the sincerity of his ministerial vocation, was above all a crowd-compeller.

When he took up his first church at Lawrenceville, Indiana, with a congregation of nineteen women and one man, he sought to build his preaching power by saturating himself with the study of the sermons of Robert South, Barrow, Howe, Sherlock, Butler, and Edwards. He always preached as well as he could, and went to bed every Sunday night with a

---

[18] *Lectures on Preaching, op. cit.,* pp. 186–187.
[19] *Ibid.,* p. 214.
[20] Rourke, *Trumpets of Jubilee, op. cit.,* p. 177.
[21] Crocker, *op. cit.,* I:274.

headache from worry because he had not been better. Then he began to develop a system. He recalled that as a child with a new gun, he had simply shot off into the bushes and hit nothing, until he learned to take careful aim. One Sunday morning he went into the pulpit with a sermon carefully prepared to start with points of view his hearers thoroughly accepted, then to proceed on that basis to his own projected conclusion. The results were so good that "I never felt so triumphant in my life. I cried all the way home. I said to myself, 'Now I know how to preach.' "[22]

Beecher's craftsmanship as a preacher was thorough. He knew that he must live and act the part as well as speak it. "A preacher is in some degree a reproduction of the truth in personal form."[23] The aim toward which all preaching should be directed is "reconstructed manhood"[24]— a vast shift from the ancient theme of salvation. As to the materials to be used, the Bible was to him of less utility than the life he saw around him. "The kingdom of God and of truth, as it is laid down in the New Testament, is a kingdom of seeds . . . . And shall I go back and talk about acorns after I have learned about oaks? . . . . You must not shut yourself up in those germ-forms, with stupid reverence merely for the literal text of the gospel."[25] Neither do the Bible commentaries and church histories supply the material for preaching. "A man's study should be everywhere,—in the house, in the street, in the fields, and in the busy haunts of men."[26] Beecher devoted one of his Yale lectures to the value and uses of illustrations, which are important because "an illustration is a window in an argument, and lets in light."[27] And he practiced what he taught.

How he used the common experiences of life to illuminate his main point may be shown in a sermon, "The Background of Mystery," which he preached late in his life:

> Once, when a boy, I stood on Mount Pleasant, at Amherst, and saw a summer thunder-storm enter into the valley of the Connecticut from the North. Before it was all bright; centerwise it was black as midnight, and I could see the fiery streaks of lightning striking down through it; but behind the cloud—for I could see the rear—it was bright again. In front of me was that mighty storm hurtling through the sky; and before it I saw the sunlight, and behind it I saw the sunlight; but to those who were under the center of it there was no brightness before or behind it.

[22] *Lectures on Preaching, op. cit.,* pp. 146, 145, 10–12.
[23] *Ibid.,* p. 3.
[24] *Ibid.,* p. 6.
[25] *Ibid.,* pp. 78–79.
[26] *Ibid.,* p. 173.
[27] *Ibid.,* p. 158.

They saw the thunder-gust, and felt the pelting rain, and they were enveloped in darkness and heard the rush of the mighty winds; while I, that stood afar off, could see that God was watering the earth and washing the leaves, and preparing the birds for a new outcome of jubilee, and giving to men refreshment and health. So I conceive that our human life here, with its sorrows and tears, as compared with the eternity that we are going into, is no more than the breath of a summer thunder-storm; and if God sees that our experience in this world is to work out an exceeding great reward in the world to come, there is no mystery in it—to Him.[28]

Beecher's ideal of public speaking was that of a close, conversational relation with his listeners, together with an impetuosity, or *lunge*, as he called it, in the speaker's manner.[29] In order to safeguard both the immediacy of contact with the audience and the spontaneity of manner, he not only spoke extempore but actually refrained from making so much as an outline until just an hour or so before he was to speak. He would select a topic early in the week. Then, "I brood it, and ponder it, and dream over it, and pick up information about one point and another but if I ever think I see the plan opening up to me I don't dare to look at it or put it down on paper. If once I write a thing out, it is almost impossible for me to kindle to it again."[30] From 1858 on Beecher had an "official stenographer" who took down his speeches as he delivered them. Most of them were promptly published; Beecher, so far from editing them for the press, could not bear to read them until they appeared in print.[31]

Illustrative both of his mode of enlivening his sermons and also of his theory of persuasion is an anecdote he included in a discourse on "The Moral Teaching of Suffering":

. . . a man of great violence of temper came to see my father and rated him with such a scolding as I had never heard. I looked at my father with amazement, as he sat perfectly still and tranquil. When the man had done, and felt relieved, father began, in the gentlest manner, to say to him, "Well, if all you say is true, I think you are right in the severity of your remarks; but I suppose that if in any regard you are not correct, you are willing to be set right." "Yes," said the man with a growl, "of course I am." "Well, will you allow me to make one statement?" said father, humbling himself before the man. "Yes." So father began with a little matter, and stated it; and then he went a little further; until, by and by, the man began to lose color, and at last broke

28 *Patriotic Addresses*, op. cit., pp. 29–30.
29 *Lectures on Preaching*, op. cit., pp. 214, 188.
30 Crocker, op. cit., I:379.
31 *Patriotic Addresses*, op. cit., pp. 6, 137.

out, "I have been all wrong in this matter; I do not understand it." After he had gone away, father said to me, in a sort of casual manner, "Give up, and beat 'em."[32]

His manner of delivery was generally suited to his audience situation and to the topic he was developing. After his death the Boston *Advertiser* paid tribute to "that gift of wellnigh magical eloquence which for forty years astonished and thrilled and held spellbound the packed thousands in that Brooklyn meeting-house . . . , that personal magnetism, that intuitive knowledge of human nature, that all-creative imagination" which made Beecher "the pulpit phenomenon of his time."[33] The themes he developed with this eloquent power were those of most significance to his time: the transformation of the church from a guardian of the doorway to eternity into a guide to moral conduct, the liberation of theology from interpretation of the Scriptures to an exposition of divinity at work in evolution and in accordance with the natural laws of science, antislavery, temperance, and women's rights. Withal, Beecher was no revolutionist; he considered Grant the greatest American President and found no reason to quarrel with the economic system which enriched many of his parishioners. He was conservative enough in his social predilections so that the liberalism of his basic ideas found all the readier and the broader acceptance.

While many of his contemporary ministers recoiled from Charles Darwin as from Satan himself, Beecher preached on "Evolution and Religion," saying, "I have hailed the evolutionary philosphy with joy."[34] When he was advised that a preacher's function is with spirituality not politics, he preached on "The Sphere of the Christian Minister," declaring, "The moment a man so conducts his profession that it touches the question of right and wrong, he comes into my sphere. There I stand; and I put God's measure, the golden reed of the sanctuary, on him and his course; and I am his master."[35] In 1863 he went to England for a vacation, and finding misunderstanding of the Civil War, in part because England's textile industry was suffering from loss of Southern cotton, with consequent high unemployment, he delivered a magnificent series of speeches defending the North as a liberator of the slaves.[36] In these talks, particularly at Manchester and Liverpool,

---

[32] *Ibid.*, p. 25.
[33] Ira V. Brown, *Lyman Abbott: Christian Revolutionist*, Cambridge: Harvard University Press, 1953, pp. 116–117.
[34] *Patriotic Addresses, op. cit.*, p. 159.
[35] *Ibid.*, p. 80.
[36] Hibben cites evidence that the speeches in England had little influence on public opinion or governmental policy, *op. cit.*, pp. 161–163. This evaluation is supported by John H. Timmis, III, "The Function and Relative Effect of Public Speaking on British Foreign Policy During the 1861 Mediation Crisis in Anglo-American Rela-

Beecher provided one of history's best examples of how to deal with a hostile audience. By patiently enduring the jeers of his foes, and by appealing to the English love of fair play, he converted noisy opposition into enthusiastic receptiveness of his message.

It was on the most sensational topic of the time, the slavery issue, that Beecher won his greatest acclaim. His biographer Hibben feels that he came to the antislavery cause late (not until 1847) and embraced it then only because he sensed a strong public support for abolitionism. Even Hibben, however, found that "on occasion" Beecher did not lack courage—as in his sermon charging that exploitation of labor in Northern factories was akin to slavery on the Southern plantations.[37] When, during the 1874 presidential campaign, Beecher proclaimed that "I became an Abolitionist the moment I was born,"[38] he grossly exaggerated. But when he did pick up the banner of abolitionism, he became virtually Garrisonian in his zeal. Denouncing the Compromise of 1850, he thundered, "If the compromises of the Constitution include requisitions which violate humanity, I will not be bound by them."[39] William Henry Seward heard Beecher preach on February 18, 1854, and, while Hibben judged that Beecher "left no intellectual impression whatever on Seward,"[40] the fact is that the Senator's doctrine of "irrepressible conflict," which he stated four year's later, emerged in this sermon by Beecher in these words: "the two great principles must come into collision and fight till one or the other is dead." Then it was that Beecher performed one of the most dramatic acts ever produced in an American church. He sent to Staunton, Virginia, for a beautiful mulatto girl who was to be sold by her own white father into prostitution "down South" and conducted a slave auction from his pulpit platform, to raise money for her purchase and maintenance in freedom. As Beecher cried, "Will you allow this praying woman to go back to meet the fate for which her father sold her? Who bids? Who bids? . . . ."

> Women became hysterical; men were almost beside themselves. For half an hour money was heaped into the contribution boxes, while those to whom the baskets seemed too slow in coming, threw coin and banknotes upon the pulpit. Women took off their jewelry and put it into the baskets. Rings, bracelets, brooches, piled one upon the other. Men unfastened their watches and handed them to the ushers.[41]

tions During the American Civil War," M.A. thesis, unpublished, The Pennsylvania State University, Sept., 1962. The British Government had already firmly decided against recognition of the Confederacy *before* Beecher's arrival in England.

[37] *Ibid.*, p. 154.
[38] *Ibid.*, p. 306.
[39] *Ibid.*, p. 117.
[40] *Ibid.*, p. 133.
[41] *Ibid.*, p. 136.

As the war was ending, Beecher suggested to Lincoln that it would be a good stroke of public relations to send a shipload of Sunday School teachers to Ft. Sumter, in Charleston harbor, to attend the raising of the federal flag on the anniversary of the firing on the fort.[42] Beecher was asked to make the speech, which was delivered April 14, 1865. He worked very carefully upon it, writing it out, as he infrequently did. In it he tried hard to define an attitude and a policy for reconciliation between the sections.

The South must accept its defeat unconditionally, he said.[43] But this meant only that slavery was forever abolished, that loyalty to the national government would be enforced. "I charge the whole guilt of this war upon the ambitious, educated, plotting, political leaders of the South," he said and added that they would be judged by God at the last judgment for their crimes. As for the South itself, he itemized seven benefits which the war had brought to it: an end to the doctrine of secession; respect for the rights of minorities; destruction of its vain belief in the personal superiority of its aristocratic sons; the revelation of the capabilities of the Negroes; conversion from an agricultural to an industrial economy; the advancement of the interests of the white laboring class; and freedom to develop education. He tried to allay the fears of the defeated: "We do not want your cities nor your fields . . . . All that we ask is unswerving loyalty." Then he pointed toward a future in which the union would be the stronger for having endured and surmounted a war to defend its institutions. And he concluded with "solemn congratulations" that God had sustained Abraham Lincoln to the completion of the task of safeguarding the nation—not knowing, of course, that even as he spoke, Lincoln was on the threshold of death.

Six months later, as Andrew Johnson was locked in conflict with Thaddeus Stevens over the issues of reconstruction, Beecher preached a bold sermon in which he declared: "There are many who desire to see the South humbled. For my own part, I think it to be the great need of this nation to save the self-respect of the South."[44] He went on to plead that the North work not against the Southern whites but with them to develop a program to improve the lot of the freed Negroes. This was Beecher at his best.

In his latter years Henry Ward Beecher became manifestly less spiritual, more secular. To one listener (as early as 1859) "He seems to me a stump-speaker who has mistaken his way and stumbled into a church."[45] His salary at Plymouth church mounted to $20,000, and he

[42] *Ibid.*, pp. 169–170.
[43] *Patriotic Addresses*, *op. cit.*, pp. 676–697.
[44] *Ibid.*, p. 718.
[45] Hibben, quoting Adam Badeau, *op. cit.*, p. 152.

was earning many thousands besides on the lecture platform. His sermons came to be more political, even partisan, and it was as natural for him to discuss problems of finance as it had been in earlier days to consider matters of individual morality. He found women attractive and underwent a sensational trial in which his own friends and supporters found it difficult not to convict him of adultery.[46] Yet so great was the magnetism of the man and the power of his preaching that the fickle and scandal-mongering public remained true to him against all charges and evidence, and his church remained crowded until his death. The long journey which he took from his birth, on June 24, 1813, to his death, March 8, 1887, has never been better depicted than in two statements by the iconoclastic critic of the church, Robert Green Ingersoll. The first was this: "Henry Ward Beecher was born in a Puritan penitentiary of which his father was one of the wardens."[47] And the other, which has already been quoted earlier, Beecher himself would probably like to have stand as his memorial: "I think Mr. Beecher has liberalized the English-speaking people of the world."[48]

Religions of Challenge and of Comfort: Charles Grandison Finney and Phillips Brooks

CHARLES GRANDISON FINNEY preached to change men; Philips Brooks to comfort and sustain them. The difference was profound, yet it was a difference in attitude and emphasis rather than in kind. Both men believed their mission was to unite their listeners more closely with God; once that was accomplished, all else that was needful would follow. Marie Hochmuth and Norman Mattis, in their study of Phillips Brooks, pointed to Brooks's "profound conviction that all improvement in society must be the product of a change in the character of the people who compose society."[1] James Robert Emmel, in his dissertation on Finney, concluded that: "[Finney] believed that basically social conditions would improve as men came to a full realization of what it means to love God and to be worthy of being loved by God."[2]

If the similarities are significant, the contrast between these two

---

[46] Robert Shaplen, *Free Love and Heavenly Sinners*, London: Andre Deutsch, 1956, had no doubt of Beecher's guilt. Hibben, *op. cit.*, pp. 101, 160, and Chapters 21–28, was equally sure that Beecher had had other affairs as well.
[47] Cramer, *Royal Bob, op. cit.*, p. 23.
[48] Rogers, *Colonel Bob Ingersoll, op. cit.*, p. 245.
[1] Marie Hochmuth and Norman W. Mattis, "Phillips Brooks," in Brigance, ed., *History and Criticism, op. cit.*, I:310.
[2] James Robert Emmel, "The Persuasive Techniques of Charles Grandison Finney as a Revivalist and Social Reform Speaker, 1820–1860," unpublished Ph.D. thesis, The Pennsylvania State University, 1959, p. 119.

preachers emerges from the study of their personalities, their careers, and the messages they preached. Their own words bring it out most clearly. To Finney, "Mere outward reform is of no avail—Reform of the heart is alone able to secure permanent good."[3] What this meant he defined in his sermons as "a change from selfishness to benevolence, from having a supreme regard to one's own interest to an absorbing and controlling choice of the happiness and glory of God and his kingdom."[4] The great revolutionary doctrine that Finney taught was that regenerated or converted man is good, not sinful, and that man has freedom of will to turn deliberately from a carnal to a spiritual life. He was interested in various reforms: particularly abolition of slavery; temperance; education for women; purification of politics; safeguarding the Sabbath for worship; and honesty in business dealings. But he said comparatively little about them and kept himself aloof from identification with any group of reformers. What he sought, he kept insisting, was a *total reform* of the whole person, starting from the heart and working outward in all directions to comprise the totality of all behavior. In a blaze of controversy with the Princeton theologians, Finney renounced the Calvinistic ideas of the all-powerfulness of God and the utter weakness or passivity of man. Instead, he argued that God's will can only be done through the active partnership of converted men. Far from being utterly depraved, men can become sanctified and "perfect," he asserted, as they accept and develop their role of partnership with God. But much—most—of what passes for religious zeal is really only selfishness dressed up in theological terminology; the essential step—surrender of self to unification with God—has not been achieved:

> Many seem to mistake light for religion. They get some new views of religious truth which produce a corresponding excitement of mind, and they bustle about, under the impression that this excitement is religion; when, at the same time, if they would narrowly watch, it would be seen that their heart is still selfish, and not benevolent—that their ruling propensity or disposition is not changed—that while they are excited by their new views of religious truth, it is *emotion* and not *will* that is active. Their business habits and transactions will soon develop the fact that selfishness is, after all, in some form, the ruling propensity of their mind. In all such cases, there is of course a radical mistake, a fatal delusion, under which the mind is laboring.[5]

In sum, Finney was first, last, and always an evangelist. His business was with the unconverted and his aim was to accomplish conversions. In his

---

[3] From a chapel talk by Finney, quoted by Robert S. Fletcher, *A History of Oberlin College*, Oberlin, Ohio: Oberlin College, 1943, I:210.
[4] Emmel, *op. cit.*, p. 103.
[5] *Ibid.*, p. 262.

view the preacher is a prophet whose mission is to bring men to God; and once this is done there is little need for further ministerial supervision over the relations between worshippers and their deity.

Phillips Brooks was equally spiritual but in a different way. Instead of underscoring the need for dramatic and dynamic change through conversion, his emphasis was upon the quiet and soulful perception and appreciation of God. Acrobatic preaching and assertive personalization in sermons were offensive to him. At the age of twenty seven, in 1863, he wrote to his father: "Henry Ward Beecher has been here this week, and spoke to a tremendous crowd at the Academy of Music. I went of course. It was very curious to see him applauded and see him petted by all the old fogies of Philadelphia."[6] What he may have thought of Finney, he apparently never said; perhaps he didn't think of him at all. There was a curious remoteness about the life and the preaching of Brooks. He felt that men needed constant ministering to nurture their spirituality. But he shrank from discussion of current affairs; his business was with eternity. Equally, he could not conceive of a dramatic moment of conversion. Man is God's creature, from beginning to end, always; only the light is dim and the flame must be tended to keep it from going out and to make it instead glow brighter. The particular meant little to him—even so large a particular as the theory of evolution, or the struggle to end slavery:

> It is not the difficulty of this or that doctrine that makes men skeptics today. It is rather the play of all life upon the fundamental grounds and general structure of faith. It is the meeting in the commonest minds of great perpetual tides of thought and instinct which neutralize each other, such as the tides of faith and providence, the tides of pessimism and optimism, the tides of self-sacrifice and selfishness.[7]

With such a view, Brooks did not seek to "win sinners to God" but tried, rather, to help his regular parishioners, Sunday after Sunday, to attain and maintain a stronger spiritual union with divinity. Even the true worshipper, he thought, "is ignorant and rebellious—the prodigal child of God; but his ignorance and rebellion never break that first relationship. It is always a child ignorant of his Father; always a child rebellious against his Father."[8] Brooks was the preacher as priest, constant in attendance to the needs of his congregation, much as a shepherd must always care for his flock.

In personality Finney and Brooks were as different as were their aims

---

[6] Allen, *Phillips Brooks, op. cit.,* I:478.
[7] *Ibid.,* II:330, quoting from Brooks's 1878 lecture on "The Teaching of Religion," delivered at the Yale Divinity School.
[8] *Ibid.,* II:346, quoting from Brooks's 1879 lecture, "The Influence of Jesus."

and their diverse messages. Finney was a child of the frontier, from an impoverished home, without education, where religion was never mentioned. He became a shrewd and effective lawyer before he was converted, near the age of thirty, by a jerking, shouting, arm-waving evangelist in a meeting that was a bedlam of agonized frenzy.[9] Shortly Finney freed himself from the camp-meeting mannerisms of "jerking sinners out of hell" and instead developed a style of preaching that resembled a lawyer's courtroom arguments to a jury. Perhaps for this reason, his evangelism was especially effective with professional men, particularly lawyers and doctors. Most of his sermons were extemporaneous, or even impromptu. They typically ran for one or two hours, and were very energetic. As Finney himself described one of them, "It was a fire and a hammer breaking the rock; and as the sword that was piercing to the dividing asunder of body and spirit."[10] He would make outlines of his sermons, not in preparation for actual speaking, but rather to remind himself what ground he might cover at another time to another audience. Since he was constantly seeking new listeners who stood in need of salvation, he could and did repeat the same message again and again. He ridiculed the idea of writing out sermons and was suspicious of any studied preparation. "We can never have the *full meaning* of the gospel," he declared, "till we throw away our notes."[11] While he presided as president for many years over Oberlin College, he was always sensitive to the charge of his critics that he lacked thoughtfulness and failed to instruct his listeners. He knew he could not win a case in court by reading a speech to a jury and he felt the same was true when he was in the pulpit.

Finney was described as "a tall, grave-looking man"; one of the students at Oberlin called him "the crossest-looking man I ever saw." He preferred to speak from a platform, or from the floor of a hall, rather than from a pulpit, and when he preached he wore a business suit rather than clerical garb. A news reporter who heard him in 1830 said, "It did not sound like preaching, but like a lawyer arguing a case before a court and jury." Then he added, "I have heard many celebrated pulpit orators in various parts of the world. Taken all in all, I never knew the superior of Charles G. Finney."[12] Another listener found him "vigorous in his delivery, dramatic in his attack, magnetic in his appeal."[13] His constant endeavor was to bring his message directly and personally to the members of his audience. How he preached was described vividly by an

---

[9] Emmel, *op. cit.,* pp. 49–51.
[10] *Ibid.,* pp. 301–302.
[11] *Ibid.,* p. 307.
[12] Stanton, *Random Recollections, op. cit.,* pp. 40–41.
[13] Emmel, *op. cit.,* p. 318, quoting Philemon H. Fowler.

Oberlin graduate, who recalled sermons Finney preached in the college chapel:

> Indeed, it almost makes one shudder, even after the lapse of years, to recall some of them—that especially from the text, "The Wages of sin is death"! The preacher's imagination was as vivid as his logic was inexorable . . . . How he rung the changes on that word "wages" as he described the condition of the lost soul: "You will get your 'wages'; just what you have earned, your due; nothing more, nothing less; and as the smoke of your torment, like a thick cloud, ascends forever and ever, you will see written upon its curling folds, in great staring letters of light, the awful word, *wages*, *Wages*, *WAGES!*"
> As the preacher uttered this sentence, he stood at full height, tall and majestic—stood as if transfixed, gazing and pointing toward the emblazoned cloud, as it seemed to roll up before him: his clear shrill voice rising to its highest pitch, and penetrating every nook and corner of the vast assembly. People held their breath. Every heart stood still.[14]

Phillips Brooks, on the other hand, was the epitome of majestic dignity and control. Standing six feet four inches tall and weighing over 200 pounds, with a richly melodious voice that poured forth its diction at the rate of 215 words a minute, he never went into the pulpit except in his meticulously clerical robes and he never spoke except to read from manuscripts that he always wrote out in full on 8″ by 6¾″ note paper.[15] In a schoolboy essay, written at the age of fifteen, he declared with italicized emphasis that "*Men like to be talked to better than to be preached at; they prefer the easy-chair to the pulpit.*"[16] The lesson was one he only partially remembered. In 1863, when he was twenty seven, he was invited to preach a trial sermon in Trinity Church, in Philadelphia. It was a hot July day, no announcement had been made of Brooks's coming, and "the congregation was so small as to seem almost invisible." However, a visitor, who "might sit where I liked, for there was scarce anybody in the church," described his preaching thus:

> When the time for the sermon arrived, a person who had been sitting silent in the chancel, muffled in a black gown, emerged—or rather projected himself—in the direction of the pulpit. A tall, thin figure rushed up the pulpit steps. Before fairly reaching the top of them a voice called out the text, and instantly broke into a speech of most astonishing rapidity, quite beyond anything I had ever experienced or imagined of human utterance . . . . As soon as I recovered from my surprise, and the mind could catch its breath, so to speak, and begin

[14] Charles P. Bush, *Reminiscences of Rev. Charles G. Finney*, Oberlin: Oberlin Press, 1876, p. 12.
[15] Hochmuth and Mattis, *op. cit.*, I:312; Allen, *op. cit.*, I:282.
[16] Allen, *op. cit.*, I:85.

to keep up with the preacher's pace, I perceived that what I was hearing was a wonderful sermon, such as would oftenest be called brilliant, perhaps, but is better described as glowing or lambent . . . and the discourse contained material for a score of sermons, so rich was it in high thought and apt illustration and illuminative turns of phrase.[17]

Quite unlike both Beecher and Finney, Brooks delighted to speak from a manuscript, enjoying both the writing and the later reading. In his first lectures on preaching, at Yale in 1877, he said: "I think that every earnest preacher is often more excited as he writes, kindles more then with the glow of sending truth to men, than he ever does in speaking; and the wonderful thing is, that that fire, if it is really present in the sermon when it is written, stays there, and breaks out into flames again, when the delivery of the sermon comes. The enthusiasm is stowed away and is kept."[18]

Finney, born in 1792, continued active as preacher, lecturer, and college administrator until his death on August 16, 1875. He was almost always engaged in conflict. He was ordained a Presbyterian but remained essentially a non-denominational layman preacher. At his ordination examination he was asked if he believed in the Westminster Confession. He had never so much as read it, but he replied unblinkingly that he believed it insofar as he understood it.[19] He thought Presbyterian theology consisted largely of "you can and you can't, you shall and you shan't, you will and you won't; you'll be damned if you do, and you'll be damned if you don't."[20] Without mincing words and with apparent joy in controversy, he spelled out his rejection of predestination and of the whole concept of man's supposed helplessness to redeem himself.[21] He also often deeply disturbed the sinners whom he drove with whiplash scorn to repentance and conversion, as in one passage in which he depicted condemned souls who had served their time in hell leaping up to the pearly gates, shouting: "Stand away, you old saints of God! . . . . And you, too, Jesus Christ, stand one side! Get out of our way! No thanks to you our being here: we came here on our merits." One of the devices he used freely, indeed, was shock. In another revival sermon he cried out:

> Why, sinner, I tell you, if you could climb to heaven, you would hurl God from his throne! Yes, hurl God from his throne! Oh, yes, if you

---

[17] *Ibid.*, I:458–459.
[18] *Ibid.*, II:309–310.
[19] Emmel, *op. cit.*, pp. 57–58.
[20] *Ibid.*, p. 86, quoting from Finney's *Lectures on Revivals.*
[21] Cf. Finney's *Sermons on Important Subjects*, New York: John S. Taylor, 3rd ed., 1836.

could but get there, you would cut God's throat! Yes, you would cut God's throat![22]

With such preaching Finney was in constant demand in Ohio, New York, New England, and in England. Normally, year after year, he would preach three times on Sunday and three or four times during the week. His enormous vitality occasionally sagged but never flagged. To the end he remained a dynamo of regenerative fire.

Phillips Brooks was a product of New England ultra-respectability—a direct descendant of John Cotton. He was educated in Harvard, loved the study more than the drawing room, and even after his ordination was seriously tempted to abandon his successful ministry, with a salary of $4000 a year and an assured future, for an obscure post as professor of theology at $1800. After six years at the Episcopal Church of the Holy Trinity in Philadelphia, Brooks accepted a call to Trinity Church, in Boston, where he remained for a quarter century, until his death, at the age of fifty nine, in 1893. He was showered with honors, a principal one being an invitation to preach before Queen Victoria, and remained remote from controversy. Of the 372 sermons he preached in Philadelphia,[23] he published only five; and from his lifetime of preaching, he printed fewer than one hundred sermons. Perhaps he was wise. Brooks possessed high intelligence and a noble serenity of spirit which illumined his speaking and enthralled his congregations. But his refusal to discuss topical issues, or even to use specific instances to illustrate his thought, gives to the printed texts a rather flaccid and sweetly hazy obscurity. Far from shocking, he soothed. Yet when he spoke, such was the power of his personality, that he won tributes such as this from a dour Scotsman, Dr. Tulloch, Principal of St. Mary's College of the University of Aberdeen, who heard him in 1874 and wrote his wife:

> I have just heard the most remarkable sermon I ever heard in my life (I use the word in no American sense) from Mr. Phillips Brooks, an Episcopal clergyman here: equal to the best of Frederick Robertson's sermons, with a vigor and force of thought which he has not always. I never heard preaching like it, and you know how slow I am to praise preachers. So much thought and so much life combined; such a reach of mind, and such a depth and insight of soul. I was electrified. I could have got up and shouted.[24]

The effect is impressive. So is the fact that Tulloch made no effort to tell his wife what Brooks said. Hochmuth and Mattis remark that in

[22] Both passages are from Weisberger, *They Gathered at the River, op. cit.,* p. 115.
[23] Allen, *op. cit.,* II:119.
[24] *Ibid.,* II:247.

1865, at a Harvard memorial service, Brooks delivered a prayer so moving that it quite dimmed the other contributions to the program; yet no word of it was preserved, not even in the memory of the enchanted listeners.[25] So it was ever to be with Phillips Brooks: the man himself was overpowering; his words flowed through the mind, and on, and were gone.

Salesmen of Salvation: Dwight L. Moody and Billy Sunday

DWIGHT L. MOODY and Billy Sunday converted religion into big business. It was Moody who reached the conclusion that "every human being on earth was a customer for salvation."[1] In the words of the historian W. G. McLoughlin, Jr., "Charles Finney made revivalism a profession, but Dwight L. Moody made it a big business."[2] Billy Sunday, following in his footsteps a generation later, added the element of sensational entertainment, declaring, "I'd stand on my head in a mud puddle if I thought it would help me win souls to Christ," but at the same time remained hardheaded about the practicalities—as when his advance agent, dickering with the ministers of Denver concerning a projected evangelistic campaign, flatly told them: "The campaign will cost you $25,000. For $25,000 you can give the devil a good run for his money."[3] Ministers from John Cotton to Phillips Brooks had studied their vocation with exhaustive care; but these titans of the revival tent sold salvation with a sizzle. Like the salesmen they were, they concentrated less on the product than on the customers. Critics may argue over how much they knew about religion; but it is obvious that they were masters of mass persuasion.

The parallels between the two men are astonishing. Both came from impoverished homes; both were semi-orphans from babyhood; in neither home was there any significant religious influence; neither received more than the crudest of educations. Both of them became quickly and highly successful in vocations far removed from the ministry: Moody as a shoe-salesman and investor, earning $5000 a year by his twenty-first birthday and boasting to his brother that he had loaned $100 at the rate of seventeen percent a day; Sunday as a professional

[25] Hochmuth and Mattis, *op. cit.,* I:294–295.
[1] Weisberger, *They Gathered at the River, op. cit.,* p. 176.
[2] William G. McLoughlin, Jr., *Modern Revivalism: Charles Grandison Finney to Billy Graham,* New York: Ronald Press, 1959, p. 166.
[3] William G. McLoughlin, Jr., *Billy Sunday Was His Real Name,* Chicago: University of Chicago Press, 1955, pp. 154 and 66.

baseball player with the Chicago White Sox, where one year he batted .359 and another year stole 95 bases. Neither of them showed early promise as a speaker. Moody all his life remained ungrammatical, and his enunciation and pronunciation always were slovenly. After he abandoned baseball to take up religion, Sunday worked for the great evangelist J. Wilbur Chapman, who tried hard to teach him to speak but gave up when Sunday stammered and stuttered and could scarcely utter a coherent sentence. Sunday took lessons in rhetoric from Dean Cumnock, at the Evanston Academy (later to be Northwestern University), but there is no evidence that these helped him much. He began to speak only when he had to—that is, when he lost his job with Chapman and got an opportunity to preach a week of revival sermons at a little town named Garner, in Iowa. Then he "borrowed" the outlines of seven of Chapman's sermons and plunged in to the week's revival. At the end, he received $68 and had one hundred converts. He was launched.[4]

Dwight L. Moody, whose speaking career is depicted in an especially helpful study by Robert Huber,[5] decided to forego his successful business career when he was twenty two and surrender himself to the intoxicating work of saving souls. To his mother he wrote: "I go to meeting every night. Oh, how I enjoy it! It seems as if God were here himself." His initial enterprise was to "go out on the streets button-holing every man that came along" to try to send him to meetings of the YMCA, or to a Methodist or a Congregational church. Very soon, however, he rented a hall in a slum area of Chicago where he started a Sunday School that quickly gained an enrollment of over a thousand, then started gospel services for adults in the evenings. At first he found other speakers, but gradually began doing more and finally all of the speaking himself.

Neither Moody nor Sunday was ever ordained. Neither identified with a denomination; neither had much knowledge of or interest in theology. To Moody heaven was a place, like Chicago, the Bible was the road-map by which to get there, and the vehicle was belief in Christ. Billy Sunday, whose modest goal was, "I want to be a giant for God," declared frequently that "I don't know any more about theology than a jack-rabbit does about pingpong, but I'm on the way to glory."[6] What both sought was to win converts—converts by the multiple thousands, men, women, and children, who would stream down the aisles at the

---

[4] *Ibid.*, p. 11.
[5] Robert B. Huber, "Dwight L. Moody," in Marie Kathryn Hochmuth, ed., *A History and Criticism of American Public Address, op. cit.*, III:222–261.
[6] William T. Ellis, *"Billy" Sunday: The Man and His Message*, Philadelphia: Universal Book and Bible House, 1914, pp. 15, 147.

close of their meetings, responding to Moody's call to "Come to Christ!" and to Sunday's invitation to "Hit the sawdust trail!" The numbers for both men were, cumulatively, in the hundreds of thousands. No one could know how many. The instruments of measurement were too indefinite. For those who added up the penitents who gasped out, "Take me, Jesus!" or "I'm coming, Lord!" the tally of conversions in single campaigns reached as many as 7000 or 10,000. Reverend J. T. Sunderland, a rather jaundiced critic of mass revivalism, pointed out the difficulty of assessing results: "If by success we mean notoriety, or the attracting of great crowds, then extraordinary success they have certainly achieved. But if by success we mean accomplishment of a work whose results are at all permanent . . . the results attained are more than doubtful."[7] Billy Sunday phrased the problem in his own forthright way when he said: "Salvation to some men is just as big a change as crawling out of a snowbank and going into a warm room. To other men, to become a Christian does not mean much of a change. Multitudes of men live good, honest, upright, moral lives. They will not have much to change to become a Christian."[8] Moody, too, believed that for some conversion came as a dramatically cataclysmic change and for others it was a slow process in which "Daily habits would be improved, chances of success increased, greater happiness attained, fear of death and the grave removed and, most important of all, the new convert would take a great interest in religious activities."[9]

Both Moody and Sunday, from initial awkwardness and fear of speaking, attained great skill in their own styles of speaking. Moody, who was short, stocky, and full-bearded, spoke with enormous rapidity—some two hundred words a minute—in short sentences, rarely using words of more than one and two syllables.[10] Billy Sunday lived up to the ideal he stated: "I want to preach the gospel so plainly that men can come from the factories and not have to bring along a dictionary."[11] Both men dominated their audiences completely, but in different ways. Moody spoke with a Bible opened in one hand, which he frequently pounded with a fist and from which he read appropriate verses. Billy Sunday won more attention by his "acrobatic preaching" than by any other charac-

[7] J. T. Sunderland, *Orthodoxy and Revivalism*, New York: James Miller, 1876, p. 105.
[8] McLoughlin, *Billy Sunday, op. cit.*, p. 129.
[9] Huber, *op. cit.*, III:236–237. Reverend Joseph B. Hennessey, Jr., "A Comparison of the Use of Theological Terms in the Speaking of D. L. Moody and Billy Graham," unpublished M.A. thesis, The Pennsylvania State University, June, 1960, concluded that "Graham has the tendency to be more orthodox than Moody and not the opposite, as one would think. Actually the shift is not away from orthodoxy, but more toward it" (p. 168).
[10] Huber, *op. cit.*, III:233, 240.
[11] Ellis, *op. cit.*, p. 69.

teristic. He would leap about the platform like a tiger pouncing on an antelope, tear off his coat and hurl it into the audience, pick up a chair and smash it across the piano, crouch on the floor like a runner about to take off on a race. Neither man would abide anything less than perfect attention. In Moody's meetings, if an exuberant worshipper would whoop out an "Amen!" the evangelist would stop, fix him with a cold eye, and declare, "I'll do all the hollering around here!" Billy Sunday put sawdust on the floor, for he said that an auditor walking across bare boards made a noise that broke the spell he sought to maintain. Both men used a squad of guards to remove disorderly or unruly auditors.

Their speaking was only the dramatic highlight of a carefully produced and highly organized total performance. Both men followed the practice of sending teams of workers into the chosen community weeks or even months in advance of their coming. Local committees were organized: of preachers, to coordinate their activities and insure harmonious cooperation; of businessmen, to raise funds, develop publicity, and insure crowds. Both men used skilled musicians to polarize the crowds with half an hour or more of group singing before the actual service began. Moody hired Ira B. Sankey and Sunday secured Homer A. Rodeheaver as soloists whose gospel hymns produced an almost hypnotic effect. Only rarely would either man speak in a church. They preferred wide open spaces and freedom from the inhibiting effects of stained glass windows, stiff oaken pews, and altars dominated by the sadly drooping figure of Christ on the Cross. Moody held his meetings in warehouses, or skating rinks, or theatres, or freight depots, or convention halls. Sunday insisted on the building of special tabernacles for his meetings, with seats crowded close together but with broad aisles for the parade of sinners, with bright lights, with a sturdy platform on which to do his gymnastics, and with "never more than two nails in any board" on the walls, so that people could kick their way out in case of fire. At the close of the meetings, Moody would invite penitents to go into the "Inquiry rooms," each of which was manned by a staff of volunteer exhorters and comforters. Billy Sunday preferred to have the converts mass at the foot of his speaking platform.

The goal of the meetings was to get as many people as possible to "testify" that they were lost in sin until the moment when they turned from their past to "accept Christ." With such an aim, the audience had to be packed with the right kinds of people. The evangelists wanted to avoid "the comfortable class who spent their leisure in running from meeting to meeting"[12] and might not be impressionable. Moody said

---

[12] George Adam Smith, *The Life of Henry Drummond*, New York: Doubleday and McClure, 1896, p. 98.

publicly in London that "It's time for Christians to stop coming here and crowding into the best seats." And to one of his audiences he said: "I see too many Christian people here. I know you. A great many of you were at my meetings in Islington. You are converted already. Now I want you to get up and go out and leave room for the hundreds of those sinners who are waiting outside for a chance to come in and hear the Gospel."[13] The appeal of both evangelists was aimed primarily toward "down-and-outers"—poor, dissolute, hopeless, uneducated, uncared for. These were the ones who needed to "straighten up." But the show was too good, and their "standing room only" appeal was too potent for them to be able to limit the crowds. Typically the halls they used would contain from 8000 to 20,000 or more; and it was almost unthinkable that there would be space left for a single additional standee. Sunday appeared to care less than did Moody if the fashionable crowded in with the fanatics. "I hate to see a man roll up to church in a limousine and then drop a quarter in the collection plate," was his comment on the quality of his audience.[14]

Money, indeed, is one of the fascinating and only partially known facets of the revival business. Moody, as has been noted, was doing well by lending money at seventeen percent a day before he turned to revivalism. His organization frequently reiterated to the newspapers that neither Moody nor his singer, Sankey, ever received any salary for their services. But the collections from various meetings ran to $40,000 in New York City, $30,000 in Philadelphia, $22,000 in Chicago, and $140,000 in London. There was no accounting, no auditing of the books, no income tax to pay. Questions about the financial aspects of the meetings were far too delicate to be raised by the believers; and who cared what the skeptics might think? What Moody did with his money is, however, much better known, for he left as permanent monuments the Northfield Seminary for Girls, the Mount Hermon School for Boys, the Northfield Summer Bible Conferences, the Bible Institute for Home and Foreign Missions, and the Colportage Library Publications.

Billy Sunday's financial involvements were somewhat more obscure. He never tired of telling his audiences that he gave up a $500-monthly job (which he sometimes forgetfully described as a $1000-monthly paycheck) in professional baseball to accept $83 a month from the YMCA. Soon he was doing better. At one meeting in Philadelphia $15,000 was donated for charity, $50,000 for local expenses, and $52,849.97 as a "gift" for Mr. Sunday.[15] Sunday always refused to answer any questions

[13] McLoughlin, *Modern Revivalism, op. cit.,* pp. 202–203; McLoughlin, *Billy Sunday, op. cit.,* p. 212.
[14] Ellis, *op. cit.,* p. 78.
[15] *Ibid.,* p. 60.

about the size of his income or what he did with it, but he was sensitively aware of the criticisms. He pointed to the enormous numbers whom he "saved for Christ," and said, "In spite of all these high figures, you kick about what I get. What I'm paid for my work makes it only about $2 a soul, and I get less proportionately for the number I convert than any other living evangelist."[16] He went on to compare his "take" with the $100,000 annually earned by William Jennings Bryan for his Chautauqua lectures and denied that his earnings were graft unless Bryan's were. Sunday's most careful biographer estimates that his average income, beyond expenses and in addition to what he gave to charities, was $80,000 a year; and Dun and Bradstreet rated him at the height of his career as "worth $1,500,000." When a meeting in Washington, D.C. netted him $16,332, it was noted as the "smallest Sunday had received in five years."[17] Meanwhile, his star singer, Rodeheaver, was paid $200 a week and other members of his staff got only $30 to $50 a week, with Mrs. Sunday carefully supervising to make sure they got no more. Sunday's method of stimulating large donations was to belittle the value of money to its possessor. He told of the death of Vanderbilt, who was reputed to have $200,000,000. When he died, Sunday pointed out, and it was asked, "How much did he leave?" the answer was, "He left it all." Then he drove the lesson home:

> Naked you came into this world, and naked you will crawl out of it. You brought nothing into the world and you will take nothing out, and if you have put the pack screws on the poor and piled up a pile of gold as big as a house you can't take it with you. It wouldn't do you any good if you could, because it would melt.[18]

As this sample shows, Sunday dramatized his speaking by direct personalization, by lavish use of specific examples, by reiteration, by use of colloquial language, and by considerable humor. He was also skilled in the coinage of aphorisms, which circulated widely and helped build his fame. For example:

> Death-bed repentance is burning the candle of life in the service of the devil, and then blowing the smoke into the face of God.
> Churches don't need new members half as much as they need the old bunch made over.
> The bars of the Church are so low that any old hog with two or three suits of clothes and a bank roll can crawl through.
> Whiskey is all right in its place—but it's place is in hell.

[16] McLoughlin, *Billy Sunday*, op. cit., p. 116.
[17] *Ibid.*, pp. 114–116.
[18] Ellis, op. cit., p. 270.

If you put a polecat in the parlor, you know which will change first
—the polecat or the parlor?

It won't save your soul if your wife is a Christian. You have got to be
something more than a brother-in-law to the Church.

Going to church doesn't make a man a Christian any more than
going to a garage makes him an automobile.

Wouldn't this city be a great place to live in if some people would
die, get converted, or move away?

There would be more power in the prayers of some folks if they
would put more white money in the collection basket.[19]

A University of Chicago professor who often heard Moody preach
described him as "incomparably the most artless preacher in the world.
. . . The particular sermon is apt to be like so much preaching cut off
from an endless reel of such. The piece cut off might be longer, or it
might be shorter, and in either case the unity and the completeness
would remain unaffected. The conclusion is where the preacher stops,
not where the treatment has reached a goal . . . . The goal has been as
much in sight all the way as it is when the sermon stops."[20] Huber
found that Moody prepared his sermons by putting an outline of a topic
into a blue linen envelope and, from time to time, adding pertinent
clippings or other materials. On the outside of the envelope he wrote
the date and place of delivery of the sermon. More than four hundred
such envelopes were left by Moody; and one of the sermons, "The New
Birth," had been delivered 193 times.[21] Despite his vast amount of
preaching to large audiences, he retained all his life the conviction and
habit of personal evangelism. He tirelessly visited homes, dropped in at
saloons, stopped people on the street, button-holed drunks, and poured
forth his message of salvation.

What McLoughlin concluded about Billy Sunday applies to Moody as
well. Both men were "a symbol of the American dream, a living embodiment of the mythical farm boy who went to the city and made good, an
orphaned bricklayer's [or farmer's] son who rose to fame and wealth,
whose name became a byword throughout the land, and who lived on
familiar terms with the leading figures of his day."[22] Perhaps both men
represented a "theology which in sober thought a man would cast away
with loathing."[23] Beyond doubt, they were master organizers of mass

[19] *Ibid.*, pp. 72–79.
[20] William C. Wilkinson, "Dwight L. Moody as a Preacher," *Homiletic Review*, 36
(August, 1898):114.
[21] Huber, *op. cit.*, III:234.
[22] McLoughlin, *Billy Sunday*, *op. cit.*, p. 297.
[23] Sunderland, *op. cit.*, p. 114.

persuasion. Moody devised the system; Sunday, and in recent years Billy Graham, have thus far been his most able American successors. When speaking becomes "big business" it incorporates a great deal that is far removed from the rhetorical arts; but its results can be incomparably "big."

XI

FORENSIC ELOQUENCE
1800 ‿ 1900

The Nature of Courtroom Oratory 📖

THE FUNCTION of a lawyer is not to decide what is right and what is wrong, or what is legal and what is illegal, or who is innocent and who is guilty. These are determinations to be made by judges and juries. The lawyer is an advocate. When he undertakes a case his business is to do what he properly can to win it. Whether he wins or loses will depend to some degree upon the facts and the evidence, upon the statute and common laws, and upon the prevailing mood and attitudes of the community within which the case is tried. But the result will also depend upon how well he marshals, arranges, and presents the evidence: upon his skill in speech. The lawyers who attain success are, in the end, those who win their cases. "Law as a philosophy," as Thurman Arnold has well said, "is the property of scholars; as a technique it is the property of lawyers."[1]

If no client of Henry Clay's was ever found guilty in a capital case, this does not mean that none of them had unjustly taken the life of a fellow man. In the only capital case in which he served as the prosecutor, Clay did secure the death penalty—for a man he believed to be innocent. Meanwhile, he was becoming wealthy primarily by winning land title cases, through his "potent art of oratory"—his "dramatic adroitness and almost mesmerizing power over juries."[2] It is not the business of a lawyer to decide in advance of the courtroom verdict upon the justice or the injustice of the cause which he represents; or at least so most lawyers have averred. It is for reasons such as these that the young Daniel Webster almost determined to become a teacher rather than a lawyer, and when he did elect the legal profession, he wrote: "I pray God to fortify me against its temptations."[3] Something of this sort

[1] Thurman W. Arnold, *The Symbols of Government*, New Haven: Yale University Press, 1935, p. 129.
[2] Bernard Mayo, *Henry Clay*, op. cit., Chapter III, "A Frontier Lawyer," particularly pp. 103, 105, 108, 110, and 111.
[3] Curtis, *Life of Daniel Webster*, op. cit., I:55. A contrary view has been stated by Judge Samuel Leibowitz:"My experience as a lawyer and judge, however, convinces me that lawyers who practice in our criminal courts are for the most part high-

was probably in the mind of Rufus Choate when, after graduation from college and entry into law school, he wrote to his best undergraduate friend, who was entering the ministry: "We go on together no longer; our paths are widely asunder already, to diverge still more at every step."[4] One of the earliest American novels (written by a lawyer) is in part a defense of the law against the many criticisms that were directed against it.[5]

A major criticism often directed against courtroom pleading is that it deals with trivial technicalities rather than with basic issues or principles. What law practice consists of was thus described by a great lawyer who had grown weary of it: "Quibbling, raising nasty little points—answering those who deal in mean decisions—reading idiotic decisions —talking about absurd statutes—hearing witnesses, who are liars, tell about things that never happened—listening to the opinions of a judge as ignorant as Balaam's jack-ass."[6] This indictment was written, of course, in a jaundiced mood. But in the heat of the courtroom battles lawyers direct much these same charges back and forth against one another. The courtly Joseph H. Choate, arguing a case in 1884, protested that the opposing counsel had gone too far. "They would introduce me to your Honor as a flippant pettifogger, who has nothing to present in behalf of his client but technicalities and possible flaws in the indictment."[7] Robert Ingersoll, at the height of his fame, in 1891, responded to a similar line of attack by saying to the jury: "Now, let us be honest about this matter—let us be fair. It is not a personal quarrel between lawyers. I never quarrel with anybody; my philosophy being that everybody does as he must, and if he is in bad luck and does wrong, why let us pity him, and if we happen to have good luck, and take the path where roses bloom, why let us be joyful. That is my doctrine; no need of fighting about these little things. They are all over in a little while anyway."[8]

Forensic eloquence would be of small avail if all cases in the courtroom were decided simply by an objective analysis of the facts and the law. Not even judges—and certainly not juries—are always objective.

minded, honest and decent people. Also I am fully convinced that our criminal courts offer the cleanest and most challenging battleground for the testing of legal knowledge and wisdom." Quentin Reynolds, *Courtroom*, New York: Popular Library, 1963, based on 1950 edition, p. 9.

[4] Samuel Gilman Brown, *The Life of Rufus Choate*, Boston: Little, Brown, 1898, p. 30.

[5] Hugh Henry Brackenridge, *Modern Chivalry*, New York: American Book Co., 1937, based on editions of 1792 to 1815.

[6] Robert Green Ingersoll, quoted by C. H. Cramer in *Royal Bob*, op. cit., p. 220.

[7] Frederick C. Hicks, *Famous American Jury Speeches*, St. Paul: West Pub. Co., 1925, p. 3.

[8] *Ibid.*, p. 220.

The facts may be obscure, or contradictory, or incomplete. The law is not a single statute but a vast maze of legislation and custom and court decisions that have accumulated through generations and centuries, each item having been interpreted and reinterpreted multiple times in terms of differing specific cases and by judicial minds having their own special biases. The lawyer must attempt to conduct the untrained minds of the jurymen, or the jaded mind of the judge, through a complex train of specific facts, while the opposing attorney may be seeking to divert their attention with such "loud reiteration of half-truths that they have neither curiosity nor energy for elaborate investigation."[9] Meanwhile, the lawyers, the clients, and the witnesses are not scientific investigators attempting to ferret out the truth; they are contestants who exercise a rather wide latitude in trying to befuddle and confuse one another and their listeners, when they think this serves their purpose.

How the mind of the lawyer works—how it must work, as it deals not only with the law, the facts and their logical connections, but also with the psychology of the jurymen—appears in the following extracts from a closing address to the jury by Robert G. Ingersoll, as he sought to get a judgment setting aside a will on the ground that it was spurious. As a general proposition he argued that:

> There is this beautiful peculiarity in nature—a lie never fits a fact, never. You only fit a lie with another lie, made for the express purpose, because you can change a lie but you can't change a fact, and after a while the time comes when the last lie you tell has to be fitted to a fact, and right there is a bad joint; consequently you must test the statements of people who say they saw, not by what they say but by other facts, by surroundings, by what are called probabilities; by the naturalness of the statement. If we only had to hear what witnesses say, jurymen would need nothing but ears. Their brains could be dispensed with; but after you hear what they say you call a council in your brain and make up your mind whether the statement, in view of all the circumstances, is true or false.[10]

Having thus laid the groundwork for a critical, or skeptical, approach to the evidence opposing counsel had presented, Ingersoll proceeded to pinpoint what he considered to be lies in the evidence:

> Do you believe that Job Davis spelled sheet—a sheet of paper— "sheat"? That is the way he spells it in this document. Now let us be honor bright with each other, and do not let the lawyers on the other side treat you as if you were twelve imbeciles. You would better be

[9] Walter Bagehot, *Physics and Politics*, ed. Jacques Barzun, New York: Knopf, 1948, p. xxv, based on 1869 edition.
[10] Hicks, *op. cit.*, pp. 217–218.

misled by a sensible sinner than by the most pious absurdities that ever floated out from the lips of man. Let us have some good, hard sense, as we would in ordinary business life. Do you believe that Job Davis, the educated young man, the school teacher, the one who attended the Normal school, would put periods in the middle of sentences and none at the end? That he would put a period at one side of an "n" and then fearing the "n" might get away, put one on the other; and then, when he got the sentence done, be out of periods, so that he could not put one there, and put so many periods in the writing that it looked as if it had broken out with some kind of punctuation measles?[11]

The law has been practiced by a great many different kinds of lawyers, some of whom have been notably fastidious in consenting to defend only clients whom they could respect. Abraham Lincoln has often been cited for a comment he made once to a colleague: "The man is guilty. You defend him; I can't. If I try to speak the jury will see that I think he is guilty, and convict him."[12] Lincoln's purpose, of course, was to try to get for the man a lawyer who could get him acquitted. When Lincoln himself was trying a case, he sought, as must all lawyers, to win the verdict by whatever proper means were available. When he was suing another lawyer to recover $200 for an elderly widow of a Revolutionary War veteran, he did not confine himself to the facts and the law but did his best to make his client's case appealing to the jury. Herndon relates that Lincoln spoke as follows:

> She was not always thus. She was once a beautiful young woman. Her step was as elastic, her face as fair, and her voice as sweet as any that rang in the mountains of old Virginia. But now she is poor and defenseless. Out here on the prairies of Illinois, many hundreds of miles from the scenes of her childhood, she appeals to us, who enjoy the privileges achieved for us by the patriots of the Revolution, for our sympathetic aid and manly protection. All I ask is, shall we befriend her?[13]

Among the other factors which complicate the problems lawyers must deal with in their courtroom speaking, a significant one is the influence exerted by public opinion. If there is so much adverse feeling concerning an indicted person that the judge feels he cannot get a fair trial in his

---

[11] *Ibid.*, p. 220.
[12] Sandburg, *Lincoln: Prairie Years*, op. cit., p. 347.
[13] *Ibid.*, p. 348. In effect, Lincoln was following a philosophy of courtroom advocacy which Clarence Darrow frankly recommended to his young associates: "The most important thing to do is to make the judge *want* to decide things your way. They are human beings, moved by the same things that move other human beings. The points of law merely give the judge a *reason* for doing what you have already made him want to do." Irving Stone, *Clarence Darrow for the Defense*, New York: Bantam Books, 1958, p. 38.

own community, the case may be tried elsewhere. Despite efforts to secure jury members who have not formed prior opinions about the case, and despite warnings to them not to discuss a case while it is pending, it is notorious that many a verdict is influenced, if not determined, by public opinion. Clarence Darrow referred to this fact in the opening of his final plea in the Loeb-Leopold case, in 1924, when he said: "Our anxiety over this case has not been due to the facts that are connected with this most unfortunate affair, but to the almost unheard-of publicity that it has received; to the fact that newspapers all over this country have been giving it space such as they have almost never before given to any case. The fact that day after day the people of Chicago have been regaled with stories of all sorts about it, until almost every person has formed an opinion."[14] Lawyers are aware that public opinion is not necessarily either intelligent or well-informed and that it may be capricious and prejudiced. What we call public opinion is, as Walter Bagehot once observed, "the opinion of the bald-headed man at the back of an omnibus."[15] But right or wrong, it is a factor that has to be dealt with very carefully. It is the atmosphere pervading the trial rather than an objective element of the trial itself. It cannot be brought to the witness stand for cross-examination. It may not even be referred to, for no judge willingly admits that the proceedings in his court are influenced by factors from outside its walls. Yet somehow an attorney whose case is adversely affected by public feeling concerning it must devise means of countering such influence in the minds of the jurors.

More than any other kind of speaking, courtroom pleading is subject to an immediate and direct test in the form of a verdict. Legislative speaking often is followed by a vote on the subject being discussed; but no one thinks the voting is determined primarily or even largely by the speeches. In the courtroom the judge charges the jury to reach a verdict upon the basis of the evidence as it has been presented and interpreted. Even though they may not always do so, this is their duty. This is not to say that courtroom speeches that win verdicts are always "good" and those that lose always "bad." But more than for most kinds of speaking,

[14] Clarence Darrow, *Attorney for the Damned*, ed. Arthur Weinberg, New York: Simon and Schuster, 1957, p. 20. How realistically Darrow sought to deal with the factor of public opinion is related by Irving Stone: "Keeping his defense plans secret, he made his first moves to quiet the public outcry against the two boys. He sent men to mingle in the crowds in the Loop and ask people whether they thought Loeb and Leopold should hang. Sixty percent of those questioned said 'Yes.' He then had the fathers of Loeb and Leopold issue a letter to the press saying that there would be no attempt to free the boys, only to prove them insane, and that they would agree to have Darrow's fee set by the Bar Association. After the newspapers had printed this letter the men went back to the Loop to ask the same question and found that sixty percent of the people were now willing to accept life imprisonment for the culprits." *Clarence Darrow, op. cit.,* p. 261.
[15] Bagehot, *Physics and Politics, op. cit.,* p. xix.

the correlation between eloquence and success is very high. For this reason the study of courtroom speeches is rewarding to those who are curious about the means by which people may be persuaded.

But it is also true that no other kind of formalized speaking—thus avoiding comparison with conversation and unsys'ematized discussion— offers such difficulty of analysis and criticism. Much that the lawyer says must be oblique, as in his handling of the effects of public opinion. Much of it is exhaustively detailed in terms of trivia which he may ingeniously make momentous in swaying the judgment of jurors. In cases a lawyer feels he will not win, much of his speaking may actually be directed to the peculiar susceptibilities of just one juror, in order to try to get a split decision. Or elaborate attention may be given to a single precedent or a series of precedents that may be cited either for the purpose of winning the case or of laying groundwork for an appeal. It is useless to expect the organization of the speech to obey the ordinary laws of composition; for the lawyer must work upon the minds of a select and identified small body of listeners and it would be fatal for him to leave a crucial point until he has won concurrence not from a majority but from every single one of the jurors. For such reasons speeches to juries normally read as though they were excessively loose-jointed, rambling, circuitous, and wearisomely repetitive.

But the great courtroom pleaders, like great speakers of other types, somehow surmount the difficulties. It is these select few whose greatest courtroom addresses become the classics of forensic eloquence.

Aside from the greatness of the speaking, however, there is yet another factor that helps determine whether or not the speeches emerge out of the mass to attain lasting distinction. This factor is the importance of the case—and of the line of argument developed in defending or prosecuting it—in terms of its lasting influence upon subsequent judicial decisions. For it is a significant fact that the courts, through their decisions, "make" laws as well as enforce them. Justice Oliver Wendell Holmes was very clear in his own mind that "The substance of the law at any given time pretty nearly corresponds, so far as it goes, with what is then understood to be convenient."[16] Bourke Cockran, in his address of July 8, 1908, to the Ohio Bar Association, was even more explicit on the same point: "The questions now arising in the pathway of the republic and of civilization cannot be settled by legislative enactment or executive action. They can be solved only by judicial decree."[17] Great forensic eloquence, like great legislative speaking, extends beyond

[16] Silas Bent, *Justice Oliver Wendell Holmes*, Garden City: Garden City Pub. Co., 1932, p. 149.
[17] James McGurrin, *Bourke Cockran*, New York: Scribner's, 1948, pp. 96–97.

the immediate cases at issue to deal influentially with the course of events. Of the great courtroom speeches it may truly be said that our life as a nation would have been different had they not been persuasively presented.

The extensive influence of an immediate case under consideration was well stated by Daniel Webster on March 10, 1818, in his great plea in the Dartmouth College case before the Supreme Court:

> This, sir, is my case. It is the case, not merely of that humble institution, it is the case of every college in our land. It is more. It is the case of every eleemosynary institution throughout our country—of all those great charities founded by the piety of our ancestors, to alleviate human misery, and scatter blessings along the pathway of life. It is more! It is, in some sense, the case of every man among us who has property of which he may be stripped, for the question is simply this: Shall our State Legislatures be allowed to take that which is not their own, to turn it from its original use, and apply it to such ends or purposes as they in their discretion shall see fit?
>
> Sir, you may destroy this little institution; it is weak; it is in your hands! I know it is one of the lesser lights in the literary horizon of our country. You may put it out. But, if you do so, you must carry through your work! You must extinguish, one after another, all those greater lights of science which, for more than a century, have thrown their radiance over our land![18]

Then he added a line that has become one of the classic gems of American oratory: "It is, sir, as I have said, a small college. And yet there are those who love it—."

There have been few among the great political orators in American history who were not also great, or at least effective, courtroom pleaders. Patrick Henry, Henry Clay, William Henry Seward, Abraham Lincoln, Stephen A. Douglas, and Robert G. Ingersoll are only a few of the many who won acclaim at the bar. By general consent, however, the greatest of them all, and the ones who will be considered in this chapter, are Daniel Webster, Rufus Choate, Jeremiah S. Black, and William M. Evarts.[19]

[18] Curtis, *Daniel Webster, op. cit.*, I:170. Curtis ascribes this version of the concluding plea to Chauncey Goodrich, who heard the speech and preserved his notes on it. The only full text for the speech is that in Webster's *Works, op. cit.*, which is merely the legal brief. Webster's speech from this brief was freely extemporized.
[19] William Norwood Brigance, in the "Preface" to *The History and Criticism of American Public Address, op. cit.*, regrets that space and the plan of his two volumes precluded discussion of "such brilliant pleaders as Seargent S. Prentiss, David Paul Brown, and Charles O'Conor." I:ix. Other historians have cited Charles Pinckney of South Carolina as indubitably one of the greatest of American courtroom orators. Nevertheless, the four whom we have selected deserve and generally receive recognition as the "big four" (before Clarence Darrow).

𝕃 Daniel Webster as a Lawyer

NEAR THE end of his life, in a speech to the bar association of Charleston, South Carolina, Webster said: "If I am anything, it is the law—that noble profession, that sublime science which we all pursue—that has made me what I am. It has been my ambition, coeval with my early manhood, nay, with my youth, to be thought worthy to be ranged under the banner of that profession. The law has been my chief stimulus, my controlling and abiding hope, nay, I might almost say, my presiding genius and guardian angel."[1] How much he was exaggerating, in compliment to his audience, and in view of the obscuring character of nostalic memory, is evidenced by the reluctance with which he let himself be pushed into the law because, as he wrote at the age of twenty, "First, and principally, it is my father's wish . . . . Secondly, my friends generally wish it."[2] What he most disliked about the law were its "propositions so abstract, distinctions so nice, and doctrines embracing so many conditions and qualifications."[3] The legal curriculum was so distasteful to him that even years later he was still rejecting it: "Why disgust and discourage a boy by telling him that he must break into his profession through such a wall as this?"[4]

Once admitted to the bar, however, Webster found the profession very much to his liking and well suited to his talents. In the village of Boscawen, New Hampshire, where he opened his first office, there was a little one-story courthouse in which he argued his first cases. One of these was observed by N. P. Rogers, who left a vivid account of the young lawyer in action:

> There was a man tried for his life . . . and the judges chose Webster to plead for him; and, from what I can learn, he never has spoken better since than he did there when he first began. He was a black, raven-haired fellow, with an eye as black as death, and as heavy as a lion's—and no lion in Africa ever had a voice like him; and his look was like a lion's—that same heavy look, not sleepy, but as if he didn't care about any thing that was going on about him or any thing anywhere else. He didn't look as if he was thinking about any thing; but as if he *would* think like a hurricane if he once got waked up to it. They say the lion looks so when he is quiet. It wasn't an empty look, this of

[1] Wilbur Samuel Howell and Hoyt Hopewell Hudson, "Daniel Webster," in Brigance, ed., *History and Criticism, op. cit.*, II:668–669.
[2] Curtis, *Daniel Webster, op. cit.*, 1:55.
[3] *Ibid.*, I:56.
[4] *Ibid.*

Webster's; but one that didn't seem to see any thing going on worth his while.[5]

Shortly Webster moved his office to Portsmouth where his real legal education commenced in his friendship and rivalry with Jeremiah Mason, who taught him to abandon his early ornate style in favor of compelling clarity. In later years Webster once said, "If you were to ask me who was the greatest lawyer in the country, I should answer John Marshall, but if you took me by the throat and pinned me to the wall and demanded my real opinion, I should be compelled to say it was Jeremiah Mason."[6] In 1816 he moved again, to Boston, primarily because in Portsmouth he was unable to earn more than $2000 a year; within a year his income from the law mounted to $15,000.[7]

The appeal to the Supreme Court on behalf of Dartmouth College was the speech which first established Webster's national reputation. For it, the legal arguments had already been adduced by Jeremiah Mason and Jeremiah Smith, who had earlier carried the appeal, unsuccessfully, to the New Hampshire Supreme Court. Webster added the eloquence. The decision which Webster won quickly became a cornerstone of American law. By 1901 it already had been cited in the *American Reports* 970 times—more than any other case. "More than that," wrote Fisher, "the vast business operations of the whole continent have been built up upon it."[8] Its principal effect was to establish the sanctity of contracts, placing them above the reach of legislative enactments. Shortly afterward, in the case of *Gibbons* v. *Ogden*, Webster succeeded in establishing another principle that was complementary, and to some degree even contradictory: namely, that a legislature could indeed rescind a contract which granted a monopoly that proved to be against the public interest. The case concerned a grant by the State of New York to Fulton and Livingston, giving them a monopoly to operate steamboat navigation upon the waters of the state. This case, too, was argued before the Supreme Court, and under circumstances peculiarly difficult for Webster. He was at the time deeply engrossed in the Congressional debates on the Tariff of 1824, and the case was announced for the next day at a time when he thought he would have two more weeks in which to prepare his argument. After a very arduous day in the Congress, he went home, took a sleeping pill, and slept until ten p.m. Then he worked for the next eleven hours, until nine a.m., to complete his brief. Without

[5] Peter Harvey, *Reminiscences and Anecdotes of Daniel Webster*, Boston: Little, Brown, 1878, p. 49.
[6] Fisher, *The True Daniel Webster*, op. cit., p. 87.
[7] *Ibid.*, p. 144.
[8] *Ibid.*, pp. 156–157.

further rest he went to court and made the plea that "released every creek and river, every lake and harbor in our country from the interference of monopolies."[9] In still another case on another similar kind of topic, the case of *Ogden* v. *Saunders*, in 1827, he established the principle that no State Legislature could enact a bankruptcy bill which frees a creditor from his obligations. "The duty of performing promises," Webster said, "is shown to rest on universal law."

Webster remained active in law throughout his life, but in his later years he served chiefly as a corporation counsel, which required little courtroom pleading. Two criminal cases in which he participated required him to unsnarl tangled evidence and scent vital clues much in the tradition of the fictional lawyer-detective. In 1816 a very respectable Major Goodridge charged that he had been robbed and shot through the left hand by two impoverished men named Kenniston and by an accomplice named Pearson. Pieces of the missing gold were found in the possession of the Kennistons and of Pearson. Webster was influenced by the fact that the accused were men of good character and, largely on the basis of reasoning, managed to convince the jury that Goodridge had faked the robbery and shot himself through the hand.

In 1830 he consented to assist the prosecution in trying John F. Knapp for the murder by stabbing of Captain Joseph White. He was enjoying tremendous public acclaim for his debates that winter in the Senate with Robert Hayne and he accepted the commission with reluctance. However, he said, he felt it a duty to aid the cause of justice in a case of such barbarous cruelty. "An aged man, without an enemy in the world, in his own house, and in his own bed, is made the victim of a butcherly murder, for mere pay," he told the jury. The case was a peculiarly complicated one, involving a number of accessories and a complex network of planning. Webster's principal contribution lay in his ability to bring the skein of facts into a pattern of clarity, so that the jury could understand them "beyond reasonable doubt." To counteract the natural reluctance of ordinary citizens to bring in a verdict of guilty which would result in a sentence of death, Webster concluded with a paean to duty that many lawyers since have found useful:

> There is no evil that we cannot either face or fly from, but the consciousness of duty disregarded. A sense of duty pursues us ever. It is omnipresent, like the Deity. If we take to ourselves the wings of the morning, and dwell in the uttermost parts of the sea, duty performed, or duty violated, is still with us, for our happiness or our misery. If we say the darkness shall cover us, in the darkness as in the light, our

[9] Curtis, *op. cit.*, I:217.

obligations are yet with us. We cannot escape their power, nor fly from their presence. They are with us in this life, will be with us at its close; and in the scene of inconceivable solemnity, which lies yet farther onward, we shall still find ourselves surrounded by the consciousness of duty, to pain us wherever it has been violated, and to console us so far as God may have given us grace to perform it.[10]

Webster was proud of his work at the bar. Rufus Choate, in his memorial address on Webster, reported that "I have myself heard him say, that for many years while still at the bar, he tried more causes, and argued more questions of fact to the jury than perhaps any other member of the profession anywhere." In Choate's judgment, "he was, by universal designation, the leader of the general American bar."[11] To his friend Peter Harvey, Webster once remarked that of all his speeches, "My forensic efforts have been those which pleased me most."[12] Another time he said he "never experienced more intellectual pleasure" than in arguing a case before Chief Justice Marshall against so able an opponent as Attorney General William Wirt, the biographer of Patrick Henry.[13] This was the kind of tussle that brought his powers to their fullest fruition. Thus it was, he felt, to truly live.

Rufus Choate: The Courtroom Wizard

To DESCRIBE and evaluate the courtroom eloquence of Rufus Choate—"that vast power which we shall see no more in action, nor aught in any degree resembling it among men,"[1]—is peculiarly difficult, for the principal reason that almost nothing of the great outpouring of his speeches in court remains even in paraphrase; and there are no verbatim reports. What has come down to us is a reputation, a computation of speeches made and fees received, and a few brief sketches of the arguments he used in his pleading of major cases. There is a compilation of Choate's occasional speeches,[2] which reveal a mind that was conservative, prone to lavish use of historical and literary references, and rather prim and prosey. But this is largely beside the point; for Choate

10 Webster, *Works, op. cit.,* XI:105.
11 *Addresses and Orations of Rufus Choate,* Boston: Little, Brown, 6th ed., 1891, pp. 225–226.
12 Harvey, *op. cit.,* p. 140.
13 *Ibid.,* p. 142.
1 Quoted in "Preface" to 2nd ed., 1869, of Samuel Gilman Brown, *Life of Rufus Choate, op. cit.,* p. x.
2 *Addresses and Orations of Rufus Choate, op. cit.*

wrote out and read his ceremonial speeches, while in the courtroom he spoke always extemporaneously and with a mesmeric power that kept Daniel Webster listening to him with wonder and the justices of the Supreme Court amazed at "the brilliancy and power of his oratory."[3]

There was a profusion of generous genius in the life span of Rufus Choate, which extended from October 1, 1799 to July 13, 1859, and his colleagues, far from envying, delighted in praising this genius. Wherever he was or whatever the occasion, he poured forth the utmost of his powers without stint or measure. "He never prepared nor reserved his good things for a grand occasion," wrote his biographer, "and to those who knew him best was as full of surprises as to a stranger. In the little office of a justice of the peace,—in a retired room of a railroad depot, in the presence of a few interested members of the corporation,—before two or three sensible, but not brilliant, referees in the hall of a country tavern, he displayed nearly the same abundance of learning, the same exuberance of language, and felicity of allusion, the same playfulness and beauty, as when he spoke before the most learned bench, or the elegant and cultivated assemblies of Boston."[4] An instance of this magical discourse is given by a politician who rode home alone with him in a coach one evening in Boston, in 1848, after Choate had finished a brilliant address, was drenched in perspiration, drooping with weariness, and suffering from a raging headache:

> As we rode home in the soft moonlight, he amazed me with his vast power of thought. I have seen men stirred with passion; men eloquent; men profound and brilliant in conversation; but in the whole course of my life I never saw a man more roused than he was. He poured out, without stopping, a torrent of conversation upon history, constitutional law, philosophy, poetry, upon Burke, Plato, Hamilton, the future of the Union. No other word could explain his style but "torrent" or "cataract"; for what he spoke in that hour would have made a small volume— brilliant and full of philosophy and learning. And I think that I never realized so much as then the power and unapproachableness of genius.[5]

This is but a sample of the impression Choate made time after time upon many associates. The pity is that he had no Boswell. Not even approximations of either his impromptu talk or of his extemporaneous courtroom addresses have been preserved. The scintillation was admired and lost; what remains is testimony—and an abundant record of the methodology by which the effects were achieved. John W. Black, who made an intensive study of Choate as a courtroom speaker, found most

[3] Brown, *Life of Choate*, *op. cit.*, p. 189.
[4] *Ibid.*, pp. 435–436.
[5] *Ibid.*, p. 190.

applicable to him Choate's own comment on John Adams: "Of that series of spoken eloquence all is perished; not one reported sentence has come down to us."[6]

The career of Choate is soon sketched. Like Webster, he adopted the law reluctantly, but wholeheartedly embraced it once the decision was made. As a student at Dartmouth he received a little instruction in speech, amidst his brilliant record in liberal arts, and early impressed his fellows with his skill in speaking. He matured early and by graduation had firmly established habits of continuous hard work and a driving power of concentration which never thereafter lessened. He served two terms in the House and four years in the Senate, rejecting further office to labor with single-minded concentration upon the practice of law. In his profession he averaged year after year seventy court cases, one every five days, and slaved assiduously upon all of them. He was careless about fees, yet at the height of his career earned $18,000 annually. From time to time he delivered lengthy, ornate, and carefully written ceremonial addresses, which were much admired but were remote from his courtroom style. He was more than six feet tall, erect, vigorous, courtly and courteous in manner, introspective, yet sociable and friendly. "For many years before his death, his countenance was haggard, and the lines became deeper and deeper with age."[7] He died in Halifax, of Bright's disease, while en route to England to seek rest.

Rest was the last thing this restless man ever sought. All his life he read with a tremendous, driving urgency. There was no kind of knowledge he would not rather possess than lack. He studied Roman and English law to trace out the sources of American jurisprudence. He read literature and the social sciences widely and avidly, both to satisfy his hunger for learning and because he thought this knowledge made him a better lawyer. For every case he took up—and they ran the gamut, for legal specialization was unknown in his time—he made detailed studies of the facts and the law, often filling several hundred pages with notes in preparation for a single case. In his study he read standing up, often all night long, always with a pen in hand to mark the margins or to take notes. No other great orator has equalled his frenzy of unleashed energy. Yet he gave time patiently to clients and friends.[8]

Despite his tremendous industry—some might think because of it— he was beset by pains and bodily misery. Before almost every appearance in court, which meant two or three times a week, he was tense, over-

[6] John W. Black, "Rufus Choate," in Brigance, ed., *History and Criticism, op. cit.*, I:436.

[7] Brown, *op. cit.*, p. 375.

[8] *Ibid.*, p. 417 and *passim*. Extensive use has also been made of the essay by J. W. Black.

wrought, and nervous. While he spoke he gestured but little and his manner was restrained, yet so intense were the fires within him that he perspired copiously. And as every speech ended, he was wracked by a splitting headache. The following account of what happened to Choate during a specific trial, written by a young legal associate, is of interest not because it was unusual but because it was typical both of what he endured and of what he accomplished:

> During the trial Mr. Choate became unwell, and was obliged to go to his hotel, while a portion of the argument of Mr. Lord was made. He requested me to write down every word Mr. Lord said, and bring it to him. I did so, and, at the same time, found Mr. Choate sick in bed, with a physician in attendance, who was prescribing calomel, and asked Mr. Choate how large a dose he was accustomed to take. Choate replied that he did not know, but said, "Give me the largest dose you ever gave a man in your life." The next day he rose from his sick bed, came into court, and began the grand argument which he made in the case, which lasted during the entire day, and nearly all the following day. While he was speaking, the perspiration, like raindrops, fell from his bushy hair all over the paper on which I was writing. Taking it altogether, that was the greatest speech I ever heard. Some of the tones of his voice were more than arguments of themselves. His classical allusions, his eloquent flights, his magnificent argument and beautiful illustrations, combined to entrance the court and auditors.[9]

The thirty five years of his law practice show few variations. He matured early both in his skill and in his methods. His cases were widely various in their subject matter, but he dealt with all of them very much alike. As Black observed, because of the richness of his knowledge and the eager questing of his mind, "one might expect his legal speeches to reflect an extraordinary versatility. On the contrary, they abound in similarities."[10] He took whatever cases were offered to him, with no bias concerning either the size of the fee or the merit of the case. When defending in criminal cases, he avoided pre-trial contacts with his clients, often not so much as speaking to them, for he did not want the question of their guilt or innocence to arise. In one of the most sensational cases he ever conducted, he did not speak to the defendant until he met him in court the day of the trial, when he said, "Well, Sir, are you ready to make a strong push for life with me today?[11] Nevertheless, he prepared exhaustively, both in assembling all available facts on the case and in searching the law books for principles and precedents.

---

[9] Enoch L. Fancher, *Albany Law Journal*, March 17, 1877. The occasion was the Methodist Church case, which was tried in May, 1851.
[10] J. W. Black, *op. cit.*, I:440.
[11] Brown, *op. cit.*, pp. 174–175.

This latter practice was original with him, for the American bar had not developed either the custom or the resources for a study of precedents. The theory was that each case should be tried on its own individual merits. Choate's practice helped to introduce the emphasis upon a uniformity of standards to be maintained through time.[12]

In still further preparation Choate would canvass his memory for literary allusions and parallels which he could cite in his speech to the jury. One reason why he used much of this type of material was to help clarify his points. But another reason was to supply periodically light, frolicsome, or irrelevant "resting places" for the minds of the jurors from time to time. It was one of his convictions that no mind can give its fixed attention to a matter for more than an hour at a time.[13]

The next stage in his preparation was to outline the approach he would use, which varied little from case to case. He would stress the importance of the case; draw a favorable character sketch of his client; show that the plaintiff was wrong, either inadvertently or by design; then conclude that his client was suffering from an ill-treatment which the jury could and should redress. After this opening exposition, Choate would examine the evidence with two aims: first, to select out of the mass the irreducibly essential considerations; and second, to interpret the facts in terms of *probabilities*. His aim was to admit as much as possible, often to the extent that he would turn in court upon his own client and shower abuse upon him. But the admissions dealt only with peripheral aspects of the case. For example, when he defended Helen Dalton against a charge of adultery, he chastised her severely for her habit of engaging in unwise and frivolous flirtations. When he defended Albert Tirrell against a charge of murder, he berated Tirrell soundly for profligacy and adultery. But from this abuse, he would turn to the jury and point out that his client was not on trial for these admitted misdeeds; the charge was something else, and of this his client was innocent. Typically he developed the claim of innocence in terms of a pattern of probabilities. Granted the accused was the kind of person he appeared to be, and considering the circumstances, wasn't it highly unlikely that he would or could have committed the crime? Finally, he carefully and emphatically reminded the jury that the burden of proof rested fully upon the prosecution. The accused is innocent unless proven guilty beyond a shadow of a doubt.

This typical line of argument may be illustrated concretely in terms of Choate's defense of Albert J. Tirrell, in March, 1846. Tirrell was a man

---

[12] J. W. Black, op. cit., I:448.
[13] E. G. Parker, *Reminiscences of Rufus Choate*, New York: Mason Bros., 1860, quoted by J. W. Black, op. cit., I:454.

of good family but of vicious character, who habitually left his wife to seek the company of prostitutes. While he was under actual indictment for adultery, he went to a house of prostitution and spent the early hours of the night there with a young woman named Maria Bickford, who was one of his established favorites. Early the next morning, other inhabitants of the house heard a scream coming from their room and then heard a sound as of a heavy body falling to the floor, after which footsteps were heard going down the stairs. A fire broke out in the room and when several persons went to extinguish it, they found Miss Bickford on the floor, with her throat cut from ear to ear, and with quantities of blood in a washstand in a distant corner of the room. Tirrell fled to New Orleans but was arrested and brought back for trial. The public was greatly exercised by the case and there was general expectation that Tirrell would promptly be found guilty and executed.

Choate's defense was that Tirrell had not been shown to have a motive for the murder: that Miss Bickford might have committed suicide; or that someone unknown may have done the murder; or that Tirrell might have done it in his sleep, in which case, of course, it would not be murder. Any one of these three explanations, he insisted, was more probable than that Tirrell would wantonly murder a woman with whom he had so casual a liaison. Choate also dwelt lengthily and wittily upon the fact that the government's witnesses, who were either inhabitants or clients of the house of prostitution, were not exactly credible. A passage from his speech to the jury, which was reported, or perhaps paraphrased, in the Boston press, illustrates his skill in use of humor and sarcasm, his ability to emphasize and dramatize the precise point he wished to make, and the light, almost frolicsome tone with which he wooed back the flagging attention of tired jurors:

> Where was this tardy and belated witness that he comes here to tell us all he knows, and all he doesn't know, forty-eight hours after the evidence for the defence is closed? Is the case so obscure that he had never heard of it? Was he ill, or in custody? Was he in Europe, Asia, or Africa? Was he on the Red Sea, or the Yellow Sea, or the Black Sea, or the Mediterranean Sea? Was he at Land's End, or John o' Groat's house? Was he with Commissioners on our north-eastern boundary drawing and defining that much-vexed boundary line? Or was he with General Taylor and his army at Chihuahua, or wherever the fleeting south-eastern boundary line of our country may at this present moment be? No, gentlemen, he was at none of these places (comparatively easy of access), but—and I would call your attention, Mr. Foreman, to the fact, and urge it upon your consideration—he was

at that more remote, more inaccessible region, whence so few travellers return—Roxbury.[14]

In another part of his speech he is reported to have injected an irrelevant bit of sentimentality that he must have hoped would help his client: "I beg leave of the court to read, as illustrative of my point of argument here, a passage from a good old book, which used to lie on the shelves of our good old fathers and mothers, and which they were wont devoutly to read." Equally sentimental were his opening lines, as the newspapers reported them: "Every juror, when he puts into the urn the verdict of 'guilty,' writes upon it also, 'Let him die' "; and his conclusion: "Under the iron law of old Rome, it was the custom to bestow a civic wreath on him who should save the life of a citizen. Do your duty this day, gentlemen, and you too may deserve the civic crown." The jury found Tirrell not guilty, after which he was tried again on a charge of arson, for having set the fire in Miss Bickford's room. Once again Choate defended, and once again the verdict was for the prisoner. As in the first trial, Choate depended heavily on argument from probability, reasoning that Tirrell had no motive to burn the woman or the house within which she plied her trade. "He was fascinated by the wiles of the unhappy female whose death was so awful; *he loved her with the love of forty thousand brothers*, though, alas! it was not as pure as it was passionate."[15] As for Choate's manner of speaking, "His addresses to the jury were singularly impassioned; every muscle of his frame quivered with emotion; the perspiration stood in drops even upon the hairs of his head. Yet he was always dignified and conciliatory, as if speaking to friends."[16] When the Tirrell trial was ended, his usual headache had more than the usual cause.

Choate's address to the jury in defense of Helen Dalton against a charge of adultery, is printed in Snyder's anthology of *Great Speeches by Great Lawyers*,[17] although with a note that disingenuously hints what is beyond doubt a fact, that the text is scarcely representative of anything more than the outline of the argument. Choate was handicapped in his plea of innocence by the fact that his client had confessed her guilt to her husband in writing. Nevertheless, he not only managed to win an acquittal from the jury but he also proved so convincing that the estranged husband wooed back his wife's affections and they were reunited.

[14] Brown, op. cit., pp. 179–180.
[15] *Ibid.*, p. 183.
[16] *Ibid.*, pp. 427–428.
[17] William L. Snyder, *Great Speeches by Great Lawyers*, New York: Baker, Voorhis and Co., 1921, based on 1881 ed., pp. 247–324.

Upon receiving news of Choate's death, the great editor Richard H. Dana, Jr., declared simply: "The age of miracles has passed. The day of inspiration is over." He said it in the presence of the best lawyers in the Boston area, yet none doubted that the man who had died was not their peer but vastly their superior. Dana put the consensus even more plainly: "He was, Sir, in two words, a unique creation."[18] To those who knew him he was the wizard at the bar. But whatever he was in his own time and among his fellows in New England, he was neither the last nor the climactic figure in forensic eloquence in the developing history of the United States. There was more greatness yet to come.

Jeremiah S. Black: Defender of Civil Liberties

No OTHER American lawyer ever defended cases of greater importance than did Jeremiah S. Black. He defended a President, Andrew Johnson, and a Secretary of War, William W. Belknap, when they were under impeachment proceedings; and before the Electoral Commission he defended Samuel J. Tilden's right to be certified as the successful candidate in the presidential election of 1876. In the bitter years of controversy following the Civil War he fought to destroy the Lincolnian policy of suspending the right of *habeas corpus*, and he opposed the Radical Republican program of ruling the South with martial law. What he said in opening his plea in the Milligan case, before the Supreme Court, could as well have been said by him in regard to still others of his principal cases: "I am not afraid that you will underrate the importance of this case. It concerns the rights of the whole people. Such questions have generally been settled by arms. But since the beginning of the world no battle has ever been lost or won upon which the liberties of a nation were so distinctly staked as they are on the results of this argument. The pen that writes the judgment of the court will be mightier for good or evil than any sword that ever was wielded by mortal arm."[1]

Black merits consideration as one of the greatest of American forensic orators not alone because of the importance of the cases which he pleaded but also because his triumphs were won more by his powers of persuasion than by his knowledge and utilization of legal technicalities. Black served for six years on the Supreme Court of Pennsylvania, was

[18] The Dana eulogy is from Brown, *op. cit.*, pp. 385–392.
[1] Chauncy F. Black, *Essays and Speeches of Jeremiah S. Black*, New York: Appleton, 1885, p. 510.

nominated for the U.S. Supreme Court, and for four critical years was Attorney General of the United States. In other words, his professional competence was of a high order. Nevertheless, it was his eloquence rather than his legal proficiency that was most admired by those who knew him. "That he was really a great lawyer," a contemporary wrote when he died, "was not so universally admitted as that he was a bold pleader and an eloquent, forcible, and most interesting speaker. If he did not always persuade the court, he never fatigued it. If his audience was sometimes unconvinced, it never failed to be delighted."[2] A. F. Faust, looking back after a space of three years, concluded that "There is a degree of skill in the constructive and destructive methods which Judge Black employs rarely to be met with in argumentation. Persuasive and eloquent as he may appear at times, all the links in the chain of his reasoning are carefully forged and welded together . . . . Every fact and every argument follow in strictest sequence and when complete exhibit both a consummate power in art and an unrivaled perfection in presentation."[3]

Black himself had no admiration for skill in speech as an end in itself. In a July Fourth oration delivered at the height of his fame, he toyed with the subject playfully, denying any "faculty of speaking readily and fluently upon any side of any case upon the shortest possible notice . . . —that is, the sort of speaking which has no particular object or purpose except that of talking."[4] Nevertheless, as an observer who sat through his speech in the Goodyear Rubber case attested, he was a master of the arts he pretended to disdain. Speaking "for three hours without notes," the account reads, he made "one of the most masterful arguments heard for years. His ridicule of Goodyear and his clients as a scientific inventor, kept the Court in constant laughter, while his splendid bursts of eloquence in reciting the benefactions to mankind of Galileo, Newton and others . . . were acknowledged by the almost breathless silence of Court and spectators. He handled the testimony with equal skill, never at loss for the name of a witness, and quoting his language so accurately, that the opposing counsel in no instance corrected him. He read no law book, but from his vast stores of knowledge cited decision after decision, giving book, title and page . . . . He enriched his argument with illustrations drawn from nature, science, history, the Bible, literature, art and poetry."[5] His daughter considered

---

[2] Editorial, *Philadelphia Press*, August 20, 1883.
[3] *Catholic World*, September, 1886, p. 759.
[4] Hollidaysburg, Penna., *Standard*, July 4, 1877.
[5] Quoted by William Norwood Brigance, *Jeremiah Sullivan Black*, Philadelphia: University of Pennsylvania Press, 1934, p. 256.

him so natural an orator that when the time came to speak, "his sentences rolled off his tongue."[6]

The encomiums so far surpass the extravagant as to compel conviction. "Who can forget the charms of his conversation?" asked Randolph Tucker. His son believed that "A book of his table-talk would be a contribution to that of literature inferior in interest and value to none of the class." J. H. Ashton of Washington, D.C. felt that "his speech and thought often recall the sagacity of Montaigne and the humor of Rabelais." In the view of Thomas J. Keenan, a Pittsburgh attorney, as a conversationalist he "needed but a Boswell to make him in that respect appear equal to Johnson." Then he added: "Talk was his kind of dissipation—his intoxicant—the means for exhilaration, like wine to the more sluggish."[7]

As a youth born (on January 10, 1810) and raised on a farm in western Pennsylvania, Black aspired to become a physician, but was diverted to the law when an opportunity arose to become a student in the office of a brilliant neighborhood attorney.[8] He was depressed when he saw the size of the law library and learned "the vastness of the knowledge" of his mentor, convinced he never could master all he needed to know. Then he encountered the works of Shakespeare and entered "almost a new world." He read and reread every play, until he could quote from memory even from obscure passages. The precise retentive grasp of his memory was to prove one of his major courtroom assets; and Shakespeare's plays were to serve him frequently for illustrative materials in his courtroom speeches. Milton, Horace, and the King James Bible also entranced him; by contrast Coke and Blackstone seemed desolate. The curriculum which his own taste prescribed was not that recommended for aspiring lawyers. But it may have been instrumental in forming his style. Senator Garland, who often heard him in later life, was impressed by his "almost boundless" learning: "his reading vast, his memory prodigious, his versatility extraordinary." He called him "a rhetorician without superior—the best phrase-maker I ever heard—he used the English language after the style of Shakespeare; . . . a logician, when he stated his case, it was more than half argued."[9] A lawyer who studied many of the 250 opinions Black wrote while Chief Justice of the Pennsylvania Supreme Court commented that "The style of Judge Black's composition is unlike any other with which we are acquainted," especially "in

[6] *Ibid.*
[7] C. F. Black, *op. cit.*, in which all the passages quoted are included in the "Biographical Sketch," pp. 30–31.
[8] Brigance, *Black, op. cit.*, p. 7.
[9] C. F. Black, *op. cit.*, p. 26.

the perfect clearness in which he exhibits his thoughts—whether right or wrong, no man can misunderstand him."[10]

For Jeremiah Black, as for so many others of our orators, his first public appearance on the platform was on a July 4th, in 1830. The speech was flamboyant and immature, though good enough to be published in the Somerset *Whig*; but it reached a high point in its dramatization of the words of Patrick Henry: "I am not worth buying, but such as I am, the King of England is too poor to do it." Then, while community praise still rang in his ears, the attorney in whose office he studied decided he was ready to commence practice, and while the attorney took off for Congress, he turned his entire clientele over to young Black. The anxiety of the youth under this sudden and heavy responsibility was "greater than I can express"; but there was no escape, "and so I kept on in the law for the mere lucre of it, until I began to love it for its own sake."[11] Shortly he was made both deputy sheriff and prosecuting attorney, and found himself inundated in a series of cases in which he was confronted by able lawyers of maturity and ability. Without adequate time to prepare the multiplicity of cases that thrust themselves upon him, he developed a technique that persisted throughout his life: that of pleading each case in terms of some fundamental maxim of general applicability. And he won his cases in part by his skill in drawing upon the already vast resources of his literary reading to illuminate and illustrate these basic principles.

In this manner he worked out his apprentice years. He was just under six feet in height, rugged, physically strong, with strongly marked features and enormously bushy eyebrows that overhung luminously expressive eyes. He was a tireless worker, preparing many of his cases while pacing rapidly back and forth, in the parlor in bad weather, in the garden when the season permitted. So intense was his concentration that his wife never called him to dinner; instead, she sent one of their children to take him by the hand and lead him in. He was so oblivious to appearances that his wife often despaired in her efforts to keep him in clean clothes; and on one occasion, when he went out on the legal circuit promising solemnly to put on a clean shirt every day, he returned home wearing four shirts, having put the clean ones over the soiled ones.[12] Then, at the age of thirty two, he was appointed President Judge of the 16th Judicial District of Pennsylvania. Shut off in this fashion from intimate social contact with the lawyers who practiced before

[10] Brigance, op. cit., p. 9.
[11] Mary Black Clayton, *Reminiscences of Jeremiah Sullivan Black*, St. Louis: Christian, 1887, p. 25.
[12] Brigance, op. cit., p. 17.

his court, he dedicated himself in meditative solitude to continuing mental growth. Another decade passed, and he was appointed Chief Justice of the Pennsylvania Supreme Court. For the strength of his intellect, the range of his knowledge, and the fascinating versatility of his conversation, he was already a legend.

As a judge he continued his insistence upon the basic importance of fundamental principles. In his first opinion from the bench, he handed down a twenty-three-line decision on a case that had been working its way through the courts for thirteen years. Black commented that a precedent decision existed and added: "Where a question has been once deliberately settled after solemn argument, it ought not to be disturbed, unless it be so manifestly erroneous that it cannot be supported without doing violence to reason and justice."[13] In another case he ruled against a brief that was filled with hair-splitting distinctions. "I think," he said, "that the domain of the law is full enough of man-traps and spring-guns without any assistance from me in setting them."[14] When Senator Seward in 1850 appealed from the Constitution to a "Higher Law," in the course of his attack upon slavery, Justice Black went out of his way to answer this philosophy, in an opinion he was handing down: "Law is a fixed and established *rule*, not depending in the slightest degree on the caprice of those who happen to administer it . . . . It is this law we are bound to execute and not any 'higher law' manufactured for each special occasion out of our private feelings and opinions."[15] Thus gradually he was helping to clarify the principle of *stare decisis*—that the meaning of a law is dependably defined by precedent decisions. Then in 1857, at the age of forty seven, he was taken from the bench and returned to the arena of forensic encounters by appointment as Attorney General in the Cabinet of his friend, President James Buchanan.

Black's four-year tenure as Attorney General possesses special interest because this was the period in which the actual secession of the Southern States took place. As the issue drew dramatically toward its climax, Black was a key figure in the administration. His advice to Buchanan was that there was no constitutional basis for secession. Neither was there any constitutional power for the coercion of any State by the Federal Government. But there was both power and responsibility for the President to take any necessary action to protect federal property and to enforce federal laws upon individual citizens. Particularly, he urged Buchanan to reinforce and defend the forts in Charleston Harbor, and

[13] *Ibid.,* p. 30.
[14] *Ibid.,* p. 33.
[15] *Ibid.,* p. 37.

threatened resignation as a means of persuading Buchanan to this position. In 1861, as Lincoln was inaugurated, Black returned to the private
practice of law, having spent fifteen years as a government official. Paradoxically, it was to be in his private capacity that he made his greatest
contributions to the public weal.

In several respects his position was difficult. He was $4000 in debt,
without resources, and needed to start at once to earn a living. But the
dignity of his preceding offices rendered ordinary legal practice unsuitable; and, as a member of Buchanan's cabinet, in the fierce feelings
generated by the Civil War, he was discredited and accused of being a
Copperhead—a Northern man with Southern sympathies. For a time he
considered an offer of $7000 to write Buchanan's biography. He was
hard-pressed by his creditors. But he did not seek to curry favor by
either changing or concealing his opinions. In his view, Lincoln was
violating the Constitution by waging war against the seceded States. In
a speech in Philadelphia as late as October 24, 1864, he was still maintaining the judgment he already had stated publicly many times: "Mr.
Lincoln four months after his inauguration declared in a message to
Congress that there was not a majority for secession in any State except,
perhaps, South Carolina. Yet war was made upon the States and the
innocent were confounded with the guilty—the friends of the United
States were compelled, in self-defense, to unite with the enemies, and
now, instead of dealing with a tenth of the people, we have a deadly and
terrible conflict with all of them."[16]

Black's financial needs were met when he was engaged to defend clients in California whose land titles were disputed by their former Mexican owners. More than eight hundred such claims were presented,
some valid, some fraudulent. Forgery and perjury were freely utilized by
some claimants. Black made an intensive study of the general problem
while he was Attorney General, including a mastery of Mexico's land
laws and the Spanish language. Naturally he was engaged as a private
lawyer to defend American owners whose land titles were in jeopardy.
In all this work he was careless about fees, keeping no records and even
forgetting what agreements had been reached on the question. The fees
he did receive varied from $250 to $180,000 (the largest fee paid to any
American lawyer during this period). Beyond his ordinary needs, however, he had no taste for or interest in money. As his son wrote, "The
rest of the golden shower was neglected. He would scarcely stoop to pick
it up, or, when he did, he gave it away, or let it run through his hands
like water."[17] Even so, he was now free to do what he wished, to live as

[16] *Ibid.*, pp. 123–124.
[17] C. F. Black, *op. cit.*, p. 25.

he wished—with no financial worries, no political ambitions, and with as much of honor attained as any man could want or hope for. So far as a man could know freedom, he had it. In this situation, he determined to serve the needs of the nation.

Perhaps the most urgent need was the restoration of basic civil rights which had been grossly suspended during the war. The *habeas corpus* was suspended by presidential proclamation throughout the four year struggle; and some 38,000 citizens were imprisoned without any charge being lodged against them, held simply as "prisoners of state."[18] One such arrest occurred in Indiana, on October 5, 1864, when by order of a military commander three men named Milligan, Bowles, and Horsey were arrested, charged with treason, and tried summarily before a military commission. They were found guilty and sentenced to be hanged the following May 19. Milligan filed a petition in the United States Circuit Court asking for discharge and the case was remanded to the Supreme Court, where three questions should be settled: "1. Was Milligan entitled to a writ of habeas corpus? 2. Ought he to be discharged? 3. Had the military commission the jurisdiction legally to try and sentence him?" Black undertook to defend Milligan "at vast expense of time and labor . . . without fee or the hope of fees."[19]

The task that confronted Black was staggering. He himself was unpopular—as a member of the discredited Buchanan administration, and as an alleged Copperhead who had criticized the conduct of the war and who championed the South against the Congressional reconstruction program. The nine Justices who would comprise his audience included three who had helped render the Dred Scott decision and five who were Lincoln appointees. To this court he must argue that Lincoln's whole plan of suspending civil rights during the war was unconstitutional, as was the Congressional plan for military rule of the South. Under these circumstances, after the government case had been presented, Black rose without a note in his hand to speak for two hours in what was "indisputably the most remarkable forensic effort" ever made before the Supreme Court.[20]

Unlike Rufus Choate, he did not attempt to shift the burden of proof but frankly, almost eagerly, embraced it. The prosecution, he said, "with all the power of their artful eloquence," maintained that the military had the right to "take and kill, try and execute," civilian prisoners:

> We, on the other hand, submit that a person not in the military or naval service can not be punished at all until he has had a fair, open,

[18] Brigance, *op. cit.*, p. 145.
[19] C. F. Black, *op. cit.*, p. 27.
[20] Clayton, *op. cit.*, p. 131.

public trial before an impartial jury, in an ordained and established court, to which the jurisdiction has been given by law to try him for that specific offense. There is our proposition. Between the ground we take and the ground they occupy there is and there can be no compromise. It is one way or the other.

Our proposition ought to be received as true without any argument to support it; because if that, or something precisely equivalent to it, be not a part of our law, this is not, what we have always supposed it to be, a free country. Nevertheless, I take upon myself the burden of showing affirmatively not only that it is true, but that it is immovably fixed in the very framework of the Government, so that it is utterly impossible to detach it without destroying the whole political structure under which we live. By removing it you destroy the life of this nation as completely as you would destroy the life of an individual by cutting the heart out of his body. I proceed to the proof.[21]

Despite the enormous importance of the case, Black did not draw upon any unusual sources of fact or legal precedents with which to bolster his case. On the contrary, he made a point of confining himself to "the mere rudiments of constitutional law, . . . the most commonplace topics of history, . . . plain rules of justice and right." Then he added: "You must not think the worse of our armor because it happens to be old-fashioned and looks a little rusty from long disuse." In a masterly effort to identify his cause with the interests of the judiciary, he pointed out that the Constitution entrusted defense of "the life, liberty, and property of every person" solely to the courts; and he added, "the highest compliment that has ever been paid to the American bench is embodied in this simple fact: that if the Executive officers of this Government have ever desired to take away the life or the liberty of a citizen contrary to law, they have not come into the courts to get it done; they have gone outside the courts, and stepped over the Constitution, and created their own tribunals." Then in quick summation he reminded the Justices of the twelve absolutely fundamental bases of Anglo-American law: that no law may be enforced retroactively, no arrest made without a warrant, no prisoner forced to testify against himself; that all trials shall be held promptly, with an open statement of an indictment that has been approved by a grand jury; that the trial must be held before a competent court, with a jury of the accused's peers, in an open court where all witnesses appear and the accused has a counsel of his own choice; that a verdict of guilty must be unanimous by the jury, that the punishment not be cruel or unusual, and that no one may twice be placed in jeopardy for the same offense. Then he added that these pro-

21 Text of the speech is in C. F. Black, *op. cit.*, pp. 510–539.

visions apply with special force in all cases where treason has been charged, for "A tyrannical government calls everybody a traitor who shows the least unwillingness to be a slave."

There was no need, he said, to "prove" the nature of the protection afforded to citizens by the law—then he proceeded to illuminate it in a remarkably dramatic historical review. Having demonstrated soundly that all law is aimed to protect the citizenry against arbitrary oppression by government, he pointed out that in this case the prosecution argued that normal rights were overthrown by the necessities of the war: "in other words, the end justifies the means." Scathingly he declared, "Nothing that the worst men ever propounded has produced so much oppression, misgovernment, and suffering as this pretense of State necessity." Necessity was an especially weak plea in this case, Black pointed out, for there was no war in Indianapolis, where the military trial was held. If the military claim the right to arbitrary power everywhere because war exists somewhere, this means "that when the Constitution is attacked upon one side, its official guardians may assail it upon the other; when rebellion strikes it in the face, they may take advantage of the blindness produced by the blow, to sneak behind and stab it in the back."

Since "necessity" was the principal element of the government's case, Black turned to history to show that this was always the plea of absolute monarchs against the natural rights of their subjects. Then he turned to his beloved Shakespeare for a crowning instance:

> Macbeth understood the whole philosophy of the subject. He was an unlimited monarch. His power to punish for any offense or for no offense at all was as broad as that which the Attorney General claims for himself and his brother officers under the United States. But he was more cautious how he used it. He had a dangerous rival, from whom he apprehended the most serious peril to the "life of his government." The necessity to get rid of him was plain enough, but he could not afford to shock the moral sense of the world by pleading political necessity for a murder. He must—
>
> "Mask the business from the common eye."
>
> Accordingly he sent for two enterprising gentlemen, whom he took into his service upon liberal pay—"made love to their assistance"—and got them to deal with the accused party. He acted as his own Judge-Advocate. He made a most elegant and stirring speech to persuade his agents that Banquo was their oppressor, and had "held them so under

fortune," that he ought to die for that alone. When they agreed that he was their enemy, then said the king:

> "So is he mine, and though I could
> With barefaced power sweep him from my sight
> And bid my will avouch it; yet I must not,
> For certain friends, who are both his and mine,
> Whose loves I may not drop."

For these and "many weighty reasons" besides, he thought it best to commit the execution of his design to a subordinate agency. The commission thus organized in Banquo's case sat upon him that very night, at a convenient place beside the road where it was known he would be traveling; and they did precisely what the Attorney General says the military officers may do in this country—they took and killed him, because their employer at the head of the government wanted it done, and paid them for doing it out of the public treasury.

Black adduced yet other instances from history, then proceeded to a *reductio ad absurdum*: if American citizens are to be killed without due protection of law, why confine the privilege to military officers; "why not employ commissions of clergymen, merchants, manufacturers, horse-dealers, butchers, or drovers, to do it?" He concluded abruptly, stating that if the military were upheld in the Milligan case, "a tyrannical government" would have the power "to trample upon innocence, to gag the truth, to silence patriotism, and crush the liberties of the country," all through the agency of secret informers—"those loathsome wretches who do their lying by the job." His final words were: "To this fearful extent is the destiny of this nation in your hands."

"Never," wrote S. S. Cox, "had the question of personal liberty been so thoroughly discussed, from the time of Magna Charta down."[22] The Justices returned their verdict in the remarkably short space of three weeks, not only freeing Milligan and his associates and restoring the right of *habeas corpus* but also going further to deny the legality of any military commissions except in actual theatres of war where the civil courts were inoperative.

A case of scarcely less importance was his defense of McCardle, a Southern editor, who had been imprisoned by the military in 1867 for writing editorials that impeded the work of Reconstruction. The case was appealed to the Supreme Court and Black argued his client's case for two days in March, during the impeachment trial of Andrew Johnson. In essence, his plea was that not even war, let alone the aftermath of

[22] Brigance, *op. cit.*, p. 155.

war, destroyed the basic legal rights of citizens. Only an imperfect text of this two-day speech remains; but it was accounted by its hearers the equal of his Milligan plea; and McCardle was freed. Another equally important case, also argued before the Supreme Court, was heard in 1872. Congress, attempting to protect the rights of Negroes in the South, had passed a Civil Rights bill granting Negroes the right to take to federal courts cases in which they might be denied their rights in the State courts. A white man named Blyew was found guilty in a federal court of entering a Negro church and brutally murdering a Negro woman. Black freely admitted the brutality of the crime but managed to convince the court that the law which granted *concurrent jurisdiction* to two different judiciary systems was unwise, unnatural, and unconstitutional.[23]

During his remaining years Black participated in many more cases in which civil or constitutional rights were to be maintained. One of the saddest experiences he ever had as a courtroom speaker was when he spoke before the Electoral Commission on January 31, 1877, on behalf of Samuel Tilden, whom Black was certain had been elected President, and who, he knew, was to be denied the office through political manipulation. Under these circumstances, he told the Commission, "I have lost the dignity of an American citizen. I, in common with the rest, am degraded and humiliated." Then he indulged in a unique burst of heroics: "I know not how I would feel if called upon to suffer death for my country. I am not the stuff that martyrs are made of, but if my life could redeem this nation from the infamy with which she is clothed, I ought to go to the grave as freely as I ever went to my bed. I see, however, no practical good that I can do, and it is mere weakness to complain."[24] Nothing, he knew, could turn the dominant political party from its deliberate course. But there would come a time when the nation would punish this electoral theft. "Wait: retribution will come in due time."

In 1881 he made a trip to Europe and when he returned it was to be welcomed all across the country with a warmth indicating that the long public prejudice against him was gone. His last forensic speech was made to a committee of the Pennsylvania Senate, in which he argued that the railway companies "are not owners of the railroads" but administer them as "public agents," who must be amenable to public regulation. He was seventy three years old, and he was near his death. On August 19, 1883, he died. His equal as a defender of civil liberties has not yet been found.

23 Text of the speech is in C. F. Black, *op. cit.*, pp. 539–557.
24 Text in *ibid.*, pp. 616–621.

William M. Evarts: Ciceronian Advocate   📖

IF JEREMIAH BLACK stood embattled upon the bulwark of the Constitution, defending it as the citadel that protected civil rights, William Maxwell Evarts reached beyond and even around the Constitution to help adjust it to the changing needs of an industrializing society. As he said to and concerning the Supreme Court in his last appearance before it: "In the long run it has made the Constitution an instrument elastic enough to provide for the country's growing pains."[1] Although he was a master of the law and a respecter of its continuity, his touchstone was social need. "Let us know and feel," he said, "that the triumphs of eloquence and intellect are vain and useless, if not positively injurious and offensive to the moral sense of men and angels, unless they tend in some degree to the welfare of our fellow men, in which service we are born, and to which service we should, to the last, adhere."[2] He took Cicero as the model for his life's endeavors,[3] both for his disposition to serve the needs of his state and for the splendor and copiousness of his style. Claude Bowers and Helen Reid, in their study of Evarts, felt he lived up to his chosen model: "It was in his great arguments in causes of far reaching consequences that he was at his best, and here the influence of Cicero is most evident. Because of his high professional ideals he approached all of these cases in a broad way, as deeply concerned with underlying principles as with facts. He viewed controversy from every possible angle, looking with unerring eye through all the non-essentials to find the pivotal point, often to his opponents' discomfiture."[4]

William Evarts was born on February 6, 1818, and reared in an atmosphere of culture and dedication to duty. He proceeded through the Bowdoin and Boston Latin Schools to Yale, receiving a sound classical education. At Yale one of his professors was the famous Professor of Rhetoric, Chauncey Goodrich, who was proud of his brilliance in debate and public speaking.[5] Richard Henry Dana, Jr., his classmate at Yale, wrote of him: "If he does not become distinguished he will disappoint more persons than any other young man whom I have ever met

[1] Chester L. Barrows, William M. Evarts: Lawyer, Diplomat, Statesman, Chapel Hill: University of North Carolina Press, 1941, p. 2.
[2] Sherman Evarts, ed., Arguments and Speeches of William Maxwell Evarts, New York: Macmillan, 1919, III:182.
[3] Barrows, op. cit., p. 283.
[4] Claude G. Bowers and Helen Dwight Reid, The American Secretaries of State and Their Diplomacy, ed. Samuel Flagg Bemis, New York: Knopf, 1927–29, Ten Vols., VI:224.
[5] Barrows, op. cit., p. 11.

with."[6] He opened his law office in New York City in July, 1841, and within two weeks was asked to defend Monroe Edwards, a notorious forger. Although Edwards was convicted, Evarts made in his behalf a two-hour speech to the jury which won applause and approval from the seasoned barristers, launching him at once upon a great career. Shortly he entered partnership with Charles E. Butler, a connection that lasted for sixty years, until Evarts's death, on February 28, 1901. Singularly devoted to his professional duties, "his life was in his speeches," according to his son, who added: "Through them can best be recalled the man, whether they were the arguments of the advocate, or political speeches, or whether they appear in the form of elaborate orations at important commemorations, or in the lighter vein of occasional addresses."[7]

Evarts was very much interested in eloquence, which on many occasions he referred to as a weapon that might be used well or ill, for good or evil, depending on the skill and the intent of the user. In 1853, when he was invited back to Yale to deliver an address in celebration of the hundredth anniversary of the Linonian debating society, he said: "Oratory, in a free state, has ever been a main instrument of public influence, and has usually been assigned the first place among the arts of public life." It is true, he went on, that Washington, Franklin, and Jefferson were "without a single gift of oratorical power." He left unsaid the parallel truth that many excellent speakers have been a bane rather than a benefit to their country; but he drew the pertinent conclusion: "The truth is that eloquence, as its greatest master has said, is a weapon, and its effect depends chiefly on the force and skill to use it. In public life this force is character, this skill is civil prudence, and when the bright weapon of oratory is thus wielded, we may limit neither our admiration nor its power. Then, indeed, . . . does oratory seem the highest form and most beneficent exercise of human abilities; then the glory of the poet and philosopher grows pale before this effulgent splendor." So much for its power. "To the 'rapt orator' we bow, as to the magician who rides upon the storm and walks unshod over burning coals." But there is also demagoguery; and "when the gift of public speech is used for exhibition, or lent to the service of mere dextrous cunning, or, double-tongued, pleads in public controversies for the private fee of office or emolument, or . . . stoops to the tricks of acting or buffoonery, or feeds the unholy fires of faction and sedition, we may yield an unwilling tribute to perverted talent, but no such homage as gives power over will or action."[8]

[6] Quoted by Paul R. Beall, "The Forensic Rhetoric of William Maxwell Evarts," unpublished Ph.D. thesis, The Pennsylvania State University, 1948, p. 23.
[7] Evarts, *op. cit.,* I:ix.
[8] *Ibid.,* III:27–28.

In tribute to a fellow lawyer, in 1856, Evarts warned his fellow attorneys against "a sharp tongue and a bitter voice." For anyone who might "take up that voice of forensic and of public eloquence," he pleaded, "Let him use his eloquence for public justice in his duty as a lawyer, as the soldier uses his sword in his duty as a soldier; and let him know that it is no part of a true soldier at the bar to brandish his weapon of eloquence in a mere gladiatorial show to wound witness and party and counsel and friend, but that it is to be directed to pierce through the joints and marrow of a cause, and there only to be employed."[9]

Regarding Evarts's own uses of speech, in the judgment of his son:

> He treated all his cases in a very large way; he made luminous the philosophy and science of jurisprudence in its application to the case in hand; he lifted the cause to a very high plane, and notably was this true in the Johnson impeachment and the Beecher trial; by remarkable clearness of statement he disentangled the greatest confusion of facts and brought them into harmony with the fundamental principles upon which the contention of his cause rested; by apt allusion and illustration, by anecdote and by a play of humor and fancy, his presentation of the driest case interested the Court, as by his forceful eloquence he drove home the principles he advocated; while his unfailing courtesy and consideration, wholly without the taint of assumed superiority, won the admiration and affection of Bench and Bar.[10]

Highly as he regarded all the skills of speech, Evarts regarded himself primarily as a stylist. In the opening of his defense of Henry Ward Beecher against the charge of adultery with the wife of Theodore Tilton, Evarts stated what he felt to be his own guiding principle: "All exhibitory or ostentatious speech has always been foreign to forensic art. We deal with realities." Then he proceeded to a brief eulogy of his own chosen model: "Cicero, easily at the head of all ancient, and easily transcending all modern, reputations in our profession—Cicero, after he had gained the credit of being the greatest lawyer among orators and the greatest orator among lawyers—Cicero, who had built up that credit which is now represented by his works on the shelves of every scholar, though he be not a lawyer, of every lawyer, though he be not a scholar . . ." He added his own ideal: "One would wish some of those fabulous powers by which poetic invention has sought to eke out the infirmities of our feeble nature."[11] Again, in his defense of President Johnson, he referred once more to Cicero as his model and revealed his own aims as

9 *Ibid.*, III:181.
10 *Ibid.*, I:xii–xiii.
11 *Ibid.*, II:6–7.

a speaker: "Cicero, I think it is, who says that a lawyer should know everything, for sooner or later there is no fact in history, in science, or of human knowledge that will not come into play in his arguments."[12]

Ciceronian, indeed, was his style. A contemporary called him "the long sentence champion."[13] Timothy Dwight, introducing him to make an afterdinner speech, said simply: "Mr. Evarts will now give us a single sentence." To which Evarts responded: "It will be a life sentence."[14] While Evarts was Secretary of State he was teased by a toastmaster for his "calm and dispassionate discussion, clothed though it be with sentences as long as the English language can supply"—to which Evarts retorted: "The only persons in this country who are opposed to long sentences are the criminal classes."[15] Yet, like Cicero, along with the complexity of his sentence structure—which mirrored a mind accustomed to considering the complications of ideas—Evarts also excelled in clarity of statement. "Under his analysis," said Chauncey Depew, "mysteries of the most complicated cases seemed simple, the legal difficulties plain, and the solution comprehensible to everybody."[16] To St. Clair McKelway:

> His was the wit, diamond-pointed, that sparkled without wounding. His was the humor as debonair as dry, and as genial as subtle. His was the power of epigram, antithesis, or characterization that gave to thought the light for its entrance into the mind, and to fancy the barb that winged its course to the recesses of the imagination and to the centre of the heart. His was the anecdotal power that united the finality of culture with the simplicity of experience, and which gilded conversation with the sheen of gold, and gave to it the charm that made listening a luxury, enjoyment contagious, imitation a failure, emulation a temerity and admiration spontaneous. And all this concurred with an involution and circumlocution of oratorical style that, whether natural or acquired, was alike the envy and despair of colleagues and rivals.[17]

From the second day of Evarts's four-day speech in the trial of Andrew Johnson, we may cite a passage which at once offers a trenchant commentary on oral style and simultaneously illustrates his own methodology. After declaring his own preference for straightforward forensic discussion, he said:

> But we have learned here that there is another form of forensic controversy which may be called the method of concussion. I understand

---

[12] Quoted by Lester Thonssen, "William M. Evarts," in Brigance, ed., *History and Criticism*, op. cit., I:494. Also in Evarts, op. cit., I:397.
[13] *Albany Law Journal*, March, 1901, p. 111.
[14] Thonssen, op. cit., I:493.
[15] Evarts, op. cit., I:xxii.
[16] Chauncey Depew, *My Memories of Eighty Years*, op. cit., p. 105.
[17] Quoted by Beall, op. cit., pp. 30–31.

the method of concussion to be to make a violent, noisy, and explosive demonstration in the vicinity of the object of attack, whereas the method of discussion is to penetrate the position, and if successful to capture it. The Chinese method of warfare is the method of concussion, and consists of a great braying of trumpets, sounding of gongs, shouts, and shrieks in the neighborhood of the opposing force, which rolled away and the air clear and calm again, the effect is to be watched for. But it has been reserved for us in our modern warfare, as illustrated during the rebellion, to present a more singular and notable instance of the method of warfare by concussion than has ever been known before. A fort impregnable by the method of discussion, that is, penetrating and capturing it, has been on the largest scale attempted by the method of concussion, and some two hundred and fifty tons of gunpowder in a hulk moored near the stone walls of the fort has been made the means and the occasion of this vast experiment.[18]

Then he made his application of the analogy, referring to the speech just delivered for the prosecution by General Butler:

The air was filled with epithets, the dome shook with invective. Wretchedness and misery and suffering and blood, not included within the record, were made the means of this explosive mixture. And here we are, surveying the concussions, and after all reduced to the humble and homely method of discussion, which belongs to "attorneys whose intellects have been sharpened but not enlarged by the practice of law."

With his theory of advocacy thoroughly in hand and well practiced, in 1860 Evarts undertook in the Court of Appeals to maintain the right to freedom of eight slaves who had been brought into New York State in 1852 by a Mr. and Mrs. Jonathan Lemmon, while en route from Virginia to Texas, and who had sued for their freedom on the ground that they became free when they were voluntarily brought into free territory. Evarts had, in 1850, upheld the validity of the Fugitive Slave Law, and he was pleased now to have an opportunity to demonstrate his opposition to slavery. He upheld the freedom of the Negroes by arguing that if New York did not have "the power of determining the political, the civil, the social, the actual condition of persons within its borders, it is because some other power has that control; . . . [and] how this admission can consist with the fundamental idea of the sovereignty, or of the separateness of a political community, it passes my intelligence to comprehend."[19]

Paul Beall has made an exhaustive analysis of two of Evarts's cases: his defense of President Andrew Johnson against impeachment; and

[18] Evarts, *op. cit.,* I:371.
[19] *Ibid.,* I:16–17.

his defense of Henry Ward Beecher against a charge of adultery, which Beall believes represent Evarts at his best. They also were two of the most important cases in this span of American history. "In one instance a vital historical precedent was in the making; in the other the social mores of the nation were under fire."[20] For both trials, hundreds of pages of verbatim recording of the attorney's summary speeches are preserved.[21] How Evarts pleaded his case before the Senate is well summarized in a contemporary news journal:

> Mr. Evarts was very long-winded, speaking for fourteen mortal hours, and coming very near tiring the Senate out before he finished. We cannot, therefore, even enumerate his points. He passed most of his time in the regions of what may be called higher expediency, and addressed himself more to the discretion of the Senate or its political sense than any of his colleagues had done, touching very slightly on questions of construction, and treating the evidence, as well he might, as trivial and unimportant. He claimed for the President the credit of having acted in good faith in disobeying the law; affirmed very strongly the doctrine that a law is not a law if it is not constitutional; that it is for the Supreme Court to say whether it is constitutional or not; that in deciding it to be unconstitutional the court does not annul a law, it simply says that something which has been passing as a law is not a law, and that, therefore, a person accused of breaking it has not been guilty of any crime. Mr. Evarts claimed for the President a large amount of responsibility to the people for the safety of the Constitution. The great merit of his speech, however, lay in the dexterity with which he turned their own weapons against the Managers, and with which he overwhelmed them with ridicule.[22]

Beall believes that Evarts's case was based not on legality nor even on logic, but on appeal to underlying moral values that must be preserved if civilized society is to endure. As Evarts said: "truth, justice, oath, duty . . . . You receive them or you neglect them; whichever way you turn you cannot be the same men afterward that you were before. Accepted, embraced, obeyed, you are nobler and stronger and better. Spurned, rejected, you are worse and baser and weaker and wickeder than before. And it is thus that by strong ideas a free government must always be held to the path of duty and to the maintenance of its own authority and to the prevalence of its own strength for its perpetual existence."[23] Barrows concluded that the address was chiefly notable for its style: "He knew how to change his pace, to combine the solid and the trivial, the

[20] Beall, *op. cit.*, p. 67.
[21] Evarts, *op. cit.*, I:340–525, for the Johnson summation; and *ibid.*, II:1–245, for the Beecher summation.
[22] *The Nation*, May 7, 1868, p. 361.
[23] Beall, *op. cit.*, p. 205.

serious and the comic . . . . When he finished a train of argument, he neatly summarized it in a terse, epigrammatic sentence . . . . Most impressive of all was the force and charm of his personality."[24] The long-range effect of the trial was properly forecast at its close by an anonymous contributor to *The Nation*: "Now that Mr. Johnson has been acquitted, we may probably take for granted that there will never be another President impeached in this country."[25]

In defense of Beecher, Evarts spoke for eight days, telling the jury he wished for the power to distill the vast mass of evidence down to its essential elements. Then, keeping to the third person, he added that "he would wish for that greatest gift, eloquence—eloquence which over-leaping even the short circuit between the voice and ear, speaks out from heart to heart as face answereth face, and what a great thinker among mankind, Lord Bacon, has said is more than eloquence, discretion of speech, that no excitements, no perversions, no enlistments, no animosities should carry him beyond the duty to his client, to justice, to truth, to his opponents, and to you."[26] The principal topic to which Evarts directed his eloquence was that Theodore Tilton, who brought the charge, was a disreputable character, and that Beecher, the accused, was a man of transparent nobility. The evidence presented against Beecher, he contended, was circumstantial and contradictory. He concluded with the admonition that on such a charge as this the accused must be found either all innocent or all guilty; there is no middle ground. He ended with a prophecy of success: "in your verdict you will find, and we shall find with joy, that truth matches all round, and your verdict will be no exception." The trial ended in a hung jury; and, in this sense, Beecher was acquitted.

Robert Shaplen, in his book on the Beecher trial, concludes that it is difficult to convict one man for what many are guilty of; and he quotes from the *London Daily Telegraph* a comment that if Beecher was not convicted of adultery, "He is not the only person in the world entitled to that negative praise."[27] Barrows, in his biography, sums up his own conclusions by saying: "Evarts showed dexterity in burying from sight testimony that was in his way and weaving a plausible story out of scanty materials."[28]

William M. Evarts served as Secretary of State and as United States Senator. He was active in a wide variety of public affairs. But to nothing did he give his mind and his heart with such clear devotion as he did to

[24] Barrows, *op. cit.*, pp. 152–153.
[25] "Marcel," in *The Nation*, June 18, 1868, p. 490.
[26] Evarts, *op. cit.*, III:8.
[27] Robert Shaplen, *Free Love and Heavenly Sinners*, *op. cit.*, p. 258.
[28] Barrows, *op. cit.*, p. 280.

the study and practice of law. His conviction of its importance was well stated in a passage from a speech made in his youth, in 1850:

> . . . let us know and feel that he who strikes at a law strikes at *the* law; . . . above all, let no one who loves his country—who reveres the memory of his fathers—who hopes for the happiness of his children— ever doubt or forget that as we citizens of this great republic acknowl- edge no superior, and bow to no master but the law, so have we no guardian of our rights, no protector of our liberties, but the law, and that every wound to its *authority*, as surely enfeebles its *protection*.[29]

[29] Evarts, *op. cit.*, II:433.

XII

THE PROFESSIONAL: ADVOCATE
AND LECTURER
1826 ‒ 1920

Professionalizing the Public Speaking Platform

BOTH THE characteristics and the quality of public speaking are inevitably affected when the speaker aims primarily toward earning a fee with his lecture. The skill and art of the speaking tend to improve from the necessity of interesting and pleasing diverse listeners. Adaptation to audience susceptibilities is accorded special consideration. The strength of conviction sometimes (though of course not always) comes to seem less important. Both the propagandizing effects of advocacy and the commercializing effects of the paid lecture circuit have debased some otherwise promising rhetorical talent. On the other hand, neither Ralph Waldo Emerson nor Wendell Phillips (to cite merely two examples) would have attained to greatness as prophets of popular appeal had not the organized lecture system offered them a ready-made agency for developing and communicating their ideas. The effects, in short, have been partly good, partly bad. Matthew Arnold, never a good speaker, profited greatly from the lecture platform but spoke ill of it.[1] Mark Twain[2] and Artemus Ward[3] mastered the commercial lecture and entranced their audiences, but resented the demands it made upon them. Meanwhile, many who were impressively successful at the box office scarcely deserve serious attention by students of the art of rhetoric. In this category are such lecturers as Russell Conwell, De Witt Talmage, Robert J. Burdette, George W. Peck, and such dialect-comics as Josh Billings, Eli Perkins, and Bill Nye.

In 1871 James Redpath, a pioneer in the lecture bureau movement, wrote that "Lecturing is becoming a distinct profession. The system has grown up without system; it has never been organized by competent managers or carefully studied by competent observers; but as it extends

[1] Wayne C. Minnick, "Matthew Arnold on Emerson," *Quarterly Journal of Speech,* 37(1951):332.
[2] Mark Twain, *Autobiography, op. cit.,* II:148.
[3] Artemus Ward continued lecturing despite the fact that he suffered from consumption, which caused his death at the age of thirty three.

itself it will be reduced to order, its attractions multiplied, its sphere widened, its popularity increased, its influence for good augmented a hundred-fold. In this era of the newspaper, it seems the only ally that science and literature can confidently count upon to make their teachings household words and their discoveries known in the homes of the American people."[4]

From the earliest beginnings of recorded time until comparatively recent years, when a man of sense and insight had also the requisite speaking skill to penetrate the indifference of his fellows, he would respond to their call to stand up and deliver the best message his mind and spirit could concoct. Often enough such speakers were also motivated by some special cause which they wished to promote. Not rarely, their aim was partly their own self-advancement. On occasion speakers have stood forth at great cost or peril to themselves to utter prophetic messages of warning or challenging calls for communal betterment. Often the speakers were leaders of their society or of some portion of it, speaking to weld together the cooperative endeavors of their chosen public. Sometimes they were paid for their efforts with office, or with influence, or with personal satisfaction for duty well done, or even with money. Their common characteristic was that as speakers they were amateurs. Speaking was for them not an end in itself but a means toward the achievement of some other end. Even when they received great applause, the proper question that accompanied it was: "but what has been the effect?"

The professionalization of public speaking converted it (on the commercial platform) into a means of earning a living. Such speaking came to be judged basically in terms of whether an audience would pay to listen; and whether they would want the speaker back. A predominant skill became that of giving the people what they liked to hear. Unpalatable messages had to be sugar-coated. Crusading speeches had to identify people not in the audience as the agents of evil. The relationships of professional lecturing to public speaking are similar to those between commercial art and painting. Some magazine illustrators come very close to greatness; and some painters are totally incompetent. Nevertheless, the two groups remain in separate spheres. A difference that makes a difference is whether the motivation comes from a commercial system or from an inner drive. This distinction was dramatized, unconsciously, by Henry Ward Beecher, when he was once asked by an enthusiastic admirer to give a lecture. Beecher's reply was: "I have nothing to do with

[4] Charles F. Horner, The Life of James Redpath and the Development of the Modern Lyceum, New York: Barse and Hopkins, 1926, pp. 187–188.

it. You must see Major Pond, who points me and fires me off according to his own programme."[5]

The difference was deliberately phrased by Clarence Day, when he wrote: "Huge seas of talk of every sort and kind, in print, speech, and writing, will roll unceasingly, involving an unbelievable waste in labor and time, and sapping the intelligence talk is supposed to upbuild. In a simian civilization, great halls will be erected for lectures, and great throngs will actually pay to go inside at night to hear some self-satisfied talk-maker chatter for hours. Almost any subject will do for a lecture, or talk; yet very few subjects will be counted important enough for the average man to do any *thinking* on them, off by himself."[6] Again, this same distinction must have been in the mind of Hippocrates, when, in the golden age of Athenian oratory, he wrote: "If for the sake of a crowded audience you do wish to hold a lecture, your ambition is no laudable one."[7]

Under the influence of professionalism, lecturers came to be collectively known as "talent," and were not unnaturally grouped with the trained dog acts, the bell-ringers, and the ventriloquists, all of whom were "sold" for the purpose of making up a program that would draw crowds. One lecturer, who was flamboyantly billed as "A new Patrick Henry," developed the technique of "serial lectures," akin to the continued story in magazines. By this suspense-technique, "he built up his curious audience from forty the first day to three thousand at the close of their third series, and for one morning session drew an unprecedented five thousand. He was tireless."[8]

The biographies and memoirs of professional lecturers have a different quality from those of the inspired amateurs. There are repetitively in them passages of cross practicality—even when the lecturer is a minister of unquestioned devotion. Russell Conwell, for example, discussing his early days on the platform, said: "I lectured at first in churches and summer hotels, and often twice a day, but for a very small fee. Once I was paid with a smoked ham, and at another time with a preacher's note for four dollars and fifty cents, which still remains unpaid. The greatest income from any one lecture was an independent lecture in Baltimore, when the receipts were $1751, above all expenses. The largest straight fee from a committee was five hundred dollars at the Mormon Taber-

[5] James B. Pond, *Eccentricities of Genius: Memories of Famous Men and Women on the Platform and Stage*, New York: G. W. Dillingham, 1900. The closeness of the relationship between Pond and Beecher is related on pp. 37–75.
[6] Clarence Day, *This Simian World*, New York: Knopf, 1920, p. 52.
[7] Hippocrates, *Precepts*, trans. W. H. S. Jones, New York: Putnam's, 1923, Chapter XII.
[8] Harry P. Harrison, as told to Karl Detzer, *Culture Under Canvas: The Story of Tent Chautauqua*, New York: Hastings House, 1958, p. 144.

nacle, Salt Lake City. One year a wealthy man in Burlington, Vermont, sent me to sixty-three different places, and paid the bill himself. The largest audience I ever had was in Madison Square Garden, New York, when upwards of fifteen thousand were present, and the next largest was in Salt Lake City, where there were twelve thousand present."[9] When Josh Billings was concocting his "Advice Tew Lectur Kommittys," the first item was: "Don't hire enny man tew lektur for yu (never mind how moral he iz) unless yu kan make munny on him."[10]

One of the effects of the professionalism was that it bred a kind of speech that aimed solely to win admiration and applause. The aim was less to communicate ideas than simply to sound impressive. The commercial lecture platform furnishes multiple examples. One such is a passage from an enormously popular lecture, called "Life and Love," which "became a pattern for other aspiring orators," delivered by Robert Love ("Fiddlin' Bob") Taylor:

> I saw the Morning with purple quiver and burnished bow, stand tip-toe on the horizon and shoot sunbeams at the vanishing darkness of night and then reach up and gather the stars and hide them in her bosom and then bend down and tickle the slumbering World with straws of light till it awoke with laughter and song. A thousand bugle-calls from the rosy fires of the East heralded her coming. A thousand smiling meadows kissed her garments as she passed. Ten thousand gardens unfurled their flowerflags to greet her. The heart of the deep forest throbbed a tribute of bird-song and the bright waters rippled a melody of "welcome." Young life and love, love radiant, radiant with hope and sparkling with the dew-drops of exultant joy came hand in hand tripping and dancing in her shining train and I wished that the Heaven of the Morning might last, forever.[11]

Mark Twain, who was one of the greatest masters of the lecture platform, albeit sometimes an unwilling one, was so distraught from hearing this kind of verbal vacuousness that he fabricated a hoax in the form of a meaningless passage, and then gleefully noted that it was praised for its beauty by listeners who took it for granted that it must mean something:

> It was a crisp and spicy morning in early October. The lilacs and laburnums, lit with the glory-fires of autumn, hung burning and flashing in the upper air, a fairy bridge provided by kind Nature for the wingless wild things that have their homes in the tree tops and would visit together; the larch and the pomegranate flung their purple and

9 Agnes Rush Burr, *Russell H. Conwell and His Work,* Philadelphia: John C. Winston, 1926, pp. 322–323.
10 Josh Billings, *His Works Complete,* New York: Carleton, 1876, p. 373.
11 Harrison and Detzer, *op. cit.,* pp. 134–135.

yellow flames in brilliant broad splashes along the slanting sweep of the woodland; the sensuous fragrance of innumerable deciduous flowers rose upon the swooning atmosphere; far in the empty sky a solitary esophagus slept upon motionless wing; everywhere brooded stillness, serenity, and the peace of God.[12]

Oliver Wendell Holmes, in his *Autocrat of the Breakfast Table* paid his dubious respects to the lecture audience: "Front seats: a few old folks—shiny-headed—slant up best ear towards the speaker—drop off to sleep after a while when the air begins to get a little narcotic with carbonic acid. Bright women's faces, young and middle-aged, a little behind these, but towards the front,—(pick out the best and lecture mainly to that). Here and there a countenance sharp and scholar-like, and a dozen pretty female ones sprinkled about. An indefinite number of pairs of young people—happy but not always very attentive. Boys, in the background, more or less quick. Dull faces, here, there—in how many places! I don't say dull people but faces without a ray of sympathy or movement of expression. They are what kill the lecturer. These negative faces with their vacuous eyes and stony lineaments pump and suck the warm soul out of him."[13] Not all audiences, of course, were of this type; but they tended to be heterogeneous because they came for entertainment, from curiosity, or from social pressure for "betterment" as well as from a genuine interest in what the speaker might have to say.

Professionalism, of course, takes many forms and produces varied effects. Women who took to the platform as earnest crusaders for equal rights had little of the professional cast except that, by and large, they gave the same speech over and over again, and their tours were organized. The temperance advocates were as much crusaders as were the earlier abolitionists—except that their subject was less vital and their need for an audience led them to develop a mode and a mood of at least partial entertainment. The Lyceum and Chautauqua movements both started with high educational and religious ideals; but both succumbed to the temptation to woo financial success through increasing popularization. The lecture bureau, on the other hand, never made any pretense of being anything but a specialized sales organization.

The lecture platform covers a spectrum as broad as that which stretches, in print, from the comic books to belles-lettres. The extent of the range is indicated in a reply that one seasoned Chautauquan, Lee Francis Lybarger, made when he was asked to sign a lecture contract:

[12] *The Complete Short Stories of Mark Twain*, ed. Charles Neider, Garden City: Hanover House, 1957, from "A Double-Barreled Detective Story," p. 436.
[13] Oliver Wendell Holmes, *The Autocrat of the Breakfast Table*, Boston: Houghton Mifflin, 1891, pp. 140–141.

"What do you want from this lecturer? What you already know, or what you do *not* know? What you believe, or what you do *not* believe? Should he make you feel good by flattery, or feel bad by advocating things you oppose? The lecturer should take none of these things into consideration. It is not his mission to flatter or irritate, denounce the old or praise the new. He simply should proclaim the truth."[14] Not all the lecturers were so particular.

Women Take to the Platform

IT WAS on a Fourth of July, 1828, that the first recorded public speech by a woman was delivered in the United States, by a Scottish immigrant educator, Frances Wright, in the communist community she had founded at New Harmony, Indiana. In justification of her unprecedentedly bold act she wrote in her newspaper, "I am not one who speaks my thoughts in whispers nor who do things in corners."[1] Her plea was not for anything so revolutionary as "women's rights," but for "rational, national" reforms in education. What she said mattered much less than that she had "with ruthless violence broken loose from the restraints of decorum, which draws a circle around the life of a woman." The newspaper editor who contemplated this awful fact proceeded confidently to his conclusion that "Miss Wright stands condemned of a violation of the unalterable laws of nature which have created a barrier between the man and the woman."[2] She was denounced for *raving* and for *fanatacism*, for questioning the system "in which woman, in obedience to her nature and the express commands of God, acknowledges man as her head," by no less a critic than Emma Wil-

[14] Harrison and Detzer, *op. cit.*, pp. 144–145.
[1] New Harmony, Indiana, *Gazette*, October 18, 1828. Frances Trollope, who heard her in Cincinnati a few months later, could scarce contain her ecstasy: "I knew her extraordinary gift of eloquence, her almost unequalled command of words, and the wonderful power of her rich and thrilling voice . . . . It is impossible to imagine anything more striking than her appearance. Her tall and majestic figure, the deep and almost solemn expression of her eyes, the simple contour of her finely formed head, unadorned, except by its own natural ringlets; her garment of plain white muslin, which hung about her in folds that recalled the drapery of a Grecian statue, all contributed to produce an effect, unlike any thing I had ever seen before, or ever expect to see again." Quoted from Mrs. Trollope's *Domestic Manners of the Americans* by William Randall Waterman, *Frances Wright*, New York: Columbia University, *Studies in History, Economics and Public Law*, Vol. CXV, No. 1, 1924, pp. 148–149.
[2] Lillian O'Connor, *Pioneer Women Orators*, New York: Columbia University Press, 1954, p. 49, quoting from the *Free Enquirer*, Dec. 10, 1828. Cf. also Doris Yoakum, "Women's Introduction to the American Platform," in Brigance, ed., *History and Criticism, op. cit.*, I:157–159.

lard.[3] Nevertheless, her speech gives her priority in a movement that was contemptuously condemned (though it could not be dismissed) as "hens trying to crow."[4]

What is little realized is that the status of women in America was actually worsened as a result of the American Revolution. The Colonial charters had restricted the voting right to church members and property owners, but made no distinction based on sex. Virginia, it is true, excluded women from the ballot in 1699. Other such restrictions, however, did not occur until 1777 in New York; 1780 in Massachusetts; and 1784 in New Hampshire. In a contrary move, New Jersey explicitly granted suffrage to women in 1790—and did not reverse itself until, in 1807, an influx of women voters at the polls frightened the men by determining the result of a local election concerning the location of a courthouse.[5] As the new society of the nation became both more formalized and less agricultural, the legal and social status of women became defined (in law and by custom) as one of basic inequality. Upon marriage, a woman's property became her husband's; their children became his wards, under his guardianship; and her testimony against him would not be received in court. The "liberal" New England school system restricted girls to such tutelage as might be given in an hour and a half each day during summer months, while the real scholars were on vacation. Only a half dozen menial vocations were open to women and these were poorly paid.[6]

The first American-born woman to speak out publicly in protest against these conditions—and also for abolition of slavery—was a Negress, Mrs. Frances Maria W. Stewart, who was born free in Connecticut in 1803. In the winter of 1832–33, she gave four public addresses in Boston, which Garrison published in *The Liberator*. She soon gave up the effort, however, feeling that "I have made myself contemptible in the eyes of many."[7]

Angelina Grimké, born in 1805 into a wealthy slaveholding family in

---

[3] O'Connor, *op. cit.*, p. 48. What the "raving" consisted of was summarized by Frances Wright in her *Course of Popular Lectures*, New York, 1829, p. 18: "I have wedded the cause of human improvement; staked on it my reputation, my fortune, and my life; and as, for it, I threw behind me in earliest youth the follies of my age, the luxuries of ease and European aristocracy, so do I, and so will I, persevere, even as I began; and devote what remains to me of talent, strength, fortune, and existence, to the same sacred cause—the promotion of just knowledge, the establishing of just practice, the increase of human happiness." Quoted by Waterman, *op. cit.*, p. 151.

[4] Sherwin, *Prophet of Liberty*, *op. cit.*, p. 241.

[5] Inez Haynes Irwin, *Angels and Amazons: A Hundred Years of American Women*, Garden City: Doubleday, Doran, 1934, pp. 3–4.

[6] *Ibid.*, p. 26. Cf. also Eleanor Flexner, *Century of Struggles: The Women's Rights Movement in the United States*, Cambridge: Harvard University Press, 1959, Chapter I, "The Position of American Women up to 1800," pp. 3–22.

[7] Flexner, *op. cit.*, pp. 44–45; O'Connor, *op. cit.*, pp. 53–55.

Charleston, South Carolina, came north in 1829 with her sister Sarah. Seven years later, in New York City, she commenced an impassioned period of speaking that lasted only two years (when her voice gave out) but that for the first time demonstrated that women need not be inferior as orators to men. Wendell Phillips said in his memorial address after her death in 1880 that "She swept the chords of the human heart with a power that has never been surpassed and rarely equalled. I well remember, evening after evening, listening to eloquence such as had never been heard from a woman."[8] Her most dramatic appearance was in February, 1838, when for three successive days she testified before a committee of the Massachusetts Legislature in support of antislavery petitions. What it meant at that time for a woman to arise to her feet in public to speak to any audience, but especially to one of men, she described in a letter to her husband:

> I was so near fainting under the tremendous pressure of feeling, my heart almost died within me. The novelty of the scene, the weight of responsibility, the ceaseless exercise of mind thro' which I had passed for almost a week—all together sunk me to the earth. I well nigh despaired, but our Lord and Master gave me his arm to lean upon, and in great weakness, my limbs trembling under me, I stood up and spoke for nearly two hours.[9]

Members of the legislature opposed her reappearance the second day, on the ground that so great a crowd would be attracted that the galleries might collapse; however, their fears were overruled.

Another decade later, in 1848, Elizabeth Cady Stanton and Lucretia Mott became so aroused by "long accumulating discontent" that they wrote out an announcement which appeared in the July 14 issue of the *Seneca County Courier* calling for a Woman's Rights Convention to discuss the "social, civil, and religious rights of woman." Eight years earlier these two women had attended the first World's Antislavery Convention in London, where they had been refused seats as delegates on account of their sex. Ever since they had been nurturing the slow boil of their wrath. Now, in a small town, without any famed names, and based upon a brief notice in an obscure country newspaper, they held their meeting with true revolutionary zeal—even reading a "Declaration of Principles" that was deliberately modelled on the Declaration of Independence, and that proved to be a rallying point and a goal for three generations of women suffragists.[10] For their opening meeting some three hundred people appeared, coming as far as fifty miles by buck-

[8] Flexner, op. cit., p. 344.
[9] Ibid., p. 49.
[10] Irwin, op. cit., pp. 84–86, gives the text of this moving document.

board. The audience included forty men, and no woman dared to open the meeting. James Mott, Lucretia's husband, called the meeting to order, but then Mrs. Stanton took charge. With most careful control of her diction, she rose to her feet and spoke evenly: "I should feel exceedingly diffident to appear before you at this time, having never before spoken in public, were I not nerved by a sense of right and duty, did I not feel that the time had come for the question of women's wrongs to be laid before the public, did I not believe that woman herself must do this work; for woman alone can understand the height, the depth, the length and the breadth of her degradation."[11] Historians generally date the beginning of the women's rights movement from this Seneca Falls Convention.

Actually the movement had many beginnings, rooted in many personalities. The gentle Lucretia Mott, a Quaker, had been speaking in meetings of Friends since 1818. Her speaking was described by a frequent auditor as "No whirlwind of passion, or lightning of eloquence; it was rather the dawn of clear day upon dark places and hidden."[12] Abbey Kelley Foster, a black-haired, sparkling-eyed Irish schoolmistress, in 1838 abandoned the schoolroom to devote herself to lecturing on behalf of abolitionism. Blistering invective was her forte. She commonly commenced her speech by saying, "I did not come intending to address you," or "I did not come to make a speech," or, "I have not been accustomed to address meetings of this kind. It is not my vocation to make speeches, or to string together brilliant sentences, or beautiful words."[13] Then she would light into her audiences, calling them thieves, liars, adulterers, murderers, pirates, and cradle-snatchers, because they tolerated slavery.[14] Another woman of great power was a Negress named Isabella, who was freed when New York abolished slavery in 1827, and who later took the name of Sojourner Truth. In 1851, at a woman's rights meeting in Akron, Ohio, when an outbreak of heckling from men in the audience threatened to break up the convention, Sojourner Truth moved slowly forward and sat on the steps of the platform until she got permission to speak. Then she rose, flexed the muscles of her arm, and cried out:

> Look at my arm! I have ploughed and planted and gathered into barns, and no man could head me—and ain't I a woman? . . . . I have born thirteen children, and seen most of 'em sold into slavery, and

[11] Flexner, *op. cit.*, pp. 76–77.
[12] Samuel Longfellow, quoted by Anna D. Hallowell, *James and Lucretia Mott: Life and Letters*, Boston: Houghton Mifflin, 1884, p. 469.
[13] O'Connor, *op. cit.*, pp. 62–63.
[14] Yoakum, *op. cit.*, I:167.

> when I cried out with my mother's grief, none but Jesus heard me—
> and ain't I a woman?[15]

This was speaking of a new sort, and the raucous men quieted to hear it. Still another Negro woman, Frances Ellen Watkins Harper, commenced speaking about the same time, creating a sensation in her own way by the quietude, gentleness, and elevated dignity of her manner.[16] These, and a growing number of others, were a part of the beginning. Women were slowly, experimentally, finding their own voice. Their effectiveness in speaking reached its greatest levels in the lecturing of Lucy Stone and Ernestine Rose. And the woman who became most influential as an organizer and director of their cause was Susan B. Anthony.

Lucy Stone (August 13, 1818–October 18, 1893) was born a few hours after her mother had milked eight cows; and when the baby was born, her mother said drearily: "Oh dear! I am sorry it is a girl. A woman's life is so hard."[17] Francis Stone, Lucy's father, was a despot who worked his girls as hard as he drove himself. There was little room for love in the family; and when Lucy, as a child, read in the first book of Genesis: "Thy desire shall be to thy husband, and he shall rule over thee," she longed to die. In any event, she determined never to marry, and she promised herself an education. Since her father would not help her get one, she was twenty five before she finally entered Oberlin, the only college in the country that would admit women. She was refused permission to attend the class in public speaking except as an auditor, and only then on condition that she sit quietly. But she studied Whately's and Blair's books on rhetoric and practiced speaking at meetings of the Young Ladies Association. When she graduated she announced boldly her plan to pursue a career of public lecturing, saying: "I expect to plead not for the slave only, but for suffering humanity everywhere. Especially do I mean to labor for the elevation of my sex."[18] She signed as an agent for the Massachusetts Antislavery Society, with the understanding that she would speak for abolition of slavery on Saturdays and Sundays, and for women's rights the rest of the week. Homely, ill-dressed, without friends, and advocating a cause with which very few had sympathy, she made her way from community to community in New York and Ohio, living as best she could. Her biography by her daughter quotes her description of these days:

> When I undertook my solitary battle for woman's rights, outside the
> little circle of abolitionists I knew nobody who sympathized with my

[15] Flexner, *op. cit.*, pp. 90–91.
[16] *Ibid.*, p. 97.
[17] Flexner, *op. cit.*, p. 69; Constance Buel Burnett, *Five for Freedom*, New York: Abelard Press, 1953, pp. 131–137.
[18] Flexner, *op. cit.*, p. 69.

ideas. I had some hand-bills printed, 12 × 10 inches. I bought a paper of tacks, and, as I could not pay for posting, I put up my bills myself, using a stone for a hammer. I did not take a fee at the door. But there was always the expense of hall and hotel. To cover this, at the close of my speech, I asked help for the great work, by a collection for expenses. Then I took a hat and went through the audience for the collection, for all were strangers to me. I always got enough to pay what was due, and sometimes more.[19]

In her twenty-eighth year, she went into a hardware store in Cincinnati and met the proprietor, Henry Blackwell, seven years her junior, who fell deeply in love with her. When they were married it was with a ceremony in which she explicitly promised *not* to obey, and she always kept her maiden name. Henry Blackwell remained true to the covenant and for the remainder of her life was her faithful attendant and supporter. Soon she had broadened her audience appeal until she was speaking all through New England, in Canada, and as far west and south as Louisville and St. Louis. Often her audiences were unruly, booing, and jeering; sometimes she was pelted with tobacco cuds, vegetables, water, or other objects. Once she was struck so hard with a hymn book that she was knocked down. But nothing stopped her lecturing until the event of which men were always reminding the suffragists: the birth of a child. Then Lucy Stone reverted from lecturing to motherhood and did not return to the platform till after the Civil War.[20]

By the time the war ended, women speakers had ceased to be a rarity and their right to speak was at least grudgingly accepted by many audiences. Even so, Lucy Stone's return to the platform led one New England minister to announce her afternoon speech as follows: "I am requested to say that a hen will undertake to crow like a cock in the town hall this afternoon at five o'clock. Anybody who wants to hear that kind of music will, of course, attend."[21] The principal objections now were not to the speakers as women, but to their topic. The abolitionists, who had been their warmest supporters, now became their violent critics, on the ground that they should drop their agitation until equal rights were won for Negroes.

Meanwhile, under all the pressures and difficulties, the women's rights advocates themselves split into two antagonistic groups. Susan B. Anthony and Elizabeth Cady Stanton organized the National Woman Suffrage Association, which restricted membership to women, concentrated upon securing a women's rights amendment to the federal Constitution, and published a journal called *Revolution*. Lucy Stone ob-

[19] *Ibid.*, p. 97.
[20] Elinor Rice Hays, *Morning Star: A Biography of Lucy Stone*, New York: Harcourt, Brace, 1961, *passim*.
[21] Burnett, *op. cit.*, p. 175.

jected to the utilization by this organization of such lecturers as Victoria Woodhull, who not only advocated free love but practiced it, and George Francis Train, an extreme eccentric who advocated his own election to the presidency, the total exclusion of imports from Europe, printing press money, and other ideas of similar value. Miss Stone accordingly founded the American Woman Suffrage Association, which welcomed men as well as women into membership, sought action first on the local and State levels, established a journal called *The Woman's Journal*, and sought to limit its lecturers to speakers of general if not genteel respectability.

In 1867, both factions participated actively in the first of fifty six State referendum battles on women's suffrage that were to take place between 1867 and 1918. This one was in Kansas, and the difficulties of travel and of obtaining accommodations were extreme. Despite their best efforts, they won only nine thousand votes in a total of thirty thousand. How hard they tried was vividly described by Lucy's husband:

> Lucy and I are going over the length and breadth of this state speaking every day and sometimes twice, journeying from twenty-five to forty-five miles daily, sometimes in a carriage and sometimes in an open wagon with or without springs. We climb hills and dash down ravines, ford creeks and ferry over rivers, rattle across limestone ledges, struggle through muddy bottoms, fight the high winds on the high rolling upland prairies and address the most astonishing (and astonished) audiences in the most extraordinary places. Tonight it may be a log school house, tomorrow a stone church; next day a store with planks for seats, and in one place, if it had not rained, we should have held forth in an unfinished court house, with only four stone walls but no roof whatsoever.[22]

Lucy Stone's manner of speaking was courageously forthright and direct. Hers was not the soft answer that turns away wrath, but the quick retort, the positive refutation. Even so, her manner was so ladylike and reserved that she won the unqualified endorsement of the gentle Quaker, Lucretia Mott, who wrote in 1858 that "Lucy Stone is worth a dozen quiet workers. Give me *noise* on this subject; a real Boanerges."[23] She wore her hair short and for a brief time adopted the short skirt and trousers advocated by Amelia Bloomer. She was only some five feet in height and weighed just a hundred pounds. Her features were not especially attractive, but she had a remarkable voice, pure, melodious, and

[22] *The History of Women's Suffrage*, edited by Elizabeth Cady Stanton, Susan B. Anthony, and Mathilda Joslyn Gage, Three Vols., New York: Fowler and Wells, 1881 and 1886, II:235. Subsequently Vol. IV appeared in 1902 and Vols. V and VI in 1922.
[23] Hallowell, *op. cit.*, p. 383.

with a capacity to carry above or through the hoots and foot-stamping of derisive crowds. Susan B. Anthony valued her eloquence so highly that she considered it a "crime" for Lucy to have a baby,[24] whereupon Lucy replied saucily that "I shall not assume the responsibility for another convention until I have had my ten daughters."[25] Even after Miss Stone accused the great Susan of spending the women's rights funds for her own personal projects, Miss Anthony still considered her "more eloquent than any other mortal woman speaker."[26] An enthusiastic supporter believed that "her solid Seward-like logic, her keen sarcasm, her earnest appeals, and volumes of facts, are wholly irresistible to every person who cares for reason or justice."[27] A clergyman abolitionist, Jehiel Claflin, summarized his critique of her speaking in glowing terms:

> The secret of Miss Stone's eloquence is, she speaks from the heart. Hers are "thoughts that breathe and words that burn." Her soul is in the subject. Her heart and mind seem all radiant and luminous with love and truth, so elevating and soul-stirring, that she holds her hearers in perfect captivity, and in the language of another, it is beautifully true, that her "words sway the multitude as pendant vines swing in the summer breeze." Under her stirring appeals, the consciences of the people have been painfully aroused.[28]

Her chief limitation was a lack of humor and an unbending earnestness. "In Heaven," she used to say with a tight little smile, "I may understand music and jokes."[29] Her last words were whispered to her daughter Alice: "Make the world better."[30] It was what she tried to do.

Ernestine Rose, a Jewess born in Poland on January 13, 1810, came as a refugee to America in 1836, where, despite the foreignism of her speech, she quickly became known as "The Queen of the Platform."[31] She had suffered religious persecution, bitter poverty, and political oppression; and her wrathful goal was the total regeneration of society. The breadth of her creed was proclaimed as liberalism itself, in one and all forms, in a debate that ran for thirteen weeks during the summer of 1837, just a year after her arrival. An organization of freethinkers called "Society for Moral Philanthropists" sponsored the debate, which drew

[24] Alma Lutz, *Susan B. Anthony: Rebel, Crusader, Humanitarian*, Boston: Beacon Press, 1959, p. 69.
[25] *Ibid.*, p. 72.
[26] *Ibid.*, p. 146.
[27] *The Liberator*, Dec. 8, 1854.
[28] *Ibid.*, Sept. 2, 1853.
[29] Burnett, *op. cit.*, p. 173.
[30] *Ibid.*, p. 176.
[31] Yuri Suhl, *Ernestine L. Rose and the Battle for Human Rights*, New York: Reynal, 1959, p. 48 and *passim*.

audiences of up to two thousand people. Frances Wright, also an immigrant, and Ernestine Rose were among the featured speakers. How they appeared to the general public was expressed by James Gordon Bennett, editor of the *New York Herald*, who heard them and reported to his readers: "What trash! what blockheads! what genuine asses!"[32] A few years later, he was describing the first National Women's Rights Convention, at Worcester, Mass., in 1850, in which Mrs. Rose was a principal speaker, as follows:

> There is not a lunatic asylum in the country wherein, if the inmates were called together to sit in convention, they would not exhibit more sense, reason, decency, and delicacy, and less lunacy, blasphemy and horrible sentiment, than this hybrid, mongrel, piebald, crackbrained, pitiful, disgusting, and ridiculous assemblage. And there we drop them, and may God have mercy on their miserable souls. Amen.[33]

Ernestine Rose was a fighter, fierce, unbridled, and unrestrained. Her coal-black hair was piled high in ringlets on her head, and her voice was resonant with power and depth of feeling. To her critical audiences she gave back in full measure the scorn she received:

> I tell you, men are overboard; the slave groans in his chains; woman groans in her supposed inferiority and in her oppression; man groans in his ignorance; men and women groan in poverty; society groans in dishonesty, in falsehood, in dissipation, in vice, in crime, in misery.[34]

While her husband earned his living in a silversmith's shop, Mrs. Rose traveled tirelessly, speaking against organized religion, for she considered the clergy the worst enemies of women's rights; for free love; for abolition of slavery; and for widespread labor reforms. After a speech in Bath, New York, the local paper commented: "She is one of the best speakers we have ever heard, and we can only regret that a woman of such brilliant intellect should be wasting her energies in a cause for which there is not a shadow of hope."[35]

Along with her associates, Mrs. Rose was delighted with the prospect of the Civil War, which she considered a war for the attainment of all

[32] *Ibid.*, p. 67.
[33] *Ibid.*, p. 114.
[34] *Ibid.*, p. 196. As an indication of the growing violence of the movement, contrast this passage with a paragraph equally radical but far more restrained, spoken by Frances Wright a quarter century earlier: "Take for your teachers experimental philosophers, not spiritual dreamers! Turn your churches into halls of science, and devote your leisure day to the study of your own bodies, the analysis of your own minds, and the examination of the fair material world which extends around you!" Waterman, *op. cit.*, p. 153.
[35] Suhl, *op. cit.*, p. 159.

her many ideals. "Whatever remains to be acquired will be easily obtained," she told a Cooper Union audience on May 12, 1860.[36] Then came disillusionment. After the war's end, the fourteenth amendment, for the first time, inserted the word "male" into the Constitution; and the abolitonists, by whose side the women had fought so long and so well, urged them to give up their own struggle in order to concentrate on civil rights for the freed slaves. Then came the defeat in Kansas, and after that the bitter split of the women's rights movement into two groups. Ernestine Rose was broken in body and went to England for a long rest. In 1876, she wrote wistfully home to Susan B. Anthony: "I would like to lecture a little more."[37] But it was too late. Two years later she went to Paris and made her last speech, a few remarks in French, in which she said: "In every country, in every nation, I have concerned myself with those subjects which touch upon reform and the improvement of mankind." This was her epitaph. She lived on, in ill health and in loneliness of spirit, until August 4, 1892. Seven years later, the aged Susan B. Anthony pondered what names should go on a "Roll of Honor" of nineteenth century suffrage leaders, and she wrote: "Generally I should begin with Mary Wollstonecraft as your first Great Champion—then Frances Wright—then Ernestine L. Rose."[38]

With the few exceptions that have been noted, the contribution of women, at least in the nineteenth century, to the public speaking platform, has largely been in numbers of passionate advocates and agitators, rather than in outstanding individual achievement. After centuries of training in submission, and from the midst of a social situation that took their subordination wholly for granted, it was too much to expect that they could quickly produce eloquent orators equal to the best of the men. Of minor figures of interest there were a great many: "Yelling Mary" Lease of Kansas, who advised the farmers to "raise more hell and less corn"; Carrie Nation—the lady who chopped up saloons with a hatchet; the Quaker preacher, Antoinette Brown; the magnetic and fiery Anna Dickinson; the scathingly denunciatory Sollie Holley; the sophisticated physiologist, Paulina Wright Davis; the oracular orator, Anna Howard Shaw; the pioneer Lyceum lecturer, Elizabeth Oakes Smith; and many more. Among them all Susan B. Anthony deserves special attention not for her superiority in speaking but because she was an expert in the organization of their joint endeavors.[39] Born on February

[36] *Ibid.*, p. 201.
[37] *Ibid.*, pp. 262–263.
[38] *Ibid.*, p. 275.
[39] Doris Yoakum Twitchell, "Susan B. Anthony," in Hochmuth, ed., *History and Criticism, op. cit.*, III:97–132.

15, 1820, into a New York Quaker family, she lived until March 13, 1906, highly honored, but with her cause still incomplete.

Near the end of her life, in 1897, she said: "It would be hard to find a city in the northern and western States in which I have not lectured, and I have spoken in many of the Southern cities. I have been on the platform over forty-five years and it would be impossible to tell how many lectures I have delivered; they probably would average from seventy-five to one hundred every year."[40] As for the quality of her speaking, an unidentified newspaper clipping which she saved judged her "angular in gesture and uncouth in phraseology."[41] A reporter writing in The Chicago Journal, for February 20, 1894, thought her "not a great speaker, although a most effective one." The Washington Star depicted her quality well when it said: "Her manner has none of the excitement of an enthusiast; never discouraged by disappointment, she keeps calmly at work, and she could give points in political organization and management to some of the best male politicians in the land."[42]

As an upstate New York schoolteacher in 1853, Miss Anthony attended an educational convention in Rochester, where the chief topic was the low esteem in which the teaching profession was held. To everyone's surprise, she arose, addressed the chairman, and asked permission to speak. A half-hour debate ended in a vote granting her this unusual privilege. In a one-minute speech she said: "It seems to me, gentlemen, that none of you quite comprehends the cause of the disrespect of which you complain. Do you not see that so long as society says a woman is incompetent to be a lawyer, minister, or doctor, but has ample ability to be a teacher, that every man of you who chooses this profession tacitly acknowledges that he has no more brains than a woman?"[43] Three of the men in the audience courageously stepped down the aisle to congratulate her; but the women, who made up the great silent majority, were outraged that she had humiliated their sex by such a public display.[44] On another occasion, when she attended a temperance meeting and had the temerity to state her views, the astounded minister who was presiding severely rapped her down, saying, "The sisters were not invited here to speak, but to listen and to learn."[45] Then it was that Miss Anthony entered upon her lifelong career as an organizer. With Elizabeth Cady Stanton, she organized a Woman's New York State

[40] Ibid., III:105.
[41] Ibid., III:130.
[42] Ibid., III:109.
[43] Katherine Anthony, Susan B. Anthony: Her Personal History and Her Era, Garden City: Doubleday, 1954, p. 112.
[44] Irwin, op. cit., p. 26.
[45] Lutz, op. cit., p. 30.

Temperance Society, carefully providing in its constitution that men might attend its meetings but that they could neither vote nor hold office.

As she commenced now to organize meeting after meeting—annual conventions in half a dozen States, a national convention, local meetings galore—someone pinned on her the tag, "The Napoleon of woman suffrage," and the title was too apt to be forgotten.[46] From that time on her life was devoted to raising money, writing letters to arrange meetings, recruiting speakers, presiding over committees, even to sweeping out halls and hunting up candles for last-minute illumination. And she also spoke, often and reasonably well. But the best picture of her role on the platform is one that stresses her management rather than her eloquence:

> Miss Anthony seldom made a stated address either in opening or closing, but throughout the entire convention kept up a running fire of quaint, piquant, original and characteristic observations which delighted the audience and gave a distinctive attraction to the meetings . . . . Perfectly at home on the platform, she would indulge in the same informality of remarks which others use in private conversation, but always with a quick wit, a fine satire and a keen discrimination. Words of praise or criticism were given with equal impartiality, and accepted with a grace which would have been impossible had the giver been any other than the recognized Mentor of them all.[47]

She early became and remained the *grande dame* of the movement—not the brightest, or the most eloquent, or the wittiest, but the one whose calm assumption of control and managerial mind gave direction, unity, and continuity to the cause. As she lay near death, she held up one hand and measuring off a little space on one finger, said: "Just think of it, I have been striving for over sixty years for a little bit of justice no bigger than that, and yet I must die without obtaining it. Oh, it seems so cruel!"[48] The nineteenth amendment, extending the vote to women, was finally ratified on August 26, 1920. But in the Capitol building in Washington, not in the rotunda but in the basement, the statue honoring the women's rights movement, with the busts of Susan B. Anthony, Elizabeth Cady Stanton, and Lucretia Mott carved in three corners, remains still unfinished, with the fourth corner rising in a jagged piece of uncarved granite, reminding all observers that there is more of the work toward equality of rights yet to be done. The last word belongs, perhaps,

[46] Irwin, *op. cit.*, p. 97.
[47] *History of Women's Suffrage, op. cit.*, IV:238.
[48] Anthony, *op. cit.*, p. 500.

to Elizabeth Cady Stanton, who said: "Lifting woman into her proper place in the scale of being is the mightiest revolution the world has yet known, and it may be that more than half a century is needed to accomplish this."[49]

Denouncing Demon Drink:
Frances E. Willard and John B. Gough

THE CAMPAIGN to control or prohibit the use of alcoholic drink began in America as early as 1651, with an ordinance at East Hampton, Long Island, which provided that youths and unemployed laborers "shall not have above one half pint at a time among four men."[1] The first temperance society of record was organized in 1789, in Litchfield, Connecticut, by farmers who wished to reduce drunkenness among their farmhands.[2] In 1826, in Boston, was organized for the first time a society that undertook to pledge its members to total abstinence and that engaged a touring lecturer, with an annual budget of $8000, to propagate this program.[3] The father of the Litchfield and Boston movements, and therefore the founder of prohibitionism, was Lyman Beecher, whose "Six Sermons on Intemperance" became a textbook of the cause. Up to this date drinking was so much a commonplace that quite as a matter of fact ministers drank copiously during their annual conferences and many were accustomed to taking a drink before and after their Sunday sermon.[4] Yet reform, when it was launched, quickly rolled up impressive results: "At the beginning of 1833 it was estimated that there were more than five thousand temperance societies in the United States, with a membership of a million and a quarter, of whom ten thousand had been drunkards. Four thousand distilleries had been stopped, six thousand merchants had given up the sale of ardent spirits, and their use had been abandoned on over four thousand vessels."[5]

The goals of the movement were early defined and thereafter were never much altered. The initial aim of fostering temperance was quickly

---

[49] Alma Lutz, *Created Equal: A Biography of Elizabeth Cady Stanton*, New York: John Day, 1940, p. 319.
[1] W. H. Daniels, *The Temperance Reform and Its Great Reformers*, New York: Nelson and Phillips, 1878, p. 6.
[2] *Ibid.*, p. 51.
[3] *Ibid.*, pp. 55–57.
[4] *Ibid.*, pp. 62–71. Cf. Constance Mayfield Rourke, *Trumpets of Jubilee, op. cit.*, pp. 25–30.
[5] Daniels, *op. cit.*, p. 59.

changed to advocacy of complete abstinence. This was to be achieved primarily by the passage of laws that were to prevent the sale of liquor. The principal appeal to be used was to religion. The audiences to be reached were two in particular: drunkards, or at least drinkers, and women. The methodology was to be the organization of societies pledged to carry on the work and the utilization of speakers who would have sufficient popular appeal to draw audiences even of people who were indifferent or positively hostile to the cause. This was the formula. It led to adoption of the first statewide prohibition law by Maine in 1846, followed by other states and many local communities, and, finally, by passage of the eighteenth amendment, which was ratified January 29, 1919. Among the many speakers who contributed to these results—including Beecher, Neal Dow, John Hawkins, Susan B. Anthony, Emma Willard, Henry A. Reynolds, Francis Murphy, Dwight L. Moody, Billy Sunday, Theodore L. Cuyler, and many more—the two who transcended all the rest were Frances E. Willard and John B. Gough. They also represented the two principal groups from whom the movement drew its vocal strength: women and drinkers. A third group, it may be added, which continuously lent considerable financial and moral support to the cause, albeit more quietly, consisted of employers—whose motivation was to keep their workers sober.

Frances Elizabeth Willard was born September 28, 1839, at Churchville, New York, of parents whose thirst for learning led them to spend five years in Oberlin College after the birth of their daughter. She was taught to read from a book called *The Slave's Friend*; and it was in the tolerant piety of her home that she imbibed the sentiments which eventuated in one of her mottoes: "No sect in religion, no sex in citizenship, no sectionalism in politics."[6] She graduated at the age of twenty from the Northwestern Female College, with an ambition that seemed a strange combination of irreconcilables: "I thought that next to a wish I had to be a saint some day, I really would like to be a politician."[7] Actually, few ambitions have been crowned by surer success. As early as 1877 she began to be known with respect as "Saint Francis"; and her quarter-century work as a national and world wide organizer was guided by her faith that "Only the Golden Rule of Christ can bring the Golden Rule of Man."[8] Aside from the enormous scope and measurably impressive effects of her work, the most notable attribute of her career was that she, almost alone among the great reformers, pursued a single-minded goal with sweetness of spirit, tolerance for the opposition she

[6] Anna Adams Gordon, *The Life of Frances E. Willard*, Evanston, Ill.: National Women's Christian Temperance Union, 1914, pp. 5, 19.
[7] *Ibid.*, p. 31.
[8] *Ibid.*, pp. 96, 147.

encountered, and unfaltering faith in ultimate success regardless of the difficulties and disappointments. Hers was a career difficult to overpraise, for it exhibits so much to admire, so little to regret.

After several years of teaching she took a trip to Paris, where, in 1868, she wrote down the goal that launched her toward, if not into, her life's vocation: "to study by reading, personal observation, and acquaintance the woman question in Europe, and, after returning to America, to study it further in relation to her own land; talk in public on the subject, and cast herself with what weight or weakness she possessed against the only foe of what she conceived to be the justice of the subject—unenlightened public opinion."[9] For a brief time (1871–74) she served as President of the school from which she had graduated, then as its Dean as it was incorporated into Northwestern University. Eventually she resigned and took the presidency of the Chicago branch of the Woman's Christian Temperance Union. The decision was momentous. "Instead of peace, I was to participate in war," she wrote; "instead of the sweetness of home, never more dearly loved than I had loved it, I was to become a wanderer on the face of the earth; instead of libraries, I was to frequent public halls and railway cars; instead of scholarly and cultured men, I was to see the dregs of saloon and gambling house and haunt of shame."[10] On her way home to tell her parents of the decision she had made, she went into a saloon in Pittsburgh, with a group of like-minded women, and "knelt on the sawdust floor, with a group of earnest hearts around me, and behind them, filling every corner and extending out into the street, a crowd of unwashed, unkempt, hardlooking drinking men."[11] This was the first of a vast number of similar experiences she was to have.

The intelligence, poise, learning, and experience which had carried her at the age of thirty two into a college presidency also propelled her promptly into the position of corresponding secretary of the Illinois WCTU, and within five years into the presidency of the National Women's Christian Temperance Union, which she helped to organize. Immediately she set out upon a tour which eventually took her into every town of consequence in the United States, travelling as much as thirty thousand miles a year, and averaging for a dozen years a speech a day.[12]

As a speaker she was something new among reformers. She had all the restrained dignity and poise of Wendell Phillips, but instead of his vitriolic denunciation she spoke always with compassion for those who

[9] *Ibid.*, p. 56.
[10] *Ibid.*, p. 90.
[11] *Ibid.*, p. 92.
[12] *Ibid.*, p. 101.

blocked the goals she sought and with radiant hope for the sure success of her cause. With her school-mistress appearance and manner, her hair drawn in a bun at the back of her head, and steel spectacles perched on her nose, and considering that her target was "demon rum," whose pleasurable effects had gone unchallenged for six thousand years of history, she seemed a natural target for ridicule. Actually, she rendered herself all the more vulnerable by insisting upon broadening her message to include suffrage for women, peace, and reduction of poverty through higher wages for laborers. Nevertheless, such was the serene confidence of her manner and her capacity for undermining opposition by assuming the best of her opponents that she met with relatively little direct attack. When her fellow temperance advocates feared that the inclusiveness of her reform program would ruin its effect by diffusion, she promptly assumed the derisive label of a "Do Everything Policy," and declared: "A one-sided movement makes one-sided advocates . . . . An all-around movement can only be carried forward by all-around advocates . . . . Let us not be disconcerted but stand bravely by that blessed trinity of movements, Prohibition, Woman's Liberation, and Labor's Uplift."[13]

The goal they must strive for, she insisted, was "home protection." They might attack drink, because "intemperance causes poverty," but they must also attack slum-conditions and exploitative labor policies, because "poverty causes intemperance."[14] They must attack the alliance between politics and business, because this alliance is a "moral chloroform . . . administered in the form of poisoned gold."[15] They must seek votes for women with which to win elections and be able to enact legislation, for "All pure and Christian sentiment concerning any line of conduct which vitally affects humanity will, sooner or later, crystallize into law."[16]

As for the method, they must aim primarily to organize the power of women. This method could scarcely fail, she argued, for "among the thousands of churches of America, with their millions of members, two-thirds are women . . . . Furthermore, nine-tenths of the teachers in this land are women."[17] To the women who crowded to hear her, who all their lives had been taught that they were helplessly dependent upon the strength of their fathers and husbands, she preached a message of their basic superiority. "First among the powerful and controlling instincts in our nature," she said, "stands that of self-preservation, and

---

[13] *Ibid.*, p. 149.
[14] *Ibid.*, p. 117.
[15] *Ibid.*
[16] *Ibid.*, p. 119.
[17] *Ibid.*, p. 127.

next after this, if it does not claim superior rank, comes that of a mother's love." This, she went on, is the power upon which they must draw. "Yes, for there is nothing in the universe so sure, so strong, as love; and love shall do all this—the love of maid for sweetheart, wife for husband, of a sister for her brother, of a mother for her son." Men, she declared, are the weaker sex. They are the ones who yield to temptation: "in the dealer, the appetite for gain, and in the drinker, the appetite for stimulants." Against these temptations, weak men desperately need support from the women who love them. "Out into the battle of life" the women "have sent their best beloved, with fearful odds against them, with snares that men have legalized and set for them on every hand. Beyond the arms that held them long, their boys have gone forever . . . . I charge you, give them power to protect, along life's treacherous highway, those whom they have so loved." Don't worry, she urged, if your numbers seem inadequate to the task. "We must not forget that for every woman who joins the Temperance Unions that have sprung up all through the world, there are at least a score who sympathize, but do not join." Therefore, she pleaded, "Roll in your petitions, burnish your arguments, multiply your prayers."[18]

Her program called constantly for organization. "Alone we can do little," she pointed out. "Separated, we are the units of weakness, but aggregated, we become batteries of power. Agitate, educate, organize— these are the deathless watchwords of success. The fingers of the hand can do little alone, but correlated into a fist, they become formidable."[19] Moreover, their aim must not be to redeem individual drunkards but to revise the laws so that society as a whole might be improved. "No legislature can bargain away the public health or the public morals," she told one audience.[20] And in a petition which she addressed to the heads of fifty nations, and for which she got seven million signatures, she said: "We know that the law might do much now left undone to raise the moral tone of society and render vice difficult."[21]

Constantly her tone was hopeful; the vision she preached was success, however long delayed it might seem to be. To counter defeatism, she lapsed into a rare passage of vaguely poetic imagery:

> The deepest billows are away out at sea; they never come in sight of shore. These waves are like the years of God. Upon the shoreline of our earthly life come the waves of the swift years; they bound and break and are no more. But far out upon eternity's bosom are the great,

18 *Ibid.*, pp. 118–133.
19 *Ibid.*, p. 104.
20 *Ibid.*, p. 114.
21 *Ibid.*, p. 158.

wide, endless waves that make the years of God; they never strike upon the shore of time. In all the flurry and the foam about us, let us bend our heads to listen to the great anthem of that far-off sea . . .[22]

Probably no one of her listeners knew what the words meant but none could miss her intent: trust, and all will work out well in due course. In other speeches she was more explicit: "No matter how near the water in the boiler comes to being steam, it will not move the locomotive one inch until it *is* steam: that elastic, invisible, impenetrable, and irresistible power. Love is like that; it cannot be withstood; its God-like flame burns away the dross of policy in the pure white light of principle . . . . There is much truth and goodness in the world already . . . and best of all the people are stirring in their sleep."[23] And always she sought to heighten the pride of the membership in the cause in which they were engaged: "More than any other society ever formed, the Women's Christian Temperance Union is the exponent of what is best in this latter-day civilization. Its scope is the broadest, its aims are the kindest, its history is the most heroic."[24]

As a speaker she was praised by Congressman Littlefield of Maine in these terms: "If true eloquence is to be measured by the effect produced upon the hearers, she had few equals and no superiors."[25] A Chicago clergyman who knew her well said in his eulogy after her death:

> Frances Willard had the gift of eloquence. She was a subtle, thoughtful, thrilling talker. Her presence was not imposing, yet it was always tranquilizing at the beginning, and afterward full of sweet surprises. Her voice was clear and melodious and strong, with a peculiar quality of blended defiance and deference, of tenderness and intrepidity, that gave it an indescribable ring. Her diction was studiously simple; her reasoning luminous and homely; her illustrations full of poetry and humor; her pathos as natural as tears to a child. She was wholly unaffected, talking her audience so deftly into her confidence that she conquered them, as Christ conquers, by self-revelation.[26]

Another minister, who considered her "one of the most eloquent of the orators of our time," praised especially "her repose of strength, the consciousness she exhibited of reserved power, her wit and wisdom, her triumphant certainty of ultimate success."[27]

No attempt has been made to depict her speaking to specific audiences, for she gave much the same speech, with minor variations, over

---

[22] *Ibid.*, p. 108.
[23] *Ibid.*, pp. 149–151.
[24] *Ibid.*, p. 139.
[25] *Ibid.*, p. 318.
[26] *Ibid.*, pp. 334–335.
[27] *Ibid.*, pp. 344–345.

and over again. Her audiences were generally much the same: composed largely or wholly of women who were members of the WCTU or were at its meetings as sympathetic guests. Aside from her early forays into saloons, she seldom had to face a hostile gathering. The reaction of her hearers may be gauged from comments that her biographer preserved. "The first time I heard her I lay awake all night for sheer gladness," one woman wrote. "It was such a wonderful revelation to me that a woman like Miss Willard could exist. I thanked God and took courage for humanity." Another woman, who lived down South, wrote of the effects of one of her talks: "It was the first ray of hope that had come into our lives since the war. We had been sitting dumb and crushed amid the wreckage of our past, and it seemed as if there were no future for us; but Miss Willard came and held out to us that little white hand, and its clasp gave us new heart and new hope."[28]

Frances Willard died on February 18, 1898. Seven years later the State of Illinois selected her statue as one of the two it could place in Washington's Statuary Hall. She was the first woman to be enshrined in this hall which is dedicated to the statesmen of the nation.

Unlike Miss Willard, John B. Gough did not address audiences of fellow enthusiasts. His favorite auditors were drunkards whom he sought to reclaim from their sodden state; and he more often found himself speaking to general audiences who paid admission and came for a combination of enlightenment and entertainment, just as they did to the Chautauqua tents. Many of his listeners were "moderate drinkers," who heard him denounce moderation as the pathway that led to degradation. Nevertheless, he proved to be a "crowd-compeller" of great power. His friend Theodore L. Cuyler praised his "extraordinary platform powers" and thought that "As an actor he might have been a second Garrick; as a preacher of the Gospel he would have been a second Whitefield."[29] His biographer called him "the most popular speaker in the English world for forty-three years."[30] Unquestionably, he possessed a magnetic power over an audience that has seldom been surpassed; but as he himself quite properly observed, he was no orator.[31] More than any other American speaker of comparable fame, he was an exemplar of that awkward but expressive term, "the gift of gab." In Platform Echoes, Gough wrote of his lectures, "I care but little for the unity of

28 Ibid., pp. 102–103.
29 Theodore L. Cuyler, Recollections of a Long Life, New York: American Tract Society, 1902, p. 52.
30 Carlos Martyn, John B. Gough: The Apostle of Cold Water, New York: Funk and Wagnalls, 1894, p. 214.
31 John B. Gough, Autobiography, Springfield, Mass.: Bill, Nichols, 1869, p. 332.

what I shall say . . . . I care but little in what direction I point or how I strike, if I can accomplish my purpose of enlisting sympathy for our cause, stimulating investigation of our statements, or exciting interest in our behalf."[32] Concerning a lecture he gave at the height of his powers in London, a report in the *British Banner* says that "His address was entirely without order of any sort . . . . His air is that of a man who never thought five minutes on the subject of public speaking; but who surrenders himself to the guidance of his genius, while he ofttimes snatches a grace beyond the reach of art."[33]

Gough definitely considered himself to be primarily a professional speaker and secondarily a reformer, subtitling one of his three auto-biographies, "Twenty-Six Years Experience as a Public Speaker." Born in England on August 22, 1817, he came to America at the age of twelve. He was a dissolute drunkard until his reformation in 1840, after which he lectured with feverish intensity in this country and in England, until, on February 15, 1886, while addressing a huge audience in Frankford, a suburb of Philadelphia, he suffered a stroke of apoplexy and died three days later.

Gough's first speech consisted of a testimonial at a Washingtonian Society, a shaky six days after he locked himself in his room to keep away from liquor while he was sobering up. This talk was so well-received that he found the audience response as pleasantly intoxicating as alcohol itself. A few days and several testimonials later, came his first public speech in a church, to a general audience:

> Not long after this, it began to be whispered about that I had some talents for public speaking; and my career as an intemperate man having been notorious, a little curiosity concerning my addresses was excited. I was invited to visit Millbury, and deliver an address there . . . . I spoke for the first time from a pulpit, and my address, which occupied but from fifteen to twenty minutes, was listened to very attentively. How queerly I felt in that pulpit, the faces all turned toward me. The strangeness of my position made me very nervous; my mouth was dry, my knees very weak; but I got on, for I had a simple story to tell. At this time nothing was farther from my intention than becoming a public speaker; in my wildest flights I never dreamed of this.[34]

Soon Gough was speaking almost every night, always to listeners who responded with enthusiastic applause to his effusions of colloquial anecdotes, mingled humor and pathos, and to his theatrical delivery.

[32] John B. Gough, *Platform Echoes*, Hartford, Conn.: A. D. Worthington, 1887, pp. 71–72.
[33] *Ibid.*, pp. 48–49.
[34] Gough, *Autobiography, op. cit.*, p. 141.

But his stage fright remained. "Often the dread of an audience has well-nigh unfitted me for the evening's service; and now, after more than twenty-six years of platform-speaking, I rarely face an audience without a dryness of my lips, and a weakness in my knees."[35] He then told of an experience in Boston, in which city alone he had already spoken 160 times, when he became so nervous that he twice turned away from the hall and had to be led back by his wife. When he finally appeared on the platform, his mind was blank. During the opening music he searched frantically for an idea but could not get one. Then he was introduced and began: "Ladies and gentlemen, I have nothing to say." He then said he wished he could feel, as some lecturers do, that the people in the audience are just so many cabbage-heads, not to be feared. But this reawakened his mind. "No, I do not wish *that*. When I look in your faces, an assemblage of rational and immortal human beings, and remember how drink has debased and dragged down the loftiest and noblest minds, I cannot feel so,—I thank God I cannot feel so."[36] Then the talk poured out, and on.

Gough never prepared his lectures, not even in outline form. He cared nothing for structure and was not a good phrasemaker. His speech was so rapid that the shorthand reports of his talks are deficient, and when he published a volume of his own selection of his lectures, he rewrote them so that they retained little resemblance to what he said. In appearance, he was five feet eight inches tall, thin as a young man, but rotund, bald, and heavily bearded in later years. He dressed soberly and was altogether without any striking features. His voice, however, was remarkable for its carrying power, its resonance, and its flexibility. And his delivery was almost as acrobatic as was that of Billy Sunday. He leaped and pounced about the platform, and his gestures were so violent that his hands were normally black and blue from pounding the rostrum, frequently they were bloodied, and once he broke a bone in his hand. Such was the man—and the message he had to deliver was no more than commonplace: the redemption of drunkards, and, later in life, a series of topics that recommended honesty, and praised common sense, and ridiculed folly, and advocated ambition. In England, the great preacher George Campbell became his reluctant admirer and wrote of him: "In what he said there was nothing new—there could be nothing new—the tale he told was as old as the hills; yet as he spoke an immense audience grew hushed and still, and hearts were melted, and tears glistened in female eyes, and the great human mass became knit together by a common spell."[37]

[35] *Ibid.*, p. 235.
[36] *Ibid.*, p. 236.
[37] *Ibid.*, p. 293.

When public enthusiasm for temperance began to lag in the late 1850's, Gough turned from reform to simple lecturing for profit. He was very sensitive to the charge of greed, and in his *Autobiography* he lists the average fee he received per lecture, from 1843 through 1867—the sum rising from $2.77 to $173.39.[38] George W. Bain, a fellow lecturer, reports that Gough's fees afterward grew to $500 per lecture.[39] Since Gough was making an average of almost a lecture a day, year after year, his income was sufficiently large. When he died he left no significant gap in American life; but as a master of the tricks and techniques of the platform, he has seldom been surpassed.

Lyceum and Chautauqua: Lecturing for Lucre

THE COMMERCIAL lecture platform in America can be and has been regarded as an agency for "the general diffusion of knowledge, and for raising the moral and intellectual taste of our countrymen"[1]; as "the most American thing in America"[2]; and as "nothing but wind and chaff and the heavy laughter of yokels."[3] Diversity has been its principal characteristic. It is no more meaningful to speak simply of "lecturing" than it is to speak simply of "magazines." The range is broad, from sensationalism to scholarship.

Commercial lecturing in America began by way of an article by a New England manufacturer, Josiah Holbrook, published in *The American Journal of Education*, in October, 1826, suggesting the establishment in every community of a *Lyceum* in which educational lectures might be presented. Within two years at least one hundred such Lyceums were in existence; and a Connecticut newspaper enthusiastically chronicled: "We doubt not that at no distant day Lyceums will be established in every section of the country, and that they will constitute the chiefest

---

[38] *Ibid.*, pp. 247–248.
[39] Robert T. Oliver, *Training for Effective Speech*, New York: Cordon, 1939, p. 33. In the 1871–72 season, Gough cleared $40,000 according to Major James B. Pond, *Eccentricities of Genius*, New York: Dillingham, 1900, p. 541.
[1] Josiah Holbrook, quoted by Carl Bode, *The American Lyceum: Town Meeting of the Mind*, New York: Oxford University Press, 1956, pp. 11–12; and John H. Vincent, *The Chautauqua Movement*, Boston: Chautauqua Press, 1886, p. 2. Mary W. Graham, a long-time student of the lecture platform, declares, "The most important educational influence affecting adult Americans in the nineteenth century was the Lyceum movement." "The Lyceum Movement and Sectional Controversy, 1860," in Auer, *Antislavery and Disunion, op. cit.*, p. 108.
[2] Theodore Roosevelt, in a speech at Lake Chautauqua, quoted by William Jennings Bryan, *Memoirs*, by himself and his wife, Mary Baird Bryan, Chicago: John C. Winston, 1925, p. 284.
[3] Sinclair Lewis, quoted by George S. Dalgety, "Chautauqua's Contributions to American Life," *Current History*, 34(April, 1931):59.

resort for amusement and knowledge among all ranks."[4] The growth
was phenomenal. This was the Jacksonian era of exuberant democracy
and Americans longed for learning and an expansion of their mental
horizons that only the lecture platform could supply. Libraries were
scanty, magazines rare and of poor quality, schools were puerilely ele-
mentary, newspapers were mostly partisan propaganda sheets. So great
was the need and so exultantly were the Lyceums welcomed that by
1835 there were three thousand of them. In Boston alone, in the winter
season of 1837–38, no fewer than twenty-six separate courses of lectures
were offered, with a total attendance of thirteen thousand.[5] In Massachusetts, the next year, there were 137 town Lyceums in operation.[6]
Then, almost as quickly as the movement commenced, it declined. The
principal reason seems to be that each Lyceum had to be organized and
directed wholly by a local volunteer committee; and the work of selling
tickets, arranging for accommodations, securing lecturers, and conducting the voluminous correspondence and negotiations was simply too
much to expect of volunteer workers. In 1839, most of the Lyceums had
disappeared.

In the fifties, however, the Lyceum movement again rose to prominence, this time with special interest centering in Ohio and beyond in
the Midwest. In 1854, Bayard Taylor wrote from Milwaukee that "The
people are infatuated. If I lecture next winter, I can spend three months
in the west and have engagements every night."[7] In this revival, the
movement turned away from the early practice of depending primarily
upon local talent—ministers, teachers, lawyers, scientists—and began to
utilize primarily a group of professional lecturers who made their living
from the platform and traveled systematically from place to place. This
group comprised a blue-ribbon listing of the ablest intellectual leaders in
the country, including Daniel Webster, Ralph Waldo Emerson, Charles
Sumner, Wendell Phillips, Oliver Wendell Holmes, Horace Greeley,
Richard Henry Dana, George W. Curtis, Carl Schurz, Theodore Parker,
Bayard Taylor, Thomas Starr King, Edward Everett, James Russell
Lowell, Alexander Agassiz, E. W. Whipple, Josiah Quincy, Andrew D.
White, Mark Hopkins, and Henry Ward Beecher. It was from the plat-
form more than from any other source that the nation was then deriving

[4] Bode, *op. cit.*, p. 18.
[5] *Ibid.*, p. 49. Cf. Victoria Case and Robert Ormond Case, *We Called It Culture:
The Story of Chautauqua*, Garden City: Doubleday, 1948, p. 23.
[6] Bode, *op. cit.*, p. 134.
[7] "Taylor was then the most popular lecturer in the country." Graham, in Auer, *op.
cit.*, p. 111. Cf. Richard Croom Beatty, *Bayard Taylor: Laureate of the Gilded Age*,
Norman, Okla.: University of Oklahoma Press, 1936, p. 148; Robert Warnock,
"Unpublished Lectures of Bayard Taylor," *American Literature*, V(1933):123–
132; and David Mead, *Yankee Eloquence in the Middle West: The Ohio Lyceum,
1850–1870*, East Lansing: Michigan State University Press, 1951.

its principal intellectual guidance. Among the gold, however, there was also dross. The great popularizer of history, John Lord, who wrote the enormously popular *Beacon Lights of History*, was a stutterer, "whose person was diminutive, whose gestures were erratic movements of the arm ignoring all coordination with his thought, and who read his notes in a frayed, unmusical voice interrupted with a periodic thoracic sneeze."[8] The perspicacious essayist, Edwin P. Whipple, famed as "the American Macaulay," lectured "in a sharp, nervous, energetic manner, with a graceful yet monotonous gesticulation, emphasizing every dozen words with a jerk of the head and a swing of the arm, as though he were pumping the blood from the vitals of the brain."[9]

Obviously some centralizing control was needed, a source from which local committees could draw platform talent of dependable quality, and a means of systematizing lecture fees and arrangements for travel. In 1867, 110 local Lyceums united to form the Associated Literary Societies, which in its first year booked thirty five lecturers who traveled a prescribed circuit from one community to another. The next year the famous Boston Lyceum and Musical Bureau was organized by James C. Redpath and George L. Fall, changing its name in 1870 to The American Literary Bureau.[10]

At first both fees and admission prices were low. Admission usually cost 25¢ for single tickets, and $1.00 or $1.50 for an entire season.[11] In the original Lyceums, speakers commonly spoke for nothing. The Concord Lyceum listed total expenses of only $33.88 for its season of 1833–34, in which half its twenty lectures were delivered by outside speakers. By the mid-forties, the average fee per lecture was $10; and a decade later it was $20.[12] Even then, however, the stars were much better paid. Beecher, in 1856, was getting $250 for single lectures; and Thomas Starr King was asserting the creed of the professionals, when he responded to a query as to why he lectured by answering, for "fame— fifty and my expenses."[13] The "King of the Lyceum," Wendell Phillips, wrote and memorized a piece of popular education which he entitled "The Lost Arts," and in a forty-year span after 1838 he delivered it some two thousand times, earning from $10,000 to $15,000 a year on the lecture platform, although he always gave his reform speeches free.[14] Beecher is estimated to have made $24,000 a year from lecturing during

[8] Bode, *op. cit.*, p. 203.
[9] *Ibid.*, p. 205.
[10] Charles F. Horner, *The Life of James Redpath*, New York: Barse and Hopkins, 1926, Chapter VIII, "Organizes Lyceum Bureau," pp. 119–139.
[11] Bode, *op. cit.*, p. 188.
[12] *Ibid.*, p. 190.
[13] *Ibid.*, pp. 196, 201.
[14] Sherwin, *Prophet of Liberty*, *op. cit.*, pp. 133, 656.

the height of his popularity—plus his $20,000 a year salary from Plymouth Church.[15] The time of really high fees, however, was yet to come.

In 1874 a new era in American lecturing commenced when John H. Vincent converted a Sunday School summer study course into the Sunday School Institute and Open Air Camp Meeting, in which lectures on diverse topics were given, at Lake Chautauqua, New York.[16] Four years later Chautauqua Scientific and Literary Circles were established in various communities, and in 1897 these were united into the Western Federation of Chautauquas, for the purpose of scheduling speakers who would travel from one to another. In 1904 Keith Vawter joined with Vincent to organize travelling Chautauquas, which moved from town to town, spending a week in each, much like a travelling circus.[17] That first year they organized thirty three towns; but the next year none at all. Disaster confronted their idea, for expenses were large and local committees not always reliable. Then Vawter and Vincent dreamed up a remarkable contract idea. They would require local committees to agree to take whatever programs they sent them; would require a flat guarantee of enough money to cover all expenses, to be paid wholly or half in advance, with this sum to be covered either through sale of season tickets or by subscription; and would require that all money received from single-ticket sales must be given to the Chautauqua management![18] The most lucrative feature of the contract was that the local committee was forbidden to sell any more season tickets than would barely cover the guarantee; all the remaining receipts must be in the form of single admission tickets, with Vawter and Vincent getting it all. Under this arrangement, they were able to provide "cheap" entertainment for the bulk of the program, and to pay a high fee—$500 to $1,000—to super-stars, such as William Jennings Bryan, who would appear late in the week and swell enormously the income from single ticket sales.

The plan required super-salesmanship to persuade local committees to sign the contracts; but the motivational appeal was to pride in the home community, and success was immediate. In 1906 the business was in full stride. One element of the Vincent-Vawter plan was to send tents along with the show, like a circus, in order not to be dependent upon local accommodations. Within a few years Chautauqua programs were being offered in ten thousand communities, with a total audience of four million in a single year. Russell Conwell, with his fabulous lecture, "Acres

[15] Bode, *op. cit.*, p. 214; Paxton Hibben, *Henry Ward Beecher, op. cit.*, p. 175; and David Mead, "Henry Ward Beecher: Eloquent Profiteer," in *Yankee Eloquence, op. cit.*, pp. 134–141.
[16] Vincent, *op. cit.*, passim.
[17] Harrison and Detzer, *op. cit.*, Chapter 6, "Vawter Has An Idea," pp. 50–55.
[18] Case and Case, *op. cit.*, Chapter 3, "There's Money In It," pp. 22–32.

of Diamonds," was earning upwards of $50,000 a year,[19] and Bryan was at least thought to earn twice that amount.[20] By 1917–20 the Chautauquas had settled down to a round of some five thousand communities, with annual audiences of about two million. Competing bureaus now numbered fifteen. In 1926 Keith Vawter cannily sold his 120-town circuit; and by the start of the Great Depression, in 1929, only five bureaus survived, providing fifteen "shows" for a total of three hundred communities. A year or two later Chautauqua all but disappeared.

Basically, the bill of fare offered to the Chautauqua audiences was remarkably like that provided in the *Reader's Digest* magazine: an ultra-respectable "home, heaven, and mother" moral tone, spiced with adventurous sensationalism and at least the appearance of great daring in the airing of liberal ideas. Bruce Bliven stressed the moral tone of the lectures, saying the illustrations and lessons were drawn: " . . . from the soldier lying on his hard pallet in the far-off Philippines . . . the Sabbath sunrise at the edge of the Grand Canyon . . . the brave Salvation Army lassie who met a gang of hoodlums in the slums of a great city . . . the famous gambler lying at the point of death . . . the silver-haired old mother of five lovely girls who asked me this question . . . and the last words of the old infidel as his little granddaughter bent over his bed."[21] Harry P. Harrison, in his volume of recollections of Chautauqua experiences, stresses that along with sheer entertainment and uplift, there also was a remarkably free forum for the development of liberal ideas.[22] A close approximation of what "went over best" in the Chautauqua tents may be gained from looking at a sample of Bryan's "Prince of Peace," which he delivered some three thousand times.[23] It was religion dressed up in the garb of science and common sense:

> I was eating a piece of watermelon some months ago and I was struck with its beauty. I took some of the seeds and dried them and weighed them, and found that it would require some five thousand seeds to weigh a pound; and then I applied mathematics to that forty pound melon. One of these seeds, put into the ground, when warmed by the sun and moistened by the rain, takes off its coat and goes to work; it gathers from somewhere two hundred thousand times its own weight, and forcing this raw material through a tiny stem, constructs a watermelon. It ornaments the outside with a covering of green; inside the

[19] *Ibid.*, p. 68.
[20] This was Billy Sunday's estimate (McLoughlin, *Billy Sunday*, *op. cit.*, p. 116). Bryan and his wife hint that such estimates were exaggerated, but they discreetly refrained from mentioning any specific sum. *Memoirs*, *op. cit.*, p. 288.
[21] Case and Case, *op. cit.*, p. 73.
[22] Harrison and Detzer, *op. cit.*, Chapter 12, "Let's Face the Issue . . . ," pp. 116–135.
[23] *Ibid.*, p. 158.

green it puts a layer of white, and within the white a core of red, and all through the red it scatters seeds, each one capable of continuing the work of reproduction. Where does that little seed get its tremendous power? Where does it find its coloring matter? How does it collect its flavoring extract? How does it build a watermelon? Until you can explain a watermelon, do not be too sure that you can set limits to the power of the Almighty and say just what He would do or how He would do it. I cannot explain the watermelon, but I eat it and enjoy it.[24]

William Jennings Bryan was even more the "King of Chautauqua" than Wendell Phillips had been of the Lyceum. Detractors called him the "Boy Orator of the Platte," and some added that he was like that river—a mile wide and a foot deep. An Iowa editor fled from a heat-drenched tent where he listened to Bryan one summer afternoon to write that: "Words flow from Bryan's lips like water over Niagara!"[25] He may have had a little more of the common touch than was needful even to merit his title, "The Great Commoner." What is indisputable is that for a long generation his was the voice, his were the words, America most wanted to hear. From the day he stood in the convention hall in Chicago in 1896 and proclaimed with youthful faith and optimism that "The humblest citizen of all the land, when clad in the armor of a righteous cause, is stronger than all the hosts of Error," it was obvious that he was a natural for the lecture platform. Audiences that were accustomed to 25¢ admission charges gladly paid $1.00 to hear Bryan. "They thought of him not as a politician, . . . not as a paid attraction, . . . but as the echo of their own inner voices refined to purest gold."[26] The role of Bryan as a political orator will be discussed in the following chapter; suffice it to say here that Chautauqua gave him the greatest audience any man had before the advent of radio. And it exacted a heavy price; for Bryan the political leader must have suffered an eclipse of his potential abilities as he devoted himself day after day, week after week, season after season, to rushing from town to town repeating over and over again in measured and memorized words a completely stereotyped message, safeguarded from any contact with immediate problems in order to preserve its flavor as a timeless restatement of what every man believed.

An almost equally astounding phenomenon of the commercial lecture platform was Russell Conwell, a Baptist minister, who founded Temple University with the profits he made from a single lecture,

[24] *Speeches of William Jennings Bryan: Revised and Arranged by Himself*, New York: Funk and Wagnalls, 1909, II:272.
[25] Harrison and Detzer, *op. cit.*, p. 157.
[26] *Ibid.*, p. 159.

"Acres of Diamonds." He delivered this lecture for the first time in a small Methodist church in Westfield, Massachusetts, in 1861, and he subsequently presented it 150–200 times a year for more than half a century, in every state of the union and in the large cities of many foreign countries.[27] Even as late as 1915, when he was seventy two, he was still travelling through the summer heat of July and August, from South Dakota through Iowa, Nebraska, and Kansas, to Pennsylvania and New Jersey, lecturing every day of the week and preaching on Sundays. During the whole period of some sixty five years, he was always a top attraction—and received top pay. While other well known lecturers were getting $100 a week and paying their own expenses, Conwell was demanding and receiving $200 for a single lecture.[28] One of his exuberant biographers estimated that if he had "kept and invested" his receipts from this one lecture, the total would have mounted to $8,000,-000.[29] Conwell himself estimated that he gave the lecture "almost five thousand times."[30]

Conwell was a large, stoop-shouldered, shambling man, who mugged and mimicked his way through his lecture with considerable physical vigor, acting out in pantomime and vocal imitations the innumerable stories and anecdotes which constituted his lecture. The theme was directly contrary to what his audiences were accustomed to hearing from the pulpit. Whereas, their own ministers were likely to tell them that wealth was unnecessary and that the love of money was the root of all evil, Conwell proclaimed the value, even the duty, of getting rich, and then went on to declare and to illustrate that making money is not difficult for those who put their minds to it. As a salve for tender consciences, he always pointed out that the money earned should be put to charitable uses—and he himself notably donated his earnings to the education of poor boys. But the major emphasis was upon the two cardinal points: you ought to get rich—and you can do so with the opportunities that lie all about you, close at hand. Audiences loved it.

Essentially the lecture was always the same, though of course there were minor adjustments from year to year; and Conwell gradually accumulated so many stories that he could and did select at random from his hoard, extemporaneously, as he spoke. In one of the latest versions of the talk, he commenced:

> I am astonished that so many people should care to hear this story over again. Indeed, this lecture has become a study in psychology; it

[27] Agnes Rush Burr, *Russell H. Conwell and His Work*, op. cit., pp. 307–308.
[28] Harrison and Detzer, op. cit., p. 22
[29] Burr, op. cit., p. 308.
[30] Russell H. Conwell, *Acres of Diamonds*, New York: Harper, 1915, p. 180.

often breaks all rules of oratory, departs from the precepts of rhetoric, and yet remains the most popular of any lecture I have delivered in the fifty-seven years of my public life.[31]

Some rules of rhetoric he did indeed break, for the speech was lacking in structure. It did not start at a given point, proceed through a regular progression, and arrive at a conclusion. Rather, it rambled. It started and stopped a dozen times, turning and twisting to gaze back upon itself. All it amounted to was a host of stories, each one illustrating the same point made by all the rest: here is a way to get rich. Its principal appeal probably lay in the fact that this was what people wanted to hear; and when they heard it from a Baptist minister it was a message they could accept without guilt. Moreover, as the lecture accumulated fame through the years, it took on a special aura of prestige. Not to hear Conwell deliver his famous lecture was akin to not seeing the reigning Broadway success or not reading the runaway best-seller book. His biographer claims that he was heard by ten million listeners.[32] As for his own concept of what constitutes good speaking, he stated it clearly: "When I address very large audiences I find it necessary to speak very slowly . . . . That is the only secret in public speaking."[33]

James B. Pond and the Rise of the Lecture Bureaus

WHAT IT meant to be a lecturer across the vast open spaces of America in the days before air travel was somewhat caustically described by Rudyard Kipling, in a letter he wrote in 1895 to Major James B. Pond, declining to sign a contract with him:

> I am much obliged to you for your letter, but . . . . There is such a thing as paying one hundred and twenty-five cents for a dollar, and though I suppose there is money in the lecture business, it seems to me that the bother, the fuss, the being at everybody's beck and call, the night journeys, and so on, make it very dear. I've seen a few men who've lived through the fight, but they did not look happy. I might do it as soon as I had two mortgages on my house, a lien on the horses, and a bill of sale on the furniture, and writer's cramp in both hands; but at present I'm busy and contented to go on with the regular writing business. You forget that I've already wandered over most of the States,

---

[31] Burr, *op. cit.*, pp. 405–438, prints the version from which this quotation is made. A variant version was published eleven years earlier, in Conwell, *op. cit.*, pp. 3–59.
[32] Burr, *op. cit.*, p. 318.
[33] *Ibid.*, p. 328.

and there isn't enough money in sight to hire me to face again some of the hotels and some of the railway systems that I have met with. America is a great country, but she is not made for lecturing in.[1]

Pond was the archetype of the successful salesmen, with no intention of having his offers declined. He purchased all twenty of Kipling's published books and sent the lot of them to be autographed by the author. Kipling melted like hot butter in the sun.

If the Lyceum and Chautauqua systems always paid at least lip service to education, reform, and moral uplift, it was Major Pond who converted the lecture business wholly and frankly to the aim of making money—for the lecturers and for himself as their manager. This aim introduced a new criterion for the selection of speakers. No longer were the fundamental questions whether they could speak effectively in delivering a message that was worthwhile; henceforth the basic question became: will the public pay to hear them? The manager of a lecture bureau has "talent" for "sale." Local program committees normally have to provide programs for which they can sell enough tickets to pay the overall costs. Audiences sometimes are attracted to a hall because the speaker is said to be eloquent; more often they come because he has a name made famous in politics, or exploring, or entertainment, or because of sensational publicity about his sex life or other pecadilloes. This was the great truth which Major Pond perceived and upon which he erected the structure of the modern lecture bureau: pick your lecturers who, for any reason, will sell.

As Pond confesses, he stumbled into the lecture business by accident. In 1873 he was working in Salt Lake City as an unwilling journalist, when, in the midst of the federal campaign to end polygamy among the Mormons, the nineteenth wife of Brigham Young, Ann Eliza Young, decided to leave him and was converted to Methodism. The Methodist minister and Pond together arranged for her to tell her story (to "testify," in the Methodist manner) to a small private gathering. Pond reported what she said and the Associated Press carried the story across the nation. The prospect of hearing an ex-wife of Brigham Young confess the orgies of the Mormon harem system proved to be an irresistible lure. Telegrams began pouring into Salt Lake City begging Mrs. Young to tell her story back East. James Redpath and P. T. Barnum were among the eager inquirers. James Pond was quick to see the possibilities. "I made a proposition that if she would go on a lecture tour, I would manage it," he wrote.[2] On the way East, they stopped over in Laramie and Denver, where Pond rented a hall, charged $1.50 for tickets, and

[1] James B. Pond, *Eccentricities of Genius*, op. cit., p. 526.
[2] *Ibid.*, p. xxi.

presented his "talent" to standing-room audiences. Then they swept through New England and the East, where Mrs. Young spoke every night to packed audiences. At the end of the season, Pond reported, she had earned $20,000. He did not report his own income from the tour, but it was sufficient to persuade him that he had at last discovered his true vocation.

The Lyceum and Chautauqua managers had concentrated upon their contracts with local program committees. Pond's principal concern was his contract with his speakers. When he had to, he accepted from them a commission of fifteen percent of the fees he could procure for them, though he was quick to raise the ante to twenty-five percent when his lecturer was unfamiliar with the business.[3] More typically, what Pond preferred, at least for his top attractions, was to promise them a set fee for each lecture, then to make for himself as much above that as he could. For example, in 1879, Pond read that the sermons of De Witt Talmage were selling in England in editions of half a million, and he promptly offered the minister $10,000, plus travelling expenses, to deliver 100 lectures in England. Talmage as promptly accepted. At first the audiences in London were enormous and Pond was making tremendous profits. Then Talmage demanded that his fees be raised to $350 per lecture. Since Pond was making some $500 profit on each lecture, he was dismayed by Talmage's threat to break his contract and go home. A compromise figure of $250 per lecture was agreed upon. Talmage, however, sulked and began giving lectures "of a secular, not religious character." The audiences were disappointed and attendance sharply dropped. By the end of the tour, Talmage had made $17,500 and Pond nothing. It was one of the few times Pond let himself be outmaneuvered. But he admired a man who could outsmart him at his own game. He concluded his recital of this tour by saying: "What cares Dr. Talmage for all this? . . . . He is said to be the richest minister in the world, and he has *earned* it all himself."[4]

Henry Ward Beecher was another minister whom Pond managed on the lecture platform; but he knew better than ever to try to best Beecher in financial matters. During twelve years (1875–1887) Beecher lectured for Pond 1261 times and the two travelled together over 300,000 miles. In January 1877, Pond scheduled Beecher to lecture in Richmond, Virginia; but when they arrived Pond found the feeling was so high against the old abolitionist that not a ticket had been sold. The legislature had even passed a resolution asking everyone to stay away from the hall. Pond had a contract guaranteeing payment of $400 by the

3 *Ibid.*, p. 465.
4 *Ibid.*, pp. 91–111.

local committee; but with a shrewd burst of insight he gratified the committee by tearing the contract up and rented the hall on his own responsibility. Then he flooded the city with handbills advertising the lecture. So great was the feeling against Beecher that Pond could hire no one to attend the door and had to sell admissions himself. Nonetheless, a huge crowd paid its money and packed the hall. Pond was warned that "the gallery was full of eggs" and that Beecher would be mobbed. However, his "pockets were stuffed with dollars," and he was determined to keep them. When Beecher stepped out on the stage he was greeted with hoots and yells, but, as he had done in England in 1863, he first waited for a lull, then launched into compliments of his audience. Shortly they were listening, and when his two and a half hour lecture ended they applauded wildly, and he was invited to stay over for another lecture the next night.[5] Beecher's penchant for making money is attested by many who knew him well. In addition to the $40,000 or so he made annually from lecturing and his salary as a minister, he also picked up odd sums for funerals and weddings. Pond tells of one occasion when Beecher found $4000 in his pocket that he didn't even know he had—a fee paid by a wealthy man for Beecher's performance of his wedding ceremony.[6] After Beecher's death, at his funeral, according to Pond, the long procession to the grave was accompanied by "the benign angel of charity, clothed in the whiteness of that purity which renders sin invisible."[7]

Besides Beecher and Talmage, the greatest platform lecturers whom Pond managed were Wendell Phillips, John B. Gough, Chauncey M. Depew, and Robert G. Ingersoll. Depew was considered by Pond to be "the peerless all-round orator of the present time"[8]; but this may have been because Depew was content to make his money in railroading and never quibbled about the lecture fees Pond offered him. Gough he admired as a genuine professional, who gave a grand total of 9600 lectures before some nine million listeners.[9] Ingersoll was a difficult lecturer to

---

[5] *Ibid.*, pp. 43–47.
[6] *Ibid.*, p. 56. A rival of Pond's, who also managed Beecher, writes: "I first came in contact with Mr. Beecher in 1872, when the Redpath Bureau, in which I was partner, engaged him to deliver seventeen consecutive lectures for $12,000, $6000 being in advance, he to have expenses paid and a special car. He went out as far as Chicago. In 1876 I took him personally. For the season 1876–77 he netted for himself $41,530; for 1877–78 $27,200; for 1878–79, $21,200; for 1879–80, when he did but little lecturing, $8500, and he has averaged about the same since, making a total of about $240,000 for the ten years for which I have his receipts. He delivered in that time over 1200 lectures, and travelled 400,000 miles." Thomas W. Knox, *Life and Work of Henry Ward Beecher*, Hartford, Conn.: Hartford Pub. Co., 1887, pp. 327–328.
[7] Pond, *op. cit.*, p. 75.
[8] *Ibid.*, p. 17.
[9] *Ibid.*, p. 5.

deal with because of his penchant for hiring his own halls, taking himself all the financial risks, and, of course, taking all the profits.[10]

Pond was the greatest of the lecture bureau managers, as well as the founder of the system, but he soon had many competitors. As Chautauqua faded, the lecture bureaus took its place. Some forty ex-Chautauqua managers established their own lecture bureaus. By the nineteen-thirties and -forties, such bureaus were grossing from three- to five-million dollars a year and their "talent" was addressing a total of some three million auditors. Fees reached a high of $3000 per lecture, which was paid to the English historian H. G. Wells. Eleanor Roosevelt received $1500; Alben Barkley and Wayne Morse, $1000. Meanwhile, the bulk of the lecturing continued to be done by retired college professors and ministers, or returned missionaries and travelers, whose fees ranged from $25 to $100.[11]

Mark Twain was indubitably one of the greatest entertainers ever to appear on the lecture platform. Pond admired him for substantial reasons: "large crowds pay higher prices to see and hear 'Mark Twain' than any other private citizen that has ever lived."[12] It was on the lecture platform that Twain first earned his fame. In 1866, after a journalistic tour of Hawaii, then known as "The Sandwich Islands," Twain decided to try his hand at lecturing and rented a hall for the occasion in San Francisco. His announcement read: "Admission one dollar; doors open at half past seven, the trouble begins at eight." When he walked out on the stage and faced his first audience, "the fright which pervaded me from head to foot was paralyzing. It lasted two minutes and was as bitter as death; the memory of it is indestructible but it had its compensations, for it made me immune from timidity before audiences for all time to come."[13] His success induced him to try again and the second time there were 1500 in his audience. Twain never had made money at this rate, and he commenced a lecture tour of California and Nevada. Then he went to New York, where Frank Fuller booked him in Cooper Union; and although Twain feared he would speak to an empty house, he found the streets blocked with people for a quarter of a mile around and the hall jammed. Even the stage was filled. "There wasn't room enough left for a child."[14]

Twain's memory was remarkable in its own peculiar way (he once

10 Ibid., p. 27.
11 Upton Close, "Lecturing Today: Successor to Chautauqua," Saturday Review of Literature, January 3, 1940. Cf. Kenneth G. Hance, "The Contemporary Lecture Platform," QJS, 30 (Feb., 1944):41–47.
12 Pond, op. cit., p. 199.
13 The Autobiography of Mark Twain, ed., Charles Neider, New York: Harper, 1959, p. 143.
14 Ibid., p. 173.

said he could remember anything, whether it ever happened or not) and his autobiographical account of his lecturing career is considerably distorted.[15] Actually, James Redpath brought him East for the lecture season of 1872–73; and from that time on, first as a lecturer, then as a reader—which he did without manuscript, and with selected passages from his works woven together much in the manner of lecturing—he continued on the platform. He loved the stimulation of an audience but he hated the discomforts and inexorable timetable demands of traveling, and disliked being away from his family. As he once wrote to Pond, who became his manager in 1895, "I like to talk for nothing, about twice a year; but talking for money is work, and that takes the pleasure out of it."[16] Pleasure or not, it was profitable. It is an interesting commentary on the lecture business that profitable as were Twain's books, he recurrently had to rescue himself from financial difficulties by making another lecture tour. In 1894, when his publishing firm, Webster and Company, failed, leaving him with debts of $80,000, he started out on a round-the-world lecture tour—and returned the next Spring with the debts substantially paid.[17]

In his lecturing as in his writing, Twain was a conscious artist who studied his technique with great care. [18] As he relates in his essay, "How to Tell a Story," on the platform he spoke slowly, with frequent and carefully calculated use of the pause. Timing, he felt, was of the first importance; and, second, it was essential to his method to tell his humorous stories deadpan, even with a suggestion of sadness. While he lectured he smoked a cigar, pausing often to light or draw upon it; and to mark transitions he would slowly and deliberately walk from one position on the platform to another. Another of his peculiarities was that, after a single season of experience with being introduced, he always thereafter insisted upon eliminating this prefatory ritual.

Other "humorous and pathetic" lecturers, who cultivated the ground Mark Twain plowed for them, included Charles Farrar Browne, known as Artemus Ward, whose specialty was satirizing the Mormons; Henry W. Shaw, billed as "Josh Billings," who concocted dialogue humor masquerading as common-sense philosophy; David Ross Locke, called "Petroleum V. Nasby," who rocked audiences with his satire of women suffragettes; Edgar W. ("Bill") Nye, who teamed up with James Whitcomb Riley, both being drunk much of the time, on and off the platform; George W. Peck, whose forte was to make light of the farm problem; and Melville D. Landon, who lectured as "Eli Perkins," telling

[15] *Ibid.,* p. 176.
[16] Pond, *op. cit.,* p. 226.
[17] Twain, *Autobiography, op. cit.,* p. 264.
[18] *Ibid.,* Chapters 32–35, pp. 161–183.

audiences the secrets of putting together a humorous lecture.[19] In the closely allied field of titillating the audiences with talks of travel and adventure, the stars were Bayard Taylor, "the most traveled American," Henry Stanley, "the man who found Livingstone," Richard Halliburton, who retraced the routes of early explorers, and Lowell Thomas, who interviewed Lawrence of Arabia and visited the hidden kingdom of Tibet. Vilhaljmar Steffanson despised lecturing but was induced by Pond to undertake it for a season and made enough money to outfit and finance his expedition to Wrangell Island. Richard Evelyn Byrd was no fonder of lecturing, but used it as a medium for raising money (partly from large contributions) for his north and south polar expeditions. Lew Wallace, F. Marion Crawford, and Ernest Seton-Thompson were among the many authors who used the popularity of their books as a springboard for reaching the more profitable lecture platform.

The Lyceum, Chautauqua, and lecture bureau each dealt with the lecturing business in a different way, to serve different ends. The Lyceums operated in the winter, were held in comfortable auditoriums, and while they professed to aim toward educating the masses, their principal appeal was to the social and educational elite. Chautauqua moved from the cities out into the rural districts, presented its programs in tents, traveled during the summer months, and reached its largest audience among the poor and the poorly educated. Both the Lyceum and the Chautauqua movements professed high moral and educational aims, even though in effect they catered without shame or question to popular taste. The lecture bureau never made any pretense of being anything except an agency for making money from speech, for the speakers and the managers. Both in print and in speech there have been practitioners whose sole aim was to "give the public what it wants" in order to reap the largest possible return; and there have been idealists and crusaders whose motivation has been to educate, inspire, and improve. Lecturing per se has been neither bad nor good. It has been an avenue through which the public has been led to vast amounts of both.

[19] Melville D. Landon, *Kings of the Platform and Pulpit*, Chicago: Werner Co., 1900, *passim*.

XIII

THE RENEWAL
OF RHETORIC
1890 ⬎ 1914

New Problems, New Voices

THE GENERATION following the Civil War has not been treated very kindly by its grandsons. Even its own more perceptive members judged the generation a failure. Ed Howe, in his *Story of a Country Town*, pictured the rural life of the time as grimly destructive of individualism; and Stephen Crane was no less harsh, in his *Maggie: A Girl of the Streets*, in criticizing life in the cities. Grover Cleveland, in his fourth annual message to Congress, in December, 1888, said: "We discover that the fortunes realized by our manufacturers are no longer solely the reward of sturdy industry and enlightened foresight, but that they result from the indiscriminating favor of the government, and are largely built upon undue exactions from the masses of the people."[1] Thorstein Veblen thought it an age of pretense, in which the newly rich sought status through "ostentatious consumption and honorific display."[2] Frederick Jackson Turner, reviewing the hatreds that rent America in the Reconstruction period, pleaded that "we shall not give up our American ideals and our hopes for man."[3] A scientist who lived through the generation was similarly disenchanted:

> Just before it I can see that while the ideals of culture were in a way still low and rather carnal, there was an eager reaching out for better things . . . . Four years of civil war . . . made an end of this and set the people on a moral and intellectual plane lower than that they occupied when they were warring with the wilderness and the savages . . . . the tide which was setting toward the better life was stayed; the thoughts of men turned toward the primitive.[4]

[1] Grover Cleveland, "Annual Message," in *Congressional Record*, Proceedings and Debates of the 50th Congress, 2nd Session, pp. 2–9.
[2] Thorstein Veblen, *Theory of the Leisure Class*, New York: Modern Library, 1934, pp. 73–74 and *passim*.
[3] Frederick Jackson Turner, *Sections in American History*, New York: Holt, 1932, p. 339.
[4] Nathaniel Southgate Shaler, *Autobiography*, New York: Houghton Mifflin, 1909, pp. 76–77.

Of course, characterizing and labelling any period of history is a hazardous enterprise. As Charles Beard said when he was inaugurated President of the American Historical Association: "Any selection and arrangement of facts pertaining to any large area of history, either local or world, race or class, is controlled inexorably by the frame of reference in the mind of the selector and arranger."[5] American historians have written and rewritten our history, depending on the fads and fashions that are currently dominant.[6] Nevertheless, since certainty is impossible in any purely evaluative enterprise, the best we can search for is a convergence of informed judgments. And the oratory of the period, like its other manifestations, as the preceding chapters have showed, reveal it as an Age of Tinsel.

There was a different tone in the generation immediately preceding World War I. No new historic period comes in like thunder, with a sharp and definite cleavage from the time before it. Mankind plods forward through the changing decades with fits and starts of idealistic yearning, but, meanwhile, it must also drag along its dead carcass of outmoded memories and discredited traditions. What is important is to try to discern the trends and tendencies that emerge into special significance.

After the Panic of 1873, the rich steadily became richer and the poor remained poor. Grover Cleveland, after two terms as President, expressed the view of many of his countrymen when he said: "I find I am developing quite a strong desire to make money and I think it is a good time to indulge in that propensity."[7] Lincoln Steffens, Ida Tarbell, and other "muckrakers" noted that this propensity was widespread, and gave it the back of their hands. The political vendetta between the North and the South cooled down from a boil to a simmer. The general white public lost interest in the unfranchised lot of the freed Negroes and were induced by eloquent spokesmen like Eugene Debs, John P. Altgeld, Samuel Gompers, and Johnny Mitchell to develop more interest in the needs and rights of labor. As land prices soared and farm marketing controls became lodged in New York and Chicago, farmers came less and less to represent Thomas Jefferson's dream of the ideal agrarian democrats. Strong voices raised in their behalf created marked reactions, but within limited spheres: "Pitchfork Ben" Tillman, the farmer's friend in South Carolina; Tom Watson, hero of the tenant farmers of Georgia; "Sockless Jerry" Simpson, scourge of the railroads; and, in a wider sphere,

[5] Henry Steele Commager, The American Mind, New Haven: Yale University Press, 1950, p. 304.
[6] C. Vann Woodward, "Our Past Isn't What It Used to Be," New York Times Sunday Book Review, July 28, 1963, pp. 1, 24–25.
[7] Hofstadter, "The Spoilsmen," op. cit., pp. 184–185.

Henry George, the apostle of a single tax, and Ignatius Donnelly, the rebellious sage from Minnesota. James G. Blaine, a "silver-tongued orator," Speaker of the House, Senator, Secretary of State, and candidate for the presidency, in a letter to James Garfield contemptuously brushed them aside as "upstarts, conceited, foolish, vain . . . noisy but not numerous, pharisaical but not practical, ambitious but not wise, pretentious but not powerful."[8]

Thomas B. Reed, the greatest parliamentarian between the eras of Henry Clay and "Uncle Joe" Cannon,[9] in a debate on May 14, 1884, tried to deal with the problems of the time in terms that had worked well before the period of rapid urbanization and industrialism:

> For my part, sir, I am heartily tired of this continual talk about this being a land where the poor man can flourish and the poor man is honored. It is neither a credit nor a discredit to a man to have been born poor. Nothing stands in the way of his advancement. He has an equal chance and fair opportunity in the race with every other citizen; and these repeated declarations are born of a suspicion on the part of some gentlemen that the poor man is not equal to the rich. I maintain that neither in our constitutions nor in the practical working of the government is there any superiority on the part of the rich over the poor man that needs the orations of Congressmen to equalize the citizens of this country."[10]

Horatio Alger agreed and wrote a series of novels to illuminate the theme that a poor boy could become rich by hard work, thrift, virtue, and marriage to the boss's daughter. But in Kansas there were half as many mortgages as there were adults in the state.[11]

A new generation of orators arose, who had scarcely more resemblance to Ingersoll, Beecher, Conkling, and Harrison than they had to the greater statesmen and spokesmen of the ante bellum years. A new tone entered into the public dialogue. The general appeals of these new speakers was to sacrifice, and duty, and patriotism. Politics came again to be evangelistic. William Jennings Bryan was the most popular of the group and his words perhaps describe best the mood and the motives of them all: "A man can be born again; the springs of life can be cleansed instantly . . . . If this is true of one, it can be true of any number.

---

[8] Ibid., pp. 176–177. For a good sampling of the views of this man who represented a dominant viewpoint in the politics of the time, see James G. Blaine, Political Discussions: Legislative, Diplomatic, and Popular, 1856–1866, Norwich, Conn.: Henry Bill Pub. Co., 1887.
[9] Neil MacNeil, Forge of Democracy, The House of Representatives, New York: David McKay, 1963, Chapter IV, "Mr. Speaker," pp. 61–86.
[10] William A. Robinson, Thomas B. Reed: Parliamentarian, New York: Dodd, Mead, 1930, p. 165.
[11] Morrison and Commager, Growth of the American Republic, op. cit., II:238.

Thus, a nation can be born in a day if the ideals of the people can be changed."[12] The politicians who rose to greatness were revivalists. Bourke Cockran had the Irishman's tendency to see eternity cradled within the particularism of his immediate topic. Albert J. Beveridge of Indiana and his friend and sometime opponent, "Battling Bob" La-Follette of Wisconsin, both shared the Bryanesque flair for talking about political issues as though they were subdivisions of religious creeds. Theodore Roosevelt always somehow felt that he was leading the hosts of righteousness as they confronted a succession of Armageddons. And even as the era faded out and a new one commenced, Woodrow Wilson picked up the thread of political evangelism which he heard preached from their lips. Rhetoric in America did not in their speaking rise to the heights of the age of Webster, Clay, Calhoun, Douglas, Seward, and Lincoln. But in strength of purpose and in dedicated zeal it was revitalized and renewed from the slough of the years of post-war reconstruction. And the people, who of old had depended first of all upon themselves, came now to listen to political promises and nostrums with a freshness of faith and a resurgence of hope.

William Jennings Bryan: Politics as Religion

WILLIAM JENNINGS BRYAN assuredly was not the greatest of American speakers, but no one else approached him in his mastery of oratory as a profession in and for itself. Hofstadter put his finger on the essential fact in saying "It was never success that he demanded, but an audience."[1] From the age of seven, when his parents placed him on a table to declaim his geography lessons, his great preoccupation was with *speaking well*. In Sunday School and high school, at Whipple Academy and at Jackson College, he was tireless in his practice and performance of public speaking. This is the more remarkable since he had few natural gifts for eloquence except a good voice and a commanding physique, and his early efforts were without much rewarding success.[2] Always he kept at it, practicing hour after hour and asking little of himself except success in speech. When he opened his law office, it was as a base from which to conduct a lecture career. And the grand climax that marked his

[12] Richard Hofstadter, "William Jennings Bryan: The Democrat as Revivalist," in *The American Political Tradition*, op. cit., p. 186, considers this statement to epitomize Bryan's political significance.
[1] Hofstadter, "Bryan," op. cit., p. 199.
[2] *The Memoirs of William Jennings Bryan*, op. cit., pp. 85–88; and J. C. Long, *The Great Commoner*, New York: Appleton, 1928, p. 30.

passage across the threshold to adult achievement came when he returned home early one morning from a lecture engagement, awakened his wife, and, sitting on the edge of the bed, told her: "Mary, I have had a strange experience. Last night I found that I had power over the audience. I could move them as I chose. I have more than usual power as a speaker. I know it. God grant that I may use it wisely."[3]

During the remainder of his life he held public office only for four years in Congress and for two years as Secretary of State. Even then, he was off lecturing whenever he could. No one knows how many speeches he delivered in his more than forty years of active speaking. "Fifteen speeches a day was a common occurrence," concluded one student of his career, "and, so far as is known, the record for a single day was thirty-six."[4] Two-thirds of his nights were estimated to have been spent on trains or in hotels. It would be conservative to estimate the total number of his speeches at ten thousand; and his audiences often were large—at least as large as fifteen thousand. He travelled two hundred miles to give two speeches on the day before his death.

Charles F. Horner, a lecture bureau manager whose shrewdness was devoted to estimating what gave speakers audience-appeal, explained Bryan's "undoubted perfection" as follows: "First, people who listened to him sensed intuitively his greatness of spirit. Second, he expressed for them their thoughts and aspirations. And finally, he reciprocated their frequently demonstrated affection for him."[5] Merrill D. Peterson, in his study of Thomas Jefferson's reputation and influence throughout our history, thought that Bryan did more to "revitalize" Jeffersonianism than any other American political figure.[6] Over the desk in his study Bryan kept a huge portrait of Jefferson, flanked by smaller pictures of Washington and Lincoln. Bryan's principal political guidebook was Jefferson's first inaugural address, and his plea to his political following was that they fight for "Jeffersonian principles with Jacksonian courage." Like Jefferson, he was first, last, and always an agrarian. Also Jeffersonian was his conviction that "It is the duty of government to protect all from injustice and to do so without showing partiality for any one or any class."[7] Unfortunately for his election prospects, he never really understood that the United States was becoming industrialized. In 1892 he campaigned (in Nebraska, among farmers) with the assurance that he was "tired of hearing about laws made for the benefit

[3] Bryan and Bryan, Memoirs, op. cit., pp. 248–249.
[4] Myron G. Phillips, "William Jennings Bryan," in Brigance, ed., History and Criticism, op. cit., II:906.
[5] Paul W. Glad, The Trumpet Soundeth, Lincoln: University of Nebraska Press, 1960, p. 21.
[6] Peterson, Jefferson Image, op. cit., pp. 259–260.
[7] Hofstadter, "Bryan," op. cit., p. 191.

of men who work in shops."[8] For similar reasons, he did not understand the nature or effects of the growing trusts. The Democratic platform in 1896 did not advocate controls over private enterprise; and in the "Cross of Gold" speech that won Bryan the nomination in that year, he said:

> When you come before us and tell us that we are about to disturb your business interests, we reply that you have disturbed our business interests by your course.
>
> We say to you that you have made the definition of a business man too limited in its application. The man who is employed for wages is as much a business man as his employer, the attorney in a country town is as much a business man as the corporation counsel in a great metropolis; the merchant at the cross-roads store is as much a business man as the merchant in New York; the farmer who goes forth in the morning and toils all day—who begins in the spring and toils all summer—and who by application of brain and muscle to the natural resources of the country creates wealth, is as much a business man as the man who goes upon the board of trade and bets upon the price of grain . . .[9]

Both his success in creating a fanatical loyalty among millions and his failure in three attempts to attain the presidency spring from the same causes; for his weaknesses and his strengths were basically identical. He could not eliminate his weaknesses without shearing away his strength; he could not exploit his strength without magnifying his weakness. For Bryan was, to a high degree, the eloquent exemplification of the average man. His deep conviction was that "Persuasive speech is from heart to heart, not from mind to mind."[10] It was less important to him to *understand* the issues than to *identify* himself with his hearers. In his Congressional campaign in 1892 he told his Nebraska constituents, "I don't know anything about free silver. The people of Nebraska are for free silver and I am for free silver. I will look up the arguments later."[11]

The intellectuals never liked Bryan; he was not their kind. Oswald Garrison Villard could try to sweep him aside, in *Prophets True and False* (1928), by a damnatory indictment: "Of all the men I have seen at close range in thirty-one years of newspaper service, Mr. Bryan seems to me the most ignorant."

But Bryan knew what his audiences knew. He knew that a farm debt contracted in 1865 that then cost one thousand bushels of wheat cost three thousand bushels to repay in 1895. He may have been, as Hofstadter called him, "intellectually a boy who never left home"; but he

[8] *Ibid.*, p. 190.
[9] *Speeches of William Jennings Bryan, op. cit.*, 1:240–241.
[10] William Jennings Bryan, *In His Image*, New York: Fleming H. Revell, 1922, p. 251.
[11] Hofstadter, "Bryan," *op. cit.*, p. 190.

was smart enough to conclude that "A dollar approaches honesty as its purchasing power approaches stability."[12] As he watched the effects of year after year of deflation debasing the lot of the debtor class, he found no difficulty in agreeing with "Coin" Harvey that what was needed was a shift away from the gold standard to free coinage of silver. In a speech at Hartford, Connecticut, in 1896, he touched a common chord with his audience when he said: "Of all the instrumentalities which have been conceived by the mind of man for transferring the bread which one man earns to another man who does not earn it, I believe the gold standard is the greatest." He heard, as did the public, many arguments in favor of a tariff that would keep out foreign products, or raise their prices on the market, in order to protect the American manufacturer. And he was shrewd enough to see and to state the effect of this tariff policy upon the American consumer: "Whenever you see the Government by operation of law send a dollar singing down into one man's pocket, you must remember that the Government has brought it crying up out of some other man's pocket."[13]

Mrs. Bryan, after his death, became wearied of the frequent charge that her husband simply lacked intellect enough to understand the complexities of modern government, and her reply was to list the causes for which he fought which eventually became law: the federal income tax, the popular election of U.S. Senators, publicity for all campaign contributions, restoration of freedom to the Philippines, prohibition, suffrage for women, an International Court and agreement to arbitrate disputes, labor representation in the cabinet, regulation of the freight rates charged by railroads, abolition of the gold standard, and utilization of the initiative and referendum in states.[14] It is an impressive list. Bryan's great strength was that on so many basic issues he was right; and his great weakness (which was also a strength) was that in order to win adherence for his program from the masses, he had to, and he could, and he did, state what he had to say in simple and often in oversimplified form.

Another element of Bryan's peculiar combination of strength and weakness was that he never greatly believed in knowledge but he greatly believed in ultra-simple moral and religious principles. He was not much of a reader, and with the exception of some speeches delivered in Congress, he did not believe in the utility of presenting to an audience either a mass of facts or a detailed analysis of a complex question. The

[12] *Ibid.*, pp. 190, 187, 188. For a further analysis of the economic plight of the Midwestern farmers in 1896, cf. Glad, *op. cit.*, pp. 44–50.
[13] *Speeches of Bryan, op. cit.*, I:42.
[14] Bryan and Bryan, *Memoirs, op. cit.*, p. 463.

one book he read and reread until he knew it thoroughly was the Bible. And his methodology in presenting his ideas was to identify them, in part, with the Biblical phraseology and imagery, and in part, through commonplace anecdotes, with the everyday experiences of his listeners. Intellectuals in general and Bryan's political opponents in particular could ridicule the transparent simplicity of his discussion of complex questions. But, with Jeffersonian insistence, Bryan declared that:

> I assert that the people of the United States . . . have sufficient patriotism and sufficient intelligence to sit in judgment on every question which has arisen or which will arise, no matter how long our government will endure. The great political questions are in their final analysis great moral questions, and it requires no extended experience in the handling of money to enable a man to tell right from wrong.[15]

It is ironic, and it is a large part of the problem Bryan (and the nation in his day) confronted, that the Jeffersonianism which he espoused was in the throes of death. "The Jeffersonian philosophy," as Merrill Peterson points out, "defined liberty largely in terms of the absence of governmental restraint."[16] But the twin bases of the Jeffersonian faith—reliance upon the simple wisdom and independent judgment of incorruptible farmers, and restriction of government to the mere minimum of police duties—were both undermined by the extent and nature of the industrialization which inundated the United States toward the close of the nineteenth century. The old liberals clung nostalgically to the principle of "leave us alone"; but as the farm boys drifted into the cities and there became dependent for jobs and livelihood upon corporations whose empires and sales extended across the continent and indeed around the world, true liberalism came to require systematic and detailed governmental controls. Bryan resisted and probably failed to understand the whole shifting situation. Theodore Roosevelt understood it only in part and sought the inadequate remedy of trying to "smash the trusts," in an effort to return to small businesses; and Woodrow Wilson, understanding it better, accepted the need for bigness and the resultant need for federal controls.[17]

Partly because of the programs Bryan sponsored, but even more because of the simplicity of his language and the old-fashioned flavor of his examples and appeals, his critics, both in his own time and since,

---

[15] Hofstadter, "Bryan," *op. cit.*, p. 191.
[16] Peterson, *Jefferson Image*, *op. cit.*, pp. 330, 332.
[17] This thumbnail summary adheres closely to the reasoning of Hofstadter, Peterson, and Commager, *op. cit.*; and of Max Lerner, *America As a Civilization*, New York: Simon and Schuster, 1957; and of Arthur M. Schlesinger, Jr., *The Crisis of the Old Order, 1919–1933*, Boston: Houghton Mifflin, 1957.

have tended generally to conclude that he was essentially simple-minded, even dull. In part this kind of criticism has stemmed from the cardinal fact that Bryan was a preacher in politics. He referred often to his Christian faith and to his active work in churches. The end of his life reached an anticlimax in the Scopes trial, where he was ridiculed by the master satirist Clarence Darrow for his stubborn insistence upon his faith in the literal truthfulness of every word of the Bible. His religion was manifestly both simple and old-fashioned. Since he himself insisted upon infusing his political campaigning with his own brand of religious revivalism, it is not strange that his critics leaped to the conclusion that his political mentality paralleled his religious thinking. What they over-looked was the curious fact that Bryan's political mentor was a religious radical—a rationalistic Deist. Bryan himself was clear-minded on the essential point: he carried into politics his faith in people, his dedication to righteousness as he understood it, and the methodology of speaking which he found effective in church and on the Chautauqua circuit. But as is indicated by the list of his major proposals, which his widow high-lighted, insofar as his political beliefs were concerned, in many respects he was not behind but ahead of his time. Thomas B. Reed waspishly quipped that "Bryan would rather be wrong than president,"[18] and perhaps in a sense he was correct. The Great Commoner surely had no intention of leading a movement to establish Big Government.

Bryan's career has always been a cause of bewilderment to cynical sophisticates. "If the fellow was sincere," H. L. Mencken exclaimed, "then so was P. T. Barnum."[19] Paxton Hibben thought that the "furniture" of his mind consisted of a "confidence that a mere sonorous recital of axioms is the equivalent of thought."[20] Richard Hofstadter concluded that "It was neither courage nor sincerity but simply steadfast and self-confident intelligence that Bryan lacked."[21] These rejections were all written after the Scopes trial, in which Bryan ended his life defending the proposition that such Biblical accounts as the swallowing of Jonah by a large fish were literally true. If this Byranesque anti-intellectualism appalled those who observed Bryan in his old age, the defenders of urban respectability and fiscal soundness were no less disturbed by the golden-voiced orator's magnetic attraction of the masses to the heresy of free silver in the 1896 campaign. After Bryan's defeat, so reputable a newspaper as the New York *Tribune* commented as follows

[18] Hofstadter, "Bryan," op. cit., p. 197. For Reed's earlier ridicule of Bryan, cf. Robinson, op. cit., pp. 279–280.
[19] H. L. Mencken, *The American Mercury*, VI(Oct., 1925):159.
[20] Paxton Hibben, *The Peerless Leader*, New York: Farrar and Rinehart, 1929, p. 87.
[21] Hofstadter, "Bryan," op. cit., p. 202.

on the demise, forever, it hoped, of the economic heresy he had espoused:

> It has been defeated and destroyed because right is right and God is God. Its nominal head was worthy of the cause. Nominal, because the wretched, rattle-pated boy, posing in vapid vanity and mouthing resounding rottenness, was not the real leader of that league of Hell. He was only a puppet in the blood-imbued hands of Altgeld, the anarchist, and Debs, the revolutionist, and other desperadoes of that stripe.
>
> But he was a willing puppet, Bryan was, willing and eager. Not one of his masters was more apt at lies and forgeries and blasphemies and all the nameless iniquities of that campaign against the Ten Commandments. He goes down with the cause, and must abide with it in the history of infamy. He had less provocation than Benedict Arnold, less intellectual force than Aaron Burr, less manliness and courage than Jefferson Davis. He was the rival of them all in deliberate wickedness and treason to the Republic. His name belongs with theirs, neither the most brilliant nor the least hateful in the list.[22]

The vindictiveness of Bryan's critics both from the radical left and from the conservative right suggests a dual conclusion that is probably correct, namely: that Bryan actually occupied a median position of moderation in most of what he advocated; and that his advocacy was skillful enough to frighten into extravagant denunciations those who feared his success. This is not to say that Bryan was either a statesman or a thinker of high calibre. The most significant fact about Bryan is that he was genuinely and impregnably representative of small-town America, particularly of the Midwest.

He was born March 19, 1860, of deeply religious, staunchly Democratic, reasonably prosperous parents, who taught him to respect education much but religion and morality even more. Judge Silas Bryan prayed in his home three times daily, earned a good living administering justice to his fellow men, and taught his son devotion to three duties: to God, to himself, and to mankind. Life in the village of Salem, Illinois, where he grew up, was not complex and this teaching seemed to provide a reliable formula for solving such problems as arose. It is but natural that young Bryan's mind became confidently formulistic. He learned to think in aphorisms; and throughout his speeches he coined them as nimbly as Ben Franklin had coined the sayings of Poor Richard. But there is a difference. Whereas Franklin's aphoristic wisdom points generally toward success, Bryan's usually points toward responsibility. Right out of his home environment comes such sayings as: "An athlete bent on mischief can do more harm than a dwarf or an invalid; and so, a well-

---

[22] Long, *Great Commoner*, *op. cit.*, p. 116.

disciplined mind, misdirected, is capable of doing more serious damage than an ignorant mind";[23] and "I fear the plutocracy of wealth; I respect the plutocracy of learning; I thank God for the democracy of the heart";[24] and "The men who have earned five million dollars have been so busy earning it that they have not had time to collect it; and the men who have collected five hundred million have been so busy collecting it that they have not had time to earn it."[25] Platitudinous though such statements may be, they are in fact Bryan's own, minted from his mind, stamped with his personality—no less truly his because they also reflect his identification with middleclass America.

Bryan did not grow up believing in the value of classical learning, or of any learning, for that matter, except thorough familiarity with and implicit confidence in the Bible. As Will Rogers was later to say of himself, he never knew a man he didn't like. He trusted the people he knew; he believed, for example, without question in free trade because the president of his college wrote a book favoring it. His mind was not complex, and he knew the same was true of the minds of people generally. He did not appeal to statistics or authority or even to argument to support the ideas he advocated in his speeches. The heart of his theory of communicative effectiveness he explained simply in one of his lectures: "If you speak to the multitude and they do not respond, do not despise them, but rather examine what you have said. If you speak from your heart, you will speak to their hearts, and they can tell very quickly whether you are interested in them or simply in yourself. The heart of mankind is sound; the sense of justice is universal. Trust it, appeal to it, do not violate it . . . . Link yourselves in sympathy with your fellowmen; mingle with them; know them and you will trust them and they will trust you."[26]

Even when Bryan was not coining phrases but was echoing his recollection of what someone else had said, the echo was likely to be not only from an American but from a very commonplace source—as in the following paraphrase of Patrick Henry, in the "Cross of Gold" address: "We have petitioned, and our petitions have been scorned; we have entreated, and our entreaties have been disregarded; we have begged, and they have mocked when our calamity came. We beg no longer; we entreat no more; we petition no more. We defy them."[27] And again, in that same speech, he reveals clearly where he was brought up and how much his early environment entered into and became the essence of his

[23] From Bryan's Chautauqua lecture, "Man"; *Speeches of Bryan, op. cit.*, II:298.
[24] From Bryan's "Faith"; *ibid.*, II:332.
[25] From Bryan's "The Price of a Soul"; *ibid.*, II:343.
[26] From Bryan's "Faith," *ibid.*, II:332–333.
[27] *Ibid.*, II:241.

character: "Burn down your cities and leave your farms, and your cities will spring up again as if by magic; but destroy our farms and the grass will grow in the streets of every city in the country."[28]

Bryan has been praised lavishly for his magnificent voice—rich, vibrant, flexible, penetrating.[29] He has been both praised and ridiculed for his delivery, which was staid, calm, dignified, with a free use of slow, widesweeping gestures. His wife spoke almost with awe of his memory which enabled him to dredge up from random reading facts and quotations when he needed them.[30] But valuable as these attributes were, his greatest source of oratorical power was his ability to put the deepest thoughts and feelings of his listeners into words at once so commonplace that they seemed their own, and yet so neatly, and rhythmically, and cleanly phrased that they became vividly memorable. The sheer bulk of his speaking gave him the largest audience any man had before radio. In the 1896 campaign alone he travelled eighteen thousand miles, speaking from 60,000 to 100,000 words a day, to a cumulative audience of some 4.8 million.[31] Perhaps the greatest of all the tributes to Bryan lies in the fact that his life reached its high point with the 1896 nomination, when he was barely thirty seven. Yet during the ensuing twenty nine years, to his death on July 26, 1925, he did not decline much in either eloquence or popularity but, rather, seemed to remain perpetually fixed upon a high plateau—until the final tragicomedy of the cruelly ludicrous Scopes trial.

Young as he was when first nominated for the presidency, Bryan nevertheless had prepared himself carefully and purposively for just that result. During his four years in Congress he not only studied the currency question thoughtfully but he undertook deliberately to connect his name in the mind of the public and of the Democratic political leadership with this issue, which he felt sure would determine the nomination.[32] He went to the Chicago Convention with a speech which he had practiced, in essence, on several lecture audiences. When his time came to address the Convention, he felt sick at his stomach (he never lost this tendency to rather severe stage fright before a speech)[33] but he regained his confidence as he gazed out at the fifteen thousand or more delegates and galleryites and listened to them roar their approval

---

[28] *Ibid.*, II:248. Herbert Hoover borrowed the "grass will grow in the city streets," phrase for use in the 1932 presidential campaign.
[29] Case and Case, *We Called It Culture, op. cit.*, p. 89; Hibben, *Peerless Leader, op. cit.*, p. 57; Bryan and Bryan, *Memoirs, op. cit.*, pp. 252–253; Harrison and Detzer, *Culture under Canvas, op. cit.*, p. 159.
[30] Bryan and Bryan, *Memoirs, op. cit.*, pp. 301–302.
[31] W. R. Werner, *Bryan*, New York: Harcourt, Brace, 1929, p. 95.
[32] Hibben, *op. cit.*, Chapter XVI, "1896," pp. 175–188.
[33] *Ibid.*, p. 184; Harrison and Detzer, *op. cit.*, p. 163.

of his measured words: "I come to speak to you in defense of a cause as holy as the cause of liberty—the cause of humanity." His conclusion was the crassest possible application of religion to politics: "You shall not press down upon the brow of labor this crown of thorns, you shall not crucify mankind upon a cross of gold." But by the time he reached this point, his audience for many minutes had been roaring a tremendous crescendo of approval for every sentence he uttered, and as his great arms spread up and out to illustrate the cross upon which labor was not to be impaled, one of the greatest ovations ever accorded a speaker broke out. Bryan's hometown newspaper described the scene with adequate ardor: "Ten acres of people . . . swayed like windswept fields; they heard the awful roar of twenty thousand voices burst like a volcano against the reverberating dome overhead; they saw a man carried upon the shoulders of others intoxicated by enthusiasm . . ."[34]

The effect of the speech indubitably was to make possible the nomination of Bryan; but it did not come about automatically. When the balloting took place the next day, "Silver Dick" Bland continued in the lead through three ballots, and Bryan did not get the necessary two-thirds until the fifth ballot. Even so, the triumph was unalloyed. A young man out of the rural West, without any real political power (though he knew more delegates personally than did any other candidate) had stolen the nomination from the professionals.[35]

So far as resources were concerned, the presidential campaign was completely one-sided. Mark Hanna raised $3,500,000 on behalf of William McKinley, as contrasted with the $300,000 Bryan was able to get.[36] The Republican strategists hired fourteen hundred speakers to counteract what Bryan was saying.[37] Bryan was opposed by Grover Cleveland, the outgoing Democratic President, who considered the free-silver program ruinously inflationary. Yet under all the handicaps, Bryan won six and a half million votes, against the seven million cast for McKinley. When the results were in, one of his Eastern opponents heaved a sigh of relief and payed him ungrudging tribute:

> The great fight is won. It was a fight conducted by trained and experienced forces, with both hands full of money, with the full power of the press and prestige—on the one side; on the other, a disorganized mob at first, out of which burst into sight, hearing and force—one man,

[34] The Lincoln, Nebraska, *News*, July 10, 1896, p. 10.
[35] See Hofstadter, "Bryan," *op. cit.*, p. 192; and Hibben, *op. cit.*, pp. 177–183.
[36] Phillips, "Bryan," in Brigance, ed., *History and Criticism*, *op. cit.*, II:904. The importance of large sums of money for the campaign, and the means by which Mark Hanna raised it, are related in Margaret Leech, *In the Days of McKinley*, New York: Harper, 1959, pp. 58–59, 75, 86–87.
[37] Glad, *The Trumpet Soundeth*, *op. cit.*, p. 56.

but such a man! Alone, penniless, without backing, without money, with scarce a paper, without speakers, that man fought such a fight that even those in the East can call him a Crusader, an inspired fanatic— a prophet! It has been marvellous. Hampered by such a following, such a platform,—and even the men whose names were our greatest weapon against him deserted him and left him to fight alone—he almost won . . .[38]

Once again Bryan was the candidate of his party in 1900, again against McKinley, but this time with the added handicap that McKinley was the President who had "won the war" against wicked, imperialist Spain, and had victoriously planted the American flag halfway around the world. His vote dropped substantially behind that of 1896; he was forty one and a badly beaten man. But, far from fading into insignificance, eight years later he again was nominated for the presidency, this time getting ninety percent of the convention votes on the first ballot. Both Bryan and his opponent, William Howard Taft, were rotund, prosperous, middle-aged, too familiar to the voters to be exciting, and too comfortable to be themselves excited. Bryan thought Taft should be defeated because he was a Unitarian who did not believe in the divinity of Christ.[39] Ruefully, in his *Memoirs*, Bryan refers to the lack of enthusiasm in the campaign. "One man told me that at a ratification meeting three cheers were proposed. The chairman gave two of them and the man who told me gave one, which made the three—the remainder of the audience refused to join."[40] Even so, in 1912 Bryan's influence within his party was still so great that he was able to swing the Baltimore Convention away from Champ Clark to accomplish the nomination of Woodrow Wilson.

The remainder of his sixty five years saw no lessening of the steady pace of his speaking, and not much decline in its quality. He moved to Florida, where he organized a Sunday School class for men in an outdoors arena, and soon had a regular attendance of some five thousand. With typical husbandly care for the practical details, he syndicated his Sunday talks to newspapers, for a payment of $2000 per month.[41] When he spoke in Detroit, three times in one afternoon, to huge overflow crowds, and was praised for his magnetic eloquence, he responded wistfully, "Please write that to Mrs. Bryan. She thinks I'm slipping." On the day before his death he made a speech, corrected page proofs on the speech he had prepared for the Scopes trial and which had not been presented in court, and travelled two hundred miles in order to be home

[38] Phillips, "Bryan," *op. cit.*, II:904, quoting Mrs. Henry Cabot Lodge.
[39] Hibben, *op. cit.*, p. 286; Glad, *op. cit.*, p. 117.
[40] Bryan and Bryan, *Memoirs*, *op. cit.*,. p. 156.
[41] Hibben, *op cit.*, p. 373.

for church on Sunday, the next day. He delivered the prayer at the service, then went home to die quietly, while napping in his chair, after telling his wife, "I never felt better in my life."[42] If he has often been underrated, he himself had an explanation that merits consideration: "They call that man a statesman whose ear is tuned to catch the slightest pulsation of a pocketbook, and denounce as a demagogue anyone who dares to listen to the heart-beat of humanity."[43]

William Bourke Cockran: The Hurrah Speaker 📖

HENRY L. STODDARD, a political reporter whose experiences in Washington stretched from Grant to Coolidge, thought there should be established a category of eloquence to be known as "hurrah oratory," to designate the splendidly impressive speakers, who arouse great admiration and enthusiasm but somehow never receive the kind of confidence that gives them genuine leadership.[1] He listed for priority inclusion in this group Henry Clay, James G. Blaine, and William Jennings Bryan, then added that it ought also to include Bourke Cockran. Like Bryan, though within a narrower range, Cockran was an orator per se; to many he was the American Burke.

It was a cold winter evening, November 26, 1905 when there stood on the stage of New York's Carnegie Hall, before an exuberant audience of three thousand Irish-Americans, a tall, powerfully built orator whose broad face was both elfin and granite-hard, and whose voice "rolled rivers of majestic diction" in tones that were organ-deep and flute-clear. With a courtly dignity that was saved from coldness by the surging tide of his Irish emotions, he spoke words that were truer of no one than of himself, though the subject of his discourse was the folk-bard who springs into eloquent song so often from amidst the villagers of old Ireland: "He has managed to lend, even to the unbending English words, something of the cadence of the Atlantic as it strikes and moans upon his rock-bound shore."[2] The speaker was William Bourke Cockran, lawyer and politician, for whom some of the most acute critics of his

[42] *Ibid.*, pp. 404–405.
[43] Quoted by Margaret Wood, "William Jennings Bryan: Crusade for the Common Man," in Loren Reid, ed., *American Public Address*, Columbia: University of Missouri Press, 1961, p. 164.
[1] Henry L. Stoddard, *As I Knew Them: Presidents and Politics from Grant to Coolidge*, New York: Harper, 1927, pp. 10–12.
[2] James McGurrin, *Bourke Cockran: A Free Lance in American Politics*, New York: Scribner's, 1948, pp. 228–229. The text of the speech is in Bourke Cockran, *In the Name of Liberty*, New York: Putnam's, 1925.

time strained to find adjectives adequate to convey their sense of his oratorical power.

T. P. O'Connor, puckish Member of Parliament, writing in the London *Chronicle* for March 7, 1923, said: "I have long held that Bourke Cockran was the most eloquent orator of his time among the English-speaking peoples, if not of all nations." Thirty years earlier, Richard Henry Dana, writing in the New York *Sun*, called him "the greatest orator of the modern world." Winston Churchill, the American novelist, in his memoirs, *Amid These Storms*, declared: "In point, in pith, in rotundity, in antithesis and in comprehension, Bourke Cockran's conversation exceeded anything I have ever heard."[3] In 1910, Archie Butt, President Taft's Military Aide, described him thus: "Leonine always in his appearance, he looks like a lion ready to spring when he is speaking. His voice is like a low rumble of thunder, then has the sweetness of the lute in it."[4] William Howard Taft said simply: "I believe Cockran is the greatest orator using the English language today."[5] Nicholas Murray Butler wrote to Theodore Roosevelt, then in the White House, that it is "enough to give anyone pause" when his presidential message was "hailed with acclaim" by Bourke Cockran.[6] The youthful William Jennings Bryan, attending his first Democratic presidential nominating convention in 1884, was disillusioned by its stodginess and bossism until he heard "the exquisite beauty of Bourke Cockran's speech." It transfused his mood from dejection to exultation:

> He listened, enraptured, to a type of oratory he had never before heard, diction, a phrasing, an elegance, a passion that might have belonged to Pitt or Fox, as distinct as day and night from the stodgy pedantism of Daniel Webster and Henry Clay in which young Bryan had been steeped. Here at last was one to match Robert Ingersoll—a very magician of eloquence, swaying like a great tree caught in a whirlwind as the tumultuous current of his words beat down resistance and swelled the hearts of those who heard him. Young Bryan watched the vast audience, alternately agitated and stilled, as a field of standing barley is swept by gusts of summer wind. There was something terrible and divine in the power of the spoken word to move men as Bourke Cockran first arrested their attention and then held them enthralled.[7]

[3] Winston Churchill, *Amid These Storms*, New York: Scribner's, 1932, p. 52. Cf. McGurrin, *op. cit.*, p. 76.
[4] Archie Butt, *Taft and Roosevelt: The Intimate Letters of Archie Butt*, New York: Doubleday, Doran, 1930, II:569.
[5] McGurrin, *op. cit.*, p. 81.
[6] Henry Pringle, *Theodore Roosevelt: A Biography*, New York: Harcourt, Brace, 1931, p. 480.
[7] Hibben, *Peerless Leader, op. cit.*, p. 104. It should be noted that the criticism of the oratory of Webster and Clay as "stodgy pedantism" was Hibben's, not Bryan's. Of course it is a piece of critical nonsense.

This was "hurrah oratory" with a vengeance; and whatever we may think of the critical standard that elevated Ingersoll above Webster, it was precisely suited to the needs of "conventionitus," and it gave Bryan ideas he nurtured as he made his own way toward 1896.

Cockran's life was seldom without drama from his arrival in New York as a penniless Irish immigrant at seventeen, in 1871, until his death at sixty nine on March 1, 1923. He quickly achieved success at the bar, earning $40,000 a year from legal fees by 1887 and $100,000 and more annually after 1895. Just as quickly he rose to political prominence. As a frequent speaker in the 1880 presidential election, he attracted wide attention with his epigram: "Democracy is a faith, Republicanism is an appetite." From that time on, his life was lived amidst storms of partisan controversy. There is surely basis for the charge made against him in 1903 by John Dalzell of Pennsylvania that he "has been at different times a Greenbacker and a Gold Democrat, a Bryanite and an anti-Bryanite, a Tammanyite and an anti-Tammanyite." No doubt Dalzell went too far in adding: "His whole political course, covering a quarter of a century, has been one of flagrant inconsistency."[8] Cockran's reply was an evasive effort to shift from the defensive to the offensive: "Once in my life I was forced to change candidates to avoid changing principles. Gentlemen on the other side have always cheerfully changed principles to avoid changing candidates."[9]

It is a fact that Cockran changed candidates on several conspicuous occasions. Nevertheless, there is truth in Churchill's observation that "never during our acquaintance of twenty years did I detect any inconsistency in the general body of doctrine upon which his views were founded."[10] Cockran's mind was too commodious, his principles too deeply seated, to permit him easily to veer and shift with the successive compromises which parade as "party loyalty" in American politics. Neither is it easy to classify him as either a conservative or a liberal. His doctrines are set forth in his speeches, in which he was always readier to explain what he believed than to try to justify why he did not believe something else. He took the political risk of acting upon the Emersonian principle that "a foolish consistency is the hobgoblin of little minds."

In 1887 he was elected to Congress as a Democrat; yet his first speech in Congress was an impassioned and successful plea for the seating of a Republican whose election was contested on technical grounds—a deviation from party regularity that five years later barred him from election

[8] McGurrin, *op. cit.*, p. 253.
[9] *Ibid.*, p. 256.
[10] Churchill, *Amid These Storms, op. cit.*, p. 53.

to the Senate. In 1892, at the Chicago Convention, he unsuccessfully opposed the nomination of Grover Cleveland, on the grounds that Cleveland was not a true Democrat and had been elected in 1884 only by votes of Republican "Mugwumps." The speech was made at two o'clock in the morning, after the delegates had been in continuous session for ten hours. The heat in the hall was excessive, the delegates were shouting for adjournment, and the nomination of Cleveland was already assured. A violent thunderstorm was pouring water through holes in the roof on the New York and Michigan delegations. Tired and ill, Cockran moved heavily down the aisle and mounted the platform to confront a hostile storm of boos. He responded not with conciliation but with a challenge launched so forthrightly that the scene quickly became as still as a country church: "God forbid," he said, "that this party of ours . . . shall be surrendered into the control of those who despise and detest it, that one man may be exalted and the Democratic hosts degraded."[11] Cockran lost the fight, as he knew he would; but he won a fame that was never thereafter diminished.

In 1893 he pleaded in Congress for "the gospel of sound money"; and in 1894 he spoke against the tariff, conjuring up a future day when trade would move without barriers through all the markets of the world. "In seeking to find the freest markets for our products," he said, "we seek the welfare of the whole human race, we seek to establish a commercial system which will make this land the fountain of civilization—this people the trustees of humanity—which will make the flag of freedom in the air above us the emblem of freedom on the land beneath us— freedom in our fields, freedom in our mines, freedom on the seas, freedom through all the world, for all the children of men."[12]

Bryan and Cockran were together on the tariff question, but not on the currency issue. During the Convention of 1896 Cockran was in Rome; but he returned to renounce Bryan, to attack him on the "issue of common honesty," and to make a whirlwind campaign around the nation on behalf of William McKinley, being more effective, so Mark Hanna said, than the whole army of Republican campaigners.[13] Two years later, still an apostate, he launched an attack against "Boss" Richard Croker, Sachem of Tammany Hall, in which he told a huge audience in Carnegie Hall: "My friends, I do not use the expression of boss in a spirit of contempt. I use it respectfully and seriously . . . . His nod can make a fortune or unmake a career. Every financial interest in this

[11] McGurrin, *op. cit.*, p. 123.
[12] Marion Mills Miller, *Great Debates in American History*, New York: Current Literature Pub. Co., 1913, XII:309.
[13] McGurrin, *op. cit.*, pp. 164–165.

great city courts his favor and dreads his hostility. If today he were to declare that he needs one million dollars for political purposes, before next Friday two million dollars would be furnished . . . . The descendants of those heroes who won their freedom from a foreign oppressor will never surrender to an assault of this character. They will never consent that chains shall be riveted on their wrists while they slumber on their arms."[14] Joseph H. Choate called it "a speech that will never be forgotten by this generation."[15] Tammany's candidates won the election; but three years later, in 1901, Boss Croker resigned and sailed to Ireland to spend the rest of his days.

Still Cockran veered from side to side on the surface stream of politics, true to the deeper current of his beliefs. He joined lustily in the crusade for justice for Cuba but fought just as hard to prevent war with Spain. After that war was fought and won, he trained all his eloquence against the crescendo of American imperialism.[16] Albert J. Beveridge, who was one of Cockran's targets, was comforted to believe that "the brilliant Celt's reputation for insincerity neutralized the effect of his eloquence."[17] In a great speech at the University of Michigan, on February 4, 1899, Cockran laid down the theme that "Improvement begins where coercion ceases," and he called it "cowardly to invade the rights of the weak while respecting those of the strong." Then he explained why imperialism of the type that would make colonies of Cuba and the Philippines was vastly different from the "Manifest Destiny" by which the United States had been extended to the Pacific: "because it would divorce the American flag from the American Constitution, by sending one where the other cannot go."[18]

Another of the "shifts" charged aginst Cockran occurred in 1900. When Bryan consented to soft-pedal his free-silver demand and to wage his campaign principally on the issue of anti-imperialism, Cockran enthusiastically supported him—meanwhile being deluged by the jeers of the Republicans that he had himself in 1896 provided the principal anti-Bryan ammunition. Speaking in Boston, on the eve of the election, Cockran thundered: "We are asked to sin against the light of our own experience, to cast over our stainless success, achieved by scrupulous regard for the rights of others and indomitable defense of our own, the sinister shadow of medieval conquest. We who have been the destroyers of oppression are asked now to become its agents. We who have been

[14] *Ibid.*, p. 183.
[15] *Ibid.*, p. 186.
[16] Claude G. Bowers, *Beveridge and the Progressive Era*, New York: Houghton Mifflin, 1932, p. 131.
[17] *Ibid.*, p. 59.
[18] McGurrin, *op. cit.*, p. 196.

the builders of freedom are asked now to become the architects of tyranny."[19] Against this appeal to conscience, the imperialist orator Beveridge was retorting with his own appeal to profit: "The Philippines are ours forever. And just beyond the Philippines are China's illimitable markets."[20] During the course of the campaign, the Boer War became a related topic of controversy; and Cockran denounced it as "one of the most barbarous wars in all the dreary annals of aggression."[21]

Not all of Cockran's political shifts are defensible in terms of his basic consistency. In 1900, on May 10, in Montgomery, Alabama, as the featured speaker at the First Annual Conference of the Southern Society for Study of Race Relations in the South, Cockran argued that Negroes faced their greatest difficulties because of the fear of their political ambitions; and he advised that the fifteenth amendment, "already nullified in effect," should be repealed. He spoke, he insisted, as a friend of the Negro but with an unquestioning assumption of the Negro's racial inferiority. The aim of the Southern whites, he counseled, should not be to try to elevate the Negroes to equality, but to hold the "weaker race by the hand."[22] Booker T. Washington's reaction was to write Cockran a letter of appreciation for "the many brave things you said in your historic address." Washington's view was that "There is no reason why every Negro who is not fitted to vote should not be disfranchised. At the same time, there is no good reason why every white man who is not fitted to vote should not also be disfranchised."[23] In a somewhat similarly questionable shift, Cockran supported William Randolph Hearst in 1906 for the Governorship of New York, after having opposed him for many years. Even though Charles Evans Hughes was Hearst's opponent, Cockran's explanation for his shift was: "I must support Mr. Hearst because as a Democrat I cannot help it. If I must choose between rottenness and riot, I must choose riot."[24]

The cause that lay dearest to Cockran's heart was independence for Ireland. With his own Irish blood astir in his veins, and through his close association with many thousands of Irish Catholic Democratic voters, his principal efforts were directed to undermining "the one defense which English rule has in Ireland . . . the extraordinary capacity for misrepresentation which has enabled English statesmen to shroud this whole Irish question in mystery."[25] In speech after speech Cockran

[19] *Ibid.*, p. 210.
[20] Bowers, *op. cit.*, p. 119.
[21] McGurrin, *op. cit.*, p. 198.
[22] *Ibid.*, p. 216.
[23] Scott and Stowe, *Booker T. Washington, op. cit.*, pp. 48–49.
[24] McGurrin, *op. cit.*, p. 268.
[25] *Ibid.*, p. 225.

served as the chief American spokesman for Irish liberty: on March 4, 1896, in a great eulogy on the young martyr, Robert Emmet; in Faneuil Hall, Boston, in October, 1902; on November 26, 1905 and again on April 22, 1913, in Carnegie Hall, in New York, in praise of the Irish literary revival; on August 30, 1919, a speech to the Senate Foreign Relations Committee which Henry Cabot Lodge called "one of the greatest speeches ever delivered inside the walls of Congress"; and in 1922, in celebration of the long-heralded establishment of the Irish Free State. But perhaps the two greatest of his Irish speeches were those delivered in Boston on March 26, 1900, and in New York on May 6, 1916.

In the Boston speech he developed the principal charge the Irish levelled against the British: that theirs was rule by the aristocracy, for the aristocracy, and of the aristocracy:

> Ever since the defeat of Harold at the Battle of Hastings, the Norman has dominated England. He has disappeared from every other part of the world from which he obtained a foothold. In England alone he has always flourished and there, to this day, he rules the court and dominates the government. The history of England for eight centuries has been the struggle of the English people to revive the institutions of Edward the Confessor, the institutions of liberty and justice, against the Norman seeking to maintain the feudalism established at Hastings. Every valuable feature of English jurisprudence, every right of the subject—the Magna Carta, the petition of right, the habeas corpus, the bill of rights—have all been wrung by the English people at the point of the sword from a reluctant or hostile Norman court. The free government established by the common people has always been the object of distrust to the Norman governing class. Compelled to profess outward respect for the liberty of the subject in England, they never cease invidious efforts to overthrow constitutional freedom (in Ireland).[26]

This is no doubt bad history; but it rationalized a means by which American Irish could be both for England and against English policies. Its tone of sweet reasonableness proved powerfully persuasive, bringing many tributes, of which the telegram from Joseph Pulitzer is typical: "You never spoke with more feeling or greater power in behalf of humanity and justice."[27]

Cockran's speech in 1916, delivered after the execution by England of sixteen leaders of the Easter Week uprising, was white with anger: "The vilest murders ever committed are fresh before our eyes. The noblest Irishmen of our generation, the fairest flowers of our civiliza-

[26] *Ibid.*, p. 200.
[27] Cockran, *In The Name of Liberty, op. cit.*, p. 202.

tion, are dead, killed by the bullets of British soldiers, shot down like dogs, for asserting the immortal truths of patriotism."[28] Like Sam Adams moving swiftly to take advantage of the opportunity to propagandize the "Boston Massacre" in 1770, Cockran helped to organize the Friends of Irish Freedom, which quickly became nationwide and politically powerful, reminiscent of Adams's "Committees of Correspondence." The time was now close at hand, Cockran exultantly promised, when Ireland would be "delivered from this body of death called English rule."

Fittingly, the passing away of Bourke Cockran was as dramatic as was his career. On February 28, 1923, he celebrated his sixty ninth birthday, in excellent health and buoyant spirits. In the afternoon session of Congress he made an eloquent forty-five-minute speech, opposing a bill to lend $600,000,000 of government funds to farmers. His speech was followed by an outburst of cheering that, in opposition to the rules, was allowed to continue for three full minutes. Cockran commented to a friend that the speech had not been planned or prepared and that its presentation left him feeling particularly exhausted. He rose, then, to ask a question; but the Speaker rapped him down, saying, "The time of the gentleman from New York has expired." It had indeed. Cockran went home to a birthday party that was distinguished by excellent conversation, went wearily to bed, and died quietly of a hemmorhage of the brain.[29]

Roosevelt, Beveridge, and LaFollette: Wielders of the Big Stick

THE THREE orators who are here grouped together had much in common. All were vociferously self-assertive: loud, cockily confident, vehemently vocal. On many basic issues they fought on the same side, sometimes harmoniously. All three were undisciplinable insurgents, armed with a courage that verged on recklessness. All would be classified on most counts as "liberals," though this kind of labelling is peculiarly difficult for this particular period, when liberalism was ceasing to espouse privacy, individualism, and liberty and instead was trumpeting for increasing governmental controls and the use of publicity as weapons to promote and protect equality. All three were richly endowed with

[28] McGurrin, *op. cit.*, p. 236.
[29] *Ibid.*, p. 330.

histrionic talent and an insatiable urge for the spotlight position of upstage center. They were also men of intelligence, whose minds were wide-ranging, receptive to new ideas, hungry for facts, and fearless in plunging ahead to new and sometimes awkward conclusions. They all shared, too, a broad streak of humanitarian philanthropy that expressed itself as a genuine concern for the public weal, sympathy for the down-trodden, and a sense of personal responsibility to rectify wrongs and uphold justice.

Since they were also sturdy and articulate individualists, their differences were at least as marked as their resemblances. Theodore Roosevelt was born into a family of wealth and high social position and became a "progressive" whose predilections were conservative.[1] Albert Jeremiah Beveridge rose from poverty into prosperity with a natural liking for the rich and the well-bred.[2] Robert Marion LaFollette was born a Wisconsin farmboy with his own way to make, and remained always in manner and in temperament a "man of the people."[3] Lahman thought LaFollette had "an almost mystical belief in the sound judgment of the rank-and-file people," and concluded that "His belief in agriculture as the cornerstone of a sound democracy was Jeffersonian in its intensity."[4]

Hostettler considered LaFollette "at once a Jeffersonian and a Hamiltonian—Jeffersonian in his idealism and concepts of democracy; Hamiltonian in his practical and specific approach to political and economic problems."[5] Claude Bowers thought that Beveridge's "deep prejudice against Jefferson and his utter devotion to Hamiltonian principles were of the very texture of his being."[6] Henry Pringle, in his Pulitzer Prize-winning biography of Roosevelt agreed with Walter Lippmann's analysis that the key to Roosevelt's political career lay in "his aspiration to combine the social and political reforms initiated by Bryan and LaFollette with a Hamiltonian affection for a strong national government."[7]

[1] Noel F. Busch, *TR: The Story of Theodore Roosevelt and His Influence on Our Times*, New York: Reynal, 1963; Carleton Putnam, *Theodore Roosevelt: The Formative Years, 1858–1886*, New York: Scribner's, 1958; George Edwin Mowry, *The Era of Theodore Roosevelt, 1900–1912*, New York: Harper, 1958; and Howard Kennedy Beale, *Theodore Roosevelt and the Rise of America to World Power*, Baltimore: Johns Hopkins Press, 1956, are all new biographies that represent the "current" (i.e., post-World War II) view of Roosevelt—favorably representing his propulsion of the United States into world leadership and his preparation of the public mind for the advent in the thirties of the New Deal.
[2] Bowers, *Beveridge and the Progressive Era*, op. cit.
[3] Robert M. LaFollette, *LaFollette's Autobiography: A Personal Narrative of Political Experiences*, Madison: University of Wisconsin Press, 1913.
[4] Carroll P. Lahman, "Robert M. LaFollette," in Brigance, ed., *History and Criticism*, II:942–943.
[5] Gordon F. Hostettler, "The Political Speaking of Robert M. LaFollette," in Reid, ed., *American Public Address*, op. cit., p. 119.
[6] Bowers, op. cit., p. 421; but on p. 57 Bowers credits Beveridge with broadly Jeffersonian views.
[7] Pringle, *Roosevelt*, op. cit., p. 540.

What must be concluded is that the terms Jeffersonian and Hamiltonian, like liberalism and conservatism, were losing their old meanings and becoming ambiguous. What all three men sought (as their political views matured) was to safeguard justice for the masses within the context of a hugely expanding industrialism.

Their differences emerge more clearly in a study of their methods. All three were pragmatists in that they sought political results; they looked toward votes, and the enactment of legislation. But Roosevelt and Beveridge were content to move a step at a time, without making too much fuss. Roosevelt fastidiously called the militant reform journalists "muckrakers," who fixed their minds "only on things that were vile and debasing, on filth alone."[8] In his *Autobiography* Roosevelt confessed that "The men I knew best were the men in the clubs of social pretension and the men of cultivated taste and easy life." According to Hofstadter, when both Roosevelt and Beveridge confronted social evils, they "held their noses, made the necessary compromises, worked their way into politics, and bided their time until the social milieu gave them a chance to ride into power."[9] LaFollette was less content to win his way an inch at a time. He was suspicious of compromise. "In legislation *no bread* is often better than *half a loaf*," he declared. "I believe it is usually better to be beaten and come right back at the next session and make a fight for a thoroughgoing law than to have written on the books a weak and indefinite statute."[10] Roosevelt's reaction to LaFollette was mixed. In 1908 he denounced "the LaFollette type of fool radicalism," and in 1910 he praised LaFollette's "wise governmental action in aid of social and economic justice."[11] Beveridge's summary view of LaFollette was similarly two-pronged: "I must say that during the hard fights we made together in the Senate, I came to believe in him and in what he stands for generally; though not in all he says. Neither are his methods mine. Yet the general tendency of the man is toward righteousness."[12]

If these men were critical of one another, later critics of the progressive movement have pretty well agreed to be disappointed with what they all accomplished.[13] As one historian writes: "The disparity between its enthusiastic discussion of issues and its meager concrete results stands

[8] Speech of April 14, 1906, in Theodore Roosevelt, *Addresses and Papers*, New York: Sun Dial Classics, 1908, p. 311.
[9] Richard Hofstadter, "Theodore Roosevelt: The Conservative as Progressive," in *The American Political Tradition, op. cit.*, p. 207.
[10] LaFollette, *Autobiography, op. cit.*, p. 268.
[11] Hofstadter, "Roosevelt," *op. cit.*, p. 233.
[12] Bowers, *op. cit.*, p. 416.
[13] Cf. Herbert Agar, *The Pursuit of Happiness*, Cambridge: Harvard University Press, 1938, pp. 310–311; John Chamberlain, *Farewell to Reform*, New York: Liveright, 1932, pp. 306–324; and Russell B. Nye, *Midwestern Progressive Politics*, East Lansing: Michigan State University Press, 1951, pp. 274–278.

out as one of the striking features of the period."[14] Such criticism is, to a large degree, ex post facto. It fails to recognize the confused state of mind of the entire generation which these men represented. Rapid urbanization and industrialization had created problems no one then knew how to cope with. Two foreign wars hurled the United States out into international affairs at a time when our domestic difficulties were particularly urgent. New questions had to be formulated before right answers could be sought. Liberalism was distinctly in a transitional phase. This much, at least, Roosevelt, and Beveridge, and LaFollette understood. If their search for solutions was sometimes groping and even blind, at least they tried; and they mapped out a direction for those who followed where they led.

Simply as biography, the life-story of Theodore Roosevelt (October 27, 1858–January 6, 1919) is a fascinating library of exciting and diverse careers. Whatever kind of man was admirable, the incomparable TR is that man: the physical weakling who made himself strong; the shy boy afraid to speak who became an eloquent orator; the explorer of continents and hunter extraordinary; the scholar and thinker who so loved the realm of books that he continued to write even on his honeymoon— even while burdened with the responsibilities of the White House; the loving husband and father who was so loyal that when he decided to remarry three years after his first wife's death, he paced the floor of his study for hours, exclaiming in an agony of remorse, "I lack constancy!" "I lack constancy!"; the internationalist who in 1897 told the students of the Naval War College that "No triumph of peace is quite so great as the supreme triumph of war"—and who in 1910 won the Nobel Peace Prize; the natural leader who could not bear retreat into private life after his tenure in the presidency, yet who could say with utmost sincerity: "I am not in the least concerned as to whether I will have any place in history, and, indeed, I do not remember ever thinking about it."[15]

The phrase for which Roosevelt is perhaps best known—"Speak softly and carry a big stick, you will go far"[16]—would be a completely misleading description of his own practice. Whether dealing with the bosses of his own Republican party, with big business or labor, or with a succession of foreign governments in a succession of crises, his method was to square away in the stance of a prizefighter, to declare belligerently what he demanded, and to dare the opposition to risk a fight.

[14] Glad, *The Trumpet Soundeth, op. cit.,* p. 176.
[15] Edward Wagenknecht, *The Seven Worlds of Theodore Roosevelt,* New York: Longmans, Green, 1958.
[16] Speech of April 2, 1903, in Chicago; from Roosevelt, *Addresses and Papers, op. cit.,* p. 116.

Henry Adams, who studied him closely at first hand, and who worried much about the "effect of unlimited power on limited mind," described him best: "Roosevelt, more than any other man living within the range of notoriety, showed the singular primitive quality that belongs to ultimate matter—the quality that mediaeval theology assigned to God—he was pure act."[17] Richard Hofstadter thought him a psychologically insecure extrovert who "fled from repose and introspection with a desperate urgency that is sometimes pitiable"; and then he quoted as an example of Roosevelt's emotional instability the following exhortation to the Strenuous Life: "Get action, do things; be sane, don't fritter away your time; create, act, take a place wherever you are and be somebody; get action."[18]

Perhaps there is a kind of instability in any man of positive and incessant action. It need not be unhealthful. In Theodore Roosevelt it took the form of words used like clubs to drive his listeners to the duty he envisioned for them. He was a Puritan preacher reincarnated in political dress. His friend and comrade Owen Wister said that if he could be analyzed down into "his ultimate, central, indestructible stuff" what would be found would be not a statesman, or hunter, or historian, or naturalist—"they'd find a preacher militant."[19] In his autobiography Roosevelt declared: "I have always had a horror of words that are not translated into deeds, of speech that does not result in action—in other words, I believe . . . in preaching what can be practiced and then in practicing it."[20] When he spoke at Freeport, Illinois, honoring Lincoln's leadership in the Civil War, he phrased the same ideal even more positively: "The word was mighty. Had it not been for the word the deeds could not have taken place; but without the deeds the word would have been the idlest breath."[21] In another speech he indicated the role he always expected of his audiences: "I am not addressing weaklings, or I should not take the trouble to come here. I am addressing strong, vigorous men, who are engaged in the active hard work of life; and life to be worth living has to be a life of activity and hard work."[22]

Roosevelt did not come quickly or easily either to progressivism or to ability as a public speaker. After being educated privately at home by a tutor, then graduating from Harvard—during which time he showed

[17] The Education of Henry Adams, op. cit., pp. 417, 418.
[18] Hofstadter, "Roosevelt," op. cit., pp. 210–211.
[19] Owen Wister, Roosevelt: The Story of a Friendship, New York: Macmillan, 1930, p. 232.
[20] Quoted by Carl A. Dallinger, "Theodore Roosevelt: The Preacher Militant," in Reid, ed., American Public Address, op. cit., p. 136.
[21] Roosevelt, Addresses and Papers, op. cit., p. 147.
[22] Ibid., p. 157.

little promise and had small experience as a public speaker[23]—he won election to the New York State Assembly at the age of twenty three, and on January 24, 1882, ventured upon his first speech in that body. Isaac L. Hunt, a fellow Assemblyman, described his voice as high-pitched, his manner as rather ludicrously earnest, and said that he spoke "as if he had an impediment in his speech, sort of as if he was tongue-tied. He would often open his mouth and run out his tongue—it was hard for him to speak. But what he said was all right."[24] What he was saying in those days seems, in retrospect, somewhat short of "all right." In 1882 he voted against a bill to place a floor of $2 a day as wages for laborers; and in the following year he voted against restricting the working day to twelve hours on the grounds that such regulation was "purely socialistic." In 1885 his political views were spelled out in a speech in Brooklyn:

> Throughout the North the bulk of the honesty and intelligence of the community is to be found in the Republican ranks. If the Republicans take a false step it is usually because the politicians have tricked them into it; while if the Democrats make a good move it is almost always merely because the astute party leaders have been able for a short time to dragoon their dense-witted followers into the appearance of deference to decent public sentiment.[25]

The progression of events that led Roosevelt to become an orator who, over a period of thirty seven years on the public platform exhorted millions of people on four continents, and that shaped him into a great progressive force in politics, was marked by a series of accidents. He was frankly and avowedly a spoilsman in politics, until President Harrison appointed him a Commissioner of the U.S. Civil Service—which experience made him a lifelong fighter for civil service reforms. As New York City Police Commissioner, he outraged many by sensational dashing about and enforcement of dozens of obsolescent laws; but he learned enough about delinquency and poverty to make him a lifetime advocate of policies and laws designed to enforce economic justice. When the Spanish-American War broke out, he led his Rough Riders into a militarily impossible situation at Kettle Hill, in Cuba; but his own dramatic imagination and his camaraderie with the newsmen converted the hapless misfit into "the hero of San Juan Hill."[26] In 1900 he was nominated

[23] Richard Murphy, "Theodore Roosevelt," in Hochmuth, ed., *History and Criticism, op. cit.,* III:329–331.
[24] Pringle, *Roosevelt, op. cit.,* p. 66.
[25] *Ibid.,* p. 109.
[26] *Ibid.,* p. 194.

for the vice-presidency, against his preferences, because of a grudge-fight between the two regnant Republican bosses, Matt Quay and Mark Hanna[27]; and seven months after his inauguration to that office, the assassination of McKinley catapulted him into the White House.

Roosevelt did an increasingly large amount of speaking as Police Commissioner and then as Governor of New York and even in the relatively anonymous post of Assistant Secretary of the Navy. But it was as vice-presidential candidate that he was launched fully and finally upon the national stage. By mid-July, in that campaign, he became worried lest Bryan might win by attracting to his cause "all the lunatics, all the idiots, all the knaves, all the cowards, and all the honest people who are slow-witted." Consequently, he hurled himself into a campaign tour that matched Bryan's great effort in 1896. In a great circle route around the country he visited twenty one States, making 673 speeches in 567 towns, to a cumulative audience of some three million people.[28] When he found himself President, he soberly reassessed his own value system and concluded that "I desire to see in this country the decent men strong and the strong men decent."[29] Furthermore, he dropped his previous tendency to belittle the public and decided that "Our average fellow-citizen is a sane and healthy man, who believes in decency and has a wholesome mind."[30]

As he confronted the responsibilities of the presidency, in his first annual message to Congress on December 3, 1901, his instinct was to not rock the boat, to stabilize things as they were: "It is not true that as the rich have grown richer the poor have grown poorer," he insisted. "On the contrary, never before has the average man, the wage-worker, the farmer, the small trader, been so well off as in this country and at the present time." Great fortunes could be accumulated, he thought, "only on condition of conferring immense incidental benefits upon others." It was no time to let reformers excite the public, as the "muckrakers" were trying to do. "The captains of industry . . . have on the whole done great good for our people." The bulk of the address was then devoted to the relatively safe, but much-needed, plea for a policy of conservation of the forestlands and waterways of the nation.[31] As

---

[27] *Ibid.*, pp. 221–222. Margaret Leech, *In the Days of McKinley, op. cit.*, p. 529, portrays a wryly humorous situation in which Roosevelt went down to Washington resolutely resolved to refuse to be drafted for the nomination—only to be told to his face by the acidulous Elihu Root: "Of course not—you're not fit for it." But although the "McKinley men" did not want Roosevelt on the ticket, the bulk of the Republican leadership demanded his nomination.
[28] Pringle, *op. cit.*, p. 225. Mark Hanna thought that Roosevelt's "spread-eagle nationalism" was of particular value to the campaign. Leech, *op. cit.*, p. 557.
[29] Roosevelt, *Addresses and Papers, op. cit.*, p. 158.
[30] *Ibid.*, p. 161.
[31] *Ibid.*, pp. 7–30.

Roosevelt grew in confidence in the presidency, he did not rush to the sponsoring of reform legislation, but preached his doctrine of individual responsibility. "In the unending strife for civic betterment," he told an audience of educators in 1902, "small is the use of these people who mean well, but who mean well feebly."[32] Later that year, justifying his seizure of the Panama Canal zone and continued American rule in the Philippines, he was at once more defensive and more assertive:

> Timid people, people of scant faith and hope, and good people who are not accustomed to the roughness of the life effort—are almost sure to be disheartened and dismayed by the work and the worry, and over-much cast down by the shortcomings, actual or seeming, which in real life always accompany the first stages even of what eventually turn out to be the most brilliant victories.[33]

Then, in addresses in Boston and in Wheeling, West Virginia, still in the first year of his presidency, he finally came face to face with the new problem that political government had somehow to solve: "there came a revolution in the means of intercourse which made a change in commerce, and in all that springs from commerce, in industrial development, greater than all the changes of the preceding thousands of years."[34] The conclusion he came to was one from which there was to be no retreat: "power must be given to the national government to exercise its full supervision and regulation of these great enterprises."[35] During the seven years of his presidency, there was to be much more along this line until he came to be known as "Teddy the Trust-Buster." He also became known as an adventurer in the dangerous realm of international power politics, notably with his intervention to settle the Russo-Japanese War. But never did he state better the essence of his religio-political faith than in a paragraph of his speech to men of his own kind, the Union League Club of Philadelphia, on November 22, 1902:

> No nation as great as ours can expect to escape the penalty of greatness, for greatness does not come without trouble and labor. There are problems ahead of us at home and problems abroad, because such problems are incident to the working out of a great national career. We do not shrink from them. Scant is our patience with those who preach the gospel of craven weakness. No nation under the sun ever played a part worth playing if it feared its fate overmuch—if it did not have the courage to be great. We of America, we, the sons of a nation yet in the pride of its lusty youth, spurn the teachings of distrust, spurn the creed

[32] *Ibid.*, p. 37.
[33] *Ibid.*, pp. 62–63.
[34] *Ibid.*, pp. 68–76, 78–84.
[35] *Ibid.*, pp. 80–81.

of failure and despair. We know that the future is ours if we have in us the manhood to grasp it, and we enter the new century girding our loins for the contest before us, rejoicing in the struggle, and resolute so to bear ourselves that the nation's future shall even surpass her glorious past.[36]

This was the preachment of such a political gospel as the United States had not heard before. Its core was an exuberantly optimistic faith in the goodness of man combined with an urgent sense of public duty. The method he came reluctantly to espouse was federal regulation of the economy; but recurrently he kept returning to the theme that fundamentally was his message to America: "In the last analysis the welfare of the state depends absolutely upon whether or not the average family, the average man and woman and their children, represent the kind of citizenship fit for the foundation of a great nation."[37] This was the real Theodore Roosevelt.

The Roosevelt who is best and most vividly remembered, however, is the restlessly ambitious man who returned to the United States from a world tour as William Howard Taft was nearing the end of his first term, and who determined to try to take the presidency back for himself. In 1909 he had had a "bully time" hunting for eleven months in Africa. In 1910 he lectured his way across Europe, quarreled publicly with the Pope, was lionized by Europe's eight principal monarchs when they all met at the funeral of Edward VII, received the Nobel Peace Prize, and decided to break openly with Taft, whom he accused of timidity. At first Roosevelt encouraged LaFollette to bid for the Republican nomination, then tried to get it himself. When the party regulars proceeded systematically to renominate Taft, Roosevelt organized the "Bull Moose" Convention in Chicago, and had Beveridge prepare a keynote address on the theme: "We stand for social brotherhood as against savage individualism," and in which he launched the slogan of the Bull Moose Party: "Pass Prosperity Around."[38] Roosevelt campaigned hard, even making a speech in Milwaukee after he had been shot by a jaundiced Republican. The Electoral College result was: Roosevelt 88; Taft 8; Wilson 435. Roosevelt fled for solace on an exploratory trip up the Amazon, but returned, after war broke out in Europe, to denounce Wilson's statement that "America is too proud to fight," and to call him "the worst president by all odds since Buchanan."[39] He spent the war years in a splutter of petulance about Wil-

---

[36] *Ibid.*, p. 92.
[37] *Ibid.*, p. 238. Essentially he repeated this same message again and again—as in passages in *ibid.*, pp. 68–69, 117–118, 127, 140, 166, etc.
[38] Bowers, *Beveridge and the Progressive Era, op. cit.*, pp. 426, 428.
[39] Pringle, *Roosevelt, op. cit.*, p. 594.

son's refusal to let him lead American troops against Germany on the battlefield, and died, finally, nine years beyond his greatness, after going to bed and politely asking his valet to "Please put out the light."[40]

As a speaker Roosevelt was neither an artist nor much of an artisan. The crowds did not come so much to hear him as to see him. For his part Roosevelt paid comparatively little attention to the craft of crowd-pleasing. He himself described his approach to speechmaking in this fashion: "I did not 'divine' how the people were going to think; I simply made up my mind what they *ought* to think, and then did my best to get them to think it."[41] On another occasion he told John Hay concerning his speeches that "he knew there was not much in them except a certain sincerity and kind of commonplace morality which put him *en rapport* with the people he talked with."[42] William Allen White, in a preface to a collection of Roosevelt's speeches, struck the right note: "This is a book of sermons . . . addressed to men in the mass . . . not rhetorically interesting."[43] What gave them power was the manifest sincerity and torrential personality of the speaker—that plus the uneasy sense of the listeners that when he challenged them to rise out of their sloth and to bear bravely and well the burdens of righteous citizenship he was saying what they needed to hear.

Quite unlike Roosevelt, more like Bryan, though without the preacher-instinct they both had, Albert Jeremiah Beveridge (October 6, 1862–April 27, 1927) seemed to be *particularly* an orator. In his book *The Art of Public Speaking*, published in 1924, near the end of his life, he wrote: "Never under any circumstances or for any reward tell an audience what you, yourself, do not believe or are even indifferent about. To do so is immoral or worse—it is to be a public liar." So far, good; but this is negative advice: don't overstep permissive bounds. For Beveridge the bounds were wide. He advocated what he believed, and some of it—notably the imperialistic mission of the United States to become a dominant world power—he believed with passionate intensity. But it is difficult to avoid concluding that for him speech was less an instrument or a weapon than an accomplishment. A reporter commented disdainfully that in the Senate Beveridge's role was "the duty of dispensing flowers of rhetoric."[44] Finley Peter Dunne's *Mr. Dooley* described his first speech in the Senate as "a speech ye cud waltz to." Like

---

[40] *Ibid.*, p. 602.
[41] Murphy, "Roosevelt," in Hochmuth, ed., *History and Criticism, op. cit.*, III:321.
[42] *Ibid.*, III:328.
[43] Hostettler, "Roosevelt," in Reid, ed., *American Public Address, op. cit.*, p. 148.
[44] Charles W. Thompson, *Party Leaders of the Time*, New York: G. W. Dillingham, 1906, p. 137.

Flaubert, he polished and repolished his manuscripts, seeking endlessly for the right word, the right phrase.

All his life, from his schoolboy oratorical contests to the end of its public life, he wrote his speeches out in full, sometimes redrafting them as many as ten times, then memorized the text word for word, and even practiced the delivery and the gestures.[45] Halbert Gulley, in his analysis of Beveridge as a speaker, thought that "his arguments seemed less important to him than his balanced, rhythmical phrasing. Apparently he gave the impression that he was straining to impress with elegant language."[46] His voice was described as "curiously clear and penetrating . . . a voice of command . . . like a trumpet."[47] An unfriendly reporter described his speaking in the Senate unfairly, but with some indication of his manner: "He wags his head, shakes his fist, slaps his hand, bangs his desk and tests the capacity of his vocal organs in a way utterly to exhaust his listeners, if not himself."[48] Even during the campaign of 1900, when he was pouring out speeches in behalf of the McKinley-Roosevelt ticket and for imperialism in Cuba and the Philippines, reporters following the texts of his speeches as distributed to them found that, though he used no notes, he seldom deviated by so much as one word from the prepared manuscript.[49] To him public speaking was an art and he was its master.

As a boy in high school Beveridge got his first induction into leadership by serving as foreman for a gang of rowdy lumbermen. And he won thus early his first laurels on the platform when he gave a much-admired hour-long speech (memorized and well practiced) on temperance. In college, at DePauw University, he studied speech from early morning, when he went into the woods to practice, until late at night, when he read the world's great orations and practiced writing speeches of his own. With this foundation laid in his freshman year, he began as a sophomore to win the oratorical prizes. As a junior, his ascendancy was so firmly established that no classmates would compete against him and he was required to compete against the standard of his own best previous performance. In his senior year, after he won the Interstate Oratorical Contest, he returned after midnight to Greencastle, Indiana. As he got off the train, "artillery roared a salute, the reception committee, headed by the president of the university, showered him with congratu-

[45] Bowers, *op. cit.*, pp. 19, 159–160, 423–424.
[46] Halbert E. Gulley, "The Speaking of Albert J. Beveridge," in Reid, ed., *American Public Address, op. cit.*, p. 177.
[47] "Beveridge the Unsquelchable," *Current Literature*, XLI(Nov., 1906):512.
[48] "The Senate's Child Laborer," *The Independent*, CXVIII(May 14, 1927):503.
[49] Bowers, *op. cit.*, p. 133.

lations, and he was marched to a carriage between lines of the Cadet Corps presenting arms."[50] Hard work and natural talent had paid off.

Beveridge became a lawyer at twenty six and ten years later, in 1898, just on the eve of the Spanish-American War, he was elected to the Senate. On September 17, to a packed and wildly enthusiastic audience in Indianapolis, he delivered a paean to imperialism in which he blandly assumed that might makes right and that America should seize the occasion to extend its rule across the globe. Then he launched into a carefully written and rehearsed passage of old-fashioned oratory—which proved just as effective with his audience as had Webster's "purple passages" in his first oration at the Bunker Hill Monument:

> The march of the flag. In 1789, the flag of the Republic waved over four million souls in thirteen States and their savage territory which stretched to the Mississippi, to Canada, and to the Floridas. The timid souls of that day said that no new territory was needed, and, for an hour, they were right. But Jefferson . . . acquired that imperial territory which swept from the Mississippi to the mountains, from Texas to the British Possessions, and the march of the flag began. The infidels to the gospel of liberty raved, but the flag swept on . . . .
>
> Those who denied the power of free institutions to expand urged every argument and more that we hear today; but the people's judgment approved the command of their blood, and the march of the flag went on.
>
> The screen of land from New Orleans to Florida shut us from the Gulf, and over this and the Everglades Peninsula waved the saffron flag of Spain; Andrew Jackson seized both, the American people stood at his back, and, under Monroe, Florida came under the dominion of the Republic, and the march of the flag went on. The Cassandras prophesied every prophecy we hear today, but the march on the flag went on. Then Texas responded to the bugle call of liberty, and the march of the flag went on. And at last we waged war with Mexico, and the flag swept over the Southwest, over peerless California, past the Golden Gate to Oregon, and from ocean to ocean its folds of glory blazed.
>
> And now, obeying the same voice that Jefferson heard and obeyed, that Jackson heard and obeyed, that Monroe heard and obeyed, that Seward heard and obeyed, that Ulysses S. Grant heard and obeyed, that Benjamin Harrison heard and obeyed, William McKinley plants the flag over all the islands of the seas, outposts of commerce, citadels of national security, and the march of the flag goes on. Bryan, Bailey, Bland, and Blackburn command it to stand still, but the march of the flag goes on. And the question you will answer at the polls is whether

[50] *Ibid.*, pp. 8–26.

you will stand with this quartet of disbelief in the American people, or whether you are marching onward with the flag.[51]

He concluded, on a note of solemnly religious piety: "It is God's great purpose made manifest in the instincts of our race, whose present phase is our personal profit, but whose far-off end is the redemption of the world and the christianization of mankind."*Amen.*

This was Beveridge in the full exuberance of his youth, stirred by the fact of a foreign and popular war. Three and a half years later, preparing to address the Indiana State Convention, he told Dr. Albert Shaw, editor of the *Review of Reviews,* his most influential speech critic, "I think that the speech should not be in any sense a rabble-rouser. I think it should be a speech of reason and instruction." Then he added what he had learned, that the total effect of a speech comes not from the response of its hearers but from the reaction of the millions who may read it in print—and that what sounds well to emotionally aroused auditors may be repellant to individuals poring silently and alone over the type-columns in their morning newspaper.[52]

His next really great address was delivered in the Senate in February 1907, and lasted through four days. Beveridge was demanding a federal law to prevent exploitation of child labor and he went about it with serious carefulness. "A more remarkable and exhaustive exposé of a crime had never before been heard in the Senate Chamber," his biographer believes. "It was more than an argument—it was a treatise of history, constitutional law, and facts. Printed in a pamphlet of one hundred and seventy pages, it was sent broadcast throughout the country to awaken the public conscience and arouse the people to action."[53]

In 1908 he had a long talk with President Taft and reported: "He impressed me as almost boyish in his simplicity and truthfulness and sincerity, and I must confess to my surprise that I liked him far better than I ever did before."[54] Four years later he rather reluctantly accepted Roosevelt's urgent request to deliver the keynote address for the "Bull Moose" Convention, thus splitting the Republican Party, and sacrificing Taft's chance for re-election. "What I have done and what I stand for has forced me into this," he wrote to his wife.[55] Then he carefully prepared an address that verged back toward the style of his youth:

[51] *Ibid.,* pp. 74–76.
[52] *Ibid.,* pp. 177–178.
[53] *Ibid.,* pp. 254–255.
[54] *Ibid.,* p. 288.
[55] *Ibid.,* p. 424.

> These special interests which suck the people's substance are bipartisan. They are the invisible government behind our visible government. Democratic and Republican bosses alike are brother officers of this hidden power . . . . The root of the wrongs which hurt the people is the fact that the people's government has been taken away from them— the invisible government has usurped the people's government. Their government must be given back to the people. And so the first purpose of the Progressive Party is to make sure the rule of the people.[56]

The next two years were unhappy ones, as Beveridge fought to save and build the new Progressive Party and Roosevelt slipped back into the ranks of the regular Republicans. In bitterness of spirit Beveridge wrote: "It is not hard to lead troops who are flushed with victory; the time when leadership really is needed is in the hour of defeat."[57] His life continued, in a way more successful than ever, for during the next decade he wrote his biographies of John Marshall and Abraham Lincoln, as well as several other books. But his career on the public platform had virtually come to a close.

Among these three, Robert Marion La Follette (June 14, 1855–June 18, 1925) was the "senior in insurgency," and was probably nearly the equal of Roosevelt as a public speaker. While in college he won, like Beveridge, the Interstate Oratorical Contest. But for LaFollette, without any doubt, speech was never an end in itself but always and simply an instrument through which he sought to persuade the public to his cause. As Congressman, Governor, Senator, and, in 1924, a remarkably successful third-party nominee for the presidency, he spoke tirelessly and almost endlessly. His great forte was an earnestness that drove him into the subject matter of his speeches with a thoroughness worthy of the reports of investigating committees. Beyond doubt his speeches were a "marvelous dramatic marshalling of facts"; and always he spoke "with great vehemence—action, action, action."[58] But he seldom knew when to stop.

In 1904, he stumped Wisconsin for forty eight days, averaging more than eight hours daily on the platform; and in 1922 he repeated the feat, speaking three and four times a day for six weeks.[59] During the summers LaFollette toured the Chautauqua circuit, where his speeches typically ran to over three hours in length, while the sun boiled down through the canvas and the listeners squirmed. "One Redpath superintendent, when asked what 'Fighting Bob' talked about, said, 'About

[56] *Ibid.*, p. 427.
[57] *Ibid.*, p. 454.
[58] *Ibid.*, pp. 324, 327.
[59] Hostettler, "LaFollette," in Reid, ed., *American Public Address, op. cit.*, p. 123.

four hours. The first two hours the farmers wanted to rush to Washington and shoot Speaker Joe Cannon. After that they were for Cannon and wanted to shoot LaFollette."[60]

As a crusader for government regulation of big business, LaFollette won a significant place in American history. As a speaker he proved enormously successful on courthouse steps and at county fairs, where the listeners were free to wander away when they had had enough. Audiences in confined quarters found him overzealous in his chosen role as an educator. Lahman admirably summed up his method: "To give them understanding he gave them facts, often unadulterated figures and statistics at great length or in unbelievable quantities."[61] His speech preparation consisted largely of persistent and arduous research to assemble mountains of data. At the end of his life, he wrote: "I have no sympathy with, nor confidence in, the fellow who pretends that he gets the best results on the inspiration of the moment. He may have a flash of mental ecstasy while under the intellectual stress of speaking, but he is more likely to have a brain fluke—with a mediocre result."[62] After his death, in his desk was found a small piece of paper on which he had left his own epitaph: "I would be remembered as one who in the world's darkest hour kept a clean conscience and stood to the end for the ideas of American democracy."[63] Woodrow Wilson, who called him one of the "little band of willful men,"—for LaFollette opposed both the entrance of the United States into World War I and our participation in the League of Nations—could not have agreed. But the Senate, in 1959, selected LaFollette as one of the five outstanding members in the history of that body—along with Robert A. Taft, Daniel Webster, John C. Calhoun, and Henry Clay.

The End of an Era: Woodrow Wilson

In a practical as well as a literal sense, history refuses to be chopped up into the beginnings and endings of eras. As was evidenced in Chapter I, our very earliest Colonial beginnings were but continuations, in a new scene, of movements well launched in England; and from that time forth influences, movements, and changes have flowed into and have paralleled and have contradicted one another with a complexity that defies orderly organization. Nevertheless, the search for meaning and for

---

[60] Harrison and Detzer, *Culture Under Canvas*, op. cit., p. 120.
[61] Lahman, "LaFollette," in Brigance, ed., *History and Criticism*, op. cit., II:946.
[62] *Ibid.*, II:951.
[63] Hostettler, op. cit., p. 129.

pattern in the events of the past is a principal reason for being interested in it. Sheer dilettantism finds history interesting as anecdote and spectacle; it becomes useful and challenging when it is studied as a guide to unfolding and forward-moving mosaics of significance.

With no more than minor violation of the disparate lawlessness of the elements of continuity and discontinuity, it may be concluded that Woodrow Wilson straddled the ending of a momentous era in American life and the commencement of another. The guidemarks pointing to such a conclusion are unmistakably influential:

1. Before Wilson's second term in the presidency, the United States was a minor nation on the periphery of the world power center—no more than an adjunct of Europe, and with only incidental ties to Asia. After our successful participation in World War I, the United States emerged as the major power center on the globe: the strongest financially, militarily, and diplomatically—even if we (naturally) fumbled away much of these advantages while trying to learn how to live in accord with them.

2. Before the formative legislative program accomplished by Wilson in his first term, the United States had neither tried consistently, nor had known how, to deal with the economics of machine production. Liberal democracy was anchored firmly to the conviction that the political ideal was to protect for all the liberty to advance in self-interest insofar as this could be done without manifest injury to the rights of others. First Cleveland and then Theodore Roosevelt had toyed with the notion of enforcing controls for the common good; but it was only in the aftermath of World War I that the general ideal ceased to be liberty and became a pragmatic search for equality.

3. The invention and rapid utilization of the radio (supplemented by the telephone, and motion pictures, and the airplane, and television), the League of Nations ideal of internationalism, and the rapid expansion of globe-circling commerce—all these combined during the twenties and thirties to bind the world together into a single audience, thus changing materially the subjects, the mood, and the motivations which governed the reactions of both speakers and their audiences.

The perceptive French critic, Père Bruckberger, in his 1959 discussion of this same theme of a climactic watershed during the Wilsonian presidency, quoted an interpretation offered by Thomas Edison in 1912—which shows that the Wizard of Menlo Park was much more than a clever mechanic:

> You see, getting down to the bottom of things, this is a pretty raw civilization of ours—pretty wasteful, pretty cruel, which often comes to

the same thing, doesn't it? And in a lot of respects we Americans are the rawest and crudest of all. Our production, our factory laws, our charities, our relations between capital and labor, our distribution—all wrong, out of gear. We've stumbled along for a while, trying to run a new civilization in old ways, but we've got to start to make this world over.[1]

Barbara Tuchman, in her monumental *The Guns of August*, chronicling the outbreak of the Great War, makes it clear that when Lord Grey remarked, "The lamps are going out all over Europe; we shall not see them lit again in our lifetime," he was really speaking the requiem of a system, a scheme of life, that was going out never to return.[2]

Thomas Woodrow Wilson (December 28, 1856–February 3, 1924) was born in a Presbyterian manse in the Old South, amid old ideas; but his mind grew more than most into an understanding of the new opportunities and the new needs of an age of productivity that offered for the first time in history the hope of well-being for all. For his education he paid special tribute to his father, who, when the young Wilson was only four or five, "would not permit me to blurt things out, or stammer a half-way job of telling whatever I had to tell."[3] As a student in Davidson College, in the University of Virginia Law School, and in his work for the Ph.D. degree at Johns Hopkins, Wilson participated actively and successfully in a variety of speech activities. As a professor at Wesleyan University and then at Princeton, he organized student debates and coached the debaters. His own study included extensive reading in the great orations—among which he was fondest of those of Edmund Burke.[4] While an undergraduate at Princeton he decided what he wanted to do and the means of doing it:

> The profession I chose was politics; the profession I entered was law. I entered the one because I thought it would lead to the other. It was once the sure road; and Congress is still full of lawyers.[5]

Despite this clear vision, he soon rejected "the scheming and haggling" practice of law and turned instead to an academic career. As a university professor, he wrote and published six books dealing with government

---

[1] R. L. Bruckberger, *Image of America*, op. cit., p. 179.
[2] Barbara Tuchman, *The Guns of August*, New York: Macmillan, 1962; especially Chapters 1–9.
[3] Ida Tarbell, "A Talk with the President of the United States," *Colliers*, 58(Oct. 28, 1916):5.
[4] His preparation for public speaking is traced by Dayton David McKean, "Woodrow Wilson," in Brigance, ed., *History and Criticism*, op. cit., II:968–974.
[5] Richard Hofstadter, "Woodrow Wilson: The Conservative as Liberal," in *The American Political Tradition*, op. cit., p. 264.

and rose steadily through the ranks to the presidency of Princeton University. Then occurred the unlikely accident: the political bosses of New Jersey needed a liberal and "clean" candidate to save their party from defeat, and in 1910 Wilson became the Democratic Governor of the State. His record and manifest appeal to the voters led him to success in the Baltimore Convention of 1912, in which he emerged as the Democratic nominee, and then, aided by Roosevelt's splitting of the Republican Party, to election that fall as President.

As a political thinker and as the chief executive of the nation, Wilson had to find his own way through the tangled underbrush of the changing concepts of the relations between individual and government. Like Bryan and Roosevelt he brought to politics the crusading faith of religion; and like them he felt that the salvation of society must come through "the insurgence of individuals."[6] With such a conviction, he could scarcely help sounding like a Jeffersonian: "What do we stand for here tonight and what shall we stand for as long as we live? We stand for setting the Government of this country free and the business of this country free."[7]

But he was also a professor, a theorist, a student. He was accustomed to analyze facts and to accept whatever conclusion they demanded. When he made his feelings submit to the mastery of his mind, he arrived at conclusions that were in form more Hamiltonian: "When I think over what we are engaged in doing in the field of politics, I conceive it this way, men who are behind any interest always unite in organization, and the danger in every country is that these special interests will be the only things organized, and that the common interest will be unorganized against them. *The business of government is to organize the common interest against the special interests.*"[8] He came, then, to accept the need for centralized governmental power (Hamilton's method) to be used to enhance the welfare of the masses of the people (Jefferson's goal). This became the essence of the "new liberalism," which was to come into full flowering under Franklin D. Roosevelt's "New Deal."

It was not easy for Wilson to develop the eloquence and persuasive appeal demanded of a leader who must bring the public to a new understanding and win its support. Much as he had practiced speaking as a child, under his father's tutelage, and strong as was his faith in oratory and debate, which had led him to organize the college students into discussion clubs and to spend his free time in teaching them the arts and

---

[6] *Ibid.*, p. 250.
[7] *Ibid.*, p. 254.
[8] *Ibid.*, p. 255.

skills of rhetoric, Wilson's personality, except in his own family, was aloof, withdrawn, and solitary. "He was utterly deficient in gregarious instinct," says one biographer.[9] "He gave the impression by his brusqueness that he was conceited, arrogant, impatient; that he knew it all, and desired no information, or advice," wrote another.[10] During Wilson's college days he himself concluded that "I am naturally extremely reserved."[11] When he first entered politics it was at the top—as candidate for the Governorship and then Governor of a rich and populous State. He suffered from the belief that he was "too much a professor and doctrinaire; that he was lacking in good-fellowship and companionship; that . . . there was a coldness and an austerity about him."[12] Ray Stannard Baker, his principal biographer, concluded that during this early period of his political life, "If the crowd was with him, well and good; if it was not, he would stand alone."[13]

Much of Wilson's fifty four years of preparation for the presidency consisted of a deliberate and systematic effort to attain to "the skill and art of the orator" as John Stuart Mill defined it—that "everything important to his purpose was said at the exact moment when he had brought the minds of his audience into the state most fitted to receive it."[14] So great was Wilson's success that by the time of his first inaugural it was said of him that "not since Lincoln has there been a president so wonderfully gifted in the art of expression."[15] An unfriendly biographer, fearing Wilson's leadership in his latter years, exclaimed, "He was hypnotizing the world!"[16] Coming right to the point of Mill's definition of oratory, Baker thought that the "essence of Wilson's genius" was that he acquired a "peculiar sense of direct contact with his hearers."[17] An unidentified observer exclaimed, "He was the only orator I ever heard who could be confidential with a crowd."[18] So it came to be that by the end of his life, "The President was like a great organist playing upon the heart emotions of the thousands of people who were held spell-bound by what he said."[19]

[9] James Kerney, The Political Education of Woodrow Wilson, New York: Century, 1926, p. 452.
[10] William Allen White, Woodrow Wilson, Bsoton: Houghton Mifflin, 1924, p. 289.
[11] Ray Stannard Baker, Woodrow Wilson: Life and Letters, Garden City: Doubleday, 1924, Eight Vols., I:243.
[12] Joseph Tumulty, Woodrow Wilson as I Know Him, New York: Doubleday, Page, Literary Digest edition, 1922, p. 74.
[13] Baker, op. cit., I:107.
[14] John Stuart Mill, Autobiography, London: Longmans, Green, Reader, and Dyer, 1874, pp. 20–21.
[15] Cleveland Plain Dealer, March 5, 1913.
[16] White, op. cit., p. 346.
[17] Baker, op. cit., III:79.
[18] Ibid., III:102.
[19] Tumulty, op. cit., p. 449.

Woodrow Wilson is, then, a peculiarly appropriate man with whom to close this study of the influence of oratory in American history. His experience demonstrates vividly that the ability to speak exceedingly well may be achieved even by one whose temperament is not natively suited to it. Further, although he was not attracted by the platform or by the magnetism of gregariousness, he nevertheless seriously set about mastering the art and the skill of eloquence because he needed it in order to succeed in the great task of governing and leading the nation. Through his experience there come into sharper focus the experiences of the great bulk of the orators who preceded him.

The essential fact about Wilson as an orator is that his eloquence was not achieved accidentally. Reserved, aloof, and introverted by nature, he sought to remake himself into what he felt he should become. As a child, under his father's guidance, he studied Daniel Webster's orations. He converted a baseball team into a debating society. He read Edmund Burke so thoroughly that he thought that all his life he "must often unconsiously have been quoting" from him. He dated his "intellectual awakening" from his happening to come upon an article on "The Orator" in his college days—and he at once began telling his college mates that the study of oratory would do them more good than anything else. He went out into the woods around Princeton to practice declaiming; and he joined the Whig Society to get practice before an audience. He founded a new debating society with the objective "that we would drill ourselves in all the arts of persuasion, but especially in oratory." His first published articles were on orators and oratory. When he became a professor of political science, he voluntarily added the onerous duties of debate coaching to his teaching. Through such deliberate and continuous effort, he developed "an absolute joy in facing and conquering a hostile audience . . . or in thawing out a cold one"; and he numbered himself among the "men who enjoy speaking as an intellectual exercise." To his fiancée he explained, "I enjoy it because it sets my mind—all my faculties—aglow; and I suppose that this very excitement gives my manner an appearance of confidence and self-command which arrests the attention. However that may be, I *feel* a sort of transformation—and it's hard to go to sleep afterwards."[20]

Wilson was the intellectual in politics, the most highly educated man ever elected to the presidency; yet he clung always to the faith that it is sympathy which binds men together and the tides of love and hate which impel their choices between good and evil. In one of his earliest writings, an essay on William Pitt, the Earl of Chatham, he declared

---

[20] Baker, *op. cit.*, I:187 and *passim*, particularly in Volume I. Cf. also, Robert T. Oliver, "Wilson's Rapport with His Audience," *Quarterly Journal of Speech*, XXVII(Feb., 1941):79–90.

that "Passion is the pith of eloquence." And in one of his mature and most thoughtful statements, his lecture on "The American College," he said: "We speak of this as an age in which mind is monarch, but I take it for granted that, if that is true, mind is one of those modern monarchs who reign but do not govern. As a matter of fact, the world is governed in every generation by a great House of Commons made up of the passions; and we can only be careful to see to it that the handsome passions are in the majority."[21] This was the conviction out of which he could say, as he led the United States into the most titanic struggle the world had then known: "I have heard it said that it required courage to stand fast for the right. As I conceive it, it would require courage to do anything else. It would require courage to turn away from the shining path and plunge again into the darkness. Do you suppose it requires courage when you have once seen the light to follow it?"[22]

Far from writing out his speeches, he was casual to the point of carelessness in preparing them. One of his most widely read speeches is that on "The Bible and Progress," which he delivered in Denver on May 7, 1911. It was virtually impromptu. Wilson had agreed to make "a little address on the Bible" when he came to Denver, by invitation of a ministerial friend. He thought the occasion would be like an informal evening prayer meeting and that no preparation would be needed. When he got off the train in Denver he was amazed to be met by a delegation of fifty leading churchmen and to be informed that his address was scheduled for the city auditorium, with all the churches in the city combining to hear him. He tried to find some time for bringing his ideas together, "since the subject was wholly outside of the field with which he was then chiefly concerned." But he had "only a moment" to himself before he stepped out on the platform to be greeted by twelve thousand people. Fortunately, there was some delay in finding a stenographer capable of taking down his speech, and during this interval the Governor made a lengthy speech of introduction while Wilson busied himself in organizing his thoughts. On a more momentous occasion, when he was under heavy public attack for having sent American soldiers into Mexico in 1916, and when he was to deliver a speech over the bodies of sailors who had been killed at Vera Cruz, in which he must seek to divert criticism from his policy and convert jingoism into patriotic wisdom, he "had not prepared anything" when he alighted from the train in New York, and had to decide what to say while riding to the Navy

[21] James Milton O'Neill, *Modern Short Speeches*, New York: Century, 1923, p. 202.
[22] Baker, *op. cit.*, III:148.

Yard.[23] Of his campaign speeches in 1916 his secretary asserts: "They were delivered without much preparation and were purely extemporaneous in character."[24] Even as he started across the country in 1919 to make the climactic fight of his career for the League of Nations, he confessed, "I am scheduled between now and the 28th of September to make in the neighborhood of a hundred speeches"—but "I have not had a single minute to prepare."[25]

In these incidents are revealed still another cardinal respect in which the history of American oratory was in Wilson's time approaching a new phase: the time was near when the President (and other political leaders as well) no longer could manage the multifarious duties that were intensified as government extended its sway into more and more aspects of private life, and still have time for the preparation of their own speeches. The new age of the ghost-writer was coming in.[26] The speaker henceforth was to be less the originator and the architect of policies and more their expositor and defender. Skill in speech would be no less important in the new day; but it would be skill of a somewhat different kind.

What Wilson talked about principally, aside from the role of government in regulating industry, business, commerce, and the problems of the people related to them, was the great issue of war and peace. He ended his first term in the White House and sought his second on the theme: "He kept us out of war." And even though he had scarcely taken the oath for his second term before he was asking the Congress to declare that war existed, nevertheless the overwhelming crusading mission he envisioned for himself was to lift the curse of warfare from the back of humanity while yet safeguarding freedom and justice. The expedition of 1917–18 was to be the "war to end war" not negatively by

---

[23] *The Intimate Papers of Colonel House*, ed. Charles Seymour, Boston: Houghton Mifflin, 1926, I:125. Apropos of Wilson's unfortunate use of the phrase, "too proud to fight," in Philadelphia, in May, 1916, Colonel House noted that "It was a fatal habit with the President, who vitiated the effect of his most important utterances, on at least four occasions, by the use of phrases subject to misinterpretation." *Ibid.*, II:299.
[24] Tumulty, *op. cit.*, p. 216.
[25] *Ibid.*, p. 430.
[26] Ernest G. Bormann, "Ethics of Ghost-written Speeches," *Quarterly Journal of Speech*, XLVII (Oct., 1961):262, deprecates the practice of ghost-writing, and it is defended by Robert T. Oliver, "Syngman Rhee: A Case Study in Transnational Oratory," *Quarterly Journal of Speech*, XLVIII(April, 1962): 125–127. The problems of ghost-writing are discussed in a series of articles in *Today's Speech*, by Walter Stelkovis, "Ghost-Writing: Ancient and Honorable," II(Jan., 1954):17–19; W. Norwood Brigance, "Ghostwriting before Franklin D. Roosevelt and the Radio," IV(Sept., 1956):10–12; Robert F. Ray, "Ghostwriting in Presidential Campaigns," *ibid.*, pp. 13–15; and Donald K. Smith, "The Speech-Writing Team in a State Political Campaign," *ibid.*, pp. 16–19.

rejecting the pains and dangers of conflict, but constructively by "making the world safe for democracy." In the effort to do this Wilson conjured up a dream of "a parliament of man, a federation of the world," which could bring law to govern the unregulated relations of sovereign nations. This was the movement that propelled him and his nation out onto the world stage, where the protagonists were Clemenceau, and Lloyd George and V. I. Lenin, and then in turn Winston Churchill, and Benito Mussolini, and Adolf Hitler, and Mahatma Gandhi, and Franklin D. Roosevelt, and Syngman Rhee, and Jawaharlal Nehru, and Charles de Gaulle, and Nikita Khrushchev—and others still, from Latin America, and Africa, and from countries and from languages of which Wilson's countrymen had never heard.

In the new age that was dawning there ceased to be an American oratory, or a British or French or Russian or German or Chinese arena of closed controversy. There opened instead a forum of the world, where the voices came to speak in accents of the Orient and Africa as well as of Europe and America, and where no leader could any longer speak of the problems of his own people without considering how they fitted into the fabric of the Great Society that spreads across all continents and among all seas.[27] History flows on, unpatterned, and sometimes as repetitious in details as a phonograph record with a broken groove. But changes also come to pass. And the words men speak, and the way in which they speak them, come to be something different.

Woodrow Wilson marked the transition from the old to the new. He was part of the one. But his greatest significance lies in the fact that he was also a guide and a prophet who helped to lead humanity toward if not yet into the other. His great vision was the same as that of America's first great universal political philospher, Benjamin Franklin, who concluded his life with a prayer:

> God grant, that not only the Love of Liberty, but a thorough Knowledge of the Rights of Man, may pervade all the Nations of the Earth, so that a Philosopher may set his Foot anywhere on its Surface, and say, "This is my Country."[28]

Many critics have derided Wilson for his impracticality, for his failure to come to terms with the Republicans in the Congress, for his visionary dream of a world to be remade into one great democracy. But the faith which motivated his life had been enshrined as an American ideal in

[27] Robert T. Oliver, *Culture and Communication: The Problem of Penetrating National and Cultural Boundaries*, Springfield, Ill.: Charles C. Thomas, 1962.
[28] Benjamin Franklin to David Hartley, December 4, 1889, quoted by Carl Van Doren, *The Great Rehearsal*, New York: Viking, 1948.

words of Abraham Lincoln, spoken in his first inaugural: "Why should there not be a patient confidence in the ultimate justice of the people? Is there any better or equal hope in the world?" If the diverse and sometimes crude strands of American oratory, in all its history, are bound together by any unifying golden thread, this is it.

BIBLIOGRAPHY

Guides to Methodology 📖

Bower Aly, "History of American Public Address as a Research Field," *Quarterly Journal of Speech,** 29(Oct., 1943):308–314.

———, "Rhetorical Theory for a History of Public Speaking in the United States," *Papers in Rhetoric*, ed., Donald C. Bryant, St. Louis: Printed by Subscription, 1940, pp. 34–38.

J. Jeffrey Auer, *Introduction to Research in Speech*, New York: Harper, 1959.

A. Craig Baird, "Opportunities for Research in State and Sectional Public Speaking," QJS, 29(Oct., 1943):304–308.

——— and Lester Thonssen, "Methodology in the Criticism of Public Address," QJS, 33(April, 1947):134–138.

Jacques Barzun and H. F. Graff, *The Modern Researcher*, New York: Harcourt, Brace, 1957.

Barnet Baskerville, "Principal Themes of Nineteenth Century Criticism of Oratory," *Speech Monographs,*† 19(1952):11–26.

———, "The Dramatic Criticism of Oratory," QJS, 45(Feb., 1959):39–45.

———, "The Place of Oratory in American Literature," QJS, 39(Dec., 1953):459–464.

Waldo Braden, "The Concept of Southern Oratory: A Selected Bibliography," *Southern Speech Journal*, XXIX (Winter, 1963):141–145.

———, "The Emergence of the Concept of Southern Oratory," *Southern Speech Journal*, 26(Spring, 1961):173–183.

W. Norwood Brigance, "The Twenty-Eight Foremost American Orators," QJS, 24(Oct., 1938):376–380.

———, "Whither Research?" QJS, 19(Nov., 1933):552–561.

Oscar G. Brockett, Samuel L. Becker, and Donald C. Bryant, *A Bibliographical Guide to Research in Speech and Dramatic Art*, New York: Scott, Foresman, 1963.

Donald C. Bryant, "Aspects of the Rhetorical Tradition," QJS, 36(April, Oct., 1950):169–176 and 326–332.

———, "Scope and Method in Rhetorical Scholarship," QJS, 23(April, 1937):182–188.

———, ed., *The Rhetorical Idiom*, Ithaca, N.Y.: Cornell University Press, 1958.

Albert J. Croft, "The Functions of Rhetorical Criticism," QJS, 42(Oct., 1956):283–291.

Dallas C. Dickey, "Southern Oratory: A Field for Research," QJS, 33 (Dec., 1947):458–463.

* *Quarterly Journal of Speech*, hereafter identified as QJS.
† *Speech Monographs*, hereafter identified as SM.

———, "Were They Ephemeral and Florid?" QJS, 32(Feb., 1946):16–21.

———, "What Directions Should Future Research in American Public Address Take?" QJS, 29(Oct., 1943):300–304.

CLYDE W. Dow, ed., *An Introduction to Graduate Study in Speech and Theatre*, East Lansing: Michigan State University Press, 1961.

HENRY LEE EWBANK, "Four Approaches to the Study of Speech Style," QJS, 19(Nov., 1931):458–465.

DANIEL FOGARTY, *Roots for a New Rhetoric*, New York: Teachers College, Columbia University, 1959.

PIETER GEYL, *Debates with Historians*, New York: Meridian Books, 1958.

LELAND M. GRIFFIN, "The Rhetoric of Historical Movements," QJS, 38 (April, 1952):184–188.

G. M. A. GRUBE, "Rhetoric and Literary Criticism," QJS, 42(Dec., 1956) 339–344.

MARIE HOCHMUTH, "The Criticism of Rhetoric," in *History and Criticism of American Public Address*, ed. M. K. Hochmuth, New York: Longmans, Green, 1955, III:1–23.

VIRGINIA HOLLAND, "Rhetorical Criticism: A Burkean Method," QJS, 39 (Dec., 1953):459–464.

RAYMOND F. HOWE, ed., *Studies of Rhetoric and Rhetoricians*, Ithaca, N.Y.: Cornell University Press, 1961.

WILLIAM C. LANG, "Public Address as a Force in History," QJS, 37(Feb., 1951): 31–34.

IRVING LEE, "Four Ways of Looking at a Speech," QJS, 28(April, 1942): 148–156.

FREDERICK GEORGE MARCHAM, "History and Speech: Collaborative Studies, Present and Future," QJS, 35(Oct., 1949):284–288.

RICHARD MURPHY, "The Speech as a Literary Genre," QJS, 44(April, 1958):117–127.

MARIE HOCHMUTH NICHOLS, *Rhetoric and Criticism*, Baton Rouge: Louisiana State University Press, 1963.

HELEN F. NORTH, "Rhetoric and Historiography," QJS, 42(Oct., 1956): 234–242.

JOSEPH F. O'BRIEN, "A Re-Examination of State and Local Oratory as a Field for Study," QJS, 37(Feb., 1951):71–76.

ROBERT T. OLIVER, "A Rhetorician's Criticism of Historiography," *Eastern Public Speaking Conference, 1940*, ed., Harold F. Harding, et al., New York: H. W. Wilson, 1940, pp. 161–172.

———, *Culture and Communication*, Springfield, Ill.: Charles C. Thomas, 1962.

———, "Ethics and Efficiency in Persuasion," *Education for World Leadership*, Evanston, Ill.: National School Boards Assoc., 1960, pp. 382–388.

———, *The Psychology of Persuasive Speech*, New York: McKay, 1942, rev., 1957.

CHARLES PERELMAN, *The Idea of Justice and the Problem of Argument*, Trans., John Petrie, New York: Humanities Press, 1963.

RONALD F. REID, "The Boyleston Professorship of Rhetoric and Oratory, 1806–1904: A Case Study in Changing Concepts of Rhetoric and Pedagogy," QJS, 45(Oct., 1959):239–257.

LESTER THONSSEN and A. CRAIG BAIRD, *Speech Criticism*, New York: Ronald Press, 1948.

KARL R. WALLACE, ed., *History of Speech Education in America*, New York: Appleton-Century-Crofts, 1954.

OTIS M. WALTER, "The Teaching of Speech as a Force in Western Culture," *Speech Teacher*, XI(Jan., 1962):1–9.

RICHARD WEAVER, *The Ethics of Rhetoric*, Chicago: Regnery, 1953.

HERBERT WICHELNS, "The Literary Criticism of Oratory," reprinted in *The Rhetorical Idiom*, ed. D. C. Bryant, Ithaca, N.Y.: Cornell University Press, 1958, pp. 5–42.

EARL W. WILEY, "State History and Rhetorical Research," QJS, 36(Oct., 1950):514–519.

ERNEST J. WRAGE, "Public Address: A Study in Social and Intellectual History," QJS, 33(Dec., 1947):451–457.

General Collections and Commentaries

American Oratory, compiled by a Member of the Philadelphia Bar, Philadelphia: E. C. Biddle, 1852.

CLEVELAND AMORY, "Free Speech: Lecture on Lecturing," *New York Times Magazine*, Jan. 31, 1960, p. 22.

J. JEFFERY AUER, ed., *Anti-Slavery and Disunion, 1858–1861: Studies in the Rhetoric of Compromise and Conflict*, New York: Harper and Row, 1963.

A. CRAIG BAIRD, ed., *American Public Address, 1740–1952*, New York: McGraw-Hill, 1956.

ALICE BALDWIN, *The New England Clergy and the American Revolution*, Durham, N.C.: Duke University Press, 1928.

GILBERT HOBBS BARNES, *The Antislavery Impulse (1830–1844)*, New York: Appleton-Century, 1933.

[THOMAS HART BENTON] *Thirty Years' View . . . From 1820 to 1850*, Two Vols., New York: Appleton, 1880.

JAMES G. BLAINE, *Twenty Years of Congress*, Two Vols., Norwich, Conn.: Henry Bill Pub. Co., 1884–1886.

CLAUDE G. BOWERS, *The Tragic Era: The Revolution After Lincoln*, New York: Blue Ribbon Books, 1929.

WALDO BRADEN, "The Lecture Movement: 1840–1860," QJS, 34(April, 1948):206–212.

GAMALIEL BRADFORD, *As God Made Them*, Boston: Houghton Mifflin, 1929.

———, *Damaged Souls*, Boston: Houghton Mifflin, 1923.

CARL G. BRANDT and EDWARD M. SHAFFER, JR., *Selected American Speeches on Basic Issues (1850–1950)*, Boston: Houghton Mifflin, 1960.

DAVID J. BREWER, ed., *The World's Best Orations*, Ten Vols., Chicago: Kaiser, 1923.

W. NORWOOD BRIGANCE, ed., *Classified Speech Models*, New York: Crofts, 1928.

————, *History and Criticism of American Public Address*, Two Vols., New York: McGraw-Hill, 1943.

R. L. BRUCKBERGER, *The Image of America*, New York: Viking, 1959.

WILLIAM JENNINGS BRYAN, ed., *The World's Famous Orations*, Ten Vols., New York: Funk and Wagnalls, 1906.

JAMES BRYCE, "American Oratory," in *The American Commonwealth*, New York: Macmillan, 1888, II:650–659.

CONSTANCE BUELL BURNETT, *Five for Freedom*, New York: Abelard, 1953.

WILLIAM VINCENT BYARS, *The Handbook of Oratory*, St. Louis: Kaiser, 1901.

HARRY CAPLAN and HENRY H. KING, "Pulpit Eloquence: A List of Doctrinal and Historical Studies in English," SM, 22(No. 4, 1955):1–159.

GLENN R. CAPP, *Famous Speeches in American History*, Indianapolis: Bobbs-Merrill, 1963.

S. C. CARPENTER, ed., *Select American Speeches*, Philadelphia: Campbell, 1815.

W. J. CASH, *The Mind of the South*, New York: Knopf, 1941.

CARRIE CHAPMAN CATT and NETTIE ROGERS SHULER, *Woman Suffrage and Politics*, New York: Scribner's, 1923.

JOHN VANCE CHENEY, ed., *Memorable American Speeches*, Chicago: Donnelley, 1907.

GEORGE FABER CLARK, *History of the Temperance Reform in Massachusetts*, Boston: Clarke and Carruth, 1888.

GLENN CLARK, ed., *The World's Greatest Debate*, St. Paul, Minn.: Macalester Park Pub. Co., 1940.

DAVID LEE COLVIN, *Prohibition in the United States*, New York: Doran, 1926.

HENRY STEELE COMMAGER, ed., *America in Perspective*, New York: Random House, 1947.

————, ed., *Documents of American History*, Two Vols. in One, New York: Crofts, 1946.

————, *The American Mind . . . Since the 1880's*, New Haven: Yale University Press, 1950.

W. H. DANIELS, *The Temperance Reform and Its Great Reformers*, New York: Nelson and Phillips, 1878.

CHAUNCEY M. DEPEW, *My Memories of Eighty Years*, New York: Scribner's, 1924.

————, ed., *The Library of Oratory*, Fifteen Vols., New York: A. L. Fowle, 1902.

PHILIP F. DETWEILER, "Congressional Debate on Slavery and the Declaration of Independence, 1819–21," *American Historical Review*, 63(April, 1958): 598–616.

DAVID MILLER DEWITT, *The Impeachment and Trial of Andrew Johnson*, New York: Macmillan, 1889.

ALICE DONALDSON, "Women Emerge as Political Speakers," SM, 18(March, 1951): 54–61.

TIMOTHY DWIGHT, et al., eds., *Masterpieces of Oratory*, New York: Colonial Press, Two Vols., 1900.

OLIVER DYER, *Great Senators of the United States*, New York: R. Bonner, 1889.

CLEMENT EATON, *Freedom of Thought in the Old South*, Durham, N. C.: Duke University Press, 1940.

JONATHAN ELIOT, ed., *The Debates in the Several State Conventions on the Adoption of the Federal Constitution*, Washington, D.C., 1854, and Philadelphia: Lippincott, 1836–1845.

MAX FARRAND, ed., *The Records of the Federal Convention of 1787*, New Haven: Yale University Press, 1911.

HENRY C. FISH, ed., *Pulpit Eloquence*, New York: M. W. Dodd, 1856.

J. T. GRAVES, ed., *Eloquent Sons of the South*, Two Vols., Boston: Chaple, 1909.

GILES W. GRAY, *Index to the Quarterly Journal of Speech*, Dubuque, Iowa: W. C. Brown, 1956.

RUFUS WILMOT GRISWOLD, *Prose Writers of America*, Philadelphia: Porter and Coates, 1870.

ROBERT G. GUNDERSON, *Old Gentleman's Convention: The Washington Peace Conference of 1861*, Madison: University of Wisconsin Press, 1961.

WARREN GUTHRIE, "The Development of Rhetorical Theory in America, 1635–1850," SM, 15(No. 1, 1948):61–71; and 16(Aug., 1949):98–113.

SAMUEL B. HARDING, *Select Orations*, New York: Macmillan, 1908.

A. M. HARRIS, *Selected Orations*, Nashville, Tenn.: Cokesbury Press, 1924.

HARRY P. HARRISON, as told to Karl Detzer, *Culture Under Canvas: The Story of Tent Chautauqua*, New York: Hastings House, 1958.

GEORGE H. HAYNES, *The Senate of the United States*, Two Vols., Boston: Houghton Mifflin, 1938.

BURTON J. HENDRICK, *Bulwark of the Republic: A Biography of the Constitution*, Boston: Little, Brown, 1937.

————, *Statesmen of the Lost Cause: Jefferson Davis and His Cabinet*, New York: Literary Guild, 1939.

FRANCIS HIGGINSON, *American Orators and Oratory*, Cleveland: Imperial Press, 1901.

MARIE K. HOCHMUTH, *History and Criticism of American Public Address*, Vol. III, New York: Longmans, Green, 1955.

RICHARD HOFSTADTER, ed., *Great Issues in American History*, Two Vols., New York: Vintage Books, 1958.

————, *The American Political Tradition*, New York: Vintage Books, 1948.

ROY FRED HUDSON, "Rhetorical Invention in Colonial New England," SM, 25(Aug., 1958):215–221.

GAILLARD HUNT and JAMES B. SCOTT, eds., *The Debates in the Federal Convention of 1787 which Framed the Constitution of the United States of America*, New York: Oxford University Press, 1920.

Inaugural Addresses of the Presidents of the United States from George Washington 1789 . . ., Washington, D.C.: Gov't. Printing Office, 1961.

INEZ HAYNES IRWIN, *Angels and Amazons: A Hundred Years of American Women*, Garden City: Doubleday, Doran, 1934.

ALLAN JOHNSON and DUMAS MALONE, eds. *Dictionary of American Biography*, Twenty Two Vols., New York: Scribner's, 1928–1958.

GERALD JOHNSON, *America's Silver Age: The Statecraft of Clay, Webster, Calhoun*, New York: Harper, 1939.

ALEXANDER JOHNSTON and JAMES ALBERT WOODBURN, eds., *American Eloquence*, Four Vols., New York: Putnam's, 1896.

EDGAR DEWITT JONES, *Lords of Speech*, New York: Willett, Clark, 1937.

MATTHEW JOSEPHSON, *The Politicos: 1865–1896*, New York: Harcourt, Brace, 1938.

JOHN F. KENNEDY, *Profiles in Courage*, New York: Harper, 1956.

HARRY P. KERR, "The Election Sermon: Primer for Revolutionaries," SM, 29(March, 1962):13–22.

———, "Politics and Religion in Colonial Fast and Thanksgiving Sermons, 1763–1783," QJS, 46(Dec., 1960):372–382.

FRANKLIN H. KNOWER, "Graduate Theses in the Field of Speech," SM, annually since 1935.

———, *Table of Contents of QJS, SM, and ST,** published annually by Speech Association of America.

LAWRENCE LADER, *The Bold Brahmins: New England's War Against Slavery* (1831–1863), New York: Dutton, 1961.

MELVILLE D. LANDON, *Kings of the Platform and Pulpit*, New York: Werner, 1900.

GUY CHARLETON LEE, ed., *The World's Orators*, Ten Vols., New York: Putnam's, 1900.

MAX LERNER, *America as a Civilization*, New York: Simon and Schuster, 1957.

JAMES S. LORING, *The Hundred Boston Orators*, Boston: Jowett, 1853.

REINHARD H. LUTHIN, "Some Demagogues in American History," *American Historical Review*, 57(Oct., 1951):21–46.

CLARENCE E. MACARTNEY, ed., *Great Sermons of the World*, Boston: Stratford, 1926.

WILLIAM MACLAY, *Sketches of Debate in the First Senate of the United States*, ed., George W. Harris, Harrisburg, Pa. : Lane S. Hart, 1880.

ALEXANDER K. MCCLURE and BYRON ANDREWS, eds., *Famous American Statesmen and Orators*, Six Vols., New York: F. F. Lovell, 1902.

FRANCIS MCCURDY, "Courtroom Oratory of the Pioneer Period," *Missouri Historical Review*, 56(Oct., 1961):1–12.

NEIL MACNEIL, *Forge of Democracy: The House of Representatives*, New York: McKay, 1963.

E. L. MAGOON, *Orators of the Revolution*, Cincinnati: Baker and Scribner, 1848.

HOWARD H. MARTIN, "The Fourth of July Oration," QJS, 44(Dec., 1958): 393–401.

ROBERT CARL MARTIN, "The Early Lyceum: 1826–1845," Unpublished Ph.D. thesis, Northwestern University, 1953.

WILLIAM MATTHEWS, *Oratory and Orators*, Chicago: Griggs, 1879.

JOHN C. MILLER, "The American Mind: Religion," in *Origins of the American Revolution*, Boston: Little, Brown, 1943, pp. 186–197 and passim.

MARION M. MILLER, ed., *Great Debates in American History*, Fourteen Vols., New York: Current Literature Pub. Co., 1913.

MELVIN H. MILLER, "Chautauqua and the Wisconsin Idea," *Transactions of the Wisconsin Academy*, 52 (1963): 159–168.

FRANK MOORE, ed., *American Eloquence*, Two Vols., New York: Appleton, 1857.

———, ed., *The Rebellion Record*, Eleven Vols., New York: Putnam, 1864.

* *Speech Teacher*, quarterly publication by Speech Association of America.

HEZEKIAH NILES, *Principles and Acts of the American Revolution*, Baltimore: W. O. Niles, 1822.

LILLIAN O'CONNOR, *Pioneer Women Orators*, New York: Columbia University Press, 1954.

JAMES MILTON O'NEILL, *Classified Models of Speech Composition*, New York: Century, 1921.

HERBERT L. OSGOOD, *The American Colonies in the Seventeenth Century*, Four Vols., New York: Macmillan, 1904.

E. G. PARKER, *The Golden Age of American Oratory*, Boston: Whittenmore, 1857.

VERNON LOUIS PARRINGTON, *Main Currents in American Thought*, Three Vols. in One, New York: Harcourt, Brace, 1930.

WAYLAND MAXFIELD PARRISH and MARIE HOCHMUTH, *American Speeches*, New York: Longmans, Green, 1954.

MERRILL D. PETERSON, *The Jefferson Image in the American Mind*, New York: Oxford University Press, 1960.

DONN PIATT, *Memories of the Men Who Saved the Union*, New York: F. F. Lovell, 1887.

MABEL PLATZ, ed., *Anthology of Public Speeches*, New York: Wilson, 1940.

BEN: PERLEY POORE, *Perley's Reminiscences of Sixty Years in the National Metropolis*, Two Vols. in One, Philadelphia: Hubbard Bros., 1886.

ROLLAND W. QUIMBY and ROBERT H. BILLIGMEIR, "The Varying Role of Revivalistic Preaching in American Protestant Evangelism," SM, 26(Aug., 1959):217–228.

CARRIE RASMUSSEN, "Who's Who of Women Orators in America from 1856 to 1930," Unpublished M.A. thesis, University of Wisconsin, 1930.

LOREN REID, ed., *American Public Address*, Columbia: University of Missouri Press, 1961.

JAMES D. RICHARDSON, ed., *A Compilation of the Messages and Papers of the Confederacy*, Two Vols., Nashville: U.S. Pub. Co., 1905.

―――――, *A Compilation of the Messages and Papers of the Presidents*, Twenty Two Vols., New York: Bureau of National Literature, 1911.

W. C. ROBERTS, *Leading Orators of Twenty-Five Campaigns*, New York: Strouse, 1884.

CONSTANCE MAYFIELD ROURKE, *Trumpets of Jubilee*, New York: Harcourt, Brace, 1927.

FREDERICK SAUNDERS, ed., *Centenary Orations*, New York: E. B. Treat, 1882.

ARTHUR M. SCHLESINGER, *The American as Reformer*, Cambridge: Harvard University Press, 1950.

H. W. SCOTT, *Distinguished American Lawyers*, New York: Griggs, 1891.

LORENZO SEARS, *The History of Oratory from the Age of Pericles to the Present Time*, Chicago: Scott, Foresman, 1903.

WARREN C. SHAW, *History of American Oratory*, Indianapolis: Bobbs-Merrill, 1928.

REV. D. SHERMAN, ed., *New England Divines*, New York: Carlton and Porter, 1860.

JOHN SHERMAN's *Recollections of Forty Years in the House, Senate, and Cabinet: An Autobiography*, Two Vols., Chicago: Werner, 1895.

NETTIE ROGERS SHULER and CARRIE CHAPMAN CATT, *Woman Suffrage and Politics*, New York: Scribner's, 1923.

T. V. SMITH, "In Honor of Oratory," QJS, 34(April, 1948): 143–149.

WILLIAM L. SNYDER, ed., *Great Speeches by Great Lawyers*, New York: Baker, Voorhis, 1881.

JARED SPARKS, *The Library of American Biography*, Boston: Little, Brown, 1855.

ELIZABETH CADY STANTON, SUSAN BROWNELL ANTHONY and MATILDA JOSLYN GAGE, *History of Woman Suffrage*, Three Vols., Rochester: S. B. Anthony, 1881–1889.

HENRY B. STANTON, *Random Recollections*, New York: Harper, 1887.

HENRY L. STODDARD, *As I Knew Them: Presidents and Politics from Grant to Coolidge*, New York: Harper, 1927.

ROBERT BRIGGS SUTTON, *Speech Index*, New York: Wilson, 1935.

ASHLEY H. THORNDIKE, ed., *Modern Eloquence*, Fifteen Vols., New York: Modern Eloquence Corp., 1932.

WINGATE J. THORNTON, *The Pulpit of the American Revolution*, New York: Sheldon, 1860.

CARL VAN DOREN, *The Great Rehearsal*, New York: Viking, 1948.

GLYNDON G. VAN DEUSEN, "Some Aspects of Whig Thought and Theory in the Jacksonian Period," *American Historical Review*, 63(Jan., 1958): 305–332.

JERRY VOORHIS, "Effective Speaking in Congress," *QJS*, 34(Dec., 1948): 462–463.

EDITH WEBBER, "Early Fourth of July Celebrations," *Annals of Iowa*, 36(Summer, 1962):374–378.

ARNOLD WHITRIDGE, *No Compromise: The Story of the Fanatics Who Paved the Way to the Civil War*, New York: Farrar, Straus, and Cudahy, 1960.

E. B. WILLISTON, ed., *Eloquence of the United States*, Five Vols., Middleton, Conn.: E. and H. Clark, 1827.

DONALD L. WOLFARTH, "John F. Kennedy in the Tradition of Inaugural Speeches," *QJS*, 47(April, 1961):124–132.

ERNEST J. WRAGE and BARNETT BASKERVILLE, *American Forum: Speeches on Historic Issues, 1788–1900*, New York: Harper, 1960.

————, *American Forum: Speeches on Twentieth Century Issues*, New York: Harper, 1962.

Individual Orators

JOHN ADAMS (1735–1826)

Charles F. Adams, ed., *Works of John Adams*, Three Vols., Boston: Little, Brown, 1856.

Catherine Drinker Bowen, *John Adams and the American Revolution*, Boston: Little, Brown, 1950.

Natalie A. Hennessy, "The Speech Education of John Adams," Unpublished M.A. thesis, State University of Iowa, 1952.

Page Smith, *John Adams*, Two Vols., Garden City: Doubleday, 1962.

JOHN QUINCY ADAMS (1767–1848)

John Quincy Adams, *Lectures on Rhetoric and Oratory,* Two Vols., Cambridge: Hilliard and Metcalf, 1810.

Samuel Flagg Bemis, *John Quincy Adams,* New York: Knopf, 1949.

Worthington C. Ford, *Writings of John Q. Adams,* Seven Vols., New York: Macmillan, 1913.

Horace Rahskopf, "John Quincy Adams' Theory and Practice of Public Speaking," Unpublished Ph.D. thesis, State University of Iowa, 1935.

L. G. Rousseau, "The Rhetorical Principles of Cicero and Adams," *QJS,* 2(Oct., 1916):397–410.

Dorothy Summers, "The Classical Basis of John Quincy Adams' Theory of Rhetorical Invention," Unpublished M.A. thesis, University of Oklahoma, 1942.

SAMUEL ADAMS (1722–1803)

Harry A. Cushing, *Writings of Samuel Adams,* Four Vols., New York: Putnam's, 1904.

James K. Hosmer, *Samuel Adams,* Boston: Houghton Mifflin, 1885.

John C. Miller, *Sam Adams: Pioneer in Propaganda,* Boston: Little, Brown, 1936.

William V. Wells, *Life and Public Services of Samuel Adams,* Three Vols., Boston: Little, Brown, 1865.

SUSAN B. ANTHONY (1820–1906)

Katherine Anthony, *Susan B. Anthony: Her Personal History and Her Era,* New York: Doubleday, 1954.

Florence Horn Bryan, *Susan B. Anthony: Champion of Women's Rights,* New York: Julian Messner, 1947.

Ruth F. Berman, "A Critical Evaluation of the Speeches of Susan B. Anthony," Unpublished M.A. thesis, University of Wisconsin, 1947.

Anna Howard Shaw, *The Story of a Pioneer,* New York: Harper, 1915.

LYMAN BEECHER (1775–1863)

Charles Beecher, ed., *Autobiography of Lyman Beecher,* Two Vols., New York: Harper, 1865.

HENRY WARD BEECHER (1813–1887)

Henry Ward Beecher, *Lecture Room Talks,* New York: J. B. Ford, 1870.

———, *Lectures and Orations,* Newell D. Hillis, ed., New York: Fleming H. Revell, 1913.

———, *Patriotic Addresses,* John H. Howard, ed., New York: Ford, Howard, and Hulbert, 1887.

———, *Plymouth Pulpit,* Lyman Abbott, ed., New York: Harper, 1868.

———, *Sermons,* Two Vols., New York: Harper, 1869.

———, *Yale Lectures on Preaching,* Two Vols., New York: J. B. Ford, 1872 and 1873.

Batsell B. Baxter, "An Analysis of the Basic Elements of Persuasion in the Yale Lectures on Preaching," Unpublished Ph.D. thesis, University of Southern California, 1944.

Roger B. Bernhardt, "Henry Ward Beecher's Application of His Own Theories of Persuasion," Unpublished M.S. thesis, University of Wisconsin, 1947.

Lionel Crocker, "Beecher and Fosdick," *Central States Speech Journal,* 12(1961):100–105.

———, "Henry Ward Beecher and the English Press of 1863," SM, 6(1939):20–43.

———, "Lincoln and Beecher," *Southern Speech Journal,* XXVI (Winter, 1960):149–159.

———, "The Rhetorical Theory of Henry Ward Beecher," Unpublished Ph.D. thesis, University of Michigan, 1933.

Royal L. Garff, "A Study of Henry Ward Beecher's Methods of Controlling Hostile Audiences," Unpublished Ph.D. thesis, University of Southern California, 1944.

Ernest H. Hendrikson, "Rhetorical Elements of Beecher's English Addresses," Unpublished M.A. thesis, State University of Iowa, 1929.

Paxton Hibben, *Henry Ward Beecher: An American Portrait,* New York: Press of the Readers Club, 1942, based on Doran ed., 1927.

L. D. McGladry, "The Changing Styles of Preaching as Revealed in the Lyman Beecher Lectures in Preaching from 1872–1935." Unpublished M.A. thesis, University of Minnesota, 1935.

C. H. Walters, "A Quantitative Study of the Oratorical Style of Henry Ward Beecher," Unpublished M.A. thesis, University of Wisconsin, 1930.

JUDAH P. BENJAMIN (1811–1884)

Speeches in *Rebellion Record,* op. cit., and *Congressional Globe,* 33rd–36th Congress, *passim.*

Pierce Butler, *Judah P. Benjamin,* Philadelphia: George W. Jacobs, 1906.

John Caylor, Jr., "A Rhetorical Analysis of Two Speeches of Judah P. Benjamin," Unpublished M.A. thesis, Texas Christian University, 1950.

Robert D. Meade, *Judah P. Benjamin: Confederate Statesman,* New York: Oxford University Press, 1943.

THOMAS HART BENTON (1782–1858)

Thomas Hart Benton, *Abridgement of the Debates of Congress,* Fifteen Vols., New York: Appleton, 1857.

———, *Thirty Years' View,* Two Vols., New York: Appleton, 1857.

William M. Chambers, *Old Bullion Benton: Senator from the New West,* Boston: Little, Brown, 1956.

Charles F. Hunter, "Four Speeches of Thomas Hart Benton, Edited with Notes and Introduction," Unpublished Ph.D. thesis, Cornell University, 1942.

———, "Thomas Hart Benton: An Evaluation," QJS, 30(Oct., 1944): 279–285.

Thomas R. Lewis, "Persuasive Techniques of Thomas Hart Benton as a Congressional Debater, 1828–1840," Unpublished Ph.D. thesis, State University of Iowa, 1948.

———, "Thomas H. Benton's Analysis of His Audience," QJS, 35(Dec., 1949):441–447.

Elbert B. Smith, *The Magnificent Missourian,* New York: Lippincott, 1958.

William E. Seelen, "A Rhetorical Criticism of Thomas Hart Benton's Expunging Speech," Unpublished M.A. thesis, University of Missouri, 1940. Summarized in SM, 8(1941):58–67.

Elizabeth Worrell, "A Study of Thomas Hart Benton's Attitude Toward the Union," Unpublished M.A. thesis, Northwestern University, 1931.

ALBERT JEREMIAH BEVERIDGE (1862–1927)

C. H. Beem, "Study of the Persuasive and Logical Elements in the Beveridge-Hoar Debates on the Philippines Question," Unpublished M.A. thesis, State University of Iowa, 1931.

Claude G. Bowers, *Beveridge and the Progressive Era*, Boston: Houghton Mifflin, 1932.

John A. Coffin, "Senatorial Career of Albert J. Beveridge," *Indiana Magazine of History*, 24(1928):159–185 and 242–295.

Mary Keirn, "A Study of the Rhetorical Style of Albert Jeremiah Beveridge," Unpublished M.A. thesis, Kent State University, 1950.

Helen R. Paulson, "Jeremiah Beveridge from 1896–1902," Unpublished M.A. thesis, University of Wisconsin, 1942.

Herold T. Ross, "Oratorical Career of Albert Jeremiah Beveridge," Unpublished Ph.D. thesis, State University of Iowa, 1932.

———, "The Education of an Orator," QJS, 18(Feb., 1932):70–82.

L. W. Sawtelle, "The Oratory of Albert Jeremiah Beveridge," Unpublished M.A. thesis, University of Southern California, 1932.

JEREMIAH SULLIVAN BLACK (1810–1883)

Chauncey F. Black, *Essays and Speeches of Jeremiah S. Black*, New York: Appleton, 1885.

William Norwood Brigance, *Jeremiah Sullivan Black*, Philadelphia: University of Pennsylvania Press, 1934.

Mary Black Clayton, *Reminiscences of Jeremiah Sullivan Black*, St. Louis: Christian, 1887.

JAMES G. BLAINE (1830–1893)

James G. Blaine, *Political Discussions: Legislative, Diplomatic, and Popular*, Norwich, Conn.: Henry Bill Pub. Co., 1887.

T. C. Crawford, *James G. Blaine: A Study of His Life and Career*, Philadelphia: Englewood Pub. Co., 1893.

Henry G. Roberts, "James G. Blaine," in *History and Criticism of American Public Address*, ed., W. Norwood Brigance, New York: McGraw-Hill, 1943, II:878–890.

PHILLIPS BROOKS (1835–1893)

Phillips Brooks, *Essays and Addresses*, New York: Dutton, 1894.

———, *Lectures on Preaching*, Grand Rapids, Mich.: Zondervan Pub. Co.

———, *Sermons*, in ten series, New York: Dutton, 1910.

Alexander V. G. Allen, *Life and Letters of Phillips Brooks*, Three Vols., New York: Dutton, 1901.

Kenneth Hance, "The Elements of the Rhetorical Theory of Phillips Brooks," SM, 5(1938):16–39, based on his Ph.D. thesis, University of Michigan, 1937.

Marie K. Hochmuth, "Phillips Brooks," QJS, 27(April, 1941):227–236.

Ardia M. Kerensenky, "The Style of Phillips Brooks' Sermons in 1878," Unpublished M.A. thesis, State University of Iowa, 1951.

Orvin P. Larson, "Phillips Brooks' Theory and Practice of Preaching," Unpublished M.A. thesis, University of Iowa, 1937.

WILLIAM JENNINGS BRYAN (1860–1925)

Memoirs of William Jennings Bryan, by himself and his wife, Mary Baird Bryan, Chicago: John C. Winston, 1925.

Eloise Ann Carrick, "The Nature of Word Concepts as Revealed in the Addresses of William Jennings Bryan," Unpublished M.A. thesis, Ohio State University, 1937.

Dorothy A. Critchfield, "The Use of Concrete Illustration as Revealed in the Speeches of William Jennings Bryan," Unpublished M.A. thesis, Northwestern University, 1931.

Elizabeth Gillilland, "William Jennings Bryan: A Study in the Psychology of Persuasion," Unpublished M.A. thesis, University of Minnesota, 1931.

Grace E. Harper, "A critical Study of the Elements of Persuasion in the Speech of William Jennings Bryan," Unpublished M.A. thesis, University of Southern California, 1929.

Paxton Hibben, The Peerless Leader, New York: Farrar and Rinehart, 1929.

Jessie H. Rutledge, "Allusions in the Speeches of Lodge, Bryan, Hoar on Colonial Expansion," Unpublished M.A. thesis, University of Wisconsin, 1930.

Charles Willis Thompson, Presidents I Have Known and Some Near Presidents, Indianapolis: Bobbs-Merrill, 1929.

M. R. Werner, Bryan, New York: Harcourt, Brace, 1929.

Wayne C. Williams, William Jennings Bryan, New York: Putnam's, 1936.

George Frisbie Whicher, William Jennings Bryan and the Campaign of 1896, Boston: Heath, 1953.

JOHN C. CALHOUN (1782–1850)

Speeches of John C. Calhoun, 1811–1843, New York: Harper, 1843.

Works of John C. Calhoun, ed., Richard K. Crallé, Six Vols., New York: Appleton. 1888.

Margaret L. Coit, John C. Calhoun: American Portrait, Boston: Houghton Mifflin, 1950.

Herbert LaVere Curry, "An Evaluation of the Debating Techniques of John C. Calhoun in Representative Pro-Slavery Speeches, 1847–50," Unpublished M.A. thesis, State University of Iowa, 1936.

Melvin H. Hansen, "An Evaluation of the Arguments of Calhoun on Foreign Affairs," Unpublished M.A. thesis, State University of Iowa, 1940.

R. M. T. Hunter, Life of John C. Calhoun (based on Calhoun's own draft), New York: Harper, 1843.

Robert T. Oliver, "Studies in the Political and Social Views of Slave-Struggle Orators: I—Calhoun," QJS, 22(Oct., 1936):413–429.

Carl Harry Pitzman, "A Critical Study of Four Representative Speeches on States Rights by John C. Calhoun," Unpublished M.A. thesis, University of Iowa, 1935.

Charles M. Wiltse, *John C. Calhoun: Nationalist,* Indianapolis: Bobbs-Merrill, 1944.

———, *John C. Calhoun: Nullifier,* Indianapolis: Bobbs-Merrill, 1949.

ALEXANDER CAMPBELL (1788–1866)

Robert Richardson, *Memoirs of Alexander Campbell,* Two Vols., Philadelphia, Lippincott, 1868–1870.

Robert F. West, *Alexander Campbell and Natural Religion,* New Haven: Yale University Press, 1948.

PETER CARTWRIGHT (1785–1872)

Autobiography of Peter Cartwright, The Backwoods Preacher, ed., W. P. Strickland, Cincinnati: Hitcock and Walden, 1856.

Paul Henshaw Boase, "Peter Cartwright: Preacher and Politician," Unpublished M.S. thesis, University of Wisconsin, 1947.

———, "Cartwright Meets Lincoln," *Western Speech,* 2(Nov., 1950): 26–34.

———, "The Education of a Circuit Rider," QJS, 40(April, 1954): 130–136.

CARRIE CHAPMAN CATT (1859–1947)

Carrie Chapman Catt and Nettie Rogers Shuler, *Woman Suffrage and Politics,* New York: Scribner's, 1926.

Ima Fuchs Clevenger, "Invention and Arrangement in the Public Address of Carrie Chapman Catt," Unpublished Ph.D. thesis, University of Oklahoma, 1955.

Ruby Lee Draughon, "A Study of Selected Speeches on War and Peace by Carrie Chapman Catt," Unpublished M.A. thesis, University of Illinois, 1951.

WILLIAM ELLERY CHANNING (1780–1842)

William Ellery Channing, *Discourses, Reviews, and Miscellanies,* Boston: Carter and Hendee, 1830.

———, *Memoirs,* Three Vols., Boston: Crosby and Nichols, 1848.

———, *Works,* Six Vols., Boston: Geo. G. Channing, 1843.

———, *Works,* Boston: American Unitarian Assoc., 1885.

Arthur W. Brown, *Always Young for Liberty,* Syracuse, N.Y.: Syracuse Univ. Press, 1956.

John W. Chadwick, *William Ellery Channing: Minister of Religion,* Boston: Houghton Mifflin, 1903.

David P. Edgell, *William Ellery Channing: An Intellectual Portrait,* Boston: Beacon Press, 1955.

Robert L. Patterson, *The Philosophy of William Ellery Channing,* New York: 1952.

RUFUS CHOATE (1799–1859)

Addresses and Orations of Rufus Choate, Boston: Little, Brown, 1878.

John W. Black, "Analytical Study of the Rhetorical Methods of Rufus Choate in His Representative Forensic, Deliberative and Demonstrative Speeches," Unpublished M.A. thesis, University of Iowa, 1930.

Samuel Gilman Brown, *Life and Writings of Rufus Choate*, Three Vols., Boston: Little, Brown, 1862.

——, *Life of Rufus Choate*, Boston: Little, Brown, 1878.

David M. Grant, "Factors and Influences in the Training and Education of Rufus Choate Accounting for His Later Effectiveness as a Speaker," Unpublished M.A. thesis, State University of Iowa, 1940.

HENRY CLAY (1777–1852)

Works of Henry Clay, ed., Calvin Colton, Ten Vols., New York: Putnam, 1904.

Anon., "Henry Clay as an Orator," *The New Englander*, 2(1944):105.

——, "Henry Clay as an Orator," *Putnam's Monthly Magazine*, 3(1854):493.

——, "The Speeches of Henry Clay," *Magazine of American History*, 16(1886):58.

Daniel Mallory, *Life and Speeches of the Hon. Henry Clay*, Two Vols., 5th ed., New York: Van Amringe and Bixby, 1884.

Bernard Mayo, *Henry Clay: Spokesman of the New West*, Boston: Houghton Mifflin, 1937.

Robert T. Oliver, "Studies in the Political and Social Views of the Slave-Struggle Orators: III—Clay," QJS, 23(Oct., 1937):409–426.

Joseph M. Rogers, *The True Henry Clay*, Philadelphia: Lippincott, 1905.

Epes Sargent, *Life and Public Services of Henry Clay*, ed., and completed by Horace Greeley, Philadelphia: Porter and Coates, 1852.

Mary Belle Smith, "An Analysis of Henry Clay's Speech on the Compromise Resolution of 1850 by Aristotelian Standards," Unpublished M.A. thesis, University of Iowa, 1935.

THOMAS L. CLINGMAN (1812–1897)

Selections from the Speeches and Writings of Thomas L. Clingman, Raleigh, N.C.: J. Nichols, 1877.

HOWELL COBB (1815–1868)

Zachary T. Johnson, *The Political Principles of Howell Cobb*, Nashville, 1928.

Horace Montgomery, *Howell Cobb's Confederate Career*, Tuscaloosa, Ala.: Confederate Pub. Co., 1959.

Ulrich B. Phillips, *Correspondence of Robert Toombs, Alexander Stephens and Howell Cobb*, Washington, D.C.: American Historical Association Report, 1911.

WILLIAM BOURKE COCKRAN (1854–1923)

Bourke Cockran, *In the Name of Liberty*, a collection of his speeches, New York: Putnam's, 1925.

Ambrose Kennedy, *American Orator: Bourke Cockran, His Life and Politics*, Boston: B. Humphries, 1948.

James McGurrin, *Bourke Cockran: A Free Lance in American Politics*, New York: Scribner's, 1948.

ROSCOE CONKLING (1829–1888)

Donald Barr Chidsey, *The Gentleman from New York: A Life of Roscoe Conkling*, New Haven: Yale University Press, 1935.

Alfred R. Conkling, *The Life and Letters of Roscoe Conkling: Orator, Statesman, Advocate*, New York: Charles L. Webster, 1889.

Venila L. Shores, *The Hayes-Conkling Controversy, 1877–1879*, Northampton, Mass.: Smith College Studies in History, IV, 1919.

MONCURE DANIEL CONWAY (1832–1907)

Addresses and Reprints, 1850–1907, Boston: Houghton Mifflin, 1909.

Autobiography: Memories and Experiences, Two Vols., Boston: Houghton Mifflin, 1909.

Mary Elizabeth Burtis, *Moncure Conway*, New Brunswick: Rutgers University Press, 1952.

RUSSELL H. CONWELL (1843–1925)

Acres of Diamonds, by Russell H. Conwell, with essay, "His Life and Achievements," by Robert Shackleton, New York: Harper, 1915.

Agnes Rush Burr, *Russell H. Conwell and His Work*, with variant text of "Acres of Diamonds" in Appendix, Philadelphia: John C. Winston, 1926.

Mary Louis Gehring, "A Rhetorical Study of the Lectures and Sermons of Russell H. Conwell," Unpublished Ph.D. thesis, Louisiana State University, 1952."

———, "The Invention of Russell H. Conwell in His Lecture, 'Acres of Diamonds,' " Unpublished M.A., thesis, Louisiana State University, 1949.

Charles A. Parker, "The Theory of Oratory of Russell H. Conwell," Unpublished M.A. thesis, Temple University, 1953.

THOMAS CORWIN (1794–1865)

Life and Speeches of Thomas Corwin, ed. Josiah Morrow, Cincinnati: W. H. Anderson, 1896.

Speeches of Thomas Corwin with a Sketch of His Life, ed., Isaac Strohm, Dayton: W. F. Comby, 1859.

J. Jeffrey Auer, "Tom Corwin: King of the Stump," Unpublished Ph.D. thesis, University of Wisconsin, 1947.

———, "Tom Corwin: Men Will Remember Me as a Joker." QJS, 33(Feb., 1947):9–14.

———, "Tom Corwin: 'King of the Stump,' " QJS, 30(Feb., 1944): 47–54.

Warren LaVerne Strausbaugh, "The Speaking Technique of Thomas Corwin in the Campaign of 1858 to 1859," Unpublished M.A. thesis, State University of Iowa, 1935.

JOHN COTTON (1585–1652)

Everett H. Emerson, ed., *Gods Mercie Mixed With His Justice, Six Sermons by John Cotton*, with introductions and bibliographic notes, Gainesville, Florida: Scholar's Facsimiles and Reprints, 1958.

DAVID CROCKETT (1786–1836)

Autobiography of David Crockett, introduction by Hamlin Garland, New York: Scribner's, 1923.

James Atkins Shackford, *David Crockett: The Man and the Legend*, Chapel Hill: University of North Carolina Press, 1956.

GEORGE WILLIAM CURTIS (1824–1892)
  Orations and Addresses of George William Curtis, ed., Charles Eliot Norton, Three Vols., New York: Harper, 1894.
  Carroll C. Arnold, "George William Curtis," in *A History and Criticism of American Public Address*, ed., Marie Kathryn Hochmuth, Vol. III, New York: Longmans, Green (McKay), 1955, pp. 133–174.
  Charles F. Lindsley, "George William Curtis," *QJS*, 5(March, 1919): 79–100.

JEFFERSON DAVIS (1808–1889)
  Jefferson Davis, Constitutionalist: His Letters, Papers, and Speeches, ed., Roland Dunbar, Ten Vols., Jackson, Miss.: Mississippi Dept. of Archives and History, 1923.
  Speeches of the Honorable Jefferson Davis of Mississippi, Delivered During the Summer of 1858, Baltimore: J. Murphy, 1859.
  Jefferson Davis, *The Rise and Fall of the Confederate Government*, Two Vols., New York: Appleton, 1912.
  Audrey W. Dreyfuss, "A Rhetorical Analysis of the Two Inaugural Addresses of Jefferson Davis," Unpublished M.A. thesis, University of Alabama, 1950.
  Hubert Ellingsworth, "The Thwarted Lecture Tour of Jefferson Davis," *QJS*, 43(Oct., 1957):284–287.
  Glenn M. Maxwell, "An Analytic Study of the Speech Style Contained in Four Public Addresses Delivered by Jefferson Davis in the Summer of 1858," Unpublished M.A. thesis, University of Michigan, 1942.
  Ralph Elvon Richardson, "The Speaking and Speeches of Jefferson Davis," Unpublished Ph.D. thesis, Northwestern University, 1950.

CHAUNCEY DEPEW (1834–1928)
  Chauncey Depew, *Life and Later Speeches*, New York: Cassell Pub. Co., 1894.
  ———, *My Memories of Eighty Years*, New York: Scribner's, 1924.
  Willard Hayes Yeager, *Chauncey Mitchell Depew the Orator*, Washington, D.C.: George Washington University Press, 1934.

STEPHEN A. DOUGLAS (1813–1861)
  Autobiography, Springfield, Ill.: Illinois State Journal Co., 1913.
  Paul M. Angle, *Created Equal? The Complete Lincoln-Douglas Debates of 1858*, Chicago: University of Chicago Press, 1958.
  Jeannette Anderson, "Man of the Hour or Man of the Ages? The Honorable Stephen A. Douglas," *QJS*, 25(Feb., 1939):75–93.
  Wallace Ashby, "The Oratorical Techniques of Stephen A. Douglas in Defense of the Union, 1860–1861," Unpublished M.A. thesis, University of Iowa, 1935.
  Arthur M. Barnes, "A Rhetorical Analysis of the Speeches of Stephen A. Douglas in the Lincoln-Douglas Debates," Unpublished M.A. thesis, State University of Iowa, 1937.
  Oneda P. Carpenter, "Stephen A. Douglas as a Speaker," Unpublished M.A. thesis, Baylor University, 1950.
  William A. Dwen, "A Rhetorical Analysis of the Alabama Speeches of Stephen A. Douglas During the Presidential Campaign of 1860," Unpublished M.A. thesis, University of Alabama, 1950.

Violet M. Hassler, "A Study of the Eulogies of Stephen A. Douglas and Thaddeus Stevens," Unpublished M.A. thesis, Northwestern University, 1935.

Harriet P. Jordon, "The Lincoln-Douglas Debates of 1858: A Presentation of the Rhetorical Scene and Setting with Pilot Film Script of the Ottawa Debate," Unpublished Ph.D. thesis, University of Illinois, 1958.

Ritav McKenna, "The Iowa Speeches of Stephen A. Douglas in the Campaign of 1860," Unpublished M.A. thesis, State University of Iowa, 1935.

George Fort Milton, *The Eve of Conflict: Stephen A. Douglas and the Needless War*, New York: Houghton Mifflin, 1934.

Kenneth M. Rock, "Relative Uses of Formal and Material Logic in the Lincoln-Douglas Debates," Unpublished M.A. thesis, University of Southern California, 1934.

Willa W. Roof, "A Rhetorical Analysis of Two New Orleans Speeches of Stephen A. Douglas, 1858–1860," Unpublished M.A. thesis, Louisiana State University, 1959.

George H. Rose, "The Use of Persuasion in the Lincoln-Douglas Debates," Unpublished M.A. thesis, University of Southern California, 1929.

Julius Slutsky, "A Rhetorical Analysis of the Lincoln-Douglas Debates," Unpublished M.A. thesis, Brooklyn College, 1939.

Forest L. Whan, "Invention in the Speeches of Stephen A. Douglas in the 1858 Campaign for the Illinois Senatorship," Unpublished Ph.D. thesis, State University of Iowa, 1938.

FREDERICK DOUGLASS (1817–1895)

Life and Times of Frederick Douglass, Boston: De Wolfe, Fisk, rev., 1895.

Philip S. Foner, *The Life and Writings of Frederick Douglass*, Four Vols., New York: International Publishers, 1950.

Frank W. Hale, "A Critical Analysis of the Speaking of Frederick Douglass," Unpublished M.A. thesis, University of Nebraska, 1951.

Frederick May Holland, *Frederick Douglass: The Colored Orator*, New York: Funk and Wagnalls, rev., 1895.

Cornelius Abraham Ladner, "A Critical Analysis of Four Anti-Slavery Speeches of Frederick Douglass," Unpublished M.A. thesis, State University of Iowa, 1947.

Benjamin Quarles, *Frederick Douglass*, Washington, D.C.: Associated Publishers, 1948.

TIMOTHY DWIGHT (1752–1817)

Timothy Dwight, *Sermons*, Two Vols., New Haven: Hezekiah Howe and Durrie and Peck, 1828.

————, *Theology Explained and Defended in a Series of Sermons*, 3rd. ed., New Haven: S. Converse, 1823.

Jared Sparks, *Library of American Biography*, op. cit., contains a listing of Dwight's sermons, IV:361–364.

JONATHAN EDWARDS (1703–1758)

Works, ed., Sereno Dwight, Ten Vols., New York: S. Converse, 1829.

Clarence H. Faust and Thomas H. Johnson, eds., *Jonathan Edwards: Representative Selections with Introduction, Bibliography, and Notes*, New York: American Book Co., 1935.

H. Norman Gardiner, *Selected Sermons of Jonathan Edwards*, New York: Macmillan, 1904.

Wilbert L. Anderson, "The Preaching Power of Jonathan Edwards," *Congregationalist and Christian World*, 88(Oct. 3, 1903):463–466.

Franklin G. Bouwsma, "A Rhetorical Analysis of Selected Sermons of Jonathan Edwards," Unpublished M.A. thesis, University of Michigan, 1950.

Orville A. Hitchcock, "A Critical Study of the Oratorical Technique of Jonathan Edwards," Unpublished Ph.D. thesis, State University of Iowa, 1936.

RALPH WALDO EMERSON (1803–1882)

Complete Works of Ralph Waldo Emerson, Medallion Edition, ed., Edward Waldo Emerson, Twelve Vols. in Six, New York: Wm. H. Wise, 1929.

Early Lectures of Ralph Waldo Emerson, eds., S. E. Whicher and R. E. Spiller, Two Vols., Cambridge: Harvard University Press, 1959, 1961.

Journals of Ralph Waldo Emerson, ed., E. W. Emerson, Ten Vols., Boston: Houghton Mifflin, 1909.

Young Emerson Speaks, ed., H. C. McGiffert, Boston: Houghton Mifflin, 1938.

Barnet Baskerville, "Emerson as a Critic of Oratory," *Southern Speech Journal*, 18(March, 1953):150–162.

Wayne Minnick, "Matthew Arnold on Emerson," *QJS*, 37(Oct., 1951):332–336.

William S. Tacey, "Emerson on Eloquence," *Today's Speech*, 6(Sept., 1958):23–27.

Willard Thorp, "Emerson on Tour," *QJS*, 17(Feb., 1930):19–34.

WILLIAM MAXWELL EVARTS (1818–1901)

Arguments and Speeches of William Maxwell Evarts, ed., Sherman Evarts, Three Vols., New York: Macmillan, 1919.

Chester L. Barrows, *William M. Evarts: Lawyer, Diplomat, Statesman*, Chapel Hill: University of North Carolina Press, 1941.

Brainerd Dyer, *The Public Career of William M. Evarts*, Berkeley, University of California Press, 1933.

EDWARD EVERETT (1794–1865)

Edward Everett, *Orations and Speeches*, 7th ed., Four Vols., Boston: Little, Brown, 1865.

Paul Revere Frothingham, *Edward Everett: Orator and Statesman*, New York: Houghton Mifflin, 1925.

John W. Keys, "The Factors in the Training and Education of Edward Everett Accounting for His Ability as a Speaker," Unpublished M.A. thesis, State University of Iowa, 1939.

Ronald Reid, "Rhetorician of Nationalism, 1824–1855," QJS, 41 (Oct., 1956):273–282.

CHARLES G. FINNEY (1792–1875)

Autobiography, Charles G. Finney, Popular Edition, New York: Salvation Army, 1903.

————, *Lectures on Systematic Theology,* Oberlin: E. J. Goodrich, 1878.

————, *Lectures to Professing Christians,* New York: John S. Taylor, 1837.

————, *Revivals of Religion,* New York: Levitt, Lord and Co., 1835.

————, *Sermons on Gospel Themes,* Oberlin: E. J. Goodrich, 1896.

————, *Sermons on Important Subjects,* New York: John S. Taylor, 1836.

————, *Sermons on the Way of Salvation,* Oberlin: E. J. Goodrich, 1891.

J. Robert Emmel, "The Persuasive Techniques of Charles Grandison Finney As a Revivalist and Social Reform Speaker, 1820–1860," Unpublished Ph.D. thesis, Pennsylvania State University, 1959.

Rollin W. Quimby, "Charles Grandison Finney: Herald of Modern Revivalism," SM, 20 (Nov., 1953):293–299.

BENJAMIN FRANKLIN (1706–1790)

Complete Works, ed., J. Bigelow, New York: Putnam's, 1887–1888.

Representative Selections, with Introductions, Bibliography, and Notes, eds., Frank Luther Mott and Chester E. Jorgenson, New York: American Book Co., 1936.

Writings of Benjamin Franklin, ed., A. H. Smyth, New York: Macmillan, 1905–1907.

Sandra Lewis, "Franklin's Advice to Speakers," *Today's Speech,* 7 (Nov., 1959):18–21.

Aita G. Shimukler, "Benjamin Franklin's Philosophy of Speech," Unpublished M.A. thesis, Temple University, 1953.

BENJAMIN FRANKLIN (1812–1878)

Ottis Castleberry, "A Study of the Nature and Sources of the Effectiveness of Preaching of Benjamin Franklin in the Restoration Movement in America, 1840–1878," Unpublished Ph.D. thesis, Pennsylvania State Univ., 1957.

————, *They Heard Him Gladly: A Critical Study of Benjamin Franklin's Preaching,* Los Angeles: Old Paths Pub. Co., 1963.

WILLIAM LLOYD GARRISON (1804–1879)

Selections from the Writings and Speeches of William Lloyd Garrison, Boston: R. F. Walcutt, 1852.

Words of Garrison, Boston: Houghton Mifflin, 1905.

John J. Chapman, *William Lloyd Garrison,* Boston: Atlantic Monthly Press, 1921.

Wendell Phillips Garrison and Francis Jackson Garrison, *William Lloyd Garrison,* Four Vols., New York: Houghton Mifflin, 1894.

Russel B. Nye, *William Lloyd Garrison and the Humanitarian Reformers,* Boston: Little, Brown, 1955.

JOHN B. GOUGH (1817–1886)
John B. Gough, *Autobiography*, Springfield, Mass.: Bill, Nichols, 1869.
————, *Platform Echoes, With a History of Mr. Gough's Life and Work*, by Lyman Abbott, Hartford, Conn.: A. D. Worthington and Co., 1887.
Theodore L. Cuyler, *Recollections of a Long Life*, New York: American Tract Society, 1902.
Harold T. Ross, "Harry Bainbridge Gough," QJS, 32(April, 1946): 193–197.

HENRY W. GRADY (1850–1889)
Dorothy Siedenburg Hadley, "Contemporary Estimate of Henry W. Grady as a Public Speaker," Unpublished M.A. thesis, Northwestern University, 1937.
Joel Chandler Harris, *Henry W. Grady: His Life and Speeches*, New York: Cassell Pub. Co., 1890.
Charles F. Lindsley, "Henry Woodfin Grady, Orator," QJS, 6(April, 1920):27–42.
Raymond Blalock Nixon, *Henry W. Grady: Spokesman of the New South*, New York: Knopf, 1943.

ANDREW HAMILTON (1676–1741)
The Trial of John Peter Zenger, London: P. Brown, 1752.

ALEXANDER HAMILTON (1757–1804)
Works of Alexander Hamilton, ed., John C. Hamilton, Nine Vols., New York: John F. Trow, 1850–1851.
Works of Alexander Hamilton, ed., Henry Cabot Lodge, Twelve Vols., New York: Putnam's, 1904.
Bower Aly, *The Rhetoric of Alexander Hamilton*, New York: Columbia University Press, 1941.
Gertrude F. Atherton, *The Conqueror: Being the True and Romantic Story of Alexander Hamilton*, New York: Macmillan, 1904.
W. M. Fulton, "Speeches of Alexander Hamilton in New York State Convention for the Ratification of the Federal Constitution," Unpublished M.A. thesis, State University of Iowa, 1930.
Clarence E. Miner, *The Ratification of the Federal Constitution by the State of New York*, New York: Columbia University, 1921.
Gale L. Richards, "Alexander Hamilton's Influence on John Marshall's Judiciary Speech in the 1788 Virginia Federal Ratifying Convention," QJS, 44(Feb., 1958):31–39.

BENJAMIN HARRISON (1823–1882)
Speeches of Benjamin Harrison, ed., Charles Hedges, New York: United States Book Co., 1892.
Gilbert L. Harney, *The Lives of Benjamin Harrison and Levi P. Morton, With a History of the Republican Party*, Providence, R.I.: J. A. and R. A. Reid, 1888.
Harry J. Sievers, *Benjamin Harrison: Hoosier Warrior, and Hoosier Statesman*, Two Vols., New York: University Publishers, 1959.

ROBERT YOUNG HAYNE (1791–1839)
W. A. Cable, "Webster-Hayne Debate: A Critical Study in Argumentation," Unpublished M.A. thesis, State University of Iowa, 1924.

Theodore Jervey, *Robert Y. Hayne and His Times*, New York: Macmillan, 1909.

Donald W. Nelson, "A Study of the Senate Speaking of Robert Y. Hayne," Unpublished M.A. thesis, University of Florida, 1949.

PATRICK HENRY (1736–1799)

William Wirt Henry, *Patrick Henry: Life, Correspondence, and Speeches*, Three Vols., New York: Scribner's, 1891.

Louis A. Mallory, "Patrick Henry: Orator of the American Revolution," Unpublished Ph.D. thesis, University of Wisconsin, 1938.

Bernard Mayo, "The Enigma of Patrick Henry," in *Myths and Men*, New York: Harper Torchbooks, 1963, pp. 13–35.

Robert D. Meade, *Patrick Henry: Patriot in the Making*, Philadelphia: Lippincott, 1957.

George Morgan, *The True Patrick Henry*, Philadelphia: Lippincott, 1907.

William Wirt, *Life and Character of Patrick Henry*, 4th ed., Philadelphia: Henry T. Coates, 1817.

BENJAMIN HILL (1823–1882)

Huber W. Ellingsworth, "Ben Hill Speaks Out," *Southern Speech Journal*, 22(Summer, 1957):233–241.

Benjamin H. Hill, Jr., *Senator Benjamin H. Hill of Georgia: His Life, Writings, and Speeches*, Atlanta: H. C. Hudgins, 1891.

Haywood J. Pearce, *Benjamin H. Hill: Secession and Reconstruction*, Chicago: University of Chicago Press, 1928.

THOMAS HOOKER (1586?–1647)

Everett H. Emerson, ed., *Redemption*, Three sermons with introduction and bibliographic notes, Gainesville, Florida: Scholar's Facsimiles and Reprints, 1956.

George Leon Walker, *Thomas Hooker: Preacher, Founder, Democrat*, New York: Dodd, Mead, 1891.

SAM HOUSTON (1793–1863)

Autobiography of Sam Houston, eds., Donald Day and Harry H. Ullon, Norman: University of Oklahoma Press, 1954.

Writings of Sam Houston, eds., Amelia W. Williams and Eugene C. Barker, Austin: University of Texas Press, 1934.

Marquis James, *The Raven: A biography of Sam Houston*, New York: Blue Ribbon Books, 1929.

Harold Marsh, "An Analysis and Criticism of the Senatorial Speaking of Sam Houston," Unpublished M.A. thesis, Louisiana State University, 1940.

Yetta G. Mitchell, "An Evaluation of Sam Houston's Oratory," Unpublished Ph.D. thesis, University of Southern California, 1945.

——, "Sam Houston: Orator," *Western Speech*, 9(Nov., 1945):9–12.

ROBERT GREEN INGERSOLL (1833–1899)

Works, ed. C. P. Farrell, Thirteen Vols., New York: Dresden, 1909–11.

C. H. Cramer, *Royal Bob: The Life of Colonel Robert G. Ingersoll*, Indianapolis: Bobbs-Merrill, 1952.

Lionel Crocker, "Robert Green Ingersoll's Influence on American Oratory," *QJS*, 24(April, 1938):299–312.

June E. deCordova, "A Study of the Style of Selected Speeches of Robert Green Ingersoll," Unpublished M.A. thesis, University of Michigan, 1942.

William Leo Finkel, "Robert Ingersoll's Oratory and Walt Whitman's Poetry," SM, 16(Aug., 1949):41–56.

Orvin Larson, *American Infidel: Robert G. Ingersoll*, New York: Citadel Press, 1962.

Jean Thelma McDowell, "Elements of Effective Oratorical Style as Found in the Lectures of Robert Green Ingersoll," Unpublished M.A. thesis, Northwestern University, 1930.

Bernard Lexro Prillaman, "A Study of the Figures of Speech as They Are Found in the Lectures of Robert G. Ingersoll," Unpublished M.A. thesis, Northwestern University, 1931.

Cameron Rogers, *Colonel Bob Ingersoll*, New York: Doubleday, Page, 1927.

Hugh F. Seabury, "Typical Deliberative and Demonstrative Speeches of Robert Green Ingersoll: A Comparative Study in Arrangement," Unpublished M.A. thesis, State University of Iowa, 1933.

Florian Vicor Viggo, "A Study of the Sources and Uses of Historical and Literary Materials in the Speeches of Robert Green Ingersoll," Unpublished M.A. thesis, Northwestern University, 1934.

ANDREW JOHNSON (1808–1875)

Speeches of Andrew Johnson, President of the United States, ed. Frank Moore, Boston: Little, Brown, 1865.

The Great Impeachment Trial of Andrew Johnson, Philadelphia: T. B. Peterson and Bros., 1868.

Lyndon Gregg Phifer, "Andrew Johnson at Cleveland and St. Louis, 1866: A Study in Textual Authenticity," QJS, 37(Dec., 1951): 455–462.

———, "Not for the Purpose of Making a Speech: Andrew Johnson's Swing Around the Circle," SM, 21(Nov., 1954):285–293.

———, "The Last Stand of Presidential Reconstruction: A Rhetorical Study of Andrew Johnson's Swing Around the Circle in 1866," Unpublished Ph.D. thesis, State University of Iowa, 1949.

Eric L. McKitrick, *Andrew Johnson and Reconstruction*, Chicago: University of Chicago Press, 1960.

Lloyd P. Stryker, *Andrew Johnson: A Study in Courage*, New York: Macmillan, 1936.

Mary Grace Walsh, "A Comparative Study of the Spoken Words of Andrew Johnson and Thaddeus Stevens," Unpublished Ph.D. thesis, University of Wisconsin, 1939.

Robert W. Winston, *Andrew Johnson: Plebian and Patriot*, New York: Holt, 1928.

RUFUS KING (1755–1827)

Life and Correspondence of Rufus King, ed. Charles R. King, New York: Putnam's 1894.

ROBERT MARION LAFOLLETTE (1855–1925)

LaFollette's Autobiography: A Personal Narrative of Political Experiences, Madison: University of Wisconsin Press, 1913.

The Political Philosophy of Robert M. LaFollette as Revealed in His Speeches and Writings, ed., Ellen Torelle, Madison: University of Wisconsin Press, 1920.

John Woodford Crawford, "A Study of the Development of Robert M. LaFollette as a Speaker," Unpublished M.A. thesis, Northwestern University, 1935.

Carroll P. Lahman, "Robert Marion LaFollette as a Public Speaker and Political Leader (1855–1905)," Unpublished Ph.D. thesis, University of Wisconsin, 1939.

Wallace S. Sayre, "Robert M. LaFollette—A Study in Political Methods," Unpublished Ph.D. thesis, New York University, 1930.

LUCIUS Q. C. LAMAR (1825–1893)

Wirt A. Cate, *Lucius Q. C. Lamar: Secession and Reunion*, Chapel Hill: University of North Carolina Press, 1935.

Paul E. Geisenof, "The Pre-Civil War Oratory of Lucius Q. C. Lamar," Unpublished M.A. thesis, Louisiana State University, 1939.

Edward Mayes, *Lucius Q. C. Lamar: His Life, Times, and Speeches*, Nashville: Pub. House of Methodist Episcopal Church South, 1896.

Donald C. Streeter, "A Rhetorical Criticism of the Major Public Addresses of Lucius Q. C. Lamar during the Period 1874–1890," Unpublished Ph.D. thesis, State University of Iowa, 1948.

———, "The Major Public Addresses of Lucius Q. C. Lamar During the Period 1874–1890," SM, 16(1949):114–124.

ABRAHAM LINCOLN (1809–1865)

Collected Works of Abraham Lincoln, ed. Roy P. Basler, et al., Eight Vols., New Brunswick, Rutgers University Press, 1953.

Complete Works of Abraham Lincoln, eds., John G. Nicolay and John Hay, Twelve Vols., New York: Century, 1894–1905.

Jay Monaghan, *Lincoln Bibliography, 1830–1939*, Two Vols., Springfield, Ill.: Illinois State Historical Library Assoc., 1945.

Abraham Lincoln: Selected Speeches, Messages, and Letters, ed. T. Harry Williams, New York: Rinehart, 1957.

Paul M. Angle, *A Shelf of Lincoln Books*, New Brunswick: Rutgers University Press, 1946.

———, *Created Equal. The Complete Lincoln-Douglas Debates of 1858*, Chicago: University of Chicago Press, 1958.

Marvin Bauer, "The Rhetorical Practice of Abraham Lincoln," Unpublished M.A. thesis, Cornell University, 1924.

Mildred F. Berry, "Lincoln the Speaker," QJS, 17(Feb. and April, 1931):25–40 and 177–190.

Godfrey Rathbone Benson, Lord Charnwood, *Abraham Lincoln*, New York: Holt, 1917.

Walfred A. Dahlberg, "A Critical Analysis of Lincoln's Use of Wit and Humor for Persuasive Effect," Unpublished M.A. thesis, Northwestern Univ., 1931.

———, "Lincoln the Wit," QJS, 31(Dec., 1954):424–427.

———, "Motivation as a Factor in Lincoln's Rhetoric," QJS, 24(Dec., 1938):615–621.

David Donald, *Lincoln's Herndon*, New York: Knopf, 1948.

Mary B. Gibson, "A Study of the Background, Occasion, and Growing Significance of Abraham Lincoln's Gettysburg Address," Unpublished M.A. thesis, University of Michigan, 1947.

Robert G. Gunderson, "Lincoln and the Policy of Eloquent Silence," QJS, 47(Feb., 1961):1–9.

B. W. Harris, "A Study of Outstanding Interest-Producing Sentences Employed in Lincoln's Speeches," Unpublished M.A. thesis, University of Southern California, 1931.

John G. Nicolay and John Hay, *Abraham Lincoln: A History*, Ten Vols., New York: Century, 1890.

James G. Randall, *Lincoln the President*, Four Vols., New York: Dodd, Mead, 1945–1955.

Carl Sandburg, *Abraham Lincoln: The Prairie Years*, Two Vols., New York: Harcourt, Brace, 1926.

———, *Abraham Lincoln: The War Years*, Four Vols., New York: Harcourt, Brace, 1939.

Junella Teeter, "A Study of the Homely Figures of Speech Used by Abraham Lincoln in His Speeches," Unpublished M.A. thesis, Northwestern University, 1931.

Benjamin P. Thomas, *Abraham Lincoln*, New York: Knopf, 1952.

Earl W. Wiley, "Criticism of the Gettysburg Address," SM, 23(March, 1956):1–8.

———, "Lincoln the Speaker 1816–1837," QJS, 20(Feb., 1934): 1–15, and 21(June, 1935):305–322.

T. Harry Williams, *Lincoln and the Radicals*, Madison: University of Wisconsin Press, 1941.

EDWARD LIVINGSTON (1764–1836)

Complete Works of Edward Livingston on Criminal Jurisprudence, ed. E. C. Wines, Two Vols., New York: National Prison Assoc. of U.S., 1873.

JAMES MADISON (1751–1836)

Writings of James Madison, ed., Gaillard Hunt, Eight Vols., New York: Putnam's, 1900.

Irving Brant, *James Madison: The Virginia Revolutionist*, Indianapolis: Bobbs-Merrill, 1941.

Adelaide Haselow, "A Rhetorical Study of James Madison," Unpublished M.A. thesis, Kent State University, 1950.

W. E. Moore, "Analysis and Criticism of Madison as a Debater in the Virginia Federal Constitutional Convention," Unpublished M.A. thesis, University of Iowa, 1932.

———, "James Madison, the Speaker," QJS, 31(April, 1945):155–162.

COTTON MATHER (1663–1728)

Diary of Cotton Mather, Two Vols., New York: Frederick Unger Pub. Co., 1957.

Magnalia Christi Americana, Hartford: S. Andrus, 1853.

Wendell Barrett, *Cotton Mather: Puritan Priest*, New York: Dodd, Mead, 1891.

William Reid Manierre, "Cotton Mather and the Plain Style," Unpublished doctoral thesis, University of Michigan, 1958.

Abijah P. Marvin, *The Life and Times of Cotton Mather*, Boston: Congregational Sunday-School and Pub. Society, 1892.

Samuel Mather, *The Life of the Very Reverend and Learned Cotton Mather*. Boston: Samuel Gerrish, 1729.

Eugene E. White, "Cotton Mather's *Manuductio ad Ministerium*," *QJS*, 49(Oct., 1963):308–319.

INCREASE MATHER (1639–1723)

Cotton Mather, *Parentator, Memoirs of Remarkables in the Life and Death of Ever-Memorable Dr. Increase Mather*, Boston: B. Green, 1724.

Increase Mather, *Testimony Against Prophane Customs*, Charlotte: University of Virginia Press, 1953 (Contains bibliography of I. Mather's publications).

Kenneth Murdock: *Increase Mather: The Foremost American Puritan*, Cambridge: Harvard University Press, 1926.

RICHARD MATHER (1596–1669)

Increase Mather, *The Life and Death of that Reverend Man of God, Mr. Richard Mather*, Cambridge: Samuel Green and Marmaduke Johnson, 1670.

JONATHAN MAYHEW (1720–1766)

Jonathan Mayhew, *Seven Sermons*, Boston: Rogers and Fowle, 1749.

Robert F. Herold, "The Rhetorical Characteristics of Jonathan Mayhew," Unpublished M.A. thesis, University of Wisconsin, 1955.

DWIGHT L. MOODY (1837–1899)

Dwight L. Moody, *Addresses and Lectures*, New York: A. D. F. Randolph, 1875.

————, *Crowning Glory*, Chicago: Laird and Lee, 1893.

————, *Fifty Sermons and Evangelistic Talks*, New York: F. M. Barton, 1899.

————, *Moody's Great Sermons*, Chicago: Laird and Lee, 1899.

————, *To the Work*, Toronto, Canada: Rose Pub. Co., 1885.

Richard K. Curtis, "The Pulpit Speaking of Dwight L. Moody," Unpublished Ph.D. thesis, Purdue University, 1954.

Rowan Lundsford, "The Evangelistic Campaigns of Dwight L. Moody," Unpublished Ph.D. thesis, Purdue University, 1954.

Roland W. Quimby, "Dwight L. Moody: An Examination of the Historical Conditions and Rhetorical Factors which Contributed to his Effectiveness as a Speaker," Unpublished Ph.D. thesis, University of Michigan, 1951.

————, "How D. L. Moody Held Attention," *QJS*, 43(Oct., 1957): 278–283.

Richard S. Rhodes, ed., *Dwight Lyman Moody's Life Work and Gospel Sermons*, Chicago: Rhodes and McClure, 1900.

William C. Wilkinson, "Dwight L. Moody as a Preacher," *Homiletic Review*, 36(Aug., 1898):110–119.

LUCRETIA MOTT (1793–1880)

Angeline Ducas, "Lucretia Mott: Woman of Eloquence," Unpublished M.A. thesis, Emerson College, 1953.

Anna Davis Hallowell, *James and Lucretia Mott: Life and Letters*, Boston: Houghton Mifflin, 1884.

JAMES OTIS (1725–1783)

James Otis, *The Rights of British Colonies Asserted and Proved*, Boston: Edes and Gill, 1764.

Jerald L. Buninga, "James Otis and the Writs of Assistance: A Textual Investigation," SM, 37(Nov., 1960):351–352.

Sheila Graham Morrison, "The Significance of the Contributions of James Otis to the Pre-Revolutionary Movement in America through the Medium of Oratory," Unpublished Ph.D. thesis, Ohio State University, 1947.

William Tuder, *The Life of James Otis*, Boston: Wells and Lilly, 1823.

William S. Smith, "James Otis' Use of Fundamental Law as a Rhetorical Argument," Unpublished M.A. thesis, Stanford University, 1949.

THEODORE PARKER (1810–1860)

Theodore Parker, *Autobiography*, Boston: American Unitarian Assoc., 1911.

———, *Speeches, Addresses, and Occasional Sermons*, Three Vols., Boston: Horace B. Fuller, 1867.

———, *Ten Sermons of Religion*, Boston: Crosby, Nichols, 1853.

———, *Works*, Centenary Edition, Fifteen Vols., Boston: American Unitarian Ass'n, 1907–1910.

Henry Steele Commager, *Theodore Parker: Yankee Crusader*, Boston: Beacon Press, 1936.

Roy Clyde McCall, "The Public Speaking Principles and Practice of Theodore Parker," Unpublished Ph.D. thesis, State University of Iowa, 1936.

WENDELL PHILLIPS (1811–1884)

Wendell Phillips, *Speeches, Lectures, and Letters*, Boston: Lee and Shepard, 1892.

———, *Speeches on Rights of Women*, Philadelphia: A. J. Ferriss, 1898.

———, *The Lost Arts*, Boston: Lee and Shepard, 1884.

———, *Toussaint L'Ouverture*, New York: E. D. Barker, 1862.

George Lowell Austin, *Life and Times of Wendell Phillips*, Boston: Lee and Shepard, 1888.

Myrtle C. Bacon, "A Behavioristic Interpretation of the Persuasive Elements in the Language of Wendell Phillips," Unpublished M.A. thesis, University of Minnesota, 1927.

R. H. Barnard, "A Study of the Control of Hostile Audiences in the Anti-Slavery Speeches of Wendell Phillips," Unpublished M.A. thesis, University of Utah, 1929.

———, "An Objective Study of the Speeches of Wendell Phillips," Unpublished Ph.D. thesis, University of Utah, 1930.

———, "The Freedom Speech of Wendell Phillips," QJS, 25(Dec., 1939):596–611.

LeRoy Brown, "A Study of Wendell Phillips' 'The Scholar in a Republic,'" Unpublished M.A. thesis, University of Illinois, 1948.

John Casteel, "Allusions to English Literature in the Speeches of Wendell Phillips," Unpublished M.A. thesis, Northwestern University, 1929.

J. H. Doyle, "The Style of Wendell Phillips," QJS, 2(Oct., 1916): 331–339.

Ralph E. Engstrom, "A Study of the Factors and Influence in the Training and Education of Wendell Phillips Accounting for His Later Ability as an Orator," Unpublished M.A. thesis, University of Iowa, 1940.

H. B. Gislason, "Elements of Objectivity in Wendell Phillips," QJS, 3(April, 1917):125–134.

Bernard I. Griffith, "Elements of the Oratory of Wendell Phillips," Unpublished M.A. thesis, Ohio Wesleyan University, 1930.

Mildred Pomeroy, "The Imagery of Wendell Phillips," Unpublished M.A. thesis, Northwestern University, 1925.

John W. Sattler, "Wendell Phillips: Speaker and Agitator," Unpublished Ph.D. thesis, Northwestern University, 1943.

Oscar Sherwin, *Prophet of Liberty: The Life and Times of Wendell Phillips*, New York: Bookman Associates, 1958.

Joseph Snyder, "An Analysis of the Epithets Used in the Speeches of Wendell Phillips," Unpublished M.A. thesis, Northwestern University, 1930.

George E. Woodberry, *Wendell Phillips: The Faith of an American*, Boston: D. B. Updike, 1912.

SEARGENT SMITH PRENTISS (1808–1850)

Dallas C. Dickey, *Seargent Smith Prentiss*, Baton Rouge: Louisiana State University Press, 1945. (Based on his Ph.D. thesis on Prentiss, at Louisiana State University, 1938).

———, "The Oratorical Career of Seargent S. Prentiss," QJS, 26(April, 1940):221–229.

Joseph Shields, *The Life and Times of Seargent Prentiss*, Philadelphia: Lippincott, 1884.

JOHN RANDOLPH (1773–1833)

Henry Adams, *John Randolph*, Boston: Houghton Mifflin, 1882.

William C. Bruce, *John Randolph of Roanoke*, New York: Putnam's, 1939.

Mason Gerald Daly, "The Political Oratory of John Randolph of Roanoke," Unpublished Ph.D. thesis, Northwestern University, 1951.

Hugh Garland, *The Life of John Randolph*, Two Vols., New York: Appleton, 1851.

Gerald White Johnson, *Randolph of Roanoke*, New York: Minton, Balch, 1929.

Russell Kirk, *Randolph of Roanoke*, Chicago: University of Chicago Press, 1951.

ROBERT BARNWELL RHETT (1800–1876)

H. Hardy Perritt, "Robert Barnwell Rhett: South Carolina Secession Spokesman," Unpublished Ph.D. thesis, University of Florida, 1954.

L. A. White, *Robert Barnwell Rhett: Father of Secession*, New York: Century, 1931.

THEODORE ROOSEVELT (1858–1919)

Theodore Roosevelt: *Addresses and Papers*, ed., W. F. Johnson, New York: Sun Dial Classics Co., 1908.

Works of Theodore Roosevelt, ed., Herman Hagedorn, Twenty Vols., New York: Scribner's, 1926.

Howard Kennedy Beale, *Theodore Roosevelt and the Rise of America to World Power*, Baltimore: Johns Hopkins Press, 1956.

William A. Behl, "Theodore Roosevelt's Principles of Invention," SM, 14(1947):93–110.

——, "Theodore Roosevelt's Principles of Speech Preparation and Delivery," SM, 12(1945):112–122.

Noel F. Busch, *TR: The Story of Theodore Roosevelt and His Influence on Our Times*, New York: Reynal, 1963.

E. M. Davis, "A Study of the Speeches of Theodore Roosevelt," Unpublished M.A. thesis, Ohio Wesleyan University, 1942.

Herbert Hildebrandt, "Theodore Roosevelt's Western Speaking Tour of 1903," Unpublished M.S. thesis, University of Wisconsin, 1955.

Henry Pringle, *Theodore Roosevelt: A Biography*, New York: Harcourt, Brace, 1931.

Carleton Putnam, *Theodore Roosevelt: The Formative Years, 1858–1886*, New York: Scribner's, 1958.

Edward Wagenknecht, *The Seven Worlds of Theodore Roosevelt*, New York: Longmans, Green, 1958.

ERNESTINE ROSE (1810–1892)

Morris U. Schappes, "Ernestine Rose, Queen of the Platform," *Jewish Life*, March, 1949.

Yuri Suhl, *Ernestine Rose and the Battle for Human Rights*, New York: Reynal, 1959.

CARL SCHURZ (1829–1906)

Reminiscences of Carl Schurz, Three Vols., New York: Doubleday, 1907–08.

Speeches, Correspondence, and Political Papers of Carl Schurz, ed. Frederic Bancroft, Six Vols., New York: Putnam's, 1913.

Speeches of Carl Schurz, collected and revised by the author, Philadelphia: Lippincott, 1865.

Claude Moore Fuess, *Carl Schurz: Reformer*, New York: Dodd, Mead, 1932.

Joseph Harr Mahaffy, "The Speaking and Speeches of Carl Schurz," Unpublished Ph.D. thesis, Northwestern University, 1951.

Joseph Schafer, *Carl Schurz: Militant Liberal*, Evansville, Wis.: Antes, 1930.

WILLIAM HENRY SEWARD (1801–1872)

William H. Seward, Autobiography, ed. and completed by Frederick W. Seward, Three Vols., New York: Appleton, 1877, and Derby and Miller, 1891.

——, *In Defense of William Freeman*, Auburn, N.Y.: Derby and Miller, 1846.

——, *Life and Public Services of John Quincy Adams*, Auburn, N.Y.: Derby and Miller, 1849.

————, Works, ed. George E. Baker, Five Vols., New York: Redfield, 1853, and Houghton Mifflin, 1884.

Frederic Bancroft, *The Life of William H. Seward*, Two Vols., New York: Harper, 1900.

T. K. Lothrop, *William Henry Seward*, Boston: Houghton Mifflin, 1899.

Robert T. Oliver, "William H. Seward on the 'Irrepressible Conflict,' October 25, 1858," in J. J. Auer, *Antislavery and Disunion, op. cit.*, pp. 29–50.

ELIZABETH CADY STANTON (1815–1902)

Eighty Years and More: Reminiscences of Elizabeth Cady Stanton, New York: European Pub. Co., 1897.

Alma Lutz, *Created Equal: A Biography of Elizabeth Cady Stanton*, New York: John Day, 1940.

Winifred Esther Wise, *Rebel in Petticoats: The Life of Elizabeth Cady Stanton*, Philadelphia: Chilton Co., Book Division, 1960.

ALEXANDER HAMILTON STEPHENS (1812–1883)

Rudolph Von Abele, *Alexander H. Stephens*, New York: Knopf, 1946.

Myrta Lockett Avary, *Recollections of Alexander H. Stephens*, New York: Doubleday, Page, 1910.

Nemias B. Beck, "The Oratory of Alexander H. Stephens," Unpublished Ph.D. thesis, University of Wisconsin, 1937.

Henry Cleveland, *Alexander H. Stephens in Public and Private, with Letters and Speeches, Before, During, and Since the War*, Philadelphia: National Pub. Co., 1866.

R. M. Johnston and W. H. Browne, *Alexander H. Stephens*, Philadelphia, 1878 (mostly a collection of his letters).

E. Ramsay Richardson, *Little Aleck: A Life of Alexander H. Stephens*, New York: Grosset and Dunlap, 1932.

THADDEUS STEVENS (1793–1868)

Fawn W. Brodie, *Thaddeus Stevens: Scourge of the South*, New York: Norton, 1959.

Richard N. Current, *Old Thad Stevens: A Story of Ambition*, Madison: University of Wisconsin Press, 1942.

Thomas A. Finley, "A Rhetorical Analysis of the Speech Delivered by Thaddeus Stevens before Congress on the Compromise of 1850," Unpublished M.A. thesis, St. Louis University, 1951.

Ralph Korngold, *Thaddeus Stevens: A Being Darkly Wise and Rudely Great*, New York: Harcourt, Brace, 1955.

Samuel W. McCall, *Thaddeus Stevens*, Boston: Houghton Mifflin, 1899.

Alphonse M. Miller, *Thaddeus Stevens*, New York: Harper, 1939.

Elsie Singmaster, *I Speak for Thad Stevens*, Boston: Houghton Mifflin, 1947 (a novel).

Mary Grace Walsh, "A Comparative Study of the Spoken Words of Andrew Johnson and Thaddeus Stevens," Unpublished Ph.D. thesis, University of Wisconsin, 1939.

William B. Whitaker, "Thaddeus Stevens: Spokesman for the Vindictives and Creator of the 'Solid South,'" Unpublished Ph.D. thesis, University of Wisconsin, 1949.

SOLOMON STODDARD (1643–1729)
Eugene E. White, "Solomon Stoddard's Theories of Persuasion," SM, 29(Nov., 1962):235–259.

LUCY STONE (1818–1893)
Alice Stone Blackwell, *Lucy Stone: Pioneer of Women's Rights*, Boston: Little, Brown, 1930.
Elinor Hays, *Morning Star: A Biography of Lucy Stone*, New York: Harcourt, Brace & World, 1961.

CHARLES SUMNER (1811–1874)
Charles Sumner, *Addresses on War*, Boston: Ginn and Co., 1902.
————, *Orations and Speeches*, Two Vols., Boston: Ticknor, Reed, and Fields, 1850.
————, *Recent Speeches and Addresses*, Boston: Ticknor and Fields, 1856.
————, *Works*, Statesman Edition, Fifteen Vols., Boston: Lee and Shepard, 1900.
David Donald, *Charles Sumner and the Coming of the Civil War*, New York: Knopf, 1960.
Edward L. Pierce, *Memoir and Letters of Charles Sumner*, Four Vols., Boston: Robert Bros., 1877.

WILLIAM ASHLEY ("BILLY") SUNDAY (1862–1927)
Frederick W. Betts, *Billy Sunday: The Man and Method*, Boston: Universalist Publishing House, 1916.
Paul R. Brees, "A Comparative Study of the Devices of Persuasion Used in Ten Sermons by Harry Emerson Fosdick and Eight Sermons by William Ashley Sunday," Unpublished Ph.D. thesis, University of Southern California, 1948.
William T. Ellis, *"Billy" Sunday: The Man and His Message*, Philadelphia: Universal Book and Bible House, 1914.
Theodore T. Frankenberg, *The Spectacular Career of Rev. Billy Sunday: Famous Baseball Evangelist*, Columbus, Ohio: McClelland, 1913.
Lawrence L. Lacour, "A Study of Revival Methods in America, 1920–1955, with Special Reference to Billy Sunday, Aimee Semple McPherson, and Billy Graham," Unpublished Ph.D. thesis, Northwestern University, 1956.
Life and Labors of Rev. William A. (Billy) Sunday, The Great Modern Evangelist, With Selected Sermons, Decatur, Ill.: Herman, Poole, 1908 (only publication of collection of his sermons—highly inaccurate and disowned by Sunday).
William G. McLoughlin, Jr., *Billy Sunday Was His Real Name*, Chicago, University of Chicago Press, 1955.
Homer A. Rodeheaver, *Twenty Years with Billy Sunday*, Winona Lake, Ind.: Cokesbury Press, 1936.

BENJAMIN RYAN TILLMAN (1847–1918)
Lindsey S. Perkins, "The Oratory of Benjamin Ryan Tillman," SM, 15(No. 1, 1948):1–18.

Francis Butler Simkins, *Pitchfork Ben Tillman, South Carolinian*, Baton Rouge: Louisiana State University Press, 1944.
————, *The Tillman Movement in South Carolina*, Durham, N.C.: Duke University Press, 1926.

ROBERT A. TOOMBS (1810–1885)

Ulrich B. Phillips, *Correspondence of Robert Toombs, Alexander Stephens, and Howell Cobb*, Washington: American Historical Assoc. Report, 1911.
————, *Life of Robert Toombs*, New York: Macmillan, 1913.
Pleasant A. Stovall, *Robert Toombs: Statesman, Speaker, Soldier, Sage*, New York: Cassell Pub. Co., 1892.

SOJOURNER TRUTH (?–1883)

Arthur Huff Fauset, *Sojourner Truth: God's Faithful Pilgrim*, Chapel Hill: University of North Carolina Press, 1938.

MARK TWAIN—SAMUEL L. CLEMENS (1835–1910)

Autobiography of Mark Twain, ed., Charles Neider, New York: Harper, 1959.
Kraid I. Ashbaugh, "Mark Twain as a Public Speaker," *Western Speech*, 14(Jan., 1950):10–14.
Stanley T. Donner, "Mark Twain as a Reader," QJS, 33(Oct., 1947): 308–311.
Jean Conyers Ervin, "Mark Twain: Speechmaker," Unpublished Ph.D. thesis, University of Missouri, 1950.
E. James Lennon, "Mark Twain Abroad," QJS, 39(April, 1958):197–200.

MARTIN VAN BUREN (1782–1862)

Autobiography of Martin Van Buren, ed. John C. Fitzpatrick, Vol. II of American Historical Assoc. Report for 1918, Washington: U.S. Gov't Printing Office, 1920.
Denis T. Lynch, *An Epoch and a Man: Martin Van Buren and His Times*, New York: Horace Liveright, 1929.
Vernon Elwood Rank, "Martin Van Buren's Political Speaking in His Rise to Political Power," Unpublished Ph.D. thesis, Pennsylvania State University, 1961.

BOOKER T. WASHINGTON (1856?–1915)

Selected Speeches of Booker T. Washington, ed., E. D. Washington, Garden City, N.Y.: Doubleday, 1932.
Booker T. Washington, *Up from Slavery: An Autobiography*, New York, 1900.
Willis N. Pitts, Jr., "A Critical Study of Booker T. Washington as a Speech-Maker with an Analysis of Seven Selected Speeches," Unpublished Ph.D. thesis, University of Michigan, 1952.
Emmet J. Scott and Lyman Beecher Stowe, *Booker T. Washington: Builder of a Civilization*, Garden City, N.Y.: Doubleday, Page, 1917.
Wofford K. Smith, "An Analysis of the Dynamic Factors in Selected Speeches of Booker T. Washington to the Students of Tuskegee Institute," Unpublished M.A. thesis, University of Alabama, 1952.

GEORGE WASHINGTON (1732–1799)

    Autobiography of George Washington, 1753–1799, ed., Edward C. Boykin, New York: Reynal and Hitchcock, 1935.

    Writings of George Washington, ed. John C. Fitzpatrick, Thirty One Vols., Washington, D.C.: U.S. Gov't. Printing Office, 1944.

    Horace Binney, *An Inquiry into the Formation of Washington's Farewell Address*, Philadelphia: Parry and McMillan, 1959.

    Paul R. Mottox, "A Rhetorical Study of Selected Speeches of George Washington," Unpublished M.S. thesis, State University of Iowa, 1958.

    Geraldine Wharry, "Study of the First Inaugural Address of President George Washington," Unpublished M.A. thesis, Bradley University, 1950.

DANIEL WEBSTER (1782–1852)

    Great Speeches and Orations of Daniel Webster, ed. with introduction, Edwin P. Whipple, Boston: Little, Brown, 1897.

    Works of Daniel Webster, Six Vols., Boston: Little, Brown, 1857.

    Writings and Speeches of Daniel Webster, National Edition, Eighteen Vols., Boston: Little, Brown, 1903.

    John W. Black, "Webster's Peroration in the Dartmouth College Case," QJS, 23(Dec., 1937):636–642.

    Howard A. Bradley, "A Study of the Structure of a Selected Group of Webster's Speeches," Unpublished M.A. thesis, Cornell University, 1927.

    George Ticknor Curtis, *Life of Daniel Webster*, Two Vols., New York: Appleton, 1872.

    Claude Moore Fuess, *Daniel Webster*, Two Vols., Boston: Little, Brown, 1930.

    Robert G. Gunderson, "Webster in Linsey-Woolsey," QJS, 37(Feb., 1951):23–30.

    Peter Harvey, *Reminiscences and Anecdotes of Daniel Webster*, Boston: Little, Brown, 1878.

    Harold M. Jordan, "An Evaluation of the Argumentative Methods of Daniel Webster in Four Representative Courtroom Speeches," Unpublished M.A. thesis, University of Iowa, 1936.

    Robert King, "Daniel Webster's Western Tour of 1837—a Critical Examination of His Speeches and Speech Techniques," Unpublished M.A. thesis, State University of Iowa, 1940.

    Mary L. Kocher, "A Critical Analysis of the Oral Style of Four Representative Occasional Speeches of Daniel Webster," Unpublished M.A. thesis, University of Iowa, 1937.

    Henry Cabot Lodge, *Daniel Webster*, Boston: Houghton Mifflin, 1883.

    John Back McMaster, *Daniel Webster*, New York: Appleton-Century, 1902.

    Ford Harry H. McCoy, "Methods of Refutation Used by Daniel Webster in His Replies to Hayne," Unpublished M.A. thesis, Northwestern University, 1931.

    Glen Mills, "Daniel Webster's Principles of Rhetoric," SM, 9(1942):124–140.

————, "Misconceptions Concerning Daniel Webster," QJS, 29(Dec., 1943):432–428.

Robert T. Oliver, "Studies in the Political and Social Views of the Slave-Struggle Orators: II—Webster," QJS, 133(Feb., 1937):13–32.

Elizabeth J. Turnell, "The Genesis of the Reply to Hayne," Unpublished M.A. thesis, University of Illinois, 1931.

ANGELINA GRIMKÉ WELD (1805–1879)

Catherine H. Birney, *The Grimké Sisters: Sarah and Angelina Grimké, the First American Women Advocates of Abolition and Women's Rights,* Boston: Lee and Shephard, 1885.

Theodore D. Weld, *In Memory: Angelina Grimké Weld,* Boston: Geo. H. Ellis, 1880.

THEODORE DWIGHT WELD (1803–1895)

Theodore D. Weld, *Slavery As It Is,* New York: American Antislavery Society, 1839.

————, *The Bible Against Slavery,* New York: American Antislavery Society, 1837.

Gilbert H. Barnes and Dwight L. Dumond, eds., *Letters of Theodore Dwight Weld, Angelina Grimké Weld and Sarah Grimké, 1822–1844.* Two Vols., New York: Appleton-Century, 1934.

Paul A. Carmack, "Theodore Weld: Orator and Schoolmaster," Unpublished Ph.D. thesis, Ohio State University, 1949.

Benjamin P. Thomas, *Theodore Weld: Crusader for Freedom,* New Brunswick: Rutgers University Press, 1950.

GEORGE WHITEFIELD (1714–1770)

George Whitefield, *Eighteen Sermons,* rev. by Andrew Gifford, Springfield, Mass.: Thomas Dickman, 1808.

————, *Fifteen Sermons,* New York: Hugh Gaine, 1794.

————, *Works of the Reverend George Whitefield, Containing All His Sermons and Tracts Which Have Been Already Published: With a Select Collection of Letters,* Six Vols., London: Edward and Charles Dilly, 1771–1772.

Stuart C. Henry, *George Whitefield: Wayfaring Witness,* New York: Abingdon Press, 1957.

Eugene E. White, "Decline of the Great Awakening in New England: 1741 to 1746," *New England Quarterly,* March, 1951.

————, "George Whitefield and the Paper War in New England," QJS, 29(Feb., 1943):32–36.

————, "George Whitefield's Preaching in Massachusetts and Georgia: A Case Study in Persuasion," *Southern Speech Journal,* 15(May, 1950):249–262.

————, "The Great Awakener: George Whitefield," *Southern Speech Journal,* 11(Sept., 1945):6–15.

————, "The Preaching of George Whitefield During the Great Awakening," SM, 15(No. 1, 1948):33–43 (based on his unpublished doctoral thesis at Louisiana State University, 1947).

————, "The Protasis of the Great Awakening in New England," SM, 21(March, 1954):10–20.

————, "Whitefield's Use of Proofs During the Great Awakening in America," *Western Speech*, 14(Jan., 1950):3–6.

FRANCES E. WILLARD (1839–1898)

Frances E. Willard, *Glimpses of Fifty Years: The Autobiography of an American Woman*, Chicago: Women's Temperance Pub. Assoc., 1889.

Mary E. Dillon, *Frances Willard: From Prayers to Politics*, Chicago: University of Chicago Press, 1944.

Anna Adams Gordon, *The Life of Frances E. Willard*, Evanston, Ill.: National Women's Christian Temperance Union, 1914.

JAMES WILSON (1742–1798)

Selected Political Essays of James Wilson, ed., Randolph G. Adams, New York: Knopf, 1930.

Works of the Honorable James Wilson, Philadelphia: Bird Wilson, 1804.

Berne William Enslin, "The Argumentative Technique in Selected Forensic and Demonstrative Speeches of James Wilson, 1775–1788," Unpublished M.A. thesis, University of Iowa, 1936.

Horace G. Rahskopf, "The Oratory of James Wilson of Pennsylvania," SM, 5(1938):40–61.

WOODROW WILSON (1856–1924)

The Public Papers of Woodrow Wilson, eds., Ray Stannard Baker and William E. Dodd, Eight Vols., Garden City, N.Y.: Doubleday, Page, 1927–39.

The Messages and Papers of Woodrow Wilson, ed., Albert Shaw, Two Vols., New York: Geo. H. Doran, 1917, 1924.

Ray Stannard Baker, *Woodrow Wilson: Life and Letters*, Eight Vols., Garden City: Doubleday, Page, 1927–1939.

Georgia G. Casebeir, "An Analysis of the Motives to Which Woodrow Wilson Appealed in His Presidential Addresses," Unpublished M.A. thesis, University of Illinois, 1942.

Hardin Craig, "Woodrow Wilson as an Orator," QJS, 38(April, 1952): 145–148.

William E. Dodd, *Woodrow Wilson and His Work*, Garden City, Doubleday, Page, 1920.

Howard Gilkinson, "A Critical Study of the Persuasive Technique of Woodrow Wilson," Unpublished M.A. thesis, State University of Iowa, 1929.

Cyril F. Hager, "Persuasion in the Speeches of the Presidential Campaign of 1916: A Study in Organized Persuasion," Unpublished Ph.D. thesis, University of Wisconsin, 1942.

Clair R. Henderlider, "Woodrow Wilson's Speeches on the League of Nations, September 4–25, 1919," SM, 13(No. 1, 1946):23–34.

W. C. Miller, "A Critical Analysis of Woodrow Wilson as a Public Speaker, 1910–1921," Unpublished M.A. thesis, University of Southern California, 1932.

Helen Margaret Mowry, "Woodrow Wilson's Concept of Democracy as Revealed in His Speeches," Unpublished M.S. thesis, Northwestern University, 1932.

Carl S. Mundinger, "The Influence of Calvinism and of French Romantic Theory on Woodrow Wilson," Unpublished M.A. Thesis,
University of Minnesota, 1931.

Marijo Wayde Oliver, "An Analysis of Woodrow Wilson's Use of Invention in His Speeches on Education," Unpublished M.A. thesis,
University of Colorado, 1952.

Robert T. Oliver, "Wilson's *Rapport* with His Audience," QJS, 27
(Feb., 1941):79–90.

Anna J. Pendleton, "Woodrow Wilson's Speeches on the Western
Tour, 1919—A Study in Argumentation," Unpublished M.A. thesis,
State University of Iowa, 1931.

Howard Runion, "An Objective Study of the Speech Style of Woodrow
Wilson," SM, 3(1936):75–94.

Joseph P. Tumulty, *Woodrow Wilson as I Know Him*, New York:
Doubleday, Page, 1921.

JOHN WINTHROP (1588–1649)

Winthrop's Journals, ed., James K. Hosmer, Two Vols., New York:
Scribner's, 1908.

Winthrop's Papers, Six Vols., Boston: Mass. Historical Society, 1931.

Joseph H. Twitchell, *John Winthrop*, New York: Dodd, Mead, 1891.

Robert C. Winthrop, *Life and Letters of John Winthrop*, Boston:
Ticknor and Fields, 1867.

FRANCES WRIGHT (1795–1852)

Alice J. Perkins and Theresa Wolfson, *Frances Wright: Free Enquirer*,
New York: Harper, 1939.

William Randall Waterman, *Frances Wright*, New York: Columbia
University, 1924.

WILLIAM LOWNDES YANCEY (1814–1863)

William L. Yancey, *For Southern Rights*, Charleston: Walker, Evans,
1860.

John W. DuBoise, *Life and Times of William Lowndes Yancey*, Two
Vols., New York: Peter Smith, 1892.

Alto L. Garner and Nathan Scott, "William Lowndes Yancey: Statesman of Secession," *Alabama Review*, 15(July, 1962):190–202.

Rexford S. Mitchell, "William Lowndes Yancey: Orator of Southern
Constitutional Rights," Unpublished Ph.D. thesis, University of
Wisconsin, 1937.

INDEX

"Ah me, what act that roars so loud and thunders in the index?"
William Shakespeare

"It is easy enough to make an index, as it is to make a broom of odds and ends, as rough as oat straw; but to make an index tied up tight, and that will sweep well into corners, isn't so easy."
John Ruskin